Food Policy
for America

FOOD POLICY
FOR AMERICA

Harold G. Halcrow

Professor of Agricultural Economics
University of Illinois at Urbana-Champaign

McGRAW-HILL BOOK COMPANY

New York   St. Louis   San Francisco   Auckland
Bogotá   Düsseldorf   Johannesburg   London
Madrid   Mexico   Montreal   New Delhi   Panama   Paris
São Paulo   Singapore   Sydney   Tokyo   Toronto

Food Policy for America

1234567890   K P K P   783210987

This book was set in Times Roman by University Graphics, Inc.
The editors were Rose Ciofalo and Michael Weber;
the cover was designed by Nicholas Krenitsky;
the production supervisor was Milton J. Heiberg.
The drawings were done by ANCO/Boston.
Kingsport Press, Inc., was printer and binder.

Library of Congress Cataloging in Publication Data

Halcrow, Harold G
    Food policy for America.

    Bibliography: p.
    Includes index.
    1. Food supply—United States. 2. Agriculture and
state—United States. I. Title.
HD9006.H2   338.1'9   76-45408
ISBN 0-07-025550-4

Contents

Preface

A shift in economic events has brought food to the center of the stage as a primary economic concern in America and around the world. This book addresses itself to this concern through discussion of the best food policy for America now and for several years ahead. The book views food policy comprehensively as it can best develop in a new era distinguished by accelerating growth in the magnitude and intensity of the world food problem, by higher costs for energy and some other food inputs, and by growing concerns over the adequacy of food resources and related issues, such as environmental protection, equity in income distribution, nutrition, and the general welfare.

Whether or not people in America will face relatively higher food prices in the future depends on decisions to be made in food policy—in foreign trade, production, and distribution. The high food prices of the early 1970s, which ushered in this new era, are viewed as one consequence of governmental policy, inadequate preparation to meet weather reverses, and unforeseen economic events around the world. To keep food prices at acceptable levels and still achieve progress and prosperity with efficiency and equity is a general goal of food policy. A discussion of the alternatives is one objective of this book.

Simultaneously, the study also presents a specific analysis of some of these alternatives and appraises both various goals in food production and distribution and the consequences of following one option or another. Both comprehensive vision and specific analysis are required to recognize the basic values and philosophical foundations underlying America's policy goals and to develop a coordinated policy that links America's farm and food system to domestic and world markets. The aim is to link food policy for America to the welfare of people at home as well as abroad and to develop new insights into policy options for this great country.

How the Book Can Be Used

The book is intended for all who are interested in public policy—citizens, legislators, public officials, farm people and people in farm service industries, food processing, and marketing, and students and teachers in the social sciences. It is designed as a comprehensive introduction for undergraduates to more advanced or more specialized courses in production, marketing, public policy, land economics, and so on; as a text for students who do not plan to take additional formal work in this area; or as a reference work for upper-division courses in public policy, where it may be supplemented with additional reading material. Also, it has been used by graduate students in a one-semester course, which can be extended to two semesters by the addition of other readings, such as those cited in the text, and more independent study.

What Is Policy?   The study conceives of food policy as a course of action to be consciously developed, involving decision and action on the part of people and their institutions, especially government. Policy, as defined in *Webster's New Collegiate Dictionary,* is:

> **1a:** prudence or wisdom in the management of affairs: SAGACITY. **b:** management or procedure based primarily on material interest. **2a:** a definite course or method of action selected from among alternatives and in light of given conditions to guide and determine present and future decisions. **b:** a high-level overall plan embracing the general goals and acceptable procedures, esp. of a governmental body.[1]

The Oxford Universal Dictionary defines one meaning of policy as: "A course of action pursued by a government, party, ruler, statesman, etc.; any course of action adopted as advantageous or expedient."[2]

How Is Policy Made?   *Food Policy for America* deals with both the long and the short view, with the processes and functions of government in making and implementing policy, with the actions of people in many roles who, by compromise and consensus, work toward their goals through political action. Policy, in essence, is a political process, with the citizen exercising political choices. It sometimes involves a wide variety of organizations or activities. Policy evolves

---

[1]By permission. From *Webster's New Collegiate Dictionary,* copyright 1975 by G. and C. Merriam Co., publishers of the Merriam-Webster Dictionaries.
[2]By permission. *The Oxford Universal Dictionary,* Oxford University Press, Oxford, England.

from the actions of governments—federal, state, and local—and from pressures of organizations that are sanctioned or encouraged by government. In a democracy it is a universal game, in which any number may play.

Why Study Policy?   There are a variety of reasons—personal interest, the enhancement of individual or group welfare, the improvement of the general welfare of society. Or the purpose of such study can be more directly conceived as how best to achieve specific goals through the political process: food abundance for America, high-level exports for trade and aid, equity in farm income, conservation, environmental protection, and a desired balance in growth between the rural and urban economy. The lessons of policy are replete with evidence of how one may gain or lose from a particular policy, how the position of an interest group may be affected, how the general welfare may be hurt or enhanced.

The General Theme

The general theme of our study is that the most effective progress toward food policy goals or their balance, as in an optimum food policy, can be attained only by more complete rural-urban understanding and interaction and a broader participation in a democracy of intellect. Only then can we achieve what is required for efficiency and equity in the food system and beyond. For a long time, food policy for America was carried out in a more narrow sphere, confined to relatively isolated questions of commodity management and income supports as supplements to farm producers. Now, production and welfare goals have a much broader range, and the answer to each policy question or the result of each policy decision affects other answers and decisions. So there must be a comprehensive view or vision as well as competent and specific economic analysis, all combined into intelligent, well-informed political action.

This theme sets the tone for our study and helps to define its style and general limits. The book attempts to cover the major issues in a comprehensive, yet meaningful way. In a real sense, however, none is covered to exhaustion. This is because the analysis of public policy is open-ended and never really complete; and each new day brings new problems, new challenges, and new opportunities. Today's new economics takes account of the broad macro questions of our time while it attempts to bring together the specific analyses that bear on individual policy choices. The book is dedicated to the improvement of our understanding of some of these questions and choices in the hope that policy-making with respect to food resources will bring higher levels of performance, with understanding and tolerance for the views of others and a greater ability to meet the varied goals of society.

Acknowledgments

Hundreds of people have contributed directly to this study, as the citations throughout the book indicate. Additionally, a large number of students have read the manuscript in the course of its development, and many have helped with questions, comments, and papers. Several students are cited in footnotes where appropriate. My colleagues at the University of Illinois at Urbana-Champaign—most notably J. W. Gruebele, H. D. Guither, S. C. Schmidt, and R. G. F. Spitze—have contributed through discussions and interchanges in teaching courses in public policy. R. W. Bartlett, C. A. Bock, Folke Dovring, D. I. Padberg, E. R. Swanson, T. Takayama, and D. L. Uchtmann reviewed important parts of the manuscript. Reviews of the material on nutrition policy were contributed by R. R. Bell, J. W. Erdman, B. E. Haskell, Z. J. Ordal, and M. F. Picciano. W. M. Bever reviewed the work on pesticide policy. General reviewers in the academic world included H. F. Breimyer (Missouri), F. M. Clydesdale (Massachusetts), L. W. Schruben (Kansas State), and L. T. Wallace (California, Berkeley). To all of these and to many others, and especially to my secretary, Gail Metheny, who has been most dedicated, I am deeply grateful. None of them is responsible, of course, for specific shortcomings, errors, or weaknesses in the argument. For these as well as the judgments expressed the author alone is accountable.

As we proceed into the subject, it is hoped that the reader will be excited by the issues that are raised. We have attempted to include the major essentials that are within the grasp of the serious reader or student but not to include anything that is unnecessarily hard or confusing. Above all, we attempt not to include anything that later must be unlearned as wrong. The basis for food policy has greatly broadened, however, and the issues that are most crucial will continue to grow in prominence in America and throughout the world. How best to meet them is the major challenge of this book.

Harold G. Halcrow

Food Policy
for America

Chapter 1

Establishing the Scope
of Food Policy

The U.S., long preoccupied with rapid urbanization, is rediscovering its economic heritage and still its biggest industry—agriculture. News of food prices, grain exports and supply and demand is in the headlines, underscoring for citizens and national leaders the tremendous influence that agriculture has on the economic, social and political well-being of America and the world.

Theme of a series in *The Wall Street Journal,* October–November 1973

America has entered a new era for food policy, in which new and sometimes different answers are desired—or, in fact, required—for the three general policy questions: What quantities of food and farm products shall be produced? How shall they be produced? And for whom?

In our vision, this era began in the early 1970s, and it stretches through at least the balance of the twentieth century. In the next few years, new answers must be developed for solutions to the world food problem, or starvation and disaster will face much of the human race. In the United States, we must have new answers in the development of our farm and food system. If our policy is to be successful, we must have appropriately coordinated answers to questions of growth and development, economic structure, environmental protection, and income distribution. What answers are made and how they are developed define the scope of food policy.[1]

THE SCOPE OF FOOD POLICY

Many people, in their broadening concern about food, are asking questions such as these: Will there be enough food? What will it cost? Do we have resources adequate for the future? Second, who will control the farm and food system? Can we have a policy that will result in the kind of agriculture and food economy that we most desire? Third, who will get the income? How will food be shared among the affluent and not so affluent consumers, among the rich nations and the poor nations? How can we best be assured that we will have good food, or food in sufficient quantity that is good for us?

All these questions—and more—are part of our study of food policy for America; and, as we have just remarked, our approach to answering them defines the scope of food policy. We begin by looking at them broadly to get a perspective on the new era, to view this as a possible third great era, in comparison and contrast with the uniqueness of the first and the second eras.

The First Era of Policy Based on Land Settlement

For 300 years, from the first settlements at Jamestown and Plymouth to about the end of the second decade of this century, America's encounter with the frontier was the dominant theme in farm and food policy. The overall policy was primarily one of land settlement, or of farm settlement, based on an abundance of land and a scarcity of labor. This policy attempted to maximize the returns from labor rather than from land and, in so doing, it was most concerned with laws, regulations, and actions to expedite land settlement, to build a transportation and marketing system, and to develop the forms and structures of democratic government, all within certain fundamental concepts of individual freedom and equality of opportunity. These concepts translated generally to fee-simple ownership of the means of production, a basic family farm policy, and a just reward determined in the marketplace according to postulates of the work ethic, the democratic creed, justice, and social reform. In the 300 years, more than 1 billion acres of land, more than half the total land area of the first 48 states, passed from public to private use for farming, grazing, forestry, and other purposes. The great bulk of this land was settled during the nineteenth century, as the index of gross farm production increased between 19 and 20 times.[2]

---

[1]This concept of the three policy questions and the general outline are traced to Prof. Frank Knight, great teacher and my first graduate advisor at the University of Chicago. For further discussion, see Don Patinkin, "Frank Knight as Teacher," *The American Economic Review,* Vol. 63, No. 5, December 1973, pp. 787–810.

[2]Marvin W. Towne and Wayne D. Rasmussen, "Farm Gross Product and Gross Investment in the Nineteenth Century," *Trends in the American Economy in the Nineteenth Century, Studies in Income and Wealth, Vol. 24, A Report of the National Bureau of Economic Research,* New York. Princeton, N.J.: Princeton University Press, 1960, pp. 255–315, especially pp. 264–271.

Within this land-based growth model, however, the farm and food economy was stagnating in terms of economic performance. Increases in aggregate farm output were closely correlated with the changes in land being farmed, with increases in man-hours worked on farms, and with growth in livestock inventories and farm capital investment. In fact, it has been estimated that near the end of the 300-year era, from 1899 to 1919, the average rate of change in total factor productivity in American agriculture was slightly negative.[3] The land use pattern of agriculture began to stabilize, with about 350 million of the 1 billion acres being in crops and the rest used more extensively for grazing, forestry, or wild life.

The Second Era of Policy Based on Science

After World War I, the policy of growth based on land gave way to a more revolutionary policy of economic change and development, largely built on science and technology, with larger scale of firm organization, more capital investment in the new technologies, more and more highly skilled management. The first impetus for this came from farm mechanization, the development of mechanical power for farming, and improvements in the food marketing system. Then came new crops, hybrid seeds, and new techniques in crop and livestock production. Finally came commercial fertilizer and a wide array of chemicals to control crop pests—weeds, insects, and various plant and animal diseases. Indexes of rates of change in factor productivity began to rise rapidly. The annual rate of gain in aggregated labor productivity, which integrates the total factor inputs in farm production, was near 1.5 percent around 1920, close to 3 percent around 1940, and as high as 6 percent around 1960. Thus, agricultural productivity did not grow by simple compound interest, but for 40 years or more the rate of increase did so.[4]

The innovations were both cost reducing and output increasing; that is, they both substituted for other, less productive inputs and complemented some inputs that remained in production. The payoff was generally high. Sometimes, as in the case of hybrid corn and a few other innovations, it was enormous.[5] In farming, on the average, whereas total factor productivity changed by only 1 percent

[3]John W. Kendrick, *Productivity Trends in the United States, A Study by the National Bureau of Economic Research,* New York. Princeton, N.J.: Princeton University Press, 1961, p. 136.

[4]Folke Dovring, *Productivity of Labor in Agricultural Production,* Urbana: University of Illinois College of Agriculture, Agricultural Experiment Station Bulletin 726, September 1967, p. 15.

[5]It has been estimated, for example, that the internal rate of return on hybrid corn research, as of 1955, with the discount rate which equates earnings from the outcome of research with costs on research, averaged about 37 percent annually. The external rate, based on percentage of annual earnings from the outcome of research to total past costs, assuming a 10 percent interest rate, averaged about 690 percent annually. The benefit-cost ratio, which is equal to the annual rate of return divided by 100 times the interest rate, was 69 percent annually. (From Zvi Griliches, "Research Costs and Social Returns: Hybrid Corn and Related Innovations," *Journal of Political Economy,* Vol. 66, October 1958, pp. 419–431.) In Mexico, the annual rate of return on wheat research from 1943 to 1963 was estimated at an external rate of 750 percent annually with a benefit-cost ratio of 75. (From L. Ardito Barletta, "Costs and Social Returns of Agricultural Research in Mexico," Ph.D. dissertation, University of Chicago, 1967.) Data taken from T. W. Schultz, *Economic Growth in Agriculture,* New York: McGraw-Hill Book Company, 1968, p. 85.

annually from the early 1920s to about 1937, total factor productivity increased by more than 3 percent annually from 1937 to 1953, by 2.5 percent annually from 1953 to 1960, and again by 3 percent annually from 1960 to 1966. Capital per unit of labor input did not change from 1919 to 1937. Then it increased by 3.4 percent annually from 1937 to 1948 and by 5.6 percent annually from 1948 to 1966. Farm output per unit of farm labor input, which had not changed from 1899 to 1919, increased by 1.2 percent annually from 1919 to 1929, and 0.8 percent from 1929 to 1937. Then it began to rise rapidly: by 3.8 percent annually from 1937 to 1948, by 6.2 percent annually from 1948 to 1953, by 4.1 percent annually from 1953 to 1960, and by 5.8 percent annually from 1960 to 1966.[6] After 1966, output per unit of labor input continued to rise, but the preliminary indications implied a slowing down in the rate of growth.

From the mid 1930s to 1970, the index of aggregate food and farm output approximately doubled. The number of people employed in farming declined by two-thirds. The number of farm operating units dropped by more than one-half. An increasingly large share of total output became concentrated in a small number of farms. The index of farm labor productivity, a measure of the marginal value product of labor, rose more than 4 times. The output per farm worker increased by a factor of 6.[7]

The marketing subsector and the farm service-supply subsector expanded, changed in economic structure, and upgraded their quality of service. Between 1930 and 1970, for example, whereas total food and farm products marketed doubled, an index of supplies purchased for farming, with quality of inputs taken into account, considerably more than doubled. Changes in economic structure involved consolidation or integration—vertically, by combining different production stages under one ownership or management, or horizontally, by combining two or more firms in one stage of production into the larger firm. The result throughout was further concentration of volume and of service in fewer firms.

Expanded Scope of Development Policy

The scope of policy had expanded to create this development experience. First, both federal and state policies supported a greatly enlarged role for research and education, primarily through the United States Department of Agriculture, the land grant system of colleges and universities, and the national system of vocational agriculture. The federal patent system encouraged private research and invention in agriculture as elsewhere. Second, federal policy assured an expanded flow of capital into agriculture through the most complete system of federally sponsored credit found in any sector of the American economy. There also were numerous direct lending and grant programs, including federal financing for irrigation, reclamation, and the like. Third, federal and state governments,

---

[6]John W. Kendrick, *Productivity Trends in the United States*, pp. 136, 148, 152, and 343–367; and Kendrick, *Postwar Productivity Trends in the United States, 1948–1969*, National Bureau of Economic Research, General Series 98, New York: Columbia University Press, 1973.

[7]*Changes in Farm Production and Efficiency, A Summary Report*, U.S. Department of Agriculture, Economic Research Service, Statistical Bulletin No. 233, June 1971, and Supplements.

after a long period of laissez faire, standardized rules and regulations in a wide array of industries and services in the food resource sector. Such rules and regulations affected grain, livestock, and other produce markets, and policy developed and controlled rail and other freight services. Fourth, government provided more specific developmental services, such as state and federal food inspection, rural free mail delivery, subsidy for rural electrification through the Rural Electrification Administration, specific stimulants to development such as the program of the Tennessee Valley Authority, and general encouragement of science and industry related to agriculture.

New Policy for Compensation

The modern scientific revolution, emerging from its embryo in the long years of the country's first great agricultural era, grew to full size in the second great era. It gathered momentum as its impact swept across the land, raising the rate of the transformation of resources into products. Some of the innovations were resource saving, especially by displacing animal power and substituting for human labor on a broad front. Some of them were more generally output increasing, a development that depressed prices for farm products relative to the returns formerly earned by the traditional inputs of human and animal power. Whereas the animals could quickly adjust, human beings could not. The returns to management and labor were depressed as farm people became the major surplus resource. As returns to human resources declined, and as continuing low income in the farm and rural community became more serious, farm and food policy evolved from the relatively simple system wherein government sought mainly to foster development by reducing the costs of land and other resources. Farm and food programs became much more diverse.

Agitation for the government to improve the economic status of farm people by reducing farm production and food marketing costs and by raising farm product prices relative to nonfarm prices had rumbled throughout most of the last half of the nineteenth century in the widespread Populist Revolt. Now the need for action could no longer be denied. The United States government became involved in a struggle of contending interests to change the terms of trade for agriculture, to increase farm product prices relative to nonfarm prices, and to improve the economic status of farm people and the rural society.

The struggle was over a new set of policies to compensate farm people more adequately for their productivity. There already were the evolving agricultural education and research, the new farm credit system, and the growing cooperative extension service aimed at more efficient agricultural production and improvement in rural life. The new struggle involved efforts to raise the prices of farm products relative to nonfarm prices; that is, to improve the terms of trade for farm people more directly. In the 1920s, farm service and marketing cooperatives were promoted as a way to grapple with the rising competitive power of the farm service and marketing sectors. And the farm leadership strove unsuccessfully for an export subsidy program to reestablish foreign markets lost through World War I and the Treaty of Versailles, which had destroyed the buying power of Central

Europe. In 1929, the Federal Farm Board was established, almost as a stop-gap measure, to strengthen farm food markets by funding an expanded storage program through farm cooperatives. When this type of support proved abortive, a whole new system for compensation came in under the Roosevelt New Deal to raise farm prices by control of crop production and more help in storage and marketing.

The new compensatory policy recognized that the increases in production arising first out of land settlement and then out of science and technology were more than just a "green revolution," the popular label for the increased productivity that comes from new land, farm mechanization, hybrid crops, fertilizers, and agricultural chemicals. Literally and actually, there was a social and economic upheaval in the American countryside. New emphasis in economic policy aimed to alleviate some of the hardship and suffering associated with the production revolution.

The various compensatory policies were designed to produce changes thought to be desirable. In the second era, the policies labored in an almost chronic food surplus situation. In our third era, we assume that there will be periodic surpluses, but because of the world's growing food requirements and higher energy costs, new types of compensatory policy will tend to be developed.

New Policy for Environment

New policies to protect and upgrade the environment are also related to this settlement, development, and compensatory experience. In each of the three eras of farm and food policy, there has been a strong wave of concern about conservation, or environmental policy. Each wave has been broader in scope than the one before it.

The 30-year period from 1891 to 1921 is generally regarded as the first conservation era in American history. The new concern with conservation arose chiefly out of interest in the preservation of timberland and the protection of some of the nation's mineral deposits. Although the land frontier had largely disappeared, soil conservation was not yet a subject for national policy.

In the 1930s there was increasing concern about possible misuse of the nation's soil resources and endangerment of the nation's food supply. Great dust storms caused by widespread drought heightened the concern about soils and brought a new emphasis to conservation policy. Although some scientists, educators, and others were worrying about the exhaustability of minerals and some other resources, conservation programs were limited chiefly to soils and timber.

The third wave of concern is far broader in scope, with more general implications for policy. It involves concerns about future sources and costs of energy and minerals, the wise use of soils and water, and the reduction of soil, water, and air pollution. The effect of these expanding concerns on food production is not entirely clear. In some cases, production may be constrained by higher costs for fertilizers or more strict regulations on use of farm chemicals. These constraints may be offset, in part at least, by new products to produce more food or by innovations to make more efficient use of traditional products used in food production. In any event, the scope of food policy includes concerns about the environment.

Social and Economic Structure

Finally, and perhaps most importantly, the scope of food policy embraces social and economic structure. Food policy for America has been built on concepts of freedom in a family-farm economy, as we have mentioned. This policy can be traced to the utilitarian concepts of classical economics, such as found in the writings of Adam Smith, David Ricardo, John Stuart Mill, and Alfred Marshall,[8] or to the philosophy of John Locke, emphasizing that the ideal world lies in a natural order of things—as opposed to collective restraints on individual actions—where human beings, because of their acquisitive instincts, are led to a utopia by the invisible hand of the perfect market. In England this philosophy was part of the enlightenment defining the rights of man, leading to the rule of reason, empiricism, and constitutional democracy. In France the idea that government would assume a significant role as servant of an egalitarian society combined with the French Physiocrat philosophy emphasizing the primacy of agriculture.

From early colonial foundations, these ideas merged into the philosophy of Thomas Jefferson, George Washington, and other founders of the republic. Perhaps the most typical tenets were, in Jefferson's words, that the tiller of the soil was the most noble of beings, and that an agricultural society built on freeholders and the family farm was the best not only for food production but for the foundation of democratic government.[9]

Now, we are not concerned so much with the family farm as a bastion of democracy. In today's vernacular, national policy is more concerned about equal rights, about bargaining power for food producers, about rights for landless laborers, and about how best to achieve the socially desirable distribution of income. In addition to questions of price supports, conservation payments, and the like, food policy for America must touch on ideas about structural reform, new arrangements for farm credit, the rights of farm wage workers, and reforms in land and water policies. The scope of policy has broadened.

Conclusion on the Scope of Policy

In terms of its scope, food policy embraces actions having to do with development, compensation, structure, and environment, and questions relating to these

[8]See Jacob Viner, *The Long View and the Short, Studies in Economic Theory and Policy,* Glencoe, Ill.: The Free Press, 1958. See especially the essays entitled "Adam Smith and Laissez Faire," "Marshall's Economics in Relation to the Man and His Times," "Bentham and J. S. Mill: The Utilitarian Background," and "Schumpeter's History of Economic Analysis."

[9]A. Whitney Griswold, *Farming and Democracy,* New York: Harcourt, Brace and Company, 1948. In this succinct and quotable study, Griswold shows that democracy has enjoyed its greatest development in nations such as England and the Low Countries where urbanization and industrialization, rather than family farms, dominate the economy. France, emphasizing family farms, almost lost democracy in the process. Germany and Italy, with large populations of family farms, did so.

areas are not easily separated. Nor should they be. In policy, the questions and the answers are related. In answering the question of what shall be produced, one influences the answers to the questions of how and for whom. Some concerns can be made more specific.

Increasing International Awareness   The United States is by far the largest exporter of the farm and food products that move in international trade. To ask what role farm products shall play in meeting the nation's critical needs for foreign exchange and what role we shall fulfill in supplying food aid is to ask, as already noted, how much shall be produced as well as how, what, and for whom, to produce. How shall the felt needs for aid be balanced against the market demand for food at home and abroad? Because of our great productivity and our success in development, we may feel that we have had more success in answering the first policy question of what shall be produced than we have in answering how and for whom. The new answers are based on increasing international awareness.

Increasing Costliness of Industrial Inputs to Agriculture   As energy costs rise, how can the food economy be best organized to conserve on energy—fuel, fertilizer, food processing—and still achieve the desired levels of production or output? Since production is becoming concentrated in ever fewer units, the question of how goods shall be produced becomes more pointed. Shall new action be taken to expand or to regulate the use of land more stringently? Shall we open new supplies of credit? How far shall we go to protect the environment? The answers are all related.

Concern over Equality of Opportunity   As concepts concerning equality of opportunity have gained in prominence, answers to questions concerning income distribution have become more urgent. Shall there be new policy to protect the small producer, to protect and regulate unionization of farm labor, to regulate bargaining between farm producers and food processors? In essence, what shall be the goals of employment and production? We know now that our great growth does not automatically solve the problems of poverty, especially as we see them in the farm and rural communities. Growth requires technical progress, and technical progress alters the composition of the labor-management force in agriculture and rural society as elsewhere. In agriculture, as growth goes on at the top among high-level management, more families are thrown out at the bottom. Under some circumstances, absolute misery and unemployment grow even though aggregate wealth increases. What shall be done about this situation? Although we do not have an adequate theory of distribution of income, we must continue to seek standards for its distribution. Part of our study is about how such standards can be developed in the farm economy and the related food sectors.

Increasing Awareness concerning Levels of Compensation   In the United States economy where prices for food and farm products are almost constantly on the move, what programs shall there be to try to stabilize prices, to define and achieve fair prices, or to maintain prices that will consistently provide a measure of economic justice? Prices allocate resources and distribute incomes. To what extent shall there be interference with resource allocation to achieve the desired level of compensation? To what extent shall we use prices rather than other means, such as direct payments, to achieve income goals? Our decisions on these questions will form the very roots of our future food policy.

THE ELEMENTS OF POLICY

The real problems in policymaking are not over the definition of policy or the statement of general questions and problems. They relate to *goals* and the respective priorities to be given them, the *means* or emphasis to be given to the programs, the agencies and powers of government to *implement* them, and the types and degrees of *constraints* used to limit them. Goals, means, implementers, and constraints are known as the elements of policymaking. It is important for our purposes to identify the meaning of each and how it is used.

Goals

The goals of public policy in a democratic society are always to some extent those that society as a whole wishes to achieve. But the public is seldom, if ever, unanimous in its opinion regarding any goal. Moreover, specific goals formed in the passion of conflict and compromise seldom, if ever, fully reflect the ideal world as seen by either a committed or a dispassionate observer. Public policy consists of a large number of individual policies, each with one or more goals, which vary from time to time in regard to their breadth, urgency, attainability, reasonableness, and so on. Although there may be wide agreement on such general goals as full employment, stable prices and incomes, growth of real income per person, equitable income distribution, and satisfactory balance of payments, specific goals for an industry have been harder to define.

In general, the ultimate goals of food policy for America include food abundance, efficiency within a democratically functioning society, equitable incomes, and some protection for the environment or assurance for the future. But if these are to be made explicit, someone must decide whether freedom, efficiency, security, or economy shall come first, since there is a conflict among these in various systems. In the United States, less than 5 percent of the people now live on farms. A mere 8 percent of our farm management units produce more than one-half of certain important commodities. Two-thirds of the nation's farms each generate less than $10,000 in annual farm sales and supply less than 10 percent of the value of farm products sold. Farming is becoming more concentrated. The $80 billion food processing-marketing industry has also become more concentrated. In the mid 1950s there were 42,000 food processors. In the mid-1970s there were fewer than 25,000. Similar growth in concentration has occurred in the firms supplying farm services and production inputs.

Food policy for America is concerned with answers for each subsector.

Who, for example, will own the resources? Who will own the land? Shall there be new emphasis on government-sponsored credit? Shall we allow tax advantages to continue to attract nonfarm capital into agriculture, thereby shifting farm ownership to a new group of people? Or, what emphasis shall be given to scientific progress and to development of human resources? What action shall be taken to assure continued access to foreign as well as domestic markets? And so on.

Formation of policy goals requires deliberative judgment about production, economic organization or structure, environmental protection, and income distribution. It is not possible to restrict the role of the policymaker to that of the social engineer or to positive economics, concerned only with alternative ways of achieving stated objectives within a prescribed policy area. Traditionally, the problems of food policy, developing especially in the Great Depression, caused most American economists to go beyond the bounds of positive economics, to make judgments about what on balance would be good or bad for the country, and to work in analysis of programs that in their judgment offered some hope of gain for agriculture and for the general welfare. In this, economists went beyond what is called the Pareto Optimum,[10] the condition where neither an individual nor a group can be made better off without making another person or group worse off, to various broader criteria for policy. Particularly, in their judgment, if the fortunes of agriculture, as conceived for many years at low ebb, could be improved by an income transfer to agriculture with the cost spread over the general society, there would be a gain in general welfare. Specifically, if it were possible to prevent agricultural production in excess of the amount required to clear the market at prices considered fair and reasonable, consumers would suffer little loss and farmers would gain immeasurably more. A balance would be restored to the economy that, overall, would be more desirable. Farmers would compensate society with a stable and predictable food supply at reasonable prices. They would not be forced off the land and into the legion of unemployed. They would not be forced, if staying in agriculture, to exploit their soils for short-run gain.

The policy of income transfer has always required the understanding, or at least the acquiescence, of the general society through the political policymaking process. To achieve some agreement on policy, economists have had to work with various groups across the political spectrum, in which their pursuit of objectivity (which is never fully achieved) is the price to pay for their license to educate and to practice their profession. As a rule, the economist relies on the articulation of various value concepts which serve as a guide in policymaking. What are some of them?

---

[10]Vilfredo Pareto (1848–1923), Italian mathematician, sociologist, and economist, was professor of economics at the University of Lausanne, Switzerland. The Pareto criterion is: "Any change which harms no one and which makes some people better off (in their own estimation) must be considered to be an improvement." From W. J. Baumol, *Economic Theory and Operations Analysis,* Englewood Cliffs, N.J.: Prentice-Hall, Inc., 1961, p. 267.

Justice as a Value underlying Goals There must be some standard of justice that will serve as a guide to policy. We find this first in the American tradition of the work ethic, that a just society will strive to reward individuals and groups according to their specific contributions to society and, at the same time, will offer to each an equal opportunity to be productive. Out of the concept of reward there comes the idea of a fair price, a fair wage, an appropriate level of income, that can be used as a measure of justice, sometimes called commutative justice, as "justice in exchange." The concept of equal opportunity for all persons, without regard to race, origin, religion, political beliefs, etc., to be productive, leads to the concept of distributive justice. The just society will strive to provide both commutative and distributive justice.

Various standards are used to define a "fair" price or "fair" return. In the evolution that started in the 1920s, farm leaders argued that a fair price for farm products was one that bore the same ratio to nonfarm prices as existed in the last five peacetime years from August 1909 to July 1914. This period was not only convenient as a standard but also had been the most favorable to agriculture since the Civil War. The idea of a fair price as a policy goal was argued strenuously throughout the 1920s. In 1929 it was used in legislation establishing the Federal Farm Board to support farm prices. In the Agricultural Adjustment Act of 1933, Congress adopted the idea as a national policy goal, to reestablish agriculture on a parity with other industry, meaning fair prices as suggested in the 1920s. Most of the political activity of farm organizations then centered on support for programs to achieve parity price, or some percentage of it, as a means of obtaining equality for agriculture.

In the second great era of food policy, from the 1920s to the early 1970s, the long struggles over price policy or parity pushed concerns over equal opportunity and distributive justice into the background. The nineteenth century land policies, intending to favor the family farm, had been designed primarily to help provide equal opportunity. Until about the end of the second decade of the twentieth century, expanding employment in industry and the open frontier provided a solution for unemployment, an opportunity for people to escape from a situation in which they felt that they were not obtaining distributive justice—that is, an equal opportunity to be productive. The substantial closing of the frontier, the shock of the Great Depression, and the rise of labor unions, which restricted entry into many of the more attractive occupations, created a new and different situation. Together, they limited opportunities to achieve distributive justice and thus had three effects in respect to agriculture. First, the poor tended to stay in farming. Second, many of those who had left farming returned, especially those who were least well equipped for successful employment and careers outside agriculture.[11] Third, since farming continued to be one of the

---

[11]One study covering 1957–60 showed that there is a very high rate of mobility both from and to agriculture, with the ratio of in-farm movers to off-farm movers averaging about 9 to 10. See Dale E. Hathaway and Brian B. Perkins, "Farm Labor Mobility, Migration and Income Distribution," *American Journal of Agricultural Economics,* Vol. 50, No. 2, May 1968, pp. 342–353.

major sectors with open entry, many without appealing opportunities elsewhere continued to migrate into this sector. This influx resulted in low returns on average to human resources, some concentration of poverty in agriculture and rural society, and many people with an inheritance that could not give them an equal opportunity to be productive.

In the just society, the problem is not only how to define a fair price and select among the measures to achieve it within a given or existing resource structure, thus to achieve commutative justice. The problem is also to define the income distribution that is tolerable and the measures that are appropriate to influence income distribution, thus to achieve distributive justice.

Creeds Underlying Goals[12]   Various creeds underlie the goals of food policy and give meaning to them. Among the most important are the democratic creed, the enterprise creed, and the creed of self-integrity.

The democratic creed rests in two value judgments: (1) that all human beings are of equal worth and dignity, and (2) that no one, however wise or good, is wise or good enough to have dictatorial power over another. It follows, as stated in the Declaration of Independence, that certain rights—life, liberty, and the pursuit of happiness—are inalienable; and, as Lincoln said at Gettysburg, that they are to be achieved through government of the *people,* by the *people,* and for the *people.* If all persons are of equal worth and dignity, all citizens of the democratic republic should have an opportunity for equal voice (e.g., one person—one vote) in shaping the rules that are deemed desirable for the general welfare. Rules of conduct in public meeting and in political debate are based upon this concept, as are some of the concepts of a free press and academic freedom. The democratic creed is a positive force, not just the mere absence of collective restraints on the individual.

The enterprise creed holds that the individual or his or her immediate family is responsible for that person's economic security. Because proprietors are so responsible, they deserve the exclusive right to prescribe the rules under which they shall organize and manage the resources entrusted to them. The prime function of government is to prevent others from forcing the burden of their security on another's enterprise or from infringing on the entrepreneur's freedom to manage. Strict adherence to the enterprise creed restricts the role of government in management or regulation of agriculture but inevitably involves it in matters of organization and protection. The line between these responsibilities is not easy to draw.

The essence of self-integrity is honesty in judgment and relates specifically to the status of dissent. In the case of conflict, an individual or a group has a

[12]For a more extensive discussion, see J. Patrick Madden and David E. Brewster (eds.), *A Philosopher among Economists, Selected Works of John M. Brewster,* Philadelphia: J. T. Murphy Co., Inc., 1970, especially part III, chaps. 5–8; John M. Brewster, "Society Values and Goals in Respect to Agriculture," *Goals and Values in Agricultural Policy,* Ames: Iowa State University Press, 1961; and M. L. Wilson, "Beyond Economics," *Farmers in a Changing World, 1940 Yearbook of Agriculture,* Washington: Government Printing Office, pp. 922–937.

responsibility to seek new modes of thought or new areas of agreement. Consistent with this judgment, the community prizes its dissenting members as sources of new knowledge, and the dissenters feel an obligation to identify themselves so that their views can be considered. A status for dissent is paramount in research and invention. Scientific inquiry is based on hypotheses that certain assumptions or revealed truths do not conform to generally accepted rules. An hypothesis, as a statement asserting an observation or truth and indicating its relevance, is a form of dissent, used in scientific inquiry, by which the researcher may either be proved wrong or discover a new truth. New inventions, new art forms, new songs, new political theories, and new public policies arise out of the status of dissent.[13]

Practically every policy in our study can be traced to the status of dissent. The typical American land policies began with the dissent of the early colonists from the feudal forms of the Old World; and land policy evolved among protests and dissent with various concepts. The typical credit system that serves the food economy in America arose out of dissent, as did the land grant educational system, farm cooperatives, and other institutions. Self-integrity, the power of dissent, is essential in expressing goals of farm and food policy.

Goals for this policy must be integrated with general economic and social goals for America. Moreover, goals need to be made reasonably explicit so that the general public as well as those responsible for administering policy can have greater understanding of the wisdom of a particular goal with respect to long-run as well as short-run considerations.

Means

The means in food policy for America include a wide variety of measures. First, there are things aimed at *growth* and *development,* such as (1) cheap land and cheap credit to reduce the cost of resources or to improve the terms on which they can be acquired; and (2) research, invention, and education to increase the rates of transforming inputs into outputs. These means are concentrated in the input markets. Second, there are measures to affect terms and levels of *compensation,* such as price supports, income payments, export subsidies, and the like—measures largely applying to the product markets. Third, these and other measures, such as income taxes, rules for inheritance, and specific aid to low-income farmers, affect *economic structure.* Fourth, all these and others, such as conservation or other types of forced saving and investment, affect the *environment* and the future of the society. It may be said that the means are developmental, compensatory, structural, or environmental in nature. Some are primarily one or the other. Some are all four at once.

The means of implementing a policy or program should be easily understood, simple to administer, and flexible in regard to local conditions, and the

---

[13]Compare Paul Tillich, *The Courage to Be,* New Haven, Conn.: Yale University Press, 1953, pp. 104–105.

costs or benefits should be consistent with the goals. The testing of means requires analysis of the output of a program in terms of its goals, measurement of program costs in terms of dollars as well as of production forgone (by land retirement, for example), not for just one year but for a series of years for which a program may be adopted. Programs involve costs which, in responsible government, must be examined and weighed in balance against the expected benefits.[14]

A distinction must be drawn between goals and means, even though they are interchangeable (one goal may be a means for achieving another goal). When criticizing a program, one must make clear whether fault is being found with the goal or the means selected for pursuing that goal. There is perhaps more confusion in public discussion on this point than on any other in the elements of policy. In the United States, much of the criticism of the distributional effects of farm price supports and income payments to farmers, for example, which is directed at how the programs operate, could be directed with more meaningful results at the goals inherent in the programs. If a program is to be successful, the equity of the goals must be evaluated as well as the efficiency of the means used to achieve the goals.

Implementers

The responsibility for implementing food policy for America is most often vested in a government department or government-sponsored agency. National policy in food research and education is implemented by land grant colleges, agricultural experiment stations, and extension services, in cooperation with private groups. Private firms, such as seed firms and machinery companies, help to implement development policy in a variety of ways. Price support, conservation, direct payments, and other means are largely implemented by or through a government agency. National farm credit policy is implemented by the federal government through direct loans and services from the Farmers Home Administration (FHA), through lending and other services by the government-sponsored federal land banks, the intermediate credit banks, and the banks for cooperatives, coordinated by the Farm Credit Administration (FCA), and through controls over commercial banking. Although the responsibility for making policy comes from the electorate through the Congress, the Executive, and the Judiciary, the government may delegate the implementation of policy to an agency of its creation, to a semipublic agency, or even to a private agency.

How to implement a policy depends on a number of considerations regarding goal type and cost. Interests may be competing or conflicting; this may be seen in the desires to minimize administrative costs, decentralize political power,

---

[14]This process, sometimes called programming, planning, and budgeting (PPB), is used as a means for helping responsible officials make decisions in respect to setting goals and selecting means for achieving goals. See Charles L. Schultze, *The Politics and Economics of Public Spending,* Washington: The Brookings Institution, 1968, especially chaps. 1 and 2. For further discussion, see U.S. 91st Cong., 1st Sess., 1969, Joint Economic Committee, Subcommittee on Economy in Government, *The Analysis and Evaluation of Public Expenditures: The PPB System, A Compendium of Papers,* Vols. 1–3.

minimize effects of political power on administrative decisions, maximize program flexibility to local conditions, and so on. The increasing importance of coordinating national food policy with other national policies favors a closely structured framework for policy development. At the same time, the political desire to make policy more sensitive and responsive to local conditions and to other felt needs favors communication systems including extension services, advisory committees, farm organizations, and an active free press.

Constraints

The possible constraints include the relevant economic, political, and social conditions within the society where policy must be applied. In a democratic society, the values and beliefs of individuals who will be, or could be, affected by a policy are of critical importance, as are the vested interests of various business organizations and political groups. The limits of national food policy in a democracy, where sooner or later almost everything must be argued in public, are far different from those in a dictatorship or in a country where freedom of expression does not exist. Limits or constraints to food policy are imposed by and through the political system.

Policy is constrained by the state of the arts and sciences, including the stage of economic development, the level of wealth or affluence. What is feasible in the United States differs vastly from what is feasible in a poor country. For several years the federal budget for agriculture included an annual outlay of some $5 billion to $8 billion, much of which was appropriated for purposes of limiting output to achieve prices and incomes more favorable to producers. This is a direction of policy and a scale of program far different from that found in most other countries, particularly in the less developed or developing nations, where policy is—or should be—to increase output. At the same time, America's farm programs impose a lesser burden on the people than is imposed by policy in many other countries. Also, because of higher productivity, the current burden on the American people is less than was imposed by some programs in earlier years. Although one may admit all these facts, the real question for the student of policy is: Can a more desirable policy be developed that is more economical with resources, more conducive to development and protection of the production system, or more equitable?

The most general of all constraints grows out of people's conceptions of need and of alternatives available to them. There is no really coordinated public policy until there is a felt need to do something specific, and until choices are defined and constraints established according to concepts of cost and benefit. In the case of pollution, for example, people have been polluting the environment— air, land, and water—since human life began. As society has developed and become more affluent, human beings have become more proficient in both consuming and wasting—that is, polluting. Policy in regard to pollution control does not become coordinated, however, until we define what is important and appropriately analyze efficiency of alternative programs. All constraints on policy reside ultimately in judgments of those involved.

THE PROCESS OF MAKING PUBLIC POLICY

The process of making public policy in a democracy involves a series of steps.[15] There is first a *felt need,* sometimes a dissatisfaction with the status quo, sometimes a feeling of hurt, sometimes a vision of a more desirable society to arise out of public action. The felt need, as transmitted into goals, may be formulated by a student, a legislator, a concerned citizen, a pressure group. There is then the development of *public awareness.* A goal or vision of a goal does not become meaningful in a democracy until there is public awareness, and then *public acceptance,* of the need for action. Study and *analysis of the alternatives* may involve a group, a research project, the scientist, the engineer, the economist, or other concerned persons. Proposals may be developed in legislative hearings, in group discussions, in the public press. Then bills may be legislated and signed into law, taxes may be levied and appropriations passed, and then—sometimes—the law may be tested in the courts. Where acts require renewal or amendment from year to year, the entire process may be viewed as a continuum, where the issues are merely laid to rest until new conditions or new circumstances require further reappraisal and action.

Such is the process of making food policy for America. The issues are never finally settled. Policymaking in this area resembles a stream or river flowing quietly at times and then becoming agitated, boiling down a narrow gorge or rushing over a precipice to some new outlet. In each area of policy relating to food resources, whether we are speaking of land, credit, human resources, prices, trade, or whatever, new situations are constantly developing, and policy—if it is to be attuned to the times—must be periodically rethought and generally changed in some way. The constant in this process is the need for a broad vision of the society and some analytical rigor in deciding what to do. The process itself narrows and broadens. It goes through various stages. It is constantly dynamic, as a part of life in the democratic experience.

The process of making our nation's food policy has broadened in recent years. In 1968, Ross B. Talbot and Don F. Hadwiger, both of Iowa State University, began their book *The Policy Process in American Agriculture* with the observation that "what was once 'farm politics' has recently become a network which can more accurately be viewed as the politics of food and fiber, relative to production, marketing and consumption. . . ."[16] Subsequently, James T. Bonnen, of Michigan State University, observed that "For decades the U.S. has been evolving from a producer dominated farm policy to an industry oriented total food and fiber policy. In the face of the political crisis generated by current inflation, the farmer and business interests of the food fiber sector are now being subordinated to those of the consumer. In effect, a consumer food policy now

[15]For further discussion, see R. G. F. Spitze, "Searching for the Educator's Role with Public Economic Policy," Urbana: University of Illinois College of Agriculture, *Special Publication No. 30,* March 1974, pp. 77–96.

[16]Ross B. Talbot and Don F. Hadwiger, *The Policy Process in American Agriculture,"* San Francisco: Chandler Publishing Company, 1968, p. xi.

exists . . . the Executive Branch [of the federal government] decision structure for agricultural policy has been transformed probably to some degree permanently. The Council of Economic Advisers, the Office of Management and Budget, the Cost of Living Council, and the Council on Economic Policy now intervene as primary forums within which all economic policy decisions are looked at from various aspects of national interest. This cuts through the classical cabinet agency-clientele dominated decision. Neither agricultural policy nor any other national economic policy decision making process will ever be quite the same again. . . ."[17]

Yet the process of policymaking remains the same in terms of structure. As Talbot and Hadwiger show, it flows from the political decisions of farmers and their organizations, through the ballot box in which all voters may register their choice, to the political parties as an instrument of power, to the strategies and tactics of legislation. It would be wrong to surmise that the executive has the last word. As Bonnen notes, in the absence of strong administrative leadership the Congress becomes more vulnerable to pressures from agricultural commodity groups as well as other interests.

The process of policymaking is not perfect; neither is it enigmatic. Understanding it is an exercise in political economy. We shall approach it as a process of infinite variety in which the task is to discover the goals, the various means, the alternative ways to implement the means, and the constraints that may apply.

LOOKING AHEAD

In looking ahead to the new third era of food policy for America, we face the general problem of finding new ways to answer the three policy questions—what quantities to produce, how, and for whom—so as to bring a more rational consensus on what is good for America and the related world community. We have suggested that a more complete rural-urban interaction is essential. The most rational policy cannot be achieved by appeasement of narrow interests. It must be built on the welfare of the whole.

One of the first tasks is to develop vision in regard to setting food production goals. Chapter 2 is concerned with population and food production in the long-run world view of a century or more as well as in the short view of the next few years. The population growth prospects in the United States and the reasons for changes in these prospects are important in food policy. Policymakers are interested in projections as well as in the theories of population growth and food production alternatives in this country and around the world.

Chapter 3, on influencing food demand, presents a classification of America's agricultural markets, the demand elasticities in domestic and export markets, and the aggregate demand for the nation's farm output. A major part of

---

[17]James T. Bonnen, "A Discussion of the 1973 Economic Report of the President, Implications for Agricultural Policy," *American Journal of Agricultural Economics,* Vol. 55, No. 3, August 1973, p. 397.

production policy is how to relate supply to demand in both domestic and export markets. Through a classification of these markets and study of elasticities, we may begin to approach major questions of how policy influences food demand.

Chapter 4, on increasing food supply, shows how the United States has increased food production. It is also intended to give a broader perspective on production policies and alternatives for the future. It provides an introduction to agricultural land use and to the policies affecting innovations that apply to land— farm mechanization, fertilizers, and farm chemicals. More detail on land policy alternatives are discussed in Chapter 8.

Chapter 5, on making national policy, discusses how the government has become involved in food and farm programs, how various interests impinge on the policymaking process, and how they tend to limit the changes that can be made. This chapter is intended as a lesson in policymaking that has much relevance for the future.

Chapter 6 shows more directly how the farm organizations making policy exert influence on the national scene. It shows how farm organizations evolved out of farm and agrarian discontent and actions of people who wished to change some of the answers, especially those concerning incomes and compensation.

The last five chapters, from 7 to 11, deal more specifically with policies in both factor and product markets. Chapter 7 takes up alternatives in product pricing, management, and trade. Chapters 8, 9, and 10 deal with the markets for agricultural land, capital and credit, and human resources and incomes. Finally, Chapter 11, on coordinating nutrition policy, brings considerations of food and nutrition together.

In summary, there is a system in making public policy. It starts with vision about where we are. It moves into questions concerning goals, or where we want to go. Then there is the process of developing means, implements, and constraints, out of which there arise various concepts of gains and losses, how to get from where we are to where we want to go.

In the next chapter (in fact, throughout the first six), the study tends to emphasize vision: where we are and where we want to go—a necessary prelude to determining how to get there. Our study therefore begins with the problem of setting food production goals in a national and world perspective.

QUESTIONS FOR DISCUSSION

1   What is policy? Who makes policy? How is policy made? Why is food policy important? Who is affected by it?
2   In what ways has the scope of food policy changed in America? Be specific in respect to both the system and the breadth of food policy.
3   It is said that food policy is either developmental or growth-oriented, compensatory, structural, or environmental. Comment.
4   Who has gained and who has lost as a result of scientific progress in American agriculture? Can we say that farmers as a class would be better off or worse off if scientific advance were not to occur? How about consumers in the United States? And those abroad?

5 What are the fundamental values and beliefs that have guided farm settlement in this country? Discuss the concept of the family farm.

6 Distinguish between goals and means. Cite examples of means that may be treated as goals, and vice versa. Is there a hierarchy of goals for food policy?

7 Discuss the values and creeds that underlie food policy for America. Is democracy a value, a creed, a goal, a means, an implement, or a policy constraint? It is said that the essence of democracy is the freedom to dissent. How can dissent be limited without losing this freedom? Comment.

8 Outline the process of policymaking. Trace at least one policy that illustrates this process.

9 What is PPB? How is it used in making policy at the national level? Is it applicable in making food policy?

10 What problems will be most important for food policy in the new third era as compared with the first and the second?

REFERENCES

Bonnen, James T., "A Discussion of the 1973 Economic Report of the President, Implications for Agricultural Policy," *American Journal of Agricultural Economics,* Vol. 55, No. 3, August 1973, pp. 391–398.

Brewster, John M., "Society Values and Goals in Respect to Agriculture," *Goals and Values in Agricultural Policy,* Ames: Iowa State University Press, 1961.

Carter, Harold O., "The 1975 Report of the President's Council of Economic Advisers: Food and Agriculture," *The American Economic Review,* Vol. 65, No. 4, September 1975, pp. 533–538.

Farrell, Kenneth R., "Public Policy, the Public Interest, and Agricultural Economics," *American Journal of Agricultural Economics,* Vol. 58, No. 5, December 1976.

Griswold, A. Whitney, *Farming and Democracy,* New York: Harcourt, Brace and Company, 1948.

Spitze, R. G. F., "Searching for the Educator's Role with Public Economic Policy," Urbana: University of Illinois College of Agriculture, *Special Publication No. 30,* March 1974, pp. 77–96.

Talbot, Ross, B., and Don F. Hadwiger, *The Policy Process in American Agriculture,* San Francisco: Chandler Publishing Company, 1968.

Wilson, M. L., "Beyond Economics," *Farmers in a Changing World, 1940 Yearbook of Agriculture,* Washington: Government Printing Office, pp. 922–937.

Setting Food Production Goals

To get land's fruit in quantity
Takes jolts of labor evermore,
Hence food will grow like one, two, three . . .
While numbers grow like one, two, four . . .

Anonymous
Song of Malthus: A Ballad of Diminishing Returns

In the broadest vision, the new third era of farm and food policy will be dominated by food production goals emphasizing food abundance and stability in supply. First, food demand in our affluent socity will be strong and stable in comparison with the historical record. Additionally, the federal government has moved, perhaps politically irreversibly, into a system of food subsidy for low-income consumers through food stamps and other means. Second, pressure to maximize exports of food, especially grains, is increased by the projected high and ever rising demand of the nation for oil, natural gas, and nonenergy minerals. Someone has coined the phrase for this trade as "food for crude." Third, the prospects for high population growth in the developing countries—sometimes called "less developed countries" (LDCs)—will bring strong pressure for food aid as well as for more economic aid in support of their development.

These factors must be taken into account in setting food production goals, and weighed in the balance. Our purpose in this chapter is to view them in a time perspective—as short, intermediate, and long-term—and to consider goals relative to prospects in production, population, world trade, and food aid. Thus we will gain perspective in the broad choices for food policy.

GOALS IN THE SHORT AND INTERMEDIATE TERMS

Food production goals are always difficult to set in the very short term, such as the next year or two. A nation's policy, moreover, must be designed with two ends in view. One is to provide some kind of cushion for the unpredictable changes in crop production and trade, thus to counteract uncertainty in food supplies and prices. The other is to set some kind of goal in an intermediate term, such as a decade or so, that will serve as a guide to agricultural planning and development.

Experience Shows the Need for Food Production Goals

The period from the early 1960s to the mid 1970s illustrates the need for food production goals that allow for uncertainties in the market. The Kennedy administration, coming to power in January 1961, reaped the legacy of policy from the 1950s, when crop surpluses had built up in government storage as a result of price supports under ineffective control programs. By the early 1960s, more than 80 million tons of feed grains, sufficient for about six months of normal feeding, were being carried over from one crop year to the next, largely in government-financed storage. The wheat carryover, at its peak on July 1, 1961, was 1.4 billion bushels, more than the average of annual production for the previous five years. The cotton carryover at the beginning of the season, although more than doubling between the early 1960s and the peak carryover in 1966, equaled about 80 percent of normal mill consumption. There were large stocks of butter, dried milk, and several other products in storage.

These stocks were not planned. For eight years the Eisenhower administration had tried to prevent their buildup, largely because of the government expense involved. But, in spite of the backlog, farm income was not at a satisfactory level. The goal of the Kennedy administration was to contain and reduce these stocks while supporting farm income by more effective production-control programs and direct payments to cooperating farmers.

By the mid 1960s, however, another situation was thought to prevail. Policymakers in the United States Department of Agriculture (USDA) and elsewhere sensed impending catastrophe as they surveyed existing and anticipated food shortages in various countries. Much of this shock was engendered by successive crop failures caused by the unusually light monsoon rains in India and other parts of South Asia, and the situation was aggravated by crop failures elsewhere. To some it appeared that widespread famine was here.[1] A greatly

---

[1]"Famine is Here," *The New Republic*, Sept. 18, 1965.

stepped-up food aid program from the United States seemed imperative.[2] The President's Science Advisory Committee viewed the world's emerging food problem as one of frightening proportions. Consequently, it presented an imposing picture of food production goals, recommending large-scale food aid from America, accelerated economic development in the populous developing counties, and more emphasis on birth-control programs.[3]

Then the situation changed again. More abundant monsoons in South Asia coincided with rapid introduction of new wheat varieties and new and improved production practices. The immediate outlook for food became more heartening. The United Nations Food and Agricultural Organization (FAO) implied, in its *State of Food and Agriculture* for 1969, that the main policy problem of the future might be managing the surplus rather than overcoming shortage.[4] Production in the developing countries was sufficient to compensate for the growth in population. The immediate need for food aid dropped off and farm exports continued low. A guardedly optimistic view of the world food problem was offered, assuming that the developing countries would make best use of known food production technologies.[5] Capital transfers from the advanced countries would be required for development and food aid for the most critical situations. In the United States, by the fall of 1970, farm product prices had fallen to the lowest levels, relative to nonfarm prices, that had existed since the 1930s. The nation's policymakers worried anew about rising food surpluses, depressed farm prices, and the high costs of government programs.

Scarcely more than a year later, however, just as these worries were gaining new force, the situation changed again. The United States government, attempting to maintain a fixed exchange rate between the dollar and other major currencies, which progressively overvalued the dollar in international trade and depressed farm exports, was faced with sharply rising trade deficits. In August 1971 the dollar was devalued with respect to gold. This and subsequent devaluations reduced the prices of U.S. farm exports in currencies of other countries, thus encouraging purchases of more food from the United States, especially in Western Europe and Japan.[6] Additionally, in 1972, the Soviet Union, plagued by a series of poor wheat harvests and committed to a policy of improving the Soviet diet, decided to purchase grain internationally; it began to buy 30 million tons, 18 million of which would come from the United States. Also in 1972, the monsoons in India and Pakistan brought less rainfall than usual. The Peru fish catch, an important source of protein in the international markets, declined

[2] James Reston, "Fight 'Em or Feed 'Em," *The New York Times,* Feb. 11, 1966.

[3] The President's Science Advisory Committee, *The World Food Problem,* Washington: The White House, May 1967.

[4] FAO, *The State of Food and Agriculture, 1969,* 1970, pp. 1–3.

[5] See Willard W. Cochrane, *The World Food Problem: A Guardedly Optimistic View,* New York: Thomas Y. Crowell Co., 1969; and review by Marion Clawson in *American Journal of Agricultural Economics,* Vol. 52, No. 2, May 1970, pp. 341–342.

[6] See G. Edward Schuh, "The Exchange Rate and U.S. Agriculture," *American Journal of Agricultural Economics,* Vol. 56, No. 1, February 1974, pp. 1–13.

precipitously. Drought and typhoons slashed the rice and corn crops in the Philippines. The Peoples Republic of China bought wheat from Canada. The Australian wheat crop was a poor one. A severe drought in the broad region of Africa south of the Sahara desert, called the Sahel, then more than six years in duration, continued. The newly formed nation states prevented large-scale migration, and some 15 to 20 million people in this vast region faced undernourishment and starvation unless large amounts of food could be brought to them.

In the spring of 1973, as United States food stocks were drawn down to levels barely sufficient to fill marketing channels, farm prices rose to unprecedented heights. Cropland diverted from crop production was reduced from 63 million acres in 1972 to 19 million in 1973; and for 1974 the national food production goal was that agriculture should produce at near full capacity. Then came the oil crisis and a dawning realization that food production in all industrialized countries would become more expensive. Short-term food production goals would have to be tempered by these higher costs. The distaste for farm surpluses was displaced by the grimmer fear of food shortages.

The lesson for food policy is that the on–again, off–again food surpluses and shortages do not provide the desired stability in domestic food prices, the necessary assurance for continued high-level commercial farm exports, or a reliable basis for emergency food aid programs. The concepts and goals that were used are a weak basis for food policy. They must be replaced by other concepts and goals.

Intermediate-Term Goals: Programming and Uncertainties

For more than 50 years, agricultural economists in the United States have been projecting the farm outlook as a basis for planning and policy; in the latter part of this period, they have projected both a short-term and an intermediate-term perspective. In the mid 1960s, for example, it was projected that on the basis of known farm technology, with trend increases in use of fertilizer and other purchased inputs, and with no substantial change in aggregate crop acreage, by 1980 total farm production would be 60 percent above the 1957–59 base.[7] About 165 million acres were being used for wheat and feed grains, with around 55 million acres being withheld from crop use. There were another 150 million acres that would move into grain production under long-term favorable prices.[8] If trends in crop yields, livestock productivity, and domestic food demand were projected, and additionally, if cropland idled by government programs were returned to use, American exports could be equivalent to 180 million acres of grain, or slightly more.[9] Based on a floating dollar, farm exports could reach $18

[7]Rex F. Daly and Alvin C. Egbert, "A Look Ahead for Food and Agriculture," *Agricultural Economics Research,* January 1966.

[8]L. M. Upchurch, "The Capacity of the United States to Supply Food for Developing Countries," *Alternatives for Balancing World Food Production and Needs,* Ames: Iowa State University Press, 1967, pp. 215–223.

[9]Martin E. Abel and Anthony S. Rojko, *World Food Situation: Prospects for World Grain Production, Consumption and Trade,* USDA, Foreign Agriculture Economic Report 35, 1967.

billion annually in terms of 1971 prices, with a net trade surplus from agriculture of more than $9 billion.[10] At current prices, the net surplus could be still larger.

Assuming trend increases in aggregate food consumption in America and no government acreage diversion, and with the availability of good cropland being the main limiting factor, a detailed linear program was drawn up. It revealed that, between 1965 and 1980, exports could increase some 2½ times for wheat, feed grains, oilmeals, and cotton, as follows:[11]

	Domestic use		Exports		Acres required	
	1965	1980	1965	1980	1965	1980
	(in millions)		(in millions)		(in millions)	
Wheat (bushels)	587.0	720.0	867.0	2,157.0	49.3	88.7
Feed grains (tons)	130.0	154.0	29.0	70.0	99.0	94.4
Oilmeals (tons)	17.0	20.0	11.0	37.0	34.6	58.6
Cotton (bales)	9.5	10.5	3.0	6.8	13.6	9.7

In this program solution, specific assumptions or requirements included an increase of 187 percent in the total use of farm capital, which emphasizes the still growing commercialization of American agriculture and its still increasing dependence on purchased inputs. But the total labor requirement for farm work would be reduced by 31 percent under these requirements, and the reduction would be about the same even if no land were diverted and the higher levels of exports were not achieved. This decline in labor needs highlights part of the problem of declining employment in rural labor markets, with the resulting hardship resting most heavily on low-income families and unskilled rural workers.

The specific solutions that are reached through linear programming do not eliminate the uncertainties inherent in setting intermediate-term goals, however. These solutions depend on estimates of changes in the input factors used in production, and policymakers must also take account of prospects in food consumption and demand. The type of uncertainty that must be faced in setting policy goals is well illustrated in the "Report of the Panel on Nutrition and the International Situation" in the U.S. Senate *National Nutrition Policy Study, 1974.*[12] Quoting a projection published by the USDA's Economic Research Service (ERS) for 1975, "the world's capacity for production of cereals will increase faster than consumption and there could be a rebuilding of grain stocks, downward pressure on prices, or possibly programs to restrict production in the

[10]USDA, Foreign Agricultural Service estimates. See *Forbes* magazine, "Can Agriculture Save the Dollar?" March 15, 1973, p. 32.

[11]Earl O. Heady, Leo V. Mayer, and Howard C. Madsen, *Future Farm Programs, Comparative Costs and Consequences,* Ames: The Iowa State University Press, 1972, pp. 50, 74, 80, 81. Feed grains are measured in terms of corn equivalent, including a small amount of wheat used as feed. Oilmeals include soybeans and cottonseed measured in terms of soybean equivalent.

[12]See *National Nutrition Policy Study, 1974,* Hearings, Select Commitee on Nutrition and Human Needs, U.S. Senate, 93d Cong., 2d Sess., June 19–21, 1974, Part II, pp. 279–371.

major exporting countries, or some combination of these. . . ."[13] The FAO, in contrast, believed that, while world food production would expand faster than the demand and while aggregate world grain supplies might be adequate, the developing countries—unless they increased their production much more rapidly than in the past—might need to import in an average year as much as 80 to 100 million tons of grain a decade hence. Some members of the Senate Panel on Nutrition viewed the relative stringency in food supplies in 1974 as more permanent in nature. Lester Brown, most notably, viewed the events of the early 1970s as the signal of a fundamental shift in the structure of the world food economy. The inability to achieve further technological breakthroughs in critical areas was emerging as a serious constraint on expansion of food supplies. For the first time in modern history, the world was facing short supplies—that is, uniquely simultaneous constraints—of all four of the critical resources in world food production—land, water, energy, and fertilizer.

In addition, a number of climatologists were expressing the belief that the earth had entered an adverse weather cycle with meteorological conditions comparable to those that dominated the planet from 1600 to 1850. If true, this could mean reduced agricultural production from widespread drought, as in Russia, the Sahel, and Western Europe, or from other regional conditions adverse for crop production. There was a consensus among climatologists that from the beginning of the 1930s to the early 1970s the world had experienced some 40 years of abnormally warm weather which was generally favorable to crop production. A shift to another phase in a transitional trend of a few years would typically bring greater temperature variability and other extremes in rainfall and crop conditions. Over several centuries the earth has experienced various short-term weather cycles of a few years and longer-term trends of a century or more.

The implication for our farm and food policy is that we did, and do indeed, face new uncertainties in regard to world food demand and the future costs of important food-producing inputs. Wider margins for error must be allowed in setting intermediate-term production goals. Abundant crops must no longer be looked upon as a national liability, as they were in the 1950s and 1960s. Instead, marketing, storage, and trade policies must be designed to prevent abundant crops from depressing farm income; these crops must be converted into positive benefits yielding satisfactory farm incomes, stable food prices at home, and a dependably substantial supply for export in trade and aid.

Goals in Food Trade and Commodity Reserves

The projection of a goal involving a large trade surplus in food and other agricultural products becomes even more critical to the United States balance of payments position, according to the economic analysts. They suggest (1) that American industry has lost much of its early postwar advantage over Western Europe, Japan, and Russia in manufacturing efficiency and technology; and (2)

---

[13]*Ibid.*, p. 280.

that, confronted by a growing demand for imports of both fuel and nonfuel minerals, a considerable export surplus in other goods will be required for a balanced trade position. In respect to the continuing energy shortage, the demand for petroleum and natural gas will increase by 60 percent between 1970 and 1980, or double between 1970 and 1985.[14] It has been suggested that to satisfy the demand for oil on the basis of a trend development in the petroleum industry, as much as $18 billion of oil imports at 1972 prices will be required by 1980.[15] Additionally, according to Department of Interior estimates, United States imports of all nonfuel minerals, costing $6 billion in 1971, will rise to $20 billion by 1985 and to $52 billion by the turn of the century.[16] The alternatives are increased domestic production and restricted use.

On a basis of such estimates, it is possible to project the goal of a very large trade surplus in food and agricultural products. Contributions of agricultural commodities to the United States balance of payments averaged about $1 billion a year from fiscal 1964 through 1971. The margin widened as agricultural exports rose from $5.7 billion in fiscal 1969 to $6.7 billion in 1970, to $7.8 billion in 1971, to $8.1 billion in 1972, to more than $12 billion in 1973, and to more than $20 billion from 1974 on. These gains were nearly all in commercial sales, as government program–financed sales remained at about $1 billion per year. The trade surplus in agricultural products rose to $3 billion for 1972 and then increased more rapidly to near the $10 billion level from 1974 on. The expansion was mainly in wheat, feed grains, and soybean products to Japan, Western Europe, and the U.S.S.R. with smaller increases elsewhere. By 1975, exports included more than half the wheat and rice crops, almost half the soybean crop, a third of the cotton and tobacco, and a fourth of the corn and grain sorghums. As was predicted, this required a substantial shift in production goals.[17]

The new trade position not only required the most substantial change in crop production goals since World War II. It also showed the necessity of shifting other world trade patterns on a more permanent basis toward further expansion of industrial exports from the developed countries that have a deficit in both food and minerals, and toward high-level exports of food and industrial products from the United States to pay for the anticipated growth in our mineral imports. Continued prosperity for American agriculture and the nation at large requires a more permanent shift in food policy away from national goals emphasizing limits of the domestic market. A policy must be developed to integrate the immense capabilities of American agriculture with the needs of both the developed food-deficit countries and the still larger potentials of the developing countries. Such a

[14]Michael Rieber and Ronald Halcrow, *U.S. Energy and Fuel Demand to 1985: A Composite Projection by User within PAD Districts* [*Petroleum Administration for Defense Districts*], University of Illinois at Urbana-Champaign: Center for Advanced Computation, CAC Document No. 108, Jan. 25, 1974.

[15] *Forbes* magazine, March 15, 1973.

[16]Nicholas Wade, "Raw Materials: U.S. Grows More Vulnerable to Third World Cartels," *Science,* Vol. 183, Jan. 18, 1974, pp. 185–186.

[17]Carol G. Brunthaver, "U.S. Agriculture Gears for Foreign Trade," *Foreign Agriculture,* Vol. XI, No. 10, March 5, 1973, p. 3.

goal structure has been expressed eloquently before.[18] What is new is the growing immensity of the population problem, the realization of stringency in energy and other minerals, and the necessity of balancing world trade at higher and more stable levels.

Although more liberal trade policy reduces the need for food reserves in various countries because the available supplies will move more readily to markets, the experience of the last decade illustrates the need for a more stabilizing policy for food reserves than one of such extremely wide shifts from shortage to surplus. The problem cannot be solved by one nation alone, although the goals established in the United States will be most critical for domestic consumption as well as for export. Various questions of the goal type must be answered. How large are the reserves that are required? Where shall reserves be held? What rules shall be followed in managing the reserves, and will farmers or consumers control them—and through what agencies of government? We will see, when examining commodity programs, that farm surpluses have accumulated largely as a result of price support programs rather than food reserve policy. This will no longer suffice. Goals in food trade and food reserves must be integrated with food production goals for the intermediate term.

Goals in the future will be more influenced by consumer interests than by strictly producer interests, as in the past. This means that programs to limit farm output or farm inputs will receive more resistance than formerly. Growth and development, within certain environmental constraints, will become more important under the envisioned conditions. The consumer's voice will remain strong as long as demand presses against supply.

A reasonable assumption must remain, however, that the discipline of the pre-1971 economic model of agriculture with surplus food has not been entirely discarded. Until some other result is demonstrated, the prudent analyst must assume that the overriding goal of an abundant food supply, with some reserve to spare, will sometimes depress farm product prices below what is acceptable to farmers, or below what is equitable or desirable for a balanced economy. To prevent such a consequence, there must be a clearly defined policy for management of food supply and distribution within goals of both abundance and equity. The basis for such policy must be considered further in respect to population growth.

LONGER-TERM GOALS RELATED TO POPULATION GROWTH

Population growth and prospects for growth are one of the basic factors in setting longer-term goals. In this respect, a world vision or perspective, as well as a national perspective, is required. In world perspective in the long term, the population-food question may well be the biggest problem ever to confront the human race. Only about one-third of the world's population, very largely in the

---

[18]See, for example, *The Annals of the American Academy of Political and Social Science,* Vol. 331, September 1960, "Agricultural Policy, Politics, and the Public Interest." Charles M. Hardin was special editor of this volume.

economically advanced or more developed countries, can be assured an adequate food supply from conventional agriculture. The remaining two-thirds of the world's people, chiefly in the late-developing countries, have at the present no such long-run assurance. Population is increasing at a rate sufficient to tax all food resources. Diets are deficient, nutritively speaking, and at best improvement comes slowly.

Population in Historical Perspective

As seen in historical perspective, the current world population picture is unique in regard to the numbers of people on the planet and the magnitude of their growth potential. Both the numbers and the potential are very large; and, because of these large magnitudes, plus the associated problems of government, no one can say with a comfortable degree of certainty whether we are near the brink of a colossal disaster or whether we are approaching the millenium of civilization's most shining hours. In the past 150 years, world population has increased about fourfold. In a little more than 200 years, it has increased about sevenfold. Under one set of population growth curves and food supply assumptions, it can be shown quite clearly that population growth will soon—before another century, perhaps before the end of another generation—far outstrip possible food resources. Thus, catastrophic starvation may result. Under another set, it can be shown with equal clarity that the population, production, and ecological problems of most nations are, with some foresight, intelligence, and effective policy, readily manageable. The food supply of most nations can become more adequate and more nutritious. The millennium of happiness and benign government can come to the people of a community of nations operating under universal law and well-recognized policy. This can be humanity's most shining hour, when many more people than ever before will live in peace, with improved nutrition and comfort, and increasing longevity.

The conditions that we are approaching, our closeness to them, and the magnitudes of change are yet to be determined. The first condition—colossal disaster—will result from immutable projection of recent trends. It is clear from projections of trends from 1960 to 1980 that most developing countries have a widening food gap or deficit, and that, in nearly all of them, food reserves sufficient to stabilize food consumption between good and bad crop years have not been maintained.[19] But with recommended changes in policy, the second condition—the millennium of humanity's greatest progress—is, in the view of this study, also possible. Part of the necessary conditions involves two sets of policies that must be appropriately developed and applied. One set must take account of population growth, theories, and policies relating to growth and control. The other must deal with future food resources and the policy options for expanding food production and trade. In the philosophical tradition of classical economics, the assumption is that the course of future events is not

---

[19]From an unpublished M.S. thesis by William C. Kokontis, "Grain Reserve Alternatives for Developing Countries." University of Illinois at Urbana-Champaign, 1975.

predetermined but can be influenced systematically by deliberative choice, that is by public policy.

World Population Growth

The present population growth experience is unique in history in regard to both the numbers of people involved and the potentials for growth. Although the human race—Homo sapiens—has existed for 3 or 4 million years, it was only in the time between the two continental glaciers, from 150,000 to 50,000 years ago, that men and women with chins, small brow ridges and small facial skeletons, and high, flat-sided skulls, probably appeared on earth.[20] From a few individuals in that era, numbers grew to between 4 and 5 million about 15,000 years ago. Then, in the Thai region of Southeast Asia, a primitive agricultural revolution began.[21] This was followed about 5,000 years later, or 10,000 years ago, by revolutionary developments in the area of the Tigris and Euphrates.[22] This, and later developments in China, in other parts of Asia, and around the Mediterranean carried the human population to about 250 million persons by the time of Christ. Then, further growth, spectacular by ancient standards but minuscule by those of the present, curtailed by all sorts of communicable deseases and other dangers, carried the population to about 400 million by the year 1000. But it took more than 700 years to add the next 100 million and to reach ½ billion slightly before 1750.

About 1750 or a little earlier, a new growth trend began in Europe, preceded about 50 years before by a new surge in China. The new European trend was related to rudimentary advances in the medical sciences, to expanding employment in the industrial revolution, and to development of new food resources in the New World as well as the Old. Although there was little improvement in working conditions, the population of Europe about doubled between 1750 and 1850. Apparently, it would have grown much more except for some of the deliberate checks on population growth. Often people married late in life and many did not marry at all. There are evidences of infanticide, and sometimes children did not survive because of neglect, abuse, and abandonment. Migration to the New World was a significant although minor restraint on European population growth. Then, starting about 1750, total population about doubled, to reach the first billion about 1830. The second billion was added in just 100 years, from 1830 to 1930. The third billion was added in just 30 years, by 1960. The fourth required only 15 years, to 1975. The fifth, according to reliable projections, will take about 10 years, to 1985. The sixth and the seventh billion could be reached around the year 2000, with a suggested range, as of that date, between

[20]Edward S. Deevey, Jr., "The Human Population," *Scientific American,* Vol. 203, No. 3, September 1960, pp. 195–204; and William W. Howells, "The Distribution of Man," *ibid.,* pp. 113–127.

[21]William G. Solheim II, "An Earlier Agricultural Revolution," *ibid.,* Vol. 226, No. 4, April 1972, pp. 34–41.

[22]Robert J. Braidwood, "The Agricultural Revolution," *ibid,* Vol. 203, No. 3, September 1960, pp. 131–148.

Table 2-1   World Population, 1970, Year 2000 Estimates, and Potential under Assumed Conditions

(In millions)

	Population			Potential under assumed conditions*		
	1970†	2000‡		Present diet	Better diet	Adequate diet
		Medium estimate	High estimate			
Less developed regions	1,749	3,523	3,936	4,378	4,180	3,825
Communist Asia	879	1,761§	1,986§	1,354	1,127	952
Developed regions	1,073	1,441	1,574	1,441¶	1,441¶	1,441¶
World	3,701	6,725	7,496	7,178	6,748	6,218

*Present diet is that projected for 1970 in the World Food Budget 1970; better diet assumes a minimum adequate caloric level; adequate diet assumes minimum adequate calories and proteins.
†Estimates from the AID-USDA Demand Studies.
‡Estimates by F. W. Notestein based on United Nations 1963 and 1966 projections in *Overcoming World Hunger,* American Assembly. Medium estimates assume some success in population control measures; high estimates assume straight-line growth rates at current levels.
§Estimates by F. W. Notestein, *ibid.,* assuming a population growth rate projected for South Asia, 2.3 percent per year to 2000 (medium projection).
¶These estimates are the same as United Nations figures for year 2000; a much larger population could be supported by food production capacity now available in these countries.
Source: USDA, Foreign Economic Development Service, cooperating with the Agency for International Development, *World Food–Population Levels,* Report to the President, April 9, 1970. U.S. Department of State, April 1970, table 1, p. 3.

6.7 billion and 7.5 billion persons. These trends can be visualized as three logarithmic growth curves (Figure 2-1), as an arithmetic growth curve since 8000 B.C. (Figure 2-2), or as a projection for major world regions (Table 2-1). What levels will future population reach?

Some Reactions to the Population Surge

Reactions to the great population surge range from expressions of concern over the alternatives for national food policy to outright alarm. Among knowledgeable persons who have sounded the tocsin are William and Paul Paddock, who projected the specific date of 1975 when a new food crisis would strike many nations in "awesome proportions." By 1975, they argued with evidence, skill, and cogency, many of some 100 or so countries in the world "will have lost the capability, even with massive American food aid, to feed themselves." The United States is "the sole hope of the hungry nations. . . . Yet the United States, even if it fully cultivates all its land, even if it opens every spigot of charity, will not have enough wheat and other foodstuffs to keep alive all the starving. *Therefore,* the United States must decide to which countries it will send food, to which countries it will not."[23]

Biologist Paul R. Ehrlich, in *The Population Bomb,* argued that "each year

[23]William Paddock and Paul Paddock, *Famine—1975! America's Decision: Who Will Survive?* Boston: Little, Brown and Company, 1967, pp. 4, 200, and 206.

Population

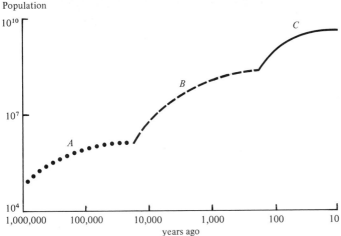

Figure 2-1 Concept of the human population on logarithmic scale. *(Source: Edward S. Deevey, Jr., "The Human Population," Scientific American, September 1960, p. 198.)*

food production in undeveloped countries falls a bit further behind burgeoning population growth, and people go to bed a little hungrier. While there are temporary or local reversals of this trend, it seems inevitable that it will continue to its logical conclusion: mass starvation. . . ."[24] Again Ehrlich, with Anne H.

[24]Garrett DeBell (ed.), *The Environmental Handbook,* New York: Ballantine Books, Inc., 1970, p. 219.

Population
(billions)

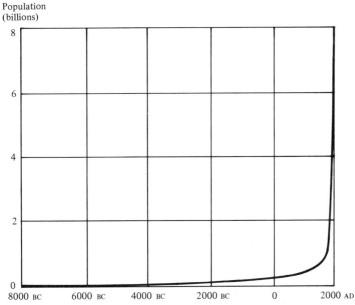

Figure 2-2 Concept of the human population on arithmetic scale. *(Source: Edward S. Deevey, Jr., "The Human Population," Scientific American, September 1960, p. 198.)*

Ehrlich, in *Population, Resources and Environment, Issues in Human Ecology,*[25] warned of the catastrophic consequences of some of the population growth trends and argued for the most stringent measures for birth control to reach levels of zero population growth (ZPG) in the near future. Former United States Senator Joseph D. Tydings, in his book *Born to Starve,* flatly asserted that "mankind is breeding itself into oblivion,"[26] and Ehrlich, in a foreword to the Tydings book, set a theme by asserting:

> No crisis faced by human beings in the four million or so years our species has walked the earth has approached the magnitude of the population-resource-environment crisis which is now upon us. Skyrocketing numbers of human beings, inadequate food resources, disappearing mineral resources, and deterioration of the ecological systems upon which all human life depends are combining in a series of interactions which pose a threat to every man, woman and child on this planet. . . . If mankind is to be saved, an unprecedented change in human attitudes will be required.

Sociologist Alvin Toffler, in the runaway best seller *Future Shock,* warned of the societal implications of accelerating change, of which the population explosion is a part.[27] Not only do people need to adjust their thought processes, value systems, and life styles to the reality of such change. The success or failure to do so will determine whether people will build more desirable societies or whether society itself will degenerate, or sharply decline, in ways that cannot be entirely foretold.

The System Dynamics Group at the Massachusetts Institute of Technology, in *The Limits to Growth,* concluded that "if present trends in world population, industrialization, pollution, food production, and resource depletion continue unchanged, the limits to growth on this planet will be reached sometime within the next 100 years. The most probable result will be a rather sudden and uncontrollable decline in both population and industry capacity."[28]

In a number of computer print-outs of the earth's ecological system, it was suggested that future levels of per capita food production, industrial output, and pollution are predictable. With no major change in the physical, economic, or social relationships that have historically governed the development of the world system, food production per capita will reach a peak shortly after the year 2000 and then decline sharply. Total population will reach a peak perhaps 25 or 30 years later and then decrease as the rapidly diminishing resource base forces a slowdown in industrial growth. Population growth will finally be halted and the world's population will decline through a rise in the death rate due to decreased

[25]San Francisco: W. H. Freeman and Company, 1970.

[26]Joseph D. Tydings, *Born to Starve,* New York: William Morrow & Company, Inc., 1970, p. 3.

[27]Alvin Toffler, *Future Shock,* New York: Random House, Inc., 1970.

[28]Donella H. Meadows, Dennis L. Meadows, Jørgen Randers, and William W. Behrens III, *The Limits to Growth: A Report for the Club of Rome's Project on the Predicament of Mankind,* a Potomac Associates Book, New York: Universe Books, 1972, p. 23.

food and medical services. But, if a number of measures are taken to recycle certain resources, control pollution, prolong the life of capital, restore and conserve soil, and eventually reach zero population growth, the equilibrium level of food consumption per capita can be maintained far above 1970 base-year levels; then industrial output per capita can be sustained indefinitely into the future at some 3 times the 1970 world average. Thus, "It is possible to alter . . . growth trends and to establish a condition of ecological and economic stability that is sustainable far into the future. . . . If the world's people decide to strive for this second outcome rather than the first, the sooner they begin working to attain it, the greater will be their chances of success."[29]

The Future Compared with the Past

Although the future will differ from the past importantly in the magnitude of population growth and the nearing exhaustion of nonrenewable mineral resources, many of the ideas have a familiar ring. Since late in the eighteenth century students, scientists, and others have doubted the future adequacy of the world's resources to sustain the growing population at desired levels of living. The first to gain lasting fame for his discussion of the subject was Thomas Robert Malthus. In 1798, during the first wave of rapid growth in Europe, he expressed what he called the "principle of population," the belief that "the power of population is infinitely greater than the power in the earth to produce subsistence for men."[30] The two postulates supporting the principle were: first, that food and sexual passion are both essential to human existence; and second, that, while food increases only in arithmetic ratio, population, unchecked, increases in geometric ratio. Malthus advocated moral restraint, that is, chastity, and late marriage.

Malthus did not go unheeded. Throughout many countries in Western Europe people married relatively late, and rather large proportions of the population did not marry at all. Birthrates generally ranged from 32 to 38 births a year per 1,000 total population, which was low compared with the rates in most other countries, although higher than in modern developed countries. Emigration to the empty Americas served as a safety valve, but it was not really very important in the total picture. Throughout Europe's nineteenth-century era of technological development, population grew by about 1 percent per year. Repeal of the Corn Laws (England's tariff on grain imports), following the arguments of Ricardo,[31] generally helped to usher in the worldwide development of the British Empire, consistent with the growth of commerce and industry on the European continent.

Still, even a 1 percent population growth in the most advanced countries was cause for some alarm. In 1898, almost exactly 100 years after Malthus's great

[29]*Ibid.,* p. 24.
[30]Thomas Robert Malthus, *On Population,* edited and introduced by Gertrude Himmelfarb, New York: The Modern Library of the World's Best Books, 1960, p. xix. The first edition (1798) was followed by a much larger edition in 1803. That edition was the basis of all later editions, of which six appeared in Malthus's lifetime, and a seventh posthumously.
[31]David Ricardo, *Protection to Agriculture,* London: John Murray (Publishers), Ltd., printed by William Clowes, 1822.

book, Sir William Crookes, president of the British Association for the Advancement of Science, keynoted his presidential address with the observation that
England and all other civilized nations stood in deadly peril of not having enough
to eat. The problem of food supply would be a life-and-death question for
generations to come.

So it is. In a number of alarmist tracts, some published shortly after World
War II, the hypothesis is presented that the population growth projected for the
future will exhaust the world's resources, most importantly those for food.[32] The
question of food sufficiency was also appraised in respect to population trends and
food production potentials in less alarming but still serious views.[33]

The great surpluses generated by American agriculture in the 1950s and
1960s, and the general return of normalcy to most of the world's agriculture,
apparently quieted some of the most disturbing fears. But not for long. The
question of food supply has now returned full force. It is not just one of physical
potential, but also one of costs. What are the economic, technological, and
institutional prospects in food production? What will be America's role in the
world food economy?

PROSPECTS IN THE WORLD FOOD ECONOMY

That the vast population upsurge has been more than matched by counterweight-
ing advances in world food production is attested in the voluminous statistics of
the Food and Agriculture Organization of the United Nations (FAO).[34] From the
1952–1956 period, when presumably agricultural recovery from World War II
was far advanced, to 1971, the world index of food production per capita moved
up 15 points. But this gain was not evenly divided between the rich and the poor
nations, or the developed and the developing countries. The increase in the
former was 32 points while the latter increased by only 6 points. Moreover, the
developing countries, after about 1960, showed scarcely any appreciable upward
trend. Small declines in food production per capita in Tropical Africa (only
slightly affected by the war in Nigeria) were offset by modest increases elsewhere. The index of aggregate world food production based on 100 in 1952–56,
stood at 161 in 1971. It was 160 in the developing countries, but their higher rates

[32]The following are listed as examples: E. Parmalee Prentice, *Food, War, and the Future,* New
York: Harper & Brothers, 1944; Frank A. Pearson and Floyd A. Harper, *The World's Hunger,*
Ithaca, N.Y.: Cornell University Press, 1945; Fairfield Osborn, *Our Plundered Planet,* Boston: Little,
Brown and Company, 1948; William A. Vogt, *Road to Survival,* New York: William Sloane
Associates, 1948. For further discussions, see C. Lester Walker, "Too Many People," *Harper's*
magazine, February 1948, pp. 97–104; Guy Irving Burch, "Conservation and Population," *American
Forests,* Vol. LV, No. 11, November 1949.

[33]Merrill K. Bennett, in a balanced, scholarly study, shows that the food and nutrition problem
in the early 1950s did not give credence to projections of disaster. See Bennett, *The World's Food; A
Study of the Interrelations of World Population, National Diets, and Food Potential,* New York:
Harper, 1954. See also, John D. Black and Maxine E. Kiefer, *Future Food and Agricultural Policy, A
Program for the Next Ten Years,* New York: McGraw-Hill Book Company, 1948, and Theodore W.
Schultz (ed.), *Food for the World,* Chicago: The University of Chicago Press, 1945.

[34]Data from *Monthly Bulletin of Agricultural Economics and Statistics,* Rome: FAO, various
issues.

of population growth offset the gain in the index of total production, resulting in practically no gain in food production per capita either then or through the 1970s.

The dimensions of the world food problem have been more specifically revealed in a series of world surveys conducted under the auspices of the FAO and the U.S. Department of Agriculture. The first of these surveys was issued in July 1946, within a year of the founding of the United Nations. As a background to this report, it may be recalled that World War II was a major watershed in world history. It saw the emergence of a new set of super powers, with the European states, temporarily at least, relegated to a secondary position. It also saw the emergence of a so-called Third World, the great band of largely tropical countries in Africa, Latin America, and Asia, including the population giants, China, India, Pakistan, and Indonesia. This Third World emergence took a number of forms—political independence for some nations, a growing concept of humanitarian need, and a general introduction of medical and sanitary advances that dramatically lowered death rates, contributing almost immediately to a substantial change in the world population growth curve. The formation of the FAO was followed shortly by development of the United States–financed European Recovery Plan, the Marshall Plan. Then came a broadening of United States foreign aid to Third World countries, which culminated in passage of the Agricultural Trade Development and Assistance Act, Public Law 480, in 1954.[35]

The first *World Food Survey,* purported to cover 70 countries and 90 percent of the world population, established the analytical pattern that has been followed in all subsequent surveys by the FAO and the U.S. Department of Agriculture.[36] In it a distinction is drawn between undernourishment and malnutrition. Undernourishment is generally accepted as such a deficiency in total calorie intake that a person cannot maintain normal bodily activity without losing weight and eventually dying. Malnutrition is a lack or deficiency of one or more of the protective nutrients—proteins, vitamins, minerals. The FAO method required the establishment of a food balance sheet based on estimates of food available to various sectors of a country's population and then a comparison of this per capita availability with accepted levels of nourishment and desired nutrition. The survey presupposes the existence of statistical data and a knowledge of food habits.

The *Second World Food Survey* was published in 1952[37] and the *Third*

---

[35]This act and its later modifications set the stage for a massive food aid program. From 1955 to 1966 a total of $15.7 billion of farm products were exported under Public Law 480. Another $2.2 billion was exported under mutual security programs. The total of $17.9 billion under these two programs compares with total farm exports of $61.2 billion during the same period. USDA, *12 Years of Achievement Under Public Law 480,* ERS, Foreign 202, Washington. Although Public Law 480 continued, recovery rates under it (including commodity costs in the United States, ocean transportation, export payments, and other costs) rose from 60 percent in 1965 to 69.5 percent in 1966, to 80.9 percent in 1967, and to 84.7 percent in 1968. Leo V. Mayer, "Estimated Net Costs of P.L. 480 Food Aid with Three Alternative Farm Programs," *American Journal of Agricultural Economics,* Vol. 54, February 1972, p. 49.

[36]FAO, *World Food Survey,* Washington: July 5, 1946.

[37]FAO, *Second World Food Survey,* Rome: November 1952.

World Food Survey in 1963.[38] The third, largely the work of Dr. P. V. Sukhatme, director of FAO's Statistics Division, covering some 80 countries and 95 percent of the world's people, concluded that "while the world food consumption level has improved over the last decade, up to half of the world's population is still hungry or malnourished or both." The study, consistent with the FAO's general data, reiterated that most of the gains in output per capita had occurred in the developed areas, whereas increases in agricultural productivity in the less developed areas were barely sufficient to maintain approximate prewar consumption levels. The U.S. Department of Agriculture, in studies entitled *The World Food Budget,* has revealed somewhat similar trends.[39]

Trends in trade between the developed and the developing countries highlight the latter's difficult problems. The developing countries were net food exporters before World War II of about 11 million tons of grain annually. By 1957–59, the net inflow had increased to about 13 million tons annually. By 1961, the net was 20 million tons, and by 1964 about 25 million. Then, with the severe droughts in India and other parts of southern Asia, imports rose rapidly. But, when food shortages became acute in these countries again in the early and mid 1970s, stronger food demands were also being felt in other developed countries including the U.S.S.R., and food aid was not so readily available. As starvation spread across the African Sahel and eastward into parts of Ethiopia, food aid from America, although greater than from all other countries combined, was little more than a trickle. In 1974 the United States Congress appropriated $100 million especially for aid to this region, whereas some 15 to 20 million people were estimated to be in acute stages of undernourishment and malnutrition. Other large populations facing critical food shortages, Bangladesh, for example, received very little food aid despite the known shortages.[40] In this case, however, the United States had to curtail its very modest aid program because of the inadequacy of grain storage and transportation in the recipient country.

The lesson for policy is that unless there are substantial new steps in development of a world food emergency-reserve program, including reliable large-scale financing, neither the short-term nor intermediate-term deficits of developing countries will be offset by food aid. The world population will not share uniform catastrophe, however, such as suggested in *The Limits to Growth.* Instead, unless food production is greatly accelerated, populations in large areas in the developing countries will not reach earlier suggested levels (such as in Table 2-1), but will cease to grow, because of either undernourishment and starvation or more regulated birth controls to achieve eventual zero population growth.

Although some have argued that only a global approach with appropriate

[38]FAO, *Third World Food Survey,* Freedom from Hunger Campaign Basic Study No. 11, 1963.

[39]USDA, *The World Food Budget, 1962 and 1966,* ERS, 1961, and *The World Food Budget, 1970,* ERS, 1964.

[40]See *War on Hunger,* A Report from the Agency for International Development, Washington: July 1975.

global actions can obviate such regional catastrophes,[41] at the present stage of world political development the makers of food policy may have to settle for something less, such as intergovernmental agreements among the nation states and cooperative financing of food programs, perhaps through the World Food Council formed in 1974. Broad world agreement will in the end prove critical, but regardless of how soon it is achieved, the setting of the longer-term production goals for the United States will be influenced by decisions concerning food aid, which in turn depend on food production prospects in developing countries.

Production Prospects in the Developing Countries

In the developing countries, although many have tended to interpret the problems in terms of the earlier experience of now developed countries, the situations are not parallel. The area of cropland per person is shrinking more rapidly than it did in the now developed countries at a similar stage in their development. Population growth rates are far higher than they ever were in the developed countries. The opportunities for emigration, such as those in Europe in the nineteenth and early twentieth centuries, are not available to the developing countries on any comparable scale. Most importantly, although the modern scientific and management technology now used in the advanced countries is available for export to the developing countries, the results of the attempts to transfer this technology have been largely disappointing. Many developmental projects have failed for want of education and technical knowledge, cheaper farm inputs, or more efficient food marketing and processing.[42]

Economic incentives, such as higher prices for farm products or lower prices for fertilizer and other farm inputs, must be introduced to enable farm people to transform traditional agriculture into more productive, more profitable enterprise;[43] and, as part of this program, the supporting infrastructure of farm service and food marketing industries must be developed. Great breakthroughs must occur in the developing countries to reduce the costs and increase the availabilities of capital inputs to all food sectors. Furthermore, marketing systems must be improved.

That the developing countries can supply more adequate diets, or even diets equal to the present low levels, may be regarded as a working hypothesis rather than a reasoned conclusion. In June 1970, a panel, organized as part of the Sixth Annual Meeting of the Association of U.S. University Directors of International Agricultural Programs and meeting at the University of Illinois, responded to

[41]Mihajlo Mesarovic and Edward Pestel, members of the Club of Rome, in *Mankind at the Turning Point*, New York: Dutton/Reader's Digest Press, 1975.

[42]See William Paddock and Elizabeth Paddock, *We Don't Know How*, Ames: The Iowa State University Press, 1973.

[43]For further discussion on this point, see Theodore W. Schultz, *Transforming Traditional Agriculture*, New Haven: Yale University Press, 1964; and *Economic Crises in World Agriculture*, Ann Arbor: The University of Michigan Press, 1965. See also Arthur T. Mosher, *Getting Agriculture Moving, Essentials for Development and Modernization*, New York: Frederick A. Praeger, Inc., 1966, for the Agricultural Development Council.

three questions: What are the major trends in agricultural production in the major world regions? What are some of the prospects for increased productivity in the next 25 to 30 years? What are the prospects for rising nutritional levels, taking into account prospective population increases?[44]

Anthony M. Tang, speaking of China and the Far East and drawing on the Japanese experience from 1880 to 1940 as a model applicable to the developing countries, suggested that the answer "may not be very reassuring to the developing nations. . . . Under today's demonstration effects on the consumption side and population growth rates prevalent in the developing nations, agricultural development of the Japanese historical pace will fall short of the requirements."[45]

John W. Mellor, speaking of India and East Pakistan (now Bangladesh), suggested that there is "concern as to whether the present rate of accelerated growth [in agricultural output] can be maintained. In West Pakistan, where growth was extremely rapid for a short period of time, there are clear signs of leveling off and there are some signs that the rate of growth in India is also leveling off after an initial surge."[46]

William O. Jones responded to the series of questions by speaking of 31 independent countries and 3 colonial territories in Tropical Africa. He said:

> My response to the first question, "What are the major trend lines in agricultural productivity in this important region?" is that they are discouraging.
>
> To the second question, "What are some of the prospects for increased productivity in the next 25 or 30 years?" I would say the possibilities are very good; the prospects, I think, rather poor.
>
> The third question is "What are the prospects for rising levels of nutrition, taking into account prospective population increases?" It might surprise you to have me say I think they are rather good.

The essential characteristic of almost all these African countries, according to Professor Jones, was a rather remarkable development in the first half of this century in the form of steady and very rapid increases in production of agricultural crops for export. Generally, except for coffee, this trend has not continued. Jones concluded, "If you examine the present policies for agriculture in the African countries, I find some encouraging spots that are cheering. I cannot find any overall achievements that are cheering. I find depressing the policies that are being advocated generally."[47]

Lowell S. Hardin, speaking of Latin America, said:

[44]Harold G. Halcrow (panel chairman), Anthony M. Tang, John W. Mellor, William O. Jones, Lowell S. Hardin and Charles B. Shuman, "Secondary and Tertiary Effects of Agricultural Development," in *Association of U.S. University Directors of International Agricultural Programs, Sixth Annual Meeting,* University of Illinois, Urbana-Champaign, June 1970, pp. 5–25. George K. Brinegar shared responsibility for organization of this panel.

[45]*Ibid.,* p. 5.

[46]*Ibid.,* p. 9.

[47]*Ibid.,* p. 12.

Most of the increased agricultural output in Latin America is still a matter of geographic expansion. What are the prospects? Technically, given the quality of human and physical resources that Latin America possesses, prospects for improvement are good. Output per person could rise substantially. I think that the bottleneck is structural; it pertains to matters of public policy. This has to do with price relationships, exchange rates, and investments in the agricultural sector, which I think will be determining. Public decisions taken will determine whether or not that which is technically possible will in fact be achieved . . . to keep up with three percent population growth rate is no small achievement."[48]

The task of achieving the desired continuing increases in the developing countries is formidable.[49] Walter P. Falcon estimated that in Asia, for example, 1969 wheat production exceeded the 1960–64 average by 30 percent and rice exceeded the 1963–67 average by 18 percent; and that in 1968–69, only about 9 percent of the rice land and only about 23 percent of the wheat land was in improved varieties. In his opinion, "There are important reasons to believe that continued rapid rates of adoption in additional areas are unlikely."[50] A first major constraint consists of the low limits thus far on adequate and controllable water supplies. The new plant varieties in most situations require controlled irrigation. Without that control, fertilizer provides only a low return. Without new seeds and fertilizers, the possibilities for increase in crop output have distinct limitations.[51] A second major constraint in Asia has been inadequate pesticide programs in most countries and an inherent difficulty in controlling migratory pests in much of the prevailing system of small land holdings.

Nearly all social scientists who are knowledgeable about development problems in the developing countries now increasingly stress at least three or four policy requirements:[52] First is the great need for expansion of agricultural research and education through long-term institutional programs. It has been viewed as wholly inappropriate that, as of 1965, only 11 percent of the world's publicly supported agricultural research was undertaken in developing areas of the world—Latin America, Africa, and Asia, excluding Japan and the Peoples Republic of China—that contained at least half the world's population. Second, the recommended research should not be limited just to improving farm production but should include designs to improve storage, transportation, and marketing, and programs to develop effective and acceptable methods for controlling

[48]*Ibid.,* p. 13.

[49]Compare, for example, "The Green Revolution: Second Generation Problems," discussion by Vernon W. Ruttan, Walter P. Falcon, Randolph Barker, Carl K. Eicher, Lowell S. Hardin, A. T. Mosher, David Hopper, John H. Schnittker, Quentin M. West, Eldon D. Smith, William K. Gamble, Dale W. Adams, Peter Dorner, John W. Mellor, G. Edward Shuh, Kusum Nair, Wyn F. Owen, *American Journal of Agricultural Economics,* Vol. 52, No. 5, December 1970, pp. 698–722.

[50]*Ibid.,* p. 699.

[51]S. C. Hsieh and V. W. Ruttan, "Environmental, Technological, and Institutional Factors in the Growth of Rice Production: Philippines, Thailand, and Taiwan," *Food Research Institute Studies,* Vol. VII, No. 3, 1967, pp. 307–341.

[52]See *National Nutrition Policy Study,* 1974, Hearings, Select Committee on Nutrition and Human Needs, U.S. Senate, 93d Cong., 2d Sess., June 19–21, 1974, part II, p. 281.

rodents, insects, crop diseases, and similar problems. Third is the need to spread opportunities for more equitable income distribution. As Kusum Nair has aptly remarked, "In a developing agriculture, it is not the aggregate increase alone that counts. Its breakdown in terms of the spread of production opportunities, resources and income is equally important."[53] In other words, structural transformations are required. Fourth is the problem of achieving adequate food reserves solely to meet emergency human needs in the developing countries. It has been recommended that the costs of such reserves should be borne by all the industrial nations and not just the major exporters; that the size of the reserves should be related to the probabilities of shortfalls in grain output of developing countries; and that the reserves—or the system of reserves—should be owned by individual governments subject to international agreement on the total amounts to be accumulated, the distribution among countries, and the rules for release.[54]

Structural Transformations Required

Hayami and Ruttan have concluded:

> It is clear that output per worker in the several LDC's can be increased by several multiples, while land area per worker remains constant or even declines slightly. To achieve increases of this magnitude will require substantial investment (*a*) in rural education and (*b*) in the physical, biological and social sciences . . . for the invention, development and extension of more efficient agricultural technology. It will also require the allocation of substantial resources to the production of the technical inputs supplied by the industrial sector, by which new technology is carried into agriculture. By and large, these changes achieve the higher levels of output per worker through increases in output per unit area.[55]

Dovring states:

> A more discouraging aspect . . . is that . . . it will be necessary to increase output per unit area with technologies that reduce the labor input per unit area. Significant reduction in labor input per unit area is likely to occur, however, only in those economies in which urban-industrial development is sufficiently advanced to absorb not only the growth in the rural labor force but also to permit a continuous reduction in employment in rural areas . . . this has occurred in Japan only since World War II. In most LDC's it seems likely that the agricultural labor force will continue to expand more rapidly than the nonagricultural demand for labor from rural areas.[56]

[53]Kusum Nair, "The Green Revolution: Second Generation Problems," *op. cit.*, p. 720.
[54]*National Nutrition Policy Study, 1974, op. cit.*, pp. 285, 286.
[55]Y. Hayami and V. W. Ruttan, "Agricultural Productivity Differences among Countries," *The American Economic Review*, Vol. 40, No. 5, December 1970, p. 907.
[56]F. Dovring, "The Share of Agriculture in a Growing Population," *Monthly Bulletin of Agricultural Economics and Statistics*, FAO, August–September 1959, p. 1–11 (quoted from Hayami and Ruttan, p. 907).

Bruce F. Johnston, of the Food Research Institute at Stanford University, and Peter Kilby, of Wesleyan University, have presented the most thorough study of the structural transformations required for an increased supply of food and for economic development in the less advanced countries.[57] They concentrated on the reciprocal interactions between agricultural development and the expansion of manufacturing and other nonfarm sectors. Poverty is a distressingly persistent problem and it is importantly farm-related. Earlier views that rapid industrialization would soon transform these economies have been discredited in the past 25 years. Although the late-developing countries can draw on the great knowledge of technology that is now available, a successful development strategy will have to avoid the pitfalls of inappropriate technology transfer, especially too heavy reliance on developments that are highly capital-intensive.

An interdependence between agriculture and the rest of society must be recognized in development of policies (1) to transfer investible resources—capital and labor—from agriculture to the faster-growing nonfarm sectors, and (2) to maintain a rate of farm productivity advance consistent with constant or falling urban consumer food prices. Since a high percentage of the total population in these countries is in farming, a policy that is successful in achieving sustained economic growth will be vitally concerned with the rates of labor transfer between the farm and nonfarm sectors, the levels of commodity flows, and their composition. Generally, the proportionate size of the agricultural labor force will fall slowly; and for many years—in some cases many decades—the absolute size of the farm labor force will grow. The volume of inter-sectorial commodity flows can be raised only as the weight of the agricultural population in the total is reduced. The progressive modernization of millions of small-scale farmers is clearly a formidable task.

Implications of the Changing Role of Fisheries[58]

As we have moved into the new third era of food policy, the role of fisheries in the world food economy, as well as the role of farming, has changed significantly. Until late in the second era, the oceans were viewed as an almost limitless source of protein. From 1950 to 1970, the world fish catch climbed steadily from 21 to 70 million tons annually, more than tripling during the 20-year period. Then, in spite of the increased efforts of the leading fishing nations, the catch declined for three years in a row; in general, this appeared to be true in fisheries as widely separated as the cod and haddock fisheries in the Northwest Atlantic and the anchovy fishing along the western coast of South America. The Peruvian anchovy fishery, the world's richest, yielded as high as 12 million tons annually in the late 1960s but then fell precipitously to scarcely 3 million tons in 1973. From there, recovery appeared to come slowly. The growing dispute between Great Britain and Iceland over the right to fish off the banks of Iceland empha-

[57]Bruce F. Johnston and Peter Kilby, *Agriculture and Structural Transformation, Economic Strategies in Late-Developing Countries,* New York: Oxford University Press, 1975.
[58]This section draws on the prepared statement of Lester R. Brown, *National Nutrition Policy Study, 1974, op. cit.,* pp. 322–339, and related sources.

sized another strain in the fish economy. Disputes arose between the United States, Russia, and Japan over efforts to control fishing in the North Pacific and, even more significant, between Russia, the United States, and Canada over fishing rights in the Grand Banks off Newfoundland.

Because of overfishing occuring in the scarcely concealed condition of anarchy under which the oceans have been fished, many marine biologists now believe that the global catch of table-grade fish is at or near the maximum sustainable level. The yield of several of the most preferred fish species has declined drastically and, in various areas, some of the most valuable species of fish and whales have been practically wiped out. Many of the 30 or so leading species of commercial-grade fish may be severely overfished, so that replacement stocks will not sustain the level of fish catch reached in the late 1960s.

The changing role of the world's fisheries has various implications for food supplies in a number of countries and for America's food policy goals. In 1970, the aggregate world fish catch averaged about 40 pounds live weight of fish per person, of which about 60 percent was fish of table grade and the remaining 40 percent was inferior species processed mainly for fish meal, used most importantly for livestock, poultry, and pet food in the developed countries.

But a world aggregate fish catch that does not increase, and thus declines relatively as the human population increases, has different implications country by country. In the United States, consumption of table fish (live weight) averages only about 14 pounds annually, in contrast with (1971 data) 50 pounds of poultry, 73 pounds of pork, and 117 pounds of beef (dressed weight). In Japan, fish consumption averages about 70 pounds annually, as a result of the traditional fish and rice diet. The main source for displacing fish in the Japanese diet is importation of soybeans, mainly from the United States. After World War II, as Soviet agriculture apparently failed to keep pace with food demand, the Soviet government turned increasingly to ocean fisheries as a major source of protein. The Soviet consumer's consumption of table fish is believed (the data are not available) to average at least double that of the American consumer. Several other countries depend heavily on fish as a direct source of protein but, among the developed countries, the Japanese and the Soviets appear to be most vulnerable to the relative declines in the yield of table fish. Consumers in the United States will be less affected.

Although a number of major world conferences under the United Nations and related agencies have attempted to develop agreements and international controls over the exploitation of ocean resources, and although some agreements have been reached to regulate fishing in disputed areas of the ocean, no general agreement has been forthcoming, Whaling, which not only destroys the most valuable species but also is exceedingly cruel, has not been controlled. Japan and the U.S.S.R. especially have resisted all international efforts at control. A world fisheries authority, which may be the ultimate solution, does not appear to be acceptable. We conclude, therefore, that although new agreements are possible, they are not likely to be effective for some time to come. The yield of world fisheries is not apt to increase unless there are both more efforts in development of fish culture and a major breakthrough in international control of fishing.

If the world fish catch has reached its zenith or is declining, the increased demand for protein must be met by agriculture, aquaculture or fish farming, or processing of algae. The last two are of minor importance, generally. In America, catfish and trout, raised under induced conditions, have become important, but the total yield still amounts to only a few ounces per person annually. Therefore, the chief implication of a stable world aggregate or a declining per capita world fish catch is to project the increase in demand for protein to the countries that are major soybean, feed grain, and livestock producers. This probability then becomes an additional factor of increase in demand for food exports from America.

As we mentioned earlier, however, food production around the world is only one of the factors to take into account in setting production goals in food policy for the United States. For a more comprehensive view, we must also recognize the possibilities for population growth and its control before turning to other matters.

POSSIBILITIES FOR POPULATION GROWTH AND CONTROL

Food production goals for America depend not just on the population and production trends but on how these may be made to vary. What accounts for changing fertility levels? For variation in growth patterns? Is there a built-in feedback situation that results in adjustments in family size according to a demonstrable economic theory or hypothesis?

America's Population and Growth Prospect

In the United States it is now demonstrated that fairly minor shifts in average family size can have significantly profound effects on the size of the nation's population. To illustrate, the United States census of 1970 recorded 204.7 million persons living in this country. At then current rates of increase, about 2 million per year were being added. It has been estimated[59] that women who were 35 to 39 years of age in 1970–71 will have borne about 320 children per 100 women by the time they complete their childbearing role. If this pattern were to continue in the next generation or two, the United States would add another 100 million people by 1997, reaching about 315 million by the year 2000! On the other hand, women who were 55 to 64 years of age in 1970–71, and who thus had lived much of their early adult life in the Great Depression, bore only 221 children per 100 women. This latter pattern, if adopted by oncoming generations, would bring the nation to nearly stationary growth in the next generation, to about 250 million by 2000 and about 275 million people by 2037.[60]

In fact, the twentieth-century birthrate in the United States looks something like a section of descending roller-coaster track: high in the early part, sinking during the twenties and thirties, rising during the forties and fifties but not so high

[59]See Calvin L. Beale, "100 Million More People Coming Up?" *A Good Life for More People, 1970 Yearbook of Agriculture,* Washington: Government Printing Office, pp. 2–7.

[60]Ben J. Wattenberg, "The Decline of the American Baby—Whatever Happened to the Population Explosion?" *World,* Aug. 29, 1972, pp. 20–23.

as earlier, and sinking again in the sixties and seventies. In 1958, after eight successive years of climbing, the general fertility rate turned downward. The annual rate fell from 120 births per 1,000 women aged 15 through 49 in 1958, to 110 in 1960, to less than 100 in 1963 for the first time in 20 years, to less than 90 in 1967, to below 80 for a six-month period in 1971, to 75 in the first quarter of 1972, the lowest rate in the nation's history,[61] and continued on down to new record-breaking lows in 1973 and later years.

Although the wide fluctuations in birthrates prevent accurate projections of future population levels in the United States, the current campaigns for zero population growth, the growing popularity of birth-control systems, the legalization of abortion, and general economic theories in regard to childbearing which we will shortly examine, all suggest that birthrates will trend lower in the last quarter of the twentieth century. If this assumption proves to be accurate, there are at least two generalizations of pertinent interest to our study.

First, in general, as the Commission on Population Growth and the American Future has concluded, is that:[62]

1 Major economic changes are on the horizon regardless of future changes in population growth rates.
2 The nation has nothing to fear from a gradual approach to population stabilization.
3 From an economic point of view, a reduction in the rate of population growth would bring important benefits, especially if the United States develops policies to take advantage of the opportunities for social and economic improvement that slower population growth would provide.

Second, however, in regard to food policy for America, the demand for food will increase less, solely because of lower domestic population growth, than appeared to be the case during most of the postwar years up to the early 1970s. Although demand will increase on a per capita basis as the level of real income continues to rise, this increase in demand will be proportionately less than the increase in real income. Given the anticipated growth curves in farm output, the terms of trade (farm prices in contrast to nonfarm prices) will swing against agriculture unless the export market is greatly expanded or unless more stringent controls are placed on farm production. American agriculture must have an expanding export market or it will experience some combination of lower prices, production controls, and consumer food subsidies. The possibilities are examined in Chapter 3.

Crude Birthrates in Other Countries

Although the population explosion in the United States (if there ever was one) is over, it is not so overseas. Although most birthrates are still lower in Europe than

---

[61]Donald J. Bogue projected a median population for America of 245 million people in the year 2000. See Bogue, *Principles of Demography,* New York: John Wiley & Sons, 1969. Reviewed by Dudley Kirk, *American Journal of Agricultural Economics,* Vol. 52, No. 1, February 1970, p. 168.

[62]*Population and the American Future: The Report of the Commission on Population Growth and the American Future,* Washington: Government Printing Office, 1972, p. 38.

in America and are just slightly higher in Japan, elsewhere birthrates are still high. In Latin America, most of Asia, and Africa, the crude birthrate (number of births per 1,000 population) ranges between 30 and 40 per 1,000, compared with a 15 to 20 range in the United States, Europe, and Japan. In many developing countries, however, the crude birthrate dropped significantly between 1960 and 1970; for example, in South Korea, from 41 to 31, in Taiwan, from 40 to 28, in Chile, from 35 to 17, in Egypt, from 40 to 37, in India, from 45 to 42, in China, from 40 to 37, and in Brazil, from 40 to 37.[63]

Thus, although birthrates are still comparatively high in most developing countries, the situation and outlook are changing. Whether or not birthrates will drop sufficiently in the last quarter of the twentieth century to enable these countries to improve their low levels of per capita food consumption cannot be foretold. In some combination still to be determined, birthrates will have to drop much lower, farm output will have to expand much more, or food imports will have to be increased substantially over what they were in the first three decades following World War II.

Economic Analysis of Fertility

It is evident that the birthrate in all developed countries is falling and that this trend, which was interrupted by temporary increases after World Wars I and II, as well as in the United States after the Civil War, has been operative for 100 years or more. There is an inverse relationship between life expectancy and the number of children per family. Although there is no satisfactory theory of all factors affecting birthrates and death rates and hence no complete theory of population growth, considerable progress has been made in explaining differences in fertility within an economic framework.

Within such a framework, T. W. Schultz has suggested that parents' decisions concerning family planning are affected by at least four relevant considerations. These are (1) the development of parents' views of what is optimum for investment of human capital in each child, such as education or training; (2) views as to the amount of time they wish to spend in raising children; (3) the positive values they place on having children; and (4) their general view of the role of the family, including both consumer choices and production decisions in bearing and raising children.[64]

Investment in human capital, involving decisions on family size, rests on the proposition that parents tend to equate the anticipated costs of their children and the benefits. The costs are of two sorts: the opportunity cost of the parents' time in bearing and rearing the child, and the cost of commodities and services in the form of food, clothes, shelter, health care, and schooling. The benefits are the psychic utility of the child, which is largely intangible, and the child's more

---

[63]FAO data.

[64]Theodore W. Schultz, "The Value of Children: An Economic Perspective," *Journal of Political Economy,* Vol. 81, No. 2, part II, March–April 1973, pp. S2–S13; and Theodore W. Schultz, *Economic Research: Retrospect and Prospect; Human Resources,* Fiftieth Anniversary Colloquium VI, National Bureau of Economic Research, New York 1972, distributed by Columbia University Press, New York and London, pp. 52–58.

tangible returns to the parents' living or real income. Parents then have a demand for children based on anticipated benefits; and they have a supply function that is related to the anticipated costs. The optimum size family is defined by the intersection of the demand and supply functions.[65]

As an economy develops, the child's tangible contributions to the parents' real living generally declines. So, to the extent that demand for children depends on the anticipated tangible benefits to the parents, their demand for children declines. Also, with an improving economy, the opportunity cost of the parents' time rises. Other opportunities become more attractive both because of the goods and services offered by the society and because of the rising value of other consumption or productive activity available to the parents. Although tangible costs of commodities and services also rise, they generally decline relative to income. Nevertheless, the supply function of children per family for the economy in general is thought to be restricted.

This formulation can lead to a number of policy propositions. If a population control problem is thought to exist, demand for children can be weakened by providing alternative sources of the parents' security, such as old-age pensions,[66] public health care, and unemployment insurance. Opportunity cost can be increased, or supply restricted, by providing equal, or at any rate, greater opportunity for women in the labor market and by removing or reducing taboos on working wives.[67] Other means of increasing supply cost, such as reducing or eliminating income tax credits for the third and each succeeding child, have more negative welfare effects.

Although many of these policy options are not generally available in developing countries, T. W. Schultz asserts that "economic explanations of completed fertility in widely different populations, using essentially the same theoretical approach, reveal comparable empirical results. . . ."[68] Increased education and increased earnings, and therefore rising opportunity costs and rising real income, result in lower fertility rates. In the developed countries, declining fertility rates are correlated with growing prosperity, improved education, greater economic security, and overall improvement in the quality of life. The same is true for minority groups as for majorities, and there is growing evidence that the generalization applies to countries in mid-stage of economic development as it does to developed countries.

Fertility rates respond to the economic incentives and penalties imposed by

[65]T. Paul Schultz, "An Economic Model of Family Planning and Fertility," *Journal of Political Economy,* Vol. 77, March–April 1969, pp. 153–180, and T. Paul Schultz, "A Preliminary Survey of Economic Analysis of Fertility," *The American Economic Review,* Vol. 63, No. 2, May 1973, pp. 71–78.

[66]Philip Neher suggests the provision of pensions for such purposes in P. A. Neher, "Peasants, Procreation, and Pensions," *The American Economic Review,* Vol. 61, No. 3, June 1971, pp. 380–389.

[67]Marianne Abeles Ferber, "Peasants, Procreation, and Pensions: Comment," *ibid.,* Vol. 62, No. 3, June 1972, p. 451.

[68]Theodore W. Schultz, *Economic Research: Retrospect and Prospect; Human Resources,* p. 56.

society. Education and growing prosperity reduce demand for children by reducing the child's contribution to the parents' level of living and security. In countries that do not have pensions, health insurance, unemployment compensation, and the like, however, the poor have little security without children. Demand for children is high and can be reduced only by providing alternative forms of security. In all countries, the opportunity cost of having children is less for poor people than for the not so poor; and an improvement in the general level of living is expected to reduce birthrates. Thus, in the United States in the late 1960s, birthrates in families with incomes of less than $5,000 per annum declined by over 15 percent more than did the rates for the rest of the society.[69] The poor still had a higher birthrate but the discrepancy was disappearing.

Economic-Sociocultural Analysis of Fertility

As discussed by Leibenstein,[70] the fall in fertility is a consequence of modernization associated with a number of related influences depending heavily on reduction of the *desired* fertility. A partial list includes the following: (1) the rise in education of women and the consequent change in their role and values; (2) the increase of female participation in the nonfarm labor force and the consequent reduction of the importance of the childbearing role; (3) sustained reduction in infant mortality rates; (4) a decline in religious beliefs that formerly supported high fertility norms; (5) urbanization with its alternatives to traditional patterns; (6) the increase in compulsory education and the decrease in the value of child labor; (7) increases in the rights of women and changes in their role outside the home; (8) weakening or alteration of the extended family system; (9) introduction of superior contraceptives; (10) development of old-age and other security systems outside the extended family; and (11) increases in social mobility.

The economic-sociocultural theory of fertility takes account of the competition between the budgetary demands of expenditure of time and other resources on children versus pressures for other expenditures as the *social* and *economic* circumstances change in the course of economic development. Human beings create standards for themselves and others. A population is divided into sociocultural groups which influence target living standards and family-size preferences. Each household in a sociocultural group belongs to a social influence group (SIG) which helps to create achievable *common* standards for its members involving commitments that household members make to themselves and to others. Each SIG has a different representative household income and a *target* standard of consumption for some important class of goods, including children. Interhousehold competition and emulation put an upward drift on commitments to family members. For the economy as a whole, the changes in fertility will

---

[69]From a statement by John R. Meyer, President of the National Bureau of Economic Research, in *The Report of the Commission on Population Growth and the American Future, op. cit.,* p. 159.

[70]Harvey Leibenstein, "An Interpretation of the Economic Theory of Fertility: Promising Path or Blind Alley?" *Journal of Economic Literature,* Vol. XII, No. 2, June 1974, pp. 457–479.

depend on the degree to which SIGs are open or closed and the movement of households among SIGs.

Implications for Policy

Economic theory and SIG analysis suggest that as countries develop economically and socially, birthrates fall and become more variable. As modern nations have developed, population growth rates have become increasingly responsive to changing economic conditions and to a wide range of conditions bearing on what is called the quality of life. The United States experience is most instructive on this point.

In regard to long-term goals for food production, the effects of lower birthrates are cumulative over time. The abortion revolution in this country is one unpredictable factor imposed on an already declining birthrate.[71] Japan, the largest single importer of American farm products, stands out among developed nations in its demonstration of the practical limits of a population abortion policy. As late as 1965, one of the most authoritative scholars cited Japan as having the characteristics of a time bomb even though the government, for more than a decade, had been carrying out a stringent population control policy.[72] Now, it appears, in America and in many other countries, that greater acceptance of family-planning ideas—sometimes but not necessarily including abortion—plus the declining economic advantages of children, will result in substantially lower birthrates.[73]

In the long term, which embraces our third policy era, world food requirements will shift more heavily toward the late-developing countries. Additionally, the emphasis on diet improvement in the U.S.S.R. and some other European countries, the Middle East, China, Japan, and others will tend to shift some of the older traditional trade patterns. As a study by Stephen Schmidt has concluded, the expanding livestock industries in some countries may widen the outlets for surplus grain supplies, both domestic and foreign; and it seems possible that future feed-grain production will be extended into areas formerly under wheat.[74]

In the third era of food policy for America, these prospects tend to displace the more pessimistic outlook for agricultural trade, which grew out of the trade restrictions imposed by developed countries, including tariff and trade restrictions by the United States, and by the disappointing slow economic growth of the

---

[71]See Lawrence Lader, *Abortion II: Making the Revolution,* New York: Beacon Press, 1973; Arlene Carmen and Howard Moody, *Abortion Counseling and Social Change,* New York: Judson Press, 1973; and "Planned Parenthood of New York City," *Abortion: A Woman's Guide,* New York: Abelard-Schuman, Limited, 1973.

[72]Georg Borgstrom, *The Hungry Planet, The Modern World at the Edge of Famine,* New York: The Macmillan Company, chap. 9, "Japan—The Time Bomb."

[73]For further discussion, see A. S. Parks, "Human Fertility and Population Growth," in *Population and Food Supply,* Cambridge, England: Cambridge University Press, 1969.

[74]Stephen C. Schmidt, *East-West Trade in Wheat: Present and Potential,* University of Illinois at Urbana-Champaign, Department of Agricultural Economics, Agricultural Experiment Station, AERR 121, September 1973.

developing countries. These had led to conclusions that, given world trends in production and consumption, potential surpluses of cereal supplies would outstrip effective demand at 1971–72 prices by some 62 million tons by 1980, with exportable supplies from the United States alone reaching some 46 million tons by 1980.[75] The subsidy and protection of agriculture in developed countries were of questionable benefit to the sectors that were the most protected.[76] In America, under assurance of stable prices, farmers were applying larger quantities of fertilizer, herbicides, and other nonfarm inputs than would otherwise by used. In Western Europe and Japan, where grain and rice prices were supported at levels from 100 to 300 percent above world price levels, uneconomic investments of long-term nature were encouraged as well as heavy use of fertilizer and other purchased inputs. American officials who were involved in trade negotiations were most concerned with restrictions placed on imports by the countries of the European Community (EC), the enlargement of the EC by the addition of four countries, and the possible further restrictions of trade through a common agricultural policy (CAP).[77]

Although many of the pressures for trade restriction still remain in the third policy era, major shifts have occurred in the world market for food and farm products. Food production goals for America need to be viewed in this broader perspective, including the prospects for population and food production around the world. For a consistent policy to emerge, however, the demand for food and farm output must be placed in an economic setting, which includes a discussion of policies influencing food demand, the subject of our next chapter.

QUESTIONS FOR DISCUSSION

1 By reference to the projections of America's capacity or ability to produce food, state your priority goals in the intermediate term for food production in reference to (a) the domestic market, (b) food export trade, and (c) international food aid. What are your reasons for the goals selected? Are the goals attainable? Comment.

2 Straight-line projection of recent trends in food production and population leads to mass starvation in some countries. What are some of the policy alternatives to this solution? In general? In food policy for America? Theoretically speaking, what is an optimum level of food production?

3 Summarize views in respect to population and food presented by Robert Malthus, Sir William Crookes, William and Paul Paddock, and Paul Ehrlich. In the light of

[75]See Stephen C. Schmidt, "An Enlarged European Community and Agricultural Trade Policy Choices for Third Countries," *Journal of Agricultural Economics*, Vol. XXIV, No. 1, 1973, pp. 141–164, especially p. 145.

[76]See D. Gale Johnson, *World Agriculture in Disarray*, London: Macmillan St. Martin's Press in association with the Trade Policy Research Centre, 1973.

[77]For a discussion of problems encountered in negotiating reductions in tariffs and trade restrictions on farm products, see *Agricultural Trade and the Proposed Round of Multilateral Negotiations*, report prepared at the request of Peter Flanigan, assistant to the president for International Economic Affairs for the Council on International Economic Policy, U.S. Senate Committee on Agriculture and Forestry, 93d Cong., 1st Sess., April 30, 1973 (sometimes called the Flanigan Report).

history, is it possible to reject the underlying hypotheses? Comment. In economic terms, is there an optimum level of population?

4 Some economists have attempted to develop an economic model or theory of population growth. What are the major elements of this theory? How well does the theory fit current growth patterns of developed and developing countries? Identify factors altering the supply and demand for children.

5 The alternative syndromes of surplus and scarcity may be rejected as an acceptable goal in food policy for the United States. Assuming such a pattern is rejected, what alternative goals are there? What will be required to implement them? Be specific in regard to value judgments concerning production and trade, food reserves and food aid, population growth, and distribution of income and wealth.

REFERENCES

Alternatives for Balancing World Food Production and Needs, Ames: Iowa State University Press, 1967.

DeBell, Garrett (ed.), *The Environmental Handbook,* New York: Ballantine Books, Inc., 1970.

Johnson, D. Gale, *World Agriculture in Disarray,* London: Macmillan St. Martin's Press in association with the Trade Policy Research Centre, 1973.

Johnston, Bruce F., and Peter Kilby, *Agriculture and Structural Transformation, Economic Strategies in Late-Developing Countries,* New York: Oxford University Press, 1975.

Population and Food Supply, Cambridge, England: Cambridge University Press, 1969.

Schickele, Rainer, *Agrarian Revolution and Economic Progress, A Primer for Development,* Praeger Special Studies in International Economics and Development, published in cooperation with the Agricultural Development Council, Inc., New York: Frederick A. Praeger, Inc., 1968.

Thorbecke, Eric (ed.), *The Role of Agriculture in Economic Development,* New York: National Bureau of Economic Research, 1969. Distributed by Columbia University Press, New York.

Tolley, G. S. (ed.), *Study of U.S. Agricultural Adjustments,* Raleigh, N.C.: North Carolina State University, School of Agriculture and Life Sciences, Agricultural Policy Institute, AP 1 Series 48 (no date).

Turk, Kenneth L. (ed.), *Some Issues Emerging from Recent Breakthroughs in Food Production,* Ithaca, N.Y.: New York State College of Agriculture at Cornell University, 1971.

Influencing Food Demand

*As if increase of appetite had grown
By what it fed on.*

William Shakespeare
Hamlet, Act I, Scene II

For whom shall food be produced? The purposes of this chapter are to discuss how government policy is influencing food demand in domestic and foreign markets and to present alternatives for the new third era. Demand is treated in the tradition of classical economics, as a measure of quantities that will be purchased under a range of prices under given conditions, or the quantity that will be purchased at a stated price under known conditions. A significant change in conditions is then, by definition, a change in demand.

POLICY INFLUENCING FOOD DEMAND

Government policy influences demand in both foreign and domestic markets. In 1963–65, in terms of value the domestic market absorbed 83 to 84 percent of America's total farm output—76.2 percent in food and feed, 4.8 percent in cotton, and 2.5 percent in tobacco. The export market, including commercial sales and food aid shipments, absorbed the other 16 to 17 percent—13.1 percent in food and feed, 2.4 percent in cotton, and about 1.0 percent in tobacco.[1] During 1966–68, as already noted, food aid shipments were increased sharply, especially because of monsoon failures in South Asia. Then, as more abundant rains came, food aid was curtailed and United States policy was shifted to recover a larger portion of the costs of aid by reducing the amount of subsidy in the total cost of aid shipments. Food aid programs were stabilized around $1 billion a year which, with higher grain prices in the early 1970s, meant another reduction in the volume of food aid.

Beginning in 1961 for feed grains and in 1964 for wheat and cotton, the United States shifted from high price supports, which restricted exports, to lower price supports, which permitted these commodities to be competitive in export trade without such large export subsidies. Direct payments were made to compensate farmers for the lower supports and to encourage them to participate in the programs of production control. Largely as a result of these policies, the nation's food prices were stabilized. By the early 1970s, consumer expenditures on food dropped below 16 percent of total income. In terms of value, the domestic market was absorbing 86 to 87 percent of total farm output, so exports of farm products were stabilized between 13 and 14 percent of the farmers' total receipts from farm marketings.

The Export Market's Effect on Food Demand

Then, starting in 1971, several things happened to shift the market shares away from this stable pattern. First and of more than temporary importance, the dollar was devalued in relation to gold by 8 percent in August 1971, and by another 10 percent in February 1973. Finally, it was allowed to float without a fixed price in gold. There were also upward revaluations of the currencies of countries that buy grains and other farm products from the United States, most importantly Japan and countries of the European Economic Community (EEC). Between May 1, 1971, and September 30, 1973, the revaluations between the United States and the EEC ranged from 33.5 percent in Germany to 23.2 percent in France, and revaluation of the dollar in respect to the yen was 25.8 percent. This devaluation of the dollar was equivalent to a price reduction for American food and farm products in the importing countries. Most of the export subsidies on U.S. farm products were soon dropped.

Second, in the spring of 1972, the U.S.S.R. decided to buy more wheat and feed grains abroad, and thus to carry out its policy of improving its own food supply. Back to 1967 at least, wheat production in Russia had generally held about steady, in contrast to the Soviet plans to increase production. Subsequent Russian purchases of wheat and feed grains in the United States totaled some 18 million tons in the next 12 to 18 months.

---

[1]USDA data as presented in annual issues of the *Handbook of Agricultural Charts, Agricultural Statistics*, and monthly or quarterly situation reports.

Table 3-1   Shares of U.S. Agricultural Exports, 1966 and 1973
(In percentage of total)

	Wheat and products		Meat and products		Rice		Feed grains	
	1966	1973	1966	1973	1966	1973	1966	1973
Developed	25	24	82	89	45	19	87	70
Developing	69	41	18	11	55	81	9	15
East Europe U.S.S.R., P.R.C.	6	35	.01	0.2	0	0	4.0	15

	Soybeans		Fats		Vegetables	
	1966	1973	1966	1973	1966	1973
Developed	95	86	89	86	89	84
Developing	3	7	10	12	11	15
East Europe U.S.S.R., P.R.C.	2	7	1	2	0.2	1

Source: What Makes U.S. Farm Trade Grow, USDA, ERS and FAS, October 1974.

As a result of these two policy changes, total farm exports expanded sharply. Between fiscal 1971 and 1973, total exports of wheat and flour in grain equivalent increased from 17 million tons to 32 million tons. Total exports of feed grains (corn, barley, grain sorghum, and oats) went from 21 million to 44 million tons. The share of wheat exports going to Russia expanded sharply, and other changes occurred in trade between the developed and developing countries (Table 3-1). The U.S.S.R. and the Peoples Republic of China (P.R.C.) accounted for a major part of the shift in world trade.

Results of Trade Policy

By 1974, the growth of the export market, combined with expansion of domestic demand, had pushed the total receipts from farm marketings to $93.5 billion, in contrast to an average of $49.3 billion in the two years 1969 and 1970, just prior to the beginning of the changes in trade. Total U.S. agricultural production averaged 9 percentage points higher in the four years from 1971 through 1974 than it had from 1967 through 1970. Thus, changes in trade and in demand in the respective markets made the big difference.

Although the quantity index of agricultural exports in 1974 was only about 50 percent above the fiscal years 1969 through 1971, the value of agricultural exports was 3 times as high. With the value of farm exports set at $21.3 billion, they were equivalent to almost 23 percent of the market for total farm output, in contrast to the 13 to 14 percent recorded earlier. By 1974–75, the export market was absorbing more than 50 percent of the wheat crop, almost half the soybeans, a third of the tobacco and cotton, and more than a quarter of total corn and grain sorghums.

During the two fiscal years 1974 and 1975, each of three products—wheat and flour, oilseeds and oilseed products, feed grains and products—averaged nearly $5 billion each, together accounting for 70 percent of all agricultural exports. Animals and animal products averaged $1.7 billion, fruits and nuts $1.2 billion, cotton about $1.1 billion, rice and tobacco each about $0.9 billion. During the three fiscal years 1972 through 1974, United States delivered 40 percent of all world wheat exports, 57 percent of all coarse grains, 24 percent of the rice, and 82 percent of all soybeans and soybean products. Also, the nation exported 26 percent of all cotton.

The years from 1972 through 1974, which are regarded in this study as the first in the new third era of food policy, mark a fundamental shift in the world food economy. Although 1973 and 1974 may be somewhat unique in terms of the effects of market changes on food prices and farm incomes in America, the more fundamental questions for policy focus on whether or not the new levels of trade will be maintained, what policies will be conducive to trade expansion or contraction, and how might such policies originate and develop. To answer some of these, it is necessary to sort out the effects of overvaluation and devaluation as well as other trade policies.

The Traditional Farm Problem Linked to Overvaluation

A traditional interpretation of the farm income problem in the second era of food policy is to suggest that, as a result of policy by the United States government and related development, there was heavy investment in new and improved production technology for the agricultural sector. This caused the supply of agricultural products generally to forge ahead of demand to push farm product prices down to levels unacceptable to producers. The politically powerful farm bloc, which was formed in Congress in the 1920s, attained some of its policy goals in the Roosevelt New Deal in the 1930s and continued to influence policy. It had some degree of success in establishing price supports for politically important farm products at levels frequently above the equilibrium market price. This success led to other measures to clear the market, most, but not all, of which were supported by the farm bloc. They included supply control, such as land retirement and other production and market restrictions to offset a too rapid advance in the farm sector, and supplements to demand, such as food stamps and school lunch programs, export subsidies, and food aid programs to maintain the traditional levels of food and farm exports.

Sometime in the 1950s and 1960s, the U.S. dollar, being tied to a fixed price in terms of gold which permitted it to serve as the common reserve currency in world markets, began to be overvalued in terms of gold and other world currencies, and this overvaluation became greater over time. Suggestive evidence is found in declining U.S. gold stocks, which fell from $24,563 million in 1949, to $19,507 million in 1959, to $10,367 million in 1969, and to $10,132 million in 1971.[2] Also, balance of payment deficits began sharply in 1950, averaging $1.8 billion annually during the 1950s, $2.7 billion annually during the 1960s, and reaching unprecedented levels of $7.0 billion in 1969, $4.7 billion in 1970, and

---

[2]*Historical Statistics of the U.S.,* and *Statistical Abstract of the U.S.,* annual reports.

$24.0 billion in 1971.[3] Since large gold outflows and deficits in the balance of trade can also be generated by other policy means, such as by a federal tax policy that favors investments by American-based businesses abroad or by war expenditures abroad, they do not provide firm evidence of the amount of overvaluation or its timing. Nevertheless, the United States was cumulatively shipping gold and drawing on dollar credits abroad to compensate for insufficient exports of industrial goods, food, and farm products.

To the extent that these insufficiencies were not offset by export subsidies and food aid programs abroad, American agriculture was forced back upon the domestic market. As a consequence, the benefits of capital growth and technical change in agriculture were distributed most importantly to American consumers and away from farm producers, who otherwise would have received a larger share of the benefits of technological advance. Under these circumstances, the main beneficiaries of the rising agricultural productivity were domestic consumers, who bought food at low prices; the more affluent family-farmers, farm corporations, and other agricultural investors, who were able to acquire farm land and real estate at depressed cost; and certain foreign countries, who were recipients of low-cost or free food aid shipments. The small-scale farmer was most adversely affected by the combination of rapid technological advance and market restriction, as seen in the statistics on farm abandonment and consolidation.

Overvaluation and Devaluation Illustrated[4]

The discontinuance of overvaluation, or devaluation—so the hypothesis develops—helped to change this, as we illustrate in Figure 3-1. Let SS and DD represent the domestic supply and demand for all farm products and I_D represent the foreign demand which, merely to simplify the illustration, is drawn as if it were perfectly elastic.

If DAI_D prevails, the domestic price will be P_1. The quantity Q_1 will be demanded in the domestic market, Q_1Q_2 will be exported, and total production will be Q_2, or OQ_2. The total earnings in foreign exchange will be Q_1ABQ_2. Or, gross income to the farm and food exporting sector will be OP_1BQ_2, with OP_1AQ_1 coming from the domestic market and Q_1ABQ_2 from the foreign market.

Viewed externally, as from a country importing food from the United States, overvaluation of the dollar raises the price of competitive food imports from the United States in terms of the importing nation's currency. This is equivalent to a reduction in demand for such imports. In Figure 3-1, let I_D decline to I'_D. The price in the United States falls to P_2, as Q_3 will be demanded domestically and

[3]*Statistical Abstract of the U.S., Balance of Payments—Statistical Supplement,* annual and periodic reports.

[4]The following discussion is based in part on G. Edward Schuh, "The Exchange Rate and U.S. Agriculture," *American Journal of Agricultural Economics,* Vol. 56, No. 1, February 1974, pp. 1–13. It also benefits from the subsequent exchange of comments between Amalia Vellianitis-Fidas and Schuh, *ibid.,* Vol. 57. No. 4. November 1975, pp. 692–700. See also Thomas Grennes, "The Exchange Rate and U.S. Agriculture: Comment," and G. Edward Schuh, "The Exchange Rate and U.S. Agriculture: Reply," *ibid.,* Vol. 57, No. 1, February 1975, pp. 134–137.

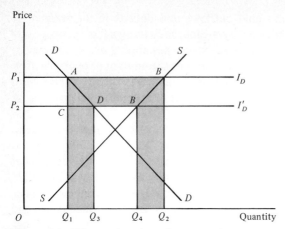

Figure 3-1 Effects of trade policy on agriculture. *(Adapted from G. Edward Schuh, "The Exchange Rate and U.S. Agriculture," American Journal of Agricultural Economics, Vol. 56, No. 1, February 1974, p. 3.)*

Q_3Q_4 will be exported. Receipts from domestic sales will be OP_2DQ_3 and earnings from export sales Q_3DBQ_4.

When devaluation occurs—or overvaluation ceases—the results will depend first on whether or not the effects are allowed to run their full course. The effects on farm exports can be offset by the United States through use of export quotas or by an embargo. An embargo was applied to soybeans briefly in 1973 and to grain sales to Russia from August to October 1975, although in both cases this was bitterly opposed by farm organizations. The effects can also be offset by new tariffs in the importing countries, to protect either their own farmers or their own exchange balances. Thus, the variable levy imposed by the EEC on grains, meats, poultry, and dairy products—except for small amounts covered in the General Agreement on Tariffs and Trade (GATT)—limits the increase in imports of these products from America, although beginning in 1973 and 1974 the levy did not increase sufficiently to fully offset the effects of currency revaluation.

Inferences for the Longer Term

The longer-term inferences for our farm and food policy are more broad, however, than the discussion has yet implied. In the longer term (in this case, anything beyond just a few years), if American agriculture, operating without acreage diversion or other production controls and with no export subsidies, responds to strong market demand, food and farm prices will recede from the intermediate-term highs, and the traditional downward pressures on farm prices will be reasserted. Whether or not this will occur, or when it will occur, depends on the strength of domestic food demand and the volume of food and farm exports.

Both trade and energy policies are closely linked to the situation for food. High levels of exports of industrial products from the EEC and Japan are required to pay for high levels of food and mineral imports. Continued large food exports to Russia will require the United States to accept other goods, such as oil and industrial products, in return. For the United States to continue high levels of food exports, a substantially larger three-way trade is required among (1) the United States, (2) the EEC and Japan, and (3) the oil-producing and -exporting countries (OPEC). The main balances involve exports of food and farm products from the United States to the EEC, Japan and the OPEC; exports of industrial goods from EEC, Japan, and the United States to one another and to OPEC; and exports of oil and natural gas from the OPEC to the EEC, Japan, and the United States.

A balance of trade at a high level among these four major market areas is required not only for agricultural prosperity in America in the current era of food policy. How freely this trade moves and how prudently the benefits are invested will have a great deal to do with whether the total world economy moves forward with balanced growth or whether it sinks into long-term stagnation. The early main lines of this trade are clearly demonstrated in the food trade developments that occurred in the first half of the 1970s. In addition to the changes in market shares traced above, agricultural imports by the OPEC increased from less than $2 billion in 1970 to more than $6 billion in 1975. Agricultural imports by the OPEC from the United States, less than $.5 billion in 1972, were $2 billion by 1975. To bring this trade to full tide, the federal government must abandon the goal of energy independence and work more successfully toward economic balance among the major trade areas. This change is of critical importance not only among these major trade areas, but also for other developed countries, and it is a matter of life and death for many people in the developing countries.

The Developing Countries' Food Trade and Aid

As we noted in Chapter 2, by the mid 1980s, according to FAO projections, the developing countries will have a food deficit in an average year equal to 80 to 100 million tons of grain, based on food consumption levels of the 1960s and 1970s and trend projections of their own food production. This deficit is in sharp contrast to imports of 20 to 25 million tons a year in the early 1970s, suggesting a growth in grain import requirements totaling 60 to 75 million tons a year. If the United States were to supply its proportionate share of this import requirement by some combination of expanded trade and aid, it would have to export at least 40 million tons more a year. Total United States exports amounted to 85 to 90 million tons a year of wheat, rice, feed grains, and soybeans during 1972 through 1974. Although the higher total of 125 million tons or more is well within the capacity of American agriculture, the question is whether a policy based on such levels would be compatible with other demand and trade projections.

Food aid programs for the developing countries have not been designed to fill a major part of this anticipated deficit. The recommendation of the World Food Conference at Rome in November 1974 was "that all donor countries accept and implement the concept of forward planning of food aid, make all efforts to provide commodities and/or financial assistance that will ensure in physical terms at least 10 million tons of grains in food aid a year, starting from

1975, and also to provide adequate quantities of other food commodities."[5] In 1975 it was proposed in pending United States legislation (H.R. 9005) that the Congress should establish a minimum of 1.5 million tons of grain for international food aid each year, with at least 1 million distributed through voluntary agencies and the World Food Program sponsored by the new World Food Council. The 1.5 million-ton commitment would be less the quantity required for famine relief or other urgent or extraordinary relief requirements. The administration's fiscal year 1976 program for "Food Aid to Poor Countries," Title II of the International Development and Assistance Act of 1975, totaled 1.3 million tons.

Since previous legislation of the Congress had not established any specific minimum for food aid requirements, the 1975 proposals may be regarded as a step forward in food aid planning. But, unless planning targets are revised drastically upward for food aid, or unless there is much more flourishing trade between food exporting nations and the developing countries, the grain deficits anticipated by the FAO in the developing countries will not be filled.

Additional United States grain exports of at least 40 million tons a year will involve a substantial change in the concepts of financial planning and programming. If the grain were mainly wheat at $4 a bushel, or $160 a ton, and if $40 a ton were allowed for transportation and distribution, the annual bill would be $8 billion. In comparison, the total value of shipments under Public Law 480 from 1955 through 1966 amounted to about $18 billion, at a lower price level and with partial recovery of the total cost. The capability or capacity of American agriculture to supply this quantity of projected exports is discussed further in Chapter 4; and some of the possible financial arrangements are discussed in Chapter 7. For now, we may conclude that it is possible and, in comparison with grain exports in 1975, it would add some 50 percent to the export demand for grain. But, if one were to judge on the basis of planning and performance thus far, this target will not be met. New institutions and new arrangements for financing must be created and a higher level of world trade must be established if the anticipated deficit is to be filled. We must emphasize expansion of trade with more modest increases in aid.

Low-Income Subsidy Policy Influences Demand

A major feature of food demand in this country has been the development of consumer subsidy programs implemented by food stamps and direct distribution programs to the poor. From 1965 to 1969, the federal expenditure on these programs grew from pilot efforts to $400 million a year, about equally divided between food stamps and direct food distribution. From 1969 to 1975, there was transitional growth to a federal expenditure level of more than $5 billion a year, with an almost complete shift to stamps except for direct distribution on Indian reservations. In mid 1975, the value of food stamps issued was running at about $7 billion a year, which was covered by the federal appropriations and partial

---

[5]From Resolution XVIII of the Conference. For further discussion, see *International Development and Food Assistance Act of 1975,* Report of the Committee on International Relations on H.R. 9005, 94th Cong., 1st Sess., House of Representatives, Report No. 94-442, Union Calendar No. 216, Aug. 1, 1975.

payments of participants. The average increase in food expenditure by participants was less than half the value of the stamp bonus.[6] So the net effect on food demand has been to add some $2 billion to $2.5 billion to the nation's total aggregate food expenditure, which was $180 billion a year in mid 1975, thus causing an increase of 1.1 to 1.4 percent in total demand for food. The difference between the value of the stamp bonus and the increase in food expenditure represented an income subsidy which was available to food stamp participants for nonfood purchases.

Food stamps have been soundly criticized as an inefficient and inequitable system of public aid.[7] Although the nationwide program has provided an important uniform standard of aid for several million participants, and the major burden has been spread uniformly via the federal tax system, very large numbers of the eligible households have not participated or received benefits from the program.[8] Administration, largely in the hands of state and local officials, has been cumbersome. Nutritional gains have been small, as food stamp bonus money has at best merely resulted in purchases of more food rather than an upgrading of diet in terms of a better balance among the essential nutrients.[9] Some recipients, lacking nutrition education, have simply spent a good portion of their increased purchasing power on more palatable or more conveniently packaged foods, such as prepared meats or prepared dinner aids. Some groups have shown no holdover effect toward higher food expenditures after the stamps were exhausted.[10]

In view of such criticism and the magnitude of the program, the idea of food stamps in lieu of other possible relief measures poses an important question for food policy with even broader implications. An examination of the alternatives requires an understanding of basic food stamp policy and the political forces involved in the evolution of the program. This leads to a more specific policy conclusion.

Basic Food Stamp Policy   Food stamp policy has evolved with two goals in view: (1) to aid the poor by shifting purchasing power to them in inverse proportion to their income, and (2) to improve nutrition among the poor by concentrating this subsidy on food. To be eligible for food stamps, households must either receive public assistance or be below certain minimum income and resource levels, and be living as an economic unit, excluding roomers, boarders, and live-in attendants. Except for disabled elderly persons, drug addicts, or

---

[6]Stephen J. Hiemstra and Sylvia Lane, *Program Evaluation Status Reports,* USDA, Food and Nutrition Service, January 1975.

[7]Kenneth W. Clarkson, with a foreword by Yale Brozen, *Food Stamps and Nutrition,* Washington: American Enterprise Institute for Public Policy Research, Evaluative Study No. 18, April 1975.

[8]*Ibid.,* p. 46.

[9]S. H. Logan and D. B. DeLoach, *The Food Stamp Program: Del Norte and Humboldt Counties, California,* Davis: California Agricultural Experiment Station, Bulletin 860, 1973, pp. 34, 35.

[10]J. Patrick Madden and Marion D. Yoder, *Program Evaluation: Food Stamps and Commodity Distribution in Rural Areas of Central Pennsylvania,* University Park: Pennsylvania State University, Agricultural Experiment Station Bulletin No. 780, June 1972.

alcoholics (who qualify for a "delivered meals" program), households must cook their food at home. All household members who are able-bodied and over 18 years of age must register for employment and accept it if offered. College or university students who are 18 or over, and who are claimed as a dependent by a taxpayer who is not a member of an eligible household, are not eligible to receive stamps.

In 1975, to obtain food stamps, participants with monthly incomes in excess of the stated minimums were required to pay a certain amount, called a purchase requirement, in order to obtain their monthly coupon allotment (Table 3-2). Family income and the number in the household determine the amount that must be paid for the stamp. A participating household is allowed to purchase one-quarter, one-half, or three-quarters of the total allotment instead of the full amount. Participants who receive welfare checks may elect to have the purchase requirement deducted from their checks and have their monthly allotment of stamps mailed to them, providing they choose to accept the full allotment. Otherwise, they can obtain stamps only at an authorized outlet. Participants are permitted to use stamps to buy any approved food, or plants and seeds used to produce food. Food stamps are not supposed to be sold, given away, or used to pay creditors. Changes in participant eligibility, according to regulations, must be reported to the agency operating the program.[11]

Political Forces in the Evolution of Food Stamp Policy   The first food stamp program, begun on an experimental basis in 1939, was designed to displace direct food distribution to the poor. Under the plan, each participating family could buy general food stamps (colored orange) in amounts equal to its normal, unsubsidized food expenditure according to a national average. Then, when the family purchased stamps, it was given additional (blue) stamps equal to one-half the value of the orange stamps. The blue stamps could be used only for the purchase of foods designated as surplus each month by the Secretary of Agriculture. Participants had to be certified by relief agencies as already on some form of relief and they had to prepare meals at home. Thus the first stamp program had the two goals of aid to the poor and increased demand for those farm products declared to be in surplus. More than 30 food commodities were included in one or more of the monthly blue-stamp lists.

The food stamp program has evolved from this depression type of innovation. Food stamps cost the U.S. Treasury $112 million in fiscal 1942, and by August 1942, a total of 1,714 counties and 88 cities were included in the program. Because of rising employment due to the war, the program was discontinued on March 1, 1943, and, although some direct food distribution was continued, the idea of food stamps virtually disappeared until the 1950s. The idea was most persistently advanced during the 1950s by Representative Leonor Sullivan, a Democrat from St. Louis, Missouri, who introduced a food stamp bill into

---

[11]See *Federal Register,* Vol. 40, Jan. 5, 1975, pp. 1882–1900, and Jan. 10, 1975, p. 2204, for more complete food stamp regulations.

Congress in at least three different sessions. In 1959, the Congress enacted Public Law 341, which authorized a two-year program. But neither Secretary of Agriculture Benson in the Eisenhower administration nor Secretary Freeman in the Kennedy administration made use of this authority, and it was allowed to expire on January 13, 1962. President Kennedy had announced, in his Economic Message to Congress on February 2, 1961, a new pilot food stamp program, which he directed Secretary Freeman to initiate. By March 1964 there were 43 pilot projects in operation in 3 cities and 40 counties in 22 states. The need demonstrated by these programs culminated in the Food Stamp Act of 1964.

During the first five years of the Food Stamp Act, however, funds increased only slightly. Appropriation requests were first screened by the agricultural committees of both houses of Congress and by the Agriculture Subcommittee of the House Appropriations Committee, all three of which were chaired by representatives from the South. Allen Ellender, an acknowledged segregationist and a conservative Democrat from Louisiana, was chairman of the Senate Agriculture and Forestry Committee. Harold Cooley, a moderate Democrat from North Carolina, chaired the House Agriculture Committee; but his vice-chairman, who was later chairman, W. R. Poage of Texas, was an outspoken segregationist and generally considered antagonistic to programs to aid the poor. Jamie Whitten of Mississippi, chairman of the House Appropriations Committee, and for years one of the most powerful members of the Congress, was a paternalistic leader, a strong proponent of farm subsidy programs, but generally against any programs to change the structure of society, especially rural society, in favor of the poor.[12]

Secretary Freeman was directed by President Kennedy and later by President Lyndon Johnson to placate the powerful Southern bloc rather than fight it, because each President in turn believed that he needed the support of these powerful congressmen for other programs that he deemed more important to the national interest. That this support was not always sufficient to obtain the needed legislation, such as new taxes to finance the unpopular Vietnam war, led to instability and then inflation. The weaknesses of presidential leadership, in the face of the dominance of Southern conservatives in Congress, not only delayed much of the progress that might have been made in aid to poor people. It built pressure for reform movements, such as the Poor Peoples' Campaign, a political movement organized by several people as a program to aid the poor.

Into this hiatus, the Poor Peoples' Campaign burst upon the consciousness of America. A so-called Citizens' Board of Inquiry, which had been formed by the campaign leaders, issued a report, *Hunger USA,* in the spring of 1968. A subcommittee of the Senate Labor and Public Welfare Committee, whose membership included Senator Robert Kennedy, heard that there was hunger in Mississippi and went to observe it first hand. A national group, brought together by several women's organizations, issued a report critical of food programs, entitled *Our Daily Bread.* In May 1968, the Columbia Broadcasting System

---

[12]For further discussion on these points, see Don F. Hadwiger, "The Freeman Administration and the Poor," *Agricultural History,* 1971, pp. 29–31, 45.

Table 3-2 Food Stamp Allotments and Purchase Requirements*

	Number of persons in household†							
	1	2	3	4	5	6	7	8
	Monthly coupon allotment (dollars)							
Monthly net income	48	90	128	162	192	222	250	278
	Monthly purchase requirement (dollars)							
$ 0–$ 19.99	0	0	0	0	0	0	0	0
20– 29.99	$ 1	$ 1	0	0	0	0	0	0
30– 39.99	4	4	$ 4	$ 4	$ 5	$ 5	$ 5	$ 5
40– 49.99	6	7	7	7	8	8	8	8
50– 59.99	8	10	10	10	11	11	12	12
60– 69.99	10	12	13	13	14	14	15	16
70– 79.99	12	15	16	16	17	17	18	19
80– 89.99	14	18	19	19	20	21	21	22
90– 99.99	16	21	21	22	23	24	25	26
100– 109.99	18	23	24	25	26	27	28	29
110– 119.99	21	26	27	28	29	31	32	33
120– 129.99	24	29	30	31	33	34	35	36
130– 139.99	27	32	33	34	36	37	38	39
140– 149.99	30	35	36	37	39	40	41	42
150– 169.99	33	38	40	41	42	43	44	45
170– 189.99	36	44	46	47	48	49	50	51
190– 209.99	36	50	52	53	54	55	56	57
210– 229.99	38	56	58	59	60	61	62	63
230– 249.99		62	64	65	66	67	68	69
250– 269.99		68	70	71	72	73	74	75
270– 289.99		70	76	77	78	79	80	81
290– 309.99		70	82	83	84	85	86	87
310– 329.99			88	89	90	91	92	93
330– 359.99			94	95	96	97	98	99

Monthly income					
360– 389.99	100	104	105	106	107	108
390– 419.99	109	113	114	115	116	117
420– 449.99	110	122	123	124	125	126
450– 479.99		131	132	133	134	135
480– 509.99		138	141	142	143	144
510– 539.99		138	150	151	152	153
540– 569.99		138	159	160	161	162
570– 599.99			164	169	170	171
600– 629.99			164	178	179	180
630– 659.99			164	187	188	189
660– 689.99				190	197	198
690– 719.99				190	206	207
720– 749.99				190	214	216
750– 779.99					214	225
780– 809.99					214	234
810– 839.99					214	238
840– 869.99						238
870– 899.99						238
900– 929.99						238

*Effective July 1, 1975 for participants in the 48 contiguous states.
†For each additional household member over 8, add $22 to the 8-person allotment.

presented an hour-long documentary, "Hunger USA," which indicted the food programs as being too little and too late, entirely inadequate in scope and coverage. The program had the widest impact, and Secretary Freeman was enraged. Instead of calling for more public support and more careful consideration in development of a relief program, however, he published a letter that he had sent to Frank Stanton, president of CBS, charging that the network presentation was a "travesty on objective reporting," and he demanded equal time to try to refute it. Stanton replied that the issue of hunger in the United States transcended the question of who was to blame, and when Freeman made a second request for equal time, Stanton's reaction was to air the program again and to make the film available to the Congress so that it might be seen first hand. The leaders of the Poor Peoples' Campaign claimed that at least $200 million was available from tariff receipts and was eligible to be spent on food programs, and they suggested ways in which the money might be used to help the poor. But Freeman replied that this money was not his to spend, apparently because of prior agreements between President Johnson and the leaders in Congress.

The issue of hunger in this country was now at full tide. Early in 1969, the influential National Planning Association issued a study on food programs,[13] and on July 15 the House Committee on Agriculture began hearings on two bills.[14] H.R. 12340, introduced by W. R. Poage (Democrat from Texas), chairman of the committee, would have continued most farm programs by indefinitely extending the Food and Agriculture Act of 1965.[15] Secondly, it would have amended the Food Stamp Act of 1964 by providing that "households shall be charged such portion of the face value of the coupon allotment issed to them as is determined to be equivalent to their normal expenditure for food. . . ." This provision could have been even more restrictive than the 1964 act, however, except that "employment, service or public work equivalent in value of such charges shall be acceptable in lieu thereof. . . ." H.R. 12222, introduced by Catherine May (Republican from Washington), Gerald R. Ford, and 23 others, would have amended the 1964 act, as the stated policy of Congress, "to promote the general welfare . . . [use] the Nation's abundance of food . . . to safeguard the health and well-being of the Nation's population and raise levels of nutrition among low-income households."[16] It authorized federal appropriations not to exceed $315 million for fiscal 1969 and $610 million for fiscal 1970, compared with expenditures of $173 million in fiscal year 1968.

All this was far below the requests of some influential writers, other politicians, and action groups. In 1969, Nick Kotz of *The Washington Post* published his book *Let Them Eat Promises*, strongly criticizing the position of both the Congress and the Nixon administration on food policy, especially in light of the

[13]See Dale M. Hoover and James G. Maddox, *Food for the Hungry: Direct Distribution and Food Stamp Programs for Low-Income Families,* Washington: National Planning Association, Planning Pamphlet No. 126, February 1969.

[14]*General Farm Program and Food Stamp Program,* Hearings, Committee on Agriculture, House of Representatives, 91st Cong., 1st Sess., Serial Q, Part 1.

[15]*Ibid.,* p. 2.

[16]*Ibid.,* pp. 2–5.

President's promise, made on May 6, 1969, to "end hunger for all time in America."[17] Although Kotz estimated that a minimum of $3 to $4 billion was required initially for an adequate food stamp program,[18] "The President indicated he sought only $1.5 billion for the food stamp program in 1971, thus underestimating by almost 50 percent the needs projected by his own planners."[19] Kotz held that households with less than $1,200 annual income should receive free stamps, that no one should pay more than 20 percent of his or her income for stamps, and that qualifications should be automatic on filing income tax returns. Somewhat more conservatively, Senator George McGovern proposed that families with less than $80 monthly income should receive free stamps. The President proposed that only those with less than $30 monthly income should receive free stamps, and the position was finally accepted by Congress. Since some 3.5 million Americans had incomes between $30 and $80 monthly, the McGovern proposals would have offered free stamps to more than twice the 2.2 million people served by food stamps in 1968.

In the new Nixon administration, which took office in January 1969, Secretary of Agriculture Clifford Hardin testified in favor of expanding the food stamp program nationwide to eliminate direct distribution,[20] as had been recommended earlier by Assistant Secretary Paarlberg.[21] But throughout the Nixon administration and later during the administration of President Ford, the emphasis from the White House was to hold the U.S. Treasury's costs of food stamps significantly below the levels authorized by Congress. In April 1971, the Nixon administration cut one-third of the welfare recipients from the food stamp roles. They were restored in July by pressure from the Congress. Again in July 1971, the administration reduced food stamp benefits by eliminating eligibility for some of the "upper-income poor." Although this eligibility too was restored under pressure in January 1972, $418 million in food stamp funds was denied in the name of preserving the budget. Finally, the pressure of Congress became more dominant. The Agricultural and Consumer Protection Act of 1973 extended the Food Stamp Program through June 30, 1977. It authorized an expansion in funds and required all states to implement the food stamp program in all their political subdivisions by June 30, 1974, unless they could show the USDA that it was impossible or impracticable for them to do so. Coverage was broadened to include the elderly in nonprofit dining facilities. Food stamps could be used to buy any food, as well as seeds or plants for home gardens. Early in 1975, however, when the Ford administration attempted to cut more than $500 million from the cost of the food stamp program through increasing the charges to recipients, the proposals were soundly defeated in the Congress.

[17]Nick Kotz, *Let Them Eat Promises: The Politics of Hunger in America*, Englewood Cliffs, N.J.: Prentice-Hall, Inc., 1969, pp. 257, 258.

[18]*Ibid.*, pp. 257, 258.

[19]*Ibid.*, p. 229.

[20]*General Farm Program and Food Stamp Program, op. cit.*, pp. 5–50.

[21]See Don Paarlberg, *Subsidized Food Consumption*, Washington: American Enterprise Institute for Public Policy Research, May 1963.

A Policy Conclusion   Strong political support has been shown for a low-income subsidy that will provide the poor with greater purchasing power for food. The underlying value expressed by the Congress is that no one in America should have to go hungry or suffer from undernourishment. Clearly, it is the poor whom they wish to help. The USDA has been under strong pressure to see that food stamps do not go to those who are, by law, not eligible to use them; and, according to USDA surveys, the great majority of those using stamps qualify strictly on grounds of low income. In 1975, for example, only 6 percent of all stamp recipients were in households with take-home pay of more than $6,000 a year, and 87 percent of these families had five or more members. In 1973, the average monthly income of participating households was only $364 a month from all sources. Although help to some recipients can be questioned on grounds of need or equity, the food stamp program has provided nationwide aid, with uniform sharing of the cost through the federal tax system. By providing this standard and by drawing national attention to the problem of hunger, it has made a contribution toward solving a major welfare problem. But, can a more satisfactory policy be designed?

Welfare in Low-Income Subsidy   A specific-purpose subsidy is of lower value to the recipient than a general-purpose subsidy of like amount, unless the benefits can be delivered in no other way. This is illustrated in Figure 3-2, where food consumption is measured horizontally in terms of a suitable index of physical volume, and money is measured vertically, as representative of consumption of all other goods and services. Each of the curved lines, called indifference curves, connects a series of points representing levels of consumption jointly of foods and nonfoods considered equally desirable by the consumer or the family. Successive indifference curves, moving from left to right, represent increasingly desirable levels of consumption.[22]

The two diagonal straight lines represent what the family can buy at two different incomes—unsubsidized and subsidized—assuming that the price of food in relation to nonfood is the same in each case. The original income determines the height of the lower line—or its intersection with the vertical axis at F—and the magnitude of the subsidy plus original income defines the point of intersection of the higher line at G. The slope of each line is determined by the price of food relative to nonfood and, since this remains the same, the two lines are parallel. At each level of income, the consumer family, acting to maximize its satisfaction or welfare, will plan to buy the quantity of food indicated by the intersection of the price line with the highest indifference curve that it reaches, thus to achieve the most desirable consumption pattern available. At the unsubsidized level of income, this will result in OD expenditures on nonfood and OA on food, when the consumer is on the indifference curve X. With a subsidized income given as a cash grant, the consumer will be able to reach the highest

[22]This diagram and discussion draw on an initial analysis by Herman M. Southworth, "The Economics of Public Measures to Subsidize Food Consumption," *Journal of Farm Economics,* Vol. XXVII, February 1945, pp. 38–66.

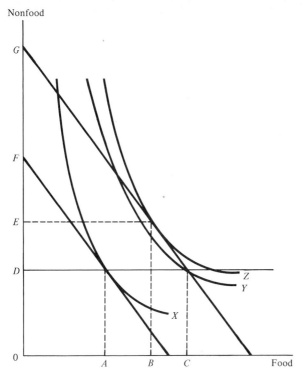

Figure 3-2 Welfare effects of food stamp programs.

indifference curve *Z*, with expenditures of *OE* on nonfood and *OB* on food. However, as in the stamp programs, if the consumer is required to accept the equivalent subsidy as a food stamp bonus and to spend it only for food, only the original amount *OD* will be spent on nonfood and *OC* will be spent on food. The consumer must accommodate expenditures on the indifference curve *Y*, which is below *Z*. This represents a loss in satisfaction or welfare as compared with *Z*, or an economic waste.

Although the food stamp program has permitted recipients under a variable purchase plan to buy only one-fourth, one-half, or three-fourths of the monthly coupon allotment, which would reduce the welfare or allocative loss resulting from the bonus being tied to food, the real loss in welfare may still be considerable. Thus, it has been estimated that a food stamp bonus of $1 averages only 82 cents in real value to the consumer.[23] Additionally, largely because of the cumbersomeness of the administrative arrangements for checking and issuing food stamps, it costs $1.09 to deliver $1 of stamp bonus money to the recipient. Also, in turning administration over to local officials, other losses in efficiency result, such as the difficulty of accurately checking the recipient's income and cross-checking with other welfare programs to verify information on eligibility. Therefore, some people receive stamps who are by law not entitled to them,

[23]See Clarkson, *Food Stamps and Nutrition, op. cit.*, pp. 63–72.

while others who can legitimately qualify go without. In the mid 1970s, the identified overissuance of food stamps from fraud or misrepresentation averaged about 1 percent of the total federal appropriations for food stamps, while only about 70 percent of the families eligible for food stamps were actually using them. Although several cases of gross negligence on the part of local authorities were cited by USDA, the recoverable amounts were apparently very small.[24]

A General Policy Conclusion   The food stamp program can be replaced by a more simple cash-grant welfare program with significant gains in both equity and efficiency, provided that the standards, conditions for eligibility, and other factors are coordinated at the federal level to attain uniform or comparable treatment across the country. This would be consistent with a reduction in special-purpose programs, which could be limited to those cases where such programs are required to deliver special benefits, such as to the aged, retarded, incapacitated, or indigent. The positive benefits from federal funding and comparable treatment across the country need not be lost in such a revision of policy.

SCHOOL LUNCH AND OTHER CHILD-NUTRITION PROGRAMS

The school lunch program, like the food stamp program, has expanded greatly since World War II. School lunch programs were started in the 1930s but languished at a low level during the war. In 1946, the school lunch was put on a permanent basis but funding levels remained very low until the end of the 1960s. In 1966, for example, the total money contributions to the program were only about $1.5 billion, of which more than half was covered by children's or family payments. The USDA contribution was scarcely a quarter of a billion, while state and local governments and school districts made up most of the rest. Slowly, the recognition of malnourishment and even undernourishment was reflected in appropriations. As late as 1970, for example, the USDA contribution was still up to barely $0.5 billion. Then the idea began to take hold, so that, by fiscal year 1975, the USDA contribution reached about $1.7 billion, children's payments rose to about $1.3 billion, state and local governments were contributing close to $0.5 billion, and other contributions brought the total to about $3.7 billion.

The legislative year of 1975 was an important milestone in the development of school food programs. Much policy debate within the Congress, and between Congress and the administration, centered on the size of the appropriation to be made and on whether to subsidize lunches for children from middle-income families. In the Ford administration's plan, free meals would go only to children from families earning $4,510 or less, and token-priced meals would go to youngsters from families earning up to $5,638. This would limit spending on child

[24]See *Statement of Richard L. Feltner, Assistant Secretary of Agriculture, before the Committee on Agriculture and Forestry, United States Senate,* Washington, D.C., November 19, 1975, pp. 146–152. See also *Summary Report* on the *Food Stamp Program, Response to Senate Resolution 58,* U.S. Department of Agriculture, Food and Nutrition Service, June 1975; *Bonus Food Stamps and Cash Income Supplements,* USDA, ERS, October 1974; and *Income Security for Americans: Recommendations of the Public Welfare Study,* Subcommittee on Fiscal Policy of the Joint Economic Committee, 93d Cong., 2d Sess., Dec. 5, 1974.

nutrition to $1.6 billion after July 1, 1975, about $600 million less than the total for all child-nutrition programs in fiscal 1975. About 15.2 million children had been paying from 40 to 50 cents daily and 9.9 million children from lower-income families were getting free or token-payment lunches and breakfasts. Under the Ford administration plan, the states would be given block grants to cover about one-third the total costs of school lunches. But, if the states did not replace the money lost through the lowered federal appropriation, the cost of school lunches would be raised as much as 21 cents a day, or $1.05 weekly. Opponents of the administration proposal saw it as a loss of $600 million from child-nutrition programs. Instead of cutting back, they proposed broadening the school lunch program and increasing its funding. Congress supported this position, authorizing some $2.7 billion for child-nutrition programs in fiscal 1976, and subsequently overriding the President's veto of the bill by an overwhelming majority: 397 to 18 in the House and 79 to 13 in the Senate (H.R. 4222—Public Law 94-105).

Apparently, although improving child nutrition was in the minds of both Congress and the President, the issue raised by the President was that of "fiscal irresponsibility," as he wrote in his veto message. "I cannot accept such fiscal irresponsibility," he said "when we face the real danger that the budget deficit could reach $70 billion instead of the already high limit of $60 billion I set earlier this year." Carl D. Perkins (Democrat of Kentucky), chairman of the Education and Labor Committee and floor manager of the bill, argued, however, that the final version was only $317 million in 1976 budget authority higher than the budget targets set earlier by Congress and $216 million higher than government estimates of the budget authority necessary to continue the program at existing levels.[25]

In giving support to school lunch and breakfast programs, the bill expanded them to include children's residential institutions, increased the income-eligibility level for reduced-price lunches (those costing a maximum of 20 cents), and made children of unemployed parents eligible for free and reduced-price lunches. In addition, the measure extended all nonschool food programs, including a supplemental feeding program for mothers and their children, and it made the school breakfast permanent.

Although the action of the Congress apparently reflected constituents' views about child-feeding programs, the action fell far short of the case presented in Chapter 11 in regard to the potential benefits of federal support for nutrition education. While the school lunch and other child-feeding programs are justified as an efficient way to provide good food and directly improve child nutrition, they have not attacked the broader policy goals of more effective nutrition education.

Review of Child-Feeding Programs   Public Law 93-50, signed November 7, 1973, authorized and directed the Secretary of Agriculture to carry out a compre-

---

[25]*Congressional Quarterly,* Oct. 11, 1975, p. 2161. Almost simultaneously, President Ford was recommending continuation and extension of a tax cut of $28 billion on grounds that this was needed to spur the economy. Apparently, he conceived that while the tax cut would have important multiplier effects, the increase in funding for school programs would not!

hensive study of the National School Lunch Act and the Child Nutrition Act which cover the national school lunch program (NSLP), the school breakfast program (SBP), the special food service program for children (SFSPFC), and the special school milk program (SMP).[26] According to the general conclusions of the study, the programs were extremely effective, being available to over 86 percent of all school children and an additional several hundred thousand children in day-care centers and other child-care institutions. About 25 million children a day participated in the programs and about 9.4 million received free or reduced-price meals. Between 1969 and 1974, the federal contribution had risen from $600 million to $1.7 billion, or to about 41 percent of total program costs. Public Law 93-326, signed June 30, 1974, guaranteed federal funds of 10 cents per lunch in food or cash in addition to administrative assistance and special aid for needy children.

The USDA made several recommendations for improvement of administration:[27] There should be better recognition of the role of states in child-nutrition programs; and policy makers were warned against further federalizing of the program, since USDA maintained that its success depended so heavily on decisions of state and local school officials. The Department requested funds for a stronger state presence in administration. The nutritional standards for the school lunch program should be continually reassessed in light of nutritional knowledge and of children's acceptability of the lunch. Studies underway should better enable the Department to design new meal standards. A single cash payment to the schools would be preferable to direct commodity distribution.

A wide range of studies was cited in the comprehensive report.[28] They generally concluded that nutrition was significantly improved among the children who participated in school food programs. There were, however, a number of problems; and many interested parties—including the National Advisory Council on Child Nutrition, the American School Food Service Association and 10 of its state affiliates, 23 state directors of school food services, the American Dietetic Association, local groups such as a YWCA, and several antihunger groups including the Children's Foundation—made recommendations for improvement of the programs.[29] They all favored strengthening and expanding food programs to place more emphasis on nutrition and nutrition education, and to reach the children not previously served by the programs. A majority of the state directors of school food services favored free programs for all students financed by federal, state or local funds. They felt that such programs would greatly simplify problems of administration, provide for more efficient service, and avoid the problem of discriminating between two classes of children according to family income. Acceptance of this recommendation would shift nearly $1

---

[26]*Comprehensive Study of the Child Nutrition Programs—July 1974,* submitted by the United States Department of Agriculture to Congress, pursuant to Public Law 93-150. 93d Cong., 2d Sess., Sept. 10, 1974.
    [27]*Ibid.,* pp. 85–87.
    [28]*Ibid.,* pp. 3–17.
    [29]*Ibid.,* pp. 71–83.

billion more of total costs to the federal government. The case for this change in policy was based on more effective programs; that is, more economical use of food and more efficient programs. Many school officials had argued for free school lunch programs that would eliminate the cumbersome and very disagreeable task of segregating children so as to collect from some and not others. This argument is consistent, of course, with the position that more of the total school budget should be supported through uniform payments from state and federal governments allocated strictly according to total school enrollment.

Conclusion Although child-feeding programs may increase the total demand for food, an accurate quantitative estimate is scarcely possible because these programs displace an unknown amount of food that would be otherwise supplied. The issue of the demand effects is comparatively unimportant, however. Questions about what can be done to provide the most efficient delivery of good food, how such programs can make their maximum contribution to good nutrition, and how the food can be most equitably distributed, are of much greater importance to food policy. We shall return to some of them in Chapter 11, which discusses coordinating nutrition policy.

INCOME AS A FACTOR INFLUENCING FOOD DEMAND

As family income increases, the amount spent on many food items goes up. People eat more and they eat better. After a certain level is reached, however, they do not increase calorie consumption; they shift away from cheap, bulky carbohydrates to more expensive meats and proteins—to fancier foods or labor-saving, prepared foods, and to more eating out. But there are limits to how much more people will spend on food as their incomes rise. Studies show that the percentage of income spent on food declines as real income increases. A general study of income expenditure was first published by the nineteenth-century Prussian statistician Ernst Engel (not to be confused with Karl Marx's friend, Friedrich Engels), and it has become popular to speak about the relationship between income and expenditures on various items as Engel curves. Conceptually, income elasticity is a measurement of this relationship. If the percentage of family income spent on an item stays the same as real income increases, the income elasticity is 1.0. If the percentage spent increases only half as much, income elasticity is 0.5. If it increases one-fourth as much, income elasticity is 0.25, and so on.

Measures of Income Elasticity for All Food

George Brandow has estimated that the income elasticity of demand at retail for all farm products consumed in the United States has varied from 0.48 to 0.23 in certain short-run periods and from 0.37 to 0.12 in the long run.[30] Because income

[30]George E. Brandow, *Interrelationships among Demand for Farm Products and Implications for Control of Market Supply,* University Park: Pennsylvania State University, Agricultural Experiment Station Bulletin No. 680, 1961.

elasticities at retail contain demands for marketing service components, the income elasticity at farm level is believed to be lower, or about 0.20 to 0.10. If the midpoint at farm level is 0.15, a 1.0 percent increase in consumer disposable income raises the demand at the farm level only 0.15 percent. If population is growing 1.5 percent annually, and per capita real income is growing by 2 percent annually, then the domestic demand for farm products will increase about 1.5 + (.15)(2) = 1.8 percent per year. If per capita real income is increasing by 2.5 percent annually, the domestic demand for farm products will increase about 1.5 + (.15)(2.5) = 1.875 percent per year. If population growth reaches zero, and the per capita real income increases by 3 percent per year, the domestic demand for farm products will increase about (.15)(3) = 0.45 percent per year, and so on.

Estimates of income elasticities are available from time series analyses as well as from cross-sectional budget studies, and the two approaches often yield divergent results. Since income is highly associated with other factors affecting demand, such as education, family size, age, and so on, it is possible that neither approach really measures the "pure" effect of income on food expenditure. Thus, alternatively, income elasticity for total food has been estimated by George Brandow as low as 0.16 from time series data, while others, using time series or cross-sectional data and other methods, have found elasticities ranging from 0.24 to as high as 0.45.[31]

In any event, as real incomes rise, the demand for food is expected to increase less than the increase in demand for nonfood services. The demand for farm-produced components will continue to increase less than the demand for food marketing services until the demand for the latter is more generally satiated. That is, with continued rising real income, the farm economy will receive less stimulus from this source than will other major sectors of the food system. Historically, in the second era of food policy, the farm sector was depressed while other sectors grew. National policy has attempted to compensate the farm sector for this situation.

Measures of Income Elasticity of Selected Foods

Income elasticity varies widely among individual foods, being generally higher for meats and other animal products, poultry, and fruit than for vegetables and cereals (Table 3-3). As real incomes have risen, there has been a shift toward the former class of foods with little change in per capita consumption of the latter. If

[31]Marguerite C. Burk, *Food Expenditures by Upper Income Families, An Analysis of Their Changing Importance in the U.S. Food Market,* St. Paul: University of Minnesota Agricultural Experiment Station in cooperation with U.S. Department of Agriculture, Tech. Bulletin 269, 1969; Robert T. Michael, *The Effect of Education on Efficiency in Consumption,* New York: National Bureau of Economic Research, Occasional Paper 116, 1972. For earlier references, see M.A. Girshick and T. Haavelmo, "Statistical Analysis of the Demand for Food," *Econometrica,* Vol. 15, No. 2, 1947, pp. 79–100; Marguerite C. Burk, "Changes in the Demand for Food from 1941 to 1950," *Journal of Farm Economics,* Vol. 33, No. 3, 1951, pp. 281–298; and James Tobin, "A Statistical Demand Function for Food in the United States," *Journal of the Royal Statistical Society,* Series A, Vol. 113, pp. 113–141.

Table 3-3   Income and Price Elasticities of Domestic Demand at Retail Level for Selected Foods and Nonfood Items, and Price Elasticities at the Farm Level

	Retail level		
	Income	Price	Farm price level
Lamb and mutton	.65	−2.35	−1.78 (sheep and lambs)
Veal	.58	−1.60	−1.08 (calves)
Beef	.47	− .95	− .68 (cattle)
Pork	.32	− .75	− .46 (hogs)
Turkey	.49	−1.40	− .92
Chicken	.37	−1.16	− .74
Eggs	.16	− .30	− .23
Cheese	.45	− .70	− .53
Ice cream	.35	− .55	− .11
Butter	.33	− .85	− .66
Fluid milk and cream	.16	− .28	− .14
Margarine	.00	− .80	−3.99 (soybean oil)*
			−6.92 (cottonseed oil)*
			−7.04 (other food oil)*
Fruit	.40	− .60	− .36
Beverages	.23	− .36	n.a.†
Sugar and syrups	.18	− .30	− .18
Vegetables	.15	− .30	− .10
Dry beans, peas, nuts	.12	− .25	− .23
Cereals, baking products	.00	− .15	‡
Nonfood	1.22	−1.03	n.a.†

*Not necessarily for use in margarine.
†Not available or not appropriate.
‡The price elasticity at the farm level for corn is −0.03, for wheat −0.02, and for barley −0.07. These are not comparable to the "cereals, baking products" category, however.

Source: George Brandow, *Interrelationships among Demand for Farm Products and Implications for Control of Market Supply,* University Park: Pennsylvania State University, Agricultural Experiment Station Bulletin 680, 1961.

there are further increases in real income, supplemented by the consumer programs that we have discussed, this shift will continue but at a decreasing rate, as larger proportions of the population reach their optimum preferences in respect to diet.

Elasticity Related to Income, Education, and Family Size

Expenditures on 52 categories of household items have been estimated by Robert Michael in respect to various levels of household income, years of formal education of the head of the household, age of the head, family size, and region, based on the 1960 and the 1950 Bureau of Labor Statistics (BLS) survey of household consumption expenditures.[32] Curves of the Engel type (expenditure

[32]Robert T. Michael, *The Effect of Education on Efficiency in Consumption, op. cit.*

lasticity Estimates for Food, Tobacco, and Alcohol Related to
cation, and Family Size, Based on the 1960 Bureau of Labor
nsumer Expenditures Survey

Item	Income	Education	Family size	$\bar{R}^{2}$*	Form†	Expenditure per person‡
Food (home)	0.526	−0.112	0.554	.95	1	$989
Food (away)	1.225	0.205	−0.319	.93	2	246
Tobacco	0.519	−0.563	0.224	.82	1	91
Alcohol	1.611	−0.584	−0.687	.90	2	78

*Since the variations are in different units, the $\bar{R}^{2}$'s are *not* comparable. Values selected were equation forms with highest $\bar{R}^{2}$.
†Equation form: 1 = linear; 2 = constant elasticity.
‡Average total family expenditure = $4,936.
Source: Adapted from Robert T. Michael, *The Effect of Education on Efficiency in Consumption,* New York: National Bureau of Economic Research, Occasional Paper 116, 1972, p. 47.

related to each variable) were fitted to the cross-sectional data for 1960 and 1950 according to an equation having the general form of

$$X_i = f_i\,(Y,\ E,\ F,\ A,\ R)$$

where X_i is the household's expenditure on the market good i, Y is the measure of the household's income level, E is years of formal education of the head, and F, A, and R are family size, age, and geographic region respectively. By use of multiple-regression techniques, estimates were obtained of the partial effects of these variables on the expenditure X_i. Findings for 1960 were consistent with those for 1950. Although family consumption patterns were not fully determined by these variables, expenditures were closely correlated with changes in income, education, and family size.

The results of the study appear to be consistent with other study estimates. By segregating the effects of the three factors—income, education, and family size—income elasticities for food were found to be higher than in most other studies. Education had a negative effect on expenditures for food eaten at home and a positive effect on food eaten away from home, while increase in family size had just the opposite effects (Table 3-4). The study suggests that use of tobacco products is positively correlated with income and family size, and negatively with education. Alcohol is correlated still more positively with income, but negatively with both family size and education.

Conclusion   The results of the Michael's study tend to reinforce the implications for policy arising out of other studies. In the third era of food policy, if there are further increases in real income, still higher levels of education and generally smaller family sizes than in the second era of food policy, then the demand for food processing and for various restaurant services in the domestic market will rise more than the demand for farm produce in the domestic market. The farm sector realizes increases in demand from expansions in exports of farm products, however, in which the food retailing sector does not share. The comparative impact on the farm and retail sectors of an increase in aggregate demand depends on whether it arises chiefly from increases in the domestic demand for food or whether it is from increased demand for farm product exports.

ELASTICITY OF DEMAND IN THE DOMESTIC MARKET

Elasticity of demand (E) represents the percentage change in quantity purchased as a result of a 1.0 percent change in price, *ceteris paribus*. Normally, all Es are negative. If E is greater than -1.0, then the demand is elastic and a change in price leads to a more than proportionate change in quantity purchased. If E is between zero and -1.0, then demand is inelastic and a change in price leads to a less than proportionate change in quantity purchased.

Elasticity of Demand for Individual Foods

The elasticity of demand for individual foods depends most heavily on the ease with which one food may be substituted for another. Foods that have close substitutes tend to be more elastic in demand, and foods that lack close substitutes are more inelastic, as is shown in Table 3-3.

In general, no distinction is made in this study between short-run and long-run elasticity. Although it has been hypothesized that there is a perceptible lag in consumer response to price, and therefore elasticity will increase as the length of time is expanded, several instances have been found where short-run elasticity exceeds long-run elasticity. This can occur if the consumers' initial reaction is to overadjust to a price change, either by altering diets in the short run or by increasing or decreasing certain food inventories in home or commercial storage. Since it is not known a priori whether the long run is more elastic or not, it is convenient to assume that in general the long-run and short-run elasticities are not significantly different.[33]

It is known, however, that demand is more inelastic at the farm level than at the wholesale or retail levels, and thus, when there are changes in supply, generally there will be relatively greater changes in price at the farm level than in retail markets. So the problem of price instability and uncertainty weighs heavily on farm managers and the makers of farm food policy.

Changes in Prices at Farm and Retail Levels[34]

Prices tend to move together between farm and retail food markets in different ways, however, depending on whether the events that cause the movement arise

[33]See George W. Ladd and John R. Tedford, "A Generalization of the Working Method for Estimating Long-Run Elasticities," *Journal of Farm Economics*, Vol. 41, No. 2, May 1958, pp. 221–233. For further discussion, see E. J. Working, *Demand for Meat*, Chicago: University of Chicago Press, 1954; and "How Much Progress Has Been Made in the Study of the Demand for Farm Products?," *Journal of Farm Economics*, Vol. 38, No. 5, December 1955, pp. 968–974.

[34]For quantitative methodology on this topic, see Bruce L. Gardner, "The Farm-Retail Price Spread in a Competitive Food Industry," *American Journal of Agricultural Economics*, Vol. 57, No. 3, August 1975, pp. 399–409.

from a shift in market demand, a change in farm supply, or a change in the supply of marketing inputs. Events that increase the demand for food will increase the percentage of total market receipts going to the farm sector if farm supply is less elastic than the supply of marketing inputs. This appears to be what happened in 1973 and 1974, for instance, when increases in farm output were slow to materialize, i.e. there was an inelastic farm supply.

Events that increase the supply of farm products, *ceteris paribus,* will depress prices relatively more at the farm level than at retail, because of the more inelastic demand at the farm level. In fact, if the demand for food stays strong in both the domestic and foreign markets, as it appeared to do in 1975, for example, and with farm supply curves shifting to the right, farm prices may show an absolute (as well as a relative) decline, even though retail food prices are still rising. The spread between farm and retail food prices may widen appreciably, not because the retail food chains have found a new element of monopoly power, but because the more inelastic demand at the farm level forces farm prices down as supply increases, whereas food prices in retail markets will move up or down depending on whether the continuing increases in demand are greater or smaller in magnitude than the continuing increases in supply.

This is not to deny that there is an oligopoly core of food distributors (food chains) and another, not wholly separate, oligopoly core of food manufacturers, each of which exercises a degree of monopoly market power. Nor is it meant to deny that this power is sometimes effectively used to widen the profits of one or the other, or both. It is simply to say that short run price changes at all levels from the farm through to the consumer are both created and constrained by the parameters of elasticity. Excess profits in the food marketing industry tend to increase the supply of marketing inputs, which then tends to reduce retail food prices relative to farm prices.

Although the marketing spread tends to be more stable from year to year than the more volatile farm share of the consumer's food dollar, this stability is of small comfort to the Congress or other food policymakers. The policy problem is to decide what action, if any, to take to stabilize farm and food prices and thus to counteract the instabilities arising out of the interactions of supply and demand.

Government Program Options

The government has essentially three major options for dealing with the farm price instabilities arising out of short-run inelasticity in supply and demand. They are (1) to restrict crop acreage and sales of farm products; (2) to support the prices of farm products above market equilibrium levels by purchase or a storage loan program; or (3) to pay farmers directly, which in effect is to subsidize a producer-consumer price differential. Since each of these possibilities will enter into our discussion of policy alternatives in the product markets (in Chapter 7), we may conveniently state them, and give illustrations, at this time.

Case 1. Supply Controls   When demand is inelastic, a small crop will sell for more than a large one; therefore, it is to the farmers' advantage to restrict

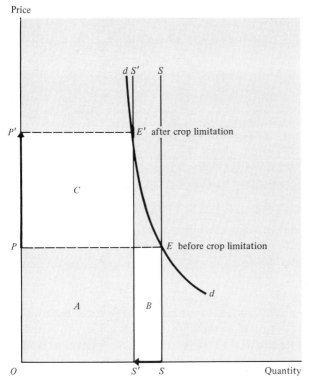

Price

P' — — — — — — — — — — E' after crop limitation

C

P — — — — — — — — — — E before crop limitation

d

A   B

O   S'   S   Quantity

Figure 3-3 Under a crop-limitation program, farm income rises because of inelastic demand. Before crop limitation, *OS* or *PE* is produced. Market is in equilibrium at price *P* and gross receipts are *OPES*, or *A* plus *B*. After crop limitation, the equilibrium is at *P'* or *E'*. Gross receipts are equal to the rectangle *OP' E' S'*, or *A* plus *C*. *A + B < A + C*. *E* = −0.25.

aggregate crop production (Figure 3-3). The basic means for reducing production is either land diversion (as to a soil bank), acreage allotments to regulate a specific crop, or marketing quotas to regulate sales. Initial support for such policies has come from farm groups. Consumers and others have been won over in sufficient numbers to permit adoption of such policy programs only when they have been convinced that the goal of higher farm prices was equitable. At almost all times when new legislation is being considered, there are long-continuing hearings and arguments about alternative levels of constraint in price support.

Supply controls are most effective in raising and stabilizing farm prices when they are placed on commodities that are highly inelastic in demand—wheat, tobacco, fluid milk, for example—and it is groups who are interested in these commodities that have led the campaigns for such policies. Although cotton farmers and their representatives in Congress supported such policies for a long time, the loss of foreign markets and the difficulty of protecting the domestic market from imports of cotton products forced a shift in policy, beginning with the Wheat and Cotton Act of 1964. This act authorized the substitution of direct payments to producers in lieu of higher price supports.

Use of land diversion or acreage allotments (Figure 3-4) while farmers are

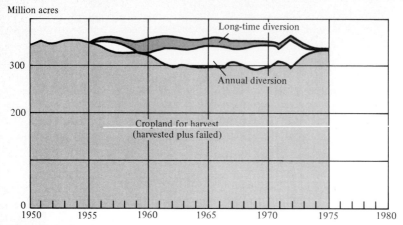

Million acres

Figure 3-4 Cropland intended for harvest and diverted acreage. Prior to 1956, acreage allotment provisions effectively limited the acreage that could be planted to basic crops, including wheat, corn, and cotton, but they had little effect on total crop acreage. Data for 1975 from July SRS crop report. *(Source: U.S. Department of Agriculture, Economic Research Service.)*

free to add more fertilizer and other inputs to the permitted acreage are not the most efficient means of crop restriction or the best way to promote efficiency in farming. In some cases, therefore, when supply control is urgent, marketing quotas have been employed, either to complement land controls or to substitute for them. Also, supply control might involve measures such as taxing or rationing other inputs to restrict production and obtain higher prices.

Case 2. Government Storage Loan and Purchase Government has supported farm prices by loaning money on crops or other farm products held in storage, thus temporarily reducing supply and generally expecting to dispose of the stocks in ways that will not equally depress market prices later. Also, the government has purchased commodities with the same idea. Unless the government can dispose of the commodities without depressing prices, however, these approaches may not have positive effects on farm incomes in the long run. Consequently, storage programs are sometimes associated with domestic food subsidy programs, such as commodity distribution and food stamp programs, or with foreign aid and export subsidy programs.

In Figure 3-5, to raise prices from OP to OP', the government must buy or put in storage an amount equal to $S'S$, or $E''E'$. The increase in farm income will be equal to the total cost of government purchases plus the net increase in market receipts. Or the government purchases may have a leverage or multiplier effect if the commodity is sold in foreign markets where at least part of the initial government expenditure may be recovered.

Whether the government will gain or lose money on this operation depends on shifts in supply and demand. The Federal Farm Board, which started in 1929 with a $500 million revolving fund, failed when it was unable to control either supply or demand. The conclusion was that the government had to control supply to make this type of program work. The Commodity Credit Corporation (CCC) accumulated large stocks in the late 1930s, even with extensive crop restriction; but these were used during World War II. Or, in other words, increases in demand saved the CCC. The Eisenhower administration in the 1950s built and carried into the 1960s CCC storage stocks that appeared to be excessive—or were they? These were reduced at great cost by more stringent controls in the 1960s, in both the Kennedy and Johnson administrations. They tended to stabilize in the first years of the Nixon administration and were sold at a profit by the government beginning in 1972 (Figure 3-6). Policy in regard to rules for government stock acquisition and disposition, and the appropriate magnitude of stocks, is discussed further in Chapter 7.

Case 3. Direct Payments to Farmers, or Producer-Consumer Price Differential   Direct payments to farmers, in lieu of price supports above market equilib-

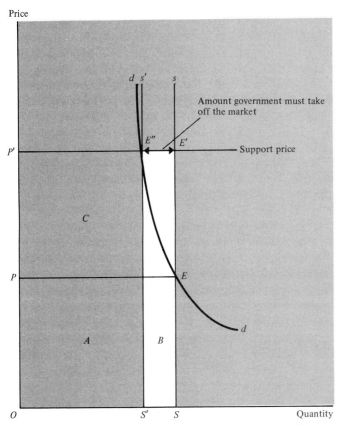

Figure 3-5 Government increases farm income by additions to storage or by taking commodity off the market. To raise market price from P, government support of price at P′ results in storage under loan or purchase equal to the quantity S′S. Total cost of acquisition is S′ E″ E′S.

$ Billions

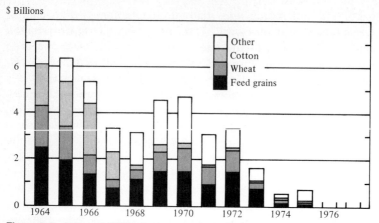

Figure 3-6   Value of CCC price support inventories and loans, year ending June 30. "Other" are primarily dairy products, soybeans, and tobacco. "Feed grains" include corn, barley, grain sorghums, oats, and rye. *(Source: U.S. Department of Agriculture, Economic Research Service.)*

rium levels, will result in a narrower market spread. In Figure 3-7, let supply and demand intersect at E as before. Then let the government attempt to support income at OP'. The gap between OP and OP' will need to be paid by the government on the quantity OS or PE. Farmers end up with payments of PP' on the quantity produced. The cost to government or to consumers through the tax system is $PP' \times PE$, or $PP'E'E$. In this case, it makes no difference whether the demand curve above the price OP is elastic or inelastic, or whether the commodities are storable or perishable.

All that is produced will be sold. This program will cost the government more and consumers directly less than a program involving purchase and disposal outside of regular market channels. If demand is elastic, it may not cost the government much more than another alternative, and since consumer prices are lower, there are some gains in welfare. Direct payments are sometimes recommended for perishable commodities, many of which are not so inelastic in demand. Secretary of Agriculture Brannan, in the Truman administration, advocated wide use of direct payments in what was called "The Brannan Plan." In the Eisenhower administration, Secretary Benson advocated direct payments for butter. They have been used widely for wool, sugar, and cotton, not because of perishability, of course, but because they are a way to provide income support and a certain level of domestic production without high tariffs. For cotton, they are also important to maintain exports and possibly recapture some of the foreign market lost through high price supports on cotton.

A Policy Conclusion   The choices among alternative government policies, which often depend on elasticities of demand and supply, also depend on agreements in respect to both goals and constraints. A free market is generally the most efficient in use of resources, and it provides normal profits to producers in the long run. Profits are often depressed in the short run, however, and policy is desired that will improve farm incomes. There are various alternative choices from among a number of possible programs.

Where demand is inelastic and producer incomes are too low, a subsidy can be provided at least cost to government by restriction of the commodities that are most inelastic in demand, such as wheat, sugar, milk, and tobacco. The main part of the cost will be shifted to consumers through the higher prices in commodity markets.

Where demand is more elastic, as in the case of cotton, crop restriction is less effective in raising prices. In the case of export crops, however, to the extent that the policy is effective, the government must subsidize exports or suffer a loss of export markets. The need for direct export subsidy may be avoided by making payments to producers in lieu of price supports.

Within the domestic market, because of poor people's higher income elasticity for food, demand can be increased by transferring income through the tax system to the poor.

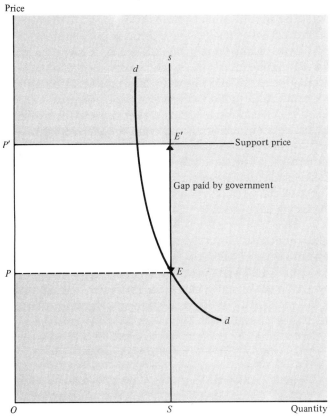

Figure 3-7 Government payments increase farm income. The government lets price to consumers remain at *P* or *E*. If the difference between *P* and *P'* is made up by direct payments, the government's cost will be *PP'E'E*. The total return *OP'E'S* is realized by farmers.

Table 3-5   Price Elasticities of Demand for Major Components of American Farm Output, Domestic and Foreign Markets, Intermediate Three-Year Term and Long Run

	Food and feed		Cotton		Tobacco	
Market	Three-year	Long run	Three-year	Long run	Three-year	Long run
Domestic	−.18*	− .10	− .65	−1.8	−.10	†
Foreign	−1.91	−6.42	−1.84	−3.7	−.50	†

*The short-run elasticity is −.25; the long-run elasticity is −.10. With 20 percent of the adjustment completed each year, then approximately 50 percent of the adjustment is completed in an intermediate run of three years.
†No estimate available.
Source: Luther G. Tweeten, "The Demand for United States Farm Output," in Stanford University, *Food Research Institute Studies,* Vol. VII, No. 3, 1967, pp. 343–369.

Comparative Elasticity in Domestic and Foreign Markets

The demand for America's food and farm output is much more elastic in the export market than in the domestic market. So farm income will be increased by price discrimination; that is, by shifting produce from the domestic to the foreign market by either subsidizing exports, thus selling at a lower price in the export market than domestically, or by paying farmers directly in lieu of domestic price support. America's food and farm exports are generally only a small portion of total supply in an importing country, and normally they can be increased by some percentage without having an equal percentage effect on prices in the importing country. Thus, it has been estimated that export demand for food and farm products is highly elastic, contrasting sharply with the inelasticity of the domestic market (Table 3-5). In this case, it is not suggested that the aggregate world demand for a commodity—wheat for example—is more elastic than aggregate domestic demand. Demand faced by exporters from the United States, or any other country, is more elastic because the shipments are only a small part of total supply in the importing countries.

Implications for Policy   Because of the greater elasticity of export demand, a policy that shifts supply into export channels will increase farm income, *ceteris paribus.* By comparing the three-year and long-run elasticities, we also can infer that such a policy will be even more effective in the long run than in the short run.

For food and feed, this inelasticity of domestic demand suggests that prices will be unstable unless supply is stabilized from year to year; and the high elasticity in the export market emphasizes the importance of having an assured or reliable supply in order to sustain a high-level export trade over the three-year term as well as the long run.

In respect to cotton, although restriction of supply in the domestic market will yield some increase in gross income to producers, it will reduce earnings in the export market. In the long run, it will greatly reduce total market receipts in both the domestic and foreign market.

The inelasticity of demand for tobacco shows why the programs to control the supply of tobacco have been able to stabilize tobacco prices so effectively. Apparently, also the control of tobacco production has not reduced receipts in the export market. The major costs of control have been transferred to tobacco users.

Although these implications and inferences are believed to be general in nature, the specific values in Table 3-5 are strictly applicable only to the conditions existing when the measurements were made. This qualification does not, however, lessen their value for policy.

Implications of Aggregate Demand   The elasticity of aggregate demand is estimated by first multiplying each commodity or group elasticity by the percentage representing the market share of each in the total output, and then by adding the products (Table 3-6).

The elasticity of $-.46$ for the three-year term suggests that during this interval restricting farm output will transfer income to farmers. A 2 percent reduction will increase farm prices 4 to 5 percent ($-.02 \div -.463 = +.045$). A 5 percent restriction will increase prices 11 percent, and so on. Since farmers are sometimes paid directly to retire land, their income payments should be added to their gain in market receipts to estimate the total effect.

Long-run elasticity of -1.106 shows that there will be no gain in market receipts in the long run from crop restriction, although farmers might gain from payments to keep them in such a program.

Table 3-6   Estimation of Aggregate Elasticity of Demand from Price Elasticities of Major Components in Table 3-5

Markets and components	Market share of each component percent	Contribution of each component to total elasticity of demand*	
		Three-year term	Long run
Domestic			
Food and feed	76.2	−.137	− .076
Cotton	4.8	−.031	− .088
Tobacco	2.5	−.002	− .012
Foreign			
Food and feed	13.1	−.250	− .841
Cotton	2.4	−.043	− .089
Tobacco	1.0	†	†
Total	100.0	−.463	−1.106

*Multiply elasticity from Table 3-5 by the corresponding market share. Thus, for example,
$-.18 \times 76.2\% = -.137$
$-.65 \times 4.8\% = -.031$, and so on
†The weight is so small for this category that its omission has little impact on the total elasticity.
Source: Luther G. Tweeten, "The Demand for United States Farm Output," in Stanford University, *Food Research Institute Studies,* Vol. VII, No. 3, 1967, pp. 343–369.

A Policy Conclusion   Farm and food policy for America has alternated between two general concepts: (1) a policy that is highly nationalistic in concept, emphasizing crop restrictions and supply control, export subsidies and tariffs, or quotas to limit imports of a few farm products; and (2) a policy that is more international in concept, with a wider range for free-market pricing, little if any production control, and efforts to have free trade in food and farm products.

To best serve the national welfare in the new third era, food policy for America must have a central theme. It must help to stabilize markets against the types of violent fluctuations that have occurred without being restrictive in regard to production and trade. A new policy in regard to food reserves must emerge, based on a new consensus between producers and consumers and involving an important new element of rural-urban understanding and cooperation. Measures must be taken to assure an export potential in bad crop years as well as in good. All these goals must be combined with policy that helps to stabilize food demand at a high level in the domestic market and provide equitable help to the poor.

To further develop the basis for this policy, we turn next to the alternatives and policy implications of increasing food supply.

QUESTIONS FOR DISCUSSION

1 There has been some disagreement about how much the demand for food and farm products was depressed by overvaluation of the dollar. Although we may not settle this question, in terms of general theory how does overvaluation affect food demand? What longer-term implications for food policy might result from letting the dollar float?

2 Do you accept the argument that the United States must abandon the goal of energy independence to enjoy the major benefits of comparative advantage in food production and trade? Give your reasons pro or con.

3 Although the food stamp program has brought an important increment of aid to several million low-income people, the program has been criticized both as to goals and as to how it operates. What is the basis for this criticism? Do you have a policy alternative that you prefer? Comment.

4 School lunch and related programs expanded rapidly in the early 1970s. What was the policy goal in this expansion? What are the arguments for a free lunch for all children? For charging children from middle- and upper-income families?

5 Define income elasticity. What are Engel's curves? The income elasticity for food tends to drop as people become more affluent, yet in the United States apparently there has been a strong increase in demand for beef, chicken, pork, etc. Also, between 1964 and 1974 the index of per capita food consumption increased by 7 or 8 points. Are these trends consistent with the accepted theory? Comment.

6 On the basis of what we know about income elasticity, compare the effects on food demand of a food stamp subsidy versus a straight cash subsidy of equal amount. How do the welfare effects compare?

7 A recent USDA report suggests that the income elasticity of demand for food in this country is near zero for a large part of the population. Distinguish as fully as you can the implications of this in terms of policy alternatives (*a*) for farm producers, (*b*) for export policy, and (*c*) for subsidies to the poor.

8 Define elasticity of demand (E). What are some typical Es for food at retail and at farm level? Why is the farm-level E lower than E at retail? What are some of the implications of these Es for price fluctuations at the retail level? At the farm level?

9 Compare and contrast the comparative costs and benefits of solving the problem of farm price instability by (a) crop restriction, (b) government storage loan and purchase, or (c) payments, as a producer-consumer price differential. Identify costs and benefits, or the welfare advantages and disadvantages of each policy. Comment on the elasticities and use diagrams to illustrate.

10 Compare and contrast Es for food and other farm products in domestic and foreign markets in the intermediate or three-year term and in the long run. In view of these Es, what will be the effects on receipts from farm marketings and on aggregate farm income (a) of crop restrictions without export subsidy, (b) of government storage-loan and purchases under alternative disposal policies in domestic and foreign markets, and (c) of a producer-consumer price differential in the domestic market? In the foreign market?

11 Resolved that food policy for this nation should attempt to stabilize food prices and producer income primarily by stabilization of food demand and a food reserve-storage program rather than by restriction of food supply. Develop the arguments for the affirmative and the negative. (a) What would be the welfare effects of each option? (b) Which would result in minimum cost to government? (c) Which would be most effective in stabilizing farm income?

REFERENCES

Brandow, George E., *Interrelationships among Demand for Farm Products and Implications for Control of Market Supply,* University Park: Pennsylvania State University, Agricultural Experiment Station Bulletin No. 680, 1961.

Clarkson, Kenneth W., *Food Stamps and Nutrition,* Washington: American Enterprise Institute for Public Policy Research, Evaluative Study No. 18, April 1975.

Gardner, Bruce L., "The Farm Retail Price Spread in a Competitive Food Industry," *American Journal of Agricultural Economics,* Vol. 57, No. 3, August 1975, pp. 399–409.

Hoover, Dale M., and James G. Maddox, *Food for the Hungry: Direct Distribution and Food Stamp Programs for Low-Income Families,* Washington: National Planning Association, Planning Pamphlet No. 126, February 1969.

Joint Economic Committee, *Income Security for Americans: Recommendations of the Public Welfare Study,* Subcommittee on Fiscal Policy, 93d Cong., 2d Sess., Dec. 5, 1974.

Kotz, Nick, *Let Them Eat Promises: The Politics of Hunger in America,* Englewood Cliffs, N.J.: Prentice-Hall, Inc., 1969.

Paarlberg, Don, *Subsidized Food Consumption,* Washington: American Enterprise Institute for Public Policy Research, May 1963.

Southworth, Herman M., "The Economics of Public Measures to Subsidize Food Consumption," *Journal of Farm Economics,* Vol. XXVII, February 1945, pp. 38–66.

Tweeten, Luther G., "The Demand for United States Farm Output," *Food Research Institute Studies,* Vol. VII, No. 3, 1967, pp. 343–369.

Increasing Food Supply

Then shall the reign of mind commence on earth,
And starting fresh as from a second birth,
Man, in the sunshine of the world's new spring,
Shall walk transparent, like some holy thing!

Thomas Moore
Lalla Rookh, "The Veiled Prophet of Khorassan," part 1

How shall food be produced? Three factors have contributed most importantly to increasing America's food supply: great land resources and the hardy bands of settlers that spread across the continent; the development of farm mechanization and power resources; and finally, a scientific revolution embodying a wide range of innovations in new or improved crops and livestock, fertilizers and farm chemicals, and improved finance and management systems. All these are now contributing to the increasing food supply as food commodities are produced by other commodities of farm and nonfarm origin; and, although there is some evidence in the 1970s of a slowing down in the rate of growth, the potential still appears to be high.

The purposes of this chapter are to provide a more secure foundation for understanding the policy problems associated with increasing food supply, to view the various factors in a more general perspective, and thus to anticipate policy problems and alternatives for the future. This foundation will also help stimulate more specific understanding of the problems encountered in making national policy (Chapter 5), the role of farm organizations in this policy process (Chapter 6), the alternatives in the product markets (Chapter 7), and the markets for factor inputs (Chapters 7 through 10), and the basis for coordinating nutrition policy (Chapter 11).

CYCLES OF INCREASING FOOD SUPPLY

Growth in American agriculture has occurred in a somewhat cyclical pattern that is related to innovations and relative prices. This pattern is illustrated in Figure 4-1, where aggregate farm output on the horizontal axis is plotted against the parity ratio (the index of prices received by farmers over the index of prices paid for commodities, interest, taxes, and wage rates) on the vertical axis two years earlier. A series or cluster of years from 1912 through 1922 is seen as a period of rather slow growth. Another, from 1923 through 1930, shows the effect of the shift from horses to tractor power. A third reflects the mixed influence of the severe drought from 1933 through 1936 and the crop control programs under the Roosevelt New Deal. But it also shows the most important jump in productivity in 1937–41, resulting from fertilizer, hybrid corn, and further mechanization. This increase tended to negate the effects of production control and to frustrate achievements in the administration's farm program. Prices plus government payments were about as unfavorable as they were in the 1920s.

In 1942 to 1951 there was a jump in production related to cancelation of acreage allotments, the transitional increase in commercial fertilizer, and the favorable prices and price guarantees of World War II and the postwar years. Contrary to popular impression, wartime productivity did not increase much from 1942 to 1946 even though prices were favorable. Farmers enjoyed a few years of good weather and good prices but, except for the release of acreage from crop control in 1942 and the development in fertilizer, very little new innovation was available. One might regard 1948 as the first year that postwar technology became available, although the production potential did not appear in full force until about 1952. By 1950, the price of fertilizer relative to the price of all farm inputs was down to 60 percent of what it had averaged from 1910 to the mid-1930s. From 1952 to 1957 there was slow growth, but a new production plateau was established, even though farm product prices dropped because of the combined force of the innovations entering agriculture, the growth in use of fertilizer, and especially the new pesticides. The years from 1958 to 1970 show the effects of the advancing productivity of the more complete system of innovations pressing down hard against the parity ratio. The price of fertilizer continued to drop relative to the price of all farm inputs, settling around 50 percent of the 1910–35 average. So, in spite of the massive effort of the Emergency Feed Grain Program and other production controls throughout the 1960s and the early 1970s, the parity ratio, including government payments,

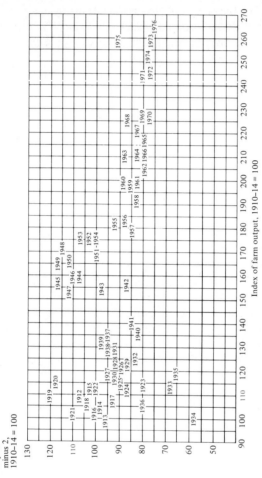

Figure 4-1 Index of farm output compared with parity ratio in year minus two, 1912–76. Parity ratio includes government payments starting in 1933. (*Source: Handbook of Agricultural Charts and related data, USDA, ERS, annual. Note:* The parity ratio for a year is calculated by dividing the index of prices received for all farm products (August 1909–July 1914 = 100) by the index of prices paid (1910–1914 = 100). See pp. 11, 151, 161 ff.)

88

averaged around the middle levels of the 1920s and 1930s. The farm programs of this era did not fail; they were simply overcome by the innovations that proved attractive to producers. Finally, the production data for the 1970s show only a relatively short upward movement in farm prices as logged against output. In spite of the great increases in food demand from 1972 on, as discussed in Chapter 3, the increases in prices of farm inputs were sufficient to offset the effects of higher food and farm product prices.

   This record of price and output raises important questions about the role of various factors in increasing food supply. We shall attempt to identify the major factors, the problems associated with their use and further development, and some of the policy alternatives for the future.

THE ROLE OF LAND

Land plays a constantly changing role in the process of increasing food supply. In the first great era, as we have noted, land settlement and development were the dominating factors in national policy. In the second era, although land use patterns continued to change, the total cropland in farms tended to stabilize at slightly less than 400 million acres. From the early 1960s on, the total cropland harvested was almost exactly 300 million acres, about 30 to 40 million acres were in summerfallow, from 37 to 65 million acres were idled by government programs, and each year 5 to 10 million acres were planted but not harvested when crops failed or were unprofitable to harvest. Then, beginning in the third era, as land diversion programs were canceled, the acreage used for crops expanded correspondingly. Questions concerning the suitability of using more land for crops, which had long been of scientific interest, became more significant for policy.

The Land Potential for Increasing Food Supply

The nation has some 2.3 billion acres of land, excluding large lakes, reservoirs, and major rivers but including about 7 million acres in small streams and ponds of 40 acres or less. Nearly 760 million acres are federally owned, including 360 million in Alaska with very little of it suitable for crops or grazing, while the other 400 million acres in the 48 contiguous states are mostly used for forestry and grazing. Some 60 million acres are in urban use, roads and highways, and other developed areas, generally precluding any use for agriculture now or in the future; and about ½ million acres—some of it the best for food production—are believed to be going into these urban and urban-related uses each year. This leaves from 1.4 billion to 1.5 billion acres of rural, nonfederal land which has not been in crops but has been used for a variety of purposes, such as grazing, forestry, wildlife, or open space.

   By assuming that the 370 million acres of cropland continue in cultivation under economical farm management and conservation policies, some policy interest has been concentrated on the question of the availability for crops of certain lands not previously in crops. In 1967, the USDA's Soil Conservation

Service (SCS) was directed to conduct a broad national inventory of soil and water conservation needs, including estimates of the potential for conversion of uncropped land to crops.[1] This study, called the Conservation Needs Inventory (CNI), revealed that there were some 265.5 million acres of potential cropland not in crops in the 48 contiguous states. Of this total, it was estimated that 95.7 million acres had a high potential for conversion to cropland, although about half this land, located in the Great Plains, would require strict conservation measures, and the balance, in the North-Central states, Florida, and the Gulf Coast, would require clearing, drainage, and some other measures, such as terracing or leveling. Some 57 million acres in the Piedmont Coastal Plain, the Atlantic Coast Lowlands, and the Southwest had a medium potential, requiring more extensive improvements if they were to be used for crops. Finally, 112 million acres, scattered more widely in almost all parts of the country, had a low potential for conversion to crops, as they were a mixture of forest land with erosion problems, farmland in small and scattered fields like those in the Appalachian and Ozark regions, and land with a short growing season as around the Great Lakes or in parts of the Northeast, or they were land limited by water shortages as in the Rocky Mountains and the Far West. According to the CNI, however, if 100 million acres of the most easily converted land were brought into production, then, compared with other estimates not involving this conversion, the acreage of grain sorghums could be doubled, cotton and citrus production could be increased by two-thirds, wheat by more than one-half, soybeans by one-third, and corn by one-fifth. Pasture acreage would be reduced by as much as 60 million acres.

Policy Problems in Converting Land to Crops

Almost all the land identified as convertible to crop use will present new or more intensive conservation problems if it becomes profitable for crops. The 50 to 60 million acres of potential cropland in the Great Plains is extremely susceptible to wind erosion, especially in years of low rainfall. In the great drought of the 1930s, several million acres of those lands were badly damaged and went out of crop production. Although much of this land subsequently was returned to crops, most of the additional land in the Great Plains identified in the CNI will require strip-cropping and other conservation measures. In the Lake States and on around into the Atlantic and Coastal Plains, much of the land identified as convertible will be subject to excessive water erosion, washing, and gullying, with attendant problems of stream pollution and sedimentation. Not only will more individual farm conservation measures be called for; the SCS or some other agency may be required to enforce new measures that are not always profitable for the farmer, such as terracing and contour farming. Finally, in the Rocky Mountains and the Far West, long-range projections of the need for water show that industrial and residential demands will be stronger than those of agriculture.

[1]*Conservation Needs Inventory, 1967,* USDA, Soil Conservation Service.

Except for a large project in the central valley of California, very little additional water can be economically supplied for increased crop production.

A Policy Conclusion

In a national policy directed at increasing food supply, public investments in land reclamation, conservation, and development can be justified only if they are the cheapest means of getting the increases in farm production that are set as a policy goal. The net increase in the marginal value of product (MVP) must exceed marginal costs (MC) during the time span taken into account in setting policy. Anticipated annual returns must be discounted and capitalized to bring them in line with investments that are planned and the opportunity costs of forgoing the alternative products. In short, to justify the public expenditure, there must be no more economical way, evaluated on a comparative basis, of obtaining the net addition to food production.[2] In addition, of course, it must be recognized that land used for crops and grazing requires certain public measures for conservation if the highest net social product is to be obtained. This is discussed further in Chapter 8. In the meantime, we shall look at other innovations for increasing food supply and their policy implications.

INNOVATIONS FOR INCREASING FOOD SUPPLY

As innovations have broadened their impact on increasing food supply, the alternatives for national policy in dealing with them have multiplied and become more varied. The first innovations that were important in the transitional growth of American agriculture were mechanical in nature. Then, early in this century, came tractor power to displace mainly horses and mules. Between 1921 and 1940, at least one-half the increase in farm marketings was due to this displacement. Between 1941 and 1960, when this transition was almost completed, about 15 percent of the increase came from this source. During this time and still later, there came science-based innovations that were largely biological—new seeds, new crop varieties, and improved strains of old ones. The most significant aggregatively was hybrid corn. Then came innovations in fertilizers, chemical pesticides, disease and weed controls, feed handling and processing, and advances in animal breeding, management, and care. Modern farming, agricultural industry, and science in the form of research and education proved to be an effective trio for increasing food supply.[3]

The effects of this transition and what may lie ahead are critical for food policy. We need to trace this evolution to see its policy impact and to identify alternatives for the future.

[2]For additional discussion, see *Food and Fiber for the Future,* Report of the National Advisory Commission on Food and Fiber, Washington: Government Printing Office, July 1967.

[3]R. P. Christensen, W. E. Hendrix, and R. D. Stevens, *How the United States Improved Its Agriculture,* USDA, ERS Foreign 76, 1964. See also Yujiro Hayami and Vernon Ruttan, *Resources, Technology and Agricultural Development: An International Perspective,* Baltimore: The Johns Hopkins Press, 1971.

Cotton Production Innovations

The first highly significant innovation in the accelerated growth of American agriculture was improvement in the process for cleaning cotton. In 1791 Eli Whitney invented a machine to remove the seeds from cotton. It was called a cotton gin. By 1845 the gin had been improved so much that with an investment of about $100, three people could clean the seeds from 600 to 2,500 pounds of cotton a day, compared with a maximum of 6 pounds a day per person prior to its invention.[4] The effect was threefold: (1) to reduce the price of cotton, bringing it within budget reach of the average consumer, (2) to make cotton the major export of the Southern states, and (3) to transfer the labor bottleneck from cleaning to picking cotton.

A large, low-cost labor force was needed to pick cotton. This requirement gave a comparative advantage to two types of farm organization in the South: (1) the small-scale farm, in which the family supplied most, if not all, of the labor; and (2) the large plantation type, with the work force at first supplied chiefly by slaves and later by low-wage labor or sharecroppers. Since the work force required for picking cotton far exceeded that required for other farm tasks, the opportunity cost for doing these other tasks was very low. The economic incentive for making laborsaving improvements in other farm practices was slight; and the agriculture of the South stagnated—we may say for at least 100 years—until invention of the mechanical cotton picker and its step-by-step improvement.

The mechanical cotton picker set in motion a new revolution in cotton production, but it aggravated an already bad income situation. Because of the highly seasonal demand for cotton pickers, the underemployment of labor in the Southern states was much more severe than in any other major region. Use of the cotton picker not only displaced a large portion of the farm labor force; by making this labor largely surplus, it contributed to an increasing skewness in the distribution of income. The people that were displaced generally had no good alternative source of employment, and those left behind in Southern communities were more destitute than they had been before.[5] Some of the surplus labor spilled off the farm, either to rural nonfarm occupations in the South or to other parts of the country.[6]

Although cotton innovations were only part of the problem, the failure to anticipate the social need of the people or to legislate effectively to meet it must be regarded as one of the major policy failures of the twentieth century. As

[4]Clarence H. Danhof, "Agricultural Technology in 1880," in H. F. Williamson (ed.), *The Growth of the American Economy*, New York: Prentice-Hall, Inc., 1946, pp. 132, 133.

[5]See *The People Left Behind*, A Report by the President's Advisory Commission on Rural Poverty, Washington: The Superintendent of Documents, September 1967.

[6]Robert Coles, *The South Goes North: Volume III of Children of Crisis*, Boston: Little, Brown and Company, 1972; Carl F. Taeuber and Alma F. Taeuber, *Negroes in Cities*, Chicago: Aldine Publishing Co., 1965; Robert E. Will and Harold G. Vatter (eds.), *Poverty in Affluence, The Social, Political and Economic Dimensions of Poverty in the United States*, New York: Harcourt, Brace & World, Inc., 1970.

pointed out by the President's Advisory Commission on Rural Poverty, the problem of poverty had not been solved by higher price supports and production payments for cotton, which had been a major direction of national policy. A recommended solution required a more comprehensive and active approach to major manpower problems of more effectively employing a retrained and relocated work force.[7] The legacy of excess labor resources from innovations in cotton, which resulted in very low average farm income in the South, as well as impoverishment, had confused the issues in cotton policy for at least a generation. The legacy gave sanction to a cotton program that greatly restricted cotton acreage to maintain aggregate income to cotton producers in the form of cotton price supports and payments. This policy largely protected and benefited landowners; and very few of the benefits ever reached the more disadvantaged labor groups.[8]

Cotton is the last major crop to complete the process of mechanization. New insecticides for control of the boll weevil, new varieties of cotton, mechanical cotton pickers, and other innovations in weed and disease control have given a great boost to cotton yields. As a result of price-support policy, however, in the early 1970s only about one-fourth as much land was in cotton as at the peak in the late 1920s. The production potential for cotton remains large, depending almost entirely on economic conditions and the price or trade policy to be followed in the cotton market.

More General Inventions and Innovations in Farm Machinery[9]

Other more general inventions and innovations in farm machinery have been adopted with wider economic effects in grain farming and, in contrast to the cotton gin and the mechanical cotton picker, they generally have given competitive advantages to the family farm. In 1797, Charles Newbold invented the cast-iron plow. Although it was heavy, hard to pull, and did not scour easily, it was a considerable advance over earlier wooden models. In 1837, John Deere used a high-grade steel, produced in Pittsburgh, to make a new plow much superior to the cast-iron model. By 1850, 1,600 steel plows were being produced annually at Moline, Illinois. The foundation for Deere and Company was firmly laid; and soon the steel plow was standard in most grain-farming regions of the United States. In 1868, James Oliver made a chilled-iron plow which would scour and wear better, and John Lane developed a soft-center steel plow with outside layers of hard steel for toughness, hardness, and scouring, and a center layer of

---

[7]*The People Left Behind*, op. cit., pp. 25 ff.

[8]*Costs of Producing Upland Cotton in the United States, 1969*, USDA, ERS, Agricultural Economics Report No. 227, June 1972.

[9]Among useful references are the following: August C. Bolino, *The Development of the American Economy*, 2d ed., Columbus, Ohio: Merrill Books, 1966; Harold D. Guither, *Heritage of Plenty, A Guide to the Economic History and Development of U.S. Agriculture*, 2d ed., Danville, Ill.: Interstate Printers and Publishers, Inc., 1972; Herman E. Kroos, *American Economic Development*, 2d ed., Englewood Cliffs, N.J.: Prentice-Hall, Inc., 1966; Douglass C. North, *Growth and Welfare in the American Past, A New Economic History*, Englewood Cliffs, N.J.: Prentice-Hall, Inc., 1966.

soft steel for durability. This was the superior principle. But a patent on it could not be protected, and the invention was widely adopted as the basic system for plows and most tillage equipment. The basic principle is in use today.

Development of grain harvesting equipment roughly paralleled the advances in tillage. In 1826, Patrick Bell, a Scotsman, invented a reaper which enabled a man with a team to harvest as much grain as was done formerly by six men. This reaper was improved in 1831 by William Manning and in 1833 by Obed Hussey. In 1834, Cyrus McCormick developed the first reaper to be widely used. It had a reel to push the grain back from the cutting bar and a platform on which the grain could fall for gathering into bunches. Although this is the basic invention that is still used in grain harvesting equipment, a really satisfactory reaper was not developed until 1855. In 1837, Hiram and John Pitts developed the first grain thresher. It had a cylinder for beating the grain out of the head and a fanning mill for separating the grain from the chaff and straw. A concave stacker was added, and it was in common use by 1860. In 1878, the first grain combine was developed, which was pulled through the field reaping and threshing at the same time. Finally, in 1880, William Deering developed a grain binder which could cut grain and automatically tie it in bundles, and E. W. Quincy got the first important patent on a mechanical corn picker.

The important point for policy is that these innovations were basic in determining the size of the family farm, and by and large they provided a competitive advantage to the family farm over larger-scale enterprise. Later modifications and improvements, plus the shift from horses to tractor power, changed the optimum size for the family farm by giving advantages to larger units. This shift is still going on. Normally, small-scale units are progressively disadvantaged and changes in economic structure occur to the advantage of large-scale units. A general question for production policy, arising frequently in policy discussion, is whether or not more deliberative policies should be adopted to preserve a family-farm structure in which the average operating unit may be smaller than the economically optimum size.

Farm Tractor Power

The development of farm tractor power lagged behind that of either tillage or harvesting equipment, and tractors did not become practical on a large scale until the beginning of the twentieth century. When the change occurred, it revolutionized the entire system of farm machinery and equipment. Although an internal combustion engine which ran on gunpowder was invented in 1678 by P.G. Hautefeuille in France, and a steam engine was invented in 1705 by Thomas Newcomen in England, it was not until 1855 that Obed Hussey in America developed a self-propelled steam engine that could be used for plowing. It was slow and cumbersome. In 1876, Nikolaus Otto in Germany developed the first practical 4-cycle internal combustion engine. In 1892, Rudolph Diesel in Germany developed the first motor to burn low-grade fuels with high efficiency—a motor that apparently will indefinitely bear his name.

Farm tractor power in America is a twentieth-century development. In 1892, John M. Froelich developed the first successful gasoline tractor, actually a forerunner of the John Deere tractor. By 1905, C. W. Hart and C. H. Parr had founded the first business to be devoted exclusively to making tractors. For several years the Hart-Parr tractors, which ran on kerosene, were important, especially in production of wheat and small grains. They were a forerunner of the Oliver tractors. Substantial economies of scale developed by the automobile industry were transferred to farm tractors. Although many firms were making farm tractors, Henry Ford emerged as the dominant manufacturer, producing about 100,000 Fordson tractors in 1925, 75 percent of the total number produced. Fordson tractors failed to keep pace, however, especially with the highly service-able John Deere "Model D" which appeared in 1923, the all-purpose McCormick-Deering "Farmall" in 1924, and the Allis-Chalmers "Model E." They all were highly adaptable, especially to the Corn Belt and the Great Plains. In some hilly areas or where soil traction was poor, new caterpillar crawl-type tractors burning distillate were an important innovation.

The age of farm tractor power swept America. In 1931, B. F. Goodrich and, soon thereafter, the Firestone Rubber Company developed rubber tires suitable for tractors. Other companies followed. By 1940, 85 percent of the wheel-type tractors were on rubber. Power takeoffs were improved, making practical a new system of motor-powered equipment. Multigear transmissions greatly increased tractor flexibility. Electric starters, new diesel motors, and air conditioning were on the way. The modern era of large-scale power and automated farming was here.

Economic Structure of the Farm Machinery and Equipment Industry[10]

Although the *1963 Census of Manufacturers* listed 1,562 establishments under "Farm Machinery and Equipment Industry," of which 555 firms had more than 20 employees, the industry has the structure of oligopoly, with a few dominant firms offering a full line of machinery and equipment and supplying the major share of the market. These firms are both price and service leaders, differentiat-ing their products through invention, innovation, nationwide advertising, and service. The core of their market for new machinery consists of fewer than 1 million commercial farms with annual sales of $10,000 or more, producing about 90 percent of the cash receipts from farming.[11] The cream of the market can be said to be about one-half million farms that have about 75 percent of the cash receipts from farming; and the best part of this group are about 200,000 farms with cash receipts well beyond $50,000 per year that now generate more than 50

---

[10]*Structure of Six Farm Input Industries,* USDA, ERS-357, January 1968.

[11]In 1969, some 1,071,000 farm families with cash receipts from farming of $10,000 or more averaged $15,560 family income including both farm and nonfarm income. These farms produced 88.5 percent of cash receipts from farming. *Income in 1969 of Families and Persons in the United States,* Washington: U.S. Bureau of the Census, Dec. 14, 1970, p. 32.

percent of total cash receipts.[12] Operators of these larger farms buy most of the new tractors and tractor-powered or self-propelled machinery and implements. Smaller farms, including many part-time farms, provide a market for some new equipment in small sizes and for some used machinery. This market continues to shrink relative to the market for large-sized machinery and equipment, thus further disadvantaging small family farms.

Manufacturers of farm machinery and equipment are sometimes classed as "full-line," "long-line," or "short line" producers. The full-line companies are those that produce a relatively complete line of tractors, tractor-powered and self-propelled equipment, various attachments, and other agricultural machines. Only seven companies are full-line firms. They are (with their 1965 percentage of the full-line market shown in parentheses): Allis-Chalmers Manufacturing Company (6.6); J. I. Case Company (6.0); Deere and Company (22.9); Ford Motor Company (17.4); International Harvester Company (24.4); Massey Ferguson, Ltd. (18.6); and White Motor Company and its two domestic operating subsidiaries, Oliver Corporation and Minneapolis-Moline, Inc. (4.1). The full-line companies were responsible for about two-thirds of all farm machinery sales in 1964, and sales of tractors and self-propelled machines together represented more than one-half the value of domestic shipments of farm machinery and equipment. Long-line companies were small in comparison and more specialized, such as the New Holland Machine Company (a division of Sperry-Rand Corporation) and the New Idea Farm Equipment Company (a division of Avco Corporation). Short-line companies were still smaller and generally more specialized, providing products and equipment to fill specific needs of farmers and homeowners, thus competing with the larger firms that were better able to promote a national brand, to provide dealer parts and services, and to offer advantages on trade-ins, all of which are factors in farmers' decisions to buy.[13]

Between 1965 and 1971, Deere and Company displaced International Harvester as the top manufacturer of farm tractors and equipment. In 1975 it was reported that Deere controlled more than 50 percent of the market for 100-horsepower and larger tractors, the most profitable and fastest-growing part of the industry. Although Harvester had improved its earnings in each fiscal year from 1972 to 1974, its total agricultural sales in 1974 were estimated at $1.5 billion to $1.6 billion, compared with $1.9 billion for Deere and Company. These figures represented an estimated 30 percent of total sales for the International Harvester Company, compared with 76 percent of the $2.5 billion total sales of Deere and Company. In 1975, Harvester executives were claiming that their company was the strongest in small tractors and internationally, where small tractors are the largest sellers, and they were moving aggressively to expand their production of four-wheel drive tractors in the 225-horsepower and larger category.[14]

[12]For current data, see *Farm Income Situation*, USDA, ERS, biannual with supplements.
[13]J. M. Bohlen and G. M. Beal, "Why Farmers Buy What They Do, Where They Do?" *Farm and Power Equipment*, Kansas City, Mo.: NRFEA Publications, Inc., February–October 1965.
[14]Joseph M. Winski, *The Wall Street Journal*, Feb. 6, 1975.

Policy Implications of Economic Structure
in Farm Machinery and Equipment

In an industry of high concentration, issues of organization, competitive conduct, and performance are of major interest in policy. In this case, interest extends to the issues of pricing policy for the industry's product, product invention and innovation, dealer performance, and services.

Most data of the farm machinery industry, such as facts collected by the Bureau of Labor Statistics, suggest that the industry is competitive as an oligopoly model with a few firms in a dominant position, that pricing is not collusive to the extent that major firms are in violation of antitrust regulations, and that the industry is a major cutting edge in development of the nation's food resources. But prices are very rigid from year to year. Although the market is very sensitive to changes in farm income, machinery firms generally do not lower prices to maintain sales when farm income falls. Because of the large cost and durability of production facilities, firms maintain their plants in slack periods and run them at a level considerably below capacity.

No longer does the industry have a clear price leader as it did before World War II, when International Harvester held that position. Harvester tried to reestablish price and product leadership after the war but was unsuccessful. Since then, the more evenly divided market shares have stimulated what may be called only modest price competition. The total number of dealers has declined to less than half those existing before the war. Reluctantly, machinery companies have become more heavily involved in dealer financing. This step makes the dealer less independent, makes entry into manufacturing more difficult, and makes the manufacturer more sensitive to changing economic conditions.

In the inflation beginning in the 1960s, farm machinery prices at first tended to lag and then began to move up sharply, with changes only loosely correlated with changes in farm income or demand. This intensified the policy issue as to whether more specific measures should be undertaken to set and control price changes in the farm machinery markets. The issue goes well beyond that of whether or not the marginal value of the product (MVP) coming from the new innovations exceeds the marginal cost (MC). It involves the broader question of specific wage and price controls in concentrated industries to provide a measure of inflation control. This problem is discussed more fully in Chapter 9.

ENERGY USE POLICY IN THE FOOD SYSTEM

Although the total food and fiber sector was estimated by the USDA to have absorbed only about 13 percent of the total energy used in the United States in 1970, policy interest in energy is heightened by the fact that the energy used by the food system has been increasing and a high percentage of that used in farming and food processing is derived from petroleum and natural gas. The chief industrial ingredient in nitrogen fertilizer is natural gas, and the bulk of farm chemicals involves a petroleum base. Not only is energy policy of major concern to the entire food system; the question of if or how the system can be changed to conserve on energy is of critical importance in the conditions projected for the third era of food policy.

Energy used within the food system approximately tripled between 1940 and 1970, with about a 50 percent increase in each of the three decades.[15] Of the total 1970 usage, approximately 24 percent was absorbed in the manufacture and delivery of farm inputs and in farming itself; 39 percent was used in food processing and transportation, and in manufacture of machinery and equipment for these purposes; and 37 percent was used in commercial and home refrigeration and cooking, and in the manufacture of equipment for these purposes.[16] A more functional breakdown for 1973, based on the total energy used outside of the farm-input industries, allocated 18 percent of this total to farming, 33 percent to food processing, only 3 percent to transporation of food and farm products, 16 percent to wholesale and retail trade in food, and 30 percent to household use, mainly refrigeration and cooking.[17]

Since the source of energy used within the food system has as much interest for policy as the comparative amounts, we wish to consider energy in this qualitative sense as well as in quantity. The manufacture of most machinery and equipment used in the food system is based primarily on coal, which is relatively abundant, whereas other functional energy uses depend more on oil and natural gas. The breakdown of energy in this qualitative sense begins with farming.

Energy Used in the Farm Sector

With allowances for imprecisions in measuring energy use, it has been concluded that in 1970 direct use of fuel for general farm work amounted to 10.7 percent of the total energy used in the food system. Pumps and other equipment used for irrigation added 1.6 percent, electricity used on farms added 2.9 percent, the manufacture of fertilizer added 4.3 percent, and the energy used in manufacture of tractor and machinery added 4.7 percent—all totaling 24.2 percent of the energy used in the food system.[18] Or, if the food system absorbs 13 percent of the total energy used in the nation, farming and the farm input industries use a little more than 3.1 percent of the total. The composition of the energy used on farms and in manufacture of commercial fertilizer is so important for policy, however, that it merits special attention.

Since the beginning of this century the energy used directly on farms has increased as much as 10 times or more. In the decade of the 1910s, if one horse is assumed to deliver one horsepower, American farmers had a maximum of 25 million horsepower available from horses and mules. Then mechanical power

[15]John S. Steinhart and Carol E. Steinhart, "Energy Use in the U.S. Food System," in Philip H. Abelson (ed.), *Food: Politics, Economics, Nutrition and Research*, a special Science Compendium, Washington: American Association for the Advancement of Science, 1975, pp. 33–42.

[16]*Ibid.*, p. 35.

[17]Samuel G. Unger, "Energy Utilization in the Leading Energy-Consuming Food Processing Industries," *Food Technology*, December 1975, pp. 33–45.

[18]Steinhart and Steinhart, "Energy Use in the U.S. Food System," *op. cit.*, p. 35.

began to grow and be substituted for horses. Total available horsepower about doubled by 1940 and almost doubled again by 1950 to 93 million. By the early 1970s it had more than doubled again to 200 million.[19] At this time, if *all* the crop output of American agriculture had been used to feed horses, the maximum amount of horsepower available from this source would have been about 125 million horsepower.[20]

Although nearly all mechanical power used by American farmers depends on petroleum and its derivatives, total farm consumption of motor fuel apparently reached a plateau in the early 1950s and then leveled off or grew more slowly. Consumption in millions of gallons was as follows:[21]

Year	1947	1953	1959	1965
Total all farm power machines	5,638	6,775	6,452	6,825
Tractors	2,820	3,271	3,370	3,515
Automobiles	1,695	2,073	1,639	1,650
Motor trucks	845	1,069	1,064	1,160
Other power units	278	362	379	500

The consumption of motor fuel by farm tractors shifted toward diesel and LP gas (liquefied petroleum gas) in millions of gallons as follows:[22]

Year	1947	1953	1959	1965
Total	2,820	2,271	3,370	3,515
Gasoline	2,245	2,738	2,669	2,535
Diesel	121	216	337	600
LP gas	—	85	300	350
All other	454	232	64	30

Consumption of petroleum in other farm uses—drying crops, brooding, killing weeds, heating water, heating and air conditioning buildings, preventing frost in orchards, and other miscellaneous uses—also leveled off by 1953 at about 450 million gallons a year.[23] Total petroleum used for farm production would then be 7,275 million gallons in 1965, which would increase to 7,900 million gallons in 1970.[24] Heating oils for farm household use leveled off around 1,800 million gallons. After 1970, the total farm fuel use leveled off at 4.0 billion gallons of

[19]*Changes in Farm Production and Efficiency,* 1970, USDA, ERS, p. 11.

[20]D. Gale Johnson, *World Agriculture in Disarray,* London: Macmillan St. Martin's Press in association with the Trade Policy Research Centre, 1973, p. 73.

[21]Data for 1947, 1953, and 1959 from P. E. Strickler and B. J. Harrington, *Liquid Petroleum Fuel Used by Farmers in 1959 and Related Data.* USDA Statistical Bulletin 344, May 1964. Data for 1965 estimated by George C. Allen and Theodore R. Eichers, *Structure of Six Farm Input Industries, op. cit.,* p. 9.

[22]*Ibid.,* p. 9.

[23]*Ibid.* By years: 456 million gallons in 1953; 421 million gallons in 1954; and 450 million gallons in 1965.

[24]Based on Steinhart and Steinhart, *op. cit.,* p. 35.

gasoline and 1.2 billion gallons of LP gas, while consumption of diesel fuel increased from 2.0 billion gallons in 1970 to an estimated 2.7 billion gallons in 1975.

In 1970 the total petroleum used directly on farms and in farm homes was slightly less than 5 percent of total national consumption; and, according to projections, the percentage will fall. In 1970, the total petroleum consumption in the United States was 5,324 million barrels, or 212,960 million gallons.[25] One energy-demand projection was 6,896 million barrels for 1975, 8,743 million barrels for 1980, and 10,982 million barrels for 1985.[26] If the direct use on farms and in farm homes were to continue leveling off, the demand for direct farm use and farm homes would drop to less than 3 percent of the total national demand by 1985.

Thus, in national perspective, in spite of the fantastic growth of horsepower available, the direct use of petroleum on farms and in farm homes is a small share of total national consumption and growing smaller.

The shift in power units on farms has a more important policy implication for economic structure of farms. More than half of all tractors sold in recent years have been diesels, whose economic advantage occurs primarily in the larger tractors of more than 35 horsepower. Below 35 horsepower, for all practical purposes, gasoline is the overwhelming choice. The average annual tractor sales for 1965–66, by fuel type, is as follows:[27]

Horsepower range	Gasoline	Diesel	LP gas
9–34	18,074	2,102	58
35–59	51,149	41,354	1,012
60–79	17,118	23,783	2,676
80 and over	4,674	45,312	3,707
Total	91,015	112,551	7,453

The economics of tractor fuel choice, based on work at the University of Illinois, shows that, under fairly normal conditions, gasoline is often an economical choice in both medium- and large-sized tractors. To produce the same amount of horsepower, a diesel engine must be larger in cubic inch displacement than a gasoline version. Diesels cost more to repair but, before an average diesel requires repair, a gasoline model on the average is in the shop about three times for repair or replacement of plugs, distributor or valves. Most important, a 90-plus horsepower gasoline tractor will use 20 gallons more fuel in a long day of heavy tillage than will a diesel.

According to the most exhaustive "Nebraska Tractor Test Data," a study conducted by the University of Nebraska Department of Agricultural Engineer-

[25]Michael Rieber and Ronald Halcrow, *U.S. Energy and Fuel Demand to 1985: A Composite Projection by User within PAD Districts* [Petroleum Administration for Defense Districts], University of Illinois at Urbana-Champaign: Center for Advanced Computation, CAC Document No. 108, Jan. 25, 1974, p. 3.

[26]*Ibid.*, pp. 4–6.

[27]*Doane's Agricultural Report*, Copyright 1971 by Doane Agricultural Service, p. 337.

ing, hours of horsepower per gallon of fuel (hp hrs/gal) delivered on power takeoff (PTO) and drawbar is fairly constant for both gasoline and diesel tractors up to the ranges of 60 to 79 rated horsepower; but the hp hrs/gal ratio consistently favors the diesel and, because of maintenance and other problems, the diesel has a clear advantage in motors of over 80 horsepower. Although the hp hrs/gal ratio continues to rise on PTO as motors are increased in size up to about 150 horsepower, the hp hrs/gal ratio for traction increases slowly on tractors of over 80 horsepower. The reason is, largely, that as tractors become more powerful, the problem of adequate traction under typical ground or soil conditions increases.[28] The problem is being solved or greatly lessened, however, by the growing use of four-wheel drives and improved tractor design.

The significance for policy is that the ongoing development of diesels and complementary equipment continues to enhance the comparative advantage of larger-sized farm-operating units. In general, hp hrs/gal efficiency ratios usually increase up to the largest size of tractor made. In addition, as size of power unit increases, the ratio of useful work to man-hours required rises almost proportionately. Although many other costs must be taken into account in defining an optimum-sized unit in terms of efficiency, modern developments in power and machinery clearly favor the large family farm with only minor additional requirements in labor and management per farm.

Energy Use and Policy in Food Processing

Food processing and related industry, identified as the Food and Kindred Products industry group, Major Group 20 in the federal government's Standard Industrial Classification (SIC), has used 7 percent of the gross energy consumed in all manufacturing industry; and 14 of the 44 industries in Group 20 use about two-thirds of the total energy in food manufacturing (Table 4-1).

The amount of energy used per dollar value of shipments varies widely among these 14 industries, however, with beet sugar processing (the least energy-efficient in terms of value) requiring more than 20 times as much energy per dollar value of product shipments as meat packing, the most energy-efficient (Table 4-2). Moreover, most of these industries obtain a high percentage of their energy from natural gas, the most dominant single fuel in all but four of these industries (Table 4-3). Because of their dependence on utility-supplied natural gas and electricity for about 76 percent of all energy consumed, their energy needs for growth in capacity, or in some cases for even sustaining current capacity, will become more critical in the new third era of policy. With the increased frequency of interruptions or curtailments in natural gas supplies, these industries will have a growing need for reserve stocks of standby fuels. But, unfortunately, the alternate standby fuels are typically wholesale-supplied middle distillates and residual fuel oils, which also are projected to be critical in future supplies.

---

[28]For a useful summary, see *Doane's Agricultural Report,* Vol. 33, No. 10-5, to Vol. 36, No. 47-6, pp. 340.1–350 (60 pp.), last dated 11/23/73; or "Nebraska Tractor Test Data," Lincoln: University of Nebraska, Department of Agricultural Engineering.

Table 4-1   Energy Use among 14 Leading Users of Energy in Food and Kindred Products, 1973

SIC No.	Industry	Energy use rank	Energy use Trillion BTU	Energy use % of total
2011	Meat packing	1	99.3	11.9
2042	Prepared animal feeds	2	86.5	10.3
2046	Wet corn milling	3	83.7	10.0
2026	Fluid milk	4	78.5	9.4
2063	Beet sugar processing	5	76.6	9.2
2082	Malt beverages	6	74.5	8.9
2051	Bread and related products	7	68.6	8.2
2037	Frozen fruits and vegetables	8	62.2	7.4
2092	Soybean oil mills	9	56.4	6.7
2033	Canned fruits and vegetables	10	52.5	6.3
2062	Cane sugar refining	11	44.6	5.3
2013	Sausage and other meat	12	25.5	3.0
2094	Animal and marine fats and oils	13	24.4	2.9
2097	Manufactured ice	14	4.5	0.5
	Total		837.8	100.0

Source: *Food Technology,* December 1975, p. 34.

The food processors that utilize energy-intensive inputs may face major readjustment problems in shifting to less critical energy sources. The policy implication of this is highlighted further by the fact that, if energy supplies are restricted for any segment of the food system, bottlenecks here also can be critical for other parts of the system. The general policy conclusion is that planning for adequate energy supplies and for efficient use of energy in food processing is critically important in food policy for America.

FERTILIZER INNOVATIONS[29]

Commercial fertilizer, specifically a product of the new industrial economy, is the most significant necessary ingredient in the increase in the nation's farm output since the late 1930s. This fertilizer consists chiefly of a wide assortment of chemical compounds, or mixtures of compounds, most often containing important mixtures of the three primary plant nutrients—nitrogen, phosphorus, and potassium; secondary plant nutrients—calcium, magnesium, and sulfur; and trace elements such as boron, cobalt, copper, manganese, zinc, iron, molybdenum, iodine, and chlorine.

Growth in the commercial fertilizer industry results from a technological

---

[29]See John F. Gale, "Note 3—Fertilizers," *Structure of Six Farm Input Industries, op. cit.,* pp. 26–41; Malcolm H. McVickar, *Using Commercial Fertilizer,* 3d ed., Danville, Ill.: The Interstate Printers and Publishers, 1970; G. W. Cooke, *The Control of Soil Fertility,* London: Crosby Lockwood & Son, Ltd., 1966; *Commercial Fertilizer Yearbook,* Atlanta, Ga.: Walter W. Brown Publishing Co., Inc.

Table 4-2 Energy Use per Dollar Value of Shipments and Rank among 14 Leading Energy-using Food and Kindred Products Industries for 1973

Industry	Energy/$ value of shipments		Total energy use rank
	BTU	Rank	
Beet sugar processing	87,600	1	5
Wet corn milling	80,600	2	3
Manufactured ice	38,500	3	14
Cane sugar refining	24,000	4	11
Animal and marine fats and oils	17,400	5	13
Malt beverages	16,400	6	6
Frozen fruits and vegetables	15,200	7	8
Canned fruits and vegetables	11,600	8	10
Bread and related products	11,600	9	7
Soybean oil mills	9,800	10	9
Fluid milk	8,000	11	4
Prepared animal feeds	7,600	12	2
Sausage and other meat	5,300	13	12
Meat packing	4,100	14	1

Source: *Food Technology*, December 1975, p. 35.

Table 4-3 Energy Use by Fuel Type for 14 Leading Energy-using Food and Kindred Products Industries for 1973

Industry	Energy use by type of fuel					
	Natural gas (%)	Purchased electricity (%)	Petroleum products (%)	Cost (%)	Other (%)	Total (%)
Meat packing	46	31	14	9	0	100
Prepared animal feeds	52	38	10	<1	0	100
Wet corn milling	43	14	7	36	0	100
Fluid milk	33	47	17	3	0	100
Beet sugar processing	65	1	5	25	4	100
Malt beverages	38	37	18	7	0	100
Bread and related products	34	28	38	0	0	100
Frozen fruits and vegetables	41	50	5	4	0	100
Soybean oil mills	47	28	9	16	0	100
Canned fruits and vegetables	66	16	15	3	0	100
Cane sugar refining	66	1	33	0	0	100
Sausage and other meat	46	38	15	1	0	100
Animal and marine fats and oils	65	17	17	1	0	100
Manufactured ice	12	85	3	0	0	100

Source: *Food Technology*, December 1975, p. 35.

revolution in production systems, which has been accompanied by strong integration among both private firms and agricultural cooperatives. Fertilizer manufacturers have attempted to gain control of raw material sources and to promote their own brand names. The fertilizer industry, like farm machinery and equipment, thus has become an oligopoly type of industry with 10 to 20 or 30 firms dominating the manufacture of the three primary plant nutrients and competing with a larger number of smaller firms. In 1966, for example, there were 63 firms, plus TVA, producing synthetic ammonia, 18 firms, plus TVA, producing triple superphosphate, and 11 firms producing potash. Only a few produced more than one of the primary materials. Also in 1966, more than 3,200 grades of mixed fertilizer were produced but only 155 grades were consumed in quantities of more than 10,000 tons annually.

Although techniques for making phosphate fertilizers have been known for some time, the rapid growth of the commercial fertilizer industry started in the early 1900s with the greatest growth dating from about World War II. In 1842, Sir John Lawes, an Englishman, developed and patented the process for making superphosphate. Originally, animal bones were treated with sulfuric acid, but a little later, Lawes used mineral phosphates instead of bones. This was the beginning of the commercial chemical fertilizer industry. In 1849, superphosphate was first made in America, and in 1850 a mixed fertilizer made from manufactured guanos was produced in Baltimore. In the next half-century, deposits of phosphate rock were discovered in several states. In 1928, anhydrous ammonia for nitrogen was used in mixed fertilizer. In 1931, the first commercial shipment of potash came from the huge deposits near Carlsbad, New Mexico; and the modern commercial fertilizer industry was, we may say, on its way. A summary of consumption in the United States, by decades from 1880, shows the rapid growth since 1940, in millions of tons, as follows:[30]

Year	Total fertilizer material	Total plant nutrients			Total
		Nitrogen (N)	Phosphates (P_2O_5)	Potash K_2O	
1880	1.1				
1890	1.9				
1900	2.2				
1910	5.5				
1920	7.2				
1930	8.2				
1940	8.2				
1950	18.3	1.0	1.9	1.1	4.0
1960	24.9	2.7	2.6	2.2	7.5
1970		7.2	4.7	3.9	15.8
1980		12.5	6.9	6.0	25.4

[30]Data from the National Plant Food Institute, USDA, and TVA. Estimates for 1970 and 1980 from TVA.

To understand the economic structure of the fertilizer industry and its importance in agricultural supply, it is necessary to know something of the manufacturing processes, at least for the three primary plant nutrients.

Nitrogen

Although about 98 percent of the earth's vast nitrogen resource is in the soil and only 2 percent is in the air,[31] the principal source of commercial nitrogen is air and, for practical purposes, is unlimited. Nitrogen from the air, combined with hydrogen under controlled conditions, produces synthetic ammonia. Natural gas is the major feedstock for this process, supplying at least 88 percent of American ammonia production. Other sources include refinery gas, naptha, fuel oil, coke-oven gas, water gas, and electrolytic hydrogen. Byproduct coke-oven ammonia (ammonium sulfate, ammonia liquor, and diammonium phosphate), natural sodium nitrate of which there are huge deposits in various parts of the world, and natural organic materials from plants and animals are additional sources of nitrogen for fertilizer.

The consideration in all cases is the matter of cost. About 10 million tons of nitrogen are contained in the 1.7 billion tons of animal excreta deposited annually in the United States, but the cost of using much of the animal excreta far exceeds the value of the nutrients and organic matter contained in it. Through various biological means, 100 million tons of nitrogen are fixed annually over the earth's surface, chiefly by algae in water and by leguminous nitrogen-fixing plants on land. Some nitrogen is fixed by growing sweet clover in crop rotations and by use of alfalfa; but it is the nitrogen supplied by commercial fertilizer that is essential for the growth in modern food production.[32]

The most rapid growth from the mid 1960s onward was in liquid fertilizers mainly carrying nitrogen.[33] Early in the 1960s, nitrogen in liquid form was found to be easier to transport and apply than nitrogen in dry form; and as products developed, chiefly under TVA experimentation, it was found that various mixes of the three primary nutrients could be handled in liquid form. Additionally, herbicides and insecticides could be combined and spread more uniformly and economically; and fluid fertilizers could be produced and applied with a minimum of air or stream pollution. Consequently, the consumption of liquid fertilizer approximately doubled in the five years beginning about 1963. In 1968, fluids accounted for about 24 percent of all forms of fertilizer; 62 percent of the nitrogen was applied in liquid form and about 12 percent of the total mixed fertilizer was in liquid form. By the mid 1970s, more fertilizer was spread as liquid than was spread dry. Because of the capital investment in technology, large farms had an increasingly greater advantage over small farms with liquid than they had with fertilizer in dry form.

[31]*Soil Nitrogen,* Madison, Wis.: American Society of Agronomy, p. 4.

[32]For further summary discussion, see George Stanford, "Nitrogen in Soils," and W. H. Gorman, "Nitrogen Facts and Fallacies," in *Plant Food Review,* Vol. 15, No. 1, 1969.

[33]Frank P. Achorn, "Status of Liquid Fertilizers," *Commercial Fertilizer Yearbook, op. cit.,* 1970, pp. 12.

Phosphorus

Phosphorus is found in all rocks but concentration is usually too low for its economic recovery. Domestic production is important in Florida, North Carolina, Tennessee, Idaho, Montana, Utah, and Wyoming, with Florida being by far the most important.

After mining, washing, benefication, and drying, the phosphate rock is ground and then routed through a chemical process. The products include ammonium phosphate, triple superphosphate, normal superphosphate, nitric phosphate, dicalcium phosphate, phosphoric acid, and phosphate rock.

Potassium

As in the phosphate rock industry, the difficulty of acquiring a commercially exploitable deposit of potash is a barrier to entry. In 1965, about 90 percent of domestic production of potassium came from mines in the Carlsbad area of New Mexico. In 1943, however, a vast reserve of ore was found in Saskatchewan, Canada, and development began in 1952. As of 1965, about 25 firms had acquired rights to potash deposits in Canada. North American producers at that time had a domestic production capacity of about 5.5 million tons. The Canadian capacity, then 1.9 million tons, is viewed as the major source of expansion for the future. Estimates of the Canadian potential were increased in the 1970s.

Process Integration

Commercial fertilizer production entails considerable economies of scale, so certain advantages go to large firms. Also, transportation costs account for considerable economies in location, so advantages go to firms that can combine fertilizer production and marketing with other petrochemical industry. As a result, it properly can be said that firms have integrated—vertically, horizontally, forward, and backward—as the industry has progressed through its technological revolution. Among the 63 firms producing synthetic ammonia in 1966, for example, about 40 percent were estimated as being owned or controlled by other firms.[34]

Although fertilizers and farm chemicals must meet certain minimum standards as provided by law, and although some testing is financed at public expense, there are differences among fertilizers and other chemicals beyond the minimum standards. These differences are highly significant economically. Accordingly, firms strive for brand identification and load into the price of their product a considerable advertising expenditure. Such practices are not necessarily all waste in terms of the public interest, however, or the worst choice for policy. The public exposure creates educational benefit or at least awareness, and technological advance is—we may assume—encouraged.

Studies in the 1960s suggested that farmers were averaging as much as $2.50 return for $1 spent on fertilizer.[35] In the 1960–64 period, for example, if farmers

[34]Gale, *op. cit.,* p. 29.
[35]D. B. Ibach, *Fertilizer Use in the United States,* USDA, Agricultural Economics Report No. 92.

had been willing to settle for a $2 return on $1 spent on fertilizer, they could have produced the 1960–64 crop output on 259 million acres, or 80 million acres less than they actually used. Although many farmers probably used fertilizer up to the point where the last dollar spent on fertilizer netted just one additional dollar of actual return,[36] their average return per unit of fertilizer still could be double or triple the outlay on fertilizer. Since commercial fertilizer continued to expand sharply, most farmers evidently were not applying fertilizer up to the point of maximum profit.

Because the aggregate short-run demand curve for national farm output is highly inelastic, however, the rapid expansion of commercial fertilizer depressed the aggregate national net farm income. Thus farmers were caught in a squeeze: It was profitable for them individually to increase fertilizer consumption but this increase was depressing on net farm income nationally. The transitional growth of the fertilizer industry added to the problem of compensatory policy with an expanded flow of funds from the federal Treasury going to farmers who— according to some economic models that could be constructed—would lose more than the equivalent of this subsidy through price-depressing effects of increased fertilizer use. The primary beneficiaries of this rapid growth were American consumers, as well as consumers in the other countries who, to varying degrees, were affected by both commercial exports and food aid financed by the American taxpayer. Among the farm producers, it can be said that some gained, that is, those relative few who were in the forefront of the technological revolution. A larger group of farmers lost as they experienced depressed prices without compensating income gains from use of fertilizer.

A Policy Conclusion

In summary, then, the commercial fertilizer industry is a strong and necessary growth factor in the expansion of the nation's agricultural supply. Without it, consumers would be vastly worse off, paying perhaps double what they now pay for their food supply. Food exports would be only a trickle of their current flow, and the output from American farms would place a heavier drain on most other resources. In the long run, if fertilizer output were lower, more farmers might be left on the land, but we cannot say whether, on the average, they would be better or worse off than they are with a strong fertilizer industry.

Since present and future food production depends so much on fertilizer, what are the prospects and alternatives for national food policy? Among the three primary materials, the sources of supply for phosphate rock and potash are enormous. Improvements in technology will force down the relative cost. But exhaustion of the most readily available supplies will tend to have a countervailing effect. Estimates vary as to the relative future shifts in costs. The situation is different for nitrogen. Since natural gas is the principle raw material in addition to air for anhydrous ammonia (the basic ingredient in all nitrogen fertilizer except

---

[36] Ibach suggests that if farmers in general had done this, they would have more than doubled crop production per acre in the mid 1960's. This statement assumes that in general farmers did not use fertilizer up to the point of MC = MR.

the organics), the future cost structure of nitrogen fertilizer is somewhat uncertain.

To produce the 12.5 million tons of anhydrous ammonia projected for 1980, plant capacity would have to be increased by 5 million tons over that of about 1973, but even so, total natural gas consumption would be only about 3 percent of the nation's total natural gas consumption.[37] In other words, if some other uses of natural gas could be restricted, meeting the physical requirements for nitrogen fertilizer would cause no problem.

The question is one of cost. It has been estimated that if prices of natural gas were to increase six times over the common price in 1971–72 (from 20 cents per thousand cubic feet (mcf) to $1.20 per mcf), the cost of gas used in anhydrous ammonia fertilizer would rise $40 per ton, about a 40 percent increase over prices of 1971–72. Although the effects of this cannot be stated precisely and there would be wide differences among the various crops, most if not all of the increased cost would be passed on to consumers.[38]

The question for policy is whether or not to let fertilizer prices reach their normal equilibrium levels. In 1973 and early 1974, the Nixon administration attempted to control fertilizer prices as part of the nationwide counterinflationary program. Fertilizer companies found the foreign markets to be increasingly attractive and fertilizer exports rose dramatically. The relaxation of price controls on fertilizer was followed by a substantial price rise in anhydrous ammonia. Exports declined to more nearly normal levels and an equilibrium was established in domestic markets at prices in some cases nearly double those of a year earlier. The attempt to control fertilizer prices without controlling exports was counterproductive as a price-control measure but, since it contributed to increased exports, it was modestly beneficial to further improvement of the United States trade balance. The reported absolute shortage of farm fertilizers in the spring of 1974 in some parts of the country,—that is, exhaustion of stocks at planting time—might, however, have reduced grain production and subsequent exports sufficiently to offset the earlier gain from increased fertilizer exports.

---

[37]For further discussion, see *Food for Crude,* reprint of speech by E. V. Stevenson, executive vice president and general manager, Farm Services (FS, Inc.), Bloomington, Ill., 61701, A-16786, Sept. 13, 1973.

[38]See Norman L. Hargett, *Fertilizer Summary Data, 1974,* Muscle Shoals, Alabama: Tennessee Valley Authority, National Fertilizer Development Center, pp. 6 and 7; *Agricultural Prices, Annual Summary 1974,* USDA, Statistical Reporting Service, Crop Reporting Board, Pr 1–3 (75), June 1975, pp. 153–158; and Luther G. Tweeten and C. Leroy Quance, "Positivistic Measures of Aggregate Supply Elasticities: Some New Approaches," *American Journal of Agricultural Economics,* Vol. 51, No. 2, May 1969, pp. 342–352. If nitrogen constitutes (say) one half of the total outlay on fertilizer and nitrogen prices increase by 40 percent, fertilizer prices may increase by 20 percent. If the elasticity of demand for fertilizer in terms of its own price is 0.6 in the short run (Tweeten and Quance, p. 350), aggregate fertilizer consumption will drop by 12 percent, *ceteris paribus.* This will bring a decline in farm output of (say) 1 percent, which will have a proportionately greater effect on farm product prices because of demand inelasticity. Whether farm income will increase or decrease depends on elasticities of demand for inputs and farm products, as well as other factors. Generally, most if not all, of the increase in cost will be passed on to consumers.

CHEMICAL PESTICIDES[39]

Chemical pesticides, broadly defined as all agricultural chemicals except those used as fertilizers, feed additives, and medicinal preparations, are in some ways even more necessary or critical in modern food production than are present-day machines, new crop varieties, and fertilizers. New cropping practices and increased crop concentrations have created an environment almost ideally suited for many pests. Chemical pesticides, along with improved cultural practices, have become an effective way of controlling them. The value of American crops saved by use of pesticides is estimated in billions of dollars annually, depending on prices and the assumptions about production relationships. Without pesticides, current food consumption levels in the United States could not be maintained even if there were no food exports, and the quality of food would be much lower. But use of pesticides presents a number of problems that must be understood and solved if there is to be a satisfactory food policy.

Pesticide Types and Problems

Five principal types of chemical pesticides have been developed, based on the target species to which they are applied:

    1 *insecticides,* for direct control or eradication of various insects or insect hosts

    2 *herbicides,* as preemergence selective weed controls or as selective poisons applied to growing weeds, such as 2, 4-D, which acts more effectively on broad-leaved plants than on narrow-leaved grasses or plants

    3 *fungicides,* for control of rusts, mildews, and molds in grains, fruits, and vegetables

    4 *rodenticides,* for control of gophers, rats, mice, coyotes, etc., and sometimes birds, by highly toxic chemicals applied as bait materials

    5 *acaricides* and *miticides,* for control of ticks and mites, which generally are not killed by most insecticides

In addition, somewhat more specialized chemicals include *nematicides,* which are chemicals usually applied as fumigants to control nematodes, the tiny, hairlike worms that live in the soil and sometimes cause damage by feeding on plant roots; *molluscicides,* for control of snails and slugs; and *bactericides,* for

[39]J. C. Headley and J. N. Lewis, *The Pesticide Problem: An Economic Approach to Public Policy,* Washington: Resources for the Future, Inc., distributed by The Johns Hopkins Press, Baltimore, 1967; Austin Fox, "Chemical Pesticides," *Structure of Six Farm Input Industries, op. cit.,* pp. 42–54; Theodore Eichers, Paul Andrilenas, Helen Blake, Robert Jenkins, and Austin Fox, *Quantities of Pesticides Used by Farmers in 1966,* USDA, ERS, Agricultural Economic Report No. 131, January 1968; Helen T. Blake, Paul Andrilenas, Robert P. Jenkins, Theodore R. Eichers, and Austin S. Fox, *Farmers' Pesticide Expenditures in 1966,* USDA, ERS, Agricultural Economic Report No. 179, April 1970; *Pest Control Strategies for the Future* (a symposium), National Research Council, Agricultural Board, Division of Biology and Agriculture, Washington: National Academy of Sciences, 1972.

control of certain undesirable bacteria. Other chemicals are sometimes used as *attractants* to lure pests to a particular location and as *repellents* to force pests away. Chemicals are sometimes used as *growth regulators,* such as to advance or retard the harvest date of a crop; or they may be used as an aid to harvest, such as *defoliants,* which induce a plant to drop its leaves but do not harm it otherwise; and as *desiccants,* which draw moisture from a plant, causing it to wither and die.

These chemicals are nearly always applied in what is called a "pesticide formulation," which is a diluted form of the pure chemical mixed with water, oil, air, or other chemically inert materials. Thus a pesticide may be applied as a solution in water or some other solvent, as an emulsifiable concentrate, a wettable or soluble powder, a thick suspension in a liquid, or a dust. Some of the chemicals are used in granules as a soil treatment, in a vapor as in a soil fumigant, in an aerosol spray, or in an attractive mixture as a poison bait.

Pesticides are poisons that differ widely in their toxicity, or capacity to produce injury or death, and their degree of hazard to humans or animals, which is related to toxicity and possible exposure in application and use. Excellent education manuals have been prepared to instruct on how to use pesticides correctly, how to avoid injury through exposure or misuse, and how to prevent food contamination which may otherwise occur through residues or other types of misuse.[40] In addition, however, extensive public input has been necessary in respect to what is licensed for manufacture and sale and how application is to be regulated so as to avoid injury to the applicator and to prevent poisoning of domestic animals and wild life or contamination of the food supply. Some chemicals have been banned because of their extreme hazard either through high toxicity or persistence in the environment. What pesticides to permit and how to control those that are permitted is the essence of the policy problem.

Policy Problem Related to Toxicity and Persistence

Pesticide poisoning may occur among applicators or field workers who have been suddenly exposed to a large quantity of a toxic material; or it may occur among those who are continuously exposed to small quantites for long periods of time. The first symptoms are usually fatigue, headache and dizziness, numbness in arms or legs, nausea and vomiting, excessive sweating and salivation, abdominal pains and diarrhea. This condition may be followed in moderate cases by general weakness, paralysis such as inability to walk or talk, twitching, and contraction of the pupil of the eye. More severe cases accentuate these symptoms, resulting in respiratory difficulties, unconsciousness, and death.

Although people may die from inhaling a pesticide vapor or from severe skin exposure, nearly all pesticide deaths in both humans and animals are caused by

---

[40]See, for example, the *Illinois Pesticide Applicator Study Guide, A Training Manual for Private and Commercial Pesticide Applicators and Operators* (1975), prepared by Wayne Bever, Loren Bode, Barry J. Jacobsen, Marshal D. McGlamery, and Stevenson Moore III. University of Illinois at Urbana-Champaign, Cooperative Extension Service, College of Agriculture, in cooperation with the Illinois Natural History Survey.

eating or drinking the product or its residue. Nearly half the accidental deaths in America from pesticide poisoning are those of children under 12 years of age. Among the cases of occupational poisoning and death, the organic phosphorus compounds, called organophosphates, are most commonly involved. These are insecticides, such as the highly toxic parathion and methyl parathions, and the somewhat less toxic malathion. The carbamates, including carbaryl (Sevin), and carbofuran (Furadan), the newest class of insecticides to be developed, may cause the same symptoms as the organophosphates, but they are generally less enduring in effect and are generally considered more safe. The chlorinated hydrocarbons, or organochlorine insecticides, consisting of DDT and its derivatives including DDD, methoxychlor, ethxychlor, methylchlor, and prolan, have been involved in only a few cases of occupational poisoning. But these materials break down very slowly in the environment or not at all—that is, they are only slowly biodegradable, if at all—they build up in the food chain, as from fish, bird, or animal to human. Because of this feature, DDT, once widely used for mosquito control, for example, has been banned in the United States for sale and use. Other insecticides, called cyclodienes, such as aldrin and dieldrin, are not manufactured for agricultural use, while still others such as endrin, heptaclor, and taxophene, have been generally restricted.

Measuring Toxicity

The policy problem in use of pesticides is related to the fact that the newest and most effective are generally most toxic to human beings and other life or most persistent in the environment and food chain. To measure toxicity, a rating scale, called the mammalian selectivity ratio (MSR), has been developed, with the hazard related inversely and geometrically to the magnitude of the number. Endrin, for example, with an MSR of 2.4, is so hazardous that it has not been manufactured for agricultural use.[41] Parathion, in comparison, with an MSR of 4.0, has been used widely in American agriculture, with production in 1966 reaching the level of 19.4 million pounds.[42] Methyl parathion, an analogue of parathion, has an MSR of 20, and 1966 production was 35.9 million pounds. But even a relatively high number does not guarantee complete safety. Malathion, for example, with an MSR of 37.7, the least toxic of this group of chemicals and widely used by gardeners and in household insecticides and in mosquito spraying, is highly hazardous if used in combination with certain other organophosphates. Malathion is relatively safe only because it is detoxified by one of the enzymes in the human liver. If something destroys this enzyme or interferes with its action, a person exposed to malathion will receive almost the full force of the poison that is generally intended for insects.

The hazard to humanity is not fully defined by the MSR but lies in the persistence of the insecticide. DDT, which has been widely used over the world

---

[41]MSR ratings are from Robert L. Metcalf, "Development of Selective and Biodegradable Pesticides," *Pest Control Strategies for the Future, op. cit.,* 1972, pp. 137–156.
   [42]*Ibid.,* p. 141.

for control of malaria without immediate adverse effects on human life, has an MSR of 59, and has been banned in America because of its persistence in a variety of ecological niches—soil, water, plant surface, animal bodies, and so on—and its slow degradation in biological systems to form DDE and DDD, all of which are highly soluble in lipids (fats) and extremely insoluble in water. Thus they may accumulate over wide limits in the food chain, as from plant to fish or bird or mammal, including humans, to establish a concentration that may become highly injurious or even lethal. DDE, although having a high safety factor, is responsible for a major portion of the adverse environmental effects of concentration and storage in animal tissues occurring after the use of DDT.[43] The other three DDT analogues, methoxychlor, methiochlor, and methylchlor, each are substantially biodegradable through oxidation, that is, the substance breaks down and disappears. When they are absorbed into living organisms, they have weak points for attack by multifunction oxidases (enzymes that promote oxidation), thus promoting rapid detoxication and elimination as water-soluble products of the metabolism. They have advantages therefore as safe, relatively stable and potentially inexpensive residual insecticides. Although they are highly preferable to the original DDT, they are still dangerous during their active life. The policy problem is how best to impose proper limits on their sale and use.

Production and Substitution Effects

Although some pesticides have been known and used for several decades and a few for centuries, the period of rapid growth in American agriculture is marked from three dates: (1) the early 1940s, when the chlorinated hydrocarbons, such as DDT, first began to be used in control of insects; (2) 1957, when other insecticides began to be used more widely; and (3) 1961, when use of herbicides for control of weeds, begun in the 1940s, entered a rapid growth stage. Whereas, during 1954–57, roughly 75 million pounds of each of the three major pesticides—insecticides, herbicides, and fungicides—were sold annually, by 1964 sales of insecticides alone were more than 200 million pounds. The total quantity of chemical pesticides produced was increased from 783 million pounds of active material in 1964 to 1,034 million pounds in 1970, with a plateau in production apparently reached about 1966.[44] In the case of herbicides alone, in 1950 there were about 15 different products. By 1960 there were more than 180 products, with some 6,000 formulations.[45] By 1964, there were more than 10,000 pesticide products packaged under about 450 company labels. Thereafter, the number of products dropped to about 8,000 by 1970, as unprofitable items were discontinued and fewer but more popular ones were introduced.

Both production and substitution effects are important and can be roughly summarized. By the late 1960s, herbicides and associated weed control technolo-

---

[43]*Ibid.,* p. 150.

[44]From highlights of papers, *The Chemical Pesticide Yearbook - Entoma,* 1972, pp. 66–237.

[45]W. C. Shaw and L. L. Jansen, "Chemical Weed Control Strategies for the Future," *Pest Control Strategies for the Future, op. cit.,* 1972, pp. 197–215.

gies had accounted for at least 10 percent of the total increase in farm production since 1940; and it was estimated that if all the cropland idled by government programs were brought back into production, the aggregate farm output could have been held constant by an 80 percent reduction in pesticide use. In other words, the increase in pesticide use after 1940 more than offset the production effect of government crop control programs. Southern cotton areas showed the lowest marginal increase from pesticides, and Corn Belt areas showed the highest.[46] In regard to substitution effects, total labor requirements for wheat, rice, and potato production were reduced by 30 to 50 percent by changes in cultural practices related to systems of chemical weed control.[47] There were somewhat similar reductions in costs of machinery and fuel in these crops and various others. In the Corn Belt, during the early years of herbicide development, a system of reduced tillage became widespread with lower costs for tillage and cultivating.[48] In 1970, about 290 million dollars in farm production costs, plus 20 million hours of family farm labor, were saved by the use of phenoxy herbicides, primarily 2, 4-D and 2, 4, 5-T, on 62 million acres of farmland devoted principally to grains, sorghums, and pasture.[49]

Marginal Returns and Price Effects

For several years almost everything that was written about pesticides was phrased in economic terms: that as a matter of national food policy, more and better pesticides are needed to grow bigger and better crops. Pesticides had proved to be a bonanza for the petrochemical industry. Farmers welcomed them and demanded more of them. Consumers enjoyed the year-by-year drop in the real cost of food and other farm products. The U.S. Department of Agriculture was encouraged by public and congressional support to expand its educational programs and to sponsor, or support through contracts, pesticide eradication programs of considerable scope. The individual state legislatures began to support pesticide research and extension programs in the land grant colleges and universities. Some state departments of agriculture were funded to carry out pest eradication projects.

Estimates by economists have documented the high marginal rates of returns. J. C. Headley, for example, estimated that on the average each $1 spent

[46]*Economic Research on Pesticides for Policy Decisionmaking,* Proceedings of a Symposium, USDA, ERS, Washington, D.C., April 27–29, 1970. From "Highlights of Papers," by Velmar W. Davis.

[47]Shaw and Jansen, "Chemical Weed Control Strategies for the Future," *op. cit.,* p. 202.

[48]On detailed cost-account farms in central Illinois, averaging 354 acres in size in 1959–60, the total number of times a field was tilled or cultivated dropped from an average of 6.3 times in 1952 to 3.8 times in 1960. The number of applications increased from 0.2 to 0.6 for fertilizer and from 0.1 to 0.6 for spray. From cost-account data assembled by R. A. Hinton, University of Illinois at Urbana-Champaign, Department of Agricultural Economics, and AERR [Agricultural Economics Research Report] 48, 1961.

[49]Austin S. Fox, Robert P. Jenkins, and Paul A. Andrilenas (agricultural economists, ERS), and John T. Holstun, Jr., and Dayton L. Klingman (agronomists, Crops Research Division, ARS), *Restricting the Use of Phenoxy Herbicides—Costs to Farmers,* USDA, ERS, and ARS, Agricultural Economic Report No. 194, November 1970.

on pesticides generated at least \$4 of additional farm output, disregarding price effects. G. A. Carlson and E. N. Castle prepared a summary which showed fabulously high returns per pound of pesticide used, as in the following table:[50]

Commodity	Insecticides	Herbicides	Fungicides
Cotton	\$ 19.25	\$ 688.55	\$896.98
Apples	23.16	*	19.00
Peanuts	49.14	93.72	16.44
Potatoes	208.54	274.12	175.52
Corn	215.19	103.19	†
Alfalfa	502.84	1,397.19‡	†
Soybeans	683.27	245.31	†
Wheat	2,322.13	259.54	†

*Mostly petroleum.
†Fungicide totals not available.
‡Includes herbicides used on all hay.

Because of the inelasticity of the short-run demand for America's farm output, however, the macroeconomic effect of the rapid growth in pesticide use was to depress aggregate national farm income by amounts running into billions of dollars annually. This effect, compounded by the rapid expansion of the fertilizer industry and the growth in farm mechanization, created an almost insuperable problem for compensatory price-support programs. The innovations intensified the chronic farm problem of the second era of food policy, the problem of low farm income and declining farm population. Although this economic problem was regarded by many as paramount, there is another side to the problem that is vitally important and almost unique in national policy: that of achieving a social optimum in pesticide use.

The Social Optimum

In almost all pesticides, but especially among insecticides, the evolution of more powerful chemicals seems to favor the use of compounds that are both highly toxic and hazardous to humans, while the more innocuous relatives of these compounds are relegated to minor applications or put back on the shelf. The most toxic pesticides are generally the most efficient in achieving a given level of control; but they are generally also the most dangerous to man and the environment.

The policy problem, then, is first to decide as a policy goal how much to limit and regulate specific pesticides; second, what means to use, such as state or federal regulation, education, or publicity; and third, what system or agencies to use for implementing the policy. Limiting or constraining the risks to the health of humans, domesticated animals, and wildlife is of fundamental concern in pesticide policy. A solution must be found that will yield the best results in terms of

[50]Gerald A. Carlson and Emery N. Castle, "Economics of Pest Control," *Pest Control Strategies for the Future, op. cit.,* p. 91.

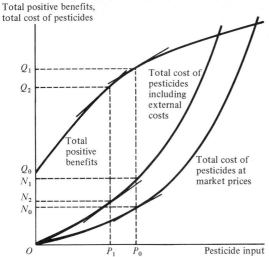

Figure 4-2 Optimum use of pesticides considering external cost. *(Source: J. C. Headley and J. N. Lewis, The Pesticide Problem, Resources for the Future, 1967.)*

society as a whole, taking full account of the values inherent in both costs and benefits. This means counting not just the costs incurred by the user, including cash outlay and possible adverse side effects of direct personal consequences, but also those costs external to the firm, including such things as loss of wildlife, possible poisoning of the food chain, contamination, and damage to the environment.

The general problem of the social optimum may be visualized as in Figure 4-2.[51] Suppose that positive benefits equal to OQ_0 or Q_0 can be produced with no pesticide. As pesticide inputs are added to a level of P_0, with other inputs held constant, total positive benefits are equal to Q_1. At this point, the distance between the "total positive benefits" curve and "total cost of pesticides at market prices" is a maximum, equal to $Q_1 - N_0$. However, if there are external costs associated with this level of pesticide use, the total cost is N_1 and the net social gain is diminished to $Q_1 - N_1$. If the external costs can be accounted for and brought into the decision framework, pesticide inputs will be reduced to P_1, which maximizes the net social gain.

Because of the magnitude of external costs and the difficulty of controlling them, biologists generally agree that good pest control does not and should not begin with a toxic chemical and work backward to the pest. Rather, first emphasis should be placed on nonchemical factors, such as breeding of pest-resistant crops and livestock, development of biological balances in nature to contain pests and crop diseases, with due consideration for social, economic, and biological limitations. Given this effort, pesticide policy then may concentrate on management of the chemical pesticides, in which the guiding rule is equalizing

[51]Headley and Lewis, *The Pesticide Problem: An Economic Approach to Public Policy, op. cit.*, p. 25.

total costs and benefits at the margin. But this problem is complicated by the fact that some of the costs are not immediately apparent and experience must be accumulated.

Experiences in Large-Scale Control Programs

Some of the experience in attempting to control some insects and plant diseases has been expensive and, for completeness of our study, should be noted as a lesson for the future. In the late 1950s and early 1960s, as the powerful effectiveness of DDT began to be recognized, the federal government was strongly urged and supported to undertake large-scale campaigns to eradicate the spruce budworm, gypsy moth, Japanese beetle, Dutch elm disease, and imported fire ant, each of which was causing widespread damage. These campaigns, except that against Dutch elm disease, essentially involved aerial spraying over wide areas with light applications of DDT or a derivative. The campaign to control the spruce budworm, which in the larvae stage is a defoliant, involved spraying possibly 20 million acres in the northeastern United States and eastern Canada, with ½ to 1 pound of DDT per acre in an oil emulsion. A plan to control or possibly eradicate the gypsy moth, which is also a defoliant, in 1957 involved spraying most of 2.5 million acres with 1 pound per acre of DDT in oil. The Japanese beetle, which causes "milky spore" disease which otherwise may be controlled by regular and timely release of a bacterium of the genus Bacillus, was slated for eradication by use of chemicals applied as a soil contaminate to attack the grub, or larvae of the beetle in soil or turf. Recommended applications ranged from 400 pounds of lead arsenate per acre, to 25 pounds of DDT, to 2 pounds of aldrin, each of which has about the same effectiveness.

The Japanese Beetle   Control involved aerial spraying of dieldrin, aldrin or heptachlor at rates of 2 to 3 pounds per acre. The beetle was first found in New Jersey in 1916. From there it spread slowly. By the 1950s it was appearing in the Midwest. Up to 1960, six states in the westward march of the beetle (Michigan, Indiana, Kentucky, Illinois, Iowa, and Missouri) had treated 96,000 acres in cooperation with the Plant Pest Control Division of the USDA. But wildlife losses were severe. In some areas, such as around Sheldon, Illinois, ground-feeding birds, muskrats, rabbits, and ground squirrels were totally, or almost totally, destroyed.[52] No one could measure the full extent of losses or the possible subsequent hazards to other birds and animals, or to human beings.

The Imported Fire Ant   The campaign to eradicate the imported fire ant was perhaps the most destructive. Although seven species of fire ants *(Solenopsis)* are distributed in warm temperate regions of the Americas and three are native to the United States, shortly after World War I a dark biologic species of fire ant *(S. saevissima),* more virulent than other known species, became established around

---

[52]T. G. Scott, Y. L. Willis, and J. A. Ellis, "Some Effects of Field Application of Dieldrin on Wildlife," *Journal of Wildlife Management,* Vol. 23, No. 4, 1959, pp. 409–427.

Mobile, Alabama. In the 1930s, a smaller reddish species appeared in the same region which, by interbreeding and internecine warfare, apparently overcame the dark species.[53] By 1956, this reddish species, which, when undisturbed, built small mounds of hardened earth 2 to 3 feet high, with as many as 15 to 25 mounds per acre, had spread to at least eleven states of the Southeast. By 1957, the USDA was under pressure to do something about the fire ant, and an appropriation was requested for an eradication program of aerial spraying. Congress approved an annual allocation of $2.4 million, providing local matching funds were made available.

A massive operation to eradicate the fire ant was set up with great speed. Although most states and many communities and even individuals responded with matching funds, controlled spraying often went forward without them. The first spraying in November 1957, begun in haste without prior consultation with local health or wildlife authorities, used 2 pounds of dieldrin or heptachlor per acre. Almost immediately, there was alarm and opposition to the program. Quickly, scientists observed catastrophic loss of wildlife.[54] The furor grew into a national controversy as the USDA found itself under attack from a new quarter. In 1958 the dosage was reduced to between 1.0 to 1.25 pounds per acre of heptachlor, then later reduced to two applications of 0.25 pound per acre. More than 2.5 million acres were treated—and the results, as in the case of the Japanese beetle program, were ecologically disastrous. The fire ant, although at least temporarily depressed, was not destroyed. In response to a huge public outcry, the USDA modified its program, substituting the much less toxic mirex for the more hazardous heptachlor.

The Dutch Elm Disease   Introduced into America about 1930, the Dutch elm disease is caused by a fungus that can live independently and is effectively transmitted by a bark beetle that thrives in the dead and dying portions of the American elm. By the late 1950s the disease had worked its way through New England and adjoining Canada, the Middle Atlantic states, and far into the North Central Region. The disease could be materially slowed, but apparently not eradicated, by quick removal and burning of infected elm trees. With development of DDT, the disease apparently might be controlled by spraying living trees with a minimum of 2.5 pounds of DDT per tree, to over 17 pounds per tree where elms were large and numerous.[55] The discovery of DDT seemed to many people to be one answer to the control problem, and large numbers of communities, especially in the Midwest, became involved in extensive spray-control programs.

Complete coverage proved almost impossible, however. Diseased trees

[53]E. O. Wilson and W. L. Brown, Jr., "Recent Changes in the Introduced Populations of the Fire Ant," *Evolution,* Vol. 12, 1958, pp. 211–218.

[54]J. L. George, *The Program to Eradicate the Imported Fire Ant,* New York: The Conservation Foundation, 1958; and J. B. DeWitt and J. L. George, *Pesticide Wildlife Review, 1959,* U.S. Fish and Wildlife Service, Circular 84, 1960.

[55]J. L. George, "Effects on Fish and Wildlife of Chemical Treatments of Large Areas," *Journal of Forestry,* Vol. 57, No. 4, 1959, pp. 250–254.

remained to host the infection for others. Worse, it was found that the quantities of DDT necessary to kill the bark beetles far exceeded the quantities sufficient to kill birds in or about sprayed trees. As R. J. Barker of the Illinois Natural History Survey explained,[56] the sprayed leaves of elm trees fell to the ground and were eaten by worms that normally lived on them; and the poisoned worms would be eaten by birds, chiefly robins. Millions of birds are believed to have been killed by this sequence.[57] In the end, although the spray programs are thought to have delayed the spread of the disease, they—like the attempts to use chemicals to eradicate the spruce budworm, the gypsy moth, the Japanese beetle, and the imported fire ant—ended in costly failure. Except for isolated elms, those in the affected areas all died.

Poisoning the Food Chain

Enthusiasm for widespread government programs to eradicate various insects was dampened, but the real lessons of danger to the environment and to humans occurred in other areas. There were a number of episodes important for pesticide and food policy.

The classic example of food chain poisoning occurred at Clear Lake, California, a shallow, warm body of water of about 72 square miles, 90 to 100 miles north of San Francisco, when attempts were made to eradicate a small, highly annoying gnat *(Chaoborus asticlopus)* with a carefully designed program using DDD. Although this gnat resembles the common mosquito, it is not a bloodsucker, and the many fishing parties who used the lake found it annoying mainly because of its large numbers. Efforts to control the gnat were fruitless until a program was begun in 1949 to apply DDD in 1 part to 70 million (1 to 70 ppm) of water. In 1954 the dosage was repeated at 1 to 50 ppm, and in 1957 was again tried.

Then ecological disaster struck, with overtones for all food supply. Prior to the first spraying in 1949, about 1,000 pairs of grebes, swanlike diving birds which resemble the loon and which fed on the abundant fish, had made their summer homes about the lake. After the spraying, they migrated elsewhere for summer breeding and rearing of their young. But they returned in the winter for feeding, and after the 1954 spraying, 100 or more died in and around the lake. After the 1957 spraying they died in great numbers. Analysis revealed that some of their fatty tissues contained as much as 1,600 ppm of DDD—a concentration 80,000 times as great as that of the .02 ppm found in the lake.[58] Microscopic plants and animal organisms had stored DDD at about 5 ppm. Fish that had eaten this food had overall DDD concentrations at 40 to 2,500 ppm in their livers, kidneys, and fatty tissues depending on the species, age of fish, etcetera, and the birds that had eaten the fish whole had absorbed a lethal dose. What loss there was to other life,

[56]R. J. Barker, "Notes on Some Ecological Effects of DDT Sprayed on Elms," *Journal of Wildlife Management,* Vol. 22, No. 3, 1958, pp. 269–279.
[57]Robert J. Rudd, *Pesticides and the Living Landscape,* Madison: The University of Wisconsin Press, 1964, p. 33.
[58]Data from Robert J. Rudd, *Pesticides and the Living Landscape, op. cit.,* pp. 138, 250–254.

such as herons, was not determined. As far as the hazard to fish-eating humans was concerned, the levels of concentration of DDD in flesh of the fish, although lower than in the vital organs, were often well above the 7 ppm set by the Food and Drug Administration as the maximum tolerance for DDD residues in marketed foodstuffs. Upon recommendations of the Lake County Mosquito Abatement District, no further applications of DDD were made to the lake; but this experience, according to Rudd, " . . . still stands as a fascinating example of the complexities of chemical transferal in living systems, and as a pointed warning to professional workers not to oversimplify their solutions to pest control problems."[59]

Another example, perhaps more pertinent for farm pesticide policy, occurred in the Klamath Basin refuges in Northern California, which are administered by the U.S. Fish and Wildlife Service.[60] In the summer of 1960, the refuge staff began to pick up dead and dying birds, and soon 307 birds were identified, all fish eaters. They were found to contain lethal doses of taxophene, DDD, and DDE, concentrated in liver, kidneys, and subcutaneous fat, ranging from as little as 2.2 ppm of taxaphene to over 600 ppm of DDT and DDD. This condition was traced to spraying, some two years before, of crops which were irrigated from the Upper Klamath Lake, just over the border in Oregon. The runoff from these sprayed fields, spreading out over the swampy refuge, carried the lethal concentration.

Pesticide Control

These and other experiences raised policy questions that could not be ignored. Although scientists were becoming more fully aware of the possible lethal chain of events and were publishing their findings in technical journals, the policymaking public was not generally aroused until publication in 1962 of Rachel Carson's book, *Silent Spring*.[61] This was the first widely read book which attempted to cover the full range of environmental problems inherent in pesticide use. Rachel Carson raised the fear that the poisons being spread mainly through the use of persistent pesticides were bringing not only an irreversible degradation of the environment but were presenting a threat to human life itself which would persist for years to come. The widespread use of some rodenticides and herbicides was further upsetting the ecological balance.

Although her warnings could not be fully substantiated, and her arguments were sometimes rejected as unscientific if not ridiculed as overalarmist, the book must be regarded as a major policymaking influence. It brought the discussion of pesticides and their effects on the environment to an audience beyond the technical and professional journals. It encouraged individual scientists with and without institutional support to undertake increased study and research on pesticide problems. It prompted both federal and state governments to take

[59]*Ibid.*, p. 254.
[60]*Ibid.*, pp. 255–259.
[61]Rachel Carson, *Silent Spring*, Boston: Houghton Mifflin Company, 1962.

action against persistent pesticides and water and air pollution several years before such action otherwise might have occurred.[62] Although the question of causality is generally moot, considerable new emphasis was given to pesticide study and research. Resources for the Future,[63] for example, decided to give special emphasis to the study of environmental quality problems. Its publications up to 1967 included: *Environmental Quality in a Growing Economy* (a forum held at Resources for the Future, edited by Henry Jarrett); *Quality of the Environment: An Economic Approach to Some Problems in Using Land, Water, and Air,* by Orris C. Herfindahl and Allen V. Kneese; *The Economics of Regional Water Quality Management* and *Water Pollution: Economic Aspects and Research Needs,* both by Allen V. Kneese.

From the University of California at Davis, biologist Robert J. Rudd, working on a comprehensive study suggested to him by officers of the Conservation Foundation in 1958, brought together most of the then known scientific information on pest biology. His study was published as *Pesticides and the Living Landscape* (The University of Wisconsin Press, Madison, 1964). Rudd concluded (p. 291) that production and protection from the adverse effects of pesticides are parts of the same cloth. They cannot be biologically separated. We can no longer afford to dismiss as piecemeal the "separate" problems that arise from uncontrolled chemicals in living environments.

At the University of Illinois at Urbana-Champaign, agricultural economists J.C. Headley and J.N. Lewis, the latter visiting professor from the University of New England, Australia, joined in the first full-scale economic study of policy for pesticide use, supported in part by a grant from Resources for the Future. Their main work was published as *The Pesticide Problem: An Economic Approach to Public Policy* (Resources for the Future, 1967). In this study, the authors attempted to develop conceptual frameworks to put economic values on the secondary and tertiary costs (externalities) of pesticide use—the effects on fish and wildlife, the effects on human health, and environment; and they attempted also to assess the consequences to agriculture of the increased output—the reduction of costs to the firm and the stimulus to output which generally results in lower prices to consumers.

As of 1963, the President's Scientific Advisory Committee on Use of Pesticides had developed a comprehensive set of pest control recommendations:[64] The Department of Health, Education, and Welfare (HEW) should (1) develop a comprehensive data-gathering program, (2) cooperate with other departments to develop a continuing network to monitor residues and provide funds to assist states in monitoring residues in foods, (3) expand the diet studies on chlorinated hydrocarbons initiated by the Food and Drug Administration and review residue tolerances, and (4) critically review and revise as necessary the

---

[62]For a friendly, comparative evaluation, see Frank Graham, Jr., *Since Silent Spring,* Boston: Houghton Mifflin Company, 1970.

[63]Located at 1755 Massachusetts Avenue, N.W., Washington, D.C. 20036.

[64]J. F. Kennedy, *Use of Pesticides,* Report of the President's Science Advisory Committee, Washington, D.C., May 15, 1963.

federal advisory and coordinating mechanisms, including educational programs, systems for hazard evaluation, and the like. Government-sponsored programs should continue to shift, as the USDA had been doing, from research on broad spectrum chemicals to research on (*a*) selectively toxic chemicals, (*b*) nonpersistent chemicals, (*c*) selective methods of application, and (*d*) nonchemical control methods such as the use of attractants and the prevention of reproduction. To strengthen public laws on pesticides the President's Committee recommended that (1) registrations of chemicals should not be permitted while the chemical was under "protest" by the FDA, (2) every pesticide formulation should carry its own number on the label, (3) fish and wildlife should be protected under law as useful vertebrates and invertebrates, and (4) operating budgets should continue to carry funds to evaluate the efficiency of pesticide programs and their effects on nontarget organisms in the environment. Finally, it was admitted that until the publication of *Silent Spring,* people were generally unaware of the toxicity of pesticides. Therefore, the federal government should have an expanded program of public education of the dangers while recognizing the value of pesticides.

To implement such policy, it is necessary to have a public commitment for research and education, in contrast to a private special-interest commitment,[65] and to make use of various economic and social strategies.[66] These might include further government control of production and marketing, more discriminating administrative regulation of pesticide use, and modification of the incentive system. A tax on externalities has been suggested, for example, the obvious difficulty being to determine the level of damage associated with each pesticide and the appropriate tax rate to apply. Other possibilities are subsidies to those who are damaged, or subsidies to public or private agencies, such as the Federal Crop Insurance Corporation, to substitute crop insurance for pesticide use. Government might (1) permit acreage allotments to be transferred to areas where pest densities are low, (2) increase the patent life of narrow-spectrum chemicals to encourage their production and use, (3) lower fruit and vegetable grades to reduce the incentive for heavy pesticide use, and (4) employ rationing or other extra-market allocation of a restricted chemical pesticide. The law already requires that some pesticides can be applied only by licensed applicators, and the range of pesticides available for private use is thereby reduced.

A commitment to support research and education must be part of a national policy on pesticide use. In the 1950s such programs were operating at a rather low level. In the early 1960s, as some problems became more evident, the rate began to soar. One estimate put the 1962 expenditure at $63 million—$30 million of public funds and $33 million of private funds—and by 1964 the outlay of public funds alone was about $48 million.[67] As of 1970, the Entomology Research

---

[65]For further discussion, see Edward H. Smith, "Implementing Pest Control Strategies," *Pest Control Strategies for the Future, op. cit.,* pp. 44–68, and H. L. Wilcke, "The Role of the Food Industry in Solving Pest Control Problems," *ibid.,* pp. 69–76.

[66]Gerald A. Carlson and Emery N. Castle, "Economics of Pest Control," *ibid.,* pp. 79–99.

[67]U.S. Senate, *Pesticides and Public Policy,* Committee on Government Operations, Subcommittee on Reorganization and International Organizations, 89th Cong., 2d Sess., Senate Report 1379.

Division of the USDA was spending only 16 percent of its research funds on conventional pesticides, with 51 percent on biological and specific control methods and 33 percent on basic and fundamental research. Thus, over the years, an increasing amount of research funds has been allocated to research on nonchemical controls and on chemicals that are more specific to their target.[68] There is continuing effort on breeding insect- and disease-resistant plant varieties:[69] Among the newer efforts is the introduction of preemptive sterile insects and other genetic control techniques,[70] biological control of parasites and predators,[71] and insect control by microbial agents.[72]

Pesticide Legislation   Pesticide policy is importantly implemented through legislation. The legislative evolution has progressed in a series of acts and rather simple regulations first set by the Federal Insecticide Act of 1910 and numerous state laws, some passed prior to 1910, dealing with (1) registration and (2) use and application, to the comprehensive and detailed Federal Environmental Pest Control Act of 1972 (P.L. 92-516; 86 Stat. 973). Because of the need to standardize regulations and to uniformly control pesticide use within states as well as in interstate commerce, the federal government has assumed a progressively larger role. The 1910 act merely prevented the manufacture, sale, or transportation of adulterated or misbranded insecticides and fungicides and authorized state regulation of sales of insecticides and fungicides. In 1946 the Council of State Governments developed a uniform insecticide, fungicide, and rodenticide act for consideration and adoption by individual states.

In 1947, the Federal Insecticide, Fungicide, and Rodenticide Act replaced the 1910 act to conform with numerous state acts and to require the following: (1) the registration of chemical pesticides before their sale or shipment in interstate or foreign commerce; (2) prominent display of poison warnings on labels of highly toxic materials; (3) coloring of insecticides to prevent their being mistaken for foodstuffs; (4) inclusion of general warnings to prevent injury to people, animals, and plants; (5) inclusion of instructions for use to provide protection to the public; and (6) furnishing of information to the administrator of the act with respect to the delivery, movement, or holding of pesticides.

In 1954, an amendment to the Food and Drug Act authorized the administrator of the Federal, Insecticide, Fungicide, and Rodenticide Act to set tolerance limits for the residues of pesticides in foods, required the pretesting of a chemical pesticide before it can be used on food crops, and required the manufacturer to provide both detailed data demonstrating the usefulness of the chemical to

[68]C. H. Hoffman, "Restricting the Use of Pesticides—What Are the Options?" *ibid.,* pp. 21–30. The Entomology Research Division of the USDA began reorienting its research in this direction in 1955 and since then has allocated about one-half its total budget for this study.

[69]*Research on Controlling Insects without Conventional Insecticides,* USDA, ARS 22-85, October 1963.

[70]E. F. Kipling, "Sterilization and Other Genetic Techniques," *Pest Control Strategies for the Future, op. cit.,* pp. 272–287.

[71]Richard L. Doutt, "Biological Control: Parasites and Predators," *ibid.,* pp. 288–297.

[72]A. M. Heimpel, "Insect Control by Microbial Agents," *ibid.,* pp. 298–316.

agriculture and scientific data on the toxicity of the chemical to warm-blooded animals. In 1959, the 1947 act was amended to include the several new types of chemicals. In 1964, further amendments eliminated provisions to use a pesticide while it was under protest, authorized each pesticide to carry a license number identification, and expedited procedures for suspending the marketing of previously registered pesticides which were found to be unsafe. Finally, in 1970, under a presidential reorganization plan, the pesticide and pure food regulatory staffs located in the Departments of Agriculture, Interior, and HEW were transferred to a new Environmental Protection Agency (EPA).[73]

The Federal Environmental Pesticide Control Act of 1972 (FEPCA) completely revised and replaced the 1947 act and its amendments under the general policy goal of regulating the use of pesticides to protect humans and the environment by extending federal regulations to cover all pesticide manufacture, sale, and use within states as well as among states. Major provisions prohibit—that is, make unlawful—sale or use of any pesticide in a manner inconsistent with its labeling and require all pesticides to be classified for general or restricted use. Those in the restricted category can be used only by or under the supervision of certified applicators or subject to such other restrictions as the administrator may determine. General or seasonal licenses, permits, or other forms of approval may be required for applicators as certified by states under a program approved by the administrator.

The 1972 act required the registration of all pesticide producers and their regular submission of information on production and sales volume. It authorized entry of establishments and other places where pesticides are held for sale or distribution for purposes of inspection and sampling of pesticides and devices. It authorized stop-sale, stop-use, and removal or seizure orders, to be enforced through civil and increased criminal penalties. It improved the procedures for registration and cancelation actions by combining scientific review and public hearings, with all questions to be submitted in writing at the beginning of a hearing. It authorized the administrator to establish pesticide packaging standards, to regulate pesticide and container disposal, to issue experimental use permits, to conduct research on pesticides and alternatives, and to monitor pesticide use and presence in the environment. States were authorized to impose more stringent regulations than those of the federal government.

A Policy Conclusion

Pesticide policy in America underwent a remarkable revolution in the ten years between publication of *Silent Spring* in 1962 and the act of 1972, without either destroying the pesticide industry, slowing down the adoption of new technologies such as aerial spraying, or reversing the strong growth in manufacture and sale of pesticides useful in crop and food production. The basic concept shifted

---

[73]For further discussion, legislative history, review of hearings, etcetera, see "Federal Environmental Pesticide Control Act of 1972," Senate Report No. 92-838, *U.S. Code, Congressional and Administrative News,* 92d Cong., 2d Sess., 1972, Vol. 3, pp. 3993–4134.

after the disastrous experiences of the late 1950s and early 1960s from that of pest eradication to that of incremental pest control. This shift was guided by the economic concept that the use of recommended pest controls can result in a social optimum and that pesticide application beyond this point will reduce social welfare. Subsequently, however, a number of events indicated that a more precise framework is needed for policy to take into account not only the contribution of chemicals to agricultural productivity but also their potentially hazardous effects on various forms of life. Although benefit-cost analysis is recognized as having relevance,[74] the crux of many decisions pertaining to the use of hazardous materials lies in balancing the risk and uncertainty of damage to human and animal life against the more certain benefits. Analytically, this may be conceived as a "hazard-benefit" analysis, to avoid the formal distinction between risk and uncertainty.[75] Thus, a policy-implementing agency may conceive of the hazard of a pesticide as a function of the average or mean damage and the variance. Conceivably, an action with a higher expected damage or mortality rate with high predictability might be preferred over one having a lower expected damage with greater uncertainty or variance.

A policy decision to limit pesticides may involve both known hazards and uncertainty. To illustrate, in the winter of 1975–76 the largest body of fresh water in Illinois, the Carlyle Reservoir, was closed to commercial fishing because of high concentrations of dieldrin in commercial species of carp and white carp. Those taking fish from the Shelbyville Reservoir, another large body of water in Illinois, were warned against eating more than one or two fish a week. This was because of the amount of mercury found in the fish. In both cases, apparently, the contamination came from the excess runoff from cropland in the watersheds. Although the ban and warning reduced the immediate danger to human consumption, a larger issue might be conceived. That is, should the pesticide in question be reduced or cut off at the source? Almost simultaneously, scientists were finding that some species of fish in Lake Superior were contaminated above levels safe for human consumption, both from DDT and from polychlorinated biphenyls (PCBs), an industrial chemical. Should more stringent controls be applied? What were the implications of more delay in implementing more stringent controls?

To illustrate further, the vast, dry and sparsely settled intermountain region, stretching from the Rocky Mountains on the east to the Sierra-Cascade Range on the west, has long been a source of conflict over grazing rights and priveleges. The range livestock ranchers have competed with one another over use of the

[74]See Allan A. Schmid, "Effective Public Policy and the Government Budget: A Uniform Treatment of Public Expenditures and Public Rules," *The Analysis and Evaluation of Public Expenditures: The PPB System,* Joint Economic Committee, 91st Cong., 1st Sess., Vol. 1, 1969, pp. 579–591.

[75]This concept has been formally developed by Earl R. Swanson, "Agricultural Productivity and Environmental Hazards: A Framework for Policy Evaluation," *The Annals of Agricultural Sciences of the Polish Academy of Sciences, 1976,* papers prepared for the 75th anniversary of the birth of Professor Richard Manteuffel, Director of the Institute of Farm Economics and Farm Management, at the Warsaw Agricultural University.

range; and their economic interest is often in conflict with that of the general public for conservation of soil and water and the preservation of wildlife and natural forest land. After many years of growing animosity over grazing rights, the Taylor Grazing Act of 1934 was passed to reorganize the use and control of the 140 million acres of "vacant, unappropriated, and unreserved lands . . . of the public domain."[76] Although the Taylor Act did not quiet all the controversies or halt many cases of overgrazing, it did offer a new approach to the problems of western land use and control. With the development of pesticides, however, some new problems arose. Until 1972, sheep ranchers were permitted to use poison bait to control predators, especially coyotes which are natural and deadly enemies of sheep. But the poison bait also killed other wildlife, including scavengers that fed on poisoned carcasses. Some scavenger birds, such as the bald eagle, were threatened with extinction. After several years of swelling protests from various individuals and groups about the damage to wildlife from the bait, the Environmental Protection Agency (EPA) banned use of the poison bait on federal lands and soon thereafter also prohibited bait shipment in interstate traffic, thus making it practically unavailable for use on private lands as well.

A great howl arose from sheep ranchers, who claimed that they were suffering large losses from predators, and soon their influence was reflected in political pressures. Twenty-one senators from Western states signed a letter accusing the Department of the Interior, which administered the EPA, of failing to protect livestock from predators. The 1974 Western Governors' Conference passed a resolution to urge the EPA to reinstate predator poisons and also to transfer the responsibility for predator control from Interior to Agriculture. In November 1974, more than 100 biologists met for four days in Denver to concentrate on possible policy solutions. But there was no ideal solution that would contain the coyote population without having other adverse consequences. Although each antagonist could make a telling point, the public interest lay somewhere between the two positions. Responsible administration required decisions that were decidedly unpopular with some groups. The hazard-benefit concept or analysis was the correct criterion for implementing the policy.

In high priority, a general policy conclusion is that the search for solutions that will be socially optimum must still go on. Research and education must play a major role. But no amount of education alone can resolve a conflict where economic interests are vitally opposed. In such instances, there is no substitute for government regulation. The best for which people can hope is a prudent balancing of costs and benefits relating to food production and the environment, accompanied by a stronger program in research and education, and more discriminating policies in respect to government controls applied to pesticides. Congress must set more specific and consistent standards for the EPA as a guide for regulatory decisions. Vendors of poisonous chemicals must carry

[76]Wesley Calef, *Private Grazing and Public Lands, Studies of the Local Management of the Taylor Grazing Act,* Chicago: The University of Chicago Press, 1960, p. x.

a heavier evidentiary burden of establishing the risk or hazard of their product. The scope of EPA economic analyses must be broadened with more extensive use of independent scientific panels to indicate and quantify the benefits and the costs of alternatives in regulatory policy. Since the quality of chemical regulatory decisions is dependent largely on the adequacy of available information, the development of an adequate data base must be emphasized, research efforts in basic clinical and environmental toxicology and epidemiology must be strengthened, and the results must be interpreted in an expanded program of economic studies. The result should be more consistent socially optimum decisions in regard to pesticides.[77]

THE FUTURE FOOD SUPPLY

The changes that have occurred in the commodities used in food production have profoundly affected the economic structure of agriculture to raise new and important issues for policy. What are the implications for future food supply? How has the structure of farming changed, and how will it be affected in the future? What is the elasticity of supply and what are the implications for policy in the future?

Implications for Future Food Supply

Periodically, economists and others have given their attention to projecting the future of agriculture and the food supply. In 1958, for example, the combined annual meeting of the Canadian Agricultural Economics Society and the American Farm Economic Association focused on the theme "Meeting the Challenge of Science in Agriculture."[78] To summarize a predominant conclusion of the more than 900 pages of discussion, the prime impact of science on agriculture and on the whole economy has been that the growth of knowledge has permitted a rapid development of economic specialization in a dynamic enterprise economy.[79] This has meant a tremendous expansion in real living standards, a growth in both supply and demand, and a new potential for productivity, savings, and investment. A survey of possible innovations recognized some of the limits to growth as well as potentials.[80] The full sequence of events in growth was not as clear then as it was later. The full impact of fertilizer and pesticides that occurred in the following years could not be foretold, for example, and the potential contribution of food science and technology was only briefly noted.[81] Later it

[77]For further discussion see *Decision Making for Regulating Chemicals in the Environment,* Washington: National Academy of Sciences, 1975. A report prepared by the Committee on Principles of Decision Making for Regulating Chemicals in the Environment, Environmental Studies Board, Commission on National Resources, National Research Council.

[78]Proceedings of the 1958 Joint Annual Meeting of the American Farm Economic Association (*Journal of Farm Economics,* Vol. XL, No. 5) and the Canadian Agricultural Economics Society (*Canadian Journal of Agricultural Economics,* Vol. VI, No. 2).

[79]See, for example, the paper by R. G. Bressler, Jr., *ibid.,* pp. 1005–1015.

[80]See papers by R. G. Bressler, Jr., Andrew Stewart, W. A. Nierenberg, T. C. Byerly, Harold G. Halcrow, H. R. Jensen, and Ben C. French, *ibid.,* pp. 1005–1056.

[81]Ben C. French, *ibid.,* p. 1053.

became more evident that revolutionary innovations in food science could be adapted to commercial use, thus expanding the food supply. Examples are new processes for preparing soybean products for direct human use, direct human consumption of high-lysine corn, and development of strains of wheat and rice that are higher in protein. These will in time tend to reduce the dependence of people on animal products.[82]

Furthermore, it is possible that new technology will unlock vast new sources of minerals, fuels, and other resources previously not even known to exist in the earth's crust. In 1974 the Earth Resources Technology Satellite (ERTS) began to put the whole earth under a gigantic microscope.[83] If some of the more imaginative possibilities are realized, some of the worry about fuel and mineral shortages will be pushed far back into the twenty-first century at least, and the energy crisis that began the new third era of food policy will be seen as a passing phase. Even though the more optimistic projections do not come true, the new technologies will make possible more accurate surveys of possible world food production, more complete acreage inventories, and a worldwide crop monitoring system. This can be of immense help in making decisions about food policy, forecasting food shortages and surpluses, and managing the world food supply.

In the intermediate term, although growth rates appear to be slower than in the 1950s and 1960s, a projection of a 25 percent increase or more in aggregate farm production in a decade depends only on the availability of purchased inputs at prices that continue to be profitable for farm investors. The initial conditions of the third agricultural era gave a powerful boost to land prices, reflecting the changes in economic rent attributable to land.[84] Although land appeared to be the most restricted of all major classes of inputs, the policy question for the future is not the physical availability of land, but what land will be profitable to farm. This decision can be measured in respect to intensity of use, total acreage and economic structure.

Changes in Economic Structure

As has been noted, the agricultural industries supplying inputs and services to the farm sector have grown, processing-marketing firms have grown in size and declined in number, and the decline in total farm population has been matched by comparable declines in numbers of farm operating units.[85] Production has been concentrated in fewer units and the percentage of total output produced by large-scale farms has increased, most significantly since the late 1920s. In 1929, for

---

[82]A computer-assisted survey of "meat substitutes" revealed 75 separate publications—bulletins, journal articles, and books—under this topic.

[83]See Gene Bylinsky (with Peter Schuyten, Research Associate), "ERTS Puts the Whole Earth under a Microscope," *Fortune,* February 1975, pp. 117 ff.

[84]Twice a year the USDA prepares and publishes an index of farm land values by states. Between November 1971 and November 1975, for example, farm land prices in the Corn Belt approximately doubled.

[85]For the most complete analysis of change up to the early 1950s, see Theodore W. Schultz, *The Economic Organization of Agriculture,* New York: McGraw-Hill Book Company, 1953. For some of the later secular trends, see John Rosine and Peter Helmberger, "A Neoclassical Analysis of the U.S. Farm Sector, 1948–1970," *American Journal of Agricultural Economics,* Vol. 56, No. 4, November 1974, pp. 717–729.

Table 4-4   Comparison of the Concentration of Number of Farms and Value of Products Sold, 1929 (Adjusted to 1964 Prices), 1964, 1969, and 1970*

1964 census class	Value of agricultural products sales	Percentage of total number			Percentage of total sales		
		1929 (adj.)	1964	1969	1929 (adj.)	1964	1970
1,2	$20,000 and over	1.2	12.7	20.2	14.9	64.4	75.8
3	$10,000 to $19,999	2.7	14.8	14.5	12.4	19.2	14.9
4	$5,000 to $9,999	7.9	16.0	14.3	17.9	10.6	5.4
5	$2,500 to $4,999	23.8	14.1	16.7	30.0	4.7	1.9
6	Less than $2,500	64.4	42.5	34.3	24.8	1.1	2.0

*Calculations for 1929, 1964, and 1969 by Leonard R. Kyle based on U.S. Census of Agriculture. Data for 1970 calculated from projections by Rex F. Daley, J. A. Dempey, and C. W. Cobb. "Farm Numbers and Size in the Future," in A. Gordon Ball and Earl O. Heady (eds.), *Size, Structure, and Future of Farms,* Ames: Iowa State University Press, 1972, pp. 314–332.

example, only 7,875 farms out of more than 6.5 million had farm sales of more than $30,000, selling an estimated 5 percent of all farm produce.[86] By 1964, there were about 126,000 farms in this sales category, reporting about 30 percent of all farm product sales.[87] In 35 years the number of farms in this sales category increased 16-fold.

A comparison of farms according to census class (adjusted to 1964 prices) shows that, between 1929 and 1969, farms selling more than $20,000 of product increased from 1.2 percent to 20.2 percent of all farms. Between 1929 and 1970, the percentage of total sales from this group increased from 14.9 percent to 75.8 percent. In 1929, 96.1 percent of all farms sold less than $10,000 of product and supplied 65.3 percent of the value of all products sold. In 1969, the small classes selling less than $10,000 of product were 65.3 percent of all farms, but supplied only 9.3 percent of the value of all farm products sold (Table 4-4).

In 1964 a special tabulation of the *Census of Agriculture* showed 31,401 large-scale farm units with farm product sales of more than $100,000, an increase of 10 percent per year since 1959.[88] By 1969 the number had increased to 52,000, again an increase of more than 10 percent per year. But the percent of total product sold by large-size farms (above $40,000 in total sales) differed widely among the various commodities (and thus by states and regions). That is, in some areas, or among certain types of farming and certain commodities, very large farms were the rule, whereas among others family farms predominated (Table 4-5).

Interpreting USDA Data on Farm Size

Because of changing definitions and concepts, the U.S. census and USDA data do not always clearly reveal the trends in farm size and concentration. A finding

---

[86]R. D. Jennings, *Large Scale Farming in the United States, 1929,* U.S. Department of Commerce Census of Agriculture, Fifteenth Census of the United States, 1930.

[87]Kenneth R. Krause and Leonard R. Kyle, "Economic Factors Underlying the Incidence of Large Farming Units, the Current Situation and Probable Trends," *American Journal of Agricultural Economics,* Vol. 52, No. 5, December 1970, pp. 748–765; and Leonard R. Kyle, "Who Will Make the Decisions in the Future?" *Illinois Banker,* Vol. 52, No. 4, October 1970.

[88]Radoje Nikolitch, *Our 31,000 Largest Farms,* USDA, ERS, Agricultural Economics Report 175, March 1970.

Table 4-5   Percent of Value of Farm Products Sold by Large-Size Farms, 1929, 1959, 1964, and 1969

Type of farm	1929 large size*	1959 Class 1†	1964 Class 1†	1969 Class 1†
		Percent		
Vegetable	20.0	73.8	81.4	85.0
Poultry	3.3	55.4	67.9	84.6
Miscellaneous	1.0	62.1	65.4	77.3
Other field crop	5.1	55.8	73.7	74.6
Ranch	29.2	59.8	64.0	72.8
Fruit and nut	19.9	45.1	67.6	68.8
Livestock	2.1	33.9	46.8	61.2
Cotton	1.4	46.8	55.2	54.4
General	.2	20.7	33.6	45.7
Dairy	3.0	15.3	23.4	41.1
Cash grain	1.8	16.7	23.9	35.4
Tobacco	. . .	3.9	8.2	18.6
Total	5.0	32.8	43.7	55.9

*Farms with over $30,000 value of products sold in 1929, which is comparable to $48,600 in 1959 and $48,450 in 1964.
†Farms with over $40,000 in gross farm product sales as listed in the *U.S. Census of Agriculture.* Data for farms with annual sales of $2,500 or more.

put forth as late as 1972 was that family farms, "those using predominately family labor, make up 95 percent of all farms and produce 65 percent of all farm products sold in the U.S. Although these percentages have fluctuated slightly, they have been substantially the same for the past 30 years, despite the decline in total farm numbers."[89] Thus, family farms accounted for the following proportions of sales in these years: 1949, 63 percent; 1959, 70 percent; 1964, 65 percent; and 1969, 62 percent.

The U.S. census and USDA data on owner-operation suggest that an increasing percentage of farms are run by owner-operators and that an increasing percentage of land is cultivated by owner-operators, as follows:[90]

Year	Percentage of farms operated by the owner	Percentage of all land farmed by owner-operators
1900	63.7	63.3
1920	60.9	66.7
1940	60.7	64.3
1964	82.4	76.7
1969	88.1	86.9

[89]R. Nikolitch, *Family-Size Farms in U.S. Agriculture,* USDA, ERS No. 499, February 1972, p. 15.
[90]See U.S. *Census of Agriculture,* 1972, USDA, Washington: Government Printing Office, 1972. Also reported in D.O. Moyer, *Land Tenure in the United States: Development and Status,* USDA, ERS, Agricultural Information Bulletin No. 338, June 1969.

But this classification of owner-operation is misleading because we do not know the percent of equity owners have in land and nonland assets and—more importantly—the census definition of "farm operator" was changed between 1964 and 1969 from "a person . . . either doing the work himself or directly supervising the work" to "the person in charge of the farm or ranch operation." This made it possible in 1969 to classify as "owners" persons who were previously classified as hired managers and absentee owners. Additionally, in 1949, plantations were counted as single units and presumably were therefore "nonfamily farms." In 1959, sharecroppers—many of whom were on plantations —were counted as operating independent family farms. This change in definitions made it appear that nonfamily farms (plantations) were disappearing and family farms (operated by sharecroppers as independent family farms) were increasing.[91]

In general, the trends toward greater concentration in farm production are proceeding more rapidly than some of the data suggest. The trend toward greater concentration is strong, as the data in Table 4-5 show, and apparently is proceeding apace. This shift is occurring only in part from internal economies of increasing scale in farm production, and more from external economies in acquiring inputs and in marketing farm products. Also (as will be discussed in more detail in Chapters 8 through 10), various policies relating to control of land, to the use of credit, to tax laws, and to employment of farm labor have given advantages to large-scale operation. What are some of the inferences for policy?

External Economies and the Growth of Large Farms

To understand the trend toward large farms, two different sets of data must be kept in mind: (1) internal economies of scale in actual management and operation of a farm, and (2) external economies in acquiring inputs and managing product sales. In respect to the first, reductions in per unit costs are widely recognized as rather modest over most of American agriculture as farms increase beyond the level of an efficient, large-size family farm. On grain farms in Central and Northern Illinois, for example, although increasing the acreage of a farm reduces the labor and machinery costs per acre, usually only small savings in costs— typically zero to $3 or $4 per acre—can be realized by increasing beyond 500 to 600 acres.[92] Somewhat similar conclusions have been reached in regard to other types of farms in various parts of the country. For example, as far as internal economies are concerned, the family farm is the most efficient.[93]

[91]For further discussion, see Ray Marshall, *Rural Workers in Rural Labor Markets,* Salt Lake City, Utah: Olympus Publishing Co., 1974, pp. 48–52.

[92]D. F. Wilken, "Costs, Investments, and Earnings by Size and Type of Farm, 1971–73," *Economics for Agriculture,* rev., Urbana: University of Illinois, Department of Agricultural Economics, FM-29, September 1974; A. G. Mueller and R. A. Hinton, "Farmers Production Costs for Corn and Soybeans by Unit Size," *American Journal of Agricultural Economics,* Vol. 57, No. 5, December 1975, pp. 934–939.

[93]Based on data for 1967. See Angus McDonald, "The Family Farm is the Most Efficient Unit of Agricultural Production," *Farmworkers in Rural America, 1971-1972,* Hearings before the Subcommittee on Migratory Labor of the Committee on Labor and Public Welfare, United States Senate, 92d Cong., 1st and 2d Sess., Jan. 13, 1972, Part 3c, pp. 2067–2073.

In respect to the external economies in acquiring inputs and managing product sales, however, a different image has sometimes emerged, based on the contention that a large farm unit can command a higher net selling price for its output and a lower buying price for many of its inputs. It was found, for example, that a 5,000-acre corn production unit in the Corn Belt had an advantage of $7.30 per acre over a 500-acre unit after federal income taxes and with a 30 percent equity. Savings of $14.04 per acre were realized in obtaining purchased inputs. There was a net marketing advantage of $5.72 per acre. Against these advantages there were increasing costs of $3.82 per acre for labor and management and increased income tax costs of $8.64 per acre.[94]

The Concentration of Large-Scale Firms

The growth of large-scale firms has been most pronounced in those parts of the food system where vertical integration—combining farm supply, farm production, food processing, or marketing—has resulted in various degrees of market control. In cattle feeding, for example, vertically integrated giant feed lots compete directly with family farms. In both fruits and vegetables large-scale firms have combined farm production with food processing and marketing. In some instances, as the economy has matured, large conglomerates have developed or bought into the food system. In 1970, the Greyhound Corporation, for example, acquired some 86 percent of the stock of Armour and Co., the meat-packing firm; and following this Greyhound added other firms in poultry and broiler production and marketing. ITT invested in a nationwide bakery system. Other large-scale firms include Dow Chemical in lettuce and the Boeing Company in potatoes and other produce. Tenneco, the oil, shipbuilding and manufacturing conglomerate, took over the holdings of the Kern County Land Company in California plus some other firms to assemble land holdings twice the size of Rhode Island. Tenneco is concentrated in fruits and vegetables, Coca-Cola and Royal Crown Cola are in fruit juices, and so on.

What position the government should adopt in regard to vertical integration or concentration in the various parts of the food system is one of the most difficult questions in food policy. Where there are real economic advantages in large-scale organization, costs can be reduced by permitting or encouraging a measure of integration or concentration. On the other hand, if large-scale firms are the result of market imperfections, tax concessions, or excessive labor exploitation, or if concentration results in monopoly pricing, then a policy to regulate or control integration and concentration may be in the public interest.

In some cases, a few large firms, through effective advertising and promotion of brand names combined with significant economies of large scale, have come to dominate almost completely a subsector. The prepared breakfast foods are an

[94]Kenneth R. Krause and Leonard R. Kyle, "Economic Factors Underlying the Incidence of Large Farming Units, the Current Situation and Probable Trends," *American Journal of Agricultural Economics,* Vol. 52, No. 5, December 1970, p. 755. See also Leonard R. Kyle, "Who Will Make the Decisions in the Future?" *Illinois Banker,* Vol. 52, No. 4, October 1970.

example. Such firms, through differentiation of their products, compete as a model of an oligopoly-type industry with minimal government controls. The main constraint is possible antitrust action by the Federal Trade Commission (FTC) and surveillance by the Food and Drug Administration (FDA). But government action to stop the trend toward monopoly is not specifically established in law. A few large firms have dominated the meat-packing industry for a long time.[95] Very large dairy firms are a result of government policy or the lack of government power to stop most mergers and acquisitions.

The Issue of Government Intervention

The issue of whether, or how and how much, the government should intervene to influence the structure of competition is far from settled. On the one hand, the growth of large-scale enterprise, brand names, and large retail food chains has brought gains in efficiency that could not be achieved in a more atomistic food industry. Some of the gains from this efficiency have been passed forward to consumers as well as backward to farm producers. On the other hand, there is a certain rigidity in the structure of competition, and it has been argued or alleged that the modern food system exploits the consumer by unnecessary and excessive advertising, by charging monopoly prices in some markets where the competition is weak or imperfect, and by sometimes promoting products that are inferior in terms of their nutritive value or deleterious to good balanced diets.[96] It has been alleged that the consumer is misled by much of the advertising and promotion that takes place, and that some food firms make an excessively high level of profit on certain product brands and food items.[97] Some authors have argued further that many food additives, and many synthetics and manufactured foods developed in this type of competition, are nutritionally deficient, if not downright bad for peoples' health.[98] The data clearly show that some important nutrients are lost by unnecessary food processing, that much of food advertising is not conducive to diet improvement, and that the average American diet has declined in terms of nutritive quality (see Chapter 11).

Representatives of the food industry argue, however, that the levels of profit, or return on investment, are not high in comparison with those in other sectors of the American economy, that costs are reduced by the amount of concentration that has been achieved, and that development of the industry is thereby enhanced. The benefits of the efficiencies of large scale are reinvested, paid to stockholders, passed on to consumers, or back to farm producers.[99] Studies have shown that

[95]William H. Nicholls, *Imperfect Competition Within Agricultural Industries,* Ames: Iowa State College Press, 1941.

[96]See William Robbins, *The American Food Scandal, Why You Can't Eat Well on What You Earn,* New York: William Morrow and Company, Inc., 1974.

[97]Jim Hightower, *Eat Your Heart Out—Food Profiteering in America,* New York: Crown Publishers, Inc., 1975.

[98]Gary Null and staff, *Body Pollution* (ed. James Dawson), New York: Arco Publishing Co., Inc., 1973.

[99]See Daniel J. McLaughlin, Jr. and Charles A. Mallowe (eds.), *Food Marketing and Distribution, Selected Readings,* New York: Chain Store Age Books, A Division of Chain Store Publishing Co., 1971.

the structure of food processing and marketing has tended to stabilize. Industry leaders have worked hard to achieve high ethical standards and exemplary conduct. Performance is generally rated as good to superior in comparison with other American enterprise.

On balance, the congressional and presidential commissions that have been formed to review the organization, conduct, and performance of the food system have not agreed on the role of government in regulation of the industry. In some cases the commissions have been dominated by the views of those representing the large and most successful food firms. Until recent years, at least, a strictly consumer interest or view—as contrasted with an industry interest or view—has not been advanced with vigor. Congressional hearings, such as those held by the Joint Economic Committee, have provided an open forum for examination of important questions. The issues are complex and they must be examined in detail. In the meantime, we close this chapter with a discussion of the elasticity of the farm food supply.

THE ELASTICITY OF THE FARM FOOD SUPPLY

Elasticity of supply generally refers to changes in output associated with changes in product price, *ceteris paribus;* or to changes in output associated with changes in prices of products relative to prices of inputs. Elasticity is generally positive, and thus an increase in product price, *ceteris paribus,* generally brings forth an increase in output. Similarly, a decrease in prices of inputs, *ceteris paribus,* also brings forth an increase. Over the 50 years of the second great era of food policy, major increases in the American food supply were importantly associated with real declines in the prices of farm inputs.

Since accurate theoretical construction and measurement of the elasticity of supply is vitally important for policymaking, as well as for other reasons, economists have been concerned with the problem for a long time. Early studies showed that farmers placed considerable emphasis on current prices in deciding what acreage to plant; but elasticities were low for aggregate crop acreage or output in respect to price.[100] In 1956, Nerlove published elasticities of supply for selected commodities, relating changes in acreage to expected prices.[101] He used the method of distributed lags, a situation in which the effect of a change in one variable, such as a change in the expected price of a product, is not felt all at once but is distributed over time. In 1958, he elaborated on the theoretical aspects of this method and concluded that, whenever such lags occur, the studies must

[100]John D. Black, "The Elasticity of Supply of Farm Products," *Journal of Farm Economics,* Vol. 6, No. 2, April 1924, pp. 145–155; F. F. Elliott, "The Nature and Measurement of the Elasticity of Supply of Farm Products," *ibid.,* Vol. 9, No. 3, July 1927, pp. 288–302; Bradford B. Smith, *Factors Affecting the Price of Cotton,* USDA Technical Bulletin No. 50, 1928; L. H. Bean, "The Farmer's Response to Price," *Journal of Farm Economics,* Vol. 11, No. 3, July, 1929, pp. 368–385; Robert M. Walsh, "Response to Price in the Production of Cotton and Cottonseed," *ibid.,* Vol. 26, No. 2, May, 1944, pp. 359–372; R. L. Kohls and Don Paarlberg, *Short-Time Response of Agricultural Production to Price and Other Factors,* Purdue Agricultural Experiment Station Bulletin 555, 1950.

[101]Marc Nerlove, "Estimates of the Elasticities of Supply of Selected Agricultural Commodities," *Journal of Farm Economics,* Vol. 38, No. 2, May 1956, pp. 496–509.

extend over the period of adjustment for accurate measurements to be made.[102] Later in the same year, Griliches, using this concept, suggested that the best way to measure elasticity of farm supply was to measure the change in farmers' use of selected inputs, such as fertilizer, farm machinery, and hired farm labor; and he showed that any supply elasticity could be expressed as a weighted average of all the elasticities of demand for individual inputs with respect to the price of the product.[103] By using factor shares as weights, assuming each factor was paid according to the value of its marginal product, an aggregate supply elasticity could be identified and related to relevant price changes. Thus, the elasticity of supply could be measured by breaking down production responses according to changes in inputs, even though no single figure could be generally accepted as the elasticity of supply in either the short or long run. In 1960, Griliches followed this with development of an aggregative supply function, with his most successful equations expressing output as a function of relative prices, weather, trend, and lagged output.[104] Nerlove and Bachman assembled an important survey article on supply estimation.[105] In 1962, Buchholz, Judge, and West published a summary of a large number of elasticity estimates of both supply and demand, in which the elasticity of supply of individual farm commodities was estimated in respect to relative prices and other factors.[106]

Heady and Tweeten used estimates of the aggregate farm commodity supply function to identify problems in adjusting farm output to market demand.[107] Based on data interpreted from this and other studies, Tweeten and Quance estimated short-run (two-year) elasticities for 1921 to 1941 and for 1948 to 1966 by three methods:[108] (1) by the method of direct least squares the best single estimate of short-run elasticity was 0.155; (2) by using separate yield and production components for crops and livestock the estimated short-run elasticity was 0.17 for crops, 0.38 for livestock, and 0.25 for aggregate farm output;[109] and (3) by using separate input contributions for eight selected categories of inputs, each weighted according to its relative importance in contributing to aggregate output, short-run (two-year) supply elasticity was 0.26 and long-run elasticity (involving

[102]Marc Nerlove, "Distributed Lags and Estimation of Long-Run Supply and Demand Elasticities," *ibid.*, Vol. 40, No. 2, May 1958, pp. 301–311.

[103]Zvi Griliches, "The Demand for Inputs in Agriculture and a Derived Supply Elasticity," *ibid.*, Vol. 41, No. 2, May 1959, pp. 309–323.

[104]Zvi Griliches, "Estimates of the Aggregate U.S. Farm Supply Function," *ibid.*, Vol. 42, No. 2, May 1960, pp. 282–293.

Marc Nerlove and Kenneth L. Bachman, "The Analysis of Changes in Agricultural Supply: Problems and Approaches," *ibid.*, Vol. 42, No. 2, August 1960, pp. 531–554.

[106]H. E. Buchholz, G. G. Judge, and V. I. West, *A Summary of Selected Estimated Behavior Relationships for Agricultural Products,* Urbana: University of Illinois, Department of Agricultural Economics, Agricultural Economic Research Report 57, 1962.

[107]Earl O. Heady and Luther G. Tweeten, *Resource Demand and Structure of the Agricultural Industry,* Ames: Iowa State University Press, 1963, especially Chapters 16 and 17.

[108]Luther G. Tweeten and C. Leroy Quance, "Positivistic Measures of Aggregate Supply Elasticities: Some New Approaches," *American Journal of Agricultural Economics,* Vol. 51, No. 2, May 1969, pp. 342–352.

[109]*Ibid.*, p. 349.

six repetitions of the short-run) was 1.52.[110] For periods of falling prices, in which only operating units were variable, the elasticities appeared to be 0.10 in the short run and 0.80 in the long run. In other words, a decrease of 10 percent in product price (*ceteris paribus*) would decrease output by 1 percent in two years and 8 percent after many years.

Although such estimates of supply elasticities provide useful averages or approximations for generalizing about policy matters, strong warnings must be observed against using them without due qualification in formulating policies and programs that are designed to pursue specific policy goals.[111] Farm production is notoriously subject to random influences, notably good or bad weather, and this makes the unveiling of supply elasticity a very difficult task. Although there is a tendency, especially in the method of least squares, for the results to be biased downward, the elasticity of aggregate farm supply may be as low as 0.1 in the short run and perhaps eight times this in the long run; or 0.10 in the short run and 0.80 in the long run for decreasing product prices, and 0.15 in the short run and 1.5 in the long run for increasing prices.[112]

Further rigor in quantification of supply elasticity is desired, but, because of the randomness of nature and other events, the most rigorous quantitative estimates must leave some degree of margin for error, and food policy must allow for this. Still, the estimates of elasticity are useful in policymaking, and they are particularly helpful in understanding certain problems, such as the persistence of low farm income and the cyclical instability in farm product markets.

Supply Inelasticity: The Persistence of Low Income

The hypothesis of supply inelasticity in respect to durable inputs can be used to account for the persistence of low income in farming. To illustrate, in Figure 4-3, let us assume that P_A is the acquisition price for human resources in farming, the price necessary to attract farm labor or farm operators into farming from the nonfarm sector. Given the marginal value product curve MVP_1, the optimum employment of human resources in farming is X.

The price P_0 in Figure 4-3 is the opportunity cost of farm labor; that is, the value of opportunities forgone, or what labor currently employed in the farm sector could earn elsewhere. The curve will fall to MVP_2 to equal opportunity

---

[110]*Ibid.*, p. 350. The price elasticity of aggregate farm supply is obtained by multiplying the percentage weight of each class of input by the elasticity of demand for that input and then aggregating the products. No significant difference was found in elasticity between 1921 to 1941 and 1948 to 1966, which may be taken to suggest that the growing importance of purchased industrial commodities in the farm input mix, which should make supply more elastic, *ceteris paribus,* has apparently been offset by the tendency for large farms to stay in full production, instead of reducing output in periods of falling product prices.

[111]See especially Harold F. Breimyer, "Nature's Felicity in Supply Response Analysis: Comment": A. J. Rayner, ". . . Comment"; and Tweeten and Quance, ". . . Reply," *ibid.*, Vol. 52. No. 1, February 1970, pp. 146–151. See also Oscar R. Burt, ". . . Comment," and reply by Tweeten and Quance, *ibid.*, Vol. 53, No. 4, November 1971, pp. 674–677.

[112]Tweeten and Quance, *ibid.*, November 1971, p. 677.

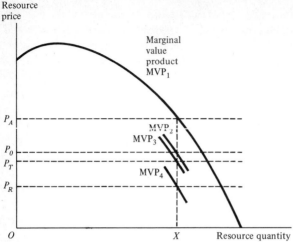

Figure 4-3 Alternative marginal value product curves and equilibrium prices for human resources in farming.

cost for quantity X. If unemployment is the alternative, P_0 is either zero or the value of unemployment compensation.

Returns must fall to the opportunity cost less transfer cost to justify the transfer of human resources from agriculture. In Figure 4-3, the opportunity cost P_0 less transfer cost is designated by P_T. In addition, however, if people place high values on farm living, or on living in the community among relatives and friends, or on rural life associated with farming, then the price that induces them to move out of agriculture will be even lower than P_T, such as P_R.[113] According to this reasoning, the low income in agriculture could not be overcome simply by more attractive urban opportunities. It would require a spread of off-farm employment to rural communities. Until this happened, not only would the supply curve for agriculture continue to be inelastic; low income would persist in farming because of the slow adjustment of the farm population.

Inelasticity and Instability: The Cobweb Theorem

The instability of agriculture is accentuated by the inelasticity in supply, or the lags that occur in the production response to price. Because it takes time to produce crops and livestock, the response to a change in price or cost is not immediate but stretches over one or more production periods. This is at least a year for most annual crops, two to three years for hogs, five to seven years for beef cattle, and so on. In their attempt to attain an efficient allocation of resources—where the value of the marginal product of a resource is equal to its

[113]Brewster called this the endodermal hypothesis of low farm income, meaning that low farm income is inherent in the value structure or value system of a declining farm population. See Patrick J. Madden and David E. Brewster (eds.), *A Philosopher among Economists*, Philadelphia: J. T. Murphy Co., 1970, Chap. 7; and John M. Brewster, "Society Values and Goals in Respect to Agriculture," in *Goals and Values in Agricultural Policy*, Ames: The Iowa State University Press, 1961, pp. 114–137.

market price in all uses—producers invest resources where favorable returns can be achieved. But, since production takes time, price or the marginal rate of return tends to fluctuate around, rather than settle at, an equilibrium.

The theory underlying this type of fluctuation was first developed by German economists, and, because of the geographic configuration described in its operation, it has been called "the cobweb theorem." In the 1930s, an imaginative American, Mordecai Ezekiel, applied the theorem in a general way in agricultural price analysis, and since then it has been used widely.[114] In substance, prices of certain commodities tend to fluctuate around a normal price, rather than settle at that price where demand and supply would be in equilibrium.

For a farm commodity to develop a cobweb pattern of behavior, it must have a rather standard period of production so that, once plans are made, significant changes do not occur in the scheduled output. Further, storage must not be practical to dampen the cycles. Producers must be so numerous that an individual decision has little influence on aggregate output, and they must operate, to some degree at least, on the assumption that current prices provide a basis for production plans.

As in Figure 4-4, the supply is the quantity produced in one period in response to a given price at the beginning. Suppose, in Figure 4-4(a), that producers expect a price of P_1. Then Q_1 is produced. Price will go to P_2. This results in production of Q_2. Then, price will fall to P_1; production will fall to Q_1, and the cycle is ready to repeat. Price and quantity then fluctuate inversely as in Figure 4-4(b). Depending on the supply-demand relationship in such cycles and the respective elasticities, the cycles may exhibit rather uniform amplitudes as in Figure 4-4(b). Alternatively, they may either dampen down, as in Figure 4-4(c), or tend to explode, as in 4-4(d), until some external force or exogenous development changes the underlying condition. Typical fluctuations for wheat, corn, beef cattle, and hogs are shown in Figure 4-5. From 1950 to 1970, the fluctuations in wheat and corn prices were moderated by the influence of government storage.

A Policy Conclusion

Various inferences for policy may be derived from the projected increases in food supply, changes in economic structure at the farm level, and the short-run inelasticity of supply. It seems clear that further increases in supply will depend most importantly on the availability and cost of all purchased farm inputs, that increases in supply will tend to come more slowly as the transitional growth in the input industries tends to stabilize, and that farm product prices will continue to be unstable because of the inelasticity of both demand and supply. These inferences suggest that farm and food policy has many options for encouraging or discouraging growth in the input industries and for influencing supply through

---

[114]Mordecai Ezekiel, "The Cobweb Theorem," *Quarterly Journal of Economics*, Vol. 52, February 1938, pp. 255–280 (reprinted in *Readings in Business Cycle Theory*, Chap. 21, New York: McGraw-Hill Book Company, 1944).

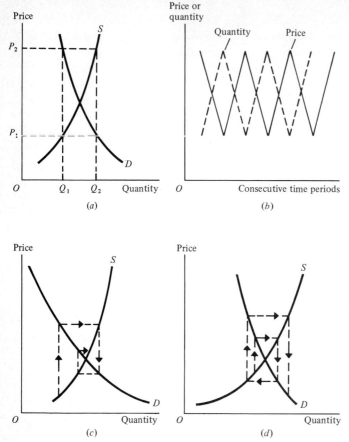

Figure 4-4 The cobweb theorem.

policy in the product markets. To more clearly visualize what some of these options are, we turn next to a study of the process in making national policy.

QUESTIONS FOR DISCUSSION

1 Since the disappearance of the land frontier in America, very little of the increase in food production has been attributed to land. In the early 1970s, however, as policy shifted into the new third era, prices for good farmland advanced sharply. What are the implications of this rise for food policy? For expansion of the acreage under cultivation? For intensity of land use?

2 As old cropland is farmed more intensively, or as new land is brought into cultivation, what are the implications for conservation? How will conservation problems differ among various areas of the country? What are the policy alternatives for solving these problems?

3 One of the features underlying the development of American agriculture is the growth of the purchased-inputs, farm supply sector. Comment on the effect of this

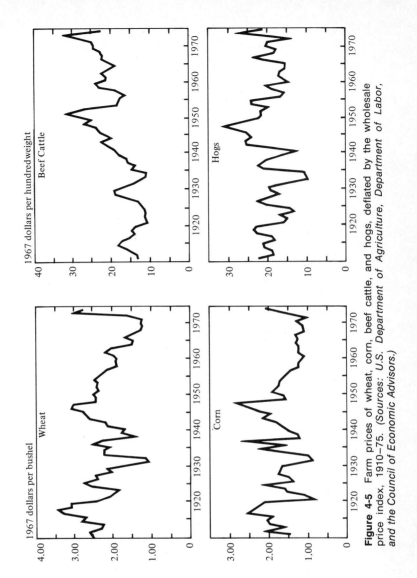

Figure 4-5 Farm prices of wheat, corn, beef cattle, and hogs, deflated by the wholesale price index, 1910–75. (*Sources: U.S. Department of Agriculture, Department of Labor, and the Council of Economic Advisors.*)

growth on (*a*) costs of food production, (*b*) size and economic distribution of farm firms, and (*c*) social effects created in the farm and rural community.

4   Trace the effects on (*a*) costs, (*b*) size of farm, and (*c*) social effects of selected innovations in cotton production, in grain production, and in fruits and vegetables. Be specific in respect to the innovations selected, for example, the cotton picker, the tomato harvester, the corn combine.

5   The production effect of farm mechanization, which though very strong, was decreasing during the second great era, will be of declining importance in the third era. Do you generally agree? Qualify the statement, stating your assumptions for costs of fuel, fertilizer, new machinery, and labor. Will it be in the farmer's interest to have relatively cheaper fuel and fertilizer? On what does your answer depend?

6   Since the demand for United States farm output is inelastic, as we have noted, increases in farm productivity per unit of labor input (*ceteris paribus*) will be price depressing. In view of this, account for the increases in prices of farm products that occurred in the 1970s. What has been the effect of improvements in fertilizer production (*a*) on aggregate receipts from farm marketings and (*b*) on net farm income, in aggregate and per farm?

7   According to Headley and Lewis, the optimum use of farm pesticides is achieved when the difference is maximized between total positive benefits and total costs, including market costs of pesticides and the external costs. What are the policy options for reducing and controlling the external costs? Review the national legislation that has been designed for this purpose by covering the major provisions of the legislation and by appraising its effectiveness.

8   Although most innovations in the nation's agriculture have been both factor saving and output increasing, the growth in output appears to be occurring at a decreasing rate. Summarize the evidence and theory on this point. What is your generalization for the future?

9   Briefly review the food system's pattern of energy use. What will be the necessary conditions to accelerate growth in the food system? The sufficient conditions?

10 Comment on the differences in elasticity of food supply between the short run and the long run, and also between relative increases and decreases in product prices. What are the major inferences for food and farm policy?

11 Growth in food and farm supply has tended to occur in cycles. What is the reason for this? What are the inferences for policy?

REFERENCES

Buchholz, H. E., G. G. Judge, and V. I. West, *A Summary of Selected Estimated Behavior Relationships for Agricultural Products,* Urbana: University of Illinois, Department of Agricultural Economics, Agricultural Economics Research Report 57, 1962.

Food: Politics, Economics, Nutrition and Research, a special Science Compendium edited by Philip H. Abelson, Washington: American Association for the Advancement of Science, 1975.

Guither, Harold D., *Heritage of Plenty, A Guide to the Economic History and Development of U.S. Agriculture,* 2d ed., Danville, Ill.: The Interstate Printers & Publishers, Inc., 1972.

Headley, J. C., and J. N. Lewis, *The Pesticide Problem: An Economic Approach To Public Policy,* Washington: Resources for the Future, Inc., 1967.

Marshall, Roy, *Rural Workers in Rural Labor Markets,* Salt Lake City, Utah: Olympus
    Publishing Co., 1974, pp. 48–52.
Pest Control Strategies for the Future (A Symposium), Washington: National Academy
    of Sciences, 1972.
Rosine, John, and Peter Helmberger, "A Neoclassical Analysis of the U.S. Farm Sector,
    1948–1970," *American Journal of Agricultural Economics,* Vol. 56, No. 4, Novem-
    ber 1974, pp. 717–729.
Rudd, Robert J., *Pesticides and the Living Landscape,* Madison: The University of
    Wisconsin Press, 1964.
Tweeten, Luther G., and C. Leroy Quance, "Positivistic Measures of Aggregate Supply
    Elasticities: Some New Approaches," *American Journal of Agricultural Economics,*
    Vol. 51, No. 2, May 1969, pp. 342–352.

Chapter 5

Making National Policy

A nation's agricultural policy is not set forth in a single law or even in a series of laws dealing directly with current farm problems. It is expressed in a complexity of laws and attitudes which, in the importance of their influence on agriculture, shade off from direct measures like the Agricultural Adjustment Act through the almost infinite fields of taxation, tariffs, international trade, and labor, money, credit, and banking policy. . . . A nation never reaches the time when it can say its agricultural policy is fixed and complete. Evolution and change are nearly the only constant factors . . . a continuous thread runs through the evolution. . . . The programs of the present become the foundations for the programs of the future.

Chester C. Davis, *Farmers in a Changing World,*
The Yearbook of Agriculture, 1940, pp. 325, 326.

Since the early 1920s the public's thinking about food and farm policy has been nearly dominated by what is popularly known as "the farm problem." This problem entails low farm prices, instability and uncertainty in farm prices and incomes, and low income in a very large part of the farm and rural community. Although the roots of the problem are found in the more than 300-year history of land settlement, broad and significant national efforts toward its solution began in the 1920s. After several decades of evolution, these efforts have now become more comprehensive in terms of national policymaking. An understanding of this evolution is essential to make rational decisions in future policy. In this chapter we trace this evolution for its important lessons for future policymaking.

THE FOUNDATION FOR POLICYMAKING

The initial spark for national policymaking in the second era was struck by the collapse of farm product prices following World War I. After a 25-year period of market growth from 1895 to the early postwar period, agriculture was suddenly confronted with a set of price relationships that meant disaster. Farm leaders quickly sensed the catastrophe and began to make proposals to correct it.

The proposals, emerging in various forms, became grouped around three main ideas for action. One was to establish a nationwide system of government-sponsored farm cooperatives that would regulate the flow of farm and food products into the market in such a way as to achieve more orderly marketing and fair and stable prices. Another was to reestablish the export market to achieve farm prices that would be in the same ratio to nonfarm prices as the prices were just before the war. The third was to withdraw farm land from crop production to balance the farm output with market demand.

The Seeds of Export Subsidy

Although many ideas were considered, popular interest in farm areas and the attention of farm leaders shifted quickly to revival of the export market, and several bills were introduced in Congress. One, sponsored by Senator George Norris (Republican of Nebraska), proposed to establish a 100-million-dollar government corporation to buy farm products in the United States and sell them abroad on liberal credit terms. Another bill proposed an appropriation of $1 billion to finance the United States Grain Corporation, which would buy up sufficient quantities of specified commodities to permit producers to sell at minimum prices covering "cost of production" plus a reasonable profit. Another bill proposed the formation of a 300-million-dollar corporation that would buy wheat at fixed prices. These and other bills were debated in Congress and in the farm areas, but they failed even to gain general farm support. The two largest farm organizations at that time, the American Farm Bureau Federation and the National Grange, considered them to involve a combination of price fixing and government in business, which was contrary to their basic principles of organization.

Fair Exchange Value

Outside of Congress, however, a plan was being developed that was to become the basis for the major agricultural political battle of the decade. In 1921, Prof. George F. Warren of Cornell University presented an analysis of farm product prices in a Department of Agriculture bulletin.[1] At that time the weighted average

---

[1]George F. Warren, *Prices of Farm Products in the United States,* USDA Bulletin 999, August 1921. For further discussion, see John D. Black, *Parity, Parity, Parity,* Cambridge, Mass.: Harvard University Press, 1942, chap. 5. Reprinted in O. B. Jesness (ed.), *Readings on Agricultural Policy,* Philadelphia: McGraw-Hill Book Company, 1949, chap. 7.

price of 31 major farm commodities was 20 percent above the prewar average, whereas the weighted average of the all-commodities index of the Bureau of Labor Statistics was 50 percent above that average. This meant that a given quantity of farm commodities would buy some 20 percent less than in the prewar period. Some of the major farm commodities, such as wheat and cotton, were relatively lower than this. Shortly thereafter, the Department of Agriculture began publishing a "purchasing power index," which compared the current purchasing power of farm commodities with their prewar purchasing power. In this index, 1913 was set equal to 100. The comparison of price trends readily showed that farm prices, although higher than in 1913, were much lower in actual purchasing power. Farm leaders argued that there was something wrong with a market system that allowed farm prices to go to such low levels and that steps should be taken to assure that farm products could be sold at a "fair exchange value."

In 1922, a conference on agricultural policy was called by Secretary of Agriculture Henry C. Wallace (father of Henry A. Wallace). One of the delegates, George N. Peek of the Moline Plow Company of Illinois, presented a resolution, which was adopted by the conference, stating that the Congress and the President should immediately take such steps as would reestablish a fair exchange value for all farm products. Then Peek and Hugh S. Johnson (later named by Roosevelt to head the National Recovery Administration) published a pamphlet entitled *Equality for Agriculture,* which showed how fair exchange value could be achieved.[2] They defined fair exchange value as a price "which bears the same ratio to the current general price index as a ten-year pre-war average crop price bore to average price index for the same period." As an example, wheat should have been $1.60 a bushel instead of $1.02.

Peek and Johnson proposed that an "ample" portion of any crop included in the program should be fed into the domestic market only in such amounts as would meet domestic demand at the fair exchange value. Any quantity produced above this amount would be sold abroad, and the losses in selling at the lower export price would be spread evenly over all producers by a general tax on sales of the commodity or by some other means.

Many farm leaders supported the plan as one that could quickly establish a "fair" price for farm commodities, a price ratio similar to the prewar ratio. The plan apparently would involve little administrative detail. Purchase operations could be restricted to the terminal markets. To its supporters, the plan did not involve price fixing in its usual sense since prices would be allowed to fluctuate according to changes in the general price level. To many farmers, the plan seemed reasonable and fair. Secretary Wallace became sufficiently interested in the idea to call a conference of businessmen to hear a discussion of the plan. They reacted unfavorably, but the Bureau of Agricultural Economics was asked

[2]George N. Peek and Hugh S. Johnson, *Equality for Agriculture,* Moline, Ill.: Privately published, 1922. See also Gilbert C. Fite, *George N. Peek and the Fight for Farm Parity,* Norman: University of Oklahoma Press, 1954, and review by Harold G. Halcrow, *Journal of Farm Economics,* Vol. XXXVI, No. 3, August 1954, pp. 546–48.

to initiate a series of studies to examine various aspects of the plan. Secretary Wallace continued to study the plan and to talk about forming an export corporation to remove "exportable surpluses" from the domestic market.

The McNary-Haugen Bills[3]

As a result of the general farm interest in the export idea, a bill was introduced in Congress on January 16, 1924, by Senator Charles McNary of Oregon and Representative Gilbert N. Haugen of Iowa. It was the first of five bills to be introduced under the McNary-Haugen sponsorship in each session of Congress from 1924 to 1928. Although their details differed somewhat in order to overcome objections raised in Congress and elsewhere, each of the bills adhered to the policy goal of fair exchange value in the domestic market and price discrimination between domestic and export sales. The first bill was defeated in the House in 1924. Southern and Eastern sections were unified in opposition. The second in 1925 never came to a vote. The third, also in 1925, even with new support from the American Farm Bureau Federation (AFBF), was defeated in both House and Senate. The fourth, with simplifying amendments and still more general farm support—especially from the AFBF—passed both houses but was vetoed by President Coolidge. The fifth bill met the same fate in 1928.

The plan of the first bill was to establish a government export corporation, to be capitalized for $200 million. It would buy designated farm commodities in sufficient amount to raise the price up to the "ratio-price," or fair exchange value. For example, wheat, the commodity that drew the most public attention, had a prewar price of 98 cents a bushel. In 1923, when the all-commodity index was at 156, the ratio price for wheat would have been $1.53 a bushel. To bring wheat up to this level, the corporation would buy wheat whenever the price fell below $1.53 and sell it at that price in the domestic market to anyone ready to buy. The price, of course, would not be fixed, but would rise and fall as the all-commodity index rose and fell. Since the corporation would buy more than it sold in the domestic market, the excess would be sold abroad. Reimports would be restricted by tariff.

The loss on exports was to be covered by use of scrip, which could be purchased by potential buyers of farm products at a slight discount and offered by them as legal tender to cover a portion of the cost of buying a farm commodity. An amount equal to the export price would be paid in cash, and the difference between domestic price and export price would be paid in scrip. The farmer could hold the scrip until it was redeemed by the corporation, generally at some fraction of its face value, depending on the losses experienced by the corporation. The farmer would not actually receive the full ratio price, however, but something between ratio price and export price. The corporation, on the other hand, would sell the commodity in the domestic market at the full ratio

[3]See Joseph S. Davis, "The McNary-Haugen Plan as Applied to Wheat: Operating Problems and Economic Consequences," *Wheat Studies of the Food Research Institute,* Stanford University, February 1927, pp. 177–234, and "The McNary-Haugen Plan as Applied to Wheat: Limitations Imposed by the Present Tariff," *ibid.,* March 1927, pp. 235–264.

price, thus to gain on domestic sales part or all of what it lost on export sales. It was argued that the plan would work for certain commodities simply because demand was more inelastic on the domestic market than on the foreign market (see Chapter 3).

Arguments on the McNary-Haugen Bills

Opinions were sharply divided in the debates that developed over the McNary-Haugen bills. Opponents argued that the plan was "unconstitutional," "unworkable," "sectional," and "price-fixing." They pointed out that the scrip would be of uncertain value until the redemption rate was set by the corporation and that farmers who needed cash might sell their scrip at a discount to speculators. Most important, the plan, if adopted, would most likely lead to tariff retaliation by other countries. Western European countries especially could not increase their purchases of American farm commodities unless they could export more into this market and, since the United States was not lowering its tariffs, other governments would have to raise their tariffs or otherwise restrict imports in order to conserve their foreign exchange.

Those in favor of the plan argued that it was not price fixing, since ratio prices would fluctuate along with changes in the general level of prices. The plan was simplified by limiting it to certain so-called basic commodities—wheat, cotton, wool, cattle, sheep, swine, and rice—and proponents argued that if the prices of these commodities were raised to the desired levels, other commodity prices would follow along. Furthermore, some contended that the general principle was basically fair since it merely provided that producers of export commodities would receive price benefits similar to the tariff protection enjoyed by producers of commodities that were on an import basis. This argument, of course, carried to an extreme the general premise that there was some ideal or "fair" price that could be statistically determined.

The Policymaking Struggle

Farmers and the farm organizations were slow to unite behind the plan. Southern farmers were more interested in development of a hydroelectric project at Muscle Shoals, which they hoped would provide them with cheaper fertilizer. Some farmers not producing the basic commodities doubted whether they would benefit in terms of price, and some farmers, such as eastern dairy farmers who bought a large part of their feed, thought that they might be hurt by any increases in the prices of feed grains. Others were more interested in supporting legislation that would provide additional credit for agriculture, particularly credit that would permit farmers to make investments with which they could diversify their farm operations.[4]

[4]This proposal refers to bills (S. 1597 and H.R. 4159, 68th Cong., 1st Sess., 1924) introduced by Senator Peter Norbeck of South Dakota and Representative Oscar Burtness of North Dakota to appropriate $50 million for loans to farmers in the Northwest Central states to aid them in shifting out of wheat into diversified agriculture. Although these bills had the endorsement of President Coolidge and the American Farm Bureau Federation, the House defeated the bill by five votes and the measure was dropped.

As a result of these diverse interests, the votes on the McNary-Haugen bills were strongly sectional. Gradually, however, the advocates of the bills picked up more support and became more skillful in presenting their views. Support that had been centered in the wheat areas was developed in the Corn Belt.[5] The American Farm Bureau Federation, which at first opposed the legislation and the whole idea of export subsidy, finally gave strong support to the fourth and fifth bills. The National Grange, which had long advocated a two-price plan and was more friendly to ideas of price discrimination, gave its support for a while to an export debenture plan that had been developed by Prof. Charles L. Stewart of the University of Illinois.[6] Under this proposal, exporters would be given debentures having a face value equal to all or part of the difference between the value of the commodity in the world market and its domestic value based on the world price plus the United States tariff. The exporters could sell these debentures to importers, who, in turn, would use them to pay the tariff on goods imported. Issuance of debentures would be regulated so that the exporter would buy in the domestic market at a price equal to world price plus the face value of the debentures. Although proponents argued that the plan would simplify actual operations and the plan may be regarded as the precedent for large-scale export subsidy in later years, it failed to generate significant support. The McNary-Haugen bills were a rallying point for the powerful coalition of senators and representatives favorable to the farm interest that came to be known as the farm bloc. This group transcended party lines, and in respect to agriculture, its members often escaped the usual party discipline. They met frequently to decide on their position on farm legislation and to organize for action.

The fifth bill, after several revisions, applied to all commodities instead of to the limited number of basic commodities. It provided that authority for the program's operation would be vested in a federal farm board, consisting of one member from each of the 12 Federal Reserve districts. Instead of using scrip to finance the export operations, a tax called an "equalization fee" would be assessed under certain conditions against each commodity either when sold by the farmer or when processed, the amount of the assessment being determined by the board's estimate of the funds needed to offset losses from sales in foreign markets. A revolving fund of $400 million was to be established to provide loans to farmers' cooperatives, which would carry out the actual market operations.

The bill had strong support. It passed the Senate by a vote of 58 to 23 and the House by 204 to 121. But the Senate, in a vote of 51 to 30, failed to muster the necessary two-thirds majority to override the President's veto. The President, in his final veto message, repeated arguments used in veto of the fourth bill. He

[5]For distribution of congressional support on the McNary-Haugen bills and for further discussion of the program, see John D. Black, "The McNary-Haugen Movement," *The American Economic Review,* Vol. XVIII, September 1928, pp. 405–427.

[6]For analysis of the plan, see Joseph S. Davis, *The Farm Export Debenture Plan,* Stanford, Calif.: Stanford University Press, Food Research Institute, 1929; and Joseph S. Davis, "The Export Debenture Plan for Aid to Agriculture," *Quarterly Journal of Economics,* Vol. XLIII, February 1929, pp. 250–277.

The Grange version of the plan is presented in a pamphlet published in 1928, *The Export Debenture Plan, A Sound Method of Restoring Agricultural Prosperity in the United States.*

maintained that the bill was unconstitutional and listed six principal objections: (1) the attempted price fixing, (2) the tax characteristics of the equalization fee, (3) the widespread bureaucracy which would be set up, (4) the probable encouragement to profiteering and wasteful distribution, (5) the stimulation to overproduction, and (6) the aid to foreign agricultural competitors.[7]

Although the second Coolidge veto brought the policy struggle over export subsidy to a close for the time being, the idea became a major policy issue again in the early days of the Roosevelt New Deal. Again it was rejected by the administration, this time as inconsistent with the reciprocal trade agreement program begun under the Trade Expansion Act of 1934. In the late 1930s and 1940s, modest export subsidies were financed out of tariff receipts.[8] In 1954, under the Agricultural Trade Development and Assistance Act, more popularly known as Public Law 480 or P.L. 480, the foundation was laid for food aid to developing countries on a concessional basis and for export subsidies sufficient to keep American farm products, wheat and feed grains especially, competitive in commercial export markets. Thus the idea of export subsidy, vigorously sought in the 1920s, rejected then and again in the mid 1930s, but expanding greatly in the post-World War II era, became imbedded in America's farm and food policy.

The Federal Farm Board

The election of Herbert Hoover in 1928 finally sealed the fate of the McNary-Haugen legislation and brought on a new compensatory price program. Hoover, in his campaign, had expressed himself as deeply concerned about the economic condition of agriculture but bitterly opposed to export subsidy in any form. The Senate, however, which had come within four votes of overriding the second Coolidge veto, had demonstrated strong support for such legislation. It was clear to the President and leaders in his administration that something had to be done, both to correct the adverse terms of trade for agriculture and to keep campaign promises.

The Federal Farm Board was established by the Agricultural Marketing Act of 1929 in June in a special session called to consider farm and tariff legislation. It received an initial appropriation of $500 million to assist cooperatives chiefly through loans to finance storage operations.[9] The Board was directed to use this money to accomplish four things: (1) to minimize speculation; (2) to prevent inefficient and wasteful methods of distribution; (3) to help producers organize

---

[7]U.S. President, *Veto Message Relating to the Agricultural Surplus Control Act,* 70th Cong., 1st Sess., S.141, May 3, 1928.

[8]See *Section 32 Handbook,* 1953, Washington: U.S. Department of Agriculture, Production and Marketing Administration.

[9]See Agricultural Marketing Act of 1929, 46 *Stat.* 11, and Federal Farm Board, *First Annual Report,* 1930, p. 1. The implementing loan provision, Section 8(a), was that "Loans to any cooperative association or stabilization corporation and advances for insurance purposes shall bear interest at a rate of interest per annum equal to the lowest rate of yield (to the nearest one-eighth of 1 per centum) of a government obligation bearing a date of issue subsequent to April 6, 1917 (except postal savings bonds). . . ." Since the Treasury borrows some of its funds on short-term notes at very low rates of

cooperative marketing associations; and (4) to aid in preventing and controlling surpluses through orderly production and distribution, to maintain advantageous markets, and to prevent surpluses from causing undue and expensive fluctuations or depressions in prices. No provision was made for controlling production or for financing sales of commodities in foreign countries.

The Board, with able, aggressive administration and high objectives but weak measures for implementation, undertook an impossible task. It began almost simultaneously with the great stock market crash, a time when the strongest price support measures might have failed. A number of national cooperative marketing associations were established to store commodities under loan at rates set by the Board.[10] In addition, the Board gave assistance to some 30 to 40 regional cooperatives handling specialty crops as well as to many more local cooperatives.[11] The main price stabilization program, carried out through the Grain Stabilization Corporation beginning in February 1930 and the Cotton Stabilization Corporation beginning in June, involved commitment of about 85 percent of the Board's total funds. The balance went mainly to finance programs for other commodities, such as dairy products, wool, and grapes.

In the wheat and cotton programs, initial loans were set at $1.15 per bushel for No. 1 Hard Winter wheat at Kansas City, $1.25 per bushel for No. 1 Northern Spring at Minneapolis, and at 16 cents a pound for cotton. The Board's action may have helped to hold prices near these levels for a few months; but, thereafter, although loans continued to be made, prices dropped sharply. In 1931 the average farm price for wheat was 39 cents per bushel as compared with $1.04 in 1929. The 1931 cotton crops sold for an average of 6 cents a pound, in contrast to 17 cents in 1929. By July 1931, wheat storage financed by the Board was 257 million bushels, about 80 percent of all wheat in storage. Cotton stocks were about 3.5 million bales, about one-quarter to one-third of an average crop. The Board had committed its funds and, before the 1931 harvest, was forced to announce that no further loans could be made. The 1931 wheat crop turned out to be the third largest in history—942 million bushels. Cotton was the second largest—17 million bales. In 1932, as President Hoover and members of his administration began their campaign for reelection, wheat and cotton prices as well as prices of most other farm products, including those in which the Board

---

interest, this meant that some cooperatives operating under the act would receive funds at very low rates of interest. The Board reported interest charges for 1929–30 ranging from 1⅝ to 3⅝ percent and an average of 2.9 percent, *First Annual Report,* 1930, p. 46; and during the 1930–31 and 1931–32 seasons, loans to the American Cotton Cooperative Association were at ⅜ of 1 percent. See *Investigation of Certain Activities of the American Cotton Cooperative Association,* U.S. Senate Report No. 2030, 75th Cong., 3d Sess., p. 4.

[10]These were the Farmers National Grain Corporation, formed in October 1929 only five days after the initial stock market break; the National Wool Marketing Cooperative, formed in December; the American Cotton Cooperative Association, formed in January 1930; the National Bean Marketing Association, organized in May; the National Pecan Marketing Association; the National Beet Growers Association, formed in August 1930; and the National Fruit and Vegetable Exchange, established in May 1931.

[11]For a complete list, see Federal Farm Board, *Third Annual Report,* 1932, pp. 3, 4.

was involved, were near the lowest levels ever experienced. But seeded acreage, the best index of farmers' production intentions, did not contract.[12]

With the coming of the Great Depression, opportunity costs for farm labor fell to almost zero. A single man's going wage for steady work in some parts of the wheat country was $15 to $20 a month plus board and room. Oats, the main ingredient for horsepower, touched a low of 5 or 6 cents a bushel in local elevators, about half of what had been charged earlier for custom threshing. As long as machinery could be repaired, the family held together, and the creditors delayed, most farmers would keep going. The only real alternative was political; and the farm revolt helped bring the 12-year stretch of Republican administration to an end.

A Policy Conclusion

Storage under the Federal Farm Board was too small and too weak a measure for the task at hand. Possibly, a much larger program could have held prices for a while—could have bought political time. But Europe was in collapse, as Keynes had predicted.[13] The farm agitators of the 1920s—the supporters of McNary-Haugenism—were being proved right. American agriculture was dependent on export trade, chiefly a strong European market. More than exports, of course, it needed domestic recovery. In spite of the low-income elasticity for aggregate farm output, the income elasticities, especially for livestock products, were high enough to reduce demand significantly. The problem was not just wheat and cotton. Hog prices fell to about $2.50 per hundred (cwt) liveweight and cattle to around $4 per cwt in the heart of the Corn Belt. Altogether, at the time of its liquidation, the Board had lost some $300 to $350 million, an outcome which might be regarded as one of the best measures of its effect in supporting farm incomes. But this, of course, was not enough. The Board, in its third and last report, concluded that "experience with stabilization . . . demonstrates that no measure for improving the price of farm products other than increasing the demand of consumers can be effective over a period of years unless it provides a more definite control of production than has been achieved so far." In the closing days of the Hoover administration, several farm relief measures were debated in Congress, but, except for a measure to expand the supply of federal credit available to farmers, the major legislation was delayed until the Roosevelt administration, with its far-reaching New Deal programs, came into power. The

---

[12]The seeded acreage of cotton, wheat, corn, and tobacco, for example, was as follows (in millions of acres):

	Wheat	Cotton	Corn	Tobacco	Total
1929	69	44	99	2.0	214.0
1933	67	40	110	1.7	218.7

[13]John M. Keynes, *The Economic Consequences of the Peace,* London: Macmillan and Co., Ltd., 1920.

Federal Farm Board was liquidated as a broader attack was made on the farm problem.

The idea of supply management or control, developed by economists and adopted by some organizations, was the basis for the first successful campaign, led by M. L. Wilson, then of Montana State College, for legislation to control agricultural output: the Agricultural Adjustment Act of 1933. The policy of the Congress, stated in the act, was declared "to establish and maintain such balance between the production and consumption of agricultural commodities, and such marketing conditions therefor, as will re-establish prices to farmers at a level that will give agricultural commodities a purchasing power of agricultural commodities in the base period.[14] Such adjustment was to be undertaken "by gradual correction of the present inequalities therein at as rapid a rate as is deemed feasible in view of the current consumptive demand and foreign markets." The consumer interest should be protected by limiting such adjustment to "such level as will not increase the percentage of the consumer's retail expenditures for agricultural commodities, or products derived therefrom, which is returned to the farmer, above the percentage which was returned to the farmer in the prewar period, August 1909–July 1914."

The policy objective as stated in the legislation set a price standard— equality of purchasing power with respect to a base period, later known as parity—and stated how it should be accomplished. The Secretary of Agriculture was granted broad authority, which in large part continued for the next 40 years, to enter into agreements with farmers; to reduce acreage or production for market; and to regulate marketing methods, prices, and margins by means of agreements, licenses, and other means. He was authorized to make rental or benefit payments to farmers in compliance with the program in such amounts as he deemed "fair and reasonable" on certain commodities defined as "basic": wheat, cotton, field corn, hogs, rice, tobacco, milk and its products, and others added later. He was authorized to levy processing taxes on these commodities to finance the program, and he could tax competing products if the processors of the basic products were at a disadvantage because of the taxes placed upon them.[15] To permit the Secretary to implement marketing agreements with processors, associations of processors, and others for controlling marketing or processing margins and prices paid to producers, the legislation provided that "the making of any such agreement shall not be held to be in violation of any of the antitrust laws of the United States, and any such agreement shall be deemed to be lawful." The Agricultural Adjustment Administration (AAA) was organized to administer the act under the Secretary's direction.

The major policy goal was to transfer income to farmers. Processing taxes would be used to make the program partially self-supporting. Such taxes were to

[14]Agricultural Adjustment Act of 1933, 48 *Stat.* 32, H.R. 3835, Public Law No. 10, 73d Cong., 1st Sess.

[15]This power was declared unconstitutional, null, and void, by the Supreme Court on January 6, 1936, in the case of *U.S. v. Butler et al.,* Receiver of Hoosac Mills Corporation, 297 U.S.1 (1936), p. 71, thus invalidating the entire act and necessitating new legislation.

be assessed, levied, and collected on the first domestic processing of the commodity. Initially, the tax was to amount to the difference between the average market price of the commodity and its fair exchange value, unless the Secretary should find, after public hearings, that this amount of tax would unduly restrict sales of the commodity. In such a case, a smaller tax could be applied. Receipts from the tax would be used to pay farmers who had signed contracts to restrict seeded acreage of the commodity according to the allotment established for their individual farms. Payments were set at so much per acre according to the normal yield of the acreage under allotment. The allotment was determined for each farm as a fixed percentage of the base acreage, defined as the average acreage seeded to the crop in the previous (usually) five-year period. Thus, the act would be financed largely by taxes, and the major cost of production adjustment would be transferred through the price system from farmers to consumers, the amount of this transfer depending on the effectiveness of the program in limiting output and the success of efforts to subsidize exports so as to hold domestic prices above world market levels.

Production Control versus Export Subsidy

An underlying policy struggle continued between proponents of export subsidy and proponents of production control. Some economists, such as M. L. Wilson and John D. Black, conceived of production adjustment or production control as the primary means of redressing the adverse terms of trade for agriculture. In part, their strategy was dictated by the weakness in world markets. The Depression was, in important respects, worldwide. Their thesis was that American agriculture was fundamentally out of adjustment, and direct action was required to right it. But men, such as George N. Peek and Hugh Johnson, who had led the battle for the McNary-Haugen legislation, conceived of production adjustment as at best a passing phase; the more enduring need was for a policy that would restore American agriculture to a more prominent position in world export trade.

Henry A. Wallace, editor of *Wallace's Farmer,* who was appointed Secretary of Agriculture, and Peek, who was appointed administrator of the AAA, personified the conflict. Peek still favored high tariffs, export dumping as proposed in the McNary-Haugen bills, and marketing agreements to limit sales of commodities which he contended would raise prices without acreage allotments or other production controls. As AAA administrator, Peek went along with the acreage allotment program on wheat and cotton, but he had his staff draw up marketing agreements for fluid milk, fruit, tobacco, and other products, setting prices to be paid producers, consumer prices, and fair trade practices.[16] He advocated directing surpluses, not marketable at parity prices, into special domestic or export channels. Wallace felt that attempts to dump products abroad through barter agreements, as Peek proposed, or through various commercial

---

[16]See Fite, *op. cit.,* p. 257, and Edwin G. Nourse, *Marketing Agreements Under the AAA,* Washington: The Brookings Institution, 1935, p. 206.

price arrangements, would lead the nation into serious international complications. He advocated lower tariffs and more free-trade policies. Although the issue was in doubt for some time, Roosevelt decided in favor of Wallace, and he made the reciprocal trade agreement program a main cornerstone of his administration policy.

The policy conflict between production control and export subsidy for agricultural commodities centered largely on the question of foreign trade policy. In 1932, the foreign export trade of the United States had dropped to $2.9 billion, in contrast to $9.6 billion in 1929. Between 1927 and 1931, the total physical volume of agricultural exports had fallen by about 35 per cent. The Smoot-Hawley tariff, passed in 1929 and raising United States import duties to the highest levels ever, had had a devastating effect on trade, as most economists had predicted, and reversal of this situation was a matter of high priority.[17]

The Trade Agreements Act, signed on June 12, 1934, permitted the President to negotiate reciprocal trade agreements and to raise or lower the tariff as much as 50 percent on unconditional most-favored-nation treatment, which simply meant that the United States, if it makes a trade agreement with one country (lowering the rates on certain imports), extends the same terms to all other nations that give United States exports most-favored-nation treatment.[18] This policy was strongly favored by Secretary of State Cordell Hull.[19] Wallace believed in it, whereas Peek favored high tariffs, individual barter, and contract agreements at negotiated prices for disposal of farm surpluses and conditional most-favored-nations treatment. Peek's view meant that import terms extended to one country could not extend to other countries unless the latter matched the first country in its import concessions granted to the United States.[20] Such conditional agreements would greatly retard the policy of reducing trade barriers to stimulate trade.

The most-favored-nation reciprocal trade agreement policy could not be consistent with an agriculture policy that depended on barter, high domestic prices on major export commodities, and export subsidies to offset low prices abroad. A consistent price policy for agriculture would permit modest reliance on price supports, major emphasis on production control, commodity agreements to assist functions of competitive markets, storage programs in concept of "the ever normal granary," and supplements to increase food purchasing power, especially for low-income consumers. These were the main elements that characterized the New Deal agricultural policy. Not all of them came into being at once.

[17]Joseph M. Jones, *Tariff Retaliation Repercussions, of the Smoot-Hawley Bill,* Philadelphia: University of Pennsylvania Press, 1934.

[18]The Trade Agreements Act, an amendment to the Tariff Act of 1930, 48 *Stat.* 943. See also Grace Beckett, *The Reciprocal Trade Agreements Program,* New York: Columbia University Press, 1941; and Henry J. Tasca, *The Reciprocal Trade Policy of the United States, A Study in Trade Philosophy,* Philadelphia: University of Pennsylvania Press, 1938.

[19]Cordell Hull, *The Memoirs of Cordell Hull,* New York: The Macmillan Company, 1948, p. 357.

[20]Fite, *op. cit.,* pp. 203–285.

Conservation was linked with allotment programs in 1936, following the great drought of 1934; and it was not until 1938 that a modest food stamp program was begun.

The New Deal, in its emphasis on trade expansion through reciprocal trade agreements and low tariffs and in its attempts at production control, turned away from the McNary-Haugen type of program and philosophy. Peek resigned as AAA administrator, and, although Roosevelt attempted to keep him in the administration, he became increasingly critical of the AAA, the trade programs, and the whole trend of recovery efforts.[21] Chester C. Davis, who had worked with Peek for the McNary-Haugen bills but who was now in agreement with Wallace, was appointed AAA administrator. From then until 1940, when Wallace resigned to campaign for the Vice Presidency under Roosevelt (then seeking his third term), the Wallace philosophy of production adjustment, as originally espoused by M. L. Wilson, W. J. Spillman, John D. Black, and others, was the guiding principle of the AAA. Thus, the food and agricultural program of the New Deal years came to involve the government in large-scale expenditures to control farm output, to store farm products, to develop conservation programs as part of the control effort, and to encourage market expansion through low-tariff trade policy.

In summary, using acreage allotments to control farm output is in principle quite simple. If it is assumed that too much of a farm commodity is being produced to clear the market at a price consistent with policy goals, the amount of surplus output can be estimated and a national allotment established at some fraction of the historic seeded acreage. The desired reduction in acreage can be achieved by funding a program to permit the Secretary of Agriculture to rent from the farmer the amount of acreage that is desired to be kept out of production. In the first AAA program and in most allotment programs that followed, the national allotment was distributed to the states, from states to counties, and from counties to individual farms. M. L. Wilson is credited with suggesting and successfully promoting the idea that the whole program should be administered from the township or community level up, with consultation from farmer committees elected by program participants.[22]

In most states, there were township committees to review information submitted by farmers, a county administrator and staff with county committees to review the acreage allocations within the county, and a state administrator and policy board. A base acreage was determined on each farm for each crop entering into the program; and the farmer who agreed to participate in the program pledged not to grow this crop on more than the acreage specifically allotted. This would result in a uniform percentage reduction in crop acreage among farms that participated in the program. In return for such an agreement, the farmer would receive a designated payment per acre, scaled according to

[21]*Ibid.,* pp. 243–303.
[22]William A. Rowley, *M. L. Wilson and the Campaign for the Domestic Allotment,* Lincoln: University of Nebraska Press, 1970, pp. 107–141.

normal yield on the base acreage. This principle, initiated in the 1933 act, has been retained in most commodity acreage allotment programs to the present day.

Regulating Supply through Storage

Pressure to raise prices by more direct means led the Roosevelt administration to an action many people hoped to avoid—initiation of nonrecourse loans on farm commodities held in approved storage, a program which would become as enduring as land retirement. So, on an autumn afternoon in 1933, Roosevelt called Jesse Jones, chairman of the Reconstruction Finance Corporation, to the White House and said, "Jess, I want you to lend 10 cents a pound on cotton."[23] With cotton selling between 8 and 9 cents a pound, up from about 5 cents in the early spring, the effect would be to encourage holding cotton in storage until prices should rise above the loan. When this occurred, cotton could be redeemed and sold. If prices did not rise to the loan, the cotton could be released to the government and the farmer's debt would be canceled, with government having no other recourse.

In an Executive order on October 16, 1933, under powers granted by the 1933 act, the Commodity Credit Corporation (CCC) was organized to issue loans to AAA participants at 4 percent interest, with initial loan rates for cotton at 10 cents a pound (then 69 percent of parity) and for corn at 45 cents a bushel (then 60 percent of parity), well above existing market prices. On June 6, 1934, Wallace proposed that the CCC be made a permanent program, to be operated as "an ever normal granary," with storage to be increased in years of large crops and low prices, and to be reduced in years of smaller crops. Soon thereafter the ever normal granary idea was merged with the new crop insurance program under which farmers might pay premiums in grain and receive indemnities in kind. The biblical parable of Joseph—the seven fat years followed by seven lean—was used by Wallace to popularize the CCC idea.[24] Acreage allotments and nonrecourse loans were coordinated to provide a comprehensive production adjustment program.

Marketing Quotas as Production Adjustment

Since capital can be increasingly substituted for land as agriculture advances in use of modern technology, acreage allotments must be supplemented with other measures, such as a marketing quota, if the most effective production control

[23]Arthur M. Schlesinger, Jr., *The Coming of the New Deal,* Boston: Houghton Mifflin Company, 1959, p. 61.

[24]Henry A. Wallace, *New Frontiers,* New York: Reynal & Hitchcock, Inc., 1934, pp. 236–238, and *Report of the Secretary of Agriculture,* 1934, pp. 20–23. Although Wallace was enthusiastic about the CCC idea, he was deeply disturbed about production control as a program that could lead to excess. In a pamphlet entitled *America Must Choose,* published in the spring of 1934, he argued that America must choose between nationalism involving strict production controls and an internationalism involving lower tariffs or free trade. Within six months of publication, 100,000 copies of the pamphlet were in print, it was being widely quoted, and excerpts were reprinted both at home and abroad. Wallace proposed moderation in both production control and trade negotiations, thus perhaps reflecting the dominant theme that has characterized policy in the years since.

system is to be created. A program of marketing quotas generally includes measures to limit a farmer's sales to a specified amount of a commodity. Various discounts or other penalties are imposed on sales in excess of the quotas.

Marketing quotas were initiated in 1934 by passage of the Bankhead Cotton Control Act and by the Kerr-Smith Act for tobacco.[25] The cotton act provided that two-thirds of the producers of cotton had to approve a quota-allotment program via referendum before it could go into effect. The tobacco act required agreement from three-fourths of tobacco growers. In case of a favorable referendum, the quota was introduced by alloting to each producer certificates which, when accompanying the crop, would exempt it from a sales tax that the Secretary of Agriculture was directed to levy.

Quota programs are generally voluntary in principle and almost compulsory in practice. Under the Bankhead Act, for example, if there were an affirmative vote on the adoption of quotas, a tax of 50 percent ad valorem would be placed on all cotton ginned. Tax-exemption certificates would be issued to growers sufficient to cover each participant's quota. Growers who did not agree to participate would not be issued exemption certificates. Under the Bankhead act, small growers were issued certificates covering all production up to 5 acres, or two 500-pound bales, since the national average yield of cotton was about 200 pounds per acre at the time. Certificates were limited to 10 million bales in 1934 and to 10.5 million in 1935, in contrast to production in 1932 of about 13 million bales. Since 1934, provisions for quotas have been included in each of the general agricultural acts, and the specific requirements have been varied according to circumstances. In all, a large number of commodities have been made eligible and provisions have been adjusted to fit the economics of the commodity (see Chapter 7).

Federal Marketing Agreements and Orders

Marketing agreements and orders have the general purpose of influencing prices by regulating the timing, volume, and sometimes the quality of commodities marketed; and they have been used most for milk, fruits, and vegetables. As provided in the 1933 act, the first federal marketing agreement, becoming effective in August 1933, covered the handling of milk in the Chicago market. The agreement was established following public hearings as provided in the law.

Commodities that could be handled in a marketing agreement were specified in a 1935 amendment to include milk, tobacco, soybeans, naval stores, pecans,

[25]The cotton program required more drastic curtailment of production than did the wheat program. The first cotton contracts, offered in June 1933, committed signatory growers to plow up before harvest 25 to 50 percent of their acreage in cotton in return for "rental payments" figured roughly on the basis of the value of potential cotton destroyed. In 1934, growers were limited to between 55 and 65 percent of their 1928–32 base acreage. The national wheat allotment was set at 85 percent of the 1930–32 planted acreage for 1934 and 90 percent for 1935. The Bankhead Cotton Control Act and the Kerr-Smith Tobacco Control Act were repealed in February 1936 to permit consideration of new legislation. See Edwin G. Nourse, Joseph S. Davis, and John D. Black, *Three Years of the Agricultural Adjustment Administration,* Washington: The Brookings Institution, 1937, pp. 92–114.

walnuts, fruits excluding apples or canning fruits other than olives, and vegetables, excluding all purchases by canners except asparagus. These exclusions resulted from opposition by canners, who could have been forced into compliance with a marketing order they opposed, and who might have found that the order conflicted with contracts previously negotiated.

The marketing agreement provisions were reaffirmed and strengthened in 1937. The 1937 act withdrew authority to levy processing taxes and redefined provisions under which a large number of marketing orders could be established under authority of the Secretary of Agriculture. These have applied to a wide range of fruits and vegetables and most generally to milk.

Federal milk orders best typify the objectives and procedures which are attuned to compromise the competing desires of producers, handlers, wholesalers-retailers, and consumers. The product is differentiated according to the market being served to achieve price stability and assured returns to producers and others, to promote an adequate supply for consumers, and generally to bring a greater degree of system and order to the industry. More specifically, federal milk marketing orders may be said to have the policy goal of raising and stabilizing prices in smoothly functioning markets, with the orders to serve four general purposes: *(1) to bring all distribution by handlers in a prescribed marketing area under the scope of the regulatory mechanism; (2) to place them all in the same competitive position in respect to a minimum price for milk entering the same use; (3) to provide for uniform participation in market sales value by the several producers; and (4) to overcome the instability of the fluid market by bringing all fluid milk entering the market under a uniform control.*[26] The terms of orders are developed through public hearings and the role of the government is to hear all arguments and proposals, to evaluate and resolve differences and to enforce the orders.

Each milk marketing order establishes minimum prices that handlers must pay for milk bought from producers or producers associations. The producer receives a "blend price" composed of two minimum prices—one price for Class I milk for fluid use and a lower Class II price for milk used in manufactured products. For many years there were just two use classes of milk—fluid and all other. In August 1973, the USDA recommended three milk use classes for 39 major federal milk marketing orders in the Central, Southern, and Southwestern parts of the United States by separating milk for manufacturing purposes into two classes depending on ultimate use.

Federal law provides that such recommendations be published in the *Federal Register*. Exceptions and comments may be filed or presented at public hearings called in the name of the Secretary of Agriculture. The regulations adopted are a supplement to a competitive market rather than a substitute for it. Surpluses occur when prices are set higher than equilibrium levels. This involves the government in direct purchase, storage, and disposal of excess milk through

[26]*Report to the Secretary of Agriculture by the Federal Milk Order Study Committee,* Washington: U.S. Department of Agriculture, December 1962, pp. 2, 3.

various domestic subsidy and export programs. At other times of relative shortage, the government is under pressure to raise prices to increase output.

Thus marketing agreements and orders are used as another policy means to influence market organization as well as the conduct and performance of marketing agents. Their desirability as policy means depends on the underlying values and the use that is made of each element of policy, the specifics of which we shall attempt to cover more fully in Chapter 7.

THE NEW DEAL EXPERIENCE

In the 1930s, the Roosevelt New Deal organized the foundation ideas into the first comprehensive farm program. The first Agricultural Adjustment Act of 1933, which established the first Agricultural Adjustment Administration (AAA), grew out of the idea that, since government policy had contributed to overexpansion of the agricultural plant, government should be used to limit output of that plant to achieve the policy goal of a fair price and equality for agriculture.[27] The goal as stated in the act was to bring agriculture to parity with other industry. The act thus elevated parity to the status of a high principle, making parity prices not only an accepted measure of economic and social performance but also an important political goal for public policy. Action to attain this goal became the inspiration of farm leaders and politicians alike. In succeeding years, although the formula would go through a number of revisions and refinements,[28] the essential idea of a fair price at the farm level has remained a tenacious but somewhat battered goal of policy. In the 1930s, the idea of using allotments to control production became professionally respectable.[29] The use of farmer-elected committees gave the program a democratic grass-roots base.[30] The New Deal experience built a foundation for farm price policy that would endure for many years to come.

Support for the AAA

In March 1933 President Roosevelt, upon sending Congress the bill which was to be signed into law on May 12 as the Agricultural Adjustment Act, commented, "I

[27]Henry C. Taylor and Anne Dewess Taylor, *The Story of Agricultural Economics in the United States, 1840–1932,* Ames: The Iowa State University Press, 1952, pp. 591–600.

[28]For those who wish to trace the history of this development, the following are helpful: Robert L. Tontz, "Origins of the Base Period Concept of Parity," *Agricultural History,* XXXII, January 1958, pp. 3–13; B. R. Stauber, N. M. Koffsky, and C. K. Randall, "The Revised Price Indexes," *Agricultural Economics Research,* Vol. 2, April 1950; James H. Shideler, "The Development of the Parity Price Formula for Agriculture, 1919–1923," *Agricultural History,* XXVII, July 1953, pp. 74–84; and B. R. Stauber, "The 1959 USDA Index Revisions and Some Related Policy Questions," *Journal of Farm Economics,* Vol. 41, No. 5, December 1959, pp. 1272–1288.

[29]Harry N. Owen, editor of *Farm, Stock and Home,* presented the basic outline of the domestic allotment plan on Feb. 1, 1926, in an article entitled "Getting the Tariff to the Farmer," which was based on the thinking of W. J. Spillman of the USDA, Bureau of Agricultural Economics. The plan, as we have noted, was given in more detail in Spillman's book, *Balancing the Farm Output,* New York: Orange Judd Publishing Co., Inc., 1927; it was outlined further in John D. Black, *Agricultural Reform in the United States,* New York: McGraw-Hill Book Company, 1929, chap. 20.

[30]See William A. Rowley, *M. L. Wilson and the Campaign for the Domestic Allotment,* Lincoln: University of Nebraska Press, 1970, pp. 107–141.

tell you frankly that it is a new and untrod path, but I can tell you with equal frankness that an unprecedented condition calls for the trial of new means."[31] The act, it was understood by many, would be pursued with greatest vigor for wheat, the crop that one writer labeled the "symbol of agricultural despair."[32] People in the wheat country were ready for it. Newspaper comment upon passage of the bill was almost all favorable, cautious but optimistic.[33]

Support among leaders of farm organizations was varied. The American Farm Bureau Federation was with some reluctance committed to the domestic allotment plan on grounds that production had to be controlled in order to obtain satisfactory prices for wheat, hogs, cotton, and some other products.[34] John Simpson, president of the National Farmers Union, condemned the plan, preferring more inflationary measures; C. E. Huff of the Farmers National Grain Corporation, which was politically aligned with the union, said no plan would work on wheat unless it controlled production. Simpson contended that control of acreage would not decrease production and that nothing short of "an army of bureaucrats" would be necessary to enforce reduction.[35] He apparently understood that the bill aimed at bringing prices (not the ratio of farm prices to farm costs) only to the 1914 level.[36] The National Farmers Union withdrew its support of the measure and failed in an attempt to get a cost-of-production amendment added while the bill was in Congress.[37] Milo Reno, president of the Farmers' Holiday Association, supported by others in that organization, openly damned the bill as inadequate, a scheme to deliver the independent farmer into the hands of a "tyrannical and conceited" bureaucracy (that is, the county agents of the Cooperative Extension Service), and an unacceptable substitute for a cost-of-production plan based on more inflationary measures. But Reno canceled a general farm strike scheduled for May 13, although he may have done so partially because he feared further violence.[38] Support in Congress, especially in the Senate, varied, with most senators apparently supporting the domestic allotment plan as the only practical source of relief available at that time. M. L. Wilson, however, who continued to be the recognized leader in the battle for its adoption, expressed the belief that members of Congress did "not get the production control idea at all."[39] He believed that only the influence of Roosevelt, placed squarely behind the concept, saved it from its enemies in Congress.

The Agricultural Adjustment Act was a three-part measure. Title I gave the Secretary of Agriculture power to employ the domestic allotment plan and to

---

[31]As quoted in Arthur Schlesinger, Jr., *The Age of Roosevelt: The Coming of the New Deal,* Boston: Houghton Mifflin Company, 1959, p. 39; and Rowley, *op. cit.,* p. 177.

[32]Rowley, *op. cit.,* p. 1.

[33]Rowley, *op. cit.,* pp. 196–197.

[34]Christiana McFadyen Campbell, *The Farm Bureau and the New Deal: A Study of the Making of National Policy, 1933–40,* Urbana: The University of Illinois Press, 1962, pp. 44–67.

[35]John L. Shover, *Cornbelt Rebellion: The Farmers' Holiday Association,* Urbana: The University of Illinois Press, 1965, p. 107.

[36]Senate Agriculture Committee Hearings, H.R. 3835, p. 126, as quoted in Shover, *op. cit.,* p. 103.

[37]Campbell, *op. cit.,* pp. 55–56.

[38]Shover, *op. cit.,* pp. 102–131.

[39]Wilson correspondence as quoted by Rowley, *op. cit.,* p. 190.

take other necessary action on certain staple or "basic" commodities to achieve for farmers an "equality of purchasing power," later called parity.[40] Title II was the Emergency Farm Mortgage Act, which authorized expanding federal farm credit, and Title III dealt with money, including the inflationary Thomas amendment which authorized the President to issue greenbacks, to remonetize silver, or to alter the gold content of the dollar.[41] Thus, while the original AAA was used as a vehicle for fundamentally altering the traditional goals of farm policy, it also carried authority for wide expansion in farm credit and for sweeping changes in monetary policy. Subsequent devaluation of the dollar was regarded as having had some effect on recovery of cotton prices, while wheat prices rose over the next three years primarily as a result of reduced U.S. output due to drought, the AAA, and changes in world supplies and carryovers.[42]

Passage of the AAA pioneered the way, or served as a catalyst, for other notable changes in the goals of farm policy. The Grazing Act of 1934 carried into grazing areas a policy goal of continuing public ownership and control of land, a goal that had been initiated as a conservation measure on forest lands some years earlier.[43] The Tennessee Valley Authority, created for multiple purposes, such as power development, flood control, and agricultural development, introduced into American policy the concept of planned development of a major region. This was in sharp contrast to traditional ideas of essentially no planning in regional development or improvement. The Soil Erosion Act, passed on April 27, 1935, authorized establishment of the Soil Erosion Service to carry out an education and action program designed to prevent soil erosion, which had been accelerated, especially in the Great Plains, by widespread drought in the early 1930s, especially in 1934.

Invalidation of the AAA

Principal parts of the AAA were invalidated as a result of a 6 to 3 Supreme Court decision, handed down on January 6, 1936, in *U.S. v. Butler,* commonly known as the Hoosac Mills Case, which held that " . . . the power to confer or withhold unlimited benefits is the power to coerce or destroy. . . . The asserted power of

---

[40]The crops originally listed as basic were wheat, cotton, field corn, rice, and tobacco. Hogs and milk and its products were also named as basic commodities to which the act applied. Later added, on April 7, 1934, were rye, flax, barley, grain sorghums, cattle, peanuts, and, on May 9, 1934, potatoes.

[41]Schlesinger, *op. cit., The Coming of the New Deal,* pp. 44–45; Henry Steele Commager (ed.), *Documents of American History,* New York: Appleton-Century-Crofts, Inc., 1958, pp. 422–426; Rowley, *op. cit.,* p. 195. The principles underlying each of these three titles had been urged upon President Roosevelt by O'Neal on authority of the AFBF board, prior to submission of the bill to Congress. See Campbell, *op. cit.,* pp. 53–54.

[42]See Joseph S. Davis, *Wheat and the AAA,* Washington: The Brookings Institution, 1935, p. 329; Henry I. Richards, *Cotton and the AAA,* Washington: The Brookings Institution, 1936, p. 280; V. P. Timoshenko, "Monetary Influences on Postwar Wheat Prices," *Wheat Studies,* Stanford, Calif.: Stanford University, Food Research Institute, April 1938, p. 286. For more general discussion, see E. G. Nourse, Joseph S. Davis, and John D. Black, *Three Years of the Agricultural Adjustment Administration.* Washington: The Brookings Institution, 1937; and M. R. Benedict, *Farm Policies of the United States, 1790–1950,* pp. 302–315.

[43]See chap. 8.

choice [given to farmers by the AAA] is illusory."[44] The power to levy processing taxes and to enter into acreage reduction contracts with farmers was nullified.
Congress reacted quickly by passing the Soil Conservation and Domestic Allotment Act of 1936, approved February 29, 1936 (49 *Stat.* 1148), technically an
amendment to the Soil Erosion Act of 1935, which set as its goal reestablishing
"the ratio between the purchasing power of the net income per person on farms
and that of the income per person not on farms that prevailed during the five year
period August 1909–July 1914. . . ." Crops were to be classified under the act as
either "soil depleting" or "soil conserving," and farmers were to be paid for
shifting specified acreages of soil-depleting crops into soil-conserving crops, the
former being largely cash crops, such as wheat, cotton, tobacco, and corn, which
it was considered desirable to reduce, while the latter were legumes, grasses, and
other forage crops. Farmers also could be paid for such soil-conserving practices
as application of lime or fertilizer and the plowing down of green manure crops.

Although soil conservation was clearly a secondary objective under the 1936
act, this act clearly created a another goal or precedent for farm policy, that of
paying farmers to carry out specified soil-conserving practices. This idea has
been continued in all major agricultural acts, usually with specifications for land
diversion for conservation, wildlife, forestry, or other land-building practices.
The definition of conservation appears to have been broadened through the years
to include actions not only to prevent diminishing the yield potential of land but
to increase potential yields.

Whereas the 1936 act had operated to some satisfaction when severe
drought sharply curtailed the 1936 crop production, a bumper crop in 1937 clearly
revealed its deficiencies. Wheat production went from a 1933–36 average of 569
million bushels to 874 million, corn from 1,913 million to 2,643 million, and
cotton from 11.4 million bales to 18.9 million. Between the 1936 and 1937 crop
seasons, the average farm price of corn declined from $1.04 a bushel to 52 cents.
Cotton declined from about 12.4 cents a pound to 8.4 cents. Wheat prices
dropped somewhat more slowly, from $1.04 a bushel in 1936, to 96 cents in 1937,
and to 56 cents early in 1938. No administration could survive in rural areas
without doing something about such prices. The Roosevelt administration and
the Congress were forced to act still more vigorously.

The AAA of 1938

The Agricultural Adjustment Act of 1938 is the most comprehensive single
legislation of the 1930s, and it set a pattern for subsequent programs. It included
the conservation provisions of the 1936 act, more specific price objectives, and

[44]*U.S. v. Butler et al.,* Receivers of Hoosac Mills Corporation, 297 U.S. 1 (1936), p. 71. In this
case a district court had ordered receivers for Hoosac Mills, then in bankruptcy, to pay certain
processing taxes required under the AAA legislation. On appeal from this decision, the Supreme
Court held that the processing taxes were null and void, or not sanctioned by the Constitution, for the
reasons stated. It was this decision, coming quickly after a decision to nullify the National Industrial
Recovery Act, that is credited with leading to Roosevelt's long and bitter fight to enlarge the Supreme
Court, in which he was soundly defeated by a Senate vote of 20 to 70.

new features including nonrecourse loans for producers of corn, wheat, and cotton under specified supply conditions if quotas were approved in referendum; the first Federal Crop Insurance Act as Title V of the bill; provisions for direct payments to producers of wheat, corn, rice, cotton, and tobacco to provide a return as close to parity as funds would permit. Section 202 of the act provided for four regional laboratories for scientific research to develop new uses and new outlets for farm products. The act authorized direct distribution of surplus farm commodities to the needy, a school lunch program, a low-cost milk program, and a food stamp program.

The plan of the 1938 act, varying somewhat from the ever-normal granary idea popularized by Wallace, would provide reserve stocks for possible emergencies. Nonrecourse loans were made mandatory for wheat and cotton within a range between 52 and 75 percent of parity. A specific formula for corn would set loans at a maximum of 75 percent of parity if supply was not expected to exceed a year's domestic consumption and exports. Loans for corn would be at not less than 52 percent of parity if supply would exceed consumption and exports by 25 percent or more. Growers approved marketing quotas for tobacco for the 1940–41 crop year. Marketing quotas were in effect for cotton, peanuts, and wheat in 1941.

In the years that marketing quotas and acreage allotments were in effect, they reduced acreages for wheat, cotton, and tobacco, but yields rose, especially for corn because of hybrid seeds. Surpluses began to accumulate rapidly. Between 1938 and 1940, the general index of farm product prices dropped by 20 percent. By 1941, the whole question of the effectiveness of supply control programs was much in doubt.

AGRICULTURE IN THE WAR ECONOMY

In 1941, however, Congress was under strong pressure, spearheaded by the American Farm Bureau Federation, to raise loan rates and provide stronger price guarantees. Loan rates for the 1941 crops of wheat, corn, rice, cotton, and tobacco were set at 85 percent of parity. An act, thereafter known as the Steagall amendment, directed the Secretary to support prices of a long list of nonbasic commodities at 85 percent of parity if he found it necessary to increase their production. The Emergency Price Control Act in early 1942 prohibited price ceilings on farm products at less than 110 percent of parity. The Stabilization Act of October 1942 raised the support rate to 90 percent of parity for wheat, corn, cotton, peanuts, rice, tobacco, and the nonbasic commodities of the Steagall amendment. Section 8 of this act provided that the prices of basic commodities would be supported at 90 percent of parity for two years immediately succeeding the first day of January following a presidential or congressional proclamation that wartime hostilities had ceased. Section 9 extended similar guarantees to the list of Steagall commodities. Subsequently, price supports on cotton were raised to 92.5 percent of parity in June 1944 and to 95 percent of parity in October; and the CCC actually paid 100 percent of parity for the 1944 and 1945 cotton crops.

Marketing quotas were retained throughout the war on burley and flue-cured tobacco, to February 1943 on wheat, and to July 1943 on cotton. Other restraints on production were all removed as efforts to increase farm output were emphasized in national planning and in policies concerning manpower allocation and distribution of fuel, fertilizer, machinery, and other farm inputs.[45]

Under the influence of strong wartime demand and the removal of most controls, both prices and production moved up (as shown in Figure 4-1). Markets moved ahead of price supports so that storage stocks of grains were reduced to near normal levels. To further encourage livestock production, a wheat subsidy of about 25 cents a bushel was paid to livestock feeders in 1943 and 1944, resulting in their feeding more than 300 million bushels of wheat in excess of normal use. Thus did farm output respond to the war demand, as reflected in market prices, and to price supports and guarantees far beyond previous levels of compensation.

But trouble was clearly brewing for farm price policy in the future. Congress in the October 1942 act, under strong pressure from the President, rescinded the inflationary provision imposing minimum price ceilings on farm products at no less than 110 percent of parity. However, the price support guarantees for the war plus two years, encouraging as they were for farm output, were to magnify the problem for compensatory policy in years to come. The cotton price policy especially, forced by the leadership of Ed O'Neal of the Farm Bureau and by the seniority power among Southern congressmen, was clearly unstabilizing. At the war's end, about 12 million bales of cotton, more than a year's consumption, were in storage and the cotton economy was inflated far beyond domestic usage and the expected exports at the price levels set. Thus the stage was set for the postwar struggle and search for reason in farm price policy.

THE POSTWAR SEARCH FOR COMPROMISE

Agricultural economists generally anticipated the problems in farm price policy that were to rule for the next 25 years. There was general disenchantment with the price support and production control programs of the 1930s, and there had to be hope that agricultural prosperity could be attained at reasonable cost, with price supports at modest levels, provided that policies favorable to structural change in agriculture were adopted. Many people felt that agriculture was out of adjustment chiefly in having excess labor resources, and that policy could concentrate best on measures appropriate to deal with this problem.

The Economists' Farm Price Policy Competition

In the spring of 1945, the American Farm Economic Association announced 18 farm price policy awards, for the best papers submitted on the topic "A Price

---

[45]John D. Black, *Food Enough,* Lancaster, Pa.: Jacques Cattell Press, 1943; *World Needs for U.S. Food and Fiber,* Washington: National Planning Association, Planning Pamphlets Nos. 25 and 26, 1943; and Walter W. Wilcox, *The Farmer in the Second World War,* Ames: Iowa State College Press, 1947.

Policy for Agriculture, Consistent with Economic Progress that Will Promote Adequate and More Stable Income from Farming."[46] The winning papers turned out to be written almost exclusively by agricultural economists. They agreed in the main that the best role for policy was to help the market work. It could do so by revising price support levels of government more in line with anticipated market requirements. For attaining the optimum allocation of resources within agriculture, 14 of the 18 essays sought to establish a system of "necessary prices" or "equilibrium prices" that would elicit only the quantities of those foods and fibers for which there would be an effective demand at full employment. Only one winning writer would use production controls and none would use marketing quotas to make good on such commitments. A majority of the papers favored storage programs for stabilization, minimum income guarantees—especially during depressions—by means of direct payments, plus a number of complementary measures. The last-mentioned would heavily emphasize monetary-fiscal policy to obtain stability and growth, broad nutrition programs, improved labor mobility through education and expanded job markets, enhancement of international trade through reduction or elimination of tariffs, limited use of quotas and export subsidies, and renewed stress on soil conservation.

Also in 1945, the American Farm Economic Association's Committee on Parity Concepts, taking as its assigment an "Outline of a Price Policy for American Agriculture for the Postwar Period," favored a policy in line with a competitive market, saying in part:

> . . . Production controls in the form of acreage quotas are ineffective for most of the crops. During the period before the war, the system of controlling the crop through acreage restrictions broke down for nearly all crops. The farmer shifted the crops to more productive land, used more fertilizer, better seed, and better methods of cultivation. The high support price gave him the incentive to produce on fewer acres as much as his too easily underrated ingenuity and resourcefulness would allow. . . . Unchanged support prices in the market in view of overloaded granaries violate the rule of good common sense. . . . The worst feature of all is that government price supports which keep prices above the free market levels tend to restrict consumption.[47]

Forward Prices and Compensatory Income Payments

Theodore W. Schultz, also in 1945, presented a system of forward prices and income payments as a solution to the farm price and income problem without resort to price floors or restrictions on output.[48] Schultz proposed a government

---

[46]*Journal of Farm Economics,* Vol. 28, No. 4, November 1945, pp. 452 ff. For a summary of the papers, see William H. Nicholls and D. Gale Johnson, "The Farm Price Policy Awards, 1945: A Topical Digest of the Winning Essays," *Journal of Farm Economics,* Vol. 28, No. 1, February 1946, pp. 267–283, and discussions by L. H. Simerl and R. F. Froker, pp. 284–293.

[47]*Journal of Farm Economics,* Vol. 28, No. 1, February 1946, p. 391. The committee members were Karl Brandt, chairman; H. R. Wellman, R. J. Eggert, H. J. Henney, Fred Waugh, and Karl Wright.

[48]Theodore W. Schultz, *Agriculture in an Unstable Economy,* Committee for Economic Development Research Study, New York: McGraw-Hill Book Company, 1945.

agency to estimate prices for farm commodities that would clear the market under conditions of full employment (defined as less than 5 percent unemployed). In principle, these were free market, predepression prices.[49] They would be announced at least one full production period ahead of their becoming official. To the extent that the prices were not achieved in the market, compensatory payments would be made to producers, *provided* that the economy was at less than full employment. Under full employment conditions, no payments would be made except to certain low-income or distressed groups.

Such a program could have many advantages. It would allow markets to clear. Payments would be countercyclical in effect. Prices would decline during depression, thus encouraging consumption. Business and labor would benefit by stabilized agricultural purchasing power.[50]

Major disadvantages were both political and economic. Politically, the plan was unappealing generally to powerful commodity groups. Since there would be no bargaining for prices or other concessions, Congress would be releasing traditional powers to the forward-price agency. The payment system might be endangered by the necessity for large federal outlays in an already unbalanced budget year; and, if payments were kept up, farm output might grow to the point where the major part of farm income was coming from the federal appropriation. Farm organizations did not favor the plan and it did not receive general support in the Congress.

The Parity Transition

Clearly, a readjustment, however painful, was in order. Provisions of the Stabilization Act of October 1942 were to end in December 1948. If new legislation were not passed, price supports for basic commodities would drop back to the range of 52 to 75 percent of parity as provided by the 1938 Act. Price supports on nonbasics would be, for the most part, discretionary.

The Agricultural Adjustment Act of 1948 established mandatory price supports at 90 percent of parity for 1949 crops of wheat, corn, rice, peanuts, cotton, and tobacco if producers in referendum had not disapproved marketing quotas. Also, similar supports were set for certain other crops and livestock marketed before December 31, 1949. Beginning January 1, 1950, a new sliding scale for price supports would become effective, with supports sliding down to 60 percent of parity if supply rose to 130 percent of normal. Before this could happen, however, the scale was reset by the Agricultural Act of 1949.

The 1949 act provided that if producers approved marketing quotas and allotments, basic commodities were to be supported at 90 percent of parity for 1950 and from 80 to 90 percent for 1951. Cooperating producers were to be guaranteed 75 to 90 percent, depending on supply, for 1952 and the years following, if marketing quotas were approved. The price support for tobacco would continue at 90 percent of parity.

[49]*Ibid.*, p. 225.
[50]For development of the theoretical argument, see D. Gale Johnson, *Forward Prices for Agriculture*, Chicago: The University of Chicago Press, 1947.

In 1950, price supports were maintained at 90 percent of parity for basic commodities; they were discontinued for hogs, chickens, turkeys, long-staple cotton, dry edible peas, and sweet potatoes. For other nonbasics they were maintained at lower levels where possible under the 1949 act. But the effect of the Korean war, being generally inflationary for food prices, obscured price effects of these actions.

A new method of computing parity prices became effective on January 1, 1950, as a result of amendments in the 1948 and 1949 acts. Prior to this, a parity price was calculated simply by multiplying the price of the commodity in the base period, usually August 1910 to July 1914, by the "parity index" of prices paid by farmers, with the period 1910–14 as a base. On January 1, 1950, the new parity was calculated (1) by dividing the average price for a commodity received by farmers in the previous ten years by the index of prices received for all commodities in the same years to find an adjusted base price, and then (2) by multiplying the adjusted base price by the index of prices paid by farmers in a particular month for all inputs and services used in farm production, plus interest and taxes on farm real estate. As an example, during the 1940–49 decade, the farmer's average price for eggs was 36.6 cents per dozen, and the index of prices received by farmers was 202. Dividing 36.6 cents by 202 yields an adjusted base price of 18.1 cents. On March 15, 1950, the index of prices paid was 250. So 250 times 18.1 yields a parity price for eggs of 45.2 cents per dozen as of March 15, 1950.

The new formula was designed to keep the same ratio between prices received by farmers for all commodities and prices paid, as in the 1910–14 base period, but to permit price relationships and supports among individual commodities to remain as they were in the most recent ten years. This stipulation intended to recognize the fact that changes occur in relative costs of production and in supply and demand, and that these changes should be reflected in price support programs. Thus parity became more firmly imbedded in the faith of farmers as a measure of fair price and justice in compensation. But the arbitrary retention of the base period and the adjustments in the new formula then perpetuated parity, however defined, as a backward-looking concept and arbitrary in its application to specific program situations.

The Brannan Plan

In the spring of 1949, as farm surpluses were mounting under the existing price supports, Secretary of Agriculture Charles Brannan advanced a program proposal in congressional hearings. In it he apparently intended or hoped to combine the best features of forward prices with other income-supporting measures. He suggested shifting to an income standard rather than a price standard as a measure of fair return to farmers. A moving base period for income would be initially 1939–48, with the earliest year dropped and a new one added each year. The general support standard would be the level of prices for individual commodities necessary to raise income to the level of the base period.

Acreage allotments, marketing agreements and orders, quotas and stor-
ages—all would be used to manage supplies to achieve the desired prices. But
most perishable commodities and some storable commodities would be supported through compensatory income payments to farmers rather than through
price supports. The proposal for such payments resembled suggestions by
Schultz in his *Agriculture in an Unstable Economy,* but the standard—the
moving base, the index keyed to past history, and the general level—was quite
different.

Price and income supports would be limited to the first 1,800 units of farm
production, where a unit was defined as 10 bushels of corn, 8 bushels of wheat,
or 50 pounds of cotton. Although this proposal was intended to aid the family
farm, the plan embraced 98 percent of the total farm operating units within its
range. There is a strong assumption that the high cost of the plan would have
precluded more effective attacks on the farm poverty problem.[51]

Although the plan would have had advantages of allowing market-clearing
prices for most nonstorable and some storable commodities, the proposed
support levels would have overpriced farm products by at least 10 to 15 percent
in the markets then anticipated. The compensatory payments required to implement the proposals could have grown astronomically, and no one could project
the budget requirements with reasonable confidence. Brannan and his economists refrained from doing so. Some farm organization leaders became convinced that the plan could impose a system of controls that would be much more
restrictive than any previously employed. As a result, the plan was strongly
opposed by the major farm organizations, except the National Farmers Union, on
grounds that it could entail great government expense, that it would discard the
more defensible price parity standard, and that it would be almost impossible to
administer because of the required control measures. The plan received little
support in Congress and was dropped from serious consideration.

The Market Revival plus Assisted Structural Change

In 1952 a report issued by the Farm Foundation, prepared by a conference
committee of 13 prominent agricultural economists, stated that, "Temporary
withholding of farm commodities from the market occupies a very limited place
in our recommendation of a farm policy for the future."[52] Two special conditions
considered appropriate for government action would be "(*a*) as a buttress to the
income supplement in time of depression and (*b*) for military stockpiling." The
committee took the position that "a general business depression is the most

---

[51]For a discussion of the Brannan Plan as originally proposed, see articles by D. Gale Johnson,
W. E. Hendrix, Harold G. Halcrow, and Roy E. Huffman, *Journal of Farm Economics,* Vol. XXXI,
No. 3, August 1949, pp. 487–519.

[52]*Turning the Searchlight on Farm Policy, a Forthright Analysis of Experience, Lessons,
Criteria and Recommendations,* Chicago: The Farm Foundation, 1952, p. 77. The committee mem-
bers were O. B. Jesness, chairman; Henry B. Arthur, George H. Aull, M. R. Benedict, E. L. Butz, T.
K. Cowden, F. F. Hill, Asher Hobson, E. J. Norton, Edwin G. Nourse, Frank L. Parsons, T. W.
Schultz, and Frank J. Welch.

serious economic threat the farmer has to face, since it undermines both the consumer and the industrial demand for his product."[53] "If the effort to equalize incomes (of farm and non-farm) groups takes the form of continuous cash supplements or subsidies rather than returns from the market, this means that resources, especially labor resources are being used in agriculture when they could be used most profitably in other lines. . . . We must, therefore, seek better means for promoting economic equality for agriculture."[54] The operational policy measures were free market-clearing prices, ready and equal access to capital (i.e., credit) for all producers,[55] free managerial choices (i.e., free from government control regulations), a safeguard against depression through "stop-loss" direct supplementary income payments if depression occurs, and a separate program for noncommercial farmers.[56]

To achieve structural change, "educational institutions should provide adequate training for workers of all grades and should use their facilities to urge the movement of farm people away from situations where labor returns in farming fall below that in other comparable occupations. . . . We need to encourage and develop prompt adaptation and flexible reduction of farmers' efforts to constantly changing conditions. . . . This principle of voluntary adjustment is basic to our system of free enterprise."[57] The Farm Foundation's report firmly stated: "The basic theme of this report is that our farm policy needs to be realistically shaped to the conditions developing for the future rather than to continue as a legacy from the past."[58]

In 1955 Murray R. Benedict's book *Can We Solve the Farm Problem?*[59] presented the market revival theme anew. Specifically in Chapter 12, which was identified as a "Report of the Committee on Agricultural Policy,"[60] the general position was "that government has an important role to play in stabilizing and strengthening the agricultural economy, that we favor as much reliance on automatic adjustments in the market as is consistent with the goals suggested."[61] These goals included full equality in the farm and nonfarm parts of the economy. Thus

> If freedom of choice to work either in agriculture or out of it can be achieved and
> maintained, real incomes to farmers should not long remain far out of balance with

[53]*Ibid.*, p. 38.

[54]*Ibid.*, p. 34.

[55]*Ibid.*, p. 63.

[56]*Ibid.*, pp. 59–82.

[57]*Ibid.*, p. 63.

[58]*Ibid.*, p. 81.

[59]Murray R. Benedict, *Can We Solve the Farm Problem? An Analysis of Federal Aid to Agriculture,* New York: The Twentieth Century Fund, 1955.

[60]*Ibid.*, pp. 483–530. The committee members signing the report were Jessee W. Tapp, chairman, John D. Black, Harry B. Caldwell, Calvin B. Hoover, Donald R. Murphy, Edwin G. Nourse, Margaret G. Reid, Quentin Reynolds, Theodore W. Schultz, Andrew Stewart, Louise Leonard Wright, and Obed A. Wyum.

[61]*Ibid.*, p. 494.

real incomes in comparable non-farm occupations, even though urban workers and industries have somewhat more direct control over prices and incomes than have farmers. . . . Some maladjustments in production and price relationships are partly an aftermath of war-expanded production and partly a result of price policies pursued by government in recent years. . . . If the problems associated with these elements in the situation can be solved, there is reason to think that agriculture's relationship to the non-farm part of the economy, even in terms of free-market trading, would now be at least as favorable as it was in the 1910–14 period. . . . [62]

The goals thus expressed would apply specifically to a full employment economy.

In times of depression, the situation is different. Agricultural workers do not then have ready access to another and much larger labor market. . . . This argues strongly for stand-by arrangements that can provide prompt and vigorous help when it is much needed. In such times, neither the public interest nor that of agriculture calls for a shift of human and material resources out of agriculture. The maladjustment is on the demand side, not on the supply side. Primary emphasis should be therefore in restoring a healthy demand . . . if agricultural production continues to exceed the amounts that can be sold at prices farmers and the Congress regard as acceptable . . . and if unused stocks build up, it is apparent that government action which continues to overstimulate the industry tends to aggravate the problem rather than to solve it. [63]

Although individual members objected to certain parts of the report, two members (Caldwell and Murphy[64]) voiced more general objections by writing, in part, that "the report . . . fails to come to grips with the major issue . . . farmers are again plagued with surpluses clear across the board . . . what the policy statement seems to lack is a realistic sense . . . of the urgent need to deal with this problem effectively and quickly in order to keep farm income in balance with the income of the rest of the economy."

The more general committee view was that minor downward adjustments in price support levels would bring the farm economy into equilibrium at reasonable levels of income. Suggestions included pricing of lower grades of wheat at levels competitive for feed use, reduction in supports for cotton of about 3 cents per pound, and a price support for corn in the order of 5 percent lower than existed in 1954.[65] Other commodities, such as butter, posed more difficult problems, although the suggested solutions were similar.

An Adaptive Program for Agriculture

In 1962, a statement on national policy made by the Research and Policy Committee of the Committee for Economic Development (CED), entitled *An*

[62]*Ibid.*, pp. 492–493.
[63]*Ibid.*, p. 493–494.
[64]*Ibid.*, pp. 529–530.
[65]*Ibid.*, pp. 497–515.

Adaptive Program for Agriculture, presented another approach for economic adjustment of the farm and food system.[66] The approach was described as seeking

> to achieve what the laissez-faire approach would ordinarily expect to achieve but to do it more quickly and with less deep and protracted loss of income to the persons involved than might result if no assistance were given. The adaptive approach requires improved knowledge of available employment opportunities, and measures to finance movement and retrain workers; that is, a generally improved labor market. It works best when there is a high rate of economic activity and employment. . . . The adaptive approach calls for action by government working with the free market, rather than against it."[67]

Thus the American farm problem was grounded in a combination of five conditions, no one of which alone could have been a causal factor for depression in the farm economy. These conditions were (1) swiftly rising productivity, (2) declining use of labor relative to capital, (3) slow growth of demand for farm goods, (4) low responsiveness of demand to price changes, and (5) inadequate flow of resources out of farming. Most basically, the outflow of resources required from agriculture had been extraordinarily large relative to the resources engaged but insufficiently large to bring labor earnings in agriculture into equilibrium with those in the nonfarm sector.[68]

Thus policy choices were primarily between leakproof control of farm production and a program to induce excess resources (people, primarily) to move rapidly out of agriculture. Between these two choices, the recommended program called for policies and programs to attract excess resources from use in farm production and for measures to cushion the adjustment for people and property. Policies should include liberalization of agricultural trade, then blocked chiefly by growing restrictions in the European Common Market, continued emphasis on research for ways to produce more farm goods with fewer resources, and use of existing surplus stocks of farm products to assist the growth of less developed countries. The adaptive approach, vigorously prosecuted, would bring production and use into balance with a level of prices that would enable farm people and land, after a reasonable period, to receive higher incomes without extensive government controls or subsidies.[69]

This conclusion, although logically consistent, was received with mixed

---

[66]*An Adaptive Program for Agriculture,* A Statement on National Policy by the Research and Policy Committee of the Committee for Economic Development, New York: Committee for Economic Development, 1962.

The Committee for Economic Development, which has headquarters in New York City, is an organization of about 200 business executives and educators. It is aided by a research advisory board of leading economists, a small permanent research staff, and advisors chosen for their competence in the field being considered. The advisors to the subcommittee of the 44-member research and policy committee which approved the report were Henry B. Arthur, Richard B. Heflebower, Dale E. Hathaway (who coordinated the research), and Theodore W. Schultz.

[67]*Ibid.,* pp. 11–12.

[68]*Ibid.,* pp. 15–19.

[69]*Ibid.,* pp. 25–60.

emotions among farm organizations and government policymakers. Representatives of some organizations, such as the National Farmers Organization and the Farmers Union, damned it openly (as discussed more fully in Chapter 6). Some other groups ignored it. Among the general farm organizations, only the Farm Bureau treated it with some kindness and respect. Thus, advocacy of the free market or market revival, in essence, a forthright attempt to find a satisfactory balance between government controls and a free market, received strong criticism and active opposition from major agricultural interests.

THE EISENHOWER-BENSON YEARS, 1952–1960

The eight-year administration of President Dwight Eisenhower and Secretary of Agriculture Ezra Taft Benson was initiated under price supports that were inconsistently high, compared with other regulations in effect. Early in 1952, President Harry Truman had asked for repeal of the sliding scale, an action just the opposite of that recommended in the Farm Foundation report *Turning the Searchlight on Farm Policy,* mentioned earlier. Congress responded by voting to set price supports for basic commodities at 90 percent of parity through April 1953, unless producers in referendum disapproved marketing quotas. In July 1952, Congress extended this provision through 1954, and both presidential candidates, Eisenhower and Governor Adlai Stevenson, promised to continue a high support level. Eisenhower, in one speech, suggested favoring farm income supports at 100 percent of parity. Thus, Secretary Benson was required to continue the 90 percent supports through 1954; and, to keep campaign pledges, the administration did not ask for their repeal. Benson's first new farm program, submitted to Congress in 1954, simply suggested that the sliding-scale provisions enacted in 1948–49 be put into effect for 1955, but that, to prevent a precipitous drop in price, Congress should authorize a set-aside of 400 million to 500 million bushels of CCC stocks. These would be ignored in setting the support level, and modernized parity, which most importantly in the case of wheat was about 10 cents below old parity, would become effective in 1956. Thus the emphasis was on gradualism in policy, in Benson's words, to improve the "functioning of market prices."[70]

Surpluses, which first became burdensome about 1949–50, began to increase again in 1953 after the end of the Korean war. Under the urging of Benson and his staff, the Agricultural Act of 1954 reestablished flexible supports for basic commodities at 82.5 to 90 percent of parity in 1955, and at 75 percent to 90 percent thereafter, except for tobacco, which was to be supported at 90 percent of parity. The Agricultural Trade Development and Assistance Act, Public Law 480, often called P.L. 480, was approved in 1954 and substantial financial assistance was provided to finance exports. The Agricultural Act of 1956 established the Soil Bank, the first large-scale effort since the 1930s to retire land either

---

[70]Testimony before the Joint Committee for the Economic Report, *Hearings on the January 1954 Economic Report of the President,* Feb. 4, 1954, p. 155.

for purposes of production control or conservation. There were two provisions. Under the Acreage Reserve, farmers were paid to reduce the planting of allotment crops—wheat, cotton, corn, tobacco, peanuts, and rice—to or below allotment levels. Under the Conservation Reserve, farmers were paid to divert all or part of their cropland to soil-conserving uses under long-term contracts. Originally, the Soil Bank was to apply to some 60 million acres or more. But it was funded at less than half this level, and therefore did not achieve the degree of crop reduction envisaged by Benson and his staff. The Democrats, gaining control of the Congress in 1956 and 1958, more stringently limited funds for the Soil Bank, thus embarrassing the Benson administration.

The Agricultural Act of 1958 made price supports mandatory for most feed grains, in addition to wheat, cotton, and tobacco. Corn farmers were given an option in referendum of choosing either (1) to terminate allotments in 1959 and thereafter, and to receive price support at 90 percent of the average price of the preceding three years, or (2) to keep acreage allotments and receive price support at 75 to 90 percent of parity, as in the 1954 act. In the referendum held in 1958, corn farmers voted for the first option, thus ending corn allotments.

Maintaining price supports at the levels set, without either allotments on feed grains or a substantial Soil Bank, continued a production level at least 5 percent more than could be sold at these prices. As a result, there was further rapid accumulation of stocks. On October 1, 1960, at the beginning of the marketing year for corn, stocks of corn on and off farms totaled 1.8 billion bushels, perhaps about 3 times as much as desired for a normal carryover. The 1960 corn crop of 3.9 billion bushels, about 1 billion bushels more than the average crop from 1954 to 1957, or 300 million more than the average for 1958 and 1959, brought the total supply for the marketing year 1960–61 to nearly 5.7 billion bushels, by a significant margin an all-time high. The 1960 wheat crop, plus stocks, totaled 2.7 billion bushels, compared with average total disappearance during 1958 and 1959 of 1.1 billion bushels annually (as food, 497 million; as feed and seed, 105 million; as exports under government programs, 337 million; as dollar exports, 137 million).

FARM AND FOOD POLICY IN THE 1960S

When John F. Kennedy was elected President in 1960, two broad goals for food policy had been discerned. One of them, mentioned by Kennedy in his campaign, was to use the current food abundance to banish hunger and malnutrition in the United States and to provide for expanded food aid abroad as part of a program for world peace. The other was to reduce the nation's farm output by more stringent production controls and payments to farmers, thus to reduce the overburdening grain stocks and other surpluses.

The Emergency Feed Grain Program
Although one of President Kennedy's first moves after inauguration was to direct his Secretary of Agriculture Orville Freeman to expand food distribution to needy persons, to increase utilization of food stamps, to expand school lunch

programs, and to promote exports in what was called Food for Peace, the first and most important legislation of the next eight years was the Emergency Feed Grain Act, approved in March 1961. It was designed to divert corn and grain sorghum acreages on a larger scale, to expand payments to farmers for this purpose, and to raise feed grain prices. Producers were eligible for price supports at 74 percent of parity if, in 1961, they diverted 20 percent of the average acreage they had devoted to corn and grain sorghum in 1959 and 1960. The national average support rate for corn was $1.20 per bushel; for grain sorghum, it was $1.93 per 100 pounds. Payments for reducing acreage by the minimum 20 percent were to be equal to 50 percent of the local support price multiplied by the normal yield of corn for the farm as recommended by the responsible committee and administratively approved. Payments were to be equal to 60 percent for additional diversions of acreage from 20 to 40 percent of the base acreage.

Although the Emergency Feed Grain Program was voluntary throughout the 1960s, the payment levels were set at generous levels to attract the large majority of eligible farmers. The CCC released corn stocks to hold prices below loan levels, a practice severely criticized at times by farm organization representatives but additionally effective in bringing cash-grain farmers, as different from grain-livestock farmers, under the program. The program of payments, plus selling corn at less than loan rates, was expensive to the government, entailing annual costs variously estimated as near the $1 billion level in most years. Although the program probably stimulated investment in corn, sorghum, and related production, it was effective in stopping the accumulation of stocks. It was reasonably popular with farmers and thus politically acceptable, and it was retained in the same general form up through 1972.

Political Action for Mandatory Supply Controls

Within the Kennedy-Freeman administration, both free market prices and the high budgetary costs of voluntary control programs were politically unattractice and thus conducive to strong mandatory controls over farm production and marketing. Willard Cochrane, chief economic advisor to Freeman, had strongly supported this position in his book *Farm Prices: Myth and Reality*[71] and in a number of journal articles and other papers. In his view, burgeoning farm production and chronically low farm prices were destroying the family farm.

Late in 1961, the administration sent a proposed bill to Congress which would establish guidelines for mandatory production control programs and procedures for giving the Secretary of Agriculture authority to set allotment levels and price supports. A commodity program would go into effect on order of the Secretary unless the Congress voted against it within 60 days after its submission to Congress. The USDA Agricultural Stabilization and Conservation Service (ASCS) would be responsible for administering programs at the farmer level and would have a stronger voice in policy formation. Since the bill would have authorized a considerable shift of power from the Congress to the administration, it was unattractive to many congressmen and did not pass.

[71]Willard W. Cochrane, *Farm Prices: Myth and Reality,* Minneapolis: The University of Minnesota Press, 1958.

In spite of this defeat, the Department of Agriculture prepared a bill to maintain farm income, control the growth of stocks, and hold down on government expenditures. Submitted early in 1962, the bill proposed to establish a comprehensive supply control system for major farm commodities, including feed grains and dairy products. Under it the Secretary would establish allotment and quota levels. Producers of a particular commodity would vote in national referendum whether or not to approve quotas and the related price supports. If two-thirds approved, quotas would be mandatory and producers who exceeded their quotas would be taxed or otherwise penalized.

The bill, strongly supported by the administration and skillfully directed by Congressman Harold Cooley, chairman of the House Committee on Agriculture, and Senator Allen Ellender, chairman of the Senate Committee on Agriculture and Forestry, passed the Senate 42 to 38 but was defeated in the House 205 to 215. Democratic congressmen and senators were under especially heavy pressure from the administration, but enough Democrats defected on the issue to defeat the bill.

The hearings and votes on this bill also revealed and perhaps magnified some deep divisions among farmers and farm organizations in regard to both the goals and means of price policy. The American Farm Bureau Federation, as well as most state farm bureaus and cattlemen's associations, especially the American National Cattlemen's Association, were bitterly against the bill on both ideological and practical grounds. Ideologically, they felt it would be the opening wedge to shift power from farm organizations to government and, perhaps ultimately, to bring all American agriculture under a government dictatorship. Practically, they expressed doubts about its achieving more satisfactory incomes in agriculture over the long run. Several other farm organizations, perhaps most influentially the National Farmers Union, were vehement in their support of the measure. The more extreme of these viewed mandatory controls as essential for justice in farm prices and salvation of the family farm. Most importantly, however, public opinion polls had shown that farmers were increasingly unwilling to tolerate mandatory controls. Subsequently, the Food and Agricultural Act of 1962 extended the 1961 Emergency Feed Grain Program and provided for a referendum by wheat growers in 1963 whether to adopt mandatory controls, essentially the issue that had been defeated earlier in Congress.

The 1963 wheat referendum provided that a 55-million-acre national wheat allotment, approved as the minimum in previous referendums, would be abolished, and that the Secretary of Agriculture would be empowered to set the allotment as low as necessary to bring production into line with utilization. Farmers were offered either one of two options: Under the first, farmers would be offered marketing certificates equal to the quantity of wheat to be used for domestic human consumption and a portion for exports. This wheat would be supported at 65 to 90 percent of parity, and the remaining wheat would go as feed. But farmers who overplanted their acreage allotments could be assessed penalties. A 15-acre exemption, which had been in effect, would be eliminated. Under the second, wheat growers complying with allotments would be eligible for price supports at 50 percent of parity, then about $1.25 per bushel. There would be no penalty for overplanting except that farmers who did so would be ineligible for any price support.[72]

The administration and the Farm Bureau chose the 1963 wheat referendum as a major test for policy. The administration, through the offices of the Agricultural Stabilization and Conservation Service and supported by the National Farmers Union and other groups, mounted a vigorous program to convince wheat farmers that they should accept the first alternative. A vote against it was variously pictured as a vote for depression, the end of the small family farm, a disaster for rural America. The Farm Bureau, on the other hand, pictured the issue as "freedom to farm" and "who will control agriculture, the bureaucrats or farmers?" If the farmer voted yes, he would be putting the country on the road to socialism, bureaucrats, big government, and the end of the traditional freedoms on which the nation was founded.

In the 1963 vote, over 1 million farmers and their wives cast ballots, more than 5 times as many as had voted in any previous referendum. The administration suffered a stunning defeat. Only 48 percent of the farmers voted for the first alternative, far fewer than the two-thirds vote required for adoption. The Farm Bureau, perhaps benefiting from farmer resentment toward government and alleged faulty administration of programs in other years, emerged triumphant. Moreover, the administration realized that it could not survive under the effects of a "no" vote, as the Farm Bureau had argued, and a new program had to be designed and promoted for 1964.

The Wheat-Cotton Act of 1964

The Wheat-Cotton Act of 1964 established a voluntary two-price certificate program for wheat which became the basis for policy for the next several years. Initially in 1964, complying farmers received $2 per bushel for 45 percent of their normal production, 70 cents of which consisted of receipts from certificates purchased by processors. Another 45 percent was supported at $1.55 per bushel. The remaining 10 percent was supported at $1.30 per bushel. In later years the domestic portion, 40 to 45 percent of normal production, was supported at parity and the balance at $1.25 per bushel. When the support was at $2 processors paid 75 cents per bushel for the certificate portion in addition to the $1.25. Later, values of the certificates rose as parity price increased relative to the basic support level. Complying farmers were also required to divert land from wheat to soil-conserving uses, for which the farmers received land diversion payments.

Under the 1964 act, all cotton farmers complying with their regular allotments were to have their cotton crops supported at 30 cents per pound, and farmers who reduced acreage to a smaller allotment level were to receive support at 33.5 cents per pound. In order to keep domestic handlers and textile mills

---

[72]For a more comprehensive discussion, see Don F. Hadwiger and Ross B. Talbot, *Pressures and Protests: The Kennedy Farm Program and the Wheat Referendum of 1963,* San Francisco: Chandler Publishing Co., 1965; and Don F. Hadwiger, *Federal Wheat Commodity Programs,* 1970.

competitive with foreign manufacturers, the Secretary was authorized to make subsidy payments to handlers or millers sufficient to reduce the effective price of cotton used domestically to the export price level.

The Food and Agricultural Act of 1965

The 1965 act, approved in November 1965, extended the wheat and feed grains programs to 1969, and in 1968 the 1965 act was extended again to 1970. The 1965 act also established a general land retirement program, supported by the Farm Bureau for several years and called the Cropland Adjustment Program. The Secretary was authorized to enter into 5- to 10-year contracts to retire cropland to conservation uses. The Congress provided that payments were not to exceed 40 percent of the value of probable production on this land, and the Secretary was initially directed not to obligate more than $225 million per year.

The 1965 act modified the 1964 act, under which cotton surpluses had begun to accumulate, by supporting cotton prices domestically at no more than 90 percent of the world price, thereby eliminating the need to subsidize cotton used in domestic mills or exported, and by setting cotton payments at an attractive level to bring farmers into the control program. Under this provision, federal payments to cotton growers replaced price supports as a means of maintaining cotton growers' incomes.

The National Commission on Food Marketing

The deepening concern in the administration and in Congress over the high costs of voluntary compensatory programs and over questions concerning the functioning of the food supply and marketing system led to the establishment of the National Commission on Food Marketing. The act establishing the commission, signed into law by President Johnson on July 3, 1964, called for a broad study of actual changes in the various segments of the food industry, principally in the preceding two decades, the changes likely to occur if present trends were to continue, and the kind of food industry that would ensure efficiency and appropriate services to consumers under acceptable competitive alternatives. Although the original bill charged the Commission with recommending actions by government, private enterprise, and individuals, this provision was deleted by the House Committee on Agriculture. The act also called for the Commission to study and appraise the changes in statutes or public policy that would be appropriate to achieve a desired distribution of power as well as desired levels of efficiency. The Commission also was to study and appraise the effectiveness of government services for the food industry and the effects of food imports. The act also directed the Commission to make interim reports as it deemed advisable and a final report of findings and conclusions by July 1, 1965, later advanced to July 1, 1966.[73]

The Commission was to consist of 15 members, 5 appointed by the President pro tempore of the Senate, 5 by the Speaker of the House, and 5 by the President

---

[73]Public Law 88-354, 78 *Stat.* 269 as amended by Public Law 89-20, 79 *Stat.* 111, 7 U.S. Code, 1621 note.

from outside the federal government. It was to be assisted by a staff headed by an executive director, who would be responsible for recruiting and organizing the staff and directing the various studies. The Congress authorized an appropriation of $2.5 million to conduct the work of the Commission.[74]

A general appraisal of the agency's work was that the hearings were well conducted, that the technical studies were competently done, and that the Commission, in its final report, was unable to present a unanimous set of conclusions.[75] The Commission broke sharply into a majority of nine and a minority of six. There were important differences over interpretations of data (the policy situation), over what the Commission was chartered to do (policy goals), and over the inferences for policy (means, implements, and constraints).

The Majority View   By drawing a fine line between recommendations and appraisals or conclusions, the majority believed that a growing concentration within the food industry needed to be more forcefully controlled by government if the public interest was to be best served. The members concluded that new legislation was therefore called for to more specifically control mergers of large firms in the food industry and acquisitions of generally smaller firms by large ones. They concluded that there should be requirements specified for intended mergers or acquisitions of firms by other firms above a certain size. A regulatory agency should have general power to issue an order to cease and desist until the economic effects of a proposal could be appraised and evaluated. Such an order should be effective for a limited time only. In event of a permanent adverse ruling, the aggrieved party should have the option of appeal to the courts.

The majority of the Commission also concluded that each public corporation in the food industry whose annual sales exceeded a certain amount should be required to report annually to the Securities and Exchange Commission, for publication, its sales, expenses, and profits in each field of operations in which the annual value of shipments was in excess of a stated minimum. Since price discrimination in the retail food industry—such as using loss-leaders or below-cost selling to eliminate competition and thus monopolize, or favoring integrated wholesale firms over independent suppliers to gain further market power—endangered the effectiveness of competition, the Robinson-Patman Act, which deals with such matters, should be specifically strengthened to include more effective enforcement. Regulatory jurisdiction over transactions in meat and poultry should be made more forceful. The Perishable Agricultural Commodities Act should be strengthened to ensure more orderly and equitable trading in fresh fruits and vegetables.

The majority held that consumers should be provided with the choices and unbiased information that they needed to get the most satisfaction for their

---

[74]Commission activities are summarized in Report of the National Commission on Food Marketing, *Food From Farmer to Consumer,* June 1966, and Technical Studies No. 1 to No. 10, 1966. Washington: Government Printing Office.

[75]See discussions by G. E. Brandow, Robert O. Aders, Charles E. French, and Kenneth E. Ogren under chairmanship of Harold Breimyer, in "The National Commission on Food Marketing," *Journal of Farm Economics,* Vol. 48 No. 5, December 1966, pp. 1319–1347.

money, including (1) consumer grades on all foods for which such grades were feasible, (2) FDA standards of identity, where practicable, for all foods belonging to a definite product category, (3) packages and labels to assist consumers in making accurate appraisals and price comparisons, and (4) a centralized consumer agency in the executive branch to be established by statute.

For farmers, the majority of Commission members concluded (1) that the government should give all reasonable support to producer cooperatives and bargaining associations; (2) that federal marketing agreements and orders should be authorized for any agricultural commodity produced in a local area or regional subdivision of the United States; (3) that new legislation should be enacted enabling an agricultural marketing board to be created upon vote of producers for the purpose of joining in the sale of farm products as they first enter the channels of trade; and (4) that new legislation should be enacted prohibiting intermediate parties from obstructing the formation or operation of a producers' bargaining association or cooperative, and from influencing of producers' understanding by dissemination of false or misleading information or other measures.

The Department of Agriculture should be empowered to improve its market information about market prices and supplies by having authority to require firms transacting business in foods to report prices, quantities bought or sold, grades, and similar information in the forms essential to prompt publication of market news. High priority also should be given to developing timely reports of prospective market supplies, forward prices, contract terms, and other potential successors of ordinary spot prices.

Additionally, the majority believed that increased effort should be given to reducing the conflicts among the profusion of state regulations regarding containers, grades, labels, product nomenclature, and the like. The FTC should investigate rates for food advertising to determine if various discounts, variations in charges, and ratemaking methods were cost-justified. The USDA should study changes in methods and costs of transporting food products, the effects on prices and the location of production, probable future trends, and their implications. The Bureau of Labor Statistics should study means by which it might improve the accuracy of its reports on food prices. The USDA should improve the accuracy of its price-spread data and the food industry should assist it to do so. There should be a periodic review of the various commissions or other bodies established by the states to increase market demand for foods. Futures trading in meats and livestock should be under the supervision of the Commodity Exchange Authority, and consideration should be given to including coffee and sugar marketing, and perishable farm foods as well.

Four individual statements from the majority called more specific attention to items of intense interest to Commission members. One was the steady trend since World War II toward increasing concentration in national food store sales. A second emphasized the imbalance of bargaining power as being largely responsible for the deteriorating economic position of producers, small manufacturers, and processors. A third called for stronger action to provide protection to producers, distributors, and consumers through improved reliability of price determinations and information. The fourth emphasized the need expressed by the majority to provide for the adequate and equal representation of consumers through the statutory establishment of an individual consumer agency.

The Minority View Six members of the Commission (two members each from among the five senators, the five representatives, the five nongovernment members) felt so strongly about what they called the unwise and untenable majority "conclusions" that they voted against submission of the report. By claiming that the majority views on concentration, competition, and farm marketing were in error, and that adoption of them as public policy would do lasting harm to the nation's economy, the minority of six suggested that the nation should applaud the impressive evidence gathered by the Commission staff and that much of the analytical material should be read with respect, but that the Congress and others should beware of accepting the conclusions.

The six minority members contended that the food industry was not as concentrated as many others (steel, automobiles, electrical appliances, etcetera), that it was highly competitive, and that ease of entry was not encumbered, especially at the local level. Farm to retail price spreads were by and large not unreasonable and the normal levels of profit in the food industry were not excessive when compared with other major sectors of the economy. They charged that the majority was misapplying the data on concentration, that breakfast cereals, for example, competed with many other food products for market position (i.e., that the demand for breakfast cereals was not highly inelastic with respect to price). In summary, the minority argued that a requirement for premerger notification would damage competition by limiting the flexibility essential for businesses to consummate important transactions. Although they agreed that the Robinson-Patman Act and other antitrust laws needed "study and reappraisal," they contended that the Commission had no evidence that the food industry lacked proper scrutiny by regulatory agencies. In broad perspective, the food industry, in responding to consumer preferences and demand, had made excellent progress in bringing high-level, integrated food services to the American public, and was continuing to do so. The minority concluded that the food industry, in offering these services at declining real cost, was contributing substantially to the national welfare and to a satisfactory rate of economic growth. Therefore, the majority "conclusions"—that there should be more reporting, surveillance, and regulation—were unjustified and could not be supported.

Economics of Food Retailing[76] Daniel I. Padberg of Cornell University, who was Project Leader for Food Retailing on the economic staff of the National Commission on Food Marketing, sought to carry the available economic data on food retailing through to logical conclusions on industry peformance. He concen-

---

[76]Daniel I. Padberg, *Economics of Food Retailing,* Ithaca, N.Y.: Cornell University, Food Distribution Program, 1968.

trated on the food retailing market structure, competitive behavior, and the kind of social performance growing therefrom. By conceiving of the food retailing industry as two markets—purchasing from suppliers and selling at retail to consumers—he was able to reach broad conclusions regarding the ongoing changes in market structure, the costs and effectiveness of competition, and public policy concerning mergers.

In regard to market structure, Padberg observed that the most significant changes have tended to occur in cycles. The chain store movement (initially, firms operating two or more stores) grew rapidly in the 1920s, and the number of stores in chain organizations reached its peak in the early 1930s at about 80,000. The four largest food chains increased their share of the food market from 5.7 percent in 1920 to 23.1 percent in 1930. Shortly thereafter, the chain movement subsided to be replaced by the supermarket movement, which affected primarily the physical presentation of merchandise at retail. Supermarkets offered a complete variety of foods, including meat products, bakery goods, and dairy products, previously sold in specialty shops, as well as many nonfood items—household cleansers, hardware, health and beauty aids, etc. With the development of supermarkets, thousands of small grocery stores were forced out of business. Many viable independents affiliated with others. Because of the increasing scale of supermarkets, however, the number of stores in chains of four stores or more dropped from 80,000 at the peak in the mid 1930s to fewer than 25,000 by the late 1940s.

From the late 1940s to the mid 1960s the supermarket irreversibly changed the market structure for food retailing. Whereas in 1948 only 27 percent of the nation's food business was done through supermarkets, by 1963 almost 70 percent went through supermarkets. Chains at first grew rapidly by internal growth and expansion through new stores and related facilities. From 1955 onward, however, as the supermarket began to saturate local communities, the chains grew mainly by acquisition and merger. Their methods included (1) horizontal merger of stores within counties and urban retail areas; (2) market extension mergers, as in markets not previously served by the acquiring firm; and (3) combinations of horizontal and extension mergers. Growth internally as well as through merger resulted in increased market concentration in the food industry; and most of the larger firms then used their superior financial resources and market power also to integrate vertically back through the wholesale structure, thus gaining control over significant parts of their supply resources.

But, in spite of this growth and merger pattern, by the mid 1960s the level of concentration in food retailing was only moderate or intermediate as compared with most other major economic sectors in the United States. The average combined market share of the four largest food retailers in the nation's market areas was slightly less than 50 percent. Between 1958 and 1963, this percentage had stabilized. There were few additional technological or merchandising advantages in larger horizontal organization. Vertical integration was not changing rapidly.

Still, despite the advantages of chains and supermarkets, gross margins in retail food merchandising had gone up as expenses had risen. For a time, increased promotion expense, including trading stamps, was the largest factor contributing to cost increases. Then, as supermarkets saturated urban and suburban communities, the outlays for advertising increased further, rivalry other than competitive pricing encouraged retailers to keep stores clean, stock a wider variety of merchandise, provide check-cashing facilities, and offer wider choices of merchandise, more convenient or attractice packages, and other consumer services.

To support these consumer-oriented services, food purchasing by retail stores became more concentrated, especially during the 1950s. Use of specialized handling equipment, large-scale computers, and other forms of automation gave economic advantages to high-volume wholesalers. As a result, a significantly greater entry barrier existed for new wholesale firms. It reduced the alternative outlets for farm producers, especially in fruits and vegetables. This placed a premium for producers on countervailing market power through producer organization, or more vertical integration by large-scale growers. The complaints of producers were indicated by numerous legal suits charging wholesale buyers with price discrimination, unfair grading, or unwarranted product rejection. The use of private labels by retailers, which permitted one supplier to be replaced by another without any break in service to consumers, strengthened the bargaining power of buyers to the disadvantage of the farmer-producer.

A Policy Conclusion   The complexity of the issues raised by the study of the National Commission on Food Marketing and the differing interpretations that could be put on these issues, as in the majority and minority views, apparently discouraged Congress and the administration from undertaking broad new legislation affecting the food industry and its competitive structure. In the next decade, according to FTC reports, mergers and acquisitions in the United States economy proceeded at a record pace, in the late 1960s reaching a high plateau unprecedented in American history. Almost all phases of the food industry were affected. Mergers and acquisitions were especially important among dairy cooperatives, meat-packing firms, bakeries, and retail food chains. New moves toward vertical and horizontal integration were important in fruits and vegetables from the producer through to the retail level. Thereafter, in the 1970s, the rate of acquisitions and mergers slowed down again. But the concern about the competitive structure of food marketing did, of course, not abate. It remained strong as an issue reaching far into the future. What is the general implication or inference for policy?

Our national policy toward mergers and the structure of competition generally grows out of the way in which market structure affects the public well-being. The Sherman Act of 1890 was intended to constrain business consolidations and holding companies, but it was not an effective deterrent to mergers. The Clayton Act of 1914, Section 7, was intended to constrain mergers through prohibitions on stock transfers; but, since firms could acquire other firms either by purchase of stock or by outright purchase of assets, the Clayton Act eventually proved ineffective in constraining mergers, such as later occurred in the food industry. In 1950, the Celler-Kefauver Act strengthened the antimerger provision of the Clayton Act to specifically prohibit acquisition of another firm's stock or assets where the effect "may be substantially to lessen competition or to tend to create a monopoly." But the action of the FTC in carrying out the stated purposes of the legislation has always been a matter of policy emphasis and court interpretation. When does an acquisition or a merger substantially lessen competition or create a monopoly?

In the 1950s, the FTC brought action against the four largest dairies, which had acquired hundreds of dairy processors or distributors, ordering them to divest themselves of many of the horizontal acquisitions in locally served markets. (Mergers in different market areas were typically considered legal). In the late 1950s and early 1960s, the FTC, primarily concerned with mergers that seemed important in lessening the degree of competition, brought suit against six major food chains. Then, in 1965, in a landmark case that eventually reached the U.S. Supreme Court, the FTC brought suit against one of the largest food conglomerates, Consolidated Foods, asking, "What are the effects of Consolidated's acquisitions on competition in the markets in which the company operates?" and also "Does the fact that the company is integrated materially affect the structure of the markets in which it operates?" Consolidated was integrated both vertically and horizontally, having acquired food processing firms, wholesale warehouses and other facilities, more than 100 supermarkets in Illinois, Iowa, Minnesota, and Wisconsin alone. Its wholesale division was contracting with independent supermarkets for them to buy all their nonperishables from Consolidated. In the Chicago area alone, 876 supermarkets had such contracts with Consolidated. The Supreme Court ruled in favor of the FTC, agreeing that Consolidated's interests in a broad range of food manufacturing and processing gave it an unfair advantage and helped it to overpower weaker competitors, that its potential for reciprocity, such as its purchases from manufacturers who were also actual or potential customers, resulted "in an irrelevant and alien factor intruding into the choice among competing products, creating at the least a priority on the business."

The ruling against Consolidated did not set a pattern for the food industry, however, or apparently, even slow down Consolidated's further growth. As noted by Padberg and others, the large food firms continued to grow as they offered more favorable services and prices to consumers. Antimerger policy based on court orders for divesture of acquired properties was not only generally ineffective in reversing the general trend toward consolidation, where divesture was carried out; it proved to be very expensive and often of doubtful value to the general public.

The broader policy recommendation of the majority of the National Commission on Food Marketing, that there be new legislation to more specifically control mergers of large firms in the food industry and acquisitions of generally smaller firms by large ones, was not carried out. President Johnson's administration was more deeply concerned with more immediate or pressing policy issues, especially the Vietnam war and the heated opposition to its continuance. Major evidences of the subsequently disastrous inflation were beginning to be felt, and this probably dampened enthusiasm for a policy such as that suggested by the majority. But even before the Commission's report could be published, its findings and conclusions were upstaged by the appointment of another commission by the President.

The National Advisory Commission on Food and Fiber

On November 4, 1965, President Johnson, in Executive Order 11256, established both the National Advisory Commission on Food and Fiber and the President's Committee on Food and Fiber. Subsequently, he asked the Commission of 30 members, whom he had appointed, "to make a penetrating and long-range appraisal of our agricultural and related foreign trade policies in terms of the national interest, the welfare of our rural Americans, the well-being of our farmers, the needs of our workers, and the interests of our consumers. . . . to construct a thorough and searching study of the effects of our agricultural policies on the performance of our economy and on our foreign relations. . . . to prepare a report which will serve as a guide and focus for future decisions and policies in the vast and diverse complex of food and fiber."[77] Between January 1966 and July 1967, according to Sherwood O. Berg, Dean of the Institute of Agriculture, University of Minnesota, and chairman of the Commission, there were 16 Commission meetings. "It sought and received testimony and assistance from scores of leaders and professional people. It had the full cooperation and assistance of many Federal, State, and private agencies and groups. It relied heavily on its staff of competent professionals, augmented by a group of expert consultants and advisers. Finally, it brought its own judgments to bear on the issues which emerged."[78] The Commission's recommendations were summarized in a report, *Food and Fiber for the Future,* appearing in July 1967.

The membership of the new Commission—like that of the National Commission on Food Marketing—was a distinguished, prestigious, influential, and able group. Of the 30 members serving at one time, 7 were from leading universities in the field of agricultural and economic research, 7 were prominent farmers or leaders of farmer and cooperative organizations, and the others were prominent in agricultural business, finance, or related activity. Among the latter group there was the chairman of General Foods Corporation; the chairman of the board of the National Cotton Council; the executive vice president of Agway, Inc.; the vice president for development of the Agricultural Group of Archer Daniels Midland Company; the assistant to the president for special projects, United Steelworkers of America; the president of Wilson and Company; the

---

[77]From the President's letter to members of the Commission, January 11, 1966, in the Report of the National Advisory Commission on Food and Fiber, *Food and Fiber for the Future,* Washington: Government Printing Office, July 1967.

[78]From the letter of transmittal of the Report, *ibid.*

executive secretary of the National Federation of Grain Cooperatives; the chairman of Deere and Company; the chairman of Safeway Stores, Inc.; the president of Campbell Soup Company; the vice president of the Amalgamated Meat Cutters and Butcher Workmen of North America, AFL-CIO; the retired chairman of the board of the Bank of America; the president of the Mechanics and Farmers Bank of Durham, North Carolina; a partner in a large implement dealership in Alabama; a prominent cotton broker in New Orleans; and a leading agricultural newspaper editor and writer. The growing consumer-activist movement was conspicious by its absence of representation.

The Commission—representing as it did a prominent cross section of food and agricultural interests, with a major, if not a dominant, group representing relatively large business—agreed that the time had arrived for a major redirection of the nation's food and fiber policy toward a market-oriented agriculture. This meant increasing the advantage of the market's ability to allocate resources and distribute incomes by reducing the overcapacity of the industry. The Commission recommended that positive steps should be taken to adjust cropland and to help the people that would be leaving agriculture anyway, under any policy, to earn more in nonfarm occupations. Government assistance to farmers would be furnished in ways that least interfere with the functioning of markets.

The Commission's concept of market orientation—reminiscent of such earlier reports as *Turning the Searchlight on Farm Policy* and *An Adaptive Program for Agriculture*—made room for programs, public and private, that would improve the operation of markets through market research and information, antitrust legislation, cooperative purchasing and selling, collective bargaining, and other means. But, in its recommendations, the report is otherwise silent on the major issue of concentration and other critical questions of economic structure that were highlighted for national attention by the majority of the National Commission on Food Marketing. The Commission on Food and Fiber did not report or offer recommendations on policy concerning the growing concentration in the food industry. There is no definite indication of the priority to give to antitrust legislation or the shape of possible changes in such laws, or the effects of further vertical and horizontal integration on the competitive structure of food manufacturing and marketing. Since the Commission looked to market orientation as the major component of policy, it did not envisage an active role for government in more specific surveillance of the food industry and increased regulation of competitive organization, structure, or performance. A hands-off policy in regard to further regulation of agricultural business and the food industry was advocated for the United States.

The members of the Commission agreed on a wide range of social and economic legislation, including social security for farm people, federal minimum-wage legislation for farm workers, federal protection and regulation for farm labor unions, stepped-up rural development programs, improved social services in rural areas, and a stated minimum annual income for rural people. On critical questions of national farm programs and on some trade issues, however, the Commission on Food and Fiber—like the Commission on Food Marketing—

split into a majority and minority view. A majority of 19 of 29 members (one member had died), including 4 of the 7 university representatives, the farm and cooperative leaders, and 1 or 2 industry representatives, generally favored continuing government commodity programs. The minority, including most of the industry leaders and 3 university representatives, recommended that the government withdraw from commodity programs to accomplish a market oriented agriculture as soon as possible.

The Majority View   The majority believed that commodity programs were consistent with a market-oriented policy and that they would not interfere with desirable resource adjustment. They endorsed marketing orders, price supports set modestly below a moving average of world market prices, direct commodity payments to implement these price supports, voluntary supply-management programs, and production quotas in bushels or pounds whenever production restraints were needed. The majority recommended a program for adjusting carryover stocks of major storable farm commodities in order to maintain reasonable stability of available supplies, with commodity loans and purchase agreements to support price levels to harmonize with the objectives of market-oriented programs.

The government should support land use or development programs only when additional farm production was needed and this was the cheapest way of getting it. Preference in water use from publicly financed irrigation projects should be given to family farms of economically viable size. Public subsidies for capacity-increasing farm practices should be discontinued and the funds redirected to projects for improving rural life.

In regard to foreign trade, the majority members recommended new legislation to permit reciprocal trade agreements with other countries, reduction and finally elimination of export subsidies, substitution of tariffs for quotas to protect the affected American producers, discontinuance of authority to impose import quotas on beef and mutton, expansion of East-West trade, and steps to permit U.S. shipping firms to operate at rates competitive with those offered by foreign fleets. The minority joined the majority in recommending that food aid programs for developing countries should be for short-term relief of famine caused by drought or other crop failure. Longer-term multinational aid should emphasize technical assistance to improve the productivity of agriculture and encourage population planning.

The Minority View   The Commission minority, largely from large firms in the food industry, felt that commodity programs should be modified to encourage major adjustments to a market-oriented agriculture, and then be gradually phased out. Government supply management was inconsistent with market orientation, and would undoubtedly interfere with resources moving to the most profitable uses and regions. Following a transition period, the United States should rely on temporary income supplements or a moderate level of price deficiency payments with the income parity concept as a gauge only, not as a program instrument.

Price supports should not be above 90 percent of the five-year average of world market prices and should be gradually phased out in favor of temporary income supplements and/or price deficiency payments. There should be a shift from nonrecourse loans to recourse loans as soon as possible, which would mean that, if market prices fell below loan levels, a farmer could not liquidate a CCC loan without incurring a loss of capital. The minority also disagreed with the majority proposals on direct payments, recommending that direct payments should not be made to achieve parity incomes, particularly if the payments were made on a price per unit of product, and independent of the farmer's net income. Acreage allotments and marketing quotas should be gradually relaxed on a specified schedule and ultimately cancelled.

To modify land use programs, the minority agreed that development projects should not be funded unless they were the cheapest means of getting increased farm production—if this were needed. In the situation then prevailing, public subsidies for capacity-increasing farm practices should be discontinued; but, instead, they should be redirected, not to rural development as the majority proposed, but to accomplish the necessary long-term shift of excess cropland to less intensive use—from wheat to livestock grazing, for example.

In regard to foreign trade, the minority agreed that there should be new legislation to permit reciprocal trade agreements, reduction of export subsidies, substitution of tariffs for import quotas, and general reduction in trade barriers. The easing of import quotas should be consistent with the needs of national security. Apart from this, the United States should take the lead in abolishing import quotas, although the minority members did not agree on abolishing authority to impose import quotas on beef and mutton. They urged the elimination of requirements for use of United States flag vessels for at least 50 percent of commercial trade, and they concurred in steps to permit United States trading firms to operate at rates competitive with those of foreign companies.

Conclusion   By avoiding the difficult questions of economic structure and concentration that so divided the Commission on Food Marketing, the Commission on Food and Fiber was able to reduce its differences largely to matters of timing and degree. But, by avoiding these more difficult questions of policy in food marketing, and by emphasizing, instead, the farm and rural problems, it not only drew attention away from the report of the Commission on Food Marketing; it probably contributed to government inaction on crucial matters affecting the food industry. The emphasis helped to veer national policy away from the difficult questions of economic structure and the effectiveness of competition in the food industry.

The two commissions largely repeated the laissez faire recommendations of the earlier studies sponsored by the Farm Foundation and the Committee for Economic Development. But even these modest recommendations for assistance in rural development and for support for adjustment of the rural labor force were not strongly approved or funded. The efforts to support farm income and stabilize farm prices resulted in a stable pattern of food prices all along the line and a decline in the real cost of food toward the lowest point in the nation's history.

POLICY IN TRANSITION

The policy transition from the conditions of the second era of food policy to those of the third was not generally led by the power of the federal government, or even encouraged by it. The policymaking initiatives came largely from various movements and groups outside the government and from the march of economic events that forced the government to change. The beginning of the transition can be seen in the awakening knowledge about hunger among the poor. Although the seeds for this awareness were sown in the Kennedy administration and were helped to germinate by the Report of the President's Commission on Rural Poverty, *The People Left Behind,* the policymaking transition did not get under-way until events such as the Poor Peoples' Campaign, the CBS documentary entitled "Hunger USA," and a number of independent studies and books, such as Nick Kotz's *Let Them Eat Promises,* drew attention to the food problems of the poor. The student movement grew more aware of the poor and it became acceptable for politicians to more openly reflect on the broader social needs of the people. Food stamps, inefficient as a policy implement to meet a vital need, became politically supportable. The school lunch followed a somewhat similar pattern.

The Transition in Food Marketing

In spite of the excellent staff work of the two national commissions, however, the leading policymakers in government apparently were persuaded by the leaders of the food industry that the people need not worry about oligopsony in food buying or about oligopoly trends in food wholesaling and retailing. The Johnson administration, of course, was floundering in its advocacy of the never popular Vietnam war, and the Nixon administration fared little better in this regard. But President Nixon openly favored big business; and, in regard to the food industry, he made it perfectly clear that he would not support guidelines or regulatory legislation such as suggested in the majority conclusions of the National Commission on Food Marketing. Nor would he sanction antitrust prosecution based solely on the basis of bigness or on questions concerning the share of the market. Statements of Attorney General John Mitchell in effect canceled the consent decree that, since 1920, had restricted meat-packing firms from vertically integrating with certain other sectors of the food economy. Thus he provided additional sanction, if any were really needed, for example, for the Greyhound Corporation to take over Armour Foods, for the conglomerate Ling-Temco-Vought to buy control of Wilson and Company, for ITT to expand into such diverse areas as Wonder Bread, Morton frozen pies and dinners, Gwaltney Smithfield ham and bacon, Pearson candies, and Hostess Twinkies. Based on 1966 data, the National

Commission on Food Marketing had warned: "Food conglomerates are likely to grow, to reduce the number of independent competitors in the industry as a whole, and to force the various segments of the industry more nearly into a single system characterized by the kind of nonprice competition in which they excel."[79] In 1968, the Federal Trade Commission had reported that "Merger activity in the current merger movement has been concentrated among the largest food manufacturers. The 50 largest food manufacturers were especially active acquirers."[80]

From 1969 on, while mergers and consolidations continued apace in food manufacturing and marketing, the study groups became even more dominated by industry. In 1969, the Consumer Research Institute was created in Washington for the stated purpose of conducting research on food issues affecting consumers, but its board of directors included representatives from Kraftco, Good Housekeeping, Grand Union Supermarkets, Heublein, J. Walter Thompson Advertising Agency, Quaker Oats, and other industry firms. In 1972–73, an 11-member committee formed in the USDA to advise on agricultural research policy had representatives from Del Monte Corporation, Crown Zellerbach Corporation, Curtice-Burns, Inc., Peavey Flour Mills, and the Nutrition Foundation, a tax-exempt organization serving as a front for firms in the food industry. There was no strictly consumer or labor representation, and only token representation from what might be called family farms. In 1973, as reported in *Supermarket News*, a nine-man industry committee, made up of representatives from Del Monte, General Foods, Greenbelt Co-op Stores, H. J. Heinz, Procter and Gamble, Red Owl Stores, Safeway Stores, and Winn-Dixie Stores, all large, integrated firms, and an attorney, wrote the code for the computerized checkout system for the retail food stores across the country. There were no independent or strictly consumer representatives.

For at least three years after the big jump in food prices in 1973, the large food firms were able to prevent government action to monitor food-price margins or counteract the growth of oligopsony-oligopoly. During this time the economic structure of the food industry tended to stabilize, but it was a stability involving considerable concentration of market power. In 1973, although nationally only 41 percent of total grocery sales were made by the 20 largest firms, and only 20 percent by the largest 4,[81] the 1973 concentration was far greater than in 1967. Out of 120 positions of market control in 30 large cities, the large supermarket chains held 101.[82] In 1973 and 1974, there were four major congressional hearings dealing with issues of imperfect competition or monopoly power in the food industry, but the committees were unable to get the leading firms to testify under

[79]National Commission on Food Marketing, *Food From Farmer to Consumer, Final Report,* June 1966, p. 95.

[80]Federal Trade Commission, "Enforcement Policy with Respect to Product Extension Mergers in Grocery Products Manufacturing," May 15, 1968, reprinted in *Food Price Investigation,* U.S. Congress, House Committee on Monopolies, Hearings, 93d Cong., 1st Sess., June, July 1973, p. 415.

[81]*Supermarket News,* July 1, 1974, p. 1.

[82]Metropolitan Market Studies, Inc., *1973 Grocery Distribution Guide,* 1973, Table II - 3.

oath as to the effects of their pricing and market-supply policies on food prices in local food market areas.[83]

The issue was not the degree of market concentration in the food industry; a sampling of the market shares in selected cities showed the concentration to be high (Table 5-1). Thus the facts on concentration were well known.

The issue was the effects of concentration on food marketing services, pricing practices, and profits of the food industry. Although 1973 was not so great a year for a large proportion of the 32,000 food-manufacturing firms, 27 of the largest food chains had an average increase in profits of 32 percent.[84] The increase in profits of a selected group of large firms was substantial, ranging from 23 percent to 147 percent (Table 5-2).

The increase in reported profits is of course only part of the picture. Various percentages of earnings could be retained by management for investment in upkeep, repair and renovation, for salary increases, for the shifting of overhead expenses among the firm's companies, or to help gain control of competing firms. The Federal Trade Commission had reported in 1966 and again in 1969 that net profits of food firms were higher where the degree of market concentration was the greatest (Tables 5-3 and 5-4).

Within a large firm, high profits in some market areas can be used to improve the firm's position in other areas, either by gaining control of competing food firms or by expansion to develop a more profitable operation. The position of leading firms at the national level need not change for the degree of market concentration to increase in local market areas.

A Policy Conclusion

The major policy issue is consumer protection, pricing, and competitive practices within the food industry. The existence of two major power blocs in the food industry—the oligopoly core of food distributors (food chains) and the oligopoly core of food manufacturers—is an accepted fact.[85] These blocs have a major focus of competitive activity involving private-label products that are price-competitive. According to 1963 data, private brands sold on the average for 20 percent less than national competitor brands.[86] Apparently, consumers are brand-conscious and responsive to product names and advertising by brand name. The question is: What consumer protection is required, and how can an effective policy for consumer protection be developed?

[83]These hearings were "Food Price Investigation," June and July 1973, House Subcommittee on Monopolies and Commercial Law, Serial No. 15; "Corporate Giantism and Food Prices," December 10, 11, and 12, 1973, Senate Select Committee on Small Business; "Federal Trade Commission Oversight," Senate Commerce Committee, March and May 1974, Serial No. 93-78; and "Hearings on the Farm-Retail Price Spread," Joint Economic Committee, Consumer Economics Subcommittee, May 1974.

[84]"1973 Profits: A Year to Remember," *Business Week,* March 9, 1974, p. 101.

[85]D. I. Padberg, "Emerging Effectiveness of Competition and the Need for Consumer Protection," *American Journal of Agricultural Economics,* Vol. 57, No. 2, May 1975, pp. 196–205, esp. p. 204.

[86]D. I. Padberg. *Economics of Food Retailing,* Ithaca: Cornell University, 1968, p. 93.

Table 5-1   Concentration of Major Food Firms in Selected Cities and Metropolitan Areas, 1973

Metropolitan area	% of area volume by top 4 grocery retailers	No. of top 4 that are chain store supermarkets	% of area volume by identified top chain store supermarkets
Akron, Ohio	64.5	3	49.0
Albuquerque, N. Mex.	74.5	2	46.0
Augusta, Ga.	59.3	all	59.3
Austin, Texas	67.7	3	51.5
Binghamton, N.Y.	51.0	all	51.0
Charlotte, N.C.	65.4	3	51.9
Cleveland, Ohio	62.7	3	53.5
Cocoa, Fla.	96.0	all	96.0
Columbia, S.C.	74.0	all	74.0
Denver, Colo.	74.3	3	62.8
El Paso, Texas	77.0	3	59.0
Eugene, Oreg.	57.4	3	52.2
Fort Worth, Texas	68.5	all	68.5
Greenville, S.C.	70.0	all	70.0
Indianapolis, Ind.	59.4	all	59.4
Johnstown, Pa.	79.0	3	68.0
Las Vegas, Nev.	57.0	all	57.0
Little Rock, Ark.	86.1	3	66.1
Louisville, Ky.	62.1	3	53.9
Miami, Fla.	60.5	all	60.5
Portland, Oreg.	74.7	3	55.7
Poughkeepsie, N.Y.	71.0	3	61.0
Raleigh, N.C.	63.3	all	63.3
Sacramento, Calif.	62.5	3	51.4
San Antonio, Texas	75.9	3	66.6
Scranton, Pa.	77.5	3	61.5
Seattle, Wash.	88.2	2	68.0
Washington, D.C.	71.8	all	71.8
West Palm Beach, Fla.	70.3	all	70.3
Wilmington, Del.	64.5	all	64.5

Source: 1973 Grocery Distribution Guide, Metro Market Studies, Inc., Greenwich, Conn., 1973.

The efforts to establish an effective consumer protective agency in the federal government have been thwarted by the food industry. On December 2, 1970, a bill to establish a consumer protection agency failed in a tie vote in the House Rules Committee, the defeat apparently the result of opposition tactics by the Grocery Manufacturers of America (GMA). In 1971, when the bill was again moving toward passage, the GMA evidently defeated it again by adding so many compromising amendments that consumer organizations withdrew their support.

Table 5-2 Increases in Reported Profits of Selected Food Firms in 1973

Food company	1973 profits (millions)	Percentage of increase over 1972
Anderson-Clayton	$24.8	40
Campbell Soup	80.7	23
Castle & Cook (Dole)	26.9	52
Del Monte	32.9	35
Federal (Holly Farms)	12.4	80
Green Giant	9.2	25
International Multifoods	11.6	23
Kane-Miller	9.5	147
Pillsbury	26.2	39
Ralston Purina	80.4	23

Source: "1973 Profits: A Year to Remember," *Business Week*, March 9, 1974, pp. 89–90.

By 1974, the public support for consumer protection had grown so strong that, even under threat of a presidential veto, the House passed a bill by a 3 to 1 margin. Although Montgomery Ward, Zenith, Polaroid, Motorola, and several other large firms switched their position to come out in favor of the bill, the GMA and the National Association of Food Chains (NAFC) were able to maintain a united opposition front in the food industry. On September 19, 1974, the Senate, by a vote of 64 to 34, failed by 2 votes to shut off a filibuster being conducted in opposition to the bill.[87]

The issues of consumer protection in the food industry—what is desired and how to get it—will be alive for a long time to come. The issues involve competitive structure and the regulations to be placed on structure. These are concerned with pricing practices, industry performance, product safety, and the

[87]Spencer Rich, "Consumer Bill Dealt 4th Defeat," *The Washington Post*, Sept. 20, 1974, p. A1.

Table 5-3 Average Net Profits after Taxes of 85 Food Firms by Degree of Market Concentration

Group	Concentration range (4 firms)	Number of firms	Net profits Simple average	Net profits Weighted average*
I	Below 40%	21	7.5%	6.2%
II	40–49%	32	9.5	9.2
III	50–59%	15	13.2	12.9
IV	60% and above	17	14.2	15.1

*Weighted by company sales.

Source: Federal Trade Commission, *The Structure of Food Manufacturing*, National Commission on Food Marketing, Technical Study No. 8, June 1966, p. 204.

Table 5-4   Profit Rates of Food Manufacturing Firms Related to Concentration and Advertising-to-Sales Ratios

Advertising-to-sales ratio (percent)	1.0	2.0	3.0	4.0	5.0
Four-firm concentration†	Associated net firm profit rates as a percentage of stockholders' equity*				
40	6.3	7.4	8.5	9.6	10.7
45	8.0	9.1	10.2	11.3	12.4
50	9.3	10.4	11.5	12.6	13.7
55	10.3	11.4	12.5	13.6	14.7
60	11.0	12.1	13.2	14.3	15.4
65	11.4	12.5	13.6	14.7	15.8
70	11.5	12.6	13.7	14.8	15.9

*Other variables influencing company profitability were held constant at their respective means. These variables were the firm's relative market share, growth in industry demand, firm diversification, and absolute firm size. Profit rates are averages for the years 1949–52.
†The average concentration ratio (weighted by the company's value of shipments) of the product classes the company operated in 1950.
Source: Federal Trade Commission, Bureau of Economics, *Economic Report on the Influence of Market Structure on the Profit Performance of Food Manufacturing Companies,* September 1969, p. 7.

adequacy of consumer information. As economists measure performance, that in the food industry has been appraised as reasonably good.[88] But a large percentage of firms are price followers and not aggressively price competitive. In many cities the dominating position of a supermarket chain apparently weakens price competition.

So, issues concerning mergers and acquisitions and the resulting structure of market power, monopoly, and oligopoly, cannot be laid to rest. With modern fabricated foods, the issue of product safety will remain important as will the problem of coordinating nutrition policy (Chapter 11). A law that establishes a consumer protection agency must be substantive in regard to these issues if it is to be effective in meeting the stated objectives of consumer organizations. In a meaningful way, policy is in transition. Issues such as these have not been covered in the comprehensive agricultural acts of the 1970s even though the Congress has included consumer protection in the title of the act passed in 1973. This policy also is in transition.

The Agricultural Act of 1970[89]

The Agricultural Act of 1970 was a compromise among farm organizations and various government interests. The American Farm Bureau Federation, which at the national level was strongly opposed to continuation of government production controls, split with most other agricultural groups, which came together in

[88]D. I. Padberg, "Emerging Effectiveness of Competition and the Need for Consumer Protection," *op. cit.,* pp. 199, 200.
[89]Based in part on discussion by R. G. F. Spitze, "Economics of the Agricultural Act of 1970," *Illinois Research,* Urbana: University of Illinois Agricultural Experiment Station, Vol. 13, No. 4, Fall 1971.

what was called the "Coalition of Farm Organizations," in support of an even stronger measure.[90] The hearings included views of individuals and organizations, and they were protracted. A series in 1969 before the House Committee ran from July 15 to December 3 and involved 1290 pages of testimony or records.[91] Hearings in the Senate from February 18 to March 23, 1970 totaled 831 pages.[92] During the closing negotiations in 1970, planeloads of farmers and farm leaders went to Washington to press their views, and the House and Senate came to a virtual impasse over the final bill.

The 1970 act included at least six key features: (1) Production control for feed grains, wheat, and cotton was by the so-called "set-aside," rather than reduction of a particular crop, whereby the amount of land retired for conservation was the same as before but farmers could plant the remaining acreage as they would choose. (2) Price supports were reduced slightly for some crops, compensatory payments were slightly higher, and both were disengaged somewhat from parity. The minimum payment for corn, for example, was 32 cents instead of 30 cents a bushel for one-half the participating farmer's normal production. (3) The total payment to any one farmer was limited to $55,000 per commodity per year. In 1970, this limit would have affected 1,100 farmers, most of them cotton producers, and would have saved $58 million out of a total $3.5 billion. (4) The target level for wool production, price plus payments, was disengaged from parity and set at 72 cents per pound for shorn wool. (5) Dairy

[90]The group, as listed in *Agricultural Act of 1970,* Hearings before the Committee on Agriculture and Forestry, United States Senate, 91st Cong., 2d Sess. on S.2524, S.3068, and a draft bill, Feb. 19, 1970, p. 239, included the following farm organizations:

The National Grange, 1616 H St., NW, Washington, D.C. 20006
National Farmers Union, 1012 14th St. NW, Washington, D.C. 20005
National Assn. of Wheat Growers, 1030 15th St. NW, Washington, D.C.
National Farmers Organization, Corning, Iowa 50841
Midcontinent Farmers Assn., Columbia, Missouri 65201
United Grain Farmers of America, Oakland, Illinois 61943
National Milk Producers Federation, 30 F St. NW, Washington, D.C. 20001
Pure Milk Products Cooperative, Box 350, Fond du Lac, Wisconsin 54935
North Carolina Peanut Growers Assn., PO Box 409, Rocky Mount, N.C. 27801
National Rice Growers Assn., Flying-J Ranch, Kaplan, Louisiana 70548
National Potato Council, 1499 Jefferson Davis Hgwy, Arlington, Virginia 22202
Virginia Council of Farmer Co-ops, Capron, Virginia 23829
Farmers Cooperative Council of N.C., PO Box H-1, Greensboro, N.C. 27402
Grain Sorghum Producers Assn., 1212-14th St., Lubbock, Texas 79401
National Corn Growers Assn., PO Box 358, Boone, Iowa 50036
Western Cotton Growers Assn., PO Box 512, Fresno, California 93709
National Wool Growers Assn., 600 Crandall Bldg., Salt Lake City, Utah 84101
Soybean Growers of America, Inc., Rt. 2, La Fontaine, Indiana 46940
Virginia Peanut Growers Assn., Capron, Virginia 23829
Peanut Growers Cooperative Marketing Assn., Franklin, Virginia 23851
American Rice Growers Co-op Assn., Lake Charles, Louisiana 70601
Webster County Farmers Organization, Guide Rock, Nebraska 68942
Vegetable Growers Assn., 226 Transportation Bldg., Washington, D.C. 20006
North Dakota Feeder Livestock Producers Assn., Ambrose, North Dakota 58833

[91]*General Farm Program and Food Stamp Program,* Hearings before the Committee on Agriculture, House of Representatives, 91st Cong., 1st Sess., Serial Z, parts 1–4, 1970.
[92]*Agricultural Act of 1970, op. cit.*

products would be supported generally, whereas formerly only butterfat was supported. (6) Finally, the federal government was called upon to give more emphasis to rural development.

In general, the act was designed to give farmers slightly more freedom in making production decisions, to support farm incomes at near the levels decreed in other recent acts, to facilitate exports by lower price supports, and to improve the public image of farm programs by limiting payments to large producers. The act made no significant effort to reduce the income spread between the poverty sector and the larger commercial farm. It did not resolve such problems as adequate education for rural youth who cannot find work on the farm, revitalization of depressed rural communities, regulation of farmer bargaining power, and improvement of food distribution to the poor (which did come later).

The compromises in the 1970 act apparently failed to satisfy almost all the contending organizations. The Farm Bureau had advocated phasing out price supports over the next three or four years, contending that government supply-management had not worked, carryover stocks were bad for farmers, the programs depended too much on political decisions. Also, it argued that farmers were too dependent on government for a substantial part of their net incomes, and that price supports were creating pressures for international commodity agreements which in themselves were not beneficial to farmers.[93] The National Farmers Union, on the other hand, called for a more workable system of supply-management, a mandatory program as the cheapest and most effective, and for the long-range an established system for collective bargaining by farmers.[94] The National Farmers Organization (NFO) proclaimed support for stronger government programs to maintain and improve farm prices and assist farmers in their bargaining efforts.[95] In between the positions of the Farm Bureau and the NFU or the NFO, various other organizations and groups called for the government to provide for more support without stringent production controls.

The Agricultural and Consumer Protection Act of 1973[96]

The 1973 act, effective through 1977, covered all basic and most nonbasic commodities with a system of nonrecourse loans and target price supports to be made effective by combining loans and deficiency payments. If the market price for a commodity were above the target price, no deficiency payments would be made. If market prices fell below the target, the Secretary was authorized to make deficiency payments to producers to offset part or all of the average of the difference. In addition, disaster payments were authorized for farmers in specific areas that had been officially declared disaster areas.

---

[93]From testimony of Charles B. Shuman, president, American Farm Bureau Federation, before the Committee on Agriculture, House of Representatives, Aug. 5, 1969. See *General Farm Program and Food Stamp Program, op. cit.,* pp. 206–7.

[94]From testimony of Tony Dechant, president, National Farmers Union, Aug. 6, 1969, *ibid.,* pp. 251–2.

[95]From testimony of Oren Lee Staley, president, National Farmers Organization, Aug. 7, 1969, *ibid.,* pp. 291–308.

[96]An amendment to the Agricultural Act of 1970, Public Law 93-86, 93d Cong., S. 1888, Aug. 10, 1973 (87 *Stat.* 225–249).

The act provided that target prices for 1974 and 1975 would be at specific levels, for example, $2.05 a bushel for wheat, $1.38 a bushel for corn, $2.34 a hundredweight for grain sorghums, and $1.13 a bushel for barley. Loan rates would be a third to a fifth lower: $1.37 for wheat, $1.10 for corn, $1.88 for grain sorghum, $0.90 for barley, and $2.25 a bushel for soybeans. It also provided that target prices and loan rates would be adjusted in 1976 and 1977 according to the index of prices paid by farmers, adjusted for the estimated change in farm productivity.

The act also set a new payment limit of $20,000 per farmer for those cooperating, and directed the Secretary of Agriculture to implement policies under the act "which are designed to encourage American farmers to produce to their full capabilities during periods of short supply to assure American consumers with an adequate supply of food and fiber at fair and reasonable prices." This might include cancellation of land diversion programs, expansion of farm credit as provided in the Farm Credit Act of 1971, and action to provide more adequate supplies of farm fuel, fertilizers, and farm chemicals. The act extended Public Law 480 and the food stamp and school lunch programs. It authorized $7 million a year for three years for rural development and made new regulations for rural environmental protection programs, which authorized the Secretary to enter into contracts of 3, 5, 10, or 25 years with landowners to develop plans for use and conservation of land and water resources.

In effect, the 1973 act removed the federal government from conducting price-support operations or from accumulating or reestablishing a food reserve. In the fall of 1974, for example, target prices were only about half of parity prices and generally less than half of market prices for wheat, corn, and grain sorghum. The loan rate for soybeans was less than a third of market price for soybeans. Although grain prices moved to lower levels in 1975, they were still far above target levels.

The extremely low levels of support apparently prompted a move by the Democratic leadership early in 1975 to raise the target prices for wheat from $2.05 to $3.10 per bushel, for corn from $1.38 to $2.25 per bushel, and for cotton from 38 to 48 cents a pound (H.R. 4296). The administration opposed this move on grounds that market prices were so strong that the change was unnecessary and also, according to ERS projections released on April 23, if the bill were to become law, declines in farm prices could cost the government as much as $1.8 billion in 1975, $5.8 billion in 1976, and $7.6 billion in 1977. Nevertheless, both houses of Congress passed the bill by substantial majorities, but the President vetoed it, and the House, by a vote of 242 to 182, failed to override the veto.[97]

A Policy Conclusion

The policy transition has carried the nation toward a broadening of goals for growth in the food supply. As part of this movement, there are new concerns also about economic structure, environment, and income distribution. But, as yet, the political forces making national policy have not come to grips with many of the

[97]See Dan Balz, "The Saga of the Farm Bill," *The Washington Monthly,* July–August, 1975.

more difficult questions implicit in these concerns. The Agricultural and Consumer Protection Act of 1973, for example, offered little real protection to either consumers or farmers. It did not propose an effective policy for farm price stability, a significant support for a food reserve program, or any price protection for consumers against monopoly in local food markets. The amounts authorized for rural development were scarcely more than a token; and subsequent appropriations were only a fraction of the sums authorized.

To bring this policy transition to maturity, there must be a broadening of understanding and more cooperation among rural and urban political interests. These developments are necessary to achieve the desired level of food abundance for domestic consumption and export, the desired level and distribution of income, and environmental protection. The United States and the world economy will suffer if these questions are approached in a narrow perspective of immediate concern. The policy must have a broad perspective while it comes to grips with specific issues. We turn next to the roles of farm organizations in making policy.

QUESTIONS FOR DISCUSSION

1 Export subsidy, loan storage, and production adjustment are the original policy means that involved the federal government in the beginning of the second era. Trace the early beginnings of these policies and, using supply-demand analysis, indicate why they were supported by farm people. Distinguish between the general and the specific policy goals.

2 Discuss the program of the Federal Farm Board. What was the policy goal? What was achieved? What lessons were learned?

3 What was the policy goal of the first AAA? What means were developed to achieve this goal? Discuss the organization of the implementing committee and the administrative structure. How was parity used as a policy constraint?

4 Discuss the political conflicts that emerged over the choices between production adjustment and export subsidy. What choices were made? On what basis were they made? Discuss the implications.

5 What is the policy reason for advocating an ever normal granary as a national program? As a world program? How does the case for such programs differ in the 1970s and the 1930s? In what ways might such programs hurt American farmers? Help them?

6 What policy goals underlie the use of marketing agreements and orders? In general? In dairy marketing? In fruits and vegetables? Are criticisms of marketing agreements and orders directed mostly at the goals, means, implements, or constraints? Comment.

7 Summarize the New Deal experience with production adjustment, loan storage, marketing agreements, and orders. What were the lessons for policy?

8 In the early postwar years, how did the proposals of agricultural economists differ from the existing policy? How did the proposals for forward prices differ from that policy? The parity transition? The Brannan Plan? "An Adaptive Program for Agriculture," issued by the Committee for Economic Development?

9 Compare and contrast the farm policy goals of the different national administrations

since World War II. How did these administrations differ in respect to the policy means that they favored? The policy implements? The policy constraints?

10 Discuss the effects of market concentration on food prices. Examine the cases for and against establishing a broad consumer protection agency. What powers might be required to constrain the growth of monopoly in retail food chains? In dairy marketing? In meat packing? In fruit and vegetable processing?

11 We have suggested that food policy is in transition. What has been accomplished? In what ways has the transition fallen short? Comment.

REFERENCES

Benedict, Murray R., *Can We Solve the Farm Problem? An Analysis of Federal Aid to Agriculture,* New York: The Twentieth Century Fund, 1955.

Black, John D., *Agricultural Reform in the United States,* New York: McGraw-Hill Book Company, 1929.

Cochrane, Willard W., *Farm Prices: Myth and Reality,* Minneapolis: The University of Minnesota Press, 1958.

Fite, George N., *George N. Peek and the Fight for Farm Parity,* Norman: University of Oklahoma Press, 1954.

Hadwiger, Don F., and Ross B. Talbot, *Pressures and Protests: The Kennedy Farm Program and the Wheat Referendum of 1963,* San Francisco: Chandler Publishing Company, 1965.

National Advisory Commission on Food and Fiber, *Food and Fiber for the Future,* Washington: Government Printing Office, 1967.

National Commission on Food Marketing, *Food from Farmer to Consumer, Final Report,* Washington: Government Printing Office, 1966.

Nourse, Edwin G., *Marketing Agreements Under the AAA,* Washington: The Brookings Institution, 1935.

Padberg, Daniel I., *Economics of Food Retailing,* Ithaca, N.Y.: Cornell University, 1968.

Schultz, Theodore W., *Agriculture in an Unstable Economy,* New York: McGraw-Hill Book Company, 1945.

Taylor, Henry C., and Anne Dewess Taylor, *The Story of Agricultural Economics in the United States, 1840–1932,* Ames: Iowa State University Press, 1952.

Farm Organizations
Making Policy

In America the liberty of association for political purposes is unbounded. . . . There are no countries in which associations are more needed, to prevent the despotism of faction or the arbitrary power of a prince, than those which are democratically constituted. . . . Americans of all ages, all conditions, all dispositions, constantly form associations. They have not only commercial and manufacturing companies, in which all take part, but associations of a thousand other kinds—religious, moral, serious, futile, general or restricted, enormous, or diminutive. . . . If it be proposed to advance some truth, or to foster some feeling by the encouragement of a great example, they form a society . . . [they] seem to regard it as the only means they have of acting.

Alexis de Tocqueville
Democracy in America, 1835[1]

Food policy for America is a product of the democratic political process in which farm organizations have played a leading role. Generally, these organizations have arisen out of discontent or protest. Consequently their activity has been aimed at improvement of economic and social conditions through political action, or the power of collective activity aimed at a policy goal. They have exerted pressure for programs or policy means such as price supports, credit,

[1]New York: Schocken Books, 1961, 4th printing 1970, Vol. I, p. 191; Vol. II, pp. 128, 129.

and other services. They have given support to commissions, regulatory bodies and service agencies to implement policy. By expressing their conviction they have helped to define the constraints that are important in food policy.

How and in what ways the policymaking farm organizations influence food policy is an important part of our study, and the purpose of this chapter is to broaden our vision in regard to this activity.

HOW THE SYSTEM WORKS

In the democratic system of the United States there will always be a role for organizations that function in policy development—to give representation to their members, to provide educational and informational services, to sometimes serve as propagandists in defining a political position, and generally to wield political power. It is not just accidental or coincidental that these same organizations in farm and related areas sometimes develop commercial interests, provide supply and marketing services, offer management aids, training programs, and so on.

The organizations are of several types. There are general farm organizations such as the American Farm Bureau Federation (AFBF), the national association representing state and county farm bureau organizations; the National Grange; the Farmers Union; and the National Farmers Organization (NFO). There are special-interest commodity organizations such as the National Cotton Council, the National Association of Wheat Growers, and the National Potato Council. Some of these are vertically integrated to represent dealers, processors, and others as well as farmers. The American Institute of Cooperation, generally not considered a directly partisan policymaking organization, lists among its membership more than 1,000 state and local organizations, associations, and societies, most of whom are active in the policy field.[2]

Although the organizations differ widely in their policymaking roles and the extent of their influence, they have a common interest in maintaining their life, membership, and structure. As a consequence, each organization attempts to define the interests of its members and, in policymaking, to speak for them. The organization maintains its vitality through the power of its appeal to members, its success in serving their felt needs and policy goals, and its recognition of the power of dissent. In a system of majority rule, if a dissenting minority believes that it cannot accept the organization position, the individual members can choose a number of alternatives, such as to discontinue their support of the organization, to work within to modify the organization's position, or to form a new organization in keeping with their position. The process of policymaking in America sharply involves dissenting individuals and groups in such activity. In such cases, the multifunctional organization has an advantage over one with a narrow special interest. Members may disagree with a policy position of the

[2]*Yearbook on the Business of Agriculture, Annual Review of Accomplishments, Goals, Problems, Business Volume and Management Techniques of Agricultural Cooperatives,* Washington: American Institute of Cooperation.

multifunctional Farm Bureau, for example, but they do not drop their membership if they wish to continue to buy fertilizer and farm supplies from the local Farm Bureau cooperative. A Farmers Union member may disagree with the stand of the national organization but may still wish to market grain through the local co-op. Members may join another organization for its policy stand but retain membership in the general organization which provides the services they want.

New organizations are formed out of discontent and protest, through exercise of the power to dissent. The result in the United States is many organizations, some agreeing on certain issues and differing sharply on others, with each organization urging policy action that is sometimes in harmony with others and sometimes diametrically opposed. There is organizational competition for membership and support. Finally, compromises among organizations in respect to legislation are sometimes developed through extensive hearings before congressional committees.[3]

The organizational system is prescribed by the nation's legal system, or the system of government which allows for organizations to emerge, gain power, and then exert an influence on government. The general rules that are the foundation of government also place limits on the self-generating organizations. How the system works, and how the organizations influence the system in making policy, can be understood best by an examination of several organizations.

Tobacco Organization as Related to Food Policy

Tobacco plays a unique role in the history and culture of this country. Since tobacco competes with food in its use of resources, the organization that has been developed for policymaking in tobacco is relevant to the policy for food. Tobacco growing reflects the classical model of perfect competition with a large number of atomistic producers. Tobacco manufacturers reflect an oligopoly organization in selling their product and an oligopsony organization in buying from farmers. The demand for tobacco is very inelastic and the big tobacco buyers have always reflected this in both their buying and selling policies. In the absence of government supply control, large crops have led to very low prices.

Good prices would draw people into tobacco production until, too typically, overproduction occurred and prices would collapse. But, because tobacco is a very intensive crop, low prices were slow to drive growers out. So great hardship was endured while growers periodically struggled to organize to control their supply. For 300 years they had only fleeting successes until the Roosevelt New Deal in 1933 created the first Agricultural Adjustment Administration (AAA) to control the tobacco crop.

---

[3]For example, 1,290 pages of close-packed text were required to record the hearings before the Committee on Agriculture, House of Representatives, 91st Cong., 1st Sess., from July 15, 1969, through December 8, 1969, under the title *General Farm Program and Food Stamp Program*. Parallel hearings before the Committee on Agriculture and Forestry of the United States Senate, 91st Cong., 2d Sess., filled 831 pages of equally close-packed text when published as *The Agricultural Act of 1970*.

Tobacco Organization prior to the AAA   Organization was not successful. As early as 1610 the colonial planters in Virginia learned tobacco culture from the Indians. Comparative advantage was so strong that tobacco soon became the colonies' major source of export earnings, with shipments going mainly to England. In 1630, however, prices fell sharply. The next year the Virginia Colonial Legislature passed a law fixing the minimum price to be paid to planters. This legislation offered temporary relief, but by 1639 production had increased so much that more direct action was taken to control production and marketing. Groups of planters were organized to curtail production by voluntary agreement, but resistance of some growers led to stronger measures. "Viewers" were employed to destroy inferior tobacco and, if necessary, to burn the crops. Some of this activity led to violence. From 1630 to the eve of the Revolutionary War in 1776, tobacco was the center of farmer protest or dissent in a continuing struggle for justice in compensation.

In 1890, after more than a century of relative quiet in tobacco policy, James B. Duke organized the American Tobacco Company, which represented five major cigarette manufacturers producing more than 90 percent of the nation's cigarettes. By agreements for the exclusive use of the best existing cigarette machines, by purchase of important companies in smoking tobacco, snuff, plug chewing tobacco, and cheroots, and by expansion through a series of fierce price wars, the company was able to carry out additions and mergers with many small firms and a few large ones, such as R. J. Reynolds and Liggett and Myers, so that by 1904 it owned or controlled some 250 formerly separate concerns and combinations in the tobacco industry. This huge company, in collaboration with a few others, exercised monopsony buying power to depress the prices received by growers.

In 1906 and 1907, farmers began to organize to try to counteract the price-depressing policies of the American Tobacco Company. The Burley Tobacco Society was organized in Kentucky to control production and raise tobacco prices. Efforts to organize were not specifically authorized by legislation, and the attempts to persuade growers to join the organization again resulted in violence. The property of growers who refused to cooperate was sometimes destroyed. Some of these growers were threatened with violence or loss of property and some were beaten. Other growers, riding horseback at night and known as "night riders," created terror and panic. In 1908, the movement was successful in forcing processors, organized in what was known as the Tobacco Trust, to agree to a large purchase contract. But the next year the Society could not control a sufficient portion of growers and the movement collapsed.

In May 1911, the U.S. Supreme Court held the Tobacco Trust a monopoly in violation of the Sherman Act because it had acted in "unreasonable" restraint of trade and had monopolized, and ordered it dissolved into a number of separate companies.[4] Subsequently, some 80 percent of the tobacco market was divided

[4]*U.S. v. American Tobacco Co.,* 221 U.S. 106 (1911).

between four major tobacco companies—American, Liggett and Myers, P. Lorillard, and R. J. Reynolds—and the balance among several others. Although the decree, before coming final, was vigorously attacked by Louis D. Brandeis and Felix H. Levy on the ground that it precluded the possibility of fair competition, it was allowed to stand.[5]

In May 1946, the Supreme Court again held that the principal cigarette manufacturers had conspired to restrain trade and to monopolize, and had monopolized as well.[6] Again the court ordered remedial action. But, although the case was clearly regarded as a legal milestone in the social control of oligopoly, the tobacco industry continued as an oligopsony-oligopoly model, under which a few major companies, in the absence of direct government intervention in the market, continued to exercise substantial market power and control.[7]

In the meantime, largely as a result of pressure from major farm organizations in the early 1920s, passage of the Capper Volstead Act permitted Burley tobacco growers to organize to form a potentially large cooperative. The cooperative would buy from growers under contract and regulate amounts sold to manufacturers with the objective of achieving higher and more stable prices. After a few years of operation the cooperative failed when it was unable to gain control of a sufficient portion of the Burley crop to attain the agreed price objective. This set the stage for more direct action by the federal government to help tobacco farmers.

Tobacco under the AAA The 1933 legislation changed the picture. Tobacco was named as one of the "basic" farm commodities in the Agricultural Adjustment Act of 1933,[8] and has been the only crop continuously under acreage allotments since that time. Allotments assigned to growers on the basis of historical records have been designed to limit the acreage that each grower can plant in tobacco, thus to regulate and obtain more stable prices at levels higher than would occur in a perfectly competitive market.

Since 1933, prices have been higher and more stable than they would have been without the program. Relative peace and stability have come to tobacco culture, along with a new measure of price stability. But in few parts of American agriculture do we find less desirable social and economic conditions within a family-farm setting. There is an unusually high proportion of small farms, and where the families rely on tobacco for their main income, poverty is widespread. In an attempt to provide distributive justice, numerous minimum-sized allot-

---

[5]191 Fed. 371 (1911), reported at 417 *et seq.* and reproduced as Defendents Exhibit 425, Record on Appeals, pp. 1747 ff.

[6]On appeal of a jury finding in the Eastern District Court of Kentucky (Criminal No. 6670), *American Tobacco Co. et. al. v. U.S.,* 148 Fed 416 (1944), 6th Circuit and U.S. Supreme Court (*ibid.,* 328 U.S. 781, 1946).

[7]For more complete discussion and analysis see William H. Nicholls, *Price Policies of the Cigarette Industry,* Nashville: The Vanderbilt University Press, 1951.

[8]The act named wheat, corn, cotton, rice, and tobacco as basic crops to which special legislative provisions for price support would apply. See *Century of Service: The First 100 Years of the United States Department of Agriculture, Yearbook of Agriculture,* 1963, p. 146.

ments have been distributed to growers. Throughout the industry the values of the allotments have been capitalized into land. Small farms have been encouraged to stay in tobacco culture.

It appears now that an income distribution that is reasonably acceptable in terms of distributive justice or of general welfare cannot be attained within the industry simply by policies in effect since 1933. Although the policies have contributed to income stability and to capital growth, especially among large growers, another approach emphasizing human resource policy (Chapter 10) must be taken if the adverse social and economic conditions among small growers are to be significantly improved. We shall return to this topic.

Shays' Rebellion: Commutative Injustice Leads to Armed Dissent, 1785–1786

What is known to history as Shays' Rebellion was an armed revolt or insurrection which, at its height in 1786, involved about 5,000 men under the command of Daniel Shays, a soldier of the Revolution.

The Articles of Confederation adopted after the Revolutionary War gave control of currency to the individual states rather than to the federal government, and soon after the war, a strong deflationary trend began. The states were ill-equipped to counter it, and prices fell sharply. But debts and taxes were not reduced. Severe hardship was brought to the people—mainly farmers—who had gone into debt when tobacco prices were high. The creditors were chiefly merchants and bankers. Many farmers who could not pay their debts were imprisoned and their mortgages were foreclosed.

The indentured farmers tried to obtain relief by a variety of means before turning to violence. They used the newspapers and legislatures to publicize their plight. They first asked for arbitration. When that request failed, they called for increased issuance of currency to induce inflation. In parts of New England they destroyed farm produce and went on market strikes to bring more attention to their situation. They burned the barns and haystacks of many who would not join their protest. In Rhode Island a law was passed requiring merchants to accept paper money at face value in place of gold. But the merchants responded by closing their shops, and farmers in turn went on strike. The law on state currency control was then rescinded.

Politicians and legislators extolled the work ethic by arguing that the unfavorable conditions would be alleviated if farmers would just work hard, be thrifty, and diversify their production in the interest of being more self-sufficient. Although this may have been good advice for less drastic situations, it was not adequate here. After a number of clashes with the state militia, the men who had gathered under Shays were defeated. Fourteen of the leaders were convicted of treason and sentenced to death in March 1787. Governor Bowdoin granted them a reprieve, however, and his successor, Governor Hancock, pardoned them all.[9]

---

[9]See Carl C. Taylor, *The Farmer's Movement,* New York: American Book Company, 1953, p. 36.

The apparent result of the rebellion was that farmers were given some concessions and a degree of leniency that they might not have obtained otherwise. But the country was ill-equipped to go much farther in respect to compensating them. Perhaps the main results were to bring attention to their situation and to show the need for a more functional or reliable monetary system.

Farm People in Agricultural Societies

Farm people as a class were without political organization, however, for many decades. Although agricultural societies began to appear almost immediately after the Revolution, and many were thriving about the time that de Tocqueville made his famous observations about democracy in America, these generally had small memberships, consisting mainly of substantial land and estate owners. The societies were mainly supportive of the existing social order, and in political influence they were developmental rather than reformist in perspective. They helped to promote the large number of local, county, and finally state fairs, for instance, which were largely agricultural in emphasis and peculiarly American in character. They favored the spread of educational opportunity, provided forums for discussion and debate, and served as a means of social organization and communication within rural communities. They were important in strengthening the basis for agricultural development in America.

The societies were generally antagonistic or at least not in sympathy with ideas such as those that sparked Shays' Rebellion or the insurrection about 1794 in the western mountain counties of Pennsylvania and Virginia known as the Whiskey Rebellion. The latter grew out of the federal excise on spirits enacted three years earlier to finance Secretary of the Treasury Alexander Hamilton's plan for the assumption of state debts. The farmers in these counties distilled most of the whiskey produced in the United States. The tax was an onerous one for them. They considered it unfair and discriminatory, and resistance to its payment became widespread. Several societies were formed in the region which served as forums for discussion of the grievance and for development of plans for resisting the federal tax agents. After several weeks of resistance, President George Washington, at Hamilton's behest, issued a proclamation in August 1794 ordering the insurgents to disperse and asking the governors of Pennsylvania, New Jersey, Maryland, and Virginia to call out 13,000 militiamen to restore order and compliance with the federal law. Resistance quickly collapsed and the authority of the federal government was reestablished, although local attempts to avoid the federal tax on small distilleries have been a characteristic of the Allegheny Mountain region down to the present day.

The tendency for the minority of people in the cities to dominate federal policy was not challenged until the election of Thomas Jefferson as President in 1800; later, with the election of Andrew Jackson in 1828, the farmers and pioneer settlers became a dominent political force. Numerous societies played an important role in development of policy positions and consensus. But a broad, strictly agricultural organization did not develop in America until after the Civil War, with the formation of the National Grange.

The National Grange

The National Grange has been notable since the early 1920s for its support of two-price plans for major export commodities of American agriculture, such as wheat, cotton, tobacco, feed grains, and rice. The first and most important of the farm organizations that developed in the post–Civil War period, it ranks as the oldest of those still active. In 1866 Oliver Hudson Kelley, employed in the office of the Commissioner of Agriculture in Washington, toured the Southern states to obtain statistical information and to reestablish statistical reporting. Apparently the deprivation, illiteracy, and lack of social life in rural communities impressed him deeply, and he resolved to do something about such conditions. After talking with a number of people, he and six men—together being "one fruit grower and six government clerks"—on December 4, 1867, founded, as a fraternal order patterned somewhat after the Masonic Lodge, the National Grange of the Patrons of Husbandry. Later Kelley resigned his government position to give full time to the organization.

Membership in the Grange grew slowly at first and then spread rapidly in the wake of falling farm prices[10] and the financial panic of 1873. By the end of that year, the Grange was organized in every state except Connecticut, Rhode Island, Delaware, and Nevada. Grange enthusiasts claimed in the next year or two "more than a million" members, and locals were being organized so rapidly that the national office could not keep track of them. The highest official figure of dues-paying members, however, was 858,050 in 1875. Other estimates have placed the real peak membership considerably lower.[11] Thereafter, membership dropped substantially to less than 100,000 by 1880, but throughout the ensuing years the Grange remained a political force and a continuing vehicle for expression of agrarian discontent.

Grange philosophy, rooted in ideas of fair prices or commutative justice, has brought the organization, in over 100 years of political action, to two main types of policy-oriented programs and legislation. The first type has to do with control and regulation of the institutions serving the farm sector: the railroads, banks, and firms performing marketing and service functions. In politics, this cast the Grange in a role in opposition to monopoly in all forms. In the early years, Grangers fought specifically against high freight costs, monopoly of transportation, and restrictive and unfair banking practices. These ideas also placed the Grange against the institutions required for development, such as finance and credit institutions, transportation, manufacturing, and even government itself. The Grange became identified with political candidates who professed a strong agrarian sympathy and who were anti-industry, antibank and antigovernment.[12]

By 1876 the Grange had won a number of legislative victories over the

---

[10]The index of farm prices (1910–14 = 100) declined from a high of 119 in 1860 to 93 in 1872 and to 67 in 1879. It rose to 95 in 1882 but fell again to 67 in 1886. The 30-year period from the end of the Civil War to the mid 1890s was the longest stretch of low farm prices in U.S. history.

[11]Robert L. Tontz estimated 451,000 members in 1875. See Tontz, "Membership of General Farmers' Organizations, United States 1874–1960," *Agricultural History,* Vol. 38, pp. 143–156, especially p. 147.

[12]See Carl C. Taylor, *op. cit.,* p. 42.

railroads. As a result, interest in the farmers' political clubs began to wane even though a high interest continued in such questions as currency inflation, better credit possibilities, the tariff, economy in government, taxation, and civil service reform.

Although the Grangers had hoped to obtain their political objectives through the established political parties, some of them decided in the early 1870s that this goal was impractical and they set out to organize their own party. In 1873 and 1874, parties expressing Granger interest appeared in several states under such labels as Independent, Reformers, Anti-monopolists, Farmer's Party, and so on. The parties died quickly, however, and for the next two decades the apparent majority of the Granger and farm or agrarian vote was loosely organized behind the Greenback movement, "free coinage" of silver, and Populism, which perhaps best expressed the strivings for various types of reform. The Grange and its related political movement fell to a low ebb with the defeat in 1896 of William Jennings Bryan, the Democratic-Populist candidate for the Presidency, and remained at a low level till the 1920s. Then its revival coalesced in the idea of export subsidy embodied in the Export Debenture Plan and the McNary-Haugen bills. We may regard this concern as the second major area of Grange policy.

Although the Grange was among the first, if not the first, to support a large amount of federal and state legislation, the primary goal, according to the Master of the National Grange, "is the realignment of those established and fully accepted government-provided protective devices so as to supply equitable income opportunites to farmers." And "the problem of just and equitable relationships . . . (between agriculture and the remainder of the American economy) could best be solved by developing specific commodity programs. . . ."[13] This tenet places the Grange in the position of supporting a "base-surplus" pricing philosophy aimed toward a "parity of income" concept, which would involve (1) voluntary supply management of basic crops, under which participation would be obtained by direct payment to producers,[14] and (2) a two-price plan for major export commodities so that they would sell for more in the domestic market than abroad. In the Grange philosophy, the parity concept should be retained as a basis for minimum pricing, and studies of cost of production should play a guiding role in determining the level.[15] The concept of compensatory justice, with strong attachment to democratic and free enterprise creeds, appears to dominate the philosophy and program proposals supported by the organization.

The Farmers' Alliance: An Amalgamation of Liberal Agrarian Movements

A movement known as the Farmers' Alliance, which embraced or incorporated a number of farmers' or agrarian groups, began in Texas in 1873. Its growth

[13]Herschel D. Newsom, "Goals and Values Underlying Programs of the Grange," *Farm Goals in Conflict,* Ames: The Iowa State University Press, 1963, p. 87.

[14]Testimony on *Agricultural Act of 1970* (Senate), *op. cit,* p. 266.

[15]For more complete statements of testimony presented by Grange officials, see *Agricultural Act of 1970* (Senate), *op. cit.,* pp. 226–280, or *General Farm Program and Food Stamp Program* (House), pp. 147–203.

coincided with the decline of the Grange in the 1870s and its membership went on expanding as farmers and other agrarian groups continued their agitation for currency inflation and their opposition to high railroad rates, restrictive mortgage practices, "soulless" corporations, national banks, and the like. The Farmers' Alliance reached its peak about 1890. It then claimed more than a million members, and 40 members of the Congress elected in 1890 were pledged to support its main principles or demands. These related to various social or political reforms, and, in the South particularly, much attention was given to cooperative buying and selling.

The Louisiana Farmers Union (not to be confused with the National Farmers Union) originated in 1880 following a discussion by 12 men who had been cleaning a graveyard. By 1887 it had grown to 10,000 members. Meanwhile, the Texas Farmers' Alliance, which had started out as an "anti-horsethief" and "anti-land-grab" organization, had gathered about 100,000 members. The two organizations merged in 1887 and were joined by the North Carolina Farmers Association in 1888.

Another group, which had started a debating club called the Agricultural Wheel, merged with the Brothers of Freedom, and they proposed reducing crop acreage to control farm production and to raise farm prices. This group also favored a graduated income tax and low tariffs. By 1887 eight states in the Southwest were organized under the merged organization. In 1889 this group and the Farmers' Alliance consolidated into what was known as the Farmers' and Laborers' Union of America. Later the name was changed to the National Farmers' Alliance and Industrial Union (not to be confused with the Farmers Union) when the Laborers' Union of Kansas joined the organization.

The Northern National Alliance, organized in Chicago in 1880, which stood for protection of farmers from the "tyranny of monopoly" and the "encroachments of concentrated capital," enlisted about 400,000 members by 1887. They were located in the Northwest Central and Great Plains states, where low prices, especially for wheat and livestock, were causing hardships and discontent.

This Alliance was closely associated with, or embraced by, other groups. The Farmers' Mutual Benefit Association, formed in Illinois in 1882 in an effort to improve wheat marketing, grew to about 150,000 members, concentrated mainly in the Midwest. Some other groups associated with the Alliance movement were the Farmers' Congress, Farmers' League, Alliance of the Colored Farmers of Texas, and the Patrons of Industry. Such groups were represented at a noteworthy meeting in St. Louis in 1889.

In 1890 the National Farmers' Alliance and Industrial Union, sometimes called the Southern Farmers' Alliance, claimed up to 3 million members, but less than 250,000 were reputed to have supported it financially. The year before, at the meeting in St. Louis, an attempt had been made to unite the Southern Alliance with other regional groups, but the effort had been only partially successful. Even more notable was the professed joining with labor "for mutual defense and protection as well as for united political action."

The Alliance movement, holding another notable convention at Ocala, Florida, in 1890, adopted the "Ocala Platform," which expressed most of the principles for which farm organizations were fighting. The Alliance movement, however, did not have a permanent organization at the national level. Its agitation was an embarrassment to the major political parties and they worked to undermine the Alliance's strength by stimulating dissension among the state groups and by attempting to absorb the membership into supporting their own platforms. Its political force consequently eroded rapidly, and in 1896 the defeat of William Jennings Bryan, with whom the Alliance groups had been largely associated, sounded the death knell of the organization.

The Alliance is important in public policy for a number of reasons. It gave the farmers and their associates a sense of worth and status. It showed, as had the Grange, that through organization a political influence can be exerted. It demonstrated the need for good management and organization, particularly at the national level; and the policies that were enunciated helped to identify meaningful areas for progress in later years. The "Subtreasury plan" of the Southern Alliance is worth noting in this context as a forerunner of the operation of the Federal Farm Board that was begun in 1929 and of the nonrecourse loan system that has been used extensively since the mid 1930s. This plan would have established a branch of the United States Treasury in each agricultural county. Owners of food commodities would deposit their products in approved warehouses and receive legal tender up to 80 percent of the market value of the commodity. The commodity could be redeemed by repaying the advance plus carrying charges or, if not redeemed within 12 months, it could be sold. The plan could be used to expand the currency system and to prevent distress sales of commodities in periods of low prices.

MODERN ORGANIZATION ACTIVITY

The early years of this century saw a turning point in farm organization philosophy and activity which may be regarded as the intellectual spawning ground of modern organization activity. This turning point at first was the center of the activities of three organizations that were strongly oriented toward attempting to obtain fair returns (commutative justice) for the American farmer. They were the American Society of Equity, the Nonpartisan League, and the Farmers Union. Later, the American Farm Bureau Federation, the largest of the organizations, was formed with a philosophic orientation more strongly favoring unregulated private enterprise (the enterprise creed), with greater faith in the benefits of research and education (personal integrity), and with an economic outlook that embodied more reliance on the competitive market (the work ethic). Still later, the National Farmers Organization, a protest organization that apparently embodied the frustrations of many groups, was established on the concept of direct action as earlier emphasized in the beginning of the American Society of Equity and in the long struggle over tobacco. Its goal was to hold farm products off the market and to regulate marketing to obtain more favorable prices (commutative justice). Finally—68 years after the founding of the American Society of Equity and the Farmers Union—the Grange, the Farmers Union, and the

National Farmers Organization joined with 21 other primarily producer-oriented organizations to form the Coalition of Farm Organizations to support passage of the Agricultural Act of 1970.[16] The American Farm Bureau Federation (AFBF), in action consistent with its long tradition of independence from other organizations of discontent and protest, held itself aloof from the Coalition and disagreed strongly with the provisions of the bill for continuance of government price support and production control.[17] The act as finally passed fell short of the wishes of the Coalition, which favored stronger government programs to regulate output and raise farm prices, and went too far for the AFBF in terms of government control over agriculture.

American Society of Equity

The American Society of Equity, founded on December 24, 1902, by Edward A. Everitt of Indianapolis, a feed and seed merchant and publisher of the journal *Up-to-Date Farming and Gardening,* was one of the first twentieth-century organizations to gain prominence and perhaps the first systematically to express some of the ideas for price support policy that have been conspicuous in public policy since the 1930s. The organization moved into a political vacuum created by the defeat of the Alliance and by the decline in political activity of the Grange which, perhaps also influenced by prosperity beginning late in the so-called Gay Nineties, had reverted to its original status as a cultural and educational body. Sometime before 1901, the Farmers' Alliance had completely disintegrated, and Populism, as expressed in the Democratic party's platform in 1896, had lost its status as an independent political movement.

Everitt thought of himself as a practical man. He believed that his objective should be to contribute to farmers' profits by forming a gigantic holding movement which would allow farmers to set prices themselves instead of permitting "the captains of industry, the promoter, the underwriter, the labor leader, and the grain gambler" to dictate to them.[18] He thought that the violent fluctuations sometimes experienced in farm produce markets were entirely unnecessary and could be prevented by controlling the "visible" supply so as to prevent excessive dumping, particularly at harvesttime. By devising simple machinery for setting prices and by keeping farm produce off the market until these prices were obtained, farmers would not only obtain relief from the ills of monopoly but would become the greatest of all monopolists. He believed that the rapid growth of the American economy and the increasing demand for food would make production control unnecessary. The founding concepts of the Society in respect to storage were very similar to those embodied in legislation establishing the Federal Farm Board in 1929, in speeches of the Secretary of Agriculture, Henry A. Wallace, in the 1930s when he was advocating establishment of the "Ever

---

[16]As discussed in Chap. 5.

[17]See testimony of Charles B. Shuman, president of the AFBF, *General Farm Program and Food Stamp Program,* House of Representatives, Committee on Agriculture, 91st Cong., 1st Sess., pp. 206–207.

[18]Edward A. Everitt, *The Third Power,* 3d ed., (1905), p. 35; 4th ed. (1907), p. vii.

Normal Granary," and in operating concepts and practices of the Commodity Credit Corporation throughout most of its history. The idea of direct holding action has been one of the main devices used by the National Farmers Organization to affect prices.

The Equity, as the Society was commonly called, was highly concentrated in structure and control; but organization at the national level, and a field force for organizing the kind of programs suggested, were nonexistent. Everitt and his journal, with its seven directors, each of whom was supposed to be an expert in some line of agriculture, were to shape the marketing policies of the organization and to provide a clearinghouse of information. Such "equitable prices" as set by this board were to be the minimum price for each commodity below which the farmers were urged not to sell. Dues, initially set at $1 a year and including a subscription to *Up-to-Date Farming,* proved to be entirely inadequate to carry out a recruiting or organizational program. Nevertheless, they were later reduced to 50 cents and then to 25 cents to curb rumors that Everitt was building a fortune at the expense of the Society. Membership, apparently having reached a peak of about 100,000 in 1906, fell to 26,259 by October 1908. By that time, however, 14 states had formed societies which were no part of the original scheme. Equity retained its greatest strength in Kentucky, Wisconsin, Minnesota, the Dakotas, and Montana.

The Burley Tobacco Society: Direct Action

From 1906 to 1909, activity, centering in Kentucky and Tennessee and involving Equity in a leading role in organizing the Burley Tobacco Society to control production and marketing of tobacco, marked the last as well as the most conspicuous effort of the Society to put its price-fixing policies into operation. This activity was directed toward forcing the American Tobacco Company, more commonly called the Tobacco Trust, to pay higher prices by improving the hopelessly unsatisfactory bargaining position of the growers, most of whom were in acute poverty and distress.[19] In 1906 Equity took the lead in a "40-day whirlwind campaign" to obtain pledges from farmers not to sell their crops at the prices being offered by the Trust. By January 2, 1907, it was reported that 58 percent of the 92,000 acres estimated to have been planted to tobacco in 1906 were pledged to the Burley Tobacco Society. On July 11, 1907, with about 103,000 acres in the pool out of an estimated 135,000 acres planted, representatives of tobacco associations from seven leading states met to organize to control the entire country. In the fall of 1907, the Burley Tobacco Society announced that it would attempt to eliminate the 1908 crop completely.

---

[19]The Trust, through a combination of purchases, mergers, and other actions, had by 1906 extended its control to 82 percent of the chewing tobacco, 71 percent of the smoking tobacco, 96 percent of the snuff, 81 percent of the little cigars, and 83 percent of the cigarettes. In 1907, Sherman Act proceedings were started against the Trust, and in May 1911, the Supreme Court held the Tobacco Trust a monopoly in violation of the Sherman Act and ordered its dissolution into a number of companies. For further history and discussion, see William F. Nicholls, *Price Policies of the Cigarette Industry,* Nashville, Tenn.: Vanderbilt University Press, 1951, Chap. 3.

The indifference or hostility of many growers toward the program resulted in a decision by some members of the Society to employ force in order to achieve conformity. This resulted in organization of the groups of men who became known as night riders, as we have noted, who attempted to coerce uncooperative growers into conformity with this program. These men assaulted tobacco buyers, set fire to tobacco sheds, sowed tobacco seedling beds with salt, and in many communities created a general state of terror. The revulsion against such tactics brought the movement into disrepute, and within a year it collapsed.

The Equity in Wisconsin and the Northwest:
The Equity Cooperative Exchange

The Equity activities in Wisconsin and the Northwest are notable as a forerunner of the activities of more modern farm organizations. Here the antimonopolistic philosophies of Equity leaders, who held that middlemen, boards of trade, bankers, and railroad interests were responsible for depressed farm prices, found fertile ground. In Wisconsin the Equity penetrated into the tobacco economy to control production, but the movement fizzled out within a year. It leveled a barrage of criticism against the Wisconsin Agricultural College as being too production-minded and urged in the Wisconsin legislature and elsewhere that more classes in marketing should be offered. It was active in promoting agricultural cooperatives. Partially as a result of its influence, the Wisconsin legislature passed a long list of progressive measures including provisions for an industrial commission, workmen's compensation, state life insurance, a state income tax, limitations on the labor of women and children, a state binder-twine plant, a cooperative-marketing law, and a state board of public affairs.[20]

Meanwhile, in Minnesota, in the Dakotas, and finally in Montana, wheat farmers were organizing under Equity leadership to form the Equity Cooperative Exchange, the first cooperative terminal marketing agency of importance in the United States. Later a livestock marketing firm was added. The Equity gained its strength from the discontent of the spring wheat growers. In eloquent prose Equity leaders denounced the grain merchants for depressing prices, underweighing, undergrading, and excessive docking of grain for foreign material. The Equity movement, although closely aligned at times with the broader progressive movement headed by Wisconsin Senator Robert (Old Bob) M. La Follette, was, in the Equity Cooperative Exchange, solely concerned with helping the spring wheat farmers to combat the organized grain exchange and achieve what they considered fairer marketing practices and more favorable prices. The complaints were widespread and support was at first enthusiastic. But, through various organizational difficulties and because the Exchange could not establish an organization of sufficient strength to achieve its purposes, its position was eroded. Within a few years after World War I, the movement was replaced by the more tightly organized Nonpartisan League and the Farmers Union. The Equity

[20]Theodore Saloutos and John D. Hicks, *Agricultural Discontent in the Middle West, 1900– 1939,* Madison: The University of Wisconsin Press, 1951, p. 131.

had helped to achieve some improvements in grading, warehousing, and credit facilities and to bring more attention to the problems of marketing and distribution.

The Nonpartisan League: Farmer Organization to Political Party[21]

The Nonpartisan League is unique among modern farm organizations in having transformed an organizational activity into a specific political party. From its beginning in North Dakota in 1915 to the present day, it has maintained a political identity and power structure in state politics in North Dakota as one of two major and generally contending branches of the Republican party, the other being known briefly as the Independent Voters' Association and in later years as the Republican Organizing Committee. Although the Nonpartisan League's influence was felt in several states, affiliated occasionally with other parties and with other farm organizations, especially the Farmers Union, it was only in North Dakota that the League developed political power sufficient at times to control a state government and to determine a state's industrial policy. It has differed from other organizations in having its greatest success in the region where it originated. It emphasized political action to achieve economic ends, being deeply influenced by the socialist movement and by organized labor.

The success of the League varied widely among the states. It came into power in North Dakota with specific and wide-ranging proposals for state financing, ownership and control of certain agricultural industries and public utilities, state hail insurance, exemption of farm improvements from taxation, and general reforms to make the state and local governments more responsive to popular mandate. In Minnesota it attempted to gain control of the Republican party, then dominant in the state. When it failed in this, it gave its support to candidates favorable to its views. These were affiliated mainly with the Farmer-Labor party. Although attempts were made to establish the League program in several other states, including Wisconsin, South Dakota, Montana, and Nebraska, the efforts were not successful. Senator La Follette, of Wisconsin, who gave some intellectual respectability to the League through his progressive leadership, came to view its program as largely impractical and in competition with his more broadly based progressive movement. Finally, except for North Dakota, the League as a strictly farmers' movement gave way to the rising influence of the Farmers Union and to the organizing efforts of the Farm Bureau Federation.

In North Dakota the League succeeded in winning state financing, construction, and operation of the Terminal Mill and Elevator at Grand Forks and in obtaining the establishment of the Bank of North Dakota. As a movement in state and national policy, however, undoubtedly the League's greatest contribution is its demonstration of how an essentially agrarian movement can exert a

---

[21]This section draws primarily on Saloutos and Hicks, *op. cit.,* chaps. 6 and 7. For further background discussion see Theodore Saloutos, "The Rise of the Nonpartisan League in North Dakota 1915–1917," *Agricultural History,* XX, January 1946, pp. 43–61, and "The Expansion and Decline of the Nonpartisan League in the Middle West, 1917–1921," *ibid.,* October 1946, pp. 235–252.

political influence within an established political party and how, through support of selected political candidates, it can influence the course of public policy. It shows also, perhaps, that an organization with a specific doctrine and program either succeeds through its own organization or gives way to movements that are more loosely or more flexibly organized for political activity.

The Farmers Union: Commutative and Distributive Justice

The Farmers' Educational and Cooperative Union of America, or the Farmers Union, as it has been called, was founded in Raines County, Texas, and was a contemporary of the Equity and the Nonpartisan League. It had its major growth as these other organizations declined. Through the years, it has emphasized organization for economic purposes, favoring the interests of the small family farm and strong action by the federal government to support prices of farm commodities. The traditional goal expressed in convention after convention, was "cost of production" for major farm commodities. Most often, since at least the early 1930s, this goal has been expressed as 100 percent of parity or some modest variation of it. This value or goal has brought the Union into sharp conflict at times with some other farm organizations, most notably the American Farm Bureau Federation, and with some national administrations, congressmen, and others who favored lower levels of support. This position, however, has also allowed the Union to join in alliances with other organizations and groups, as was demonstrated in 1970 by the Coalition of Farm Organizations (mentioned earlier). Its position has also given the Union a strong appeal in many areas, most notably in the Great Plains and Western states, where the main coalescing force has been price policy for wheat and feed grains.

The Union has strongly supported national administrations that favor its general viewpoint; for example, it gave strong support to Secretary of Agriculture Charles Brannan of the Truman administration and Secretary Orville Freeman of the Kennedy and Johnson administrations. It gave substantial backing to the Brannan Plan for high-level support of farm prices and incomes while other general farm organizations opposed the plan. It was vigorous in its advocacy of the Emergency Feed Grain Program in the Freeman years. It has fought long and hard against policies, such as those of Secretary Ezra T. Benson in the Eisenhower administration, that would decrease the role of government through lower support of farm prices and incomes.

The Farmers Union describes itself in the legislative field as "the only national farm organization representing the liberal point of view" and as the champion of the small, family-type, marginal farmer. Union literature states, "The economic and social aim of the Farmers Union is full parity of living for family farmers. High farm prices can make but a partial contribution to this goal. For this reason Farmers Union asks for an economy of abundance, federal aid to education, ample credit for production adjustment, an active program to limit corporation farms and assure family farmers of economic units of land."[22]

---

[22]From statements of policy provided in Farmers Union reports of annual meetings and other sources.

One of the general policy leaflets summarizes the belief in the family farm as the best-suited economic organization for American agriculture as follows:[23] "The Farmers Union believes that (1) family farming (*a*) is the most efficient method of food and fiber production; (*b*) provides greatest protection for the consumer since family farmers ask only to be allowed to earn parity of income with other groups; (*c*) is essential to a truly democratic way of life. (2) The small business nature of farming is a strong bulwark against Communism or Fascism, but it leaves the family farmer without protection in the market place."

The Farmers Union stresses a strong role for government in public policy, frequently asserting that "farm prices are made in Washington" and that it is the obligation of government to see these prices are made at parity levels. This approach has brought the Union into close alignment with organized labor on many matters, and in some instances into formal coalition with the CIO. George Patton, who was national president of the Union from 1940 to 1967, served for several years as vice president of the CIO's Political Action Committee. The Union, along with labor unions, is credited with being one of the chief forces in the enactment of the Employment Act of 1946, which set up the Council of Economic Advisers to the President. The Farmers Union was one of the organizations sponsoring the Farm Security Act of 1937, which was designed to improve the lot of marginal farmers. The Union has been a consistent supporter of the loan and subsistence program of the Farmers' Home Administration and of the federal Rural Electrification Administration through which money has been made available at relatively low interest rates for power development. The Union support for government development programs and its alignment with organized labor has brought it into conflict at times with the Farm Bureau and the Grange. The Union philosophy on price supports has been consistently at odds with the philosophy of the Farm Bureau except for some in the 1930s. Thus the basis exists for continuing conflict on important issues.

Farmers Union Business Cooperative Enterprise

The Union—in contrast with the Farmers' Alliance, the Grange, and some of the Equity movements—has always emphasized the business approach to problems of buying farm services and selling farm products. In fact, to a considerable extent, the Union was built on the ruins of the Farmers' Alliance. Its founders felt that the decline of both the Grange and the Alliance was largely due to excessive involvement in political crusades with not enough attention given to economic matters.

The Union built its organization through the establishment of cooperative enterprises of many kinds—cotton gins, warehouses, grain elevators, fertilizer buying pools, petroleum cooperatives, and in the early years, occasionally a bank, hotel, or livery stable. As early as 1910, its officers claimed to have a system of warehouses in every cotton-growing state in the South. By the 1920s, Union cooperatives were highly successful in Nebraska and to a lesser extent in

---

[23]*The Modern Family Farm*, Farmers Union Policy Leaflet No. 10, p. 3, as quoted by Gilbert Rohde, "Goals and Values Underlying Programs of Farmers' Union," *Farm Goals in Conflict*, Ames: The Iowa State University Press, 1963, p. 81.

Kansas. The big growth in Union activities occurred in the spring wheat states of the North as the power of the Equity disintegrated and as organizing efforts of the Nonpartisan League largely ceased in every state but North Dakota.

The one cooperative that contributed most importantly to the Union growth and stability of membership was the system of grain elevators headed by the Farmers' Union Grain Terminal Association with headquarters in St. Paul, Minnesota. The Association continues to expand and now has country elevators in more than a dozen states and large terminal elevators on the Great Lakes, the Mississippi, and the West Coast. In addition, Union-sponsored cooperatives are important in petroleum, livestock, dairy operations, and the insurance field. The Association derives its success from sound business practices applied in a competitive situation where the organization is able to gain the confidence and loyalty of farmers and farm groups.

There are three economic doctrines that exert an overpowering influence on the Union's position with regard to policy:

The first, related to the democratic creed, is that the maintenance and safeguarding of democracy depends on building an economic system that provides potential abundance for all instead of controlled production and controlled distribution for the specific purpose of price fixing. This is a basis for its support of cooperatives.

The second, related to ideas of commutative justice and somewhat at odds with the democratic creed, is the premise that farmers are entitled to cost of production, or, as frequently stated, 100 percent of parity. In an agriculture that is advancing rapidly in technology, these prices generally will be above the prices realized in a competitive market. This, however, defines the organization's position with respect to price support legislation requiring either significant control over production and marketing, or heavy government subsidy payments to producers, or strong government action to subsidize consumption both domestically and abroad.

Third, the self-identification of the Union as the only general farm organization representing the liberal point of view aligns it with the interests of the small family-type farmer, with the problems of farm labor, and with the underprivileged. Thus it establishes the organization as a leading champion of distributive justice.

This combination of values and creeds places the Union strongly in favor of big government programs to expand markets, to bring about development, and to help the low-income sector. An important conflict exists in farm production policy. Although support is given to concepts and programs of an expanding economy, the Union has favored strict control of farm output to raise prices.

Union Antagonism to Agricultural Research and Education

Union members and organizations at both state and national levels have often looked with disfavor, if not outright antagonism, at agricultural research and educational programs. The land grant universities have received the special brunt of the Union's antagonism for their work in increasing agricultural output. Starting in the 1920s and continuing with varying intensity throughout the years,

Union members and particularly those in the Midwest displayed a belligerent attitude toward the efforts of the agricultural colleges to help farmers become more efficient.[24] By drawing on the concept that the demand for farm output is highly inelastic, the Union has interpreted agricultural progress in output-increasing technology as depressing farm prices and incomes. The Union is of course correct in this view, provided that the advances in technology are not fully balanced with adjustments mainly toward fewer and larger farms. Strong support for this type of adjustment cannot be offered by the Union without bringing it into sharp conflict with its basic support for the small family farm. The only way out of this dilemma is a "proper" mix of policies to "balance" technical progress and adjustment.

Although the Farmers Union has played a leading role among organizations of discontent and protest, its actions have not always been sufficiently militant to meet the felt needs of many farmers. More militant organizations have risen and gained political following, namely the Farmers' Holiday Association in the 1930s and the National Farmers Organization (NFO), starting in the late 1950s.

The Farmers' Holiday Association[25]

In the history of farm policy, the most aggressive upheavals have been led by newly organized groups that were formed in situations of adversity and that grew as a result of actions proposed to deal with misfortune. Shays' Rebellion, the tobacco "riots," and the Nonpartisan League are examples previously discussed. The most aggressive upheaval of the twentieth century was the Farmers' Holiday Association movement. It had its roots in the late 1920s, reached its peak of activity in 1932–34, and died out about 1937. The other, perhaps in some respects equally aggressive and certainly better organized, was the National Farmers Organization, widely known as NFO. This movement began in 1955, achieved its most active moments with all-out farm-product holding actions in 1962 and 1968, and continued as an active organization in the 1970s. In each case the organization began at a community or county level and grew in farmer discontent with falling prices and adverse market conditions. This discontent was heightened by the slow response or seeming indifference of existing organizations.

The Farmers' Holiday Association is conceived as an attempt, somewhat desperate at times, by family-type farmers from better than average communities to save their farms and homes. The roots of the movement can be traced to two quite different episodes.

One was the formation in 1925 of a loose confederation of 24 farm groups in

---

[24]For examples beginning in the 1920s, see Saloutos and Hicks, *op. cit.*, pp. 226–239.

[25]Much of the discussion on the Farmers' Holiday Association is taken from John L. Shover, *Cornbelt Rebellion: The Farmers' Holiday Association*, Urbana: The University of Illinois Press, 1965. See also Christiana M. Campbell, *The Farm Bureau and the New Deal, A Study of the Making of National Policy, 1933–1940*, Urbana: The University of Illinois Press, 1962, and William D. Rowley, *M. L. Wilson and the Campaign for the Domestic Allotment*, Lincoln: University of Nebraska Press, 1970.

the so-called Cornbelt Committee. The purpose was to achieve harmony in support of a federal agricultural program and to bring pressure for its approval. The initiative came from the National Farmers Union, where the idea had first been suggested by Milo Reno, President of the Iowa Farmers Union. The committee functioned for several years and gave strong support to the McNary-Haugen movement. The second veto of these bills followed by establishment of the Federal Farm Board caused a rift in the committee. One faction favored cooperation with the new Board to press for additional legislation. The other, which came to dominate the committee, opposed the Board as an ineffective policy implement, and argued instead for a strong drive for immediate cost-of-production prices through inflation and direct government support of farm prices. As a last resort, this group would have had farmers withhold produce from the market as a pressure tactic to obtain higher prices. In 1931, several of the members of the committee resigned in protest against the proposal, and the committee disintegrated.

The second root of the Farmers' Holiday Association came from a more isolated event in 1931—the so-called Cow War which centered in Cedar County, Iowa, and surrounding counties.[26] This was a protest against compulsory testing of cows for tuberculosis. Iowa law required slaughter of cows that tests showed to be tuberculous. Since high-producing dairy cows sold for slaughter brought only a fraction of their real value as dairy animals, the program resulted in considerable loss and sometimes financial ruin to some dairy farmers. Many were not convinced that the program was necessary or justified, and determined farmer resistance halted it. Sixty-five additional sheriffs' deputies were sworn in to protect the veterinarians doing the testing and to permit the program to continue; but finally 450 farmers, armed with clubs, fought through tear gas to rout the deputies. Several were injured, the state officials' automobiles were smashed, and one veterinarian was painfully bruised. Governor Dan Turner declared martial law and sent three regiments of the Iowa National Guard, about 2,000 men, to preserve order. Within a week, the testing program was completed in Cedar and four neighboring counties where resistance had also occurred.

Although the Cow War was a rather isolated event, it is important because it indicated the temper of the time and it was a catalyst for events to follow. The break in farm prices that started in 1929 began a downward spiral in April 1931 that went unchecked until June 1932, at which time hogs sold for $3 and cattle around $5 per hundred pounds, and corn was about 10 cents per bushel. Such prices, if continued, would bring economic disaster. By early 1932, plans were being discussed for organizing to withhold farm produce from market in order to obtain higher prices. From February to June 1932, the *Iowa Union Farmer* devoted nearly all its editorial space to consideration of plans for a withholding action, while Milo Reno and other Union leaders toured the counties of western Iowa to discuss the plans for withholding. Appeals for support were extended to

---

[26]Frank Dileva, "Frantic Farmers Fight Law," *Annals of Iowa,* XXXII, October 1953, p. 88 as cited in Shover, *op. cit.,* pp. 29–32.

surrounding states. On May 3 about 2,000 farmers from Iowa and seven other states met at the Iowa fairgrounds to form the Farmers' Holiday Association as a national organization.

The next two years saw the heights of the Association's activity. It involved strikes to withhold produce—primarily milk and hogs—from market, Holiday backers hoped such strikes would become nationwide, but they were largely limited to the Midwest. Also, foreclosures on farm property were prevented by intimidation of bidders at farm auctions so that chattels were bid in for a few cents or a dollar or two and returned to the farmer. Furthermore, the Association promised active agitation and threats of revolution unless Congress took more drastic action to inflate the currency or in some way to guarantee farmers cost of production. Passage of the Agricultural Act of 1933, which established the Agricultural Adjustment Administration (AAA), was considered a sellout by the Holiday leaders. The legislation, however, helped to blunt the organization's drive, and by 1934 the attempts at strikes and withholding actions, and the violence and picketing that had accompanied them, were largely over. By 1934 the only part of the Association's legislative program that remained viable was a bill introduced by Senator Lynn J. Frazier and Congressman William J. Lemke, both of North Dakota, for inflation and cheaper farm credit. The Holiday movement splintered and faltered, in part discredited by attempts of the Communist party of the United States to take over leadership of the Association, somewhat diverted into support of third-party campaigns, and perhaps most effectively diluted by the initial successes of the Agricultural Adjustment Administration, more adequate credit programs, and rising farm prices. The Holiday Association may be remembered for having expressed the hopes of many farm people for economic and social reform in a period of hard times when the terms of trade were highly adverse, but more importantly it may have been one of the most influential farm organizations to force Congress and the administration to act on national farm policy legislation.

The National Farmers Organization[27]

The National Farmers Organization (NFO) began in 1955 as a farmers' protest against declining farm prices and the farm policies of Secretary of Agriculture Ezra T. Benson, in the Eisenhower administration, which called for lowering price supports to get the government out of agriculture. The NFO also arose because of a void in farm organization activity in the western Corn Belt when farmers found themselves in trouble. Although the Farmers Union had long advocated strong federal action to control farm output to raise prices, the Union as well as the Grange had relatively little influence in the Corn Belt as compared with the Farm Bureau, which generally supported the Eisenhower-Benson farm program philosophy. Farmers who were dissatisfied, or who felt that farm prices

[27]For further background, see George Brandsberg, *The Two Sides of the NFO's Battle,* Ames: The Iowa State University Press, 1964; Charles Walters, Jr., *The Biggest Farm Story of the Decade* (37-page pamphlet), *Holding Action,* and *Angry Testament,* Kansas City: Halcyon House.

were too low, provided a fertile source of support for a new organization having a more militant program.

The NFO program was built on the central idea—also found in the Equity and Farmers' Holiday movements as well as in the Sapiro plan for cooperatives—that farmers, through concerted action to hold produce off the market, could have a substantial effect in raising prices. The organizing technique was to set a target price well above current market levels and to get farmers to sign a membership agreement to withhold products from market when called to do so by the NFO. The original protest action as envisaged, to petition the government with a list of grievances and demands, brought few results and, in its search for a different approach, the NFO adopted almost exclusively a program of collective bargaining. The old idea of a farmers' strike or "holiday" was thus revived as a holding action.

The NFO's action plan was simply that of organizing farmers to hold products off the market until buyers and processors were willing to pay the prices the NFO demanded. Before the NFO would sell, however, it planned to force buyers to sign contracts to assure that price levels would remain up to the agreed level. The success of the program depended on organizing enough farmers to make the collective bargaining effective. If this action succeeded, a plan would be put into effect for production and marketing quotas to bring supply and demand into balance at the desired price.

The NFO attracted numerous farmers to meetings that were called to initiate holding actions. On August 28, 1962, after three limited "test holding actions" had been tried, an estimated 20,000 people met at the Veterans Memorial Auditorium in Des Moines, Iowa, to vociferously register their approval of an "all-out holding action" to start on August 31. Enthusiasm for this meeting had been increased through protests and publicity against a report, *An Adaptive Program for Agriculture,*[28] by the Research and Policy Committee of the Committee for Economic Development (CED). This report defined the farm problem as a need for "massive adjustment" of resources, especially human resources, through reduction of the farm labor force by about one-third, or 2 million workers, in the next five years. "The adaptive approach," as stated in the report, called for immediate reduction of government price supports for wheat, cotton, rice, and feed grains so that farmers would not be misled or encouraged to keep excessive resources in agriculture. The CED stressed vocational training other than in farming in agricultural areas and called for more federal aid to education, thus to prepare young people for nonfarming careers before they became committed to agriculture.

The CED report thus proposed a completely different solution to the problem of low farm income than that planned by the NFO. The NFO leaders used the report as a target for their antagonism to the society that they claimed was oppressing them. Membership of the Research and Policy Committee of the

[28]New York: Committee for Economic Development, July 15, 1962. See chap. 5 for further discussion.

CED included 47 highly prominent men of the American business community. The NFO decided to boycott some of the firms represented on the committee, especially the Ford Motor Company and Sears, Roebuck and Company,[29] although it announced that the ensuing action was not an organized boycott, but spontaneous and simultaneous efforts by farmers to let people know how they felt. During so-called catalog marches, which occurred in at least seven cities, Sears Roebuck catalogs were piled in front of the firm's stores. About the same time in at least six cities, caravans of Ford cars and trucks were driven around Ford firms to demonstrate displeasure with the CED report. Both Sears and Ford subsequently announced that they did not officially endorse the report and that the members on the committee were advocates of the plan solely as private citizens. This quieted the demonstrations, but they had served to draw national attention to the NFO and its plans for withholding.[30]

The NFO Withholding Actions

The NFO withholding action that followed was the most extensive effort of its type up to that time. It began on September 4 on hogs and cattle, with plans to continue for six months; but it "recessed" as a result of a national board meeting the night of October 2. Apparently, during the action the NFO had almost unanimous support of its membership, but there was opposition from outside the organization that took two or three forms.

First, some major farm organizations were openly hostile and, in one way or another, urged against cooperation. The National Livestock Feeders Association, headquartered in Omaha, issued a statement calling for orderly marketing, observing that interference with the flow of livestock to market, when ended, would cause bunched shipments and depressed prices. The president of the Iowa Farm Bureau said that his organization recognized the right of farmers to market when and how they chose and that legal action should be taken against any interference or intimidation.[31] The American National Cattlemen's Association, headquartered in Denver, stated that it represented thousands of breeders, ranchers, and feeders through nearly 150 affiliated organizations, none of which was involved in the holding action, and that its members traditionally favored

[29]Theodore O. Yntema, chairman, Finance Committee, Ford Motor Company, was chairman of the Research and Policy Committee, and Theodore V. Houser, director, Sears, Roebuck and Company, was one of the two vice-chairmen of the Research and Policy Committee and chairman of CED's board of trustees.

[30]A report, issued in 1952 by the Farm Foundation, and containing strikingly similar recommendations, was apparently ignored by the NFO. See *Turning the Searchlight on Farm Policy, A Forthright Analysis of Experience, Lessons, Criteria, and Recommendations,* Chicago: The Farm Foundation, 1952. This report was prepared by a 13-man conference committee of prominent agricultural economists. Recommendation No. 7 in the report (p. 77) states: "Temporary withholding of farm commodities from the market occupies a very limited place in our recommendation of a farm policy for the future." Two special conditions considered appropriate for government action would be "(a) as a buttress to the income supplement program in time of severe depression and (b) for military stockpiling."

[31]*Omaha World-Herald,* Aug. 31, 1962, and Brandsberg, *op. cit.,* p. 104.

supply and demand marketing and opposed withholding or management of livestock marketing.[32]

Second, acts of violence either by NFO proponents or by others aroused fears and public opposition to the withholding action. Violence included burning three barns in Missouri, throwing bottles, rocks, tomatoes, or paint at trucks presumably on their way to market, and in two or three cases shots were fired at livestock trucks.[33] Attempts by NFO members or sympathizers to picket livestock auctions and to slow down market operations by bringing one or two animals at a time to livestock markets aroused opposition of market personnel. The executive director of the St. Paul Retail Food Dealers Association said he thought the NFO was violating Minnesota law in its holding action.[34]

Public reaction came quickly. Missouri Governor Dalton stated that 50 incidents had been reported to the Missouri highway patrol and that "we are going to try to stop these law violations."[35] The Colorado Cattle Feeders Association said that "mob rule" cannot substitute for orderly and efficient marketing of livestock.[36] The National Livestock Feeders Association claimed that it was "emphatically evident" that the bulk of feeders wanted "no part of any movement that would disrupt the orderly flow of meat animals."[37]

Although the holding action had been planned to last six months and to include milk, which was not done, recessing the action on October 2 may be interpreted as a reaction to such public opposition or to other factors. NFO President Oren Staley claimed that the action was a success in terms of participation and price effects, that the acts of violence had not been advocated or recommended by NFO, and "tremendous strength" had been shown by the organization.[38] A comparison of prices for hogs and cattle suggests that the holding action had some effect on prices in the second and third weeks,[39] but by the first week in October hog prices were more than a dollar per hundredweight lower in Chicago and in interior markets in Iowa and Minnesota than they had been in the week ending September 1, just prior to the holding action. The average price of choice slaughter steers at Chicago was $29.08 per hundredweight in the week ending October 6, 17 cents higher than during the week ending September 1.[40]

The NFO's September 1962 holding action showed that the volume of farm

[32]American National Cattlemen's Association, Denver, news release, Sept. 12, 1962, and Brandsberg, *op. cit.,* p. 117.

[33]Brandsberg, *op. cit.,* pp. 108–124.

[34]Sioux Falls *Argus-Leader,* Sept. 12, 1962, and Brandsberg, *op. cit.,* p. 118.

[35]*Kansas City Star,* Sept. 17, 1962.

[36]*The Stockman's Journal,* Sept. 19, 1962.

[37]*Ibid.*

[38]Brandsberg, *op. cit.,* p. 132.

[39]The average price of choice slaughter steers at Chicago reached a peak of $29.91 per hundredweight in the week ending September 15, compared with $28.91 in the week ending September 1. Hogs reached a peak of $19.56 in the week ending September 22, compared with $18.71 in the week ending September 1. From USDA data quoted by Brandsberg, *op. cit.,* pp. 134–135.

[40]*Ibid.*

marketing can be altered, and some price effects may have occurred during the action. Also, NFO had demonstrated political power and the allegiance of members and their sympathizers had been tested. But apparently the long-run price effect was negligible, and the change in the direction and amount of gross farm income was and still is indeterminate.

While the holding action was in process, the Farmers Union released a policy statement blaming the Congress, the Farm Bureau, the American Meat Institute, chain stores, and "other like-minded groups" for the farmers' frustration and economic distress that led to an organization such as NFO. The statement, while implying that holding actions were futile, reiterated the need for "a Federal legislative program for achieving a sound and effective bargaining position for the American farmer."[41] The Farm Bureau and the Grange held aloof from the argument, but statements from officials of each organization, given six months later, indicated that they were skeptical of the effectiveness of the holding action.[42]

The NFO annual meeting held in December 1962 witnessed a three-way, all-out battle for the presidency by two candidates in opposition to Staley, the incumbent president. The two challengers advocated limited instead of general all-out action. Staley argued for general holding actions as the continuing basis for policy and, apparently on the basis of this stand, he was reelected by a large majority.

The NFO's policy to base its program on general or all-out holding actions seemed to be affirmed at the 1962 annual meeting. In pursuit of this policy, emphasis shifted to enrollment of dairy farmers and to attempts to develop agreements with processors of dairy products to buy under contract with the NFO. Apparently, contracts were much easier to obtain with dairy firms since markets were more localized and dairy processors were familiar with purchasing under federal milk marketing orders. The dairy processors were largely cooperatives with farmer members on their boards, some of whom would be sympathetic to the NFO.

Sporadic "wild-cat," limited holding actions in the summer of 1963 for soybeans, grains, and livestock apparently had little effect on markets as the NFO prepared for another all-out action which finally began on August 19, 1964. President Staley announced target prices of $32.25 per hundredweight for choice grade cattle, $22.75 for hogs, and $29.45 for choice wooled lambs, compared with prices in Chicago of $24 to $26 per hundredweight for cattle, $16.40 to $17.50 for hogs, and $23 for lambs. Opposition was encountered again from some of the same sources as in 1962, but in this case there was practically no violence. Also, the holding action was apparently less effective and was soon "recessed." In 1964, prices received by farmers averaged lower for beef cattle than in any year

---

[41]*Official Statement of the National Farmers Union Executive Committee,* Denver: National Farmers Union, Sept. 7, 1962, mimeographed release.
[42]Brandsberg, *op. cit.,* p. 229.

since 1957, and for hogs the price was the lowest since 1959.[43] In 1965 both markets began a strong upward trend.

The membership drive continued to enlist milk farmers and to obtain contracts with milk processors for purchase of milk through the NFO. On March 15, 1967, a milk holding action was begun. In this case, the NFO undertook its own publicity through its home office in Corning, Iowa. Strategy involved dumping milk and, where dairy plants had contracts with NFO, processing milk into powder, butter, and cheese, with farmers retaining title. Although thousands of pounds of milk were poured on the ground, serious shortages were prevented by diverting milk formerly used to produce butter and cheese to fluid uses. On March 29 the federal government filed an anti trust suit in the Federal Court at Des Moines, Iowa, for the purpose of obtaining an injunction to halt the holding action. Since NFO is organized under the Capper-Volstead Act of 1922, which permits farmers to combine in cooperative organizations for purposes that include bargaining, the holding action was adjudged legal and court action was limited to issuing a restraining order against violence.

The holding actions seemed to be heading for complete failure when two unions, the Meat Cutters and the Teamsters, decided to honor NFO picket lines in Nashville, Tennessee. This action effectively cut off milk to Nashville for all but emergency uses, and the NFO action was saved here by unions the NFO had earlier rejected. Finally, on April 11, federal hearings were begun to review the levels of fluid milk prices in Midwest markets. There may be a moot point whether these hearings were prompted by the holding action or were held sooner than had been planned. The farm and wholesale prices for milk showed a general advance over the next three years, which occurred without a substantial increase in government storage stocks.[44] The NFO milk holding action may be viewed as instrumental in affecting milk prices even though no comprehensive solution had been developed for handling the excess supplies that would be developed by setting prices above market equilibrium levels.

The events of the milk holding action apparently encouraged the NFO to try an "all commodity" holding action that started on January 11, 1968. An estimated crowd of 34,500 had gathered in Des Moines in August 1967 to vote for an all-out action on all commodities as soon as suitable arrangements could be made. After this meeting, statements became increasingly threatening, and after the action began, Staley was quoted as saying that NFO planned to "shut down the agricultural plant of America" unless farm prices improved.[45] He announced plans for an NFO "grain bank" with minimum selling prices of $1.50 per bushel for corn, $2 for wheat, and $3 for soybeans. The effect desired would be to centralize in NFO the nationwide selling of grain. Also, he stated, "We are organized from the Pennsylvania border to the west coast, and from Canada to

[43]U.S. Department of Agriculture data.
[44]From USDA data.
[45]*St. Louis Post-Dispatch,* Jan. 17, 1968.

the Tennessee-Kentucky border—and we mean business. . . . We want all commodities to reach a climax of effect at the same time. This will give us a strong bargaining position."[46]

Whether the NFO holding action had a positive effect on grain prices is again a matter of some dispute. United States Department of Agriculture data list the U.S. farm prices for the 1967–68 crop year, which includes the holding action, as $1.03 per bushel for corn, $1.39 for wheat, and $2.49 for soybeans, compared with respective 1966–67 prices of $1.24 for corn, $1.63 for wheat, and $2.75 for soybeans. Corn recovered in 1968–69 and further in 1969–70, a trend that may be correlated with strengthened livestock markets, while wheat and soybeans continued to decline in 1968 and 1979 but began to recover in 1970.

NFO Bargaining Power: A Policy Conclusion

Politically, the NFO has attempted to maintain a position of nonpartisanship, as have most other farm organizations of the twentieth century. Since the NFO has concentrated almost exclusively on price policy, however, it has fought against any position of moderation in this policy and has supported programs that promised higher prices. A major stimulus for the beginning of the NFO is found in the policies of the Eisenhower-Benson administration, which was avowedly for getting the government out of agriculture by reducing reliance of the farm sector on price support programs. NFO leaders used Benson's efforts to reduce support levels as evidence of the need for their program. During Secretary Freeman's initial appearance as featured speaker at the NFO's annual meeting in December 1961, a crowd of 6,000 NFO members and sympathizers howled and whistled their enthusiastic support of his proposals for "managed abundance" through producer adjustment and producer marketing programs which would be designed and administered by farmers themselves. They roared approval of his statement, "Our greatest problem is that we don't have enough bargaining power in the market place."[47] It was quite clear that the NFO, in the tradition of the American Society of Equity, wanted agriculture to be one big monopoly, believing that if enough government support could be given to this goal, surely it would succeed. The 1961 meeting was probably the high point of the organization's rapport with a national administration. From then on, although Freeman received NFO's support as the lesser of two (or more) evils, the main criticism of government by the NFO spokesmen was that programs were too little and too late. This justified direct action.

The NFO program depends substantially on farmers' dissatisfaction with prices. Thus the strength of the NFO movement has been directly correlated with adversity in the terms of trade for agriculture—growing when prices are adverse and declining when they are favorable. The NFO continued a high level of agitation throughout the 1960s and the early 1970s, threatening at times more vigorous holding actions. The sharp rise in farm product prices in 1972 and 1973

[46]*Ibid.*
[47]Brandsberg, *op. cit.,* p. 87.

blunted its activity but did not destroy the organization's basic structure. The seeds of discontent lay somewhat dormant but ready to sprout again whenever conditions were deemed to be appropriate for direct action.

What does the NFO accomplish? It has served as a representative for a political and economic point of view. It has demonstrated some of the limits of direct action in bargaining by a voluntary organization (although there appears to have been some coercion in obtaining membership). It was more successful in the dairy industry, where markets are more localized, than in the livestock and grain industries; and most successful of all when it combined in a local market (Nashville) with existing labor organizations. To significantly affect prices in grain and livestock for a sustained time, however, the organization is clearly insufficient for the tasks at hand. Finally, therefore, it may demonstrate, as did the Alliance movements, the American Society of Equity, and the Farmers' Holiday Association before it, that an organization must have the means to implement its goals, and that the goals must be realistic in terms of the political power structure, if the organization is to survive as a continuing political force in American society.

THE AMERICAN FARM BUREAU FEDERATION[48]

The American Farm Bureau Federation (AFBF), by far the largest of general farm organizations, is in origin and basic philosophy strikingly different from most of the others. It originated in county organizations called farm bureaus that were formed to teach better farming methods. These were the basis for state organizations, which came together to form the national organization, the AFBF, and to move quickly into national policy. To provide services to farmers, the organization helped to establish cooperatives at county, state, regional, and national levels. The diversity of this movement and its business success help to account for the growth and stability of the organization.

The farm bureau movement has embraced a more conservative philosophy than most other organizations, emphasizing the enterprise creed or private enterprise, to create "conditions whereby farmers may earn and get a high per-family real income in a manner that will preserve freedom and opportunity."[49] A

---

[48]The literature on the Farm Bureau is extensive. Some of the most useful references are: An original and penetrating analysis of policymaking in the 1930s is presented by Christiana McFadyen Campbell in *The Farm Bureau and the New Deal, A Study of the Making of National Policy, 1933–40,* Urbana: The University of Illinois Press, 1962. This book won the 1961 award of the Agricultural History Society. Early formation of bureau activity and policy is described in M. C. Burritt, *The County Agent and the Farm Bureau,* New York: Harcourt, Brace and Company, Inc., 1922. A comprehensive study is presented by Orville M. Kile, *The Farm Bureau Through Three Decades,* Baltimore: The Waverly Press, 1948. A good discussion of the problems appears in Theodore Saloutos and John D. Hicks, *Agricultural Discontent in the Middle West, 1900–1939,* Madison: The University of Wisconsin Press, 1951, chap. 9. Changes in relationship that occurred mainly in the late 1950s are presented by William J. Block, *The Separation of the Farm Bureau and the Extension Service, Political Issues in a Federal System,* Illinois Studies in the Social Sciences, Vol. 47, Urbana: The University of Illinois Press, 1960.

[49]W. E. Hamilton, *Farm Goals in Conflict,* Ames: The Iowa State University Press, 1963, p. 71.

strong faith in the ability of the market to bring about these conditions, plus the responsibility of being the most powerful of the various farm groups, has encouraged a generally conservative attitude among the leadership.

The Farm Bureau organization attempts to develop its position on policy through locally organized discussion groups, state resolutions committees and state conventions, and annual meetings of delegates to the national convention. The AFBF board, sometimes called the American, seeks to maintain the image that the Bureau is a grass-roots organization representing some 1.8 million families and that it "speaks" with a democratic and unified voice in respect to their interests.[50] Although most states have an educational program in public policy, and positions are developed on issues in which grass-roots opinions are frequently solicited, the articulation of policy depends heavily on state and national officers through various media, including county and state publiciations, and the national magazine *The American Farmer* (formerly *The Nation's Agriculture*).

Throughout the history of the organization, the positions on national policy have depended importantly on views of the president and other national officers. Beginning in the 1930s, Edward A. O'Neal of Alabama, who was president of the AFBF from 1931 to 1947, and Earl C. Smith of Illinois, who was vice president, *were* Farm Bureau as far as policy was concerned. They pushed hard for the New Deal and its price-raising programs; and it was common knowledge that the resolutions committee for the annual meeting, appointed by O'Neal and dominated by Chairman Smith, was a major force in determining the Bureau's policies.[51] From 1947 to 1970, under the presidencies of Allan Kline of Iowa (1947 to 1954) and Charles B. Shuman of Illinois (1954 to 1970), AFBF statements were inspired by a common philosophy of minimum government involvement in agriculture. This principle brought the AFBF into opposition to the farm programs of the Truman, Kennedy, and Johnson administrations and into giving general support to the Eisenhower-Benson philosophy of getting the government out of agriculture.[52] Whereas O'Neal and Smith encouraged a strong role for government but a more conservative one than that favored by the more active farm protest groups, Kline and Shuman were averse to production controls, subsidy payments, storage programs, international trade agreements, direct government lending as through the Farmers Home Administration, etcetera. Shuman especially liked to argue that government supply management did not work and that government-owned stocks were bad for farmers. In his view, the operation of government supply-management programs depended on political rather than economic decisions, which was bad for farmers. Such programs made farmers too dependent on government for a substantial part of their

[50]See testimony of Charles B. Shuman, president of AFBF, Aug. 5, 1969, before the Committee on Agriculture, House of Representatives, 91st Cong., 1st Sess. on *General Farm Program and Food Stamp Program,* Serial Q, Part 1, pp. 205–249. Membership was listed by Shuman at 1,796,641.

[51]See Campbell, *The Farm Bureau and the New Deal, op. cit.,* p. 16.

[52]See Wesley McCune, *Who's Behind Our Farm Policy,* New York: Frederick A. Praeger, Inc., 1956, pp. 15–33.

income, and they created pressures for international commodity agreements, which he also viewed as unfavorable for farmers.[53] A similar policy orientation, although perhaps less adamant, continued under William Kuhfuss of Illinois, who was elected president of the AFBF in 1970. The election of Allan Grant of California as president and of Robert Delano of Virginia as vice president, to take office in 1976, presaged a change in emphasis in the AFBF toward more government involvement in production and marketing.

Early Growth and Development

In the spring of 1911 a pioneering pattern for educational work under Bureau auspices was set when the Chamber of Commerce of Binghamton, New York, organized the Binghamton County Farm Bureau. It was agreed that the Bureau would hire an agent to help the farmers in the county develop better farming methods, that the U.S. Department of Agriculture and the railroad company serving Binghamton would finance the project, and that the state college of agriculture at Cornell University would give advice and encouragement to the agent and the farmers involved.[54]

This pattern, or a variation of it, was soon repeated by groups in other states. Minnesota, North Dakota, Wisconsin, and Illinois quickly adopted legislation allowing supervisors affiliated with county farm bureaus or developmental associations to raise money for educational purposes. The earliest group to set a pattern for the Middle West was the Better Farming Association of North Dakota, organized in November 1911. The Association received financial support from counties, districts, railroads, wholesale houses, and the North Dakota Bankers' Association. Cooperative supervision was supplied by the state agricultural college. Soon thereafter, Sears, Roebuck and Company provided $1 million for experts to advise and demonstrate in 100 counties throughout the United States. The International Harvester Company and the Chicago Board of Trade were each reported to have set aside $1 million for similar purposes. Finally, the Smith-Lever Act of May 8 and June 30, 1914, committed the federal government to aid the county agents with matching grants to states, to be administered through the land grant college in each participating state and the new federal-state Cooperative Extension Service.

A pattern had been set. Success of county bureaus created a need for state organizations to coordinate the work of the counties, to enable them to discuss mutual problems, to profit from their varying experiences, and to give farmers a power and an influence, as was sometimes said, commensurate with the importance of agriculture. The Missouri Farm Bureau, established in March of 1915, was the first state organization, and by the fall of 1918, there were 10 or 12 more state organizations.

The first meeting of the farm bureaus of the Middle West gave support to

[53]From Charles B. Shuman's statement opposing major provisions of the Food and Agriculture Act of 1965 and the Agricultural Act of 1970, in *General Farm Program and Food Stamp Program, op. cit.*, p. 206.

[54]Saloutos and Hicks, *op. cit.*, p. 262.

cooperative marketing, and when, under the initiative of the New York Farm
Bureau Federation, the states came together in 1919 and 1920 to form a national
organization, a pattern for educational work had been established. A need was
recognized for development of cooperative marketing as a conservative, busi-
nesslike approach to the economic problems of agriculture. Although a few
wanted a national policy favoring arbitrary price fixing based upon "cost of
production" plus a "reasonable profit," and the building of public warehouses to
serve public needs, the more modest principle favoring cooperative marketing
prevailed. A crucial, broad and somewhat conflicting resolution asserted the right
of every group of people to organize for its own material benefit and the right of
every American citizen "to the free and unhampered privilege of disposing of his
labor or products thereof as he may individually require."[55] Thus the AFBF was
born with, and has continued, a distinctly conservative enterprise creed or
philosophy quite different from the protest movements of the Grange, the
Farmers Union, and the Nonpartisan League.

The founders of the AFBF hoped that all or nearly all other farm groups
would join in the federation. At least two other organizations with a similar idea
had preceded it—the Farmers' National Headquarters in 1910, which had plans
for a "temple of agriculture" in Washington, and the National Board of Farm
Organizations, formally organized in Washington in 1917 to bring unity to the
various farm groups through a broad-ranging action program. At an AFBF
meeting in July 1920, called for the purpose of organizing for marketing work in
grain, the representatives of the National Board of Farm Organizations, who
were largely from the Farmers Union, requested the right to name half the
marketing committee. Their request was denied and they left the conference. The
Missouri Farmers' Association, which was to become the largest independent
state farmers' organization in the country, also declined to federate with the
AFBF when it was denied a request for preferential treatment in grain marketing.
The Nebraska Farmers Union, which had had considerable success in cooperative marketing, also demanded preferential treatment, as did the Equity Cooperative Exchange and the Farmers' National Grain Dealers Association, the educational and service agency for state grain marketing associations in the Middle
West.

The seeds were sown for a rift in farm organization activity which has
continued to the present time and, seemingly, will continue indefinitely into the
future. The Farmers Union became an outspoken and sometimes vitriolic critic
of the Bureau. The Union considered the AFBF an auxiliary of the U.S.
Chamber of Commerce, big business, and the agricultural colleges. The officers
of the American Society of Equity bitterly assailed the ties of the Farm Bureau
with county agents and the agricultural colleges. More importantly, officers of
the Equity held as suspect the Bureau's acceptance of support from the Chicago
Board of Trade, which gave $1,000 to each of the first 100 counties to organize a
farm bureau. The Equity alleged that the Bureau was antilabor, that it received

[55]Saloutos and Hicks, *op. cit.*, p. 269.

money from packers who opposed control of meat packing, that it was reactionary in failing to endorse proposals for a progressive federal inheritance tax, that its support of federal farm credit did not meet the need for fairer farm prices, and finally that it was out to crush other farm organizations by its links with the U.S. Department of Agriculture and the Cooperative Extension Service. The Nonpartisan League looked upon the Bureau as "an unholy alliance" with country bankers and alleged that the Bureau had been organized specifically to check the League.

Farm Bureau: Production, Education, and Research

Farm bureaus received a strong impetus during World War I under the slogan "Food will win the war and write the peace," and they were primarily production oriented. Under the Emergency Food Production Act, passed August 14, 1917, federal funds were supplied to extend the county agent system as rapidly as possible. In the early postwar years, as county appropriations and farm bureau membership dues made up a larger and larger proportion of the funds used for county agents' salaries and expenses, the farm bureaus took over more of the general management functions. They became involved in commercial activities such as cooperative buying of farm supplies and selling of farm produce; and as these activities grew in a number of states, the bureau rather than the county agent tended to become the dominant factor. Soon opposition from competing merchants made it necessary for the Secretary of Agriculture to rule that the county agents must limit their activities to educational work and, although agents might go as far as to give actual assistance in organizing cooperative groups, they were to have nothing to do with the ordering of goods, handling of funds, or other business transactions.[56] Their main function was expected to be education through meetings, demonstrations, and farmers' institutes, with support from the state agricultural colleges and the state and federal extension organizations.

This general policy for extension education and cooperative activity not only differentiated the farm bureaus from other farm organizations; to a significant degree, it delineated the programs and policies of the state agricultural colleges and extension services. While cooperative marketing was an important part of bureau philosophy, the major thrust of county agent work and of the county farm bureaus was to help farmers in production. Although high-level farm production depressed farm prices, the county farm bureaus and individual farmers correctly recognized that an individual farmer might improve his own situation by increasing his farm's productivity or by being more efficient in lowering costs of production. As Jonathan Swift stated in *Gulliver's Travels,* the accepted gospel to farm prosperity was to "make two blades of grass to grow upon a spot of ground where only one grew before." The county farm bureaus were important as local sponsoring agencies for educational work to spread this gospel of scientific agriculture.

The close working and contractual relationships between farm bureaus and

---

[56]See O. M. Kile, *The Farm Bureau Through Three Decades, op. cit.,* p. 44.

the agricultural college extension services, however, were strongly protested for some 35 years by other farm organizations, the Grange and the Farmers Union especially, until the contractual ties were broken by Secretary of Agriculture Ezra Taft Benson, in Memorandum No. 1368, November 24, 1954.[57] It specified that no Department of Agriculture employee, such as a county extension worker, should accept the use of free office space or contributions for salary or traveling expense from any general or specialized organization of farmers. It also stated that no employee should advocate any one organization for working with the Department of Agriculture, solicit members for any such organization, or approve contracts for the Department with it.

Issuance of the memorandum was preceded by a power struggle between Farm Bureau and other groups. In 1939, the independently organized Rural Electrification Administration and the Farm Credit Administration were both transferred to the Department of Agriculture. This shift aroused fears of farm organization leaders that Department controls over these agencies could build political machines that would greatly reduce the power of their organizations. To counteract this possibility, the AFBF presented a plan for reorganization of the Department of Agriculture to put more power in the hands of the Cooperative Extension Service and to allow more state and local control. But, because of the close relationship between farm bureaus and extension services, this was not acceptable to other farm organizations and the plan was dropped. Then, attacks by the AFBF on the Farm Security Administration, which had a direct lending and family assistance program for low-income farmers, which was regarded by the AFBF as too independent and ambitious, widened the area of conflict between the Farm Bureau and the Farmers Union, especially. The AFBF's criticism of a land use planning program of the Bureau of Agricultural Economics in the USDA, which it also regarded as too ambitious or ''socialistic,'' brought further charges that the Farm Bureau was dictating USDA and extension policy. In 1946, an AFBF proposal that the Soil Conservation Service be ''coordinated'' with the Extension Service further heightened opposition to the ties between the Farm Bureau and the Extension Service.[58] Finally, after several proposals to legislate a separation had failed, largely because of Farm Bureau opposition, Secretary Benson took administrative action to effect the split despite the objections of both Farm Bureau and various college deans and state extension directors.

The long struggle demonstrated some of the political power of the Farm Bureau. It exposed the many degress of competition that exist among farm organizations as well as the stresses within some of them. It had shown how organizations under attack will rally to their own defense and how different they are in their effectiveness in resisting such attack. Although certain agreements

[57]William J. Block, *The Separation of the Farm Bureau and the Extension Service, op. cit.,* pp. 214–277.

[58]For an excellent discussion of the conflicts over soil conservation policies, see Charles M. Hardin, *The Politics of Agriculture,* Glencoe, Ill.: The Free Press, 1952, chap. 3.

were terminated, in most states Farm Bureau still continued a closer working relationship with colleges and extension services than did most other farm groups.

The emphasis upon the application of scientific agriculture through county programs and close cooperation with the state agricultural colleges and the Cooperative Extension Service at all levels has had an important effect on the development of education and research. In most states the Farm Bureau has been credited with influential support of youth and adult agricultural education programs and with obtaining appropriations for land-grant colleges and state universities for teaching, extension, and research. The AFBF has contributed significantly to maintaining and increasing federal appropriations to the federal-state Cooperative Extension Service.[59] Additionally, consistent with the belief that educational and scientific progress will produce generally desirable results, Farm Bureau has played a leading role at the county and state level in promoting fairs and exhibits that emphasize agriculture, family living, and rural life. This activity builds on a tradition that started in American with the founders of the early colonies and that prospered in the popular acceptance of ideas stressing the work ethic, private property, individual initiative, and so on.

Farm Bureau: Cooperative Marketing

The first AFBF meeting, in November 1919, plunged almost at once into a struggle, which the Bureau has waged ever since, to solve what was called "the marketing problem"—a term covering complaints of low prices as well as high handling charges and various trade abuses, both real and fancied. Many members were inclined to believe that cooperative marketing would be a major part of the solution, especially if used as a collective bargaining device. To permit cooperatives to be used for bargaining purposes, the members felt that agricultural cooperatives should be freed from the restraints of the Sherman Antitrust Act. The meeting therefore adopted a resolution somewhat at odds with the assertion that each individual should have the privilege of disposing of his labor or products "as he may individually require," declaring "We demand that State and National legislative bodies grant agriculture the rights and privileges of collective bargaining."[60]

The possiblities of collective bargaining or some other means to affect farm prices were in the minds of many. At the first permanent organization meeting in March 1920, Henry C. Wallace, soon to be named Secretary of Agriculture, succinctly expressed what he thought should be the purpose of the organization:

> Now, people, if the purpose of this organization is to carry on the sort of work which the Farm Bureaus have been doing heretofore, which is for the purpose of education, for the purpose of stimulating production, the general line of work that has been carried on, then the Farm Bureau organization as you have started it now will serve

[59]Campbell, *op. cit.,* p. 82.
[60]Kile, *op. cit.* p. 82.

no great useful purpose; in fact, it will do harm. But if this is anything at all it is a business organization, to secure economic justice for the farmers.[61]

At a general conference of grain growers, called by AFBF President Howard in July 1920, Aaron Sapiro, the legal representative of several successful California cooperatives including the prune growers and some of the nut growers, created high excitement by his description of the successes of their cooperatives in marketing their crops.[62] He precipitated a heated argument by asserting that all growers should be bound by ironclad contracts under the regulations of an authorized cooperative. The idea was implanted that such cooperative control must be along commodity lines. That is, grain growers would need one organization, livestock producers another one, and so on. A grain committee of 19 members, appointed as a result of this meeting, diligently reviewed the situation and reported, in February 1921, that "the fundamental reason for lack of adequate profits in farming is a faulty system of marketing farm products. All other great industries merchandise their products under one direction. . . ."[63] The committee proposed a nonstock, nonprofit organization to consist exclusively of grain growers, each to pay a $10 entrance fee and sign a contract to sell his grain for a period of five years through one or more specified ways to be determined by a national selling agency. An organization called the U.S. Grain Growers was formed. A year was spent in soliciting membership at heavy expense and against the strong opposition of the organized grain trade. Failure to set up a sales agency caused the AFBF, in August 1922, to ask for the resignation of the entire board of directors. A new board controlled by Midwestern farm bureaus was formed, but dissension, mounting debts, and the growing realization that the organization could provide little more than moderate savings in commissions and handling charges lessened enthusiasm. Two years later, the U.S. Grain Growers was liquidated without loss to its backers.

Experience with other committees was less ambitious and, overall, more productive. A livestock committee's recommendation resulted in the formation of the National Livestock Producers Association for policy direction, and in time this led to Bureau-sponsored marketing cooperatives in various terminal livestock markets and to producer groups in many states. A division of dairy marketing was established in the AFBF to stimulate and guide marketing organization work. Wool pools were organized in producing states. The American Cotton Growers' Exchange was organized. The Federated Fruit and Vegetable Growers, Inc. was organized, with sales agencies in 140 markets. It operated for several years with fair success only to fail in the economic crash of 1930.

These activities were the beginning of Bureau-sponsored cooperatives, which have since grown to large size in various states. Some states have been successful in certain activities and some in others. The largest state organization,

[61]As quoted by Campbell, *op cit.,* p. 31, from AFBF, *Minutes of the Annual Meeting* (organization meeting), March 3–4, 1920, p. 224.
    [62]Kile, *op. cit.,* pp. 82–84.
    [63]Kile, *op. cit.,* p. 86.

the Illinois Agricultural Association, sponsored Farm Services, Inc., which has been outstandingly successful in service organizations, including full lines of both insurance cooperatives and farm supply cooperatives. The FS, Inc., combined with its Iowa counterpart in the mid 1960s to form one of the largest farm cooperative groups in the United States. In addition, the Illinois Agricultural Association has given support to agricultural education and has been very influential in the Illinois legislature on agricultural questions and as a leading sponsor of other measures, such as the Illinois income tax and revision of the state constitution.

In New York State, the Farm Bureau has separated the three functions— education, legislation, and cooperative business enterprise. The emphasis has always been on agricultural education, in cooperation with Cornell University and the county agents. Cooperative or business activities have been conducted through the Grange League Federation, composed of representatives of the state Farm Bureau, the Grange, and the Dairymen's League.

The Ohio Farm Bureau has been noted for its emphasis on serving farmers as consumers, with a highly successful insurance program being its most outstanding service. Participation in this program is not limited to Bureau members, but a percentage of the net income is retained for financing other Bureau activities.

Cooperatives sponsored by the Farm Bureau have spread widely over the United States, largely as farmer-patron, business-managed enterprises but, most significant for policy, except for instances of fluid milk and some fruits and vegetables, none of these has developed into a national bargaining cooperative as visualized by Sapiro and some Bureau founders. A tacit but real "states' rights" doctrine limits the AFBF, or the American, to advice and persuasion. Although the American has the residual right to audit state associations and some of their sponsored enterprises, it does not as a matter of policy do so. The cooperatives are businesses operated under state and local authority, and, with the exception noted, they do not bargain collectively in national markets. Although representatives of cooperatives are frequently heard in regard to matters of policy, as in congressional hearings and in numerous instances in state and local affairs, the cooperatives are more appropriately regarded as primarily business organizations offering a variety of commerical services in competition with other private and corporate firms.

For several years the major policy issue involving cooperatives, including Farm Bureau cooperatives as well as others, has been the question of taxation of dividends to patrons. The cooperatives have successfully defended the position that such dividends are refunds of money due patrons, rather than income to the cooperative, and that this money should not be subject to corporate income taxes. Competing noncooperative businesses have contended that all income from business operations should be subject to tax regardless of its ultimate disposition, that is, withheld for growth and development, distributed to stockholders, or returned as a dividend to patrons. Businesses not organized as cooperatives also have contended that exemption of dividends constitutes discriminatory taxation and offers an unfair advantage to the cooperative enterprise. The success of cooperatives in defending their position attests both to their political power and to the broad acceptance of the cooperative principle in American business enterprise.

The principle of cooperative bargaining by farm producers with companies purchasing farm products under contract has been extended by the Farm Bureau in sponsoring the American Agricultural Marketing Association (AAMA) and its subunits. The Bureau, serving as a parent organization, has assisted groups of farmers to organize an association, to establish by-laws and rules for operation, and so on. Farmers who agree to hold membership in an association then may receive the benefits of any marketing contract negotiated by their association with contracting parties, such as fruit or vegetable processors and meat packers. Although the AAMA has proved itself to be significant alongside the NFO, its bargaining position has been weakened by several factors: Initially at least, membership has been voluntary; the benefits of this type of organization have been hard to substantiate; and generally it has not been possible to gain control over a significant portion of the total supply. The great bulk of grain and livestock commodities produced by Farm Bureau members does not benefit from the type of bargaining inherent in the AAMA. So the Association has retained a generally low profile in the organization of the AFBF, even though the principle has been a useful if somewhat surprising extension of Farm Bureau operations.

The AFBF in National Policymaking

The prime function of the American Farm Bureau Federation from the beginning has been to make or influence national policy on a broad front. Although the major and consistent concern of the American has been farm price policy, it has taken positions on a wide variety of issues including monetary and fiscal policy, tariff policy, and antimonopoly measures. The AFBF has been consistent in urging responsibility in monetary and fiscal matters, generally favoring, at least since the end of World War II, balanced budgets, fiscal responsibility, and monetary restraint. During the New Deal period the American aligned itself with urban labor groups in favor of spending and against what O'Neal called "the economy boys." This position was broadly supported within the Farm Bureau, thus continuing an agrarian tradition, going back to the 1870s, of monetary expansion in times of low or depressed farm prices.

The Farm Bureau position on tariff policy has not been so consistent. During the 1920s the organization turned for salvation, under Midwest proddings and then through a Midwest-South alliance, to work for a more protective tariff and to support the McNary-Haugen bills for export subsidy. The breakdown of world trade following the adoption of the highly protective Smoot-Hawley tariff in 1930 brought considerable disillusionment within Bureau ranks. But, the organization was slow to change and the adoption of the original Roosevelt reciprocal trade program owed little to Farm Bureau support. Under the goading of O'Neal, a Southerner steeped in heredity and tradition and by conviction a free trader, the Bureau came to support the reciprocal trade program, although considerable opposition continued especially in the Midwest. During World War II the unfilled food demands of the Allies obliterated the traditional issues. Almost continually since then, the position has been one of urging support for expansionist trade policy. Under the leadership of Kline, Shuman, and Kuhfuss, the policy was to work for moderate tariffs and expansion of trade. From 1972–73 on, the demonstrated importance of exports to farm prosperity in America helped to assure continued support for a strong trade policy.

Although it is widely recognized among the Bureau's membership that an expansionist trade policy is in the economic interest of American agriculture, strong conflicting interests must also be acknowledged. Domestic cotton textile millers, who were placed at a competitive disadvantage with foreign millers through domestic price supports on cotton that were above world market prices, ardently urged restriction on imports of cotton textiles. Especially, they wish for a firm quota on imports from Japan. The beef cattle industry, perhaps the strongest element of the enterprise creed in American agriculture, represented by the National Livestock Feeders Association and the American National Cattlemen's Association, which include many Farm Bureau members, has long favored limitations on beef imports. Other commodity interests also reflect the conflict. Sugar and wool are major commodities that owe their level of domestic production to systems of quotas, tariffs, and subsidy payments. Most of the tropical fruits and products are represented by strong protectionist sentiment which has been highly successful through the years in limiting or absolutely preventing imports. Cotton, until the 1930s the strongest traditional home of free trade sentiment in agriculture, came to be protectionist-minded in order to support the price structure that had been created.

Within the Bureau membership the interests for protection contend with a long-dominant interest, primarily centered in the Midwest, that advocates freer trade and export expansion. Such support is gained and held together by the necessity of maintaining large exports of feed grains and wheat. The Bureau policy has been to favor pricing of corn and other feed grains at levels near the competitive market, to balance the wheat economy by allowing price supports to fall to near competitive levels, and by paying wheat farmers in forms of a negotiable certificate for participating in an acreage limitation program.[64] In its general policy position the Bureau has differed from most other farm organizations in favoring a lower support level for feed grains especially and eventual withdrawal of government from feed grain programs.

The main policy interests as well as the major conflicts within the Bureau organization have centered on price policy and the means or programs by which prices are affected. The activity falls into three major periods: the pre-New Deal era up to about 1932, when the Bureau fought for a number of reforms and finally was persuaded to join the battle for export subsidy; the New Deal era and

---

[64]The value of the certificate was periodically adjusted as necessary to bring the total support for the proportion of wheat sold in the domestic market to the price support level established by law. This method for direct payments was long opposed by the American as undesirable reliance on congressional favor.

postwar years up to about 1947, during the administration of O'Neal and Smith, when the major policy effort was directed at raising prices; and the years after 1947, under Kline, Shuman, and Kuhfuss, when the Bureau's major direction was to disengage from government programs and move agriculture toward the free market.

The first major political accomplishment of the American was leadership, through its Washington representative Gray Silver (the "Silver Eel" or the "Gray Fox"), to form the farm bloc, an informal, nonpartisan coalition of senators and representatives, mainly from the Midwest and South, who shared a common interest in agricultural legislation.[65] The farm bloc functioned most effectively during 1920–23 and was responsible for sponsoring or successfully supporting a large amount of legislation that has been crucial in shaping important institutions relating to policy. A prime goal was legislation to regulate the meat packers and stockyards. The Packers and Stockyards Act, passed during this period, prohibited packers engaged in interstate commerce from resorting to unfair, discriminatory, or deceptive practices, manipulating or controlling prices, or otherwise creating a monopoly and restraining commerce.[66] The Capper-Volstead Act, which legalized cooperatives engaged in interstate commerce by exempting them from prosecution under the antitrust laws, was the basic legislation which set the stage for the remarkable growth of agricultural cooperatives during the 1920–32 period. The Grain Futures Act of 1922 established rules and guidelines for regulation of the grain exchanges. The Agricultural Credits Act of 1923 established the Federal Intermediate Credit Banks which are the major banks of discount for the Production Credit Associations (PCAs).

Although the leadership of the Farm Bureau was at first either opposed to, or only mildly supportive of, the McNary-Haugen bills, beginning in 1925 the Bureau's support was critical for their eventual approval by Congress. Bureau members in both the winter and spring wheat areas supported the bills almost from the beginning. Members in the Corn Belt and the South were finally persuaded to join in support and this combination, together with scattered support from the West, created sufficient strength for passage. The Farm Bureau members in the Northeast continued to oppose the legislation as did nearly all the members of Congress from this region. Coolidge's vetoes in 1927 and 1928 could not be overridden, and, almost as a last resort, the Bureau then supported the Federal Farm Board in 1929. Collapse of the Board program set the stage for Bureau support of the more sweeping legislation during the 1930s for production control.

The Bureau's price policy during the New Deal era, aggressively influenced by O'Neal and Smith on the board of the American, was merely to raise farm prices. O'Neal and Smith did not develop this policy in sophisticated terms. In

---

[65]See Saloutos and Hicks, *op. cit.*, pp. 321–341.

[66]As Professor Nicholls has shown, however, this act did not prevent the concentration of meat packing in a small number of large firms involving a type of imperfect competition (oligopsony and oligopoly). See William H. Nicholls, *A Theoretical Analysis of Imperfect Competition with Special Application to the Agricultural Industries,* Ames: Iowa State College Press, 1941.

their view, farm prices were simply too low. A policy to raise them was imperative and it could be justified on grounds of national welfare as well as equity. The idea took root that the Depression was farm bred and farm led. Although the idea of production control did not originate within the Farm Bureau, its officers were persuaded to lead the political campaign for it. Early in this campaign, M. L. Wilson worked closely with the president of the Montana Farm Bureau, persuading him to write letters to bureau presidents in other states and others whose support would be critical.[67]

The Agricultural Adjustment Administration was dominated by a Midwest-Southern alliance of the Bureau membership, a fact credited with bringing on a near revolt by the Northeast. The claim was made by Bureau members in the Northeast that the AAA and the AFBF were controlled by Midwestern and Southern farmers, that the Bureau had been diverted from more fundamental problems such as cutting down the cost of food distribution, increasing consumption, and securing monetary reform (that is, a "permanently honest dollar"), and that through Bureau support the AAA had become a tremendous bureaucracy, intent mainly on saving its job and its own face.[68] Although price policy under the AAA continued to be designed primarily for the Midwest and South, a revolt in the Northeast was prevented in large part through O'Neal's compromising skill, the traditional loyalty of Bureau members, and the decentralized structure of the Bureau.[69] The threatened revolt is significant in retrospect because it illustrates an important constraint on Farm Bureau policy that is imposed by the broad comprehensive structure of the Bureau. That is, there are diverting or competing commodity and sectional interests that have to be taken into account in defining the position of the national organization, especially in regard to compensatory policy.

In the late 1930s, the leadership of the Bureau, led by officers of the American, broke with the Roosevelt administration over the issue of wage control—the Bureau wanting more strict control over wages—and the strong support that had been given to the administration was broken in the 1940 election. In essence, the Bureau returned to the more traditional Republicanism that had provided its initial strength in the 1920s.

During World War II a threatened split between Southern and Midwestern farm bureaus over the issue of price supports was averted, when Congress adopted a compromise resolution for support at 85 percent of parity. The South wanted higher supports for cotton and tobacco, and got them in amendments to the basic price support legislation. As noted in Chapter 5, however, this provision led to accumulation of large stocks of cotton by the end of the war.

---

[67]See William A. Rowley, *M. L. Wilson and the Campaign for the Domestic Allotment, op. cit.,* pp. 50–106.

[68]Campbell, *op. cit.,* pp. 68–84. These charges were presented in detail by Howard E. Babcock in the *American Agriculturalist,* an outstanding New York farm paper. They were answered by Clifford Gregory, editor of the *Prairie Farmer,* then, with the possible exception of *Wallace's Farmer,* the nation's most influential farm paper.

[69]Campbell, *op. cit.,* p. 84.

A painful transition to lower prices after the war was anticipated.[70] But the AFBF, now led by the more conservation Allan Kline, opposed the proposals of Secretary of Agriculture Brannan, made in 1949, for the so-called Brannan Plan providing for higher-level support of farm prices and incomes. The Bureau leadership worked closely with Secretary Benson during the Eisenhower years, as the line was laid down by the administration to "get the government out of agriculture." They generally fought against the policies of Secretary Freeman, during the Kennedy and Johnson administrations, to obtain higher prices through more strict production control and supply management. The most critical turning point in farm policy was reached in 1963 when the AFBF led the fight against the referendum to adopt a marketing quota for wheat. Throughout the 1960s the major crop reduction proposal supported by the Bureau was a long-term land retirement plan, called the Cropland Adjustment Program. Bureau representatives contended that this would lead to an orderly overall adjustment of land and non-land resources used in agriculture. During the five-year period, beginning January 1, 1971, and ending December 31, 1975, according to the statement of AFBF President Shuman, "acreage controls, base acreages marketing quotas, processing taxes, and direct payments for wheat, feed grains, and cotton would be phased out."[71] This position held throughout the hearings on the Agriculture and Consumer Protection Act of 1973 and the amendment proposed in 1975 as H.R. 4296, discussed in Chapter 5.

A Policy Conclusion

As seen in historical perspective, the policy of the Farm Bureau represents the position of a large organization, embracing a number of competing and sometimes conflicting commodity and regional interests and adapting to a national and international market. The necessity of keeping American agriculture competitive in export markets has forced the Bureau to adopt a rather moderate posture in respect to price policy. The heavy representation among the economically stronger part of commercial agriculture has made the enterprise creed popular among the membership. A strong faith in the ability of market prices to bring about desired adjustments, and an image of the main organization speaking for farmer interests, brings the organization to favor minimum government interference with the market. This faith has also prevented the organization from turning aggressively to government for help in time of crisis. Furthermore, this approach has created the necessary conditions for the rise of more militant protest organizations.

More generally, income and welfare programs applying to food policy for America have gained their vitality from a system of values and beliefs and policy-oriented creeds, which have found expression in activities of politically influen-

---

[70]See O. M. Kile, *The Farm Bureau Through Three Decades, op. cit.,* pp. 306–403.

[71]*General Farm Program and Food Stamp Program,* Hearings, Committee on Agriculture, House of Representatives, 91st Cong., 1st Sess., Serial Q, Part 1, p. 218; see also statement by William J. Kuhfuss, *ibid.,* pp. 222–224, Aug. 5, 1969.

tial organizations. Although the basic beliefs, values, and creeds are widely accepted, their different interpretation leads to a continuing appraisal and reappraisal of policy action. This reevaluation is what underlies the organizational activity discussed in this chapter. It also gives substance and variety to the policies in the product markets and in the various input or factor markets, which we shall discuss in the following chapters.

QUESTIONS FOR DISCUSSION

1   Discuss the roles of the general policymaking farm organizations. How have most organizations originated? What are the common characteristics of those that have survived and grown? Of those that have failed? In what ways is the American Farm Bureau Federation unique?

2   Most farm organizations have combined goals of economic justice with service to members and political action. How has justice generally been defined, and what actions have been supported to achieve it?

3   Account for the fact that certain commodities, such as tobacco, wheat, and milk, have played an extremely crucial role in farm organization activity.

4   Compare and contrast the nineteenth-century development of policy by the National Grange and the various movements of the Farmers' Alliances. These movements are generally regarded as part of the Populist Revolt. What conditions were they protesting or revolting against? How do these conditions differ from those generally experienced in the second great era of food policy? In the third era?

5   Discuss similarities in proposals of the American Society of Equity, the Nonpartisan League, the Farmers' Holiday Association, and the National Farmers Organization. Discuss the economic conditions associated with the development of these organizations. What assumptions did they generally make about supply and demand? What economic propositions relative to collective bargaining are generally consistent with their actions? On what economic grounds have other organizations protested or refused to join in their programs?

7   The National Farmers Union has been linked with programs to favor the family farm and to obtain cost of production in the market. What policy means would the Farmers Union use to obtain these goals? What economic problems would these programs generate? How would the programs be constrained?

8   The general policy goal of the American Farm Bureau Federation has been described as favoring the creation of "conditions whereby farmers may earn a high per-family real income in a manner that will preserve freedom and opportunity." Outline the general assumptions concerning markets and agricultural adjustments in the AFBF programs. How does this program differ from that of the Farmers Union, the NFO, and the National Grange?

9   Discuss the experience of the AFBF in establishing marketing and service cooperatives, in setting up producer-bargaining cooperatives and in establishing insurance companies and cooperatives.

10 Trace the shifts in price policies and price support programs favored by the AFBF from the early 1920s to the present, relating them especially to (a) the basic philosophy of leading national officers, (b) assumptions concerning foreign trade, and (c) conditions in the domestic market.

11 It is sometimes suggested that the major farm organizations should be united in

their policy proposals for the good of agriculture. What prevents them from being so? Discuss. Distinguish between issues in which they appear to be united and those upon which division seems to persist. Is the continuing disagreement more over goals, means, implements, or constraints?

12 We have argued that the national welfare will be benefited by a more complete rural-urban interaction in making food policy. Which of the general farm organizations' ideas are compatible with this presumption? Which are incompatible? Are the conditions of the new third era of food policy more, or less, conducive to conciliation and rural-urban cooperation than were conditions in the second era?

REFERENCES

An Adaptive Program for Agriculture, New York: Committee for Economic Development, 1962.

Block, William J., *The Separation of the Farm Bureau and the Extension Service, Political Issues in a Federal System,* Illinois Studies in the Social Sciences, Vol. 47, Urbana: The University of Illinois Press, 1960.

Brandsberg, George, *The Two Sides of the NFO's Battle,* Ames: The Iowa State University Press, 1964.

Breimyer, Harold F., *Individual Freedom and the Economic Organization of Agriculture,* Urbana: The University of Illinois Press, 1965.

Campbell, Christiana M., *The Farm Bureau and the New Deal, A Study in the Making of National Policy, 1933–1940,* Urbana: The University of Illinois Press, 1962.

Farm Goals in Conflict, Ames: The Iowa State University Press, 1963.

Gardner, Charles M., *The Grange—Friend of the Farmer,* Washington: The National Grange, 1949.

Kile, Orville M., *The Farm Bureau through Three Decades,* Baltimore: The Waverly Press, 1948.

Matusow, Allen J., *Farm Policies and Politics in the Truman Years,* Cambridge, Mass.: Harvard University Press, 1967.

Nicholls, William H., *A Theoretical Analysis of Imperfect Competition with Special Application to Agricultural Industries,* Ames: Iowa State College Press, 1941.

Nicholls, William H., *Price Policies of the Cigarette Industry,* Nashville: Vanderbilt University Press, 1951.

Rowley, William D., *M. L. Wilson and the Campaign for the Domestic Allotment,* Lincoln: University of Nebraska Press, 1970.

Saloutos, Theodore, and John D. Hicks, *Agricultural Discontent in the Middle West, 1900–1939,* Madison: The University of Wisconsin Press, 1951.

Shover, John L., *Cornbelt Rebellion: The Farmers' Holiday Association,* Urbana: The University of Illinois Press, 1965.

Taylor, Carl C., *The Farmers' Movement,* New York: American Book Company, 1953.

Policy in the Product Markets

The food economy must be managed. What is needed is some coherent policy that will have to consider many diverse purposes, not only price rises for consumers and producers, but also the needs of exporting food to help our international financial situation. The market need not be destroyed, merely guided in a purposeful direction. We must move to prevent the frequent violent eruptions that have become so common, for, to switch metaphors, without careful planning, our food economy is balanced scarcely more securely than a heap of jackstraws, and as we have recently learned, it doesn't take much to upset the whole thing.

Thomas Redburn, "Beets, Beef and Henry Wallace,"
The Washington Monthly, April 1975

We oppose the creation of a government-controlled food reserve in the United States and U.S. participation in any internationally-controlled reserve.

The best food reserve for America and for the people of the world is the productive capacity of our land, the ability of the American farmer, and the profit incentive system. . . .

We favor programs to encourage and assist farmers to increase their storage capacity in order to provide opportunity for more orderly marketing and to avoid government controlled reserves.

> *To meet emergency needs throughout the world, we favor the establishment of an international fund to be used for the purchase of agricultural commodities only in the amounts, and when, needed. All nations of the world should support such a fund and should share in its control in proportion to their contributions. . . .*
>
> *We urge AFBF to assume leadership in the creation of this fund.*

American Farm Bureau Federation
Farm Bureau Policies for 1976[1]

After many years of programs designed mainly to limit or constrain the production of farm commodities, food policy for America has a new and sharply different dimension. Whereas formerly large carry-over stocks of grains and a few other commodities were available to offset production shortfalls and planning errors, suddenly, in what we call the third food era, these no longer existed. Instead of a commodity-by-commodity approach to problems of price and production, policy in the product markets must be formulated under conditions with far more widespread consequences for every decision, where each decision interacts with almost all others.

The purpose of this chapter is to develop a comprehensive approach to this situation, to outline the major dimensions for policy that are assumed to exist in the third era, and to appraise the consequences of some of the alternative choices.

GOALS IN THE PRODUCT MARKETS

In broad view, the third era projects a large population increase in the world as a whole, with by far the largest growth in the developing countries, with the market demand depending primarily on economic development, and with food production around the world constrained by continued high costs of energy, fertilizer, and other agricultural technologies. In the United States, food markets will continue to reflect the traditional conditions of short-term uncertainty but, as we have seen already, the results of uncertainty will be magnified by the new dynamics of the domestic and foreign markets. A policy for all situations is required to cope with the intermittent excess demand and excess supply that will characterize agriculture and the food economy in the years ahead. What shall the goals of such policy be?

Four Policy Goals

It may be said that a policy is desired for America that will

1 Contribute to economic stability by providing a stable supply of food for domestic markets

---

[1]*Farm Bureau Policies for 1976, Resolutions on National Issues Adopted by Elected Voting Delegates of the Member State Farm Bureaus to the 57th Annual Meeting of the American Farm Bureau Federation,* St. Louis, Mo., January 1976, p. 10.

    2 Help to protect and guarantee the nation's position as an exporter of food and farm products

    3 Permit us to meet an appropriate and agreed share of food emergencies abroad

    4 Protect United States farmers from potential income losses in the event of possible collapse of world and domestic markets due to slower industrial growth or substantial increase in supplies.

Defense of these goals, which may appear to be self-evident, rests on a number of propositions that we shall try to make more explicit.

Comment on the Goals

Although economic theory can demonstrate that consumers may gain from price instability in some goods, especially where inventories can be accumulated and costs of storage, including deterioration, are low, consumers have much to gain from price stability in food markets. Modest price fluctuations, involving, let us say, one or two percentage points in the proportion of consumers' expenditures laid out for food, are not very damaging to household budgets, but wide swings are undesirable. Large food-price increases contribute substantially to the inflationary spiral when one exists. They enter into cost-of-living escalator clauses, thus contributing to the cost-push type of inflation. They cut into the living standards of people living on fixed incomes. They increase uncertainty in budgeting for food stamps and other food subsidy programs. They can be an important factor leading to other reductions in economic activity, thus tending to intensify stagnation or depression. Altogether, a stable and reasonably ample food supply is accepted as a major goal of national policy.

    Protection of the position of America as a major food exporter is desired for a number of reasons. In national self-interest, the main one is that foreign exchange must be earned if goods are to be imported into the United States over the long term. Anything that damages the ability to earn exchange in a free market is potentially damaging to the national welfare, as well as to the interests of farmers who desire to maintain a strong export market for farm products. Thus, in 1973, for example, farm organizations strongly voiced their objections to a temporary embargo on exports of soybeans and soybean products. Farm leaders argued (in both public and private) that such an embargo was damaging to the confidence that foreign governments had in the United States, that it would encourage importing countries to try harder to find alternative sources of protein, and that American agriculture was being forced to carry a disproportionate share of the costs of inflation. The importance of a consistent supply for export has been brought home to national policymakers.

    To meet an appropriate share of food emergencies abroad is an ethical goal with humanitarian overtones. The simple proposition is that where there are hungry, undernourished people in the poorer countries, the rich countries should help to feed them. America, as the wealthiest of all countries with the largest potential for food export, should—so the argument goes—take the lead in international food aid and provide a major part of such aid. In addition—the thesis may be expanded—such aid will contribute to world peace and tranquility. Thus the nation's food aid program under the umbrella of Public Law 480 has been called "Food for Peace" and promoted in support of a thesis of peace. The thesis, although untested in a meaningful way, is nevertheless appealing.

The fact of worsening undernourishment and malnutrition in some less developed countries cannot be denied,[2] nor does one wish to deny that emergency food aid will save lives. Neither, however, does one—at least not this writer—wish to propose that food aid from the rich countries will solve the long-term problem. Economic development, more equitable property and income distribution, and more effective birth control are generally recognized as the necessary, but not always sufficient, conditions for improvement in the late-developing countries. The role for food aid, given this proposition, is intermittent and supplementary to economic development.

The more difficult and almost immediate question facing food policy for America is whether to hold as a firm goal the filling of a proportionate share of the grain deficit of 80 to 100 million tons projected by the Food and Agriculture Organization (FAO) for the developing countries a decade hence. Although the nation's food production capacity may be adequate to the task, the acceptance of the goal could imply longer-term commitments for both trade and food aid. A task is suggested for a national commission, working in cooperation with FAO and other international agencies, to draw up long-range plans, to define conditions under which food aid will be offered, and to specify operating rules and procedures. We do not regard this as utopian, but rather as a practical proposal for attaining a very difficult, ethical policy goal. A successful food aid program cannot be just a matter of surplus disposal. Instead, it must be programmed on a long-term basis with stocks built up when world production is above the long-term trends and drawn down when such production falls below these trends.

To protect the interests of American farmers, policy in the product markets must have a system for counteracting the effects of excess supply either by price support, by government payments, or by both. The traditional goal has been parity price. Efforts by economists to substitute parity income as the policy goal, to lessen the distortive effects of parity prices on the allocation of land and other resources, were only partially successful. More effective have been the efforts to substitute direct payments to farmers to lessen the reliance on price supports. But policy in the product markets has not been aimed at the goal of distributive justice among farms of various sales classes. Government payments—with variations among commodity programs—generally are distributed proportionately to the value of farm sales and the skewness of income from farming is not thereby reduced (Figure 7-1 and Table 7-1). Policies in the input markets, discussed in Chapters 8 to 10, significantly affect the distribution of income among farm and food firms.

[2]See, for example, Richard W. Franke, "Miracle Seeds and Shattered Dreams in Java," *Challenge, The Magazine of Economic Affairs,* July–August 1974, pp. 41–47.

Income in $ thousands

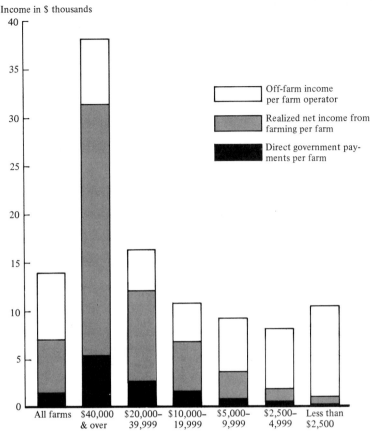

Figure 7-1 Direct government payments, realized net income from farming, and off-farm income, by farm sales classes, 1972. *(Source: Farm Income Situation, USDA, ERS, FIS-222, July 1973, pp. 68–73.)*

More equal distribution of income among farm operator families also depends heavily on receipts from off-farm income. A trend in this direction was clearly discernible as early as 1954, when off-farm income averaged $1,682 per farm operator family.[3] The trend was greatly accelerated during the decade of the 1960s (Table 7-2).

In our new third era of food policy, the income goals of farm families will be easier to attain than ever before; but, in this study, if we assume that American farmers will work under a policy in the product markets that is directed toward achievement of the first three of the four policy goals cited earlier, then farmers have a legitimate claim to a policy that protects them from periods of excess supply. Part of our purpose in this chapter is to expand on the topic of alternatives for such policy.

[3]H. G. Halcrow, "Part-time Farming," *U.S. Census of Agriculture: 1954,* Vol. III, Special Reports, Part 9, Farmers and Farm Production in the United States, chap. 8. Washington: Government Printing Office, 1956, pp. 7, 48, 49.

Table 7-1   U.S. Farm Income Distribution by Sales Classes, 1972

Value of farm product sales	All farms	Farm sales class					
		$40,000 and over	$20,000– 39,999	$10,000– 19,999	$5,000– 9,999	$2,500– 4,999	Less than $2,500
Number of farms (000)	2,870	297	404	353	359	420	1,037
Percentage distribution	100.0	10.3	14.1	12.3	12.5	14.6	36.2
Realized gross income per farm*	$23,988	$135,566	$34,068	$18,436	$9,798	$5,241	$2,496
Direct government payments per farm	1,380	5,138	2,498	1,694	978	581	225
Realized net farm income per farm†	6,856	31,310	11,927	6,736	3,533	1,929	1,061
Off-farm income per farm operator family	6,759	6,673	4,000	3,895	5,568	6,140	9,496
Total income including non-money income from farm food and housing†	13,615	37,973	15,927	10,631	9,101	8,069	10,557

*Includes value of products used in home consumption.
†Includes government payments.
Source: Farm Income Situation, FIS-222, U.S. Department of Agriculture, Economic Research Service, July 1973, pp. 68–73.

Table 7-2   Average Off-Farm Income of Farm Operator Families, by Farm Sales Class in Selected Years 1960–1973

Year	Farm sales class						
	All farms	$40,000 and over	$20,000– 39,999	$10,000– 19,999	$5,000– 9,999	$2,500– 4,999	Less than $2,500
1960	2,139	2,177	1,658	1,258	1,573	1,849	2,730
1965	3,733	4,453	2,496	2,296	3,200	3,425	4,614
1970	5,876	6,153	3,603	3,448	4,884	5,340	7,815
1973	8,249	7,120	4,325	5,500	7,294	8,361	13,930

Source: Farm Income Situation, FIS-222, U.S. Department of Agriculture, Economic Research Service, July 1973, p. 72 and July 1974, p. 71.

Problems of Goal Evaluation[4]

Since the four goals are competitive and there is no clearly established hierarchy, the problems of goal evaluation are very difficult. The trade-off between domestic food consumption goals and export markets, for example, raises a number of questions: Shall the government continue a policy of agricultural export expansion, and at what level, when success in this effort leads to more expensive food for American consumers? Since many importing countries isolate their food markets by tariffs, quotas, and other devices, the United States must absorb a good part of the adjustments that are required to offset the fluctuations in world agricultural production. To what extent shall the nation's food policy be designed to protect domestic consumers against these fluctuations rather than to provide guarantees to our export customers? Can any long-term assurances be given to developing countries? Against what contingencies and at what magnitudes shall such assurances be given? Since these questions and others like them were unnecessary in the past because of the huge surpluses carried in the United States, there are few precedents and few guidelines that have been tested politically.

The answers are not easy. The felt needs of Bangladesh alone, for example, could absorb all the food aid that America reasonably might expect to have available for all developing countries.[5] The Agriculture and Consumer Protection Act of 1973, which in its title reflects the evolving concerns for consumer food goals, fails to provide meaningful standards for protection of American consumers, let alone those millions around the world who look to America for some assurance. Although the Secretary of Agriculture is given authority to set target prices and to cancel land retirement programs, no meaningful food reserve policy

---

[4]This section draws on some of the proceedings papers presented at the meeting of the American Agricultural Economics Association, December 27–30, 1973. See Don Paarlberg, "The World Food Situation in Perspective"; Leo V. Mayer and Gary L. Seevers, "Food Policy Issues in the United States"; Luther Tweeten and James Plaxico, "U.S. Policies for Food and Agriculture in an Unstable World"; and discussions by D. E. Hathaway and Howard W. Hjort, *American Journal of Agricultural Economics,* Vol. 56, No. 2, May 1974, pp. 351–376.

[5]Claire Sterling, "Bangladesh," The *Atlantic,* September 1974, pp. 4–16.

is articulated. There is little if any policy guideline established against price instability, uncertainty, and associated economic problems at home and abroad.

Congress has been showing increasing concern about the role of the consumer in food policy. There were the Agricultural Acts of 1961, 1964, and 1970. Interspersed among them were the Food and Agricultural Acts of 1962 and 1965. Then food and consumer protection was more explicitly recognized as a policy goal in 1973. Although farmers may be indifferent or uncertain about whether (1) crop restriction and high market prices, or (2) little or no acreage restrictions and lower prices, are in their best interest, consumers are not. At issue are the short-term encouragements and guarantees to be given to farm producers, the amount or degree of reserve capacity to be held in storage stocks, the rules under which these stocks will be held, and the agencies or associations that will administer the programs. To what extent shall the United States share the power and responsibility for decisions on international food aid? The whole range of policymaking and administration must pass under review.

THE POLICY MEANS

To cover the range of policymaking in the product markets, we arrange the policy means and programs into four categories: (1) policies involved in free or competitive markets; (2) programs involving product management and price manipulation without production control, such as tariffs and import quotas, export subsidies, and food aid; (3) product management through such means as acreage allotments or marketing quotas; and (4) consumers' food subsidies. What mix of these policies is desired? What will each accomplish and at what cost? Where do the trade-offs occur? And so on.

In the conditions assumed to exist for the third era as compared with the second, the free market can extend to a larger sector of the product markets, given comparable welfare objectives. The reasons are that (1) there is less overcapacity in American agriculture, especially in respect to human resources; (2) under flexible exchange rates, the export market will be more dynamic; and (3) the food and population prospects suggest that a broader world food program has become a more vital necessity. But it should be clear that the free market cannot guarantee food price stability in America or stable farm prices and incomes in the short run. The inelasticity of supply and demand (discussed in Chapters 3 and 4) will maintain a situation of price volatility which can be somewhat lessened by food management programs that are both national and international in scope. Let us start with the latter—a world food program.

A World Food Program

The remarkable feature of the world food situation, in retrospect, has been its general stability. Yet, as we suggested in Chapter 2, the food situation shifted in just one decade from surplus to gloom, to optimism, and then to pessimism again. In the short run, the situation is highly changeable, almost unpredictable, and not necessarily self-correcting. The timetable of food shortages and surpluses varies from nation to nation. After 1963, per capita supplies increased in most developed countries but barely held even in most of the developing countries. Although we may be optimistic about producing enough food to maintain present per capita food consumption throughout the remainder of this century, it appears doubtful that we can produce enough food in the right places to sustain rapid rates of economic growth for the expanding world population without substantial changes in agricultural and population policies in many countries. Increased cooperation among major countries in programming world food supplies and increased effort by developing countries to control population and increase food production are at least necessary conditions. In looking ahead, the problem is to define what we mean by a world food program and visualize how it can work. When we have thus defined the problem, we can then consider America's role in solving it.

David Lubin, an American, was the first to bring about formal international cooperation in food and agriculture. He held a somewhat Physiocratic view that agricultural prosperity is the basis of industrial and commercial prosperity and that an international agency is required to promote and coordinate the interests of agriculture. Through his persistent efforts, the International Institute of Agriculture was founded in 1905. The King of Italy provided commodious quarters in Rome. A staff of about 100 trained men and women was recruited and various countries contributed to the costs. Their activities included collection, analysis, and distribution of economic data on food, studies of agricultural cooperation, and promotion of measures to improve farming. Up to World War II, the Institute played an important role in world food and agricultural conferences, in drafting international agreements, and in developing information on food. In World War II, the Allied Nations withdrew their support and the Institute continued on a limited scale, supported only by the Axis countries, until 1946, when it was absorbed into the United Nations Food and Agriculture Organization.[6]

During the interwar period from 1920 to 1940, attempts to coordinate national activity on major world food problems centered in the Health Organization of the League of Nations. In 1925, Yugoslavia proposed that this organization should examine the world food situation in all its aspects, and in 1935 a report was issued giving the first account of the extent of hunger and malnutrition around the world. S. M. Bruce, Prime Minister of Australia, introduced this subject to the Assembly of the League of Nations. In a three-day debate, it was argued that increasing food production to meet human needs would bring prosperity to agriculture which would overflow into industry and induce the expansion of the total economy that the world needed. Thus the vicious spiral of declining world trade, with its increasing economic distress, would be converted

---

[6]This discussion draws on John Boyd Orr and David Lubbock, *The White Man's Dilemma, Food and the Future,* 2d ed., London: George Allen & Unwin, Ltd., 1965, chap. 10.

to an ascending spiral, with economic prosperity. Bruce epitomized the new outlook in a phrase which became famous: "the marriage of food and agriculture."

A "mixed" committee of leading authorities and eminent people was established, and about two years later, it issued a comprehensive report on developing the world's food supplies and the benefits that would accrue. A conference attended by representatives of 22 nations considered what joint action could be taken to implement the recommendations of the report; but the outbreak of war in 1939 ended this promising movement for the collaboration of nations in such peaceful and beneficient activity. As is sadly reported, "the voice of wisdom was drowned in the roar of the guns."[7]

Some of the participants in this work of the League of Nations and others in the United States came to Washington to talk with Henry Wallace, then the Vice President, and other American officials. Mr. McDougall, economic advisor to the Prime Minister of Australia, in a conference with President Roosevelt, suggested that as food is the first want of man, a world food policy would be the best way to begin to fulfill the promise of freedom from want for all men that was made in the Atlantic Charter. The President was persuaded to call a conference of several nations to meet at Hot Springs, Virginia, to consider ways and means of international cooperation to raise standards of nutrition throughout the world, including the level of living of the two-thirds of the world's population then in abysmal poverty. This conference recommended setting up an international organization to achieve this goal.

The new organization, the Food and Agriculture Organization, was established at a conference convened at Quebec in October 1945, attended by 44 nations including the U.S.S.R. and chaired by Lester Pearson, subsequently Foreign Minister and later Prime Minister of Canada. John Boyd Orr, a career-long agricultural economist then knighted for his vision and work, was named the first Director-General. He and his staff took the position that the FAO, to attain its objective, would have to do more than just collect data, hold conferences, and publish reports. It would need to have funds and authority to take action itself, or to be able to promote an international agency which would take action.[8] As the first move, the International Emergency Food Council was organized, staffed, and financed through the FAO to influence the allocation of exportable food in accordance with the needs of various countries and to take measures to prevent the inflation of food prices. The latter task was carried on with very modest resources until the most acute phases of the postwar emergency were passed. The Economic and Social Council of the United Nations was established to provide a vehicle to help direct industry and trade to useful ends, and the World Bank for Reconstruction and Development was created to arrange credits.

What was needed additionally, in the Director-General's view, was an international development authority that would first focus on agriculture, the

[7]*Ibid.*, p. 86.
[8]*Ibid.*, p. 87.

basic industry, and have real power to coordinate the activities of other agencies directly to influence agricultural development and world food trade. Almost immediately after the FAO was created, and apparently with a feeling of urgency, a plan was drawn up to deal with the longer-term problem of food and agriculture. The main feature of the plan was cooperation of major nations on a World Food Board, which would coordinate the work of the FAO, the Economic and Social Council, and the World Bank, and have funds and authority to carry out two main functions: (1) to assist with credits, industrial products, and technical assistance to countries asking for help to develop their agriculture and auxiliary industries and (2) to buy and hold in reserve storable food and other agricultural products which, after a bumper harvest or for other reasons, could not be sold immediately; to release, from the world reserve, food or other products in short supply after a bad harvest in any area; and by these and other measures to stabilize prices in the world market within given limits, and so provide a guaranteed world market for agricultural products at a price fair to producers and consumers.[9]

According to the plan, international trade in food products would be carried out through normal business channels, with the Board intervening only when necessary to prevent wide fluctuations in prices. Credits given by the Board, or advanced by the World Bank with Board recommendation, would be on a long-term business basis, at low rates of interest. The countries receiving loan funds would be committed to begin refunding as soon as their national resources were developed sufficiently to enable them to do so without seriously halting the rise in the living standards of their people.

The benefits from the World Food Board were visualized as: (1) the allaying of social unrest leading to revolution in poverty-stricken countries, (2) a guaranteed world price within certain limits, (3) the doubling of food supply in the next 25 years (as compared with 61 or 62 percent subsequently attained), (4) expansion of the world market for industrial products, and (5) benefits to the wealthy as well as the poor countries, which would bring a better understanding and make international cooperation easier in other spheres. This new relationship would serve as a step toward evolution of the United Nations into a world government, without which there seemed to be little hope of permanent world peace.

The second annual conference of the FAO, which met in September 1946 in Copenhagen, debated the proposals for the World Food Board, but the United States delegation was split in regard to basic policy.[10] Although representatives of the Department of Agriculture expressed support for the Board as a useful device for management of potential surpluses and food aid, the Department of State viewed it as inimical to the basic policy of free trade which was considered crucial for the postwar world. Consequently, the World Food Board was not established, the Department of Agriculture's alternative proposals for inter-

---

[9]*Ibid.,* pp. 90–93.
[10]See Allen J. Matusow, *Farm Policies and Politics in the Truman Years,* Cambridge, Mass.: Harvard University Press, 1967, pp. 79–109.

national wheat agreements, specifying minimum and maximum prices, were inadequately supported, and the United States failed in its goal of an International Trade Organization (ITO) to more actively support the principles of free trade.

The United States Policy on Aid and Trade

The government of the United States, as we have seen, instead of programming the nation's great food surpluses through an international agency, used food as an instrument of international diplomacy, aiding its friends and denying help to its enemies. Food was an important part of the European Recovery Program, often called the Marshall Plan, and the success in recovery of Western Europe was spectacular. Out of this came the North Atlantic Treaty Organization (NATO), to be followed by various other regional blocs, justified by the United States and other Western democracies as bulwarks against the military forces of communism.

But no grand design emerged for a coordinated world food program. Public Law 480 and other export programs were conceived—so we may say—primarily as emergency relief, both to rid the U.S. government of burdensome surpluses and to aid needy countries. Few large storage facilities were built by governments at strategic points around the world. No world food reserve program was seriously programmed. The exporting countries, the United States most of all, remained vulnerable to price-depressing surpluses. The needy countries remained with inadequate facilities to handle large-scale food aid efficiently if and when it was offered. World agriculture entered the 1970s without either free trade in most food commodities or any coordinated administrative design for allocating scarce world resources to areas of most productive potential, thus to encourage development of comparative advantages for trade. National policies and regional policies such as those of the European Economic Community (EEC) were mainly protectionist for agriculture. That agriculture, in almost any country, was better off under this circumstance could not be proved by economic theory or statistical inference. Consumers were, perhaps vastly, worse off. In short, as one percipient economist observed, world agriculture was in disarray.[11] The developed countries, as food aid was then programmed, could not expect to solve their domestic surplus problems primarily by increasing the volume and value of food aid.[12] Since the "green revolution" was restricted among the developing countries by technical difficulties and social dislocation,[13] the disarray could be ended only by a broad revival of freer trade in agricultural products.[14]

The general move toward freer trade would reduce or eliminate the effect of import levies (tariffs and quotas) and export subsidies on major agricultural products entering into world trade. As shown theoretically in Figure 7-2, we

[11]D. Gale Johnson, *World Agriculture in Disarray,* London: Macmillan St. Martin's Press in association with the Trade Policy Research Centre, 1973.

[12]*Ibid.,* p. 175.

[13]*Ibid.,* p. 173.

[14]*Ibid.,* pp. 249–266.

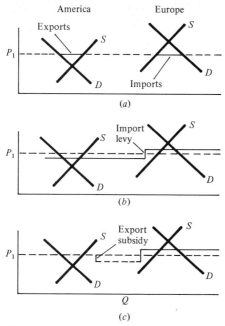

Figure 7-2 Illustrating effects of import levy and export subsidy between Europe and America.

assume that there were only two countries, called America and Europe. The supply and demand curves intersect in America at lower prices than in Europe, and these prices prevail if there is no trade between the two countries. If free trade is established, in (a), America exports to Europe until a new equilibrium price is established at P_1 (ignoring transportation costs for sake of simplicity), at which point exports from America equal imports into Europe. In (b), if an import levy is introduced into Europe, as is common under the EEC program where import levies are variable to meet internal target prices in the various countries, the effect is similar to increasing the cost of transport. A differential is created, causing prices to be reduced in America and raised in Europe, and trade between the two countries is reduced as suggested. As in (c), America can counteract the effect of the import levy, at least in part, by instituting an export subsidy.

If there is a third group of countries (not shown in Figure 7-2) to which America exports food, the export subsidy will have the effect of holding prices in America above prices on the free world market. The EEC nations imposing the import levy may maintain their own food and agricultural prices above world prices, thus protecting their own agriculture. America will export more to the Third World countries and less to Europe than it would do under free trade.

The theoretical example in Figure 7-2 is not far removed from what happened with the formation of the EEC. Until Great Britain's entry into the Common Market, the continental European countries protected their agriculture by import levies, which were usually variable to achieve a certain threshold price at point of entry. American policy until 1964 was to maintain an internal price for many agricultural products (most importantly wheat, feed grains, cotton, tobacco, and a few others) by means of crop restrictions and export subsidies. In 1964 a new system was introduced in American policy under which market prices were allowed to drop in steps toward free market levels. Crop restriction programs were continued primarily under the incentive of direct payments to program participants. The 1964 shift muted foreign criticism that America was dumping crop surpluses, thus damaging the cause of freer trade. The system was in general not merely a form of concealed subsidy, since for the most part the marginal production that was exported was produced at world prices. To the extent that government payments stimulated investment in American agriculture that would not occur otherwise, however, America's agricultural supply was expanded above the free market model. Crop restriction, on the other hand, provided a year-to-year restraint. Thus, most importantly, what was subsidized was the excess capacity which was available for release in 1972, 1973, and 1974 as we entered our third era of food policy.

In the meantime, international negotiations centered on trying to achieve a general reduction in tariffs and trade barriers. The first round, beginning in the 1950s and aiming to establish the General Agreement on Tariffs and Trade (GATT), was hardly relevant to agricultural commodities employing such devices as variable import levies and deficiency payments. The GATT procedure of agreeing not to raise tariff rates and of bargaining for their mutual reduction did not generally apply where there were no fixed tariff rates.

In the second round of GATT negotiations from 1964 to 1967, called the Kennedy Round, the United States government, after first leaning toward the generally liberal solution of freer trade, came down in favor of a market-sharing agreement guaranteeing American exports a certain share of the EEC market. In addition, American negotiators proposed that the EEC and other countries of Western Europe should participate to a greater extent in costs of holding food stocks and financing aid to developing countries. The EEC, however, proposed that the levels of agricultural price support in the United States and other exporting countries should be fixed and that the governments should bind themselves not to raise those levels. But this goal was not possible for American negotiators to accomplish. Attempts to freeze levels of protection in this country have not been successful, as policymaking is subject to the varying pressures of the political process.

The Kennedy Round ended in May 1967 with an agreement on an international scheme to donate 4.5 million tons of cereals in food aid annually to meet emergencies in the poorer developing countries. The cost would be shared by the developed countries (the United States, 42 percent; the European Economic Community, 23 percent; Canada, 11 percent; the United Kingdom, 5 percent; and so on). An agreement to raise the minimum price under the International Wheat Agreement by 21½ cents to $1.73 for hard winter wheat at Gulf of Mexico ports, instead of setting the price in terms of Canadian wheat at Fort William, proved to be unimportant. World prices soon lay above this level.

The Role of Buffer Stocks

Although the move toward freer trade is very important, alone it is inadequate for minimum world food security in an era where stocks comparable with past ones are not expected to be financed by the major exporting countries, especially the United States and Canada. There is now greater need for a buffer stock plan and coordination of efforts for worldwide financing of agricultural development in the developing countries somewhat like the plan envisaged by the proponents of the World Food Board. Within this framework we discuss the role of buffer stocks as food reserves.

The classic method of price stabilization for agricultural products or of providing food reserves for consumer use is the use of buffer stocks, the first reported case of which is described in the Book of Genesis, 41:29–36. The handsome and talented Joseph, interpreting the dreams of Pharaoh, King of Egypt, foresaw seven years of good crops followed by seven poor crop years. The able Pharaoh, commissioning him to conduct an extensive buffer stock program, reaped large rewards for the people of Egypt and the surrounding territory. Joseph, the Bible says, was successful because he knew in advance the exact lengths of the periods of surplus and shortage, an advantage not shared in the twentieth century by secretaries of agriculture or their advisors. A buffer stock program requires some attention to problems of uncertainty.

Considerable attention has been given to the desirable levels of food reserves apart from the programs carried out by the Commodity Credit Corporation (CCC). In 1945, 317 papers were submitted in a contest sponsored by the American Farm Economic Association on the topic "A Price Policy for Agriculture, Consistent with Economic Progress, that Will Promote Adequate and More Stable Income from Farming."[15] Among the 18 prizewinning papers, 9 emphasized storage as a means to stabilization, 5 took stabilization of physical supplies (mainly a consumer food orientation) as their primary objective, one proposed stabilization of feed grain supplies and income stabilization for wheat and cotton, one advocated storage to stabilize prices of nonexport durable products, and one suggested stabilizing prices of durable products.[16]

William H. Nicholls, winner of the first prize in the contest, developed a proposed storage policy for cotton, corn, wheat, and oats.[17] He proposed:

> . . . that, for each storable commodity, Congress should designate (1) an operating range in terms of specific minimum and maximum carryovers; (2) five-year moving averages of production as the criteria of storage policy within this range; and (3) specific percentages of the excess of actual production above (or the deficit below) this average by which year-end total stocks, private and public, would be increased (or diminished) by CCC operations.[18]

[15]*Journal of Farm Economics,* Vol. XXVII, No. 4, November 1945, pp. 737–902.
[16]William H. Nicholls and D. Gale Johnson, "The Farm Policy Awards, 1945: A Topical Digest of the Winning Essays," *Journal of Farm Economics,* Vol. XXVIII, No. 1, February 1946, pp. 267–283.
[17]*Journal of Farm Economics,* November 1945, pp. 752–756.
[18]*Ibid.,* p. 752.

When, in any year, the actual production of (say) cotton exceeds the five-year moving average ending with that year, the corporation should purchase sufficient cotton so that the aggregate increase in stocks, public and private (including stocks under loan), equals (say) 60 percent of the excess of actual production over the average. Conversely, when actual production falls short of the moving average, the corporation should sell that amount necessary to decrease total stocks by (say) 60 percent of the production deficit. . . .[19]

Under this rule, in a period of years when cotton production was gradually rising, stocks would rise too, but not to the extent of the amount of increase in production, and supply would be somewhat stabilized.[20] For corn, the proposed change in carry-over equaled 75 percent of the difference between the actual production and the moving average, when the latter was larger; thus, unless the carry-over were already at the minimum, the change would provide a heavy counterweight to a single bad crop year in the Corn Belt. If actual production were larger than the five-year average, only 50 percent of the difference would go into storage, thus minimizing the increase in stocks that would otherwise occur in several years of strong upward trends in production. For wheat and oats, the proposed rule for change in carry-over was 75 percent of the difference between actual and the five-year moving average production.[21] Suggested operating ranges were set at 150 to 850 million bushels for corn, 100 to 400 million for wheat, and 100 to 350 million for oats.[22] In a bad crop year, stocks would not be drawn down below the minimum by government action, or in a good crop year, raised above the maximum.

Although such rules, if followed, would have had the merit of helping to stabilize supply, this is not the direction taken by Congress or the Department of Agriculture. Until the early 1970s, price support rather than supply stabilization was the dominant policy goal for corn, wheat, oats, and several other crops, a producer-oriented rather than a consumer-oriented goal. In view of the excess demand created by the European Recovery Program in the last half of the 1940s, and then the increasing restriction on demand for America's farm exports brought about by growing overvaluation of the dollar from about 1952 onward (see Chapters 3 and 9), a policy of supply stabilization in the 1950s would have required heavier subsidies to obtain equivalent farm income. Once the stocks were built up, at the end of the 1950s, to levels well above those suggested by Nicholls, the question was, what policy should be followed in their management.

In 1959, it was hypothesized that prices for some commodities (corn was used as the example) were approaching free market equilibrium levels and, inferentially, then a policy of stock maintenance under normal weather conditions could be carried out without heavy expenditure on production controls.[23]

[19]*Ibid.*, p. 747.
[20]*Ibid.*, p. 753.
[21]*Ibid.*, p. 754.
[22]*Ibid.*, p. 755.
[23]H. G. Halcrow and T. A. Hieronymous, "Parity Prices in Their Economic Context," *Journal of Farm Economics*, Vol. XLI, No. 15, December 1959, pp. 1289–1300.

Storage policy might emphasize supply stabilization rather than stock reduction. In light of the rising world population, the existing surpluses in the developed countries, and the growing food deficits of some developing countries, this could have been an optimum time to revive a policy such as the proposed World Food Board. But, with such large surpluses in the United States, Canada, and other countries, a policy for a world food program emphasizing consumer welfare and security gave way before the more immediate problems of price supports and subsidies for producers.

The Policy Questions

If policymakers had the insight and the clairvoyance of Joseph and if government policy could be carried out under a decree of a beneficent Pharaoh, buffer stock policy would need to take account of only the food goals to be served and the production anticipated. Since this supposition is not the case, a world food program requires attention to at least the following questions:

1 What magnitude of stocks shall be carried on the average? As a maximum or minimum? Related to this are questions of goals, cost allocation, etcetera. The food deficit in India, for example, generated by the monsoon failures of the mid 1960s, was on the order of 20 million tons annually, plus or minus 5 or 6 million, for a period of two to three years. If and when a similar failure occurs, shall the goal be to compensate to the extent of one-quarter of the deficit? One-half? Three-quarters? A correlative question concerns the magnitude of food aid. The 4.5 million tons of food aid, as agreed in the Kennedy Round, would be grossly inadequate to provide the assumed requirements for relief.

2 What rules shall be followed for increasing and decreasing world food stocks? One answer might be a model for the world patterned after Nicholls's proposals, discussed above, for the United States. That is, world food stocks in a good (poor) crop year might be increased (decreased) by an agreed fraction of the amount by which this crop exceeded (or fell short of) the five-year moving average, projected to allow for trend.

3 Where shall stocks be held? To minimize the combined costs of world transport and storage, there must be a compromise between two factors: (a) To minimize transportation costs, a rather even flow of commodities would need to be shipped from the exporting food surplus areas to those of food deficit. This factor would suggest a proportionately large volume of stocks to be held in food deficit areas. (b) To minimize storage costs, stocks would be held in areas of food surplus. In time of need the shipments could go directly to the areas of most acute distress. The aggregate world storage capacity could be less than if stocks were held in areas of expected need. But this policy would require more emergency capacity in oceangoing ships and in port and distribution facilities.

4 Who shall control the stock increase or decrease and the allocation? Traditionally, the exporting countries—the United States, Canada, Australia, etcetera—have reserved this role to themselves. But Australia apparently has assumed this responsibility with some reluctance. The Canadian Wheat Board has carried this role, apparently reflecting the interests of the government of

Canada and farmers in the prairie provinces. In the United States, the Congress and the administration, evidently most willing of all, have assumed this role. American farm organizations apparently have not wished it otherwise. But, is this in their best interests or in the best interest of the nation? Would not a more comprehensive programming of world food supply through a World Food Board, in which the United States would have a major role, be able to provide a more desirable solution in the food era ahead?

A Policy Conclusion

The expansion of international trade and efficient programming of food aid requires cooperative action among the nations, especially among those that are in position to give aid and to benefit from trade. This responsibility places the United States in the most critical and influential position among the nations. A world trade board, programming food-reserve buffer stocks, could be an effective instrument in bringing about a sustained expansion in world trade, a more efficient plan of world development, and more equitable and more efficient programming of food aid.[24] Before developing this further, however, we need to clear away a number of policy questions concerning individual commodities.

POLICY FOR SUGAR, WOOL, AND BEEF LINKED TO TRADE

Tariffs and import quotas are policy instruments applied to several imported agricultural commodities which are competitive with domestic production in the United States. Most important among these are sugar, wool, beef, and dairy products. In addition, production payments have been used chiefly for sugar and wool to achieve policy goals for domestic production. What are the general policy effects? What alternatives are suggested for the future?

The United States Sugar Program

For many years the program for sugar production and marketing carried out by the federal government has had two major policy goals: (1) to maintain a healthy and competitive domestic sugar industry, and (2) to assure adequate sugar supplies for consumers at reasonable prices. To achieve these goals, a marketing quota system has been established which limits the total sugar available to American consumers and allocates production and marketing privileges among domestic producers and foreign countries. This quota system, first enacted into law in 1934, replaced a system of protection based solely on a tariff of 2½ cents per pound on imports of raw sugar. Under the depression prices then prevailing, it was felt that the tariff alone did not give sufficient support to farm income or protect consumers from the wide fluctuations in sugar prices on world markets. During the 1930s, the new system brought growth in the American sugar indus-

---

[24]Students may wish to compare these conclusions with those of F. F. Elliott of the Bureau of Agricultural Economics (BAE), "A Proposed World Trade Board for Expanding International Trade," *Journal of Farm Economics,* Vol. XXVII, No. 3, August 1945, pp. 571–590.

try, stabilized supplies, and transferred additional income from consumers to farmers. Under the prices and price guarantees of World War II, quotas were suspended to encourage further expansion in domestic production by American farm producers and to further the orderly growth of the domestic sugar industry.[25] It was followed by major amendments in 1965, 1971, and other years.[26] Under this system, the Secretary of Agriculture sets the total quota in December for the ensuing year, allocating the quota according to the statutory formula established by the Congress. Generally it has been increased from one year to the next to meet the increase in demand expected in the domestic market, taking account of production trends, visible stocks at the beginning of the year, expected receipts from foreign and offshore domestic areas, trends in domestic disappearance, and per capita consumption (Table 7-3). Following a sharp rise in sugar prices in 1974, quotas were suspended—as in World War II—to increase domestic production.

Economic Rationale The economic rationale for this policy rests in part on the fact that the demand for sugar is very inelastic (see Chapter 3) and so is supply. Sugarcane, the main source of the world sugar supply, requires 18 months to mature and, in most countries, farmers do not readily shift acreage to or from cane production. Sugar beet production requires special land preparation and a separate line of farm equipment. Although the labor requirement is heavy even under full mechanization, the fixed costs are high and variable costs are low, so that farmers, even on a free market and without quotas, change output very slowly in response to a given price change. Additionally, beet sugar factories, raw cane sugar mills, and refineries converting raw cane sugar into refined sugar, all require long-term capital investment which is used only part of the year. Under free market conditions, the high risks and uncertainties of investment tend to encourage caution in investment and maintenance of manufacturing schedules once plants are built. In a free market, these conditions create great instability in prices from year to year, very high prices during periods of unusually strong demand, such as wartime, or when alternative supplies are restricted, and sometimes very low prices, which can prevail over several years under such inelastic supply and demand. The quota system was adopted to serve the national interest in price stability and to protect the financial interests of domestic producers.

Quota Costs and Benefits To make the quota system function smoothly, both foreign and domestic producers must be subsidized so that sugar production is a preferred alternative. The subsidy to foreign producers comes through the

---

[25]For a general summary of sugar legislation to August 10, 1973, see *United States Code,* Title 7, Agriculture, chap. 34, Sugar Production and Control, pp. 4–75, sec. 1100 ff.

[26]Sugar Act Amendments of 1965, Public Law 89–331; 75 *Stat.* 1271, and Sugar Act Amendments of 1971, Public Law 92–138; 85 *Stat.* 379, *U.S. Code, Congressional and Administrative News,* 89th Cong., 1st Sess., 1965, pp. 1290–1302, 4145–4170, and 92d Cong., 1st Sess., 1971, pp. 403–416, 1530–1566.

Table 7-3 Sugar Quotas, Production and Consumption, Selected Years, 1950–1974

(In thousands of short tons, raw value, except per capita consumption in pounds, refined)

Item	1950	1955	1960	1965	1970	1972	1973	1974 (prel.)
Quota charges by supplying areas*	8,274	8,402	9,526	9,920	11,552	11,840	11,676	11,176
United States	3,412	3,349	3,629	5,261	6,375	6,402	6,343	5,430
Beet	1,749	1,797	2,165	3,025	3,569	3,511	3,512	3,025
Mainland cane	518	500	619	1,099	1,308	1,630	1,613	1,253
Hawaii	1,145	1,052	845	1,137	1,146	1,113	1,142	995
Puerto Rico and Virgin Islands	1,064	1,090	903	834	352	148	76	157
Foreign areas	3,798	3,963	4,994	3,825	5,177	5,438	5,333	5,746
Production	2,466	2,386	3,076	4,152	4,712	4,896	4,931	4,618
Visible stocks, beginning of period	1,759	1,930	2,005	2,700	2,799	2,687	2,710	2,583
Receipts from foreign sources	3,783	4,027	4,885	4,027	5,296	5,458	5,329	5,787
Receipts from offshore domestic areas	2,173	2,155	1,748	1,972	1,500	1,262	1,221	1,147
Domestic disappearance total	8,282	8,443	9,336	10,151	11,459	11,528	11,538	11,273
Per capita consumption†	100.6	96.3	97.6	96.6	102.5	103.0	102.1	97.0

*Sugar quotas govern the supply of sugar from all sources, foreign and domestic, available to the conterminous United States. The formulas for allocating the quotas among the supplying areas are established by Congress, the size of the quotas is determined by the Secretary of Agriculture.

†Adjusted for changes in invisible stocks (estimated) held by manufacturers, wholesalers, and retailers.

Source: U.S. Department of Agriculture, Statistical Reporting Service, *Agricultural Statistics,* annual; and U.S. Agricultural Stabilization and Conservation Service, *Sugar Reports,* monthly.

Reprinted from *Statistical Abstract of the United States, 1973,* p. 613 and 1975, p. 641.

effects of the quota, which normally holds import prices in the United States well above those in unsubsidized world markets. During 1965–69, for example, import prices at New York for raw unrefined sugar wholesale averaged 4 cents per pound (or $80 per ton) above prices in unsubsidized world markets. Foreign producers, although subtracting a tariff of 0.625 cents per pound, gained a net advantage on the American market of about $60 to $65 a ton for sale of raw sugar.[27] Domestic producers received this price advantage, thus benefiting from the tariff protection as well as quotas, plus direct payments which in 1971 ranged from 80 cents per 100 pounds of recoverable sugar on small farms (equivalent to about $3.20 per ton for sugar beets or $1.30 to $1.50 per ton of sugarcane, depending on sugar yield) to a low of 30 cents per 100 pounds of recoverable sugar on farms producing in excess of 30,000 tons of raw sugar per year. This payment system—which makes sugar the only commodity program discriminating against farm size—was financed by an excise tax of 0.53 cents per pound on all sugar manufactured in, or imported into, the United States. From 1937 to 1970, revenues from this tax exceeded payments to farmers by $634 million.[28]

Except in unusual circumstances, the quota system has maintained a stable price for sugar in America at a transfer cost to consumers generally ranging from about $500 million to $1 billion annually over what they would pay for sugar under free trade. To illustrate, in 1965–69 the world price for sugar in unsubsidized markets averaged 2.66 cents per pound wholesale. The wholesale price for sugar at portside in New York averaged about 4 cents per pound (or $80 per ton) more, making a net increase in cost to American consumers under the quota system of $840 million annually, assuming average disappearance of 10.5 million tons annually. The excise tax of 0.53 cents per pound (or $10.6 per ton) would have added an additional $111 million ($10.60 × 10.5 million tons), the incidence of which would fall on consumers unless the direct payments to farmers permitted setting a higher quota than otherwise. If we assume, however, that world prices in unsubsidized markets would be higher under free trade than under the quota system, the cost of quotas to American consumers would be reduced. Conceptually, for every 1-cent increase in world price in unsubsidized markets, *ceteris paribus,* the net cost to consumers would be reduced by $210 million, on the basis of average disappearance of 10.5 million tons during 1965–69.[29]

[27]*Sugar Act Amendments of 1971,* p. 1550.

[28]*Ibid.,* p. 1535.

[29]For comparative estimates and further discussion, see D. Gale Johnson, *World Agriculture in Disarray,* pp. 157–159; D. Gale Johnson, *The United States Sugar Program: Large Costs and Small Benefits,* Washington: The American Enterprise Institute, 1974; Richard A. Snape, "Sugar: Costs of Protection and Taxation," *Economica,* London School of Economics, February 1969, pp. 29–41; D. Gale Johnson, "Sugar Program: Costs and Benefits," *Foreign Trade and Agricultural Policy,* Technical Papers, Vol. VI, Washington: National Advisory Commission on Food and Fiber, 1967, pp. 37–50; and Clayton Ogg, "Johnson and Johnson on Sugar Policy," unpublished paper, University of Minnesota, 1971. Ogg estimated the cost of the sugar program during 1965–69 to be $648 million annually, based on a world price of 4.70 cents per pound in world markets, and $1,048 million, based on the price of 2.66 cents per pound.

It has been estimated that under free trade in sugar only about 15 to 20 percent of the total domestic sugar supply would be produced in the United States, coming mainly from sugarcane out of Louisiana, Florida, and Hawaii.[30] If this had been the case, additional foreign exchange of $300 million to $500 million annually (depending on the world price assumed) would have been needed during 1965–69 to compensate for the reduction in domestic production. This requirement could have been more than offset, however, by exports of other commodities produced under favorable comparative advantage.

Domestic Production and Employment   The domestic sugar industry is highly concentrated. Only about 28,000 farms produce cane and sugar beets. In 1971, some 150,000 workers were employed on farms on a highly seasonal basis and 52,000 people were employed in 59 beet sugar factories, 93 raw cane sugar mills, and 28 refineries converting raw cane sugar into refined sugar.[31] Without the quota, tariff, and sugar payments, there would be practically no beet sugar industry and the domestic cane production would be greatly reduced. The outlay for sugar by American housewives and food processors, about $2.2 billion annually up to 1970,[32] was perhaps one-third more than it would have been under free trade.

The conditions for sugar production in America vary widely. In most areas of the North and West, when sugar beets are grown they are an important stabilizing enterprise for predominantly family-sized farms. In many of the irrigated valleys of the Great Plains and the Mountain states, sugar beets are the main enterprise for most of the farms. Capital costs have been incurred on the basis of the sugar program and farmers look to sugar beets for income and stability. Harvesting as well as most other field work is completely mechanized. Fertilizers and other farm chemicals have greatly increased yields. Sugarcane is largely a plantation type of enterprise, with large farms employing workers on a seasonal-wage basis.

Although sugar production and marketing have been covered—the only farm commodity so covered—by federal wage and employment statutes beginning with the Jones-Costigan Act of 1934, conditions for employment of family and wage workers vary widely. Sugar beets, as we have mentioned, are largely a family-type farm enterprise, with a mixed economy of family and wage workers. Much of the hard labor in thinning, hoeing, and harvesting that existed previously has been eliminated. As of 1970, about two-thirds of the sugarcane was mechanically harvested and hand labor in planting and cultivating had largely given way to mechanical planters and cultivators.

---

[30]Thomas H. Bates, "The Long-Run Efficiency of U.S. Sugar Policy," *American Journal of Agricultural Economics,* Vol. 50, No. 3, August 1968, pp. 521–535; and Donald C. Horton, "Policy Directions for the United States Sugar Program," *American Journal of Agricultural Economics,* Vol. 52, No. 2, May 1970, pp. 185–196.

[31]*Sugar Act Amendments of 1971,* p. 1536.

[32]*Ibid.,* p. 1536.

In Hawaii, worker conditions have been greatly improved as a result of the strong bargaining position established by the International Longshoremen's and Warehousemen's Union (ILWU). This powerful union has obtained for Hawaiian sugar workers the highest agricultural wages in the world, fringe benefits that include paid vacations and holidays, retirement pensions, health insurance, unemployment compensation, and workmen's compensation.[33] The natural comparative advantage enjoyed by Hawaii for growing sugarcane, plus the American quota system, which provides a price for Hawaiian producers comparable with that of producers in the continental states, has been combined to bring significant benefits to Hawaiian sugar workers. The strength of the ILWU was demonstrated in 1974 when a strike closed the Hawaiian sugar plantations from March 9 through April 16. As a result, production of cane sugar in Hawaii from January 1 through June 29, 1974, totaled only 390,764 short tons, raw sugar, compared with 542,331 tons for the same period in 1973.[34]

In Louisiana and Florida, sugar workers are largely nonunion, and conditions for a large part of the field labor force involve an "almost unbelievable degree of exploitation, deprivation, poverty, and shameful mistreatment of field workers in some of the sugar plantations."[35] Senator Fred R. Harris (Democrat of Oklahoma), quoting a 1970 survey in Louisiana by the National Sharecroppers Fund, listed the following conditions and abuses:[36]

1   The average family of six earned $2,635 annually as of January 1970, which is below the national poverty level.

2a   Seventy-six percent of the households surveyed had only outdoor sanitation facilities.

b   Fifty-two percent had only cold water inside.

c   Sixty-two percent had holes or gaps in the walls.

d   Fifty percent had leaky roofs.

3 Seventy-six percent of the households surveyed had no company help in paying for medical expenses, and thirty-seven percent had at least one chronically ill family member.

Senator Harris offered amendments to the 1971 bill to correct some of the most glaring inequities and abuses; but it is not clear that the amendments that were adopted have gone very far in correcting most of the abuses. In other words, the Congress has not been able to legislate directly to establish conditions for all workers that are comparable with those obtained in Hawaii by action of a strong labor union.

[33]*Sugar Act Amendments of 1971*, p. 1557.

[34]*Sugar Reports*, U.S. Department of Agriculture, Agricultural Stabilization and Conservation Service, No. 266, July 1974, p. 4, and *Sugar Market News*, monthly reports issued by the USDA, Argicultural Marketing Service (AMS), beginning August 1, 1975.

[35]From statements of Representative Spark Matsunaga (Democrat of Hawaii), *Sugar Act Amendments of 1971*, p. 1557.

[36]*Sugar Act Amendments of 1971*, p. 1557.

The sugar acts and amendments specify in considerable detail the rules and regulations under which the Secretary of Agriculture must function in administering the laws. One important price regulation establishes "price corridor limits," which define both an upper and a lower limit for a monthly price objective as specified in Sections 201 and 202 of the Sugar Act of 1948, as amended in October 1971. Until near the end of 1973, the spot price for raw sugar generally stayed within the price corridor limits which, in December 1973, had an upper limit of 11.07 cents per pound for raw sugar duty paid at New York. But, starting in that month, the daily spot price quotation for raw sugar duty paid at New York began to exceed the upper corridor limit, and by mid-July 1974, the daily spot price was nearly 30 cents per pound. The quota system was failing in one of its two major objectives—to assure adequate sugar supplies for consumers at reasonable prices. How did this happen and what is the lesson for the future?

The policy up to 1974 was to control sugar stocks so that the visible stocks at the beginning of the marketing period were down to less than 30 percent—in the early 1970s, in one year as low as 24 percent—of the expected domestic disappearance in the ensuing year (Table 7-3). In an inflationary year, when there may have been some heavier buying by housewives and food processors in anticipation of higher sugar prices, this policy was inadequate to prevent an upward spiral in sugar prices. In the first five months of 1974, deliveries of refined sugar reported by states of destination totaled 4.4 million tons, an increase of 5.4 percent over a year earlier. As of June 30, 1974, stocks totaled 1.95 million tons, or 0.34 million tons less than a year earlier,[37] and a higher rate of delivery could not be maintained for very long, based on a draw-down of stocks.

As we have noted, the Secretary of Agriculture announces in December the quotas for the coming year. Typically he sets the quantity required at near the lower edge of the limits set by Congress, realizing that he cannot be sure just how much sugar the market will take and knowing that it is usually easier to revise the estimate upward rather than downward. Then, if the allotments have somewhat shorted the market supply and the price begins to rise (a typical situation), the Secretary revises the estimate upward and lets a little more sugar on the market.[38] In 1974, available stocks were not sufficient to hold the price at the goal set by legislation. The rule, as an operating policy, failed to protect consumers, who in 1974 more than doubled their normal $2.2 billion outlay on sugar. The lesson for the future is that in order to assure reasonable prices to consumers under the quota system, larger stocks must be carried as a means to dampen down price fluctuations arising from unusual demand or from restrictions in supply, such as may be caused by strikes, hurricanes, or other unusual events.

[37]Data from *Sugar Reports, op. cit.,* July 1974.
[38]Don Paarlberg, *American Farm Policy,* New York: John Wiley and Sons, 1964, pp. 249, 250.

Alternatives and Constraints   The broad alternatives for sugar policy are (1) to continue with the quota program without substantial change, (2) to expand the direct payments program to domestic producers with a relaxation of quotas on imports, or (3) to move essentially to free trade.

On the average, when world supplies are normal, continuation of the first alternative will cost American consumers at least $500 million annually more than the third alternative, with or without an expansion in storage stocks. The excess costs of this program are largely concealed from consumers in the sugar price, and, apparently, consumers have "accepted" the program only because these costs are concealed. Total excess costs can be constrained somewhat by adopting a no-growth policy in domestic production and by allocating increases in quotas to foreign producers, most importantly Cuba. The Congress in the 1971 amendments, however, opted for one of the most expensive alternatives by specifying that 65 percent of the increase in future quotas must go to domestic continental producers.

The second alternative has several possible variations. Quotas for off-shore producers could be eliminated and market price, as modified by tariff and storage policy, could be allowed to prevail. Sugar from foreign sources would come chiefly from developing countries enjoying a comparative advantage. The level of payments to domestic producers could be set to achieve stabilization of a desired level of domestic production. The costs of such an alternative would be considerably less than the full quota program, and the subsidy would not be concealed.

The third alternative of free trade would under projected estimates almost wipe out the domestic beet sugar industry and greatly reduce continental production of sugarcane. Unless domestic producers were compensated for capital costs previously incurred, this solution would not be equitable for either cane or beet producers. Alternatively, a move toward freer trade, as in the second alternative, appears economical to consumers and less damaging to producers.

The difficulties inherent in choosing among these alternatives are revealed in the experience from 1973 to 1976. The high sugar prices in the early months of 1974 prompted cancellation of domestic quotas and between 1973 and 1975 sugar producers, in a classic cobweb-type reaction (see Figure 4-4), increased the land seeded to sugar beets in the United States from 1,280,100 to 1,590,900 acres.[39] The domestic production of cane and beet sugar increased by nearly one-fifth;[40] while from 1971 to 1975 world production expanded by about one-sixth.[41] In 1976, sugar prices dropped sharply from the earlier peaks.[42] In the meantime, the per capita consumption of sugar in the United States, which had been 102 pounds in 1973 and 97 pounds in 1974, dropped to 90 pounds per capita

---

[39]*Sugar and Sweetener Report,* USDA, ERS and AMS, Vol. 1, No. 4, May 1976, p. 9.
[40]*Ibid.,* p. 8.
[41]*Ibid.,* p. 6.
[42]*Ibid.,* pp. 14–23.

in 1975, the lowest since World War II.[43] The 1975–76 world sugar production at 83.4 million metric tons, raw value, was about 4.8 million tons above 1974–75 production and some 2.3 million tons above the expected 1975–76 world sugar consumption.[44] Although the low level of carry-over in 1976 of 14.5 million tons would be improved by the excess production, the growth in supply indicated that 1974 and 1975 offered only a brief respite of high prices for sugar producers.

A Policy Conclusion   The demonstrated elasticity of supply under quota suspension plus the jump in world sugar production indicated that the traditional problem of sugar subsidy and production control is chronic. Unregulated production and free trade will lead to ruinously low producer prices in the United States. However, subsidy and production control incurs unnecessary consumer costs. A reduction in size of the domestic sugar industry can provide a gain in general welfare, even if the federal government is required to buy up or liquidate investments in sugar production. D. Gale Johnson, for instance, estimated that as of 1974 the upper limit of compensation sufficient to cover all economic costs of liquidating the entire mainland sugar industry would be at the outside about $2.25 billion, or the estimated excess cost to consumers of continuing the United States sugar quota program for four years under the supply and demand conditions existing prior to 1974.[45] A more modest but still generous estimate set the cost at $2.1 billion.[46] Although this does not suggest that it would be prudent policy to eliminate the domestic sugar industry, it does suggest that a limit on growth with liquidation of the higher cost production areas could be done without undue hardship to domestic growers and with a net gain in the public welfare.

In between free trade with compensation for losses and the past policy, there is the possibility of a transitional program, involving such components as (1) elimination of import quotas, domestic market allocations, and proportionate shares; (2) direct compensation to producers to cover the difference between market prices and some target price level, such as that set by the Sugar Act of 1948 as amended in October 1971; or (3) payments permitting producers to phase out of sugar production in, say, a five-year period. A more modest proposal would be to freeze the total mainland quota at 1971 levels to discourage opening up additional producer areas that can be supported only through further subsidy. In any event, there appears to be a case for a more carefully designed inventory policy to offset fluctuations in demand and supply and to stabilize the price to consumers.

The United States Wool Program

The nation's wool program, which in principle and theory bears a close resemblance to policy for sugar, has been designed to maintain domestic wool produc-

---

[43]*Ibid.*, p. 11.
[44]*Sugar Market News, op. cit.*, Vol. II, No. 1, January 1976, p. 5.
[45]Johnson, *The Sugar Program: Large Costs and Small Benefits, op. cit.*, p. 82.
[46]*Ibid.*

tion competitive with wool imports and to encourage domestic consumption of wool as competitive with other fibers.

Policy Goals and Means   In the National Wool Act of 1954, the parent legislation for at least the next two decades, the Congress recognized wool as an essential and strategic commodity not produced in sufficient quantity or grade in the United States to meet domestic needs. It declared a national policy to encourage the annual domestic production of approximately 300 million pounds of shorn wool, grease basis, and mohair (about one-third of domestic consumption) "at prices fair to both producers and consumers in a manner which will have the least adverse effects on foreign trade."[47] The Secretary of Agriculture was directed to support the prices of wool and mohair by means of loans, purchases, payments, or other operations, using the Commodity Credit Corporation (CCC) as the implementing agency. Payments were used as the means for price support each year from 1955 to 1972, with the payment per pound set to bring the total return from wool production up to the incentive or support level— 62 cents per pound for shorn wool, grease basis—until 1965, then a transition to 72 cents per pound from 1970 onward.[48] In 1973, a sharp, worldwide increase in wool prices made payments unnecessary. From 1955 through 1972, total payments to American wool growers were $987 million, paid out of receipts from a tariff of 25½ cents per clean pound on raw wool, excepting certain coarse wools for carpets and felt, and equivalent ad valorem duties on wool manufactures.[49] Payments began again in 1974, averaging 12.9 cents per pound, to bring the return to growers up to the support level.

Implements and Constraints   The payment system for domestic wool production was adopted in lieu of either (1) higher tariffs to yield higher prices to growers, under which it was thought domestic use of wool would have declined even more rapidly than it did, or (2) free trade in wool, under which the domestic wool industry would have failed to be competitive with range cattle and other competitive resource uses. During World War II, wool had been supported at an incentive level to maintain high-level production, partially, we may say, for strategic purposes, and under the Agricultural Act of 1949, wool had been consistently supported at 90 percent of parity. In spite of this support, domestic wool production continually declined. The National Wool Growers Association, representing the wool industry, was asking for more protection in addition to the tariff of 34 to 35 cents per pound on raw wool, grease basis. In 1947 the wool growers were successful in getting Congress to increase the tariff by 50 percent,

[47]*United States Code Annotated,* Title 7, Agriculture, chap. 44, Wool Program, pp. 618–624, secs. 1781–87; *U.S. Code Congressional and Administrative News,* chap. 1041, Public Law 690, 83d Cong., 2d Sess., 1954, pp. 1047–1067, 3419–3420.

[48]*Wool Situation,* TWS-106, U.S. Department of Agriculture, Economic Research Service, May 1974, p. 20.

[49]*Ibid.,* p. 21 and *Agricultural Statistics, 1975,* USDA, p. 336.

but the act was vetoed by President Harry Truman as an embarrassment to his administration and potentially damaging to negotiations then underway to reduce tariffs and expand trade.[50] By the early 1950s, however, although, a few years before, the United States had produced most of the wool used domestically, the production by American wool growers had dropped to less than one-third of domestic consumption, and the trend was still downward.

The goal of the Congress in the National Wool Act of 1954 was to make possible a high-level support program for domestic wool without increasing the cost to consumers. To do this, the emphasis in policy was put on production payments to producers, to be financed out of the tariff. But, in large part, the policy failed to achieve the major goals. Between the early 1950s and the early 1970s, the number of stock sheep on farms in the United States declined by almost one-half. Between 1963 and 1973, domestic production of wool declined by one-third while imports of wool and wool textile products dropped even more (Figure 7-3). By 1974 total production of wool in the United States had dropped to 139 million pounds, or less than half of the production target in the act of 1954 and only 2.5 percent of total world production of wool.[51]

A Policy Conclusion   Although the tariff has restricted imports of textile wools, while carpet-grade wools and mohair have been admitted duty free, both classes of wool have been much more strongly affected by competition with cotton and manmade fibers, which have been improved in texture and quality and reduced in price as compared with wool. In such a situation the tariff is a weak means for protecting the wool industry, and questions must be raised about future policy. Clearly, consumers will be best off if wool prices are allowed to seek their equilibrium level in a competitive market, but the policy moves in this direction have been modest indeed. In May 1976, for example, a bill was introduced in the House of Representatives to remove import duties on coarse wool, very little of which was produced in the United States. But support of the National Wool Growers Association was apparently dependent on a clear understanding that the measure was not to establish a general principle of tariff removal on wool and wool products.[52] In view of the small size of the American wool industry, by far the most economical way to stabilize it would be a system

---

[50]The President's veto message read in part as follows: "The enactment of a law providing for additional barriers to the importation of wool at a very moment when this Government is taking the leading part in a United Nations Conference at Geneva called for the purpose of reducing trade barriers and of drafting a charter for an international trade organization in an effort to restore the world to economic peace, would be a tragic mistake. It would be a blow to our leadership in world affairs. It would be interpreted around the world as a first step on that same road to economic isolationism down which we and other countries traveled after the First World War with such disastrous consequences. I cannot approve such an action." From veto of "The Wool Act of 1947," June 26, 1947, To the Senate of the United States. For discussion, see J. K. Galbraith, Meyer Kestnbaum, and Theodore Schultz, *The Wool Veto and the Crisis in Foreign Trade,* The University of Chicago Round Table, No. 484, June 29, 1947.

[51]*Agricultural Statistics, 1975,* pp. 334 and 335.

[52]*Cotton and Wool Situation,* USDA, ERS, July 1976, p. 19.

Million pounds

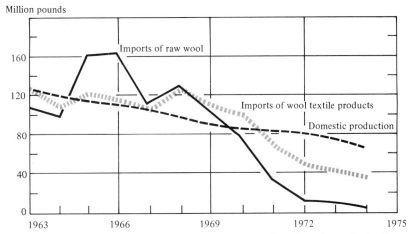

Figure 7-3 Domestic production and imports of wool and wool textile products. *(Source: Handbook of Agricultural Charts and Cotton and Wool Situation, USDA, ERS, various issues.)*

of direct payments. If an assured reserve supply of wool is desired for strategic purposes or to maintain domestic wool mills, this goal can be accomplished by a modestly programmed reserve-stock program.

Additionally, as we noted in Chapter 4, the wool industry and certain environmental goals have been in sharp conflict. For example, should cattle or other resource uses be permitted to further displace what is left of the wool industry? It is clear that for a small, one-time public expenditure, most wool growers could be compensated equitably while America shifted to a free trade policy for wool, mutton and lamb.

Beef Policy as Related to Trade

Beef, with high income elasticity of demand, is one of the most highly favored farm commodities in an increasingly affluent society. It enjoys a policy position where free market pricing and limitation of imports have resulted in the most massive shift of resources within the entire farm subsector. Between 1950 and 1969, for example, the number of beef cattle and calves on farms more than doubled. The number of beef cows and heifers two years and older increased by 116 percent while the number of dairy cows and heifers declined by 41 percent. The number of sheep decreased, as we have noted, while the number of hogs remained practically the same.[53] This massive resource shift, dependent on the trend increase in demand for beef and veal growing out of high income elasticity and increasing consumer affluence, was expected to continue. The most authoritative estimate in 1970 was that "the industry still needs to increase its output by a third to keep pace with trends in population and in per capita consumption over

[53]*Agricultural Statistics,* 1960 to 1970.

the next 10 years."[54] By the mid 1970s, there were 18 to 20 percent more cattle on farms than in 1970.

Policy Goals and Means   The traditional policy for the beef cattle industry is to rely on competitive enterprise and free market pricing with protection from imports by quotas and tariffs. Relatively high income elasticities (.47 for beef and .58 for veal in Table 3-2) lead to the inference that demand will continue to increase as the economy grows and as people become more affluent. High price elasticities (−.95 for beef and −1.60 for veal, in Table 3-2) suggest that, under usual circumstances, free market pricing, rather than price supports and production restrictions, will maintain near-maximum returns to cattle producers and maximize consumer welfare. Growth of the industry has been favored by the private ownership of range land and leasing of public lands under conditions generally favorable to sustaining high-level carrying capacity of range land. Price supports and price controls generally have been regarded as inimical to the interests of cattle producers as well as consumers.

Control of imports to avoid excessive competition from foreign cattle producers, however, is a basic tenet of American cattle owners. The important economic rationale is the belief that foreign producers have lower costs, or are willing to accept lower rates of return on labor, land, and other inputs. The working hypothesis for policy is that free trade in beef and veal will restrict earnings from cattle and inhibit growth of the nation's cattle industry to the long-run disadvantages of cattle producers and consumers. Additionally, since many foreign countries have not eradicated the dreaded hoof-and-mouth disease, all imports of meat or live cattle must meet United States sanitary regulations.

Imports and Policy Constraints   In 1964, the Congress adopted an act (Public Law 88-482; 78 *Stat.* 594) to provide for the imposition of quotas on the importation of certain meat and meat products, basically limiting imports of fresh, chilled, or frozen cattle meat or meat of goats and sheep (except lambs) in any quarter to no more than 4 percent of domestic beef and veal production.[55] The Secretary of Agriculture was directed to impose quotas whenever imports were projected to exceed this amount, but quotas might be suspended if, in the opinion of the President, he found that it was the overriding interest of the United States to do so, taking account of economic and national security interests, domestic prices, and other possible superseding trade agreements. The formula for imposing quotas was then based on the average production of beef and mutton in the previous three years, as compared with production in a base period,

---

[54]Ronald A. Gustafson and Roy N. Van Arsdall, *Cattle Feeding in the United States,* U.S. Department of Agriculture, Economic Research Service, Agricultural Economic Report No. 186, October 1970, p. iii.

[55]*U.S. Code Congressional and Administrative News,* 88th Cong., 2d Sess., 1964, pp. 680–682, 3070–3080.

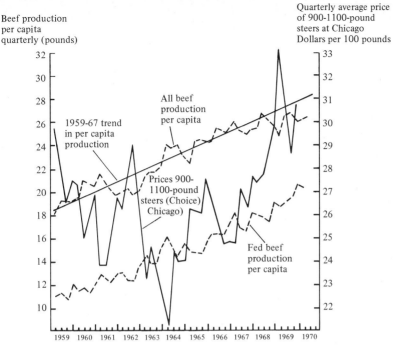

Figure 7-4 Beef production and prices. (*Source: Handbook of Agricultural Charts, Livestock Situation, and National Food Situation, USDA, ERS, various issues.*)

multiplied by the base level of imports. Thus, the quota for imports was programmed to increase in proportion to expansion in domestic production.

The basic policy goal in limiting meat imports is to prevent unregulated imports from creating excessive hardship in the cattle and sheep industry. Prior to legislation enacted March 31, 1964, beef cattle prices were 76 percent of parity, a cyclical low. Prices were protected by a tariff of 3 cents per pound on most imports of fresh, chilled, or frozen beef or comparable ad valorem duties. Imports of beef had increased from 200 million pounds (carcass weight) in 1956 to 1.7 billion pounds in 1963. During the same period, consumption of beef rose from 15.7 billion to 18.6 billion pounds. Thus, foreign beef accounted for one-half the total increased domestic use of beef over the eight-year period 1956–63.[56] This growth in imports was regarded by cattlemen and their representative organizations—the American National Cattlemen's Association and the National Livestock Feeders Association especially—as a major factor in what was then a depressed cattle market (Figure 7-4). They supported the legislation as a protection against further growth in imports.

The fact is, however, that the break in cattle prices in 1963–64 was associ-

[56]*Ibid.*, p. 3071. Imports of beef from most communist countries were subject to a tariff of 6 cents per pound or equivalent ad valorem duties.

ated mainly with a rising rate of liquidation of breeding stock preceding an inventory peak in 1965 (Figure 7-4). During the next three or four years, the price effects of the liquidation were strong enough to depress beef imports in the United States below the levels set in the quota legislation. Not until 1970, following the price peak of 1968–69 (Figure 7-4), did imports become large enough to warrant imposition of quotas.[57] The quota then announced was suspended by proclamation of the President on June 30. Although the parity ratio in the autumn months of 1970 was at its lowest level since the early '1930s, the reason given for the suspension was the high level of beef cattle prices (Figure 7-4) and the priority given to control of inflation. Subsequently, imports tended to level off at near the quota level and then began to decline under dollar devaluation and relatively lower cattle prices.[58] For ten years after the quota law was passed, the occasion had not been appropriate for its use. The tariff of 3 cents per pound on imports of beef and veal apparently was effective in holding beef imports generally below quota levels, with temporary increases in imports going slightly above. The continually increasing demand for beef in the United States, which was primarily responsible for domestic growth in beef production, was also strong enough to draw in increased imports. By 1972 the imports of 2 billion pounds of beef (carcass weight) was 7.5 percent of total domestic beef consumption and 27.5 percent of the total lower-quality, nonfed beef. Following a price break in the fall of 1974 which carried over into the first months of 1975, cattlemen again called for imposition of the quota, only to be denied again on the same basis, that the quota would contribute to inflation.

Tariff and Quota Effects   The tariff of 3 cents a pound tends to depress cattle prices most substantially in Australia and to support them in the United States; but precise estimates are very difficult to establish. Would dropping the tariff result in more beef from Australia being shipped into America? Or would other importing countries continue to demand their traditional share? Since beef cattle supply functions in Australia and other exporting countries are believed to be highly inelastic, and since the demands of some importers are also inelastic, the market shares do not change rapidly. If the tariff were fully effective in protection of beef prices in tbe United States, could it affect retail prices of hamburger and other processed meats as much as 3 cents a pound? The answer probably is no, because both elasticities of supply and demand must be taken into account. The incidence of the tariff is shifted back to beef exporters in Australia as well as forward to American consumers. At the farm level in the United

---

[57]The formula for determining the import quota in 1970, then set at 1,097.7 million pounds, was as follows: (*a*) average domestic production of beef, goats, and sheep in 1968–70, divided by (*b*) average domestic production of beef, goats, and sheep in 1959–63, multiplied by (*c*) 110 percent of 725.4 million pounds (the base quota set in 1964). Thus: (*a*) divided by (*b*) multiplied by (*c*) equals the quota for imports.

[58]*Statistical Abstract of the United States,* 1973, p. 787.

States, the incidence of the tariff is normally probably less than 1 cent a pound. Its impact on the market for fed beef is probably much less than this.[59]

J. W. Freebairn and Gordon C. Rausser have concluded that, since 1960, the actual changes in the annual levels of beef imports into the American market have had only a modest effect on performance of American cattle producers and the livestock industry.[60] Beef imports only modestly influence the retail price of all meats, with the most direct influences being exerted on the lower-quality, manufacturing beef products. Specifically, it is estimated that based on 1972 data,[61] an increase of 200 million pounds in beef imports, *ceteris paribus,* would reduce retail prices of choice beef by less than 1 cent per pound in the current year and by 1.31 cents in the long term. An increase of 700 million pounds would reduce choice beef by 3.47 cents in the current year and 4.59 cents in the long term. Also, in the long term, with a 200-million pound increase, hamburger would be reduced by 2.29 cents, pork by 0.20 cents, and chicken by 0.31 cents.[62] Farm prices would decline by 60 cents per 100 pounds for slaughter steers, $1.09 per 100 pounds for cull cows, and $1.16 per 100 pounds for feeder calves. The number of cows on farms would not drop in either the current year or the long term, but would increase slightly because of the slightly lower opportunity cost of keeping cull cows for another year. Since the number of cattle on feed declines slightly, the main price effect of increased imports falls on those keeping chiefly beef-cow herds for the growing of feeder calves.

A Policy Conclusion   Questions of policy in regard to the beef import quota go beyond these direct price effects. Typically, beef imports have risen to quota levels or somewhat beyond only when domestic retail meat prices were high; and imports generally have declined rapidly when there was a major break in cattle prices, especially one as severe as that of 1964. After such a break, or even after a shorter one such as in the winter of 1974–75, cattle growers have typically called for increased protection. But, since beef imports are usually falling rapidly at such times, this is not the element that is depressing the market. Rather, it is the liquidation of livestock herds. The import quota is not effective under these circumstances and offers no protection to the livestock industry. In times of high

---

[59]See especially J. W. Freebairn and G. C. Rausser, "An Econometric Model of the U.S. Livestock Sector with Emphasis on Beef Imports," University of California at Davis, 1973 (mimeographed). See also G. P. Houck, "The Short Run Impact of Beef Imports on U.S. Meat Prices," *Australian Journal of Agricultural Economics,* Vol. 18, 1974, pp. 60–72.

[60]J. W. Freebairn and Gordon C. Rausser, "Effects of Changes in the Level of U.S. Beef Imports," *American Journal of Agricultural Economics,* Vol. 57, No. 4, November 1975, pp. 676–688.

[61]The 1972 retail prices were, per pound, choice beef, 113.8 cents; hamburger, 74.4 cents; pork, 83.2 cents; and chicken 41.4 cents. The 1972 farm prices per 100 pounds were: slaughter steers, $35.83; cull cows, $25.21; and feeder calves, $46.54. *Ibid.,* p. 687.

[62]For fed beef, other beef, pork, and chicken respectively, the accepted price elasticities of demand were -0.83, -0.43, -0.84, and 0.85; and the income elasticities were 1.61, -0.21, 0.46, and 0.75. *Ibid.,* p. 678.

beef prices, on the other hand, when imports tend to go higher, it has been demonstrated that the national administration is reluctant to activate the quota, or to keep it in effect. So it is of little help to cattle growers in this circumstance either.

If the quota is ineffective, the broader benefits of the 3-cent tariff are in doubt. Because of the limited nature of beef imports and the American cattle producers' response to the fed-beef market, the retail market is not protected to the full extent of the tariff. Farm prices for fed beef are only slightly affected by it, and there are other policy questions of still broader importance.

Only in a very few beef-exporting countries are cattle prices lower than in the United States.[63] If free trade in food and farm products were more general, especially in the EEC, Japan, and other expanding markets, cattle prices would rise in these exporting countries as more of their beef exports were diverted to other countries. So a more general tariff reduction would be of interest to the American cattle industry, and a shift to this point of view would have wide implications for farm and food policy. Such a shift would need to be coordinated with other policy and other possible changes, however, especially policy in the dairy industry.

POLICY IN THE DAIRY INDUSTRY[64]

Because of the multiple-product nature of the dairy industry and the uniqueness of the market as divided between fluid milk and manufactured products, policy in the dairy industry is characterized by an unusual amount of government intervention. This is true not only in America, but in other developed countries and many developing countries as well.

The Policy Goals

Three general goals dominate the policy of intervention in dairy product markets. One is to bring orderly marketing to these markets in place of chaotic conditions that existed prior to federal legislation and that presumably would exist in its absence. The second is to assure an adequate supply of high-quality milk and dairy products for consumers at prices that are high enough to assure this supply but not so high as to create unnecessary surpluses of fluid milk. The third goal is to maintain a market that is efficient in transferring income to dairy farmers, providing income stability from season to season and from year to year.

---

[63]For further discussion, see D. Gale Johnson, *World Agriculture in Disarray, op. cit.,* pp. 56, 144–148.

[64]James W. Gruebele has contributed importantly to this section through advice and criticism. Also, see especially James W. Gruebele, "An Economic Analysis of Government Price Support and Federal Order Programs, 1949–1971," *Dairy Marketing Facts,* AE-4304, December 1972; and *Proceedings, the 1974 Dairy Marketing Forum* (James W. Gruebele and Roland W. Bartlett), University of Illinois at Urbana-Champaign.

The Policy Means

To achieve these goals, federal marketing agreements and orders have been developed and applied to all the large regional markets in the United States, sometimes called "milk sheds," to regulate the flow of milk that is sold as fluid. This milk must meet certain sanitary and quality standards which qualify it as USDA Grade A. The portion of this milk that is required to meet the demand for fluid consumption is classified, as to price, as Class I. The balance of Grade A milk that is not sold as Class I, and other milk that does not qualify as Grade A, have for many years been sold as Class II. More recently, milk for some uses has gone as Class III. All the milk that is not sold as Class I is manufactured into butter, cheese, nonfat dry-milk powder, and evaporated milk. The price for Class I milk is regulated by control of supply and the price of Class II milk has been stabilized through federal price supports, which involve government purchase, storage, and diversion of the quantity that is in surplus. A milk market that is regulated by a federal marketing agreement and order is called a federal order market.

Although the Agricultural Adjustment Act of 1933 first authorized the use of marketing agreements and orders under federal authority, and although there were a number of state milk boards for several years both before and after 1933, the parent law for practically all milk legislation is the Agricultural Marketing Agreements Act of 1937. Under this act, order was restored to Class I milk markets that had become chaotic during the Great Depression owing to the destructive competition of unregulated production and sales. Under the Agricultural Act of 1949 and subsequent legislation, the Secretary of Agriculture was authorized and directed to support the price of Class II milk generally between 75 to 90 percent of parity, depending on supply and demand. In the Agricultural and Consumer Protection Act of 1973, the minimum support was raised to 80 percent, and the range of discretion for the Secretary narrowed from 80 to 90 percent. In 1976, the Congress passed a bill to raise the minimum to 85 percent of parity, then $7.69 per 100 pounds. This was vetoed as too costly to the government, too restrictive to consumption, and too strong a stimulus to excess milk production. On October 2, 1975, the Secretary had raised the floor to $7.24, up from $6.57 since April 1, 1974.

Under this policy of classified pricing, order has long been restored to American milk markets and consumers have been assured of an abundant supply of high-quality milk. But, under the law, according to data published by the Department of Agriculture,[65] per capita consumption of all milk on a milk-equivalent basis declined steadily from 653 pounds in 1960 to 557 pounds in 1973. At the same time, fluid milk declined from 278 to 213 pounds, fluid cream from 9.1 to 5.6 pounds, butter from 7.5 to 4.8 pounds, and evaporated milk from 11.2 to 4.8 pounds. Although low-fat milk increased from 8.5 to 14.9 pounds and ice

---

[65]*Dairy Statistics Through 1960,* Statistical Bulletin 303, pp. 380–381; *Dairy Situation,* March 1974, p. 17, and subsequent issues.

cream held steady, the lowering of total consumption of dairy products contributed to a deterioration in the American diet (as discussed more fully in Chapter 11). Between 1956 and 1962, per capita consumption of fluid milk had declined by 7 percent, or about 1 percent per year.[66]

Implementing Class I Prices

As a result of widespread mergers and consolidations of dairy market cooperatives that climaxed in the late 1960s, which were legal under the Capper-Volstead Act of 1922, dairy markets became more highly concentrated. The supply of Class I milk apparently became easier to control, and monopoly prices could more easily be passed on to consumers. In 1972, it was estimated that Class I prices in 25 federal order markets exceeded the extra costs of supplying this milk by an average of $1.11 per 100 pounds of milk, or 2.4 cents per quart when the hauling rate was 35 cents per 100 pounds, and by 1.3 cents per quart when the hauling rate was 60 cents per 100 pounds.[67] An estimate for 1973 was 2 cents per quart, which would be more than $400 million charged for Class I milk above the extra costs of supplying milk of the necessary grade.[68] Although these estimates must be regarded as only approximations, the fact is that under the influence of Class I pricing and according to data published by the Department of Agriculture, 77 percent of the 115.4 billion pounds of milk produced in 1973 met Grade A standards and only 57 percent of this milk was required for Class I uses. In other words, the Class I price differential was creating an unnecessary surplus of fluid milk—defined as the amount of milk left after deducting from total milk receipts the Class I sales, a necessary reserve of 20 percent, and the seasonal surplus. From 1952 to 1972, as the result of a widening differential for Class I prices, the unnecessary surplus in 15 of the largest federal order markets increased from 8 percent to 23 percent of total milk receipts in these markets.[69] The proportion of milk received in all federal order markets that was used to fill Class I market sales fell from 65 percent of total milk receipts in 1969 to 60 percent in 1972 and to 58 percent in 1974.[70] In 1974, in the Chicago federal order market, out of total receipts of 8.1 billion pounds of milk, only 39 percent was used as Class I, down from 54 percent in 1969.[71] In the same year, in the New York–New Jersey

---

[66]Roland W. Bartlett, "Fluid Milk Sales as Related to Demand Elasticities," *Journal of Dairy Science,* Vol. 47, No. 12, December 1964, pp. 1314–1321.

[67]Roland W. Bartlett, "Bringing Federal Order Class I Pricing Up-to-date and in Line with Antitrust Regulations," *Illinois Agricultural Economics,* Vol. 14, No. 1, and *Dairy Marketing Facts,* AE-4335, University of Illinois at Urbana-Champaign; Department of Agricultural Economics, January 1974; and *Proceedings, The 1974 Dairy Marketing Forum,* University of Illinois at Urbana-Champaign, pp. 22–23.

[68]Roland W. Bartlett, paper presented at the Conference on Milk Prices and the Market System, sponsored by the Community Nutrition Institute, Washington, Dec. 4, 1975.

[69]J. W. Gruebele, "The Changing Conditions in the Dairy Industry," *The 1974 Dairy Marketing Forum,* University of Illinois at Urbana-Champaign, p. 18.

[70]*Federal Milk Order Market Statistics,* annual summaries published by the U.S. Department of Agriculture for 1969, 1972, and 1974.

[71]*Federal Milk Order Market Statistics,* Agricultural Stabilization and Conservation Service, FMOS—188, October 1975.

federal order market, out of total receipts of 9.4 billion pounds, only 51 percent was used as Class I, down from 54 percent in 1969. This left 4.6 billion pounds of Grade A milk (Grade A equivalent) to be manufactured into butter, cheese, or other products in this so-called milk "deficit" and indisputably high-cost area. An unnecessary cost of at least 2 cents a quart for fluid milk was being passed on to consumers in the New York–New Jersey milk market and surrounding area.

Implementing Federal Price Supports

To stabilize the price of milk that is diverted to manufactured uses, the government has to purchase marginal amounts of milk so that markets will clear at the designated support levels. From fiscal year 1949–50, under the Agricultural Act of 1949 and subsequent legislation, to 1972–73, when increased demands made government supports unnecessary, the net price support purchases and related costs for buying, processing, transporting, and storing, less the proceeds of sales to commercial buyers for domestic use and export, totaled $5.4 billion. Additionally, $1.1 billion of tariff receipts (Section 32 funds) was used to buy milk for school lunch and welfare uses and $1.6 billion was expended under specific legislative authority in special milk programs for children in schools, child-care centers, and similar institutions. The total came close to $8 billion.[72]

From 1953 to 1973, the government purchases of butter and cheese were the chief means for implementing price supports. Total purchases in terms of milk equivalent varied from year to year within a range of 1.9 to 8.5 percent of the total milk produced. From 1960 to 1973, the average was close to 5 percent of the total production.[73] With one or two exceptions, supports were lowered to 75 percent of parity following years of large purchases and then raised again when government inventories were reduced. Although practically all the government purchases were diverted outside of regular market channels to school lunch and welfare programs, foreign aid, U.S. military and veterans hospitals, this market-clearing operation was sufficient to offset only about one-half the decline in the per capita consumption of fluid milk. In other words, in the 20 years from the mid 1950s to the mid 1970s, in spite of the government price support and diversion programs, dairy farmers were forced to adjust to a market of almost zero growth or, at best, very slow growth as per capita consumption declined under the influence of unnecessarily high prices for Class I fluid milk and related support programs.

Effects on Dairy Producers

Grade A dairy producers selling in federal order markets receive a blend price which is a weighted average of the price paid for fluid milk going into Class I use

[72]*Dairy Price Support and Related Programs,* U.S. Department of Agriculture, 1949–68, Agricultural Economics Report No. 165, July 1969; and *Dairy Situation,* Economic Research Service, DS-340, May 1972, and related sources.

[73]*Dairy Price Support and Related Programs, 1949–68,* U.S. Department of Agriculture, Agricultural Stabilization and Conservation Service, Agricultural Economics Report No. 165, July 1969, pp. 67–72.

and the milk that is sold for manufactured uses; this price moves up or down as necessary to keep the market in equilibrium. From 1964 to 1973, for example, the blend price for 3.5 percent milk in the Chicago market moved from $3.55 to $6.75 per 100 pounds, and in the St. Louis market, from $4.10 to $7.58.[74] But, as we have noted, the pricing policy for Class I milk not only resulted in an increase in the unnecessary surplus, but also it attracted an oversupply of Grade A milk. The diversion of the excess Grade A milk to manufacturing then depressed the market for Grade B milk, which must all go into manufacturing uses.

Although a number of new technologies, such as innovations in milking systems and bulk-tank milk collection, favored larger dairy herds, the relatively depressed market for Grade B milk created an additional disadvantage for farmers with small dairy herds, where the bulk of Grade B production was concentrated.[75] Between 1949 and 1969, the number of dairy herds with less than 30 cows fell from 3,618,000 to 435,000, while the number of herds with 30 cows or more, where most Grade A producers were concentrated, rose from 64,000 to 132,000, with the greatest relative growth in herds of 50 cows or more.[76]

Although the disadvantage of small producers is related to a number of factors, to stabilize the competitive position of the remaining small dairy farmers who are Grade B producers, the price disadvantage to this market must be reduced. This will require lowering the Class I differential so as to stop the growth of the unnecessary surplus of Grade A milk being diverted to manufacturing uses.

Collective Bargaining in Dairy Processing and Marketing

Collective bargaining between labor and management has become well established in dairy product markets, especially in the larger plants, so that by 1969–71, four-fifths of the fluid milk volume packaged and delivered at the wholesale level was handled by unionized workers. Both wholesale and retail milk-truck drivers are largely unionized, and increasingly large proportions of drivers and other workers are represented by unions that are regionally or nationally organized. As a result, the wide differences that used to exist among firms and markets in regard to wages, commissions, and working conditions have been reduced. The largest share of the industry is organized by Teamster locals and the Teamster organization has expanded area bargaining at the Teamster Conference level. This move is intended to improve labor's bargaining position while keeping pace with the declining number and increasing size of dairy processing plants.

---

[74]J. W. Gruebele, "The Changing Conditions in the Dairy Industry," *op. cit.*, p. 5.

[75]Ronald D. Knutson, J. L. Blum, S. Cohen, E. H. Krebs, F. A. Lasley, A. C. Manchester, R. W. March, H. C. Williams, and J. B. Siebert, *Milk Pricing Policy and Procedures, Part I: The Milk Pricing Problem,* Report of the Milk Pricing Advisory Committee, U.S. Department of Agriculture, 1972.

[76]*1969 Agricultural Census,* "Livestock, Poultry, Livestock and Poultry Products," Vol. 2, chap. 5, Washington: U.S. Department of Commerce, March 1972, p. 14.

To gain advantages for unionized labor commensurate with those in other industries, however, a number of restrictive practices of the make-work or slow-down variety have been employed. A significant question for policy is whether action should be taken to force a relaxation of some of these restrictions.[77] For example, in 1970, warehouse delivery was permitted by union contract in only 20 percent of the nation's milk markets. Deliveries at store docks were permitted in only 41 percent of the markets. In 40 percent of the markets, six-day delivery on wholesale routes was required (a make-work, cost-increasing regulation). In 46 percent of the markets, five-day deliveries were required. In only about 10 percent of the markets were three-day wholesale deliveries permitted (a minimum-cost situation). Some of the contracts permitting five-day deliveries also specified higher wage rates. In a few markets, graduated commissions for milk drivers were highly significant. In 1972, in the Chicago market, for example, the average wage plus commission and other fringe benefits for a driver came to $26,243.90 on a 6,000-point route, whereas, without commissions and fringe benefits, the average milk driver's earnings would have been $14,147.53.[78] Although not all driver contracts are as lucrative as those in the Chicago market, some of the wholesale milk drivers' contracts could, if continued, act as a trade barrier and help clog the flow of milk to potential buyers.[79] The mass distribution of fluid milk to city stores has served in most cities to provide an alternative outlet to home delivery.

Cost savings from low levels of restriction on innovation may or may not be passed on to consumers, however, in the form of lower retail prices.[80] Depending on the competitive conditions and business practices of the firms in the market, cost savings may be retained as larger profits of fluid milk processing firms or food retailers, or both. Some labor contracts have provided for "productivity bargaining" so that the results of increased productivity may be shared between management and labor. Thus, severance pay or increased compensation for early retirement may be used as a way to offset the human cost of laborsaving innovations.[81] But whether consumers will share in these savings depends on how wholesale and retail markets are organized and managed.

[77]For further discussion, see James W. Gruebele and Lynn G. Sleight, *Labor-Union Restrictions on Innovations in Fluid-Milk Delivery and Their Relationship to Market Performance,* University of Illinois at Urbana-Champaign, College of Agriculture, Agricultural Experiment Station Bulletin 751, July 1975.

[78]A. L. Parks, "The Effects of Wage Contract Provisions in the Contracts of Wholesale Milk Drivers on Total Wage Payments and Per Unit Delivery Costs in the Fluid Milk Industry," unpublished Ph.D. dissertation, University of Illinois at Urbana-Champaign, 1973, p. 93.

[79]R. W. Bartlett, "An Economic Analysis of Wage Contracts of Wholesale Milk Drivers as Related to Efficiency of Milk Distribution," *Dairy Marketing Facts,* AE-4320, University of Illinois at Urbana-Champaign, Department of Agricultural Economics, February 1970, p. 4.

[80]Gruebele and Sleight, *op. cit.,* pp. 39–40.

[81]Lynn G. Sleight and James W. Gruebele, "Compensating the Human Costs of Increased Productivity of Fluid Milk Drivers," *American Journal of Agricultural Economics,* Vol. 56, No. 3, August 1974, pp. 594–599.

Concentrations in Market Structure

Between 1948 and 1971 the number of fluid milk plants declined from 8,527 to 2,080,[82] and at the same time there was a growing concentration and a shifting of market power among dairy cooperatives, private companies, and chain stores. In the 1960s, dairy cooperatives grew very rapidly through mergers and increases in membership of the larger cooperatives and federations. In December 1970, at least 70 percent of the dairy producers in 41 of 62 federal order markets were members of the largest cooperative operating in each market.[83] In the North Central region, by about this time, some 80 percent of the supermarkets and 60 percent of the smaller stores were supplied with milk on a centralized basis; and some milk processors had to increase in size just to serve the chain account.[84] Some food retailers had established their own processing facilities.[85] Some processor-distributors had turned to captive-store outlets as a form of vertical integration;[86] and they had grown by selling milk at a lower price than supermarkets in their competitive area.[87]

Although dairy cooperatives and private firms are not exempt from the various antitrust provisions of the Clayton Act of 1914, Section 6 of that Act provides that: "Nothing . . . in antitrust laws shall . . . forbid the existence and operation of . . . agricultural or horticultural organizations . . . not having capital stock . . . , or . . . forbid or restrain individual members of such organizations from lawfully carrying out the legitimate objects thereof."[88] The Capper-Volstead Act of 1922 provided that dairymen, among other agricultural producers, may "act together in associations, cooperatives or otherwise, with or without capital stock, in collectively processing, . . . handling and marketing . . . have marketing agencies in common and . . . make the necessary agreements to effect such purposes."[89] The Cooperative Marketing Act of 1926 permits exchanges of price information among cooperatives,[90] and such exchanges as well as merger of

---

[82]Alden C. Manchester, *Market Structure, Institutions, and Performance in the Fluid Milk Industry,* U.S. Department of Agriculture, Economic Research Service, Agricultural Economic Report No. 248, Washington, 1974, p. 3. See also *Market Structure of the Food Industries, ibid.,* Marketing Research Report No. 971, Washington, 1973, p. 23; G. T. Devino, "Economics of Size in Fluid Milk Installations," *American Dairy Review,* August 1969, p. 71; and G. T. Devino, *Economics of Size in Large Fluid Milk Processing Plants,* MP 62, Vermont Agricultural Experiment Station, 1969, p. 9.

[83]R. D. Knutson, *Cooperative Bargaining Developments in the Dairy Industry,* 1960–70, U.S. Department of Agriculture, Farmer Cooperative Service, Research Report No. 19, Washington, August 1971, pp. 8–9.

[84]Richard F. Fallert, *A Survey of Central Milk Programs in Midwestern Food Chains,* U.S. Department of Agriculture, Marketing Research Report No. 944, Washington, 1971, p. 5.

[85]J. W. Gruebele, "Increasing Efficiency in the Distribution of Milk Through Vertical Integration," AE-4272, University of Illinois at Urbana-Champaign, March 1971, pp. 1–9.

[86]Manchester, *op. cit.,* p. 7.

[87]Demetrios Haseotos, "Efficiency Milk Distribution Through Captive Dairy Stores," and R. W. Bartlett, "Are Supermarkets Charging Consumers Too Much for Milk?" *The 1973 Dairy Marketing Forum Proceedings,* University of Illinois at Urbana-Champaign, AE-4325, pp. 1–8, 15.

[88]15 United States Code, chap. 17.

[89]*Ibid.*

[90]44 *Stat.* 802 (1926), 7 USC 451–457, chap. 18, Cooperative Marketing, pp. 324–329.

one or more cooperatives are not regarded as illegal unless the actions result in monopolization or restraint of trade.[91]

Although a large concentration of power is permitted in dairy marketing, the courts have held that these rights are not absolute or boundless. The general policy goal of the 1937 Marketing Agreements Act and subsequent legislation, as interpreted in the courts, is to provide a balance among farmers, marketing-processing firms, and consumers. In one of the early landmark cases in 1939, the Supreme Court indicated that only the practices covered by an agreement or order have protection from the reach of antitrust laws. It rejected any notion that agricultural marketing was exclusively the regulatory domain of the Secretary of Agriculture.[92] The Secretary is protected from prosecution to the extent that what is validly agreed is covered under the act, but the legislation does not confer general authority to monopolize or operate in restraint of trade. In 1960 the Supreme Court reaffirmed this general position: that, although there is a right to associate and a right to take milk to market through an association including pricing at market, these rights are not absolute and boundless.[93] Lawfully obtained power cannot be unlawfully used for the purpose of controlling prices to processors.[94]

In spite of these legal constraints, under provisions of the Capper-Volstead Act successful firms have been able to enhance their market position by a variety of practices: standby pools, over-order payments or premiums, pool riding and pool loading. Establishment of a standby pool of reserve milk has been permitted so that a cooperative may have an assured supply for its handlers in months when milk production is low. But, by use of a standby pool, large aggressive firms have been able to dry up the source of milk for other firms, thus forcing the competing firms or their handlers to join the cooperative. Over-order payments or premiums have been approved at times to obtain adequate supplies of Grade A milk; but strong cooperatives have been able to gain power by using over-order payments to attract dairy farmers away from other firms. By pool riding, a strong cooperative has been able to siphon off Grade A milk from the periphery of a large market, thus forcing up the price that other firms must pay for the milk they need to supply their handlers. By pool loading, a strong firm may have been able to "load" the market with a higher proportion of Grade A milk than is called for by the order, thus lowering the blend price that the firm pays to producers. This has also reduced the receipts of competing firms who were forced to seek another "home" for their milk. The "homeless" milk may have become a source of loss for some firms.

[91]Edna Lindgren, "Antitrust Considerations for the Dairy Industry—A View from the Department of Justice," *Proceedings of the Twenty-Seventh Annual Midwest Marketing Conference*, Ames: Iowa State University, 1972, pp. 11–19; and George J. Devlin, "Application of Antitrust Laws to Agricultural Cooperatives," *Dairy Marketing Facts*, University of Illinois at Urbana-Champaign, AE-4294, July 1972, p. 5.

[92]*United States v. Borden*, 308 U.S. 188 (1939).

[93]*Maryland and Virginia Milk Producers Association v. United States*, 362 U.S. 458 (1960).

[94]*Bergjans Farm Dairy Company v. Sanitary Milk Producers*, 241 F. Supp. 476 (1965).

Any or all of these practices—not all of which are illegal—may be used to increase the market share of a successful firm and, if a sufficiently dominant position is achieved, this position may be used to increase profit margins chiefly by passing on higher Class I prices to consumers. The evidence that this has occurred now appears to be substantial in a number of markets; and the growing policy issue is whether or not the Capper-Volstead Act should be amended to more specifically prohibit certain kinds of mergers or break up some of those that have occurred.

Between 1971 and 1974, for example, the Associated Milk Producers Incorporated (AMPI) of San Antonio, Texas, the largest of the giant milk cooperatives, gained a dominant position in the Chicago market by acquisition and merger. On May 1, 1971, stockholders of the Pure Milk Products Corporation (PMPC), one of Chicago's two largest cooperatives, voted to merge with AMPI. The AMPI also gained control of the Chicago-based Central Milk Producers Cooperative (CMPC). Since the PMPC and CMPC had the major share of the Chicago market, AMPI thus gained dominant control over Class I milk in the Chicago market as well as power to improve its position in surrounding markets by some of the practices mentioned here.

The results were almost immediately apparent. Between 1969 and 1974 in the Chicago regional order market, the Class I sales dropped from 54 to 39 percent of total sales. In spite of growth in population, in the first 10 months of 1974, Class I sales were 9 percent less than they had been in the first 10 months of 1971. Between January and June of 1974 the differential between the Minnesota-Wisconsin manufacturing price and the Chicago Class I price widened by 4.6 cents per quart.[95] In this situation, the Department of Justice brought suit against AMPI, alleging that the AMPI had used its market power to subvert the regulations of the Chicago Regional Order and by various illegal means—including bribery and misrepresentation—it had consummated mergers that were in violation of antitrust regulations. After considerable court hearing and plea bargaining, the case was settled by a consent decree in which the AMPI agreed not to engage in such predatory practices as pool loading, use of over-order payments, and the like. But the policy question remained: Should the Capper-Volstead Act be amended to break up the concentration in dairy markets and largely prevent reacquisitions and mergers that would reestablish concentration?

A Policy Conclusion

Proposals for reform in dairy marketing include amendments to the Capper-Volstead Act of 1922 to subject dairy cooperatives to the same antitrust provisions that apply to corporations not under this act. The provision in the act authorizing farm producers to organize cooperatively to sell their products was never intended to exempt cooperatives from the antitrust laws applicable to

---

[95]Monthly Superpool Price Announcements of the Central Milk Producers Cooperative (CMPC), January to August 1974, and Monthly Report of the National Milk Producers Federation (NMPF), Washington, January to October 1974.

private corporations. The standby pool as used by AMPI and a few other large cooperatives to effect a milk monopoly would be clearly illegal if subject to the same laws as those applying to private corporations. An amendment is needed to delineate more specifically the powers of the Federal Trade Commission (FTC) to control acquisitions and mergers in the dairy industry, especially to prevent monopoly pricing in Class I milk markets.

If the Capper-Volstead Act were amended in this way, then amendments to the Agricultural Marketing Agreements Act of 1937 could assure market stability through more general regulations in regard to Class I pricing, standby pools, and other factors. By limiting the Class I price differential to cover the net additional costs over and above the Minnesota-Wisconsin manufacturing price, for example, the unnecessary surpluses of Grade A milk could be reduced, if not eliminated. Prices paid to the smaller Grade B producers could become more profitable; and, most important for good nutrition, the downtrend in per capita consumption of fluid milk could be reversed. Reforms such as these are vitally needed to meet the general goals of policy in the dairy industry.

MARKETING AGREEMENTS AND ORDERS
IN FRUITS AND VEGETABLES

Agreements and orders have been used extensively to regulate marketing of fruits and vegetables as a supplement to competitive markets rather than as a substitute for them. Generally an order applies to a specified production or marketing area and, in contrast to an order for fluid milk, it is normally covered by a prior voluntary agreement, a contract entered into by the Secretary of Agriculture with the handlers of a particular commodity to regulate the marketing of that commodity. Since an agreement is binding only on those who sign it, however, an agreement alone is seldom effective and is useful mainly as a basis for promulgating an order. A marketing order is binding on all handlers of a commodity in the specified production and marketing area, regardless of whether they have signed an agreement, providing it has been approved in referendum by at least two-thirds of the producers or by those who produce at least two-thirds of the total volume of a commodity. The Secretary may propose an order without a prior agreement, although—for political reasons—he normally would not wish to do so.

A federal agreement and order for a fruit or vegetable may permit or provide for any one or all of the following:[96]

1 Specifying grades, size, quality, or maturity of the commodity that handlers may ship to market
2 Allotting the amount which each handler may purchase or handle on behalf of any and all producers

[96]*Self-Help Stabilization Programs with Use of Marketing Agreements and Orders,* U.S. Department of Agriculture, Agriculture Stabilization and Conservation Service, PA-479, November 1961, p. 4.

3 Establishing the quantity of the commodity that may be shipped to market during any specified period

4 Establishing methods for determining the extent of any surplus, for control and disposition of the surplus, and for equalizing the burden of surplus elimination among producers and handlers

5 Establishing a reserve pool of the product

6 Inspecting the commodity

7 Fixing of the size, capacity, weight, dimensions, or pack of the container used in handling of the commodity

In addition, miscellaneous provisions may authorize actions to prohibit certain unfair trade practices in interstate commerce or to coordinate federal orders with those of individual states. Although controls over marketing vary somewhat among the states, in general the states with enabling legislation do not attempt to control the volume of supplies going to market but limit their activity to quality, size, or pack regulation, to control of advertising and sales promotion, and to support of research and investigation. The federal legislation is restricted primarily to fruits and vegetables for fresh shipment. Most production for canning or freezing is excluded. Enforcement of sanitary and other standards for consumer protection is not, of course, dependent on the existence of an agreement or order.

In general, it may be said that the wise design of programs for a marketing agreement and order rests on the staff of the Secretary of Agriculture and on the corresponding state officials. Positive benefits must be weighed against the various costs and disruptions that an order imposes. Usually, orders are most applicable and most popular where the quantity or quality of a perishable crop varies from season to season; where production is highly localized; when demand is relatively inelastic; where production is not dominated by a few large firms who may combine as oligopolists or vertically integrate through the marketing chain; or where a strong cooperative has much influence on the marketing of the product and growers thus want the protection of an order. Where surplus diversion is to be undertaken, an order is sometimes helpful for attaining market order and stability.

Goals and Means

The general policy goals are (1) to establish and maintain orderly marketing and thus to aid in price stability at the farm level; (2) to protect consumers by rate-of-flow regulations so as to level out alternating periods of glut and scarcity in markets for perishables; (3) to establish certain grade, size, and quality regulations, thus to reduce interstate shipment of "inferior" portions of perishable crops; and (4) to establish surplus controls by diverting "excess" quantities from normal channels to secondary outlets through food stamp, school lunch, and other special-purpose programs.

Marketing agreements and orders were first authorized in the Agricultural Adjustment Act of 1933, at which time many looked upon them as temporary devices to boost farm prices and incomes in the Great Depression. Later they were regarded more as aids in dealing with marketing problems through good as well as bad times. The Marketing Agreements Act of 1937 put them on a more regular basis and served as the parent legislation for succeeding amendments (7 U.S.C. 602). In the early years, control over volume was stressed, but in later years, less than one-third of the orders employed volume control or provided for diversions to secondary markets. A number of agreements have done little more than keep products of inferior quality off the market. A few California and Arizona citrus agreements simply allocate shipments by weeks throughout the shipping season, thus avoiding waste and spoilage and excessive bulges in market flows.

Implementing an Order Program

To implement a program, a proposed agreement is developed at the request of industry representatives, discussed in various industry groups, and reviewed by professionals in the Department of Agriculture. A public hearing is scheduled to hear evidence and arguments for or against the proposal. If the results appear to be favorable and consistent with the purposes of the Marketing Agreements Act and have substantial industry support, a proposed agreement may be submitted to a vote by the producers unless their views have been obtained in other ways.

Each agreement establishes an administrative organization and specifies the controls to be used and other regulations to be followed, including the mechanics of operation. For each agreement a control board, appointed by the Secretary of Agriculture from nominees chosen by the industry, acts as an intermediary between the Secretary and the industry, works up regulations, and recommends them to the Secretary for issuance as an order. For some programs a second committee, composed largely of handlers, serves in an advisory capacity and furnishes information on marketing conditions. The control board selects a program manager and staff to collect information, report alleged violations for possible enforcement action, collects assessments, and disburses monies to pay expenses of the program.

Constraints and Evaluation

An order deliberately grants monopoly power to a private sector of the economy with strict limitations on its use, including government and industry approval for each action that is taken. Generally, it is believed that incomes of producers are improved to some degree and that there are positive gains to consumers in attaining more stable prices and preventing waste, such as unnecessary spoilage of fresh fruits and vegetables, which may be prevented by more orderly marketing and regularity. Success seems to be related to the fact that the powers granted are generally mild. Orders appear to be most useful where there is a long production interval and variable harvests; and they have worked best where production is concentrated geographically. Even though agreements and orders confer some monopoly power, there is no reason to believe that perfectly competitive markets would exist in their absence. Each agreement and order must be appraised on its own merits.

Murray R. Benedict and Oscar C. Stine developed the first general summary of the results of agreements and orders in fruits and vegetables from 1933 through 1955.[97] Accurate quantitative evaluation was, and still is, limited by the fact that most agreements do not stay in continuous operation for more than a few years. More importantly, a continuing problem is that there is no dependable basis for judging what prices and marketing conditions would be if no program were undertaken. Market conditions, demand, production, and timing vary greatly from year to year and even from season to season. Hence, any attempt to relate prices and other factors to conditions that might have prevailed in the absence of an agreement is beset with great difficulties. Although proof was lacking, the general conclusion presented by Benedict and Stine was that some of the orders at least resulted in increased returns to growers and that there was some gain in the form of more stable markets.[98] A frequent contention has been that because order programs engender greater certainty, they tend to induce larger plantings than would otherwise occur. But the proof of this has not been developed with any consistency. To the extent that it is true, of course, consumers would gain. Producers might not be hurt; in fact, they could gain over time by wider acceptance of their product and a larger national market.

As Harold F. Breimyer has noted,[99] the future role of marketing agreements and orders must be related to questions of producer organization and market structure. An evaluation of whether an agreement is good or bad may depend on its effect on the structure of the market. At issue is not only whether an agreement favors marketing cooperatives; often it will. Also of concern is whether it helps smaller independent firms to survive and whether it helps the family farm in competition with large-scale producers, some of whom are highly integrated in producing, processing, and marketing.

In regard to fruits and vegetables, and in contrast with dairy products, marketing agreements and orders may reduce some of the imperfections in the market in favor of independent marketing firms and family farms, or at least they can be made to do so. As they have been used in the past, however, this effect appears to be slight and far too weak to counteract the tendencies toward concentration and monopoly in fruit and vegetable production and marketing. Further, it is hard to see how they could be adapted for this purpose in other markets, such as turkeys and broilers, where efforts to develop orders were unsuccessful.[100] Although marketing agreements and orders can be—and have

[97]Murray R. Benedict and Oscar C. Stine, *The Agricultural Commodity Programs, Two Decades of Experience,* New York: The Twentieth Century Fund, 1956, pp. 380–415.

[98]*Ibid.,* p. 412.

[99]*Individual Freedom and the Economic Organization of Agriculture,* Urbana: The University of Illinois Press, 1965, pp. 166–9, and 293–295.

[100]In 1961 and 1962, Secretary of Agriculture Orville Freeman called several hearings on applying agreements and orders to broilers and turkeys. Little support was found for an order on broilers and no order was presented for referendum. An order for turkeys, submitted to a referendum

been—used to improve the functioning of the market economy, and although they can be modestly helpful in meeting some of the structural goals of food policy, to reverse the trends toward greater concentration, stronger measures will have to be taken in the input markets for land, capital, and farm labor, as we discuss in Chapters 8 through 10.

The hundreds of marketing agreements and orders that have been promulgated for fruits and vegetables appear to have modestly improved producer returns in the short run without causing long-run damage to expansion of the industry. They generally have not damaged processors and handlers. Only a very modest amount of income has been transferred from consumers to producers. Of far greater concern is the tendency toward monopoly in some fruits and vegetables, as we note in Chapters 8 through 10; and of far greater consequence are the policies that are to be followed in the future in regard to land, taxes, labor unions, and the like.

MAJOR EXPORT COMMODITIES

As we have noted in earlier chapters, in the second great era of food policy the struggle over policies for commodities competing in major export markets dominated the scene. Whereas policy settled into a mold for the major commodities that are import-competitive—sugar, wool, beef, and dairy—as we have just noted, policy was more varied and often contentious for those that are export-competitive—wheat, feed grains, soybeans, rice, cotton, tobacco. The national policy fluctuated between four general choices:

1   Free markets, as largely prevailed up to 1929
2   Price support without government control of production, as under the Federal Farm Board from 1929 to 1931 and then periodically under other programs after World War II
3   Price support and production control, as under the Agricultural Adjustment Administration in the 1930s, or land retirement and acreage allotment programs as in the 1950s and 1960s, with direct payments and sometimes marketing quotas
4   Market subsidy
    a   to keep feed grains, wheat, cotton, etc. competitive in commercial export markets
    b   under Public Law 480, to share the cost of food aid programs
    c   as consumer subsidy, food stamp programs, and other means to clear markets and aid low-income families

In the third era of food policy, the question will be again—as it was before—what combination of these four policies shall be followed? What will be the

---

held on June 18 and 19, 1962, received a vote of only about 50 percent instead of the two-thirds required. It called for a rather aggressive, far-reaching, nationwide program, which was opposed by some farm organizations, most notably the American Farm Bureau Federation.

changing situation? What values and rules shall apply? This section is organized around these four categories of policy choices, using commodities as illustrations.

The Free Market

Our general assumption is that the free market, or freely competitive markets with less control of product and less export subsidy, will be more acceptable in the third era than they were in the second. Surpluses will not be as massive as they were in the 1930s, 1950s, and 1960s. The market will be closer to equilibrium in terms of prices that are acceptable to American farmers. Short-run profits cannot be maintained anywhere near the levels of 1973, however. In fact, economic theory as well as all our experience suggests that excess profits cannot be maintained over the long run. This means that the models for storage, for production and product management, or for export and domestic food subsidy cannot be ignored as viable policy alternatives. The free market, although generally desired as optimum for efficient use of resources, does not provide an optimum simultaneous solution for maximizing consumer welfare, stabilizing foreign trade, and reducing farmers' uncertainty in regard to prices and incomes.

The Roles for Storage Policy

Government storage may be used (1) to stabilize supply; (2) to stabilize prices by accumulating stocks in times of price weakness and liquidating stocks in times of price inflation; or (3) to stabilize flows of commodities for domestic consumption and export. These may be seen as various roles for storage and general alternatives for storage policy. Theoretically, storage per se is not conceived as either raising or depressing food prices consistently or substantially throughout a business cycle.

National policy never has been really settled, however, on questions such as the following: Which goals or which roles are to be emphasized, stability of supply, price, or flow? What rules shall be followed in distribution of stocks? Who shall own the stocks? Where shall they be located? What shall be the magnitude of the program, or what constraints shall apply?

In order to suggest answers for the future, we may summarize some experiences of the past and the lessons they convey. Let us look at three periods: (1) the Federal Farm Board experience 1929–33, (2) the CCC from 1933 to 1941, and (3) the post-World War II period from 1949 to 1972.

The Federal Farm Board   As we noted in Chapter 5, the Farm Board was charged with the goal of placing agriculture on a basis of equality with other industries. This it would do by (1) minimizing speculation, (2) preventing inefficient and wasteful methods of distribution, (3) encouraging the organization of producers into effective associations or cooperatives, and (4) aiding in preventing and controlling surpluses in any agricultural commodity, through orderly production and distribution, in order to maintain advantageous markets and prevent surpluses from causing undue and expensive fluctuations or depressions in prices. A tall order indeed! The Board was also directed to promote education in the principles and practices of cooperative marketing and to encourage the organization, improvement in methods, and development of effective cooperative associations.[101]

The Board began loan-storage operations at a time when it would have been difficult to stabilize farm prices by any means, just before the stock market crash of 1929. In the next two years the Board committed almost all its $500 million revolving fund to loans on commodities in storage, 85 percent of which went to wheat and cotton. It lost between $300 and $500 million. Of this, about $200 million of wheat and cotton was donated to the Red Cross for relief activities, presumably increasing consumption. The balance of the loss represents sale of commodities at prices below the initial loan levels.

The price effects of Board storage operations are not easily determined. Wheat prices in the major United States markets, compared with prices at Liverpool, were about 20 cents a bushel higher than their normal world relationship for about six months. This was during the most rapid storage buildup. For the entire two-year period in which the Board was acquiring wheat, prices averaged about 10 cents above the normal export ratio. During this period, farmers probably received a higher price than they would have received otherwise. During the period when stocks were being liquidated, however, wheat prices probably were depressed, and farmers sold wheat at a lower price than they would have if stocks had not been previously accumulated.

The general conclusion of the Federal Farm Board economists was that farm income could not be supported effectively by storage unless there also was control of production. From 1929 to 1933, although the acreage seeded to wheat and cotton declined by a total of 6 million acres, corn production increased by 11 million acres. In the face of this increase in supply and presumably declining demand, storage failed to stabilize price. The net effect on aggregate farm income or on consumer outlay for food is not clear, although it may be surmised that the shift was not large either way. The increases and decreases canceled over time. The conclusions of the Board economists probably influenced the passage of the Agricultural Adjustment Act in 1933.

CCC Experience, 1933–1941   The Commodity Credit Corporation (CCC) was established independently by Executive order of President Roosevelt in October 1933, under general powers granted to him under the National Recovery Act (NRA). Originally financed with funds from the Reconstruction Finance Corporation (RFC), it operated as an independent agency until 1939, when it was transferred to the Department of Agriculture. During this time the CCC loaned money on cotton, wheat, corn, and certain other farm commodities held in storage to raise prices and stabilize them against fluctuations in production or demand.[102]

---

[101]*Annual Report of the United States Federal Farm Board,* June 30, 1930.

[102]For discussion of the FRC's part in refinancing the CCC, see Jesse H. Jones with Edward Angly, *Fifty Billion Dollars, My Thirteen Years with the RFC (1932–1945),* New York: The Macmillan Company, 1951, pp. 88–104.

It seems clear now that Roosevelt, to implement the CCC programs, intended to rely on the production control programs of the AAA to bring supplies into equilibrium with demand at about the level of the loan rates established. To carry out storage policy, the device of the nonrecourse loan was developed, under which loans would be made at stated price support levels to farmers who cooperated in the acreage-control production-adjustment programs of the AAA. Under the nonrecourse loan, federal funds were lent to farmers on commodities in approved storage that were eligible for price support. Under this system, which has been continued to the present day, if the price of the commodity rises above the loan rate, the farmer may sell the commodity and pay off the loan, and if the price remains below the loan rate, the farmer may liquidate the loan by surrendering the commodity to the government.

The CCC policy to base loans higher than market prices became evident almost at once. The initial loan rate on cotton, set at the President's direction, was 10 cents a pound. This was almost twice the average price received by farmers in 1931 or 1932, and 2 or 3 cents higher than the prices then current. The initial loan rate for corn was 45 cents a bushel, in contrast to average farm prices of about 32 cents in 1931 and 1932. Loans were not made on wheat because unfavorable weather had cut the 1933 crop to 552 million bushels, about 60 percent as large as the 1931 crop, and wheat prices were almost double what they had been a year earlier.

During the first four years of CCC operations, when loans were financed from RFC funds, market conditions were improving. Presumably, there was an increase in demand for food. National income recovered from the extreme lows of 1931–33. The wholesale price index rose by 30 percent. Employment outside of agriculture increased. Supply, on the other hand, was restricted by the severe droughts of 1934 and 1936. By the beginning of the 1937 crop year, total carry-overs of wheat, cotton, and corn were reduced to less than the 1933 levels, and the CCC storage stocks were small.

From 1933 to 1937, loan rates were set, at the President's direction, usually above existing market prices. Since market prices were trending up, stocks were liquidated on a rising market. In the Agricultural Adjustment Act of 1938, however, Congress provided that the CCC must establish loan rates for wheat, cotton, and corn at specified levels between 50 and 75 percent of parity, thus setting a precedent for future years.

From 1938 to 1940, loan rates were high enough to bring wheat into storage in rather large volume, thus raising market prices higher than they would have been otherwise. Wheat stocks were increased further in 1941, and a record 600 million bushels was carried over to 1943, at which time Congress voted to subsidize wheat for livestock feed by 20 to 40 cents per bushel, thus liquidating a large part of the wheat carry-over by the end of the war.

The CCC loans on corn had had little effect on prices during 1933–37 because the drought raised prices above loan rates and storage operations were small. From 1938 to 1940, however, corn storage was increased by about 500 million bushels and corn prices were about 18 cents a bushel higher than usual or expected in relation to (1) the supply of corn, (2) the prices received for other commodities, and (3) the total number of animal units.[103] These stocks also served to expand livestock production during the war.

In the case of cotton, the CCC inherited about 2 million bales from the Federal Farm Board and continued to make loans on cotton during the 1933–41 period, liquidating some stocks and assuming ownership of other stocks released under the nonrecourse loan program. By 1939 the CCC had almost 7 million bales of cotton under storage, and the total carry-over on August 1, 1939, was 13 million bales, or more than a normal year's crop. In 1941 it was concluded that during 1933–41, cotton prices had been raised an average of eight-tenths of a cent a pound by increases in storage.[104] Throughout the war, as a result of high loan rates and restrictions governing sale and disposal of cotton, the carry-over never dropped below 10 million bales. On August 1, 1945, more than 12 million bales were in store. These stocks represented a diversion of resources that the nation could ill afford in wartime and that was unnecessary to meet any foreseeable postwar demand.

In summary, the CCC programs after 1933 and through World War II (1) stimulated farm production by price or loan guarantees; (2) assured larger carry-overs than would have occurred otherwise; (3) increased farm income on balance, since stocks were accumulated at times when markets were weak; and (4) benefited consumers when grain stocks were liquidated in times of great market strength.

Storage Policy, 1946–1972 The storage policy from 1946 through 1972 does not appear so fortuitous. Depletion of grain stocks by the end of the war eliminated the cushion that otherwise might have been used in postwar recovery, especially in Europe. Continuation of high-level price supports through the early 1950s stimulated farm production and restricted export growth, thus adding to the apparent surplus and increasing the difficulties of adjustment in the late 1950s and the 1960s.

The failure to integrate U.S. storage policy with any world food stock program placed the burden of adjustment on the programs to restrict production of feed grains, wheat, and cotton. Thus the United States government entered the 1970s without any plan for world food stability or any program for systematic aid to needy countries. This failure was dramatized in the food price escalation that occurred in 1973 and 1974 and by various food shortages abroad to which the government of the United States could not respond.

A Policy Conclusion The lesson is that to prevent calamities of this sort in the future, storage must be programmed according to probabilities of need at

---

[103]Geoffrey S. Shepherd, *Controlling Corn and Hog Supplies and Prices,* U.S. Department of Agriculture Technical Bulletin 826, 1942.

[104]Maurice Cooper, *Some Effects of the Government's Cotton Loan Program,* U.S. Department of Agriculture, Bureau of Agricultural Economics, Division of Statistical and Historical Research, June 1941.

home and abroad, rather than as a primary means for farm price support. On balance, it appears that storage per se will be largely neutral in its effect on farm income. Storage can be beneficial to farm income if stocks are accumulated in times of market weakness and liquidated in times of great market strength, as from 1933 through World War II. It can be depressing to farm income if stocks are liquidated, as they were in the late 1950s and 1960s, at a time when markets are already well supplied. Under a similar situation in the future, a world food stock could be created to implement a comprehensive world food program. Until such a stock can be created and a more comprehensive world food plan is developed, various country populations will have to adjust mainly on the basis of their own resources, with help, such as it may be, dependent on fluctuating and unpredictable annual crop surpluses.

PRICE SUPPORT AND PRODUCTION CONTROL FOR EXPORT COMMODITIES

Since 1933, price support accompanied by production control of the major export-competitive commodities, or the broader concept of production and supply management to achieve certain price objectives, has been the most distinguishing feature of farm and food policy for America, but success of the policy, as it may be measured among these commodities, has differed widely. Tobacco, for example, has been easy to control and the market has been stabilized. Cotton has been so effectively controlled that it has lost its once preeminent position as king of the agricultural exports. Wheat, for political as well as economic reasons, has not been so effectively controlled. Corn, in the Emergency Feed Grain Program, proved difficult and expensive to control by voluntary means. Many livestock farmers found it more profitable to maintain full production, selling their entire crop through livestock markets. Soybeans, the great production alternative to corn, enjoyed an expanding world market and never were subjected to control.

The record is spotty. But, there are lessons for the future, which may be viewed commodity by commodity or by product market.

Tobacco[105]

America's oldest export crop is inelastic in domestic demand, labor-intensive in production, high in value per acre. Nationally, it ranks fifth in total cash value among the crops, behind only wheat, corn, cotton, and soybeans. Highly concentrated in certain states, it accounts for 40 percent of farmers' cash income in North Carolina and Virginia, and about 10 percent in Tennessee and Georgia.

Acreage allotments for tobacco have been in effect continuously since 1934 (in 1933 there was an emergency program to plow down about a third of the crop). From 1934 to 1946, the harvested acreage of tobacco varied from 1.3

---

[105]James D. Johnson, graduate student in agricultural economics, University of Illinois at Urbana-Champaign, has contributed to this section through individual research.

million to 2 million acres as allotments and other programs were adjusted to support farm income. Starting in 1947, harvested acreage was periodically moved downward to adjust supplies to market demand, until by the early 1970s the annual harvested acreage was less than one-half of what it had been in the 1940s and early 1950s (Table 7-4). Because of substantial increases in yields, total production increased a little until the early 1950s, but since then the reduction in total acreage has been proportionately greater than increases in yields and production has dropped by one-fifth. Also, since the early 1950s the total man-hours used on farms for tobacco production have dropped by at least one-third because of increased use of mechanical transplanters, chemical "suckering" controls, and small cub tractors for cultivation.[106]

The acreage allotment is essentially a right to produce tobacco, since the amount of land suitable to grow this crop always has been much greater than the acreage used for that purpose, and there never has been any restriction on the use of land removed from tobacco production. Prior to 1963, this right could be transferred only by sale and purchase of the land to which the allotment was attached; but since then, allotments can be rented or transferred to another farmer on an annual basis. Unlike most other crops, tobacco has brought no direct payments to producers under the program, and until mid 1966, when the United States began an export subsidy program, there was practically no cost to the Treasury except for export sales under Public Law 480. The objective always has been to use acreage allotments and marketing quotas to increase market prices and stabilize farmers' incomes. What are the effects?

First, tobacco prices are raised by perhaps as much as one-quarter to one-third over what they would be in a free market. Various studies have shown that the *annual* rental value of an acre of tobacco allotment was equal to, or greater than, the market price of the land on which the tobacco was grown if that land did not have a tobacco allotment. In 1966 and 1967 in North Carolina, the major tobacco-producing state, rents paid for a tobacco allotment were one-fourth to one-third of the selling price of tobacco. In other words, increased returns from price supports were being transferred into values of tobacco allotments, or to values of land to which the allotment was attached.[107]

Second, by comparing hourly earnings of sharecroppers and family members in tobacco production with those of other occupational groups, it has been estimated that all, or virtually all, the income gains from allotments were returned to landowners or holders of the tobacco allotments.[108] In Virginia and

---

[106]*Potential Mechanization in the Flue-Cured Tobacco Industry, with Emphasis on Human Resource Adjustment,* U.S. Department of Agriculture, Economic Research Service, Agricultural Economic Report No. 169, 1969; O. K. Shugars and E. G. Garrett, "Changing Technology in Tobacco Production," in *Social and Economic Issues Confronting the Tobacco Industry in the Seventies,* Lexington: University of Kentucky, College of Agriculture and Center for Developmental Change, February 1972.

[107]James A. Seagraves, "Capitalized Values of Tobacco Allotments and the Rate of Return to Allotment Owners," *American Journal of Agricultural Economics,* May 1969, pp. 320–324.

[108]T. L. Hedrick, "Factor Returns Under the Tobacco Program," in George S. Tolley (ed.), *Study of U.S. Agricultural Adjustments,* Raleigh: State University of North Carolina, 1970.

North Carolina in 1960, if the tobacco program were to be abolished, the rent per unit of land used to produce tobacco would be reduced by 85 percent.[109]

Third, the tobacco allotment program has essentially stabilized tobacco prices from year to year. Between 1960 and 1968, for example, the average yearly farm price ranged between 57.7 cents and 69.5 cents per pound, a very narrow range considering the inelasticity of domestic demand. After 1968, tobacco prices tended gradually upward to offset rising costs. According to the price effects imputed to the program, as much as $250 million to $400 million annually was transferred from tobacco users to tobacco farmers.[110] Tobacco manufacturers have raised little objection to this transfer because they evidently can pass it on to consumers with little if any loss in sales.

Fourth, through the combination of price supports and export subsidies averaging about 9 percent of market value, the export of American tobacco was essentially stabilized from 1960 to 1971, while the export of cigarettes increased by 50 percent. Export subsidies were used to maintain the net trade balance at a rather constant level (Table 7-4).

Fifth, the reported statistical associations between cigarette smoking and the rates of incidence or death rates from several diseases including cancer, cardiovascular diseases, chronic ailments of the lungs, and others,[111] apparently have had sufficient impact to reduce per capita consumption by almost 25 percent from the highs established in 1952 and 1953 (Table 7-4).

Sixth, in the long run the opportunity to rent or buy and sell allotment rights without rent or purchase of land will transfer allotments to the larger farmer. In 1969, the average allotment was only 3.1 acres, down from 6.25 acres in 1956, and 58 percent of the allotments were less than 2 acres. Instead of rationing poverty, as some claim that the program has done, the net rents from the program will trend toward larger allotment holders as advantages of modern technology accrue to larger farmers.

In conclusion, although farm prices in America might be higher in a free market if major importing countries allowed free trade in tobacco, under existing trade regulations the program functions efficiently to hold tobacco prices at least 25 percent higher than they would be in its absence. Also, this price is stable, highly predictable, and therefore efficient in allocation of resources. But family labor incomes are notoriously low among the majority of tobacco growers. Excess labor resources have been retained in tobacco production. Efforts to protect the small farm by assurance of a minimum allotment have perpetuated this situation.

Although legislation permitting the buying and selling or renting of tobacco

---

[109]*Ibid.*, pp. 264–266.

[110]From 1960 to 1972, the annual farm value of the tobacco crop never fell below $1.2 billion or rose above $1.4 billion. Data from *Tobacco Situation,* U.S. Department of Agriculture, Economic Research Service.

[111]Robert C. Hackett, "The Tobacco Health Issue: An Evaluation of Medical Research," *Social and Economic Issues Confronting the Tobacco Industry in the Seventies, op. cit.,* p. 29.

Table 7-4   Tobacco Production, Consumption and Trade, 1947–1973

Year	Acres harvested (1,000s)	Yield per acre (lbs.)	Production (million lbs)	Per capita consumption (lbs.)*	Export trade balance Quantity (million lbs.)	Value ($ million)
1947	1,852	1,138	2,107	11.95		
1948	1,554	1,274	1,980	12.12		
1949	1,623	1,213	1,969	11.93		
1950	1,599	1,269	2,030	11.96		
1951	1,780	1,310	2,332	12.48		
1952	1,772	1,273	2,256	12.92		
1953	1,633	1,261	2,059	12.90		
1954	1,668	1,346	2,244	12.11		
1955	1,495	1,466	2,193	11.93	467.2	331.2
1956	1,364	1,596	2,176	11.47	427.7	303.9
1957	1,122	1,486	1,668	11.41	416.8	332.1
1958	1,078	1,611	1,736	11.54	387.9	330.8
1959	1,154	1,560	1,800	11.53	362.3	332.0
1960	1,142	1,703	1,944	11.82	385.5	355.4
1961	1,174	1,755	2,061	12.00	387.9	380.1
1962	1,224	1,891	2,315	11.80	362.1	387.0
1963	1,176	1,994	2,344	11.78	393.8	420.1
1964	1,078	2,067	2,228	11.53	407.2	429.3
1965	977	1,898	1,855	11.51	344.2	370.5
1966	972	1,939	1,885	11.12	432.1	477.9
1967	960	2,050	1,968	10.79	436.0	499.2
1968	879	1,945	1,710	10.59	448.3	533.6
1969	918	1,964	1,803	10.04	433.3	555.8
1970	898	2,122	1,906	9.68	366.3	534.1
1971	839	2,034	1,708	9.52	311.6	524.8
1972	843	2,068	1,754	9.65		
1973	899	1,958	1,754	9.58		

*Consumption of tax-paid tobacco products by persons 18-years-old and older. Represents un-stemmed equivalent of tobacco used in the manufacture of cigars, cigarettes, smoking and chewing tobacco, and snuff.

Sources: Bureau of the Census; Internal Revenue Service and Department of Agriculture. Agricultural Statistics, 1975, pp. 96–111.

allotments independent of the ownership of land will increase the efficiency of tobacco production by concentrating allotments in the most efficient producing units, the low-income problem of the small farmer is not necessarily alleviated by this trend. In fact, at least in the short run, it may be worsened. The policy problem for the future is to decide what more direct action shall be taken to help these families. Although several possible measures come readily to mind, such as training and employment programs for alternative use of their labor, the problem is a more general one which we take up in a more general framework in Chapter 10.

Cotton

Nowhere in our area of study has public policy had a more pervasive or wide-ranging effect than in the case of cotton.[112] In 300 years, during our first great era of food policy, the Cotton Belt of America spread across the South from Virginia to Texas. Then, in the latter years of that era and the first years of the next, in the 1920s, it stretched out to some of the newer irrigated lands of the Southwest. From 13 to 17 million bales of cotton, weighing on the average 500 pounds gross or 480 pounds of lint, were being produced on about 40 million acres in an average crop year. In many states of the South, cotton was the most important crop, a key to the economy of the rural community. The American cotton crop was more than one-half of total world production. It was the largest of the nation's agricultural exports, constituting more than two-thirds of the total cotton moving in international trade and competing freely at competitive world prices.

At the end of the second era, from 1966 through 1971, although the average yield per harvested acre for America's cotton crop was more than 2½ times what it had been in the 1920s, the annual harvest averaged less than 10 million acres, production was less than 10 million bales, and exports averaged 3.6 million bales (Table 7-5). Cotton production outside the United States had increased approximately 4 times, and United States production had fallen to less than one-fifth of total world production. The U.S.S.R. had risen through subsidy to its cotton farmers to rival America in total production. Together, these two industrial countries were producing about 40 percent of the world's cotton. Almost all the remaining 60 percent was being produced in less developed countries. But America had shifted from the role of world price leader and dominant international trader to that of price follower and residual supplier. What had brought about this transition and what are the lessons for the future?

Cotton Goals and Means   In abandoning free trade, cotton policy emphasized price supports, acreage allotments and marketing quotas, export subsidies and restrictions on imports, and, finally, heavy production payments in lieu of high price supports to implement the cotton program. The realized Treasury cost of the cotton program, in the late 1960s and early 1970s, reached well over $750 million annually. Initiation of acreage allotments and marketing quotas in the Agricultural Adjustment Act of 1933 brought an immediate reduction of 6 million acres in harvested acreage and a more than corresponding decrease in cotton exports, followed soon by an expansion in production in other countries. Throughout the 1940s, cotton production was strongly influenced by the war. High price supports discouraged cotton consumption at home and restricted exports; and, in the 1950s and 1960s, these effects were accentuated. The high domestic prices apparently encouraged the growth of the synthetic fiber industry. Reduction in the level of exports evidently served as an umbrella to stimulate cotton production in other countries as well as growth of other fibers (Table 7-6).

[112]For basic sources of data, see *The Cotton Situation, Cotton and Wool Situation,* USDA, ERS (various issues), and *Cotton, Monthly Review of The World Situation,* Washington: International Cotton Advisory Committee.

Modern cotton policy is a product of a number of programs enacted follow-ing World War II.[113] The Agricultural Adjustment Act of 1948 made price supports on the basic farm commodities, including cotton, mandatory at 90 percent of parity. In addition, as of January 1, 1950, parity prices were to be computed to take into consideration not only the 1910–14 base, but the average prices received for the previous 10 years, thus further escalating the price support for cotton. The Agricultural Act of 1949 provided that support for the 1950 cotton crop would be mandatory at not more than 90 percent of parity nor less than certain minimums based on the supply at the beginning of the year. The Act of 1952 for the first time made price supports mandatory on extra-long-staple cotton. The Act of 1954 substituted flexible supports at 82½ to 90 percent of parity. The Act of 1956 created the Soil Bank which authorized a program of annual acreage diversion for wheat, corn, rice, cotton, peanuts, and tobacco.

Under the Agricultural Act of 1958, producers of upland cotton were given a choice of supports for their 1959 and 1960 crops. Under Choice A, a producer who complied with his acreage allotment was assured of support at not less than 80 percent of parity for his 1959 crop and not less than 75 percent for his 1960 crop. Under Choice B, a producer who complied with an allotment that might be, at the Secretary's discretion, as much as 40 percent larger than his regular allotment was assured of support not less than 15 percent below that established for producers electing Choice A. A no-choice program was specified for subse-quent years with supports set at 75 to 90 percent of parity for 1961 and at 65 to 90 percent thereafter.

The Agricultural Act of 1964 set a support price at 30 cents per pound for upland cotton and a price support payment for 1964 and 1965 of not more than 15 percent of the basic level of support for those producers planting within their domestic allotment, defined as that portion of the national allotment needed to produce the cotton for domestic consumption. Payments in kind, known as cotton equalization payments, were authorized to persons, other than producers, in amounts that would make upland cotton available for domestic use at a price not exceeding that of cotton made available for export. Payments and diversion programs were extended to cotton under the Food and Agriculture Act of 1965. It also provided for market support of cotton through price support loans and payments.

In the Agricultural Act of 1970 a limitation of $55,000 per crop was set on payments to producers of upland cotton, wheat, and feed grains, with the limitation to consider all payments that were made for price support, set aside, diversion, public access, and marketing certificates. Marketing quotas and penal-ties were suspended for three years. A cropland set-aside program, not to exceed 28 percent of the cotton allotment, was added as a condition for eligibility. The Act was to provide payments for an approximated 11.5 million acres in 1971. Payments were to be the difference between the higher of 65 percent of parity or

[113]*Price Support and Related Legislation Through the Years,* U.S. Department of Agriculture, Agricultural Stabilization and Conservation Service, Background Information No. 11, December 1970.

35 cents, and the average market price for the first five months of the marketing year beginning August 1. In no event would payments be less than 15 cents per pound. Farmers would also receive payments for not planting (1) if natural disasters or other conditions beyond the producers' control kept them from doing so, or (2) if not less than 90 percent of the allotment was planted.

The Upland Cotton Program, announced in November 1972, reduced the national base acreage allotment down to 10 million acres from 11½ million in 1972, set a national production goal of 12.1 million bales, nearly 1 million below 1972, and dropped the cropland set aside as a condition for eligibility. A payment of 15 cents per pound and a national loan rate of 19½ cents per pound were set as in 1972.

Table 7-5 Cotton Production and Exports, 1929–1975

Year beginning Aug. 1	Harvested acreage (million acres)	Yield per harvested acre (pounds)	Production in United States	Carry-over Aug. 1	Exports year beginning Aug. 1	Production outside United States
			(million bales, 500 pounds gross, 480 pounds net)			
1929	43.2	164	14.8	2.3	6.7	12.0
1930	42.4	157	13.9	4.5	6.8	12.3
1931	38.7	212	17.1	6.4	8.7	10.7
1932	35.9	174	13.0	9.7	8.4	11.3
1933	29.4	213	13.0	8.2	7.5	13.9
1934	26.9	172	9.6	7.7	4.8	14.2
1935	27.5	185	10.6	7.2	6.0	16.9
1936	29.8	199	12.4	5.4	5.4	20.0
1937	33.6	270	18.9	4.5	5.6	20.1
1938	24.2	236	11.9	11.5	3.3	18.0
1939	23.8	238	11.8	13.0	6.2	17.8
1940	23.9	252	12.6	10.6	1.1	18.6
1941	22.2	232	10.7	12.2	1.1	17.2
1942	22.6	272	12.8	10.6	1.5	14.5
1943	21.6	254	11.4	10.7	1.1	14.2
1944	19.6	299	12.2	10.7	2.0	12.6
1945	17.0	254	9.0	11.1	3.7	12.1
1946	17.6	236	8.6	7.3	3.7	13.0
1947	21.3	267	11.9	2.5	2.0	13.4
1948	22.9	311	14.9	3.1	5.0	14.3
1949	27.4	282	16.1	5.3	6.0	15.2
1950	17.8	269	10.0	6.8	4.3	18.2
1951	26.9	269	15.1	2.3	5.7	20.6
1952	25.9	280	15.1	2.8	3.2	20.7
1953	24.3	324	16.5	5.6	3.9	22.7
1954	19.3	341	13.7	9.7	5.6	24.9
1955	16.9	417	14.7	11.2	2.3	28.0
1956	15.6	409	13.3	14.5	7.9	28.9
1957	13.6	388	11.0	11.3	6.0	30.6
1958	11.8	466	11.5	8.7	2.9	32.9
1959	15.1	461	14.6	8.9	7.4	32.1

Table 7-5   Cotton Production and Exports, 1929–1975 (*Continued*)

Year beginning Aug. 1	Harvested acreage (million acres)	Yield per harvested acre (pounds)	Production in United States	Carry- over Aug. 1	Exports year beginning Aug. 1	Production outside United States
			(million bales, 500 pounds gross, 480 pounds net)			
1960	15.3	446	14.3	7.6	6.6	32.9
1961	15.6	438	14.3	7.2	4.9	31.5
1962	15.6	457	14.9	7.8	3.4	34.4
1963	14.2	517	15.3	11.2	5.7	34.9
1964	14.1	517	15.1	12.4	4.1	36.3
1965	13.6	526	14.9	14.3	2.9	38.2
1966	9.6	480	9.6	16.9	4.7	37.9
1967	8.0	447	7.4	12.5	4.2	40.4
1968	10.2	516	10.9	6.5	2.7	40.8
1969	11.1	434	10.0	6.5	2.8	41.7
1970	11.2	438	10.2	5.8	3.7	46.9
1971	11.5	438	10.5	4.3	3.2	46.7
1972	13.0	507	13.7	3.2	5.0	47.8
1973	12.0	520	13.0	3.9	5.7	49.2
1974*	12.6	442	11.5	3.7	3.7	51.7
1975*	8.8	453	8.3	5.7	3.5	—

*Preliminary.
Sources: U.S. Department of Agriculture, Statistical Reporting Service, Economic Research Service, and Agricultural Marketing Service, *Agricultural Statistics* and *Cotton and Wool Situation.*

The Agriculture and Consumer Protection Act of 1973 initiated a guaranteed target price of 38 cents per pound for 1974 and 1975, to be adjusted upward in 1976 and 1977 to reflect changes in production costs and the national yield. The new program set a production goal of 14.8 million bales and raised the national base acreage allotment to 11 million acres. Payment limits were reduced to $20,000 per crop. Producers who planted above their allotments were still eligible for price support loans but not for government payments. No cropland set aside nor any conserving base was set as a condition for program eligibility. If the average price received by farmers was above the target price, no payments would be made to them, and, in such a strong market, cotton farmers would be freed from production controls. If market prices dropped below the target price, payments could be made and acreage allotments reimposed. Thus, the program allowed for quick expansion of cotton acreage in a strong market and a return to government controls if this expansion were vigorous enough to drive market prices below target levels (Table 7-6).

Costs and Constraints   In the 40 years from 1933 to 1972, the cotton program raised and stabilized the returns per pound to American cotton producers either through price support or payments, or a combination of the two. But in so doing, the United States failed to maintain its traditional share of the world cotton market (Table 7-5), and over the years billions of dollars were lost in export earnings forgone. From 1968 through 1972, for example, when world production of cotton averaged 55.8 million bales per year, U.S. production averaged only 11 million bales. If this nation had been supplying one-half the world market, even at a lower world price level, export earnings from cotton would have been $1 billion to $2 billion more annually. For this reason, it is not clear whether the cotton program increased or decreased aggregate returns—either gross or net—to American cotton producers.

Additionally, the postwar development of the synthetic fiber industry in the United States compounded some of the effects imputed to the cotton program.

Table 7-6   Cotton Support Price, Production Payments, and Season Average Price Received by Producers, 1929–1974

| Year | Support price | | Production payments, cents per pound | Season average price received by producers, cents per pound* |
	Percent of parity	Cents per pound		
1929	No support			16.79
1930	No support			9.46
1931	No support			5.66
1932	No support			6.52
1933	69			10.17
1934	76			12.36
1935	62			11.09
1936	No support			12.35
1937	53			8.41
1938	52			8.60
1939	56			9.09
1940	57			9.89
1941	85			17.03
1942	90			19.05
1943	90			19.90
1944	95–100			20.73
1945	92.5–100			22.52
1946	92.5			32.64
1947	92.5			31.93
1948	92.5			30.38
1949	90	27.23		28.58
1950	90	27.90		40.07
1951	90	30.46		37.88
1952	90	30.91		34.59
1953	90	30.80		32.25
1954	90	31.58		33.61
1955	90	31.70		32.33
1956	82.5	29.34		31.75
1957	78	28.81		29.65
1958	81	31.23		33.23
1959	65–80†	30.40		31.66

Table 7-6 Cotton Support Price, Production Payments, and Season Average Price Received by Producers, 1929–1974 (Continued)

| Year | Support price | | Production payments, cents per pound | Season average price received by producers, cents per pound* |
	Percent of parity	Cents per pound		
1960	60–75†	28.97		30.19
1961	82	31.88		32.92
1962	82	31.88		31.80
1963	78	31.72		32.02
1964	80	32.80‡	3.50§	29.62
1965	71	32.60‡	4.35§	28.03
1966	73	29.63‡	9.42§	20.64
1967	74	31.00‡	11.53§	25.39
1968	—	31.93‡	12.24§	22.02
1969	—	34.44‡	14.73§	20.94
1970	—	36.95‡	16.80§	21.86
1971		35.00‡	15.00¶	28.07
1972	65	35.85‡	15.00¶	27.20
1973	65	41.52	15.00	44.60
1974	—	38.00	—	41.70

*Includes an allowance for unredeemed loan cotton.
†Higher rate for growers selecting Choice A and lower rate for growers selecting Choice B.
‡Includes production payments in lieu of price support.
§To producers who planted within domestic allotment.
¶On production from acreage planted within the farm base acreage allotment.
Sources: U.S. Department of Agriculture, Economic Research Service, *Agricultural Statistics* and *Cotton and Wool Situation.*

Whereas in 1959 cotton consumption of 24.5 pounds per capita compared with 14.2 pounds of other fibers, by 1972 the per capita consumption of cotton had declined to 18.4 pounds and the other fibers had increased to 34.5 pounds, including most importantly the noncellulosic fibers—nylon, acrylic, modacrylic, polyester, and other fibers of the chemical industry (Table 7-7). With a lower growth of this industry, an alternative cotton policy aimed at keeping a larger share of the total fiber market could have maintained larger aggregate receipts for American cotton producers. The cotton policy that was followed, however, assures that in the future the American cotton industry will have to compete with the chemically produced domestic fibers as well as the inflated capacity of producers of cotton and other fibers in other countries. Perhaps the wonder is not the loss of foreign and domestic markets but that they have been maintained at the current level. As seen in this light, the shift to production payments in lieu of price supports which began in 1964 (Table 7-6), is the most critical of developments in cotton policy.

Finally, the equivalent of much of the 30 million acres diverted from production of cotton eventually became available for other crops, such as feed grains, soybeans, and pasture crops, thus helping to offset the effects of the Soil

Table 7-7 Cotton, Wool, Silk, Rayon, and Noncellulosic Manmade Fibers: Consumption (Total and Per Capita), United States, 1959–1972.

Year	Total (million lbs.)					Per capita (lbs.)				
	Cotton	Wool[1]	Silk[2]	Rayon and acetate[3]	Non-cellulosic fibers[3]	Cotton	Wool[1]	Silk[2]	Rayon and acetate[3]	Non-cellulosic fibers[3]
1959	4,334.5	435.3	8.0	1,293.8	770.9	24.5	2.5	(⁴)	7.3	4.4
1960	4,190.9	411.0	6.9	1,081.7	793.0	23.2	2.3	(⁴)	6.0	4.4
1961	4,081.5	412.1	6.7	1,155.6	899.0	22.2	2.2	(⁴)	6.3	4.9
1962	1,188.0	429.1	6.5	1,291.2	1,121.6	22.5	2.3	(⁴)	6.9	6.0
1963	4,040.2	411.7	6.4	1,471.0	1,304.0	21.4	2.2	(⁴)	7.8	6.9
1964	4,244.4	356.7	6.7	1,555.8	1,606.4	22.1	1.9	(⁴)	8.1	8.4
1965	4,477.5	387.0	5.8	1,593.3	2,020.8	23.1	2.0	(⁴)	8.2	10.4
1966	4,630.5	370.2	4.6	1,623.2	2,366.9	23.6	1.9	(⁴)	8.3	12.0
1967	4,423.0	312.5	2.8	1,520.4	2,724.9	22.3	1.6	(⁴)	7.7	13.7
1968	4,146.5	329.7	4.0	1,710.8	3,594.7	20.7	1.6	(⁴)	8.5	17.9
1969	3,933.0	312.8	3.3	1,623.8	3,928.4	19.4	1.5	(⁴)	8.0	19.4
1970	3,814.6	240.3	1.8	1,426.1	4,075.2	18.6	1.2	(⁴)	7.0	19.9
1971[5]	3,916.3	191.5	1.7	1,509.8	5,024.2	19.1	.9	(⁴)	7.3	24.1
1972[5]	3,841.3	219.2	2.0	1,428.3	5,572.9	18.4	1.0	(⁴)	6.8	26.4

[1]Apparel and carpet wool, scoured basis.
[2]Imports for consumption.
[3]Domestic shipments plus imports for consumption. Includes producers' waste consumed by mills. Non-cellulosic fibers also include textile glass fiber.
[4]Less than 0.05 pound.
[5]Preliminary.

Source: Economic Research Service. Data on manmade fibers from *Textile Organon.* Calendar year data divided by population on July 1, including Armed Forces overseas, to calculate per capita consumption. Data for 1929–58 in *Agricultural Statistics, 1972,* table 108.

Bank and Emergency Feed Grain Program. Costs of these programs were thereby increased. The total adjustment of agricultural supply was made more difficult.

A Policy Conclusion   In the third food policy era, as higher costs are projected for synthetic fibers made from petroleum and related resources, and as food crops compete directly with cotton in most countries, America's cotton economy will come closer to favorable terms of trade for producers under free markets than it would have during most of the second era. Because of modern technology, accelerated growth of large-scale cotton production will be experienced in the absence of production restraints. The small cotton farmer in the Old South might gain absolutely, but not relative to the large, mechanized producer. Again as in the case of tobacco, in a society concerned with human welfare, the plight of the small cotton farmer, in a continuing transitional stage, merits some special attention beyond that which is feasible in the product market.

Although the decline in the United States share of the world cotton market has been due to a number of factors, under a policy approaching free trade this share would increase. To make such a policy attractive to American cotton farmers, however, it would not be prudent to completely discard the policy that was initiated, in 1964, to substitute production payments for a program emphasizing market price supports, export subsidies, and import quotas. America's cotton production potential is so large that high cotton prices, such as those of 1973 and 1974, can lead again to overproduction and disastrously low prices. Since the development of synthetic fibers, the elasticity of aggregate world supply and demand for cotton has not been determined. A prudent cotton policy, therefore, will involve a deliberative program of income protection for cotton producers, stocks to help even out the flow of commodity from year to year, and maintenance of cotton exports.

By the late 1960s the cotton program had become the most expensive of all commodity programs in terms of Treasury cost or outlay. From the end of World War II in 1945 to 1956, the realized net cost of programs for supporting cotton price and income was only $119 million, or less than $12 million annually. But, in the late 1950s the program cost escalated rapidly to average more than $500 million annually for the next several years. In the late 1960s, the cost of payments alone was more than $750 million annually. Since these payments were distributed according to cotton production, the very high payments to a few large cotton producers became the subject of much criticism. The limitation on payments voted in the Acts of 1970 and 1973 was in response to this criticism, which centered largely on cotton. Without the payment program or its alternative—price supports, export subsidies, and subsidies to ginners to purchase domestic cotton—the production control program cannot be effective. But the continuation of unlimited payments raises an ethical question about income distribution. How much shall the taxpayer subsidize the large cotton producer?

Prudent cotton policy calls for something in addition to a freely competitive market. Although the pressure for price support and massive acreage restriction should be less in the third era of food policy than it was in the second, complete reliance on a free market will expose American cotton producers to a high degree of price variability which, we may assume, is politically intolerable. One answer is a less restrictive production policy, a more modest level of price support, a somewhat lower target for storage policy than the high points of the past, a basic free trade policy, and a lower level of production payments than in the late 1960s, with payments per bale or per pound scaled inversely to size of farm. Furthermore, the rural economy associated with cotton presents one of the strongest cases in America for human resource programs, as discussed in Chapter 10.

Wheat Commodity Programs

In the second policy era, wheat commodity programs emphasized the goal of raising and stabilizing wheat prices and incomes above world market levels by means of storage, export subsidy, and production control, using acreage allotments, nonrecourse loans, and production payments as implementers, with constraints generally expressed in terms of parity. Among the regular three major world wheat exporters—the United States, Canada, and Australia—the United States took the lead in restricting wheat acreage, subsidizing wheat exports, and accumulating stocks as a means of price support. Argentina, the fourth major export nation, forced on its wheat farmers a price significantly below world export levels. That price was achieved by multiple exchange rates, overvaluation of the Argentine peso, and, in 1970, an export tax of about 20 percent.[114]

As we discussed in Chapter 5, in the development of compensatory price policy, wheat usually led and often dominated the commodity field. From the standpoint of supply, although the wheat program was generally intended to restrict production, it has had some aspects encouraging production. Although the cropland devoted to wheat was periodically controlled well below pre-1933 levels, increased yields more than offset the reductions in acreage, resulting in a general increase in production. To regulate the flow of wheat, large carry-over stocks were controlled through the CCC. On the demand side, exports were responsive to market conditions abroad and to export subsidy and aid programs which generally increased during and following increases in wheat carry-over. Domestic use of food was very stable, reflecting nearly zero income elasticity and very low price elasticity (-0.15) for cereals and baking products (Table 3-2). The domestic use of seed was very stable (about three-fourths of a bushel per seeded acre). Feed use, generally a small component of demand, was more variable and wheat for feed use was subsidized during World War II (Table 7-8). Because of these supply-demand factors, wheat commodity programs concentrate on three things: (1) wheat production control, (2) supply management through storage and price support, and (3) export subsidies and food aid.

Wheat Production Control   Wheat price and income support has required production control. When this principle has been breached by land retirement

---

[114]D. Gale Johnson, *World Agriculture in Disarray, op. cit.*, p. 131.

without special reference to wheat, as in the Soil Conservation and Domestic Allotment Act of 1936 or the Soil Bank Act of 1956, wheat growers were not fully satisfied with the results. The political power of wheat interests has been marshaled to obtain stronger supports.

In most years, however, the interests of wheat growers have generally limited the effectiveness of control. For several years, the minimum national allotment was set at 55 million acres and the seeded acreage seldom fell below this level (Table 7-8). Farmers, most of whom were in the Corn Belt, were allowed to grow 15 acres of wheat without having an allotment history; and they were permitted to share in price support and payment programs. About 100 million bushels a year were grown on these 15-acre allotments.

Wheat Price Supports, Payments, and Reserves   Under the Wheat-Cotton Act of 1964, farmers were paid on about 45 percent of their anticipated production to bring the return on this part of their crop up to the support level, which fluctuated a little below $2 per bushel (Table 7-9). The average loan level, which tended to set the minimum market price, was allowed to drop to $1.30 for the 1964 crop and to $1.25 thereafter. Under this plan, the quantity of wheat put under support and that part acquired by the CCC through loan cancellations and purchases were drastically reduced. The nation's food reserve, as represented by wheat stocks owned by the CCC on June 30, was significantly lowered (Table 7-9).

The main burden of income support for wheat growers thus shifted from price support, storage, and export subsidy to direct payments. The U.S. Treasury outlay in direct support of the wheat program rose rapidly to more than $600 million annually by the late 1960s, not counting smaller supplementary payments for land retirement. About one-third of the gross farm income going to wheat growers came directly from such payments. Then, as we shifted into the third era of food policy, market prices rose above support levels. Acreage diversion programs were canceled. In 1974 the payments ceased. In our view, however, the underlying problem of price stability for wheat remains.

The role of wheat in a food reserve policy still needs to be defined. If stability in supply is the policy goal, then reserves must be built up or maintained in years of good crops, such as in the 1967–71 period, to be reduced in years of world wheat shortage, such as 1964 through 1966 or 1972 through 1974. As we read the record, summarized in Tables 7-8 and 7-9, this has not been the policy, except for the very modest buildup in stocks in 1969 and 1970.

Wheat Exports and Aid Programs   America has maintained the capacity and potential for large wheat exports either to commercial markets abroad or for aid. In spite of control programs, wheat production, in contrast to cotton, has kept pace with world production. What shall be the export policy?

Beginning in 1954, under Public Law 480 wheat became the most important commodity in development of foreign aid. The volume of aid shipments reached a plateau in the first half of the 1960s and then averaged lower in succeeding

Table 7-8 Wheat Production and Support Operations, 1932–1976

Year	Total seeded acreage[a] (million acres)	Yield per seeded acre (bushels)	Production	Total carry-over	Controlled by CCC[b]	Net exports[c]	Food[d]	Seed and feed[e]	Total
					July 1		Year beginning July 1		
			Millions of bushels						
1932	66.3	11.4	756	375[f]	—	35	492	227	719
1933	69.0	8.0	552	378	—	28	448	181	629
1934	64.1	8.2	526	273	—	-2	459	196	655
1935	69.6	9.0	628	146	—	-28	473	188	661
1936	74.0	8.4	630	140	—	-22	478	212	690
1937	80.8	10.8	874	83	—	103	475	226	701
1938	79.0	11.6	920	153	—	109	481	233	714
1939	62.8	11.8	741	250	6	48	475	188	663
1940	61.6	13.2	813	280	2	34	479	196	675
1941	62.3	15.1	943	385	169	28	488	180	668
1942	52.2	18.6	974	632	320	33	537	414[g]	951
1943	55.1	15.3	841	619	260	-93	543	697	1,210
1944	66.2	16.0	1,060	317	99	7	627	464	1,091
1945	69.2	16.0	1,108	279	104	318	569	400	969
1946	71.6	16.1	1,152	100	—	328	596	264	860
1947	78.3	17.4	1,359	84	—	340	636	270	906
1948	78.3	16.5	1,295	196	1	326	656	201	857
1949	83.9	13.1	1,098	307	227	177	612	192	804
1950	71.3	14.3	1,019	425	328	322	535	190	625
1951	78.0	12.6	988	396	196	438	502	180	682
1952	78.6	16.6	1,306	256	143	294	491	173	664
1953	78.9	14.9	1,173	606	470	210	489	146	635
1954	62.5	15.7	984	934	775	269	487	125	632
1955	58.2	16.1	937	1,036	976	336	481	122	603

1956	60.7	16.6	1,005	1,033	951	542	482	105	585
1957	49.8	19.2	956	909	824	392	486	105	591
1958	56.0	26.0	1,457	881	835	435	497	111	608
1959	56.7	19.7	1,118	1,295	1,147	503	496	103	599
1960	54.9	24.7	1,355	1,313	1,195	654	496	110	606
1961	55.7	22.1	1,232	1,411	1,243	713	500	127	527
1962	49.3	22.2	1,092	1,322	1,192	638	500	80	580
1963	53.4	21.5	1,147	1,195	1,179	852	503	85	588
1964	55.7	23.1	1,283	901	892	724	509	135	644
1965	57.4	22.9	1,316	817	682	866	515	216	731
1966	54.4	24.1	1,305	535	340	742	502	171	673
1967	67.8	22.5	1,522	424	201	760	519	114	633
1968	62.5	25.2	1,576	539	323	541	520	215	735
1969	54.3	26.9	1,460	817	516	605	521	251	772
1970	49.5	27.7	1,370	885	732	736	520	249	769
1971	53.8	30.1	1,618	732	561	632	526	329	855
1972	54.9	28.1	1,545	863	701	1,185	528	257	785
1973	59.0	29.0	1,705	438	211	1,148	528	224	752
1974	71.4	25.2	1,796	247	—	1,039	525	155	680
1975[h]	75.1	28.4	2,134	327	—	1,200	540	180	720
1976[h]	78.4	25.9	2,025	543	—	1,050	540	220	760

[a]Includes acreage seeded to winter wheat in the previous year for harvest in the year indicated, plus total spring wheat and durum.

[b]Includes wheat owned by CCC, under loan on July 1 from year-earlier crop, reseal from previous years, and small quantities in some years sealed under bond. Also includes 1957–1961 estimates of wheat to be delivered to CCC.

[c]Exports of wheat, wheat flour, and other products (semolina and macaroni products, bulgar, and rolled wheat) less imports of full-duty wheat, wheat imported for feed, and dutiable flour and macaroni products. Does not include wheat imported for milling in bond and export as flour, or transshipment of U.S. wheat through Canada.

[d]Includes shipments to U.S. territories and wheat for military food use at home and abroad. Military takings for civilian feeding in occupied areas measured at time of procurement and not at time of shipment overseas.

[e]Includes quantities of less than 1 million bushels per year of wheat ground into granular flour for alcohol production, together with wheat grain used for that purpose. Includes wheat used as commercial feed as well as that used on farms.

[f]From 1932 to 1936, some new wheat was included in carry-over inventory. Beginning with 1937, only old crop wheat is shown.

[g]From 1942 to 1947, increased use reflects effect of subsidy varying from 20 to 40 cents per bushel for use of 350 to 400 million bushels of wheat as feed for livestock plus 1942–1945 diversion of about 300 million bushels of wheat for manufacture of industrial alcohol.

[h]Preliminary or projected.

Source: U.S. Department of Agriculture, Economic Research Service, Agricultural Statistics and Wheat Situation.

Table 7-9 Wheat Price and Income Supports and CCC Operations, 1949–1976

Year (beginning July)	Support price		Average price per bushel received by farmers[c]	Put under support		Acquired by CCC under support program[d] (million bu.)	Owned by CCC, June 30 (million bu.)
	Price per bushel[a]	Percentage of parity[b]		Quantity (million bu.)	Percentage of production		
1949	$1.95	90	$1.88	380	34.6	248	328
1950	1.99	90	2.00	197	19.3	42	196
1951	2.18	90	2.11	213	21.5	91	143
1952	2.20	90	2.09	400	35.2	398	470
1953	2.21	91	2.04	553	47.1	486	775
1954	2.24	90	2.12	430	43.7	392	976
1955	2.08	82	1.98	318	34.0	277	951
1956	2.00	83	1.97	252	25.1	148	824
1957	2.00	80	1.93	256	26.8	194	835
1958	1.82	75	1.75	609	41.8	511	1,147
1959	1.81	77	1.76	317	28.3	182	1,195
1960	1.78	75	1.74	424	31.3	261	1,243
1961	1.79	76	1.83	271	22.0	120	1,097
1962	2.00	83	2.04	300	27.2	245	1,082
1963	2.03	81	2.06	172	15.0	85	829
1964	1.78	71	1.85	206	16.1	87	608
1965	1.72	67	1.82	173	13.1	11	262
1966	1.90	74	2.28	133	10.2	12	124
1967	1.85	71	1.99	282	18.7	83	102
1968	1.83	69	1.82	453	29.1	178	163
1969	1.94	70	1.93	408	28.3	96	301

Year							
1970	2.00	71	2.09	254	18.8	5	370
1971	1.79	61	1.88	438	27.1	35	367
1972	1.72	—	2.23	143	9.6ᵉ	24	144
1973	1.46	—	4.16	60	3.5ᵉ	—	19
1974	1.37	—	4.09	36	2.0ᵉ	—	1
1975ᶠ	1.37	—	3.52	—	2.2ᵉ	1	—
1976ᶠ	1.50	—	—	—	—	—	—

[a]Actual support price 1949–62; beginning in 1963, price includes $1.82 for the 1963 crop, $1.30 for 1964, and $1.25 thereafter, plus the average marketing certificate payment per bushel paid to program participants. Beginning in 1970 support price includes national average loan rate $1.25 plus support payments $.75 for 1970, $.54 for 1971, $.47 for 1972, and $.21 for 1973. Beginning in 1974, national average loan rate was $1.37 for 1974 and 1975 and $1.50 for 1976. Support payments were suspended in 1974.

[b]Percentage of the parity price at the beginning of the marketing year.

[c]Represents the season average market price received by farmers plus, beginning in 1963, the average marketing certificate payment per bushel paid to program participants.

[d]Acquisitions through loan cancellations and purchases (under agreement and direct) from crop harvested in the year indicated and not acquisitions during that year.

[e]From 1972 to 1976 nearly all of the wheat put under price-support loan was redeemed by farmers.

[f]Preliminary or projected.

Source: U.S. Department of Agriculture, Agricultural Stabilization and Conservation Service and Economic Research Service, *Agricultural Statistics* and *Wheat Situation*.

years, as the Wheat-Cotton Act of 1964 helped in expansion of commercial exports (Table 7-10).

There seems to be no criterion by which policymakers can judge what is optimum for designing wheat export, aid, and reserve stock programs. To minimize the government cost of a wheat production-control export-subsidy program, exports will be subsidized up to the point where the per bushel subsidy is equal to the per bushel cost of land retirement or other control.[115] If there is no production control program, the cost of foreign aid is a net cost to government. Minimum government cost is not a meaningful criterion for policy. Decisions must be made on other values and considerations.

As a minimum for a consistent aid program, it appears that a level should be set for emergency stocks and food exports. There might be, for example, buildup of 600 to 700 million bushels in years of good crops abroad and a draw-down to 100 to 150 million bushels in years of poor world crops. For the United States to be a consistent commercial exporter, stocks somewhat larger than this might be accumulated in times of good crops and drawn down in years of poor ones. The specific rules are not easy to formulate and they cannot be detailed here. But the belief can be expressed that, in a world where America has most of the excess capacity for alleviation of food catastrophe at home or abroad, we would be less than responsible to ignore the requirements of the necessary food reserve policy. It is of course appropriate that some of the costs of food reserves be shared among the nations and that the stocks be managed in a way that does not penalize American farmers. An appraisal of the full scope of such policy is not a simple task. If world wheat stocks are smaller in the third food policy era than they were in the second, more deliberative choices must be made about priorities in various aid contingencies. If total wheat reserves should be larger at their peak than in the second era, which position our view supports, these stocks should also be programmed to meet food needs rather than to serve as adjuncts to income support for producers, which function they have served with questionable benefit to producers in the past. Policy must be constrained by agreement among the nations as to the role of wheat in a world food program.

Feed Grain Program

As we see it now, in the years following World War II the wheat and cotton programs shifted a major part of the burden of adjustment to the feed grain and livestock economy. By the latter part of the 1950s, the combined acreage used for wheat and cotton was some 35 million acres below the post-World War II peak (Tables 7-5 and 7-8). In comparison, the combined seeded acreage for the feed grains—corn, sorghums, oats, and barley—and soybeans was near an all-time high (Table 7-11). Because of rising yields, total production was averaging more than 1.5 billion bushels larger than it had been in 1950 (Table 7-12). The effort to

[115]Leo V. Mayer, "Estimated Net Costs of P.L. 480 Food Aid with Three Alternative U.S. Farm Programs," *American Journal of Agricultural Economics,* Vol. 54, No. 1, February 1972, pp. 41–50.

Table 7-10 Wheat Exports under Specified Government Programs, 1954–1973
(Millions of Bushels)

Year beginning in July	Public Law 480						Total specified government programs	Total commercial net exports	Total net exports
	Sales for foreign currency[a]	Credit sales, convertible currency[b]	Government disaster relief and development[c]	Donations through voluntary agencies[d]	Barter for strategic materials[e]	Mutual security, AID[f]			
1954	24		17		46	69	156	113	269
1955	94		11	4	67	63	239	97	336
1956	203		12	13	87	67	382	160	542
1957	179		14	19	10	34	256	136	392
1958	232		12	21	20	25	309	126	435
1959	303		11	25	26	13	378	125	503
1960	344		33	29	34	34	474	180	654
1961	392	7	29	32	42	3	504	209	713
1962	418	6	34	29	6	1	494	144	638
1963	393	12	30	30	20	1	485	367	852
1964	446	60	17	29	4	—	556	168	724
1965	385	81	33	25	5	—	530	336	866
1966	215	40	24	16	2	2	299	443	742
1967	225	118	27	13	—	1	383	377	760
1968	83	112	36	10	—	2	242	299	541
1969	69	155	34	11	—	—	269	336	605
1970	47	143	30	11	—	1	233	503	736
1971	23	153	38	13	—	1	228	404	632
1972	—	88	36	13	—	—	137	1,048	1,185
1973	—	26	11	8	—	11	56	1,089	1,145

[a]Authorized by Public Law 480, Title I.
[b]Shipments, under agreements signed, through Dec. 31, 1966, authorized by Public Law 480, Title IV. Shipments, under agreements signed, from Jan. 1, 1967, authorized by Public Law 480, Title I, as amended by Public Law 89–808.
[c]Authorized by Public Law 480, Title II.
[d]Authorized by Sec. 416 of the Agricultural Act of 1949 and Public Law 480, Title III, Sec. 302, through Dec. 31, 1966. Authorized by Public Law 480, Title II, as amended by Public Law, 89–808, effective Jan. 1, 1967.
[e]Authorized by Public Law 480, Title III, Sec. 303, and other legislation. Includes some shipments in exchange for goods and services for U.S. agencies before 1963.
[f]Sales for foreign currency, economic aid, and expenditures under development loans authorized by Public Laws 165, 665, and 87–195.
Source: U.S. Department of Agriculture, Economic Research Service, *Agricultural Statistics* and *Wheat Situation.*

Table 7-11   Acreage of Feedgrains and Soybeans, 1949
(Millions of Acres)

Year	Corn[a]	Sorghum[b]	Oats[c]	Barley[d]	Soybeans[e]	Total
1949	86.7	11.1	37.8	11.1	12.5	159.2
1950	82.9	16.1	39.3	13.0	15.6	166.9
1951	83.3	15.0	35.0	10.8	15.7	159.8
1952	82.2	12.3	37.0	9.2	16.4	157.1
1953	81.6	14.6	37.5	9.6	16.7	160.0
1954	82.2	20.1	40.6	14.7	18.9	176.5
1955	80.9	23.9	39.0	16.3	20.0	180.1
1956	77.8	21.4	33.3	14.7	22.0	169.2
1957	73.2	26.9	34.1	16.4	22.2	172.8
1958	73.4	20.7	31.2	16.2	25.4	166.9
1959	82.7	19.5	27.8	16.8	23.3	170.1
1960	81.4	19.6	26.6	15.5	24.4	167.5
1961	65.9	14.3	23.9	15.6	27.8	147.5
1962	65.0	15.1	22.4	14.4	28.4	145.3
1963	68.8	17.5	21.3	13.5	29.5	150.6
1964	65.8	16.8	19.8	11.7	31.7	145.8
1965	65.2	17.1	18.5	10.1	35.2	146.1
1966	66.3	16.4	17.9	11.2	37.3	149.1
1967	71.2	18.9	16.1	10.1	40.8	157.1
1968	65.1	17.8	17.7	10.5	42.3	153.4
1969	64.3	17.2	17.9	10.3	42.5	152.2
1970	66.8	17.0	18.6	10.5	43.1	156.0
1971	74.1	20.8	15.8	11.1	43.5	165.3
1972	66.8	17.3	13.5	10.6	46.9	155.3
1973	71.6	19.2	14.1	11.2	56.7	173.0
1974	77.7	17.7	13.2	9.0	53.5	171.1
1975[f]	77.9	18.3	13.6	9.5	54.6	173.9
1976[f]	80.8	18.6	12.6	9.2	49.0	170.2

[a]Includes corn for grain, silage, and forage.
[b]Acreage planted for all purposes: grain, forage, and silage.
[c]Oats harvested for grain, rather than seeded acreage to eliminate acreage sown to oats for cover crop and not harvested under the Emergency Feed Grain Program.
[d]Barley sown for all purposes, including barley sown in the preceding fall.
[e]Acres grown alone, plus one-half the interplanted acres.
[f]Preliminary or projected.
Source: U.S. Department of Agriculture, Economic Research Service, *Agricultural Statistics, Feed Situation* and *Fats and Oil Situation.*

support prices without effective production control resulted in record stock carry-over, with more than six months' supply of feed grains in store (Table 7-13). In 1961 the total grain stocks were more than three-fourths of total stocks in the four major exporting countries. Only the rapidly rising demand for animal products, beef especially, was preventing a more disastrous decline in incomes of feed grain and livestock producers. In sharp contrast to the situation in the early 1960s, the combined effect of the Emergency Feed Grain Program and the systematic reduction of feed grain stocks from 1961 to the early 1970s then helped create the high prices and food debacle of the mid 1970s. Although world

Table 7-12 Production of Feed Grains and Soybeans, 1949–1973
(Millions of bushels)

Year[a]	Corn	Sorghum	Oats	Barley	Soybeans
1949	2,946	149	1,220	237	234
1950	2,764	234	1,369	304	299
1951	2,629	162	1,278	257	284
1952	2,981	91	1,217	228	299
1953	2,882	116	1,153	247	269
1954	2,708	236	1,410	379	341
1955	2,873	243	1,496	403	374
1956	3,075	205	1,151	377	449
1957	3,045	568	1,290	443	483
1958	3,356	581	1,401	477	580
1959	3,825	555	1,051	420	533
1960	3,907	620	1,153	429	555
1961	3,598	480	1,010	392	679
1962	3,606	510	1,012	428	669
1963	4,019	585	966	393	699
1964	3,484	490	852	386	701
1965	4,103	673	930	393	846
1966	4,168	715	803	392	928
1967	4,860	755	794	374	976
1968	4,450	731	951	426	1,107
1969	4,687	729	966	427	1,133
1970	4,152	683	917	416	1,127
1971	5,641	876	881	464	1,176
1972	5,573	809	692	423	1,271
1973	5,647	930	667	422	1,547
1974	4,664	629	614	304	1,215
1975[b]	5,757	758	657	383	1,521
1976[b]	—	758	655	370	—

[a]Marketing year beginning October 1 for corn and sorghum, July 1 for oats and barley.
[b]Preliminary or projected.
Source: U.S. Department of Agriculture, Economic Research Service, *Agricultural Statistics.*

feed grain stocks were almost as high in 1970 as 1961, there was no coordinated stock program.

As we noted in Chapter 5, the Emergency Feed Grain Program adopted early in 1961 was designed as a response to excess supply. Under the legislative provisions, farmers were eligible for price supports at 74 percent of parity if, in 1961, they diverted to soil-conserving uses 20 percent of the average acreage they had devoted to corn and sorghum in 1959 and 1960. Payments for reducing the minimum acreage were set at 50 percent of the support price times the normal yield of the farm. Payments for reducing an additional acreage from 20 to 40 percent of the base were paid at 60 percent of the county support rate. Payments were so generous that farmers were strongly induced to enter the program and, in addition, the government began a systematic reduction of CCC stocks which tended to depress market prices below loan levels, thus apparently giving a

Table 7-13   Stocks of Feed Grains and Wheat in Principal Exporting Countries, 1959–1973

(Millions of Metric Tons)

July 1	United States	Canada	Argentina	Australia	Total
1959	100.7	22.7	10.9	5.4	139.8
1960	107.6	22.5	8.7	4.9	143.6
1961	118.5	22.8	7.5	5.2	154.1
1962	105.9	14.9	6.5	3.5	130.8
1963	83.9	19.3	6.6	5.2	125.1
1964	92.4	20.9	10.1	4.3	127.6
1965	76.8	19.7	11.3	5.1	113.0
1966	67.2	18.6	8.6	4.1	98.6
1967	63.1	22.3	6.6	8.0	100.0
1968	78.0	24.7	9.0	5.0	115.8
1969	85.4	31.0	7.2	12.8	136.3
1970	86.4	36.6	9.0	14.1	146.1
1971	71.4	28.1	10.1	10.5	120.0
1972	91.5	25.2	7.6	6.9	131.3
1973*	71.5	18.8	10.3	3.3	103.9

*Preliminary.

Source: U.S. Department of Agriculture, Foreign Agricultural Service, *Agricultural Statistics, 1974*, p. 50; *1972*, p. 63.

further incentive for farmers to be in the program, especially those selling feed grain rather than feeding it to livestock. The initial loan rate was $1.25 per bushel for corn and $1.93 per hundredweight for grain sorghum.

Ten years later, the provisions of the feed grain programs, with a little higher price support for corn and grain sorghum, were essentially as adopted in 1961 (Table 7-14). In the tenth year (in 1970), farmers diverted 37.4 million acres from feed grain production, nearly 2 million less than in 1969, but except for that year the largest on record. The total payment to farmers participating in the program was a little more than $1.5 billion, roughly $40 per acre for the land diverted, totaling $739 million in price support payments and $771 million in acreage diversion payments. Starting in 1971, as America entered the third policy era, market prices dropped and payments escalated. Then, as the market quickly expanded, prices for feed grains rose sharply (Table 7-15). These prices combined with price support and diversion payments created short-term windfall gains for those farmers who sold rather than fed their grain. The livestock feeders were disadvantaged. Price support payments and the set-aside program were suspended in 1974, while a few feed grain, cotton, and wheat producers received payments under the disaster provisions of the Agricultural and Consumer Protection Act of 1973 (see Chapter 5). In 1975 and 1976 the price support levels for feed grains remained far below market prices.

Conclusion   According to the elasticities of demand given in Tables 3-3 to 3-6, the reduction in feed grains as a result of the Emergency Feed Grain Program would only modestly increase the aggregate market receipts from the livestock sector in a three-year term; and the market gain from the program would be in doubt in the long run, with much depending on how well deliveries of feed grains were maintained in the foreign market. However, since diversion of feed grain acreage was in addition to that for wheat and cotton, the feed grain program helped to balance the aggregate grain-cotton economy at a higher level of farm income than would have existed in its absence. Thus, given the policy of crop restriction, the Emergency Feed Grain Program was a consistent but expensive part of the total policy. If cotton had continued to claim its traditional share of the world market and if wheat exports had been priced at more competitive levels prior to 1964, however, the gross market receipts of the feed-livestock sector in a free market might have been close to that experienced under the Emergency Feed Grain Program. Government payments could have been made without crop restrictions, although without the program they would have been more difficult to sustain politically.

A CONCLUSION ON POLICY CONSTRAINTS

Although it is logical and helpful to build the macroeconomic policy in the product markets commodity by commodity, the conclusion on policy constraints must encompass the total market. What is done in one product area affects another, until the total product market is seen as an integrated whole. If one starts with the concept of an integrated world market, one can see that such needs as there are for price supports, payments, and production controls depend on how dynamic this market is. It is known that the demand for food around the world is rising, as we discussed in Chapters 2 and 3. America has food production capacity exceeding the demands of its own domestic market, as we suggested in Chapters 4 and 5. As we view the record of the second food policy era, America's capacity to produce grain at the approximate prices of that period, without any production control or land retirement, could have resulted in several billion tons of grain in excess of domestic requirements. Alternatively, this grain might have been (1) subsidized in export sale; (2) stored as a reserve for future use; (3) given to people in poorer countries for improvement of their low-level diets, either (a) as a contribution to direct aid or (b) as part of a cooperative world food program; (4) fitted into a domestic food stamp program; or (5) simply moved in competitive markets, which in some years would have meant very low prices for American farmers. The fact that none of these was wholly satisfactory brought the nation to its policy of production control. As we view the third food policy era, all these alternatives remain, although the cumulative magnitude of excess grains may be believed to be not so large. Still the excess over domestic demand is expected to be large. Under a full-production policy in the United States, the excess in some years will be larger than the peak potentials of the second era. How is this level of production to be programmed and managed?

A Free Trade, No Government-Reserve Policy

The policy shift in transition from the second to the third food era revealed the preference of the federal government for a free-trade, no-reserve policy, while at

Table 7-14 Summary of Provisions of the 1969–1971 Feed Grain Programs

Item	1969 program			1970 program			1971 program		
	Price support loan	Price support payment	Total support	Price support loan	Price support payment	Total support	Price support loan	Set aside payment	Guarantee support
Price support									
Corn, per bu.	$1.05	$0.30	$1.35	$1.05	$0.30	$1.35	$1.05	Corn & sorghums difference between Oct.– Feb. average price received & the price guarantee	$1.35
Grain sorghum, per cwt.	1.61	.53	2.14	1.61	.53	2.14	1.73		2.21
Oats, per bu.	.63	.00	.63	.63	.00	.63	.54		—
Barley, per bu.	.83	.20	1.03	.83	.20	1.03	.81		—
Production eligible for price support	Price support loan on total production	Price support payment on projected production of the smaller of the acreage planted to feed grains or 50% of base		Price support loan on total production	Price support payment on projected production of the smaller of the acreage planted to feed grains or 50% of base		Price support loan on total production	Set aside payment on production from 50% of the base. Payment made if planted to feed grains, some other crop or left idle.	
Preliminary or advance	50% of payment for additional diversion only (no advance on price support payment)			None			Preliminary set aside payment made soon after July 1 depending on set-aside percentage:[a] 20%		
Corn				"			$0.32 per bu.		
Grain sorghum							0.29 per bu.		
Yield used for determination of payments	Projected for 1969 (Based on 1963–67 average adjusted for trend)			Projected for 1970 (Based on 1964–68 average adjusted for trend)			Based on yield established for the farm for the preceding year with necessary adjustments to be fair and equitable		
Acreage diversion or set aside									
Grains included	Corn, grain sorghum, and barley			Corn, grain sorghum, and barley			Corn and grain sorghum		
Base period	1959 and 1960			1959 and 1960			1959 and 1960		

Acreage to be diverted			
Minimum[b]	20% of base	20% of base	Set-aside 20% of base
Maximum	50% " " (or 25 acres if larger)[c,d]	50% " " (or 25 acres if larger)[c,d]	no additional diversion for payment[e]
Limitation on acreage planted	Not more than 80% of base plus eligible substitution	Not more than 80% of base plus eligible substitution	No limitation after meeting set-aside requirement and maintaining conserving base.
Payment rates for acreage diversion	County total support rate times:	County total support rate times:	
First 20% diverted	No payment (except small farms)	No payment (except small farms)	No direct payment—set-aside payment considered payment for required set-aside. No additional diversion for payment.
Diversion of 20 to 50%	45% of projected production	40% of projected production	
Small producer: 25 acres of feed grains or less	May divert entire acreage. Payment on first 20% based on 20% of projected production; additional diversion based on 45% of projected production[f]	May divert entire acreage. Payment on first 20% based on 20% of projected production; additional diversion based on 40% of projected production[f]	No special provision. Unlike 1970, producers receive set-aside payment even if no feed grains are planted.

[a] If the final set-aside payment proves to be less than the preliminary payment, producers will not be asked for a refund. If set-aside percentage is less than 20 percent, the preliminary payment will be reduced proportionately.
[b] Minimum diversion to be eligible for diversion payments and price support.
[c] Maximum acreage that can be diverted: no payment for minimum (required) diversion except on "small farms."
[d] Producers could divert for payment up to 25 acres if no feed grains are planted.
[e] Set-aside percentage tentatively set at 20%. Final determination will be announced prior to sign-up.
[f] Producers with bases of 26 through 125 acres may elect to have the base temporarily reduced to 25 acres and be paid as a small producer, provided no corn, grain sorghum, or barley is planted.
Source: *Feed Situation*, USDA, ERS, February 1971.

Table 7-15 Corn, Grain Sorghum, and Barley: Price Support Payments, Season Average Prices and Average Prices including Payments, 1965–1973

Item	Price support payments earned by program participants		All U.S. farmers				Participants in Emergency Feed Grain Program		
	Total (million dollars)	Rate[a] (per bu.)	Production (million bu.)	Season average price (per bu.)	Average payment per bushel produced	Season average price plus payment (per bu.)	Production[b] (million bu.)	Average payment per bushel produced	U.S. season average price plus payment (per bu.)
Corn									
1965	$333.9	$0.20	4,103	$1.16	$0.08	$1.24	1,956	$0.17	$1.33
1966	449.0	.30	4,168	1.24	.11	1.35	1,775	.25	1.49
1967	428.5	.30	4,860	1.03	.09	1.12	2,175	.20	1.23
1968	514.4	.30	4,450	1.08	.12	1.20	2,146	.24	1.32
1969	584.9	.30	4,687	1.15	.13	1.28	2,434	.24	1.39
1970	583.1	.30	4,152	1.33	.14	1.47	2,091	.28	1.61
1971	893.1	.32	5,641	1.08	.16	1.24	4,791	.19	1.27
1972	1,468.9	.40[c]	5,573	1.57	.26	1.83	4,612	.32	1.89
1973[d]	910.0	.32[e].15[e]	5,643	2.37	.16	2.53	5,137	.18	2.55
Barley									
1965	$16.8	$.16	393	$1.02	$0.043	$1.06	146	$0.12	$1.14
1966	20.6	.20	392	1.06	.04	1.10	123	.17	1.23
1967	0	0	374	1.01	f	1.01	f	0	1.01
1968	0	0	426	.921	f	.92	f	0	.92
1969	23.9	.20	427	.885	.045	.93	159	.15	1.04
1970	26.5	.20	416	.973	.047	1.02	158	.17	1.14
1971	0	0	464	.993	f	.99	f	0	.99
1972	107.2	.32[c]	423	1.22	.23	1.45	296	.36	1.58
1973[d]	78.0	.26[e].12[e]	424	2.04	.15	2.19	322	.24	2.28

Grain Sorghum	(Dollars per cwt.)			(Dollars per cwt.)			(Dollars per cwt.)
	$.35	673	$1.76	$0.21	$1.97	444	$0.32	$2.08
1965	$80.5							
1966	116.1	.53	715	1.82	.29	2.11	463	.45	2.27
1967	113.9	.53	755	1.77	.27	2.04	559	.36	2.13
1968	113.9	.53	731	1.70	.27	1.97	476	.43	2.13
1969	119.1	.53	730	1.91	.28	2.19	465	.45	2.36
1970	129.3	.53	684	2.04	.33	2.37	431	.53	2.57
1971	167.0	.52	876	1.87	.31	2.18	873	.34	2.21
1972	289.3	.57^c	809	2.45	.36	2.81	690	.42	2.87
1973[d]	183.0	.54^e.25^e	937	3.80	.20	4.00	876	.21	4.01

[a]Made on projected production of 50 percent of participant's base acreage.
[b]Production computed on the basis of acreage planted on participants' farms and U.S. average yield. Includes grain equivalent of silage and forage.
[c]Payments earned for minimum set-aside requirements; program contained options for additional voluntary set-aside acreage at higher payment rates.
[d]Preliminary.
[e]Two set-aside options were in effect for the 1973 crop.
[f]Barley not included in acreage diversion program and not eligible for price support payments.
Source: *Food Situation*, February 1974.

the same time political pressure, largely outside the Department of Agriculture, brought a huge expansion in the domestic food stamp program. After many years of criticism of the budgetary costs of price support and farm income programs, the administration was eager to reduce excess stocks down to almost a pipeline minimum. Although given authority to do so by the Agricultural Act of 1970, the administration did not move to expand production by release of diverted acres at the first clear signs in 1971 of growing food shortages abroad. By not acting promptly, the administration exposed itself to criticism that subsequently rose to vitriolic levels.[116] The critics charged that the high prices for grains in 1973 and 1974 were a direct consequence of this policy of stock depletion in lieu of more prompt production expansion. Specifically, it was charged that the administration ignored the broader implications of cumulative short wheat crops in Russia; it did not move promptly in the early 1970s to cancel the acreage-reserve and set-aside programs, and to more generally assume the principal role in foreign marketing operations.[117]

The record seems clear, however, that neither the USDA nor the major American companies in the grain export trade had advance knowledge of the potential demand of the U.S.S.R.—that is, the decision of the Soviet Union to buy grain—and they did not anticipate the magnitude of the subsequent purchases.[118] Consequently, no action by the Department of Agriculture to counteract a possible reduction in grain stocks was consistent with long-standing policy. Unfortunately, before the wheat sales to Russia began, the CCC owned only 367 million bushels of wheat,[119] which might be regarded as a relatively small reserve for any time. The Soviet secrecy in not revealing its full intention to buy caused domestic prices to remain low until considerable quantities of wheat had been bought. Many farmers in the winter wheat states sold their wheat prior to the rise in price and then, since government payments under the Agricultural Act of 1970 were based on the first five months of the marketing year, or on an average of market prices from July to November, their direct payments were reduced. When domestic wheat prices rose, however, the wheat export subsidy had to be increased, finally up to 47 cents per bushel in late August, to protect the export target price of $1.65 per bushel. Thereafter, export prices were allowed to rise and the subsidy was reduced and finally discontinued.

The lesson for the future is not that the USDA was less than clairvoyant in anticipation of future export demands; it is that the United States government did not have a grain reserve policy, or a positive incentive production policy sufficient to serve the fast-growing export demand. With the exception of

[116]See, for example, Roger Morris and Hal Sheets, "Why Leave It to Earl?," *The Washington Monthly,* November 1974.

[117]Carl J. Schramm, "The Perils of Wheat Trading without a Grains Policy," *Challenge, The Magazine of Economic Affairs,* March–April 1975. For comments critical of this article, see letters by James Vertrees and Robbin S. Johnson and a reply by Schramm, *ibid.,* July–August 1975, pp. 60–64.

[118]*Sale of Wheat to Russia,* Hearings, Subcommittee on Livestock and Grains, Committee on Agriculture, House of Representatives, 92d Cong., 2d Sess., Sept. 14, 18, and 19, 1972, Serial No. 92-KK.

[119]Carroll G. Brunthaver, *ibid.,* p. 155.

Secretary of Agriculture Henry A. Wallace in the mid 1930s, who, as we recall, boldly proclaimed the principle of "the Ever Normal Granary," whereby stocks would increase in years of good crops and decrease in years of poor crops, every USDA Secretary including Butz, since the time of President Herbert Hoover, had attempted to follow the policy: Reduce government-held stocks; let farmers and the grain trade carry the reserves. The representatives of grower organizations were not concerned with possible grain shortages, but with possible overproduction resulting from a too-quick response by government in releasing land for expansion in grain production.

Eugene Moos, president of the influential National Association of Wheat Growers (NAWG), expressed concern that

> (1) The size of the Russian grain sale relates more to a shortfall in Soviet production because of adverse weather conditions than it does to sales of a continuing nature. . . . (2) World wheat stocks as well as U.S. stocks will be pulled down to a manageable level by the Russian demand this year. . . . (3) There still exists the threat of overproduction . . . pressure is already building to force USDA to relax production controls in 1973. NAWG sincerely believes that to relax production controls in 1973 would be to court disaster by inviting back the low prices and surplus stocks of just a few months ago. NAWG strongly recommends that the USDA stick with the 1973 program provisions recently announced. . . . Given careful production management by the USDA, grain producers could continue to receive a larger share of their income return from the market place. . . . Reasonable returns to producers will help keep rural people in rural areas, strengthen the rural social structure and at the same time reduce the need for rural development programs. . . . NAWG calls on the USDA to cooperate in maintaining existing world wheat prices.[120]

Mr. Moos, Weldon V. Barton of the National Farmers Union, Cleo T. Duzan of the United Grain Farmers of America, and Charles L. Frazier of the National Farmers Organization (NFO) all criticized the USDA for not having officially warned farmers earlier in 1972 of possible increases in wheat prices.[121] Government payments to farmers would not compensate those farmers who had sold prior to the increase in price. It was alleged that the major exporting companies would gain large windfalls from increases in grain prices, although this assertion is apparently still unsubstantiated. The need for grain reserves to protect food prices to consumers attracted little attention.

The policy of no government-held grain reserves was strongly supported for several years after the 1972 hearings. As late as January 1976, as noted in the second epigraph at the beginning of this chapter, the American Farm Bureau Federation still opposed government-held grain reserves, while it favored the establishment of an International Monetary Food Fund, to be supported by all the world's nations, whether or not they were food exporters, to meet disaster needs, such as starvation, malnutrition, and other emergencies. In time of food

---

[120]*Ibid.,* p. 104.
[121]*Ibid.,* pp. 92–122.

shortages, money could be withdrawn from the Fund to purchase needed food from any nation where it was available. Presumably, the unstated hypothesis was that the desired amount of grain would always be available if the managers of the Fund would bid sufficiently high for it. Grain prices in world markets would reflect the season-to-season and year-to-year strengths of supply and demand.

Worldwide Buffer Stock Programs

The argument for intergovernmental cooperation in establishing worldwide stocks of wheat and other grains rests on the proposition that this policy will provide at relatively small cost an additional element of price stability, especially a degree of protection against extreme shortfalls in grain supplies. More traditionally, as in farm price support programs, the accumulation of government stocks in years of large crops is a means of forestalling very low farm prices. Both extreme shortfalls in grain supplies and very low farm prices are regarded as conditions to be avoided in a comprehensive food and farm policy.

As Turnovsky has shown in an important article, the distribution of gains among producers and consumers depends heavily on how producers' price expectations are generated as well as on the source and properties of the price fluctuations that might occur in the absence of a buffer stock program.[122] Earlier, Waugh had pointed out that consumers may generally gain from price instability as they shift purchases among commodities to take advantage of periodic downward fluctuations in price or to stock up when prices are low.[123] Although this condition generally holds, extreme food shortages are to be avoided because of health and welfare considerations; and the prevention of both food waste in years of large crops and forced liquidation of livestock in years of poor crops is also desired for reasons of both equity and efficiency. The welfare ranking of stabilizing production and consumption depends on the relative size of the demand and price response coefficients, however, and under given assumptions, consumers generally have most to gain from stabilization of production or supply.[124]

In regard to producers, although Oi demonstrated that producers maximizing short-run profits at each point in time would gain from price instability arising out of fluctuations in demand,[125] Massell showed that if price instability is due to fluctuations in supply, then producers will be hurt by this instability, or they will benefit from price stabilization such as might occur from a buffer stock program.[126] When both producers and consumers are considered simultaneously, price stabilization will always improve total welfare even though one or the other may be adversely affected at some time.[127] Thus, overall price stabilization is to

[122]Stephen J. Turnovsky, "Price Expectations and the Welfare Gains from Price Stabilization," *American Journal of Agricultural Economics,* Vol. 56, No. 4, November 1974, pp. 706–716.

[123]Frederick V. Waugh, "Does the Consumer Gain from Price Instability?" *Quarterly Journal of Economics,* August 1944, pp. 602–614; and "Consumer Aspects of Price Instability," *Econometrica,* Vol. 34, No. 2, April 1966, pp. 504–508.

[124]Abraham Subotnik and James P. Houck, "Welfare Implications of Stabilizing Consumption and Production," *American Journal of Agricultural Economics,* Vol. 58, No. 1, February 1976, pp. 13–20.

[125]Walter Y. Oi, "The Desirability of Price Instability under Perfect Competition," *Econometrica,* Vol. 29, No. 1, January 1961, pp. 58–64.

[126]B. F. Massell, "Price Stabilization and Welfare," *Quarterly Journal of Economics,* Vol. 83, May 1969, pp. 284–298.

be preferred, with appropriate attention being given to total costs of storage, capital, and administration.[128] Finally, Turnovsky has concluded that even where price instability results from fluctuations in demand, producers may gain if their production plans are adapted to market expectations rather than based on current prices. Thus, whether producers facing an uncertain demand will gain or lose from price stabilization policy depends on the properties of the disturbance, that is, whether it is independent or correlated with other events, as well as on the lags in responding to expectations and the comparative slopes of the demand and supply curves.[129]

The static models of supply and demand (with no population growth, no taste changes, no income effect, and no technical innovation) in a single commodity market must be readdressed for policy purposes to take account of the interrelationships among commodities and the interdependence among the nations. This has led to a number of policy propositions for buffer stocks and to a new emphasis in policy study of which we shall hear more in the future.

Empirical Studies of World Buffer Stocks

Shlomo Reutlinger, for example, has estimated that a world wheat storage scheme of 20-million-bushel capacity, which operates under "insurance-oriented" storage rules where grain is released only in years of extremely poor harvests, could reduce the probability of grain shortages by more than 5 percent of the mean from 13.6 percent to 4.6 percent.[130] Alternatively, it could reduce a shortfall in excess of 7.5 percent of the mean from 4.0 percent to 0.5 percent. The annual negative net benefits or net costs of storage—that is, the annual insurance premium of such a program—would run from about $50 million to $150 million, within the range of elasticities assumed, based on storage costs of $7.50 a ton. In terms of the world's expected wheat production, this amounts to an insurance premium of 20 to 50 cents per ton per annum.

In the Reutlinger model, if world production is above a prespecified level (and the price is below a certain level), the surplus grain is put into storage. If production is below a prespecified level (and the price is above a certain level), grain is withdrawn from storage to augment total world supplies up to a prespecified level. The actual amounts to be added or withdrawn are determined by simulating sequences of annual production and inventory levels, based on an index of production and prespecified storage capacity that covers a 30-year period.

Under such a program, since the demand for wheat is assumed to be more inelastic at high prices than at low prices, consumers generally gain by stabilizing

---

[127]B. F. Massell, "Some Welfare Implications of International Price Stabilization," *Journal of Political Economy,* Vol. 78, March–April 1970, pp. 404–417.

[128]Massell, *ibid.*

[129]Turnovsky, "Price Expectations and the Welfare Gains from Price Stabilization," *op. cit.,* pp. 711, 715.

[130]Shlomo Reutlinger, "A Simulation Model for Evaluating Worldwide Buffer Stocks of Wheat," *American Journal of Agricultural Economics,* Vol. 38, No. 1, February 1976, pp. 1–12. See also Reutlinger, *Simulation of World-Wide Buffer Stocks of Wheat,* International Bank for Reconstruction and Development, World Bank Staff Working Paper No. 219, November 1975.

supply and producers tend to lose. That is, the denial of very high prices to producers, which would occur without the program in periods of extreme crop shortages, is not fully compensated by the effects of increases in buffer stocks in years of large crops. Although the estimated benefits to consumers generally exceed the losses to producers, the net benefits do not become large until supply stabilization is combined with food aid. Then, the reduced cost for food aid in years of short crops more than offsets the cost to government of the storage program. Or, to put it another way, the nations that are consistent grain importers tend to gain from a world buffer stock, whereas nations that are consistent exporters tend to lose unless buffer stocks are used to augment export trade.

The costs and benefits of a worldwide buffer stock program will depend substantially on the conditions for trade and the role of food aid. Although a buffer stock, as suggested above, can have a strong price effect if there is free trade, the more trade is restricted the larger the stocks must be to achieve individual country goals of price stability.[131] On the basis of trade patterns of the 1970s, it has been suggested that an international reserve stock program of 50 to 75 million tons during 1975 to 1985 would be required to hold world grain price oscillations within a range of, say, plus 10 percent and minus 5 percent of trend, with a probability of 85 to 90 percent.[132] The most costly way to achieve stability in production or supply would be to have each nation try to assure for itself adequate grain reserves without regard to the needs of other countries. A worldwide buffer stock, operating under insurance-oriented rules and approximating free trade, can have the most beneficial effect on consumer price stability and assurance of supply.

Even with a buffer stock, however, considerable price instability could still exist. The elasticity of world demand for wheat, for example, is believed to be near -0.1. A decline of 5 percent in world wheat supply will bring a 50 percent increase in price, *ceteris paribus*. Or a 5 percent increase in market supply could cause farm prices to fall by one-half. Since such an increase in supply is well within the parameters of American agriculture—or if production increases in the United States and in other exporting nations—additional questions may be raised about the role of a buffer stock program in America based on the principle of the ever normal granary.

An Ever Normal Granary for America

In spite of the projections of continuing expansion in the production capacity of American agriculture, under a policy of no government-held grain reserves another food price explosion of uncertain magnitude or a collapse in farm prices of almost unpredictable severity is only a matter of time. Although the combination of crops and livestock that is characteristic of American agriculture provides

[131]D. Gale Johnson and Daniel Sumner, "An Optimization Approach to Grain Reserves for Developing Countries," *Policy Analysis of Grain Reserves,* U.S. Department of Agriculture and the National Science Foundation, 1976.

[132]Willard W. Cochrane and Yigal Danin, *Reserve Stock Grain Models, The World and the United States, 1975–85,* University of Minnesota, Agricultural Experiment Station, Technical Bulletin 305, 1976.

great flexibility for short-run adjustments, the nation's ability to counteract continued severe drought by livestock liquidation is definitely limited. Likewise, the capacity to dispose of unusually large crops is limited by the inelasticity of demand in domestic food markets and by the inability of the foreign market to absorb large percentage increases in grain imports from the United States in the short run. In the latter case, American grain exports can severely depress world grain prices; whereas, in the former, valuable livestock production capacity might be lost, American farm exports might be restricted, and high food prices might help set off another round of inflation. Instability in grain prices leads to instability in livestock production and to higher costs. This is the general argument for an ever normal granary for America.

The policy problem is one both of concept and of magnitude and rules of operation. If the United States is to have a consistent policy, there must be a statement of goals in quantitative terms, development of financial means, organization of implementing agencies, and a further definition of constraints and how and under what conditions to apply them. For there to be consistency in the nation's food policy, there must be satisfactory answers to four general policy questions: Shall reserves be held? How shall they be managed? Who shall hold them? How shall the government acquire and dispose of stocks?[133]

Shall Reserves Be Held?   Four different bills were introduced in 1976 in the 94th Congress, 1st Session, to establish agricultural commodity reserves.[134] These generally would have increased the levels of target prices and price supports for grains. They would use either target prices or changes in carry-over levels as triggers for acquiring and disposing of stocks, in some cases using price triggers for sales so as to prevent an excessive runup of grain prices and quantity triggers for acquisitions in good crop years or to define the increase in carry-over.

The argument for such legislation is that a reserve program can contribute to price stability, provide a cushion for meeting unusually large export demands, help to stabilize livestock production, and assure a normal level of exports in years when grain production is low. From 1951 to 1972, the grain stocks carried by the CCC largely achieved these purposes, although farm prices, deflated by the wholesale price index, trended generally down (Figure 4-5). Although some studies have linked these low prices to the magnitude of stocks in storage, under an alternative model prices might have been still lower without storage. Since total supply was augmented by the efforts of the administration to reduce stocks from 1961 through 1972, prices were depressed not by the holding of stocks but by their release, especially in good crop years.

A national buffer stock program must play a limited role in the implementation of farm price supports. Such a program is not a means for dealing with

[133]For further discussion, see Robbin S. Johnson, "Analysis of a Grain Reserve Plan," *Policy Analysis of Grain Reserves,* USDA and the National Science Foundation, 1976.

[134]S. 513 by Senators Humphrey, Mondale, and McGee, which was similar to S.2005, 93d Cong., 2d Sess.; S. 549, by Senator McGovern; S. 2274, by Senator Bellman; and H. 1036, by Representatives Neal Smith and Robert Bergland. For more general discussion, see *Grain Reserves: A Potential U.S. Food Policy Tool,* Report of the Comptroller General of the United States, United States General Accounting Office, OSP-76-16, March 26, 1976.

chronic surplus or chronic shortage, and, although stocks are a cushion, they are not a fixed cushion for insulating consumers in America from world market conditions. They are a means for softening periodic fluctuations in grain supplies by leveling off the peaks of surplus production and filling the troughs of short crops or large export demand. In this concept, reserves can be seen as shock absorbers—limited stocks of grain to rise or fall as needed. A domestic grain reserve can be a stabilizing mechanism for the domestic market, while demonstrating to other countries the use of a buffer stock strategy rather than a hand-to-mouth food policy.

How Shall Reserves Be Managed?   Reserves to stabilize supplies must be insulated from the market in order to achieve the specific objective of making the United States a reliable supplier of domestic and foreign demands in bad years as well as good. They should not be used to create artificially high prices or to depress prices to implement crop restriction or other policies. From 1956 to 1973 the nation experienced a run of very favorable weather.[135] This, according to the criteria suggested, would have resulted in maximum carry-over stocks of, say, 80 to 100 million tons of feed grains and 50 million tons (2 billion bushels) of wheat by 1971, involving a maximum carry-over cost of about $1 billion a year. This grain would have been isolated from the market and then partially released in the early 1970s to meet the increase in purchases of some 60 million tons by the Peoples Republic of China, the U.S.S.R., and the rest of Europe (Table 3-1) and to offset the short crops in the United States, such as in 1974 and other years.

According to the hypothesis presented by Louis M. Thompson,[136] if the cooling trend of the 35 years from the mid 1930s to the early 1970s is projected to the year 2000, this will be only slightly detrimental to the production of grain in the middle latitudes, such as most of the United States. But any further cooling will have serious consequences detrimental to grain production at higher latitudes—such as the U.S.S.R., Western Europe, and Canada—because of the decrease in the length of the growing season, or possible rainfall variations. A further cooling might be favorable to crop production in the tropics. A number of policy considerations must be taken into account in deciding whether to include such possibilities as hypotheses in the management of a buffer stock program.

Who Shall Hold Reserves?   Because of the expense involved in holding grain stocks, the reserves voluntarily held by the trade (producers, grain handlers, processors, etcetera) will generally be inadequate to meet the nation's objectives of stable food prices.[137] Private parties will hold some grain stocks, at

[135]See Louis M. Thompson, "Weather Variability, Climatic Change, and Grain Production," *Food: Politics Economics, Nutrition and Research,* Washington: American Association for the Advancement of Science, 1975, pp. 43–49.

[136]*Ibid.,* pp. 47–49.

[137]See discussion by G. E. Brandow, "Grain Reserves and the U.S. Economy: A Policy Perspective," in *Policy Analysis of Grain Reserves,* U.S. Department of Agriculture and the National Science Foundation, 1976.

least enough to meet pipeline needs. But they will hold them in quantities close to pipeline needs, unless a larger stock is necessary to avoid losses from unforeseeable events.

Government must hold the reserves to meet future events that cannot be clearly anticipated or foreseen but that are at times inevitable. In this country, only the federal government is in a position to finance and withhold the necessary grain supplies from the market. If stocks are to be held outside the United States, other governments must share in the burden, or there must be international agreement on jointly held stocks. This is the lesson of the 1970s.

How Shall the Government Acquire and Hold Stocks?   In the past, the CCC has acquired grain stocks through default under the nonrecourse loan programs. It has disposed of stocks in foreign markets, sometimes with the aid of export subsidies and direct aid under Public Law 480. Disposal in domestic markets generally has not been permitted unless prices were well above support levels.

This is unsatisfactory for a grain reserve program. Acquiring stocks at loan levels does not assure the desired buildup in commodity stocks; it places too much of the cost on farmers; and, once stocks are depleted, it creates pressures for more drastic measures to hold down prices, such as export controls, embargoes, or other measures.

A second approach is to link acquisition to specific quantity triggers and sales to price targets, limiting the changes made in reserves to specific amounts designed to offset production above or below trend. Although this may be an improvement over past programs, it has the disadvantage that it may not take account of changes anticipated in foreign demands, and it cannot provide for both supply and demand without becoming hopelessly complex and uncertain in administration. It does not eliminate the risk of premature release of stocks such as occurred in 1972, for example, and it may involve unnecessary uncertainty about government actions, leading to both inequitable administration and misallocation of resources. Although specific triggers can be used as guides, there must be some administrative discretion in setting price targets, in operating within a range of prices that allows for forward prices set at least a production period in advance.

Research must establish the degree of stability that can be expected from different levels of reserve stocks and the alternative storage strategies. Domestically generated shocks from weather and other factors must be taken into account. Instability arising from changes in the commercial export market must be incorporated into reserve plans. If the policy is to be most responsive to world conditions, allowance must be made for emergency aid, cooperatively financed among nations in a world plan. If reserve programs in the United States are to be coordinated on a world scale, there must be international agreements involving cooperative financing of food aid, with the World Food Council or some related agency serving as a neutral arbiter in distribution of the established grain reserves.

As an integral part of food policy for America, a grain reserve policy keyed to both commercial exports and food aid is long overdue. In deciding how far to go, what dimensions to establish, and how to support the policy, however, a distinction must be made between two types of costs: real resource costs, which are, in fact, opportunity costs, and budgetary transfer costs.

Real Resource Costs and Budgetary Transfer Costs   In time of large crops and low farm prices, the opportunity cost of building a grain reserve can be measured in terms of the costs involved in not building it; for example, low farm income in the event of a free market policy, export or domestic food subsidy, or crop production control. During the 1950s in America, the real costs of building the grain reserve could have been measured in these terms, and in real terms the costs were very low. The excess grain stocks, which peaked in 1961, were built out of what was, in essence, unwanted production. The real cost of holding them was measurable in physical terms, the costs of resources used to build granaries, country and terminal elevators, and the resources used to keep the grain in storage from going out of condition. Once the facilities were built under a condition of excess supply, the real costs of maintaining the reserve would be very small. A national grain reserve policy carried through the 1960s and early 1970s, with grain stocks fluctuating around the 1961 level, for example, rather than reducing stocks below it, would not have been very expensive in real terms, even though it might have required as much as $1 billion annually in budgetary transfer costs. To go much beyond the peak grain carry-over of the past will require building additional storage facilities involving real resource costs.

Grain Reserves for Survival   Finally and most crucially it is prudent to link grain reserve policy to plans for surviving a nuclear bomb attack. If there is suitable protection from radiation and effective relocation from high-risk target areas, some 90 percent of the nation's population would be saved; and an adequate supply of food would be crucial.[138] If an attack occurred in June or July, when the possibility of fallout damage to crops is near maximum, then much of the nation's growing crops and livestock would be inedible for human consumption. A reserve of some 2.5 billion bushels of wheat and other grain mainly on farms and in country elevators would be required for a 300-day grain supply based on an average of 2 pounds or 3,000 calories per day. Although the nation's transportation system would be adequate even if severely damaged,[139] past storage policy would not. In most years, total grain stocks on July 1 (Table 7-13) would have been barely adequate, even if fully available; and July 1 stocks of wheat would have been inadequate even at their peak in the early 1960s, and grossly inadequate in most years since (Table 7-8). An adequate reserve will require raising the minimum carryover, especially for food grains, and more

[138]Clark David Garland, *Economic Alternatives and Policy Implications of a Strategic Commodity Reserve for National Security Considerations,* Oak Ridge, Tenn.: Oak Ridge National Laboratory, ORNL-TM-3741, March 1972; C. M. Haaland, C. V. Chester, and E. P. Wigner, *Survival of the Relocated Population of the U.S. After a Nuclear Attack, ibid.,* ORNL-5041, 1976.
   [139]William A. Hamberg, *Transportation Vulnerability Research: Review and Appraisal, 1959–1969,* Menlo Park, Cal.: Stanford Research Institute, January 1969.

complete integration of policy in the product markets with that in the input markets, the topic to which we turn next.

QUESTIONS FOR DISCUSSION

1 Discuss the general goals for policy in the food product markets. Are they competitive or complementary? Neither, or both? Is there a hierarchy of goals? If there is not, how are choices made among the goals? Discuss some of the problems of goal evaluation.

2 What policy means are there to use as alternatives in food product markets? In broad scope, what are the advantages and disadvantages of (a) free markets, (b) trade restrictions such as tariffs and import quotas, and trade stimulants such as export subsidies and food aid, (c) product management, such as through acreage allotments and marketing quotas, and (d) consumer food subsidies? Select one of these alternatives and discuss who gains and who loses by it. What are the general welfare effects?

3 Discuss the advantages and disadvantages of a world food program as conceived by David Lubin, Sir John Boyd Orr, S. M. Bruce, and others. Would such a program be advantageous to all the people of the United States? To American farmers? Define the conditions under which advantages or disadvantages might occur.

4 How did the U.S. food aid program following World War II differ from the previously proposed world food program in respect to (a) organization and management, (b) probable effects on U.S. markets and food prices, (c) probable magnitude, and (d) political gains to the United States?

5 Illustrate and discuss the price effects in exporting and importing countries of export subsidies and import quotas. How much have internal prices for wheat in the European Economic Community countries differed from the prices at Liverpool? What is the effect of the variable import levies of the EEC countries on exports and prices of American feed grains and wheat?

6 Discuss the roles of buffer food stocks and, more specifically, the alternative roles suggested for reserve stocks of feed grains and wheat. Comment on the proposals presented by William H. Nicholls in the *Journal of Farm Economics,* February 1946. Theoretically, would these rules result in higher farm prices, lower farm prices, or about the same? Why? How might the application of such rules be coordinated with the administration of a world food board or a world food program?

7 Discuss the United States sugar program in terms of (a) goals, (b) means, (c) implements, and (d) constraints. Who gains and who loses from it? What is the aggregate magnitude of loss? How does this occur? Who bears this cost? What would be the advantages and disadvantages of free trade in sugar?

8 Compare the United States wool program with that for sugar in terms of goals and means. Discuss the system of constraints in the wool program. What are the alternatives to the present policy? Who would benefit from free trade in wool? How would these benefits compare with the probable losses?

9 Discuss the recent trends in beef cattle prices, cattle production, and beef imports into America. Review the provisions of Public Law 88-482. How effective is it in protecting the American cattle industry? Would an alternative policy be more beneficial to American consumers? To cattle ranchers? To livestock feeders?

10 Discuss the basic elements of American—federal and state—price policy for dairy

products. What is the general effect of this policy on (*a*) fluid milk prices, level and stability, (*b*) the volume of manufactured dairy products, (*c*) aggregate market receipts of dairy farmers, (*d*) the economic structure, size, and distribution, of dairy farms and fluid milk manufacturing plants?

11 What are the most important criticisms made of the dairy product price and order programs? Distinguish between criticisms of goals and those of program means or constraints. What improvements do you suggest? Who would gain or lose? What are the means for compensating the losers? Give arguments for and against using such compensation.

12 What are the general policy goals for use of marketing agreements and orders in fruits and vegetables? How do they operate? What are their general effects on prices, farm incomes, market structure, and stability?

13 What are the alternative policies for management of the major export commodities? What are some of the lessons growing out of the experience with the storage policies that have been followed? What are the various roles for domestic storage?

14 Summarize your conclusions in regard to the effectiveness of the production control and price support programs for tobacco. What has been the effect on (*a*) tobacco acreage, (*b*) tobacco prices, (*c*) distribution of market receipts among growers, (*d*) earnings of tobacco processors and manufacturers, and (*e*) tobacco users? Distinguish between the benefits to tobacco workers and to the landowners who have allotments.

15 We say that "nowhere in our area of study has public policy had a more pervasive or wide-ranging effect than in the case of cotton." Summarize the general trends that may be used in support of this statement. What have been the general goals in cotton policy? The means and implements for carrying them out? Discuss the general alternatives and constraints for cotton programs in the future.

16 In the development of compensatory supply policy, wheat has usually led and often dominated the commodity field. Account for this situation in both economic and political terms. Generally, those asking for government aid have favored three types of programs: (*a*) production control, (*b*) loan storage or direct payments, and (*c*) export subsidies and food aid. In terms of the economics of the wheat market, discuss the advantages and disadvantages of each to wheat producers; to American consumers; to commercial importers; and to countries asking for food aid.

17 For a given level of net income support for wheat growers above free market levels, what policy will minimize costs to government? Maximize production efficiency? Be least disturbing to domestic consumers? Be most favorable to aid recipients abroad? Be most acceptable to foreign purchasers? What are the major trade-offs?

18 Discuss the effects of the wheat and cotton programs on the feed grain sector. Compare the acreage trends among wheat, cotton, feed grains, and soybeans from World War II to the present. What have been some of the major substitutions that have taken place? Is it true that in the years following that war, the wheat and cotton programs shifted a major burden of adjustment to the feed grain and livestock economy? Discuss.

19 Comment on the probable effects of the Emergency Feed Grain Program on market receipts from feed grains and livestock in the short term of two or three years and in the long run. What would be the effect of having, or not having, a significant export subsidy for feed grains? For soybeans, or soybean meal and oil? For grain sorghums?

20 Discuss the arguments pro and con for a significant grain reserve to be managed by the United States government. Do you feel that the fears of producers in respect to government grain reserves are justified? Comment in terms of both economic theory and political problems. Discuss the costs of holding grain reserves by government, comparing and contrasting (a) real or opportunity costs and (b) budgetary transfer costs.

21 What is the basis for recommending the establishment of an international monetary food fund? What considerations might be held uppermost in building and administering such a fund? What are the advantages for the United States government? For American consumers? For American grain producers? What are the disadvantages?

REFERENCES

Abelson, Philip A. (ed.), *Food: Politics, Economics, Nutrition, and Research,* A special Science compendium, Washington: American Association for the Advancement of Science, 1975.

Benedict, Murray R., and Oscar C. Stine, *The Agricultural Commodity Programs, Two Decades of Experience,* New York: The Twentieth Century Fund, 1956.

Comptroller General of the United States, United States General Accounting Office, *Grain Reserves: A Potential U.S. Food Policy Tool,* OSP-76-16, March 26, 1976.

Dvoskin, Dan, and Earl O. Heady, *U.S. Agricultural Production Under Limited Energy Supplies, High Energy Prices and Expanding Agricultural Exports,* Ames: Iowa State University, The Center for Agricultural and Rural Development, February 1976.

Freebairn, J. W., and Gordon C. Rausser, "Effects of Changes in the Level of U.S. Beef Imports," *American Journal of Agricultural Economics,* Vol. 57, No. 4, November 1975, pp. 676–688.

Galbraith, J. K., Meyer Kestnbaum, and Theodore Schultz, *The Wool Veto and the Crisis in Foreign Trade,* Chicago: The University of Chicago Round Table, No. 484, June 29, 1947.

Gruebele, James W., "An Economic Analysis of Government Price Support and Federal Order Programs, 1949–1971," *Dairy Marketing Facts,* Urbana: University of Illinois, AE-4304, December 1972.

Heady, Earl O., Leo V. Mayer, and Howard C. Madsen, *Future Farm Programs, Comparative Costs and Consequences,* Ames: The Iowa State University Press, 1972.

Johnson, D. Gale, *The United States Sugar Program: Large Costs and Small Benefits,* Washington: The American Enterprise Institute, 1974.

———, *World Agriculture in Disarray,* London: Macmillan St. Martin's Press in association with the Trade Policy Research Centre, 1973.

Manchester, Alden C., *Market Structure, Institutions, and Performance in the Fluid Milk Industry,* U.S. Department of Agriculture, Economic Research Service, Agricultural Economic Report No. 248, 1974.

National Advisory Commission on Food and Fiber, *Food and Fiber for the Future,* Washington: Government Printing Office, 1967.

National Commission on Food Marketing, *Food from Farmer to Consumer,* Washington: Government Printing Office, 1966.

National Planning Association, *Feast or Famine: The Uncertain World of Food and Agriculture and Its Policy Implications for the United States,* Washington: February 1974.

Orr, John Boyd, and David Lubbock, *The White Man's Dilemma, Food and the Future,* 2d ed., London: George Allen and Unwin, 1965.

Policy Analysis of Grain Reserves, Washington: U.S. Department of Agriculture and the National Science Foundation, 1976.

Reutlinger, Shlomo, *Simulation of World-Wide Buffer Stocks of Wheat,* Washington: International Bank for Reconstruction and Development, World Bank Staff Working Paper No. 219, November 1975.

Sharples, Jerry A., Rodney L. Walker, and Rudie W. Slaughter, Jr., *Managing Buffer Stocks to Stabilize Wheat Prices,* Washington: USDA, ERS, Commodity Economics Division, Agricultural Economic Report No. 341, July 1976.

U.S. Congress, *Sale of Wheat to Russia,* Hearings, Subcommittee on Livestock and Grains, Committee on Agriculture, House of Representatives, 92d Cong., 2d Sess., Sept. 14, 18, and 19, 1972, Serial No. 92-KK, Washington: Government Printing Office, 1972.

Chapter 8

Land Use
and Conservation Policy

Our lands . . . were originally very good; but use and abuse have made them quite otherwise.

George Washington

It is high time to realize that our responsibility to the coming millions is like that of parents to their children, and that in wasting our resources we are wronging our descendents.

Theodore Roosevelt, 1909

The social lesson of soil waste is that no man has the right to destroy soil even if he does own it in fee simple. The soil requires a duty of man which we have been slow to recognize.

Soil, The 1957 Yearbook of Agriculture

Future austerity will be perennial and it will become progressively more severe. What then? . . . Within each of the beleaguered "developed" countries there will be a bitter struggle for the control of their diminished resources. . . .

Arnold Toynbee
Conservation Foundation Letter, January 1975

Although we observed in Chapter 4 that, since the beginning of the second great era of food policy, land has been relatively unimportant in development and expansion of America's food supply, agricultural land policies are very important in farm and food policy. The distinctive structure of agriculture depends largely on how we organize land. Future food supplies depend on the continued productivity of land and on the choices that are made in land policy. These largely determine who will own and control the resources used in agriculture, how these resources will be used and exploited or preserved for the future, how farm firms will be organized in respect to size or scale and type of organization, tenant- or owner-operation, and private firms, corporations, or cooperatives. Land policy will also have much to do with whether the food economy continues to become more concentrated, whether food resources are further developed, and whether the pattern of income distribution is altered one way or another in the future.

Land policy is also important because we are experiencing, perhaps without knowing it, what has been called a "quiet revolution" in land use control.[1] In some states, the target is the system under which the pattern of land development has been controlled almost exclusively by local governments, each seeking to maximize its own tax base and minimize its social problems without much regard to what happens elsewhere. Local ordinances have proved inadequate to deal with a wide variety of problems related to land that are of regional, state, or national concern. Many new state laws have been enacted, and there are strong movements at the national level to introduce more comprehensive land policies and programs.

The policy issues relate to the goals in shifting land from one use to another, the investments to be made in land development and conservation, possible changes in rules concerning ownership and tenure, transfer and inheritance, and various possible land reforms. The approach to land policy has broadened as people have become more anxious about their environment and the adequacy of their institutions for dealing with it. Rising interest in the adequacy of future food supplies transfers much of this concern to agricultural land policies. To see how this concern has evolved, we begin with land distribution policy in historical perspective.

LAND DISTRIBUTION POLICY

Land distribution through various government acts, regulations, and administrative actions has set the land pattern for American agriculture, broadly defined its economic structure, and helped to shape the problems that are part of national food policy. This has been an evolving experience that may be viewed as a series of historical periods. The first was from the beginning of settlement at Jamestown and Plymouth to about 1780, the end of the Revolutionary War. During this time the basic rules governing land distribution, ownership, and use were laid down.

[1] Fred P. Bosselman and David Callies, *The Quiet Revolution in Land-Use Control,* Washington: Government Printing Office, 1972.

The second ran from the 1780s to the adoption of the Homestead Act in 1862, during which time the nation moved from a policy emphasizing land sales in the new public domain to one of free land for the settler. In the third period, occurring between 1862 and the early 1890s, a number of acts were passed to implement the policy of free land, and the best farm land was either given away or sold at low prices to encourage settlement, national growth, and development. The 30-year period from 1891 to 1921 was the first conservation period in the United States with emphasis on forestry, mining, and minerals, rather than soils. Then, in the 1920s, as it became evident that American agriculture was overexpanded in respect to available markets, a broad reappraisal of land policy began. In the 1930s, land assumed a new role as a tool of agricultural adjustment. From this stage, the national policy broadened to encompass new concepts and programs regarding land conservation and use. Finally, new questions have arisen concerning the concentration of land ownership, conservation and environmental policy, pollution control, and government controls over land use.[2]

To see how the various policy alternatives may be formulated, it is useful to deal more specifically with the related acts, policy actions, and their consequences. What was attempted, what were the accomplishments and failures, and what are the lessons for the future?

The Colonial Foundation

In the colonial era, a goal of land policy was to develop owner-operated farms as a means of achieving other goals of democracy and food abundance. In New England, the "town system" was developed, with individual towns democratically organized and land distributed to settlers in family-sized lots. In the Middle Atlantic colonies, as a result of grants from the Crown and their distribution, small farms also predominated, although intermixed with some rather large holdings. In the Southern colonies, a tract of land of 40 to 50 acres or more, called a headright, was commonly given to a settler on which he and his family were expected to settle and make a living. The distribution of headrights to settlers resulted in numerous small farms. In addition, those who provided transportation for settlers from Europe sometimes obtained title to the headrights of immigrants as payment for passage. Sometimes a planter who paid the fare and a settler, who would be indentured to the planter, might each be given a

---

[2]A partial reading list for this section includes the following: Benjamin H. Hibbard, *A History of the Public Land Policies,* New York: The Macmillan Company, 1924; John D. Hicks, *The American Nation,* Boston: Houghton Mifflin Company, 1941; Roy M. Robbins,. *Our Landed Heritage,* Princeton, N.J.: Princeton University Press, 1942; Leonard A. Salter, Jr., *A Critical Review of Research in Land Economics,* Minneapolis: The University of Minnesota Press, 1948; Henry C. Taylor and Anne Dewees Taylor, *The Story of Agricultural Economics in the United States, 1840–1932,* Ames: Iowa State College Press, 1952, chaps. 28, 29; Murray R. Benedict, *Farm Policies of the United States, 1790–1950, A Study of Their Origins and Development,* New York: The Twentieth Century Fund, 1953, especially chaps. 1, 4, 15; Marion Clawson, *The Land System of the United States, An Introduction to the History and Practices of Land Use and Land Tenure,* Lincoln: University of Nebraska Press, 1968; and Harold D. Guither, *Heritage of Plenty: A Guide to the Economic History and Development of U.S. Agriculture,* 2d ed., Danville, Ill.: The Interstate Printers and Publishers, Inc., 1972.

headright. The planter might obtain both of the headrights and combine them with other land holdings. Thus the foundation was laid for the plantation system which became characteristic of the South, as well as for many small farms based on headrights.

During the colonial period, the trend was toward giving landowners the right to use their land as they saw fit—a concept that was to affect American land policy for generations—although the terms of land distribution varied among the colonies. The rights of government to control land title and to regulate the terms of use and tenure were firmly established. The individual colonies imposed taxes on land. The right to take private lands for public purposes upon payment of appropriate compensation was established in legislation and court decision. Laws were enacted in regard to hunting, fishing, and fencing of land for private use. Rights of inheritance were recognized. When no will was left, laws generally required equal inheritance among children in place of the English concept of restricted inheritance, usually by the eldest son. Farming of land by the owner rather than by tenants was generally preferred, and this became the ideal of land policy, although leasing grew more common as the colonies matured. The object of land policy was to achieve settlement on terms favorable for good farming.

From Independence to the Homestead Act

In 82 years from the granting of independence in 1780 to passage of the Homestead Act in 1862, the United States assembled the vast public domain stretching from coast to coast (Table 8-1), and, after trying for several years to sell land to settlers, the government finally adopted the policy of free land in family-sized tracts (Table 8-2). During this era, arguments over land policy absorbed much of the attention of Congress. But the family-farm philosophy triumphed, and free land as a national policy became the critical element in future settlement and growth.

Policy under the Articles of Confederation   On October 10, 1780, a congressional resolution provided that all unappropriated lands should be ceded by the states to the federal government. States with land claims gave them up because states without recognized claims insisted on their doing so as a condition for their entry into the Union; it was agreed that defense of the public domain would require protection of the federal government. Federal ownership of the public domain became a fundamental principle of national land policy.

The first policy guidelines for settling the public domain were proposed almost immediately. In 1781, Pelatiah Webster, a Philadelphia merchant, suggested that the land be surveyed in townships of 6, 8, or 10 miles square, to be laid out in tiers, and only when one tier was sold would another be put on sale. In 1783, the Army came forward with another plan that all surplus lands should become property of the states yet to be created, with no land to be owned by the federal government. Grants would be made free to ex-soldiers, but if the land was not settled and cultivated within a specified time, it would be forfeited. Slavery would be excluded. Common lands would be used to establish schools and

Table 8-1 Acquisition of the Public Domain of the United States

Means of acquisition	Land area, acres*	Water area, acres*	Total acres*	Amount paid	
				Total	Cost per acre†
State cessions (1781–1802)	262,482,560	3,944,960	266,427,520	$ 6,200,000	2.3¢
Louisiana Purchase (1803)	523,446,400	6,465,280	529,911,680	27,267,622	5.1
Purchase from Spain (1819)	43,342,720‡	2,801,920	46,144,640	6,489,768	14.1
Oregon Compromise (1846)	180,644,480	2,741,760	183,386,240		
Mexican Cession (1848)	334,479,360	4,201,600	338,680,960	15,000,000	4.4
Purchase from Texas (1850)	78,842,880	83,840	78,926,720	16,000,000	20.3
Gadsden Purchase (1853)	18,961,920	26,880	18,988,800	10,000,000	52.7
Total in the states	1,442,200,320	20,266,240	1,462,466,560	$80,957,390	5.5¢
Alaska Purchase (1867)	365,481,600	9,814,400	375,296,000	7,200,000	1.9
Grand total	1,807,681,920	30,080,640	1,837,763,160	$88,157,390	4.8¢

*J. R. Mahoney, *Natural Resources Activity of the Federal Government*, Public Affairs Bulletin 76, Washington: The Library of Congress Legislative Reference Service, January 1950.
†Computed.
‡Includes 33,920 acres of water area subsequently recognized as part of the state of Texas, which is not a public land state.

Source: All areas, except that of Alaska, were computed in 1912 by a committee representing the General Land Office, the Geological Survey of the Department of the Interior, the Bureau of Statistics, and the Bureau of the Census of the Department of Commerce and Labor. The area of Alaska was recomputed in connection with the 1940 decennial census.

Table 8-2   Methods of Disposal by Land Acts, 1784 to 1862

Land act	Minimum sale price	Method of sale or disposal	Size of tract	Terms of sale
Ordinances of 1785 and 1787	$1 an acre; discount of one-third to companies and acceptance of government paper	Auction	Half of townships offered entire area, other half by 640-acre tracts	Cash until 1787, then one-third cash and rest in 3 months
Act of 1796	$2 an acre; evidence of public debt accepted at face value	Auction	Half of tracts 5,760 acres, the rest 640 acres	One-twentieth cash, credit of 30 days on balance of first half, and 1 year on second half
Act of 1800	$2 an acre	Auction	Minimum of 320 acres	8 percent discount for cash; liberal credit system inaugurated
Act of 1820	$1.25 an acre	Auction	160 acres or 80 acres	Cash
Act of 1841 (Preemption)	$1.25 an acre; grants to railroads and canals at $2.50	Selection and settlement, then purchase at minimum price	Not more than 160 acres	Cash
Act of 1854 (Graduation Act)	Price graduated. For example, if on market 10 to 14 years, $1 an acre; 20 to 24 years, 50¢; over 30 years, 12½¢	Offered for sale at stated minimum price		Cash
Act of 1862 (Homestead Act)	Free homesteads of 160 acres; only payment, a fee ranging from $26 to $34	Settle and "prove up"	Not to exceed 160 acres	Only nominal fee, but certain conditions had to be met

Source: Benjamin H. Hibbard, *A History of the Public Land Policies,* New York: The Macmillan Company, 1924; Roy M. Robbins, *Our Landed Heritage,* Princeton, N.J.: Princeton University Press, 1942.

academies, and possibly for support of the ministry. Bland of Virginia proposed that 10,000 acres of every 100,000 should be reserved for founding seminaries of learning.

In 1784, two committees headed by Thomas Jefferson made reports. One proposed a rather complete system of government for lands between the Ohio and Mississippi Rivers: There should be 10 states divided by meridians and two parallels of latitude, with each state embracing a system of counties and townships having elected officials; land should be divided into hundreds of tracts 10 miles square and these into lots 1 mile square; and the states should be prohibited from interfering with disposal of land by the United States or with ordinances passed by the Congress. The other committee recommended that land surveys precede sales, that proceeds of sales go into a sinking fund, that payment for land be made either by specie or by certificates of indebtedness, and that settlers be allowed to purchase warrants and then locate the land they would settle.

The first effective action by the Confederacy on land disposal—the Ordinance of 1785—developed out of these proposals. It provided for lands to be divided into townships of 6 square statute miles, with their borders running due north-south and east-west, and with lots 1 mile square numbered from 1 to 36. Formation of states was not a prerequisite for sale of lands. Half the townships were to be sold intact, the other half in sections of 640 acres each. Section 16 in every township was to be retained for the support of schools.

The Ordinance of 1787 provided for the form of government in what was then called the Northwest Territory (consisting of what is now Ohio, Indiana, Illinois, Michigan, and Wisconsin). Townships and counties were to be laid out. Territorial governments were authorized, and when a given area came to have 60,000 inhabitants or more, a constitutional convention could be called to establish a state. The ordinance prohibited slavery in the Northwest Territory, provided for equal division of property when a person died intestate, and directed that schools and religious training be encouraged. But the main struggles over land settlement policy were still ahead.

Evolution of a Free Land Policy   In 1789, in the first Congress of the United States of America, Scott of Pennsylvania led the opposition to sales of million-acre tracts to land companies and to the high cost of surveys. He proposed that land should be sold in small units and that purchasers should pay for the cost of survey. Land offices should be opened convenient for sales, certificates of indebtedness should be accepted as payment, and preemptors—that is, illegal settlers or squatters on lands not yet open for settlement—should be given the first opportunity to buy lands on which they had settled.

In 1790, Alexander Hamilton presented an extensive document which he entitled "Report of a Uniform System for Disposition of the Lands, the Property of the United States." By virtually ignoring the Ordinance of 1785 and views such as those of Scott, he recommended that land be sold in three types of tracts—one of 500 acres or more, to be available to subscribers to a government loan then under consideration, one limited to 100 acres for actual settlers, and one for sale in townships 10 miles square, for possible subdivision. The price would be 30 cents per acre, with surveys to be paid for by the purchaser, and with no credit to be given on tracts of less than 100 square miles. No credit was to run for more than two years. Private sales would be preferred to auctions. A commission of three members would administer the program.

The ordinances and these related proposals raised fundamental issues in land policy. Should land be sold in small lots to actual settlers as proposed by Jefferson, Scott, and their associates? Or, as suggested by Hamilton, should individuals be allowed to come between the government and settlers to buy up large tracts for speculative gain? If sold, should the price be set in competitive markets or controlled at nominal levels? Should the government extend credit? What restrictions, if any, should be placed on land title?

The settlers wanted free land, but changes in the policy developed slowly. The Land Act of 1796, relating to the Northwest Territory, somewhat resembled the 1785 ordinance in that it divided land into townships of 6 square miles, half of which were to be divided into sections of 640 acres each. A minimum price was set at $2 per acre without any provision for credit, a proposition almost out of reach of the average settler. The Harrison Land Act of 1800 liberalized credit only slightly, an auction plan was continued, but the minimum price of $2 per acre was retained. The Ohio Enabling Act of 1802 authorized the establishment of a state government, provided that one-twentieth of the proceeds of the land sold by the federal government in Ohio could be used for laying out and constructing public roads and that one section out of each township should be granted to the state, the proceeds to be used for the establishment of schools. Credit was extended to five years, and the state was to exempt all lands sold by the federal government from property taxes for a period of five years.

In 1804, Albert Gallatin, Secretary of the Treasury, recommended that the minimum size of units put up for sale be reduced to one-quarter section and that the prices be reduced to $1.20 per acre for whole and half sections and to $1.50 for quarter sections. In the Indiana Territory Act of 1804, all land either north or south of the Ohio was to be sold in quarter sections. Although credit terms were liberalized, most settlers still could not meet them, and altogether, between 1809 and 1820, the Congress passed 12 separate measures for credit relief of settlers. The Land Act of 1820, applying to all public lands of the United States, set a minimum price of $1.25 per acre and provided that lands might be sold at auction in half or quarter sections, or in private sale, in as much as a section or as little as 80 acres. Some preemption rights were recognized for settlers who paid for part of their lands and gave up part; but no provision was made for credit.

In the meantime, acquisition of the Louisiana Territory in 1803 and purchase of Florida from Spain in 1819 was opening up additional lands. Settlers were pushing westward and taking up land not yet legally open for settlement. By 1828, when Andrew Jackson was elected President, the westward tide was beginning to reach flood stage. Whereas, up to 1820, Treasury receipts from sale of land was averaging about $1 million to $1½ a year, in the seven years between

1831 and 1837 more than 57 million acres were sold, and more and more people were preempting land ahead of surveys, thus creating an ever-growing problem for the general land office.

Finally, pressure from the West began to overcome the commercial leadership of the East, which favored revenues and slower settlement, and the Preemption Act of 1841 was passed. Any settler, citizen or alien who had improved land and owned no more than 320 acres elsewhere could obtain title to 160 acres so improved by paying the minimum $1.25 per acre. Preemption was made legal ahead of survey in six of the new states, except on lands reserved for schools. Grants were made to states for internal improvements and additional land offices were established.

This was the settlement policy when the public domain was expanded again. The Pacific Northwest Territory, including the present states of Washington, Oregon, Idaho, parts of Montana, and Wyoming, was added in 1846. This addition came after acrimonious argument and threats of war, which were finally settled in the treaty with Britain called the Oregon Compromise. The treaty following the war with Mexico in 1846 gave the United States the area which now includes the states of California, Nevada, Utah, and large parts of Arizona, New Mexico, Colorado, and Wyoming. Agreement on admitting Texas as a state was concluded in 1850. A strip of land across southern Arizona and New Mexico, known as the Gadsden Purchase, was bought from Mexico in 1853 (Table 8-1).

Although the Graduation Act of 1854 provided for lower prices for certain lands that had been in the market for several years, more general legislation for free land was delayed until passage of the Homestead Act in 1862 (Table 8-2). By this time the slave states of the South, whose representatives in Congress had consistently voted against free land for settlers as upsetting to the balance between free and slave states, had seceded from the Union. A free land plank had been included in the Republican party platform in 1860. Lincoln favored it, and the states of the Northeast, which previously had joined with the South to defeat it, were anxious to bind the West into the Union. So the Homestead Act was passed with little opposition. Henceforth, free land to the settler would be the settlement policy for America.

The Homestead Era

The homestead period, which stretched from 1862 to the early 1920s, was a natural evolution of policy based on the beliefs that (1) the nation's land would be used in such a way as to provide an adequate supply—it was hoped an abundant supply—of food and other farm products, and (2) there would be nearly universal family-farm ownership. The various acts that were passed fall into a remarkably clear pattern or policy. The Homestead Act provided for the grant of full title for 160 acres to the actual settler after five years of residence. Or, a settler might acquire title to 160 acres through the commutation privilege, after six months, by paying $1.25 to $2.50 per acre. The act was supplemented by the Timber Culture Act of 1873 (sometimes called the Tree-Claim Act), which provided that a settler could claim title on an additional 160 acres by planting 40 acres of trees—later reduced to 10 acres—provided that at least 675 trees per acre were still alive and thriving at the end of eight years. The Desert Land Act of 1877 provided that a settler could acquire 640 acres—later reduced to 320 acres—by irrigating one-eighth of it. The Timber and Stone Act of 1878, passed ostensibly to permit purchase of timberland to be used in homemaking, was used principally by purchasers serving large lumber companies, usually buying at the minimum price of $2.50 per acre. In addition, land could be purchased under the Preemption Act of 1841, which remained in effect until 1891. Under these acts, most of the best farmland in America was claimed by 1890. The United States census specifically pronounced that a land frontier no longer existed, and 1890 is often mentioned by historians as effectively marking the end of the frontier.

There was still a strong demand by settlers for additional land, and to meet this, Congress moved in two directions. One was the development of a federal irrigation policy, chiefly through the Carey Act of 1894 and the Federal Reclamation Act of 1902. The other was expansion of the homestead policy into dry-land farming and grazing areas. The Kincaid Act of 1904 opened up new areas for homesteading. The Forest Homestead Act of 1912 authorized homesteads in timbered areas. The Three-Year Homestead Act of 1912 reduced the required residence for proving a homestead claim to three years. The Stock-raising Homestead Act of 1916 permitted homesteads of 640 acres in designated live-stock grazing areas.

Results of the Homestead Acts

Under these acts, by the early 1920s, when homesteading was virtually complete, 1,029.1 million of the original 1,442.2 million acres of public domain and Indian lands had passed into private or corporate ownership via grants to states or directly by sales or grants to individuals, railroads, and others (Table 8-3). About 413.1 million acres were retained as public and Indian lands, of which 179.5 million were being administered in grazing districts in 1943 under federal grazing laws, and the balance of 233.6 million acres had been retained or withdrawn from entry under the public land laws. The 365.5 million acres of land in Alaska was largely reserved as public lands, some of which would be transferred or leased to private interests.

When tested against the recognized goals, the distribution policy resulted in a mixed record. First, there was an abundance of food and fiber. In this respect, the policy of land distribution was highly successful, even though low farm prices would dominate national policymaking for the next 50 years. Second, there was a predominance of family farms. Of the 6.7 to 6.8 million farm-operating units listed in the 1920s, at least 90 percent would fall within the definition of a family farm. But owner operation was only partially achieved, and the large majority of farm units were too small to provide an adequate living for a farm family. In 1929, the last year of post-World War I prosperity, 88.2 percent of all farm-operating units had farm product sales of $5,000 or less. The policy of free land in the homestead era pushed settlement far beyond what was acceptable in terms of income distribution in a free enterprise economy. Henceforth, agricultural reform in the United States would require substantial readjustment of the number of farms, total farm output, and land use.[3]

A major part of the policy problem was and is related to land ownership. As based on the U.S. census classification of full owners, part owners, and tenants, the farms operated by full owners were and still are generally small. As late as 1969, although 62.5 percent of all farms were operated by full owners, only 35.3 percent of the farm land was operated by them. At the other extreme, tenants operated 12.9 percent of the farms and also 12.9 percent of the land. Part owners operated 24.6 percent of the farms and 51.8 percent of the land. For years, one of the problems of land policy was how best to achieve an efficient size of farm-operating unit while still recognizing the advantages of owner operation. The problem was only partially solved by turning to farm tenancy.

Farm tenancy as a land policy has permitted many families to operate farms who could not do so otherwise. In some parts of the country, it has led to efficiency-sized family units, as in the heart of the cash-crop areas of the Corn Belt. Here equitable farm leases have been developed, based on the principles of cost sharing by landlord and tenant and just compensation for agreed inputs.[4] Although similar examples can be found in other parts of the country, all too often farm tenancy has meant substandard farms, low income, and exploitation of land and other resources for a quick return. The share-crop system in the Old South has permitted and encouraged continuation of large land holdings. The policy goal of a universal family-farm owner-operated farm economy has been only partially achieved, leaving a long heritage of social and economic problems for policymakers.

Although the principles embodied in the various settlement acts were generally sound, that is, consistent with the stated goals, most of the legislation was loosely drawn and badly administered. Immense acreages of the best timber and mining lands passed into the hands of large corporations, whether through dummy homesteaders and employees or by purchases under the commutation privilege. Once this happened, the government had little or no control over conservation, yield, and harvest practices. Relinquishing federal rights over nonnavigable streams in the West, although of some merit at the time, prevented or greatly delayed the development of a coordinated national policy for water use and water quality. Competing demands for the water have been allowed to build without federal constraint in this huge water-short region. The seriousness of this oversight has begun to be felt, and the question of how best to meet the most critical demands will be of increasing concern in the years ahead.

---

[3]For the most comprehensive study of the time, see John D. Black, *Agricultural Reform in the United States,* New York: McGraw-Hill Book Company, 1929.

[4]See, for example, F. J. Reiss, *Farm Leases for Illinois,* University of Illinois at Urbana-Champaign, College of Agriculture Cooperative Extension Service Circular 960 (rev.), September 1972; and *Landlord and Tenant Shares,* an Agricultural Economics Research Report, published annually.

Formulation of Irrigation Policy

Legislation passed in the homestead period set the foundation for national irrigation policy. When arid lands in the Great Plains, the Mountain states, and on the Pacific Coast began to be taken up under the Homestead Act, it soon became evident that a grant of 160 acres was too small to support a family without irrigation, and irrigation involved such a heavy commitment of labor and equipment that few people could manage it. The rectangular survey was not well

Table 8-3 Disposition of the Public Domain
(In Million Acres)

Approximate area of public lands disposed of under the public-land laws, June 30, 1943:*	
Granted to states for:	
Support of common schools	77.5
Reclamation of swampland	64.9
Construction of railroads	37.1
Support of miscellaneous institutions	20.6
Purposes not elsewhere classified	16.0
Construction of canals	4.6
Construction of wagon roads	3.3
Improvement of rivers	1.4
Total	225.4
Disposed of by sales and other methods not elsewhere classified	300.0
Granted or sold to homesteaders	285.0
Granted to railroad corporations†	88.9
Granted to veterans as military bounties	61.0
Confirmed as private land claims	34.0
Sold under timber and stone laws	13.9
Granted or sold under timber-culture laws	10.9
Sold under desert-land laws	10.0
Total	1,029.1
Area of public and Indian lands in the public-land states, estimated, June 30, 1943:*	
Area subject to general disposition under public-land laws:	
Vacant land outside grazing districts	42.8
Vacant land within grazing districts	136.7
Area not subject to general disposition under public-land laws:	
Reclamation withdrawals	14.0
Indian reservations	53.6
National parks and monuments	11.5
Wildlife refuges and game ranges	5.1
Oregon and California revested lands	2.6
Stock driveways	4.7
Power and water reserves	6.1
National forests	137.5
Other withdrawals and reservations	19.2
Area in unperfected entries	0.7
Estimated total area of public and Indian lands (excluding overlap)	413.1
Grand total, United States	1,442.2

Table 8-3 *(Continued)*

Area of public, Indian, and other lands in Alaska:‡	
Vacant public lands	270.0
Oil and gas reservations (including naval)	48.8
National forests	20.9
Fish and wildlife reservations	7.9
National parks and monuments	6.9
Native reservations	3.9
Military and naval reservations	4.1
Other withdrawals, reservations, and uses (including private)	3.0
Total	365.5§
Total public domain, United States and Alaska	1,807.7

*Land Management in the Department of the Interior, U.S. Department of the Interior, July, 1946.

†A deduction of 2.4 million acres has been made to cover recent restoration of certain lands or cancellation of claims of lands by railroads.

‡Special tabulation of withdrawals and reservations of public land in Alaska, June 30, 1949, by the Bureau of Land Management, U.S. Department of the Interior, subject to revision.

§Areas estimated in part.

suited to irrigation or to stock raising, which added to the complications. The Congress tried to provide relief by an act, passed in 1866 and amended in 1870, which relinquished federal control over the nonnavigable streams of the West and acknowledged water rights based on local customs and laws. In retrospect, this was unfortunate, creating many problems having to do with land monopoly, but it was a logical policy at the time the acts were passed.

Previously, in loosely drawn acts in 1849, 1850, and 1860, the Congress had transferred to the states in fee-simple various lands subject to overflow, designated as swamplands, with the provision that proceeds from the sale of the lands should be used for reclaiming them by means of levees, drains, etcetera. More than 64 million acres were transferred under these laws to states (Table 8-3). The states' subsequent distribution of this land was usually at very low prices. Millions of acres were transferred at less than $1 an acre, and large acreages— sometimes thousands of acres—were acquired by a single individual. The grant of swampland was vague, depending merely on the land being designated as swamp, and in some states, when this land was brought under irrigation, it became the most valuable farmland in America. Thus the land laws were the basis for founding large fortunes through land monopolization and irrigation development.

When settlement of the arid regions was first begun, small irrigation systems were developed by individual farmers who took water from streams adjoining or running through their land. Even earlier, modest developments had been undertaken by the mission fathers in California and by the Mormons in what is now the state of Utah. Individual farm irrigation systems became common along the streams and in the valleys of the Mountain states. Numerous small water systems were developed by miners after the gold discoveries in California, and much of the custom and law regarding water grows out of the experience of mining rather than agriculture. But the amount of land that could be developed under these rudimentary arrangements was limited and small indeed, and the Congress attempted to offer help in irrigation development.

The Desert Land Act of 1877, as has been mentioned, provided that a settler could acquire 640 acres of land—later reduced to 320 acres—by irrigating one-eighth of it. This act, signed by President Grant on his last day in office, waived the residency requirement common to all other acts, on grounds that the so-called desert lands could not be inhabited until reclamation projects were completed. The act offered no financial or other development help to homesteaders and did nothing to correct the basic problem of financing irrigation development. Although original claims under the act were more than 32.5 million acres by 1925, and proof of compliance had been filed on more than 8.5 million acres,[5] it is not known how many bona fide homesteads were developed under it. Indeed, the waiving of the residency requirement opened the way for flagrant abuse.

Giant Farms Created

An example of the type of abuse possible under the Desert Land Act occurred in Kern County, California, in the San Joaquin Valley.[6] Starting about 1870, two San Francisco financial manipulators, who controlled considerable resources, and a politically influential vice president of Southern Pacific Railroad, moved into this area with plans to acquire land holdings. In less than 20 years, they gained title to nearly 400,000 acres of land, which they used primarily for grazing and some dry-land wheat farming. First, they were able to buy 100,000 acres directly from the Southern Pacific Railroad at nominally low prices, when no other sales were being made by this company. To this holding they were able to add another 62,000 acres indirectly through other buyers. They entered another 30,000 acres with forged soldiers' land scrip. When title to this land was clouded, they reentered their claims under the Desert Land Act by hiring individuals to file claims, which were then turned over to them. Finally, an additional 70,000 acres were entered under the act simply by hiring people to file claims which were also turned over to them.

In 1890, in order to perpetuate their operation, the holdings were incorporated under the Kern County Land Company (KCL). Until the 1930s, most of these vast holdings were used for cattle grazing. In 1936, oil was discovered on the property, and in order to reduce taxes through investment credit, the KCL began to develop irrigation on a large scale. By 1965, a share of KCL stock, which had sold for $33 in 1933, was worth (after splits totaling 40 to 1) $2,680— and paid $1,883 in dividends. Finally, in 1967 KCL was bought by Tenneco, Inc., then one of the fastest growing of United States conglomerates.

[5]Ray P. Teele, *The Economics of Land Reclamation in the United States,* New York: McGraw-Hill Book Company, 1927, p. 64.

[6]*Farmworkers in Rural America,* Hearings, Subcommittee on Migratory Labor, Committee on Labor and Public Welfare, U.S. Senate, 92d Congress, 1st and 2d Sess., in five parts from July 22, 1971, to June 20, 1972, pp. 1–4046. See especially statement by Paul Taylor, Part 3A, pp. 783–842, and articles by Peter Barnes (first published in the *New Republic,* June 5, 12, and 19, 1971), Part 3C, pp. 1949–1974.

Tenneco, which had 1970 sales of $2.5 billion and assets of $4.3 billion in such fields as shipbuilding, manufacturing, and oil production, announced that its goal in agriculture was complete integration from seedling to supermarket. It did not need to own all the land required for such production—only about 20 percent of its marketings were produced on land which it owned. By establishing a national brand called Sun Giant, and with an integrated processing-marketing organization with many growers under contract, it could integrate the system on a large scale.

Although KCL was one of the largest of the agricultural firms that could trace their lineage to the questionable land policies of the 1870s and earlier, it was not unique. In the early 1970s, the Southern Pacific Railroad still held 201,000 acres in the San Joaquin Valley. The Boston Ranch Company, owned by J. G. Boswell, who collected the record sum of $3.3 million in federal price support and other payments in 1966, held some 37,000 acres. Also under Boswell's control were Crockett-Gambody, 28,503 acres; Tulare Lake Land Company, 10,392 acres; and Miller and Lux (by lease), 25,313 acres. The Tejon Ranch, with 50 percent control under the *Los Angeles Times,* held 168,000 acres in Kern County and another 100,000 acres south of the Kern County line. In 1969, an estimated 1,673 corporations in California were operating 6.1 million acres of land, an average of more than 3,600 acres per unit.[7]

Most of these large holdings can be traced to the early Mexican land grants, inherited from Spanish rule, which were augmented by various strategies. When the land was ceded by Mexico, the terms provided that previously issued Mexican land grants would be respected. In California under Spanish rule, only about 30 land grants had been made, but, in 1848 when the United States took possession, more than 8 million acres of land in California alone were held by some 800 grantees, an average of more than 10,000 acres each. These grants, rushed through the California state land offices on the eve of United States occupation before the federal government could take control, were vaguely defined and in dispute for many years. These vast holdings, which under a prudent land policy should have been bought by the federal government for resettlement, were generally not broken up. Most have been kept intact to the present day and many have been increased by acquisition of additional acreages. Thus, much of the good land of California and some in adjoining states has been held in large trusts, and some of the most valuable of it has greatly appreciated by the development of irrigation. Then the government, either through failure to pass effective legislation or by legislation such as the Desert Land Act, has subsidized large landholders at the expense of the general public.

The issue that has been emphasized in many studies and in extensive congressional hearings is whether these larger holdings are consistent with the goals of America's farm and food policy or with the broader goals of community, state, and national welfare.[8] It has been pointed out that the big, integrated

[7]C. V. Moore and J. H. Snyder, "Corporation Farming in California," *California Agriculture,* March 1970.

[8]See *Farmworkers in Rural America,* 1971–1972, *op. cit.,* especially Parts 3A and 3B.

operations have some natural advantages of large-scale organization. On the other hand, it has been argued that such types of organization have strong disadvantages in social costs—that is, less desirable communities—a large migrant-worker population, concentrated wealth, etcetera, and much of the vaunted efficiency is due to tax advantages (as we shall discuss in Chapter 9) and to exploitation of an unorganized and disadvantaged labor force (to be discussed in Chapter 10). Furthermore, to the extent that such large-scale organizations use irrigation water from federally subsidized projects, their survival in some cases depends on lack of enforcement of what is called the 160-acre limitation.

Federal Water Policy and the 160-Acre Limitation

In a series of acts following the Desert Land Act, the federal government attempted to implement a family-farm irrigation policy. In 1888, an act was passed providing for surveys by the U.S. Geological Survey to determine which lands in arid regions could be reclaimed by irrigation. Also, the act reserved as property of the United States certain lands designated as suitable for reservoirs, ditches, and canals, but controversy over this clause was so vigorous that it was withdrawn in 1890, thus leaving the field open for unrestricted entry.

The Carey Act of 1894 granted 1 million acres to each state containing arid lands, on condition that the state provide for reclamation. Usually a state entered into a contract with a construction company to reclaim specified areas and the state sold land at minimal prices to settlers who had contracted for purchase of water rights from the company. This was far from satisfactory because, more often than not, neither the settlers nor the construction company could raise sufficient capital to complete such a project.

The Reclamation Act of 1902, an early accomplishment of President Theodore Roosevelt's administration, provided for direct federal funding of irrigation, thus marking a fundamental shift in policy. The act established a revolving fund to be derived from the sale of public lands and to be drawn upon to construct large dams for power and irrigation and canal systems for delivery of water. Settlers were to receive lands free as available under the Homestead Act but they were to repay within 10 years, without interest, their appropriate part of the cost of the irrigation system. By 1915, some 15 projects had been initiated under the act, and the federal government had invested more than $80 million in them. But settlers found it difficult to pay the charges for irrigation, and several of the projects ran into trouble even before farm prices dropped in the early 1920s. The price collapse brought further restrictions on irrigation development and heavier federal subsidy for existing projects.

Under the 1902 act, to further assure the priority of a family-farm policy and to limit the amount of subsidy that an individual landowner might lawfully receive from federally funded irrigation, Congress provided "that no right to the use of water for land in private ownership shall be sold for a tract exceeding 160 acres to any one landowner, and no such sale shall be made to any landowner unless he be a bona fide resident upon such land, or occupant thereof residing in the neighborhood . . ." (43 U.S. Code 431). According to the law, a single farmer could buy federally funded irrigation water for 160 acres of land, or a husband and wife could buy 320 acres. Owners holding land to be irrigated in excess of this amount generally would be given up to 10 years to dispose of it. If the land was not disposed of in this time, the federal government might purchase the excess land at prewater prices adjusted for changes in price levels and interest charges. The intent of Congress was apparently to carry out the traditional family-farm policy and limit the amount of subsidy going to any one owner, thus to spread the benefits of federal irrigation expenditures widely among family-type farms. The subsidy would amount, in some cases, to well over $1,000 per acre.

The Reclamation Act of 1902 has been both widely ignored and, in fact, sometimes nullified by administrative action or decree, although the Congress, after four days of debate in 1959–60, voted not to repeal it. The Boulder Canyon Project, for example, which provides irrigation water for very intensive farming in both the Imperial Valley and the Coachella Valley in Southern California, via the giant Hoover Dam and the All-American Canal System, was originally exempted from the residency requirement and the 160-acre limitation in a ruling by Secretary of the Interior Roy Lyman Wilbur on February 24, 1933, in the next-to-the-last week of the Hoover administration. The ruling was based on a 1926 statute[9] which provided for organization and sale of water to irrigation districts instead of to individuals, and for delivery of water to privately owned lands according to rules established within the district. Subsequently, in 1940, when water began to be delivered, the 1902 limitations were not applied. In 1964, the solicitor for the Department, Frank J. Berry, responding to a request from Senator Clinton P. Anderson, chairman of the Senate Committee on Interior and Insular Affairs, concluded that Secretary Wilbur's 1933 opinion was erroneous and that the Boulder Canyon Project should come under the limitations of the act of 1902. On November 22, 1971, the U.S. District Court for the Southern District of California ruled that the act of 1902 (Section 5) had not been superseded and therefore was still in force, and that, therefore, the residency requirement was a prerequisite for receiving water from the project.[10] After further appeal and argument, the U.S. Supreme Court upheld the ruling of the District Court and unanimously reaffirmed the constitutionality of the act of 1902 (357 U.S. 275). Pending final disposition of the question and possible reorganization of the valley, water was still being delivered to some 233,000 acres in the Imperial Valley alone, estimated to exceed the limits of the act of 1902.[11] In the Central Valley Project in California, which provides irrigation water to the San Joaquin Valley, the 160-acre limit has been under attack since 1937, when the project first

[9]Cited as the Omnibus Adjustment Act of May 25, 1926, 44 *Stat.* 649, 43 U.S.C.A., Section 423 a.

[10]Ben Yellen, et al., v. Walter J. Hickel. For a partial summary of the judgment, see *Farmworkers in Rural America, op. cit.,* Part 3c, pp. 1744–50. The United States of America, as plaintiff, had held that, since Congress knew of the Wilbur ruling and had done nothing to counteract it, the land limitation provisions of the 1902 reclamation law did not apply in the Imperial Valley (*ibid.,* pp. 1750–63).

[11]An estimate published by Paul Taylor in the *Bay Guardian,* San Francisco, series beginning May 19, 1967; reproduced in *Farmworkers in Rural America, op. cit.,* pp. 783 ff.

came under reclamation law. More recently in what is called the State Water Project, jointly funded by the United States government and the state of California, with land development in the late 1970s scheduled to cover almost the entire west side of the San Joaquin Valley in the Westlands Water District, more than two-thirds of the vast 500,000-acre tract eligible to receive water under the development will be in excess of the 160-acre limit. In 1967 there were about 240 landowners in this district, holding an average of more than 2,000 acres each. In the entire valley, 36 large landowners averaged 22,000 acres apiece.[12]

The State Water Project was designed to bring water to landowners by two routes: (1) by canal on the surface, and (2) by raising the water level in the landowners' wells through a combination of percolation from surface delivery and a reduction of overdraft, as fewer pumps will be required as the water level rises. Owners of excess land can escape the 160-acre limit and keep their holdings intact if they can get enough water from underground sources. The Department of the Interior under Stewart Udall, instead of getting compliance from owners of excess lands to dispose of their excess "before any contract is let or work begun" as provided in a 1914 statute, held, according to the 1926 statute, simply that excess lands not in compliance shall not "receive water." This was interpreted to mean surface water only, which, on this project (as well as some others) since 1937, has enabled owners of excess land getting water via underground flows to escape the restrictions of the 160-acre limitation.

Even prior to development of the Westlands District there were, according to estimates of the AFL-CIO cited by Paul Taylor, some 900,000 acres of land in California alone that were in excess of the 160-acre limitation. In some cases, to get around the 160-acre limit, water has been delivered to a district instead of to individuals, and the district has been allowed to deliver water according to its own agreements. In other cases, the legal requirement of getting agreements on disposal of excess lands prior to construction has been ignored, as in the Westlands District; and owners have been allowed unlimited time thereafter to dispose of their excess lands. To correct this, legislation has been introduced in the Congress to provide for purchase of federally irrigated lands in excess of the 160-acre limit by the federal government at pre-water prices. The government would then resell some of the lands on liberal terms to small farmers at prices somewhat below that of fully developed lands. Some lands might be retained for urban development or open space.

Political opposition to such legislation and to enforcement of the 160-acre limit and proposals for its repeal has been supported by various interests favoring large land holdings. In California this movement was highlighted in Governor Ronald Reagan's administration as it led the drive for development of the Westlands Water District; in 1970 a federal commission, called the Public Land Law Review Commission, recommended repeal of the 160-acre limitation as well as the residency requirements of the homestead laws. This proposal apparently reflected the views of the California Farm Bureau, the large growers, and the

---

[12]*Ibid.*, p. 811.

giant corporations such as Tenneco. Several other organizations and groups recommended strict enforcement of the 160-acre limitation including the AFL-CIO, Common Cause, the Sierra Club, the National Education Association, the National Grange, and the National Farmers Union.

Although the 160-acre limitation on federal water sales may be regarded as a somewhat localized or regional policy issue, the inferences that can be drawn for policy are national in scope and they go beyond questions of land reform. As we discuss in Chapters 9 and 10, the issues cannot be separated from questions of federal tax policy on the one hand and farm labor organization on the other. If tax laws were made more equitable, that is, if the capital gains loophole were closed especially, and if there were federal protection and supervision of farm labor unions, the issue of land reform would be somewhat less critical. Large farms would be on a level more competitive with family farms.

A Policy Conclusion

Land distribution policy, primarily family-farm in origin and concept, was generally implemented under laws that favored the family-farm agricultural economy. Although 3 or 4 times as many farm units were created as have yet proved to be economic, in most parts of the country the increasing scale of family farms assures that the bulk of agriculture will be of this type. In the Midwest particularly, although in some areas very large bonanza farms thrived for a while,[13] land taxes and capital costs, including lack of significant economies for very large-scale operations, have tended to favor the family farm, and grain farms or combination grain-livestock farms of more than 2,000 acres or so have not yet become very common. Large livestock ranches, on the other hand, are favored by the open range and by the need to integrate dry-land range with land resources capable of producing winter feed. Very large-scale livestock-feeding enterprises and large broiler producers, not depending on any fixed land base, have generated important economies of scale.

If very large farms did not provide a tax haven or loophole for avoiding taxes, and if they offered competitive wage and working conditions equivalent to those of either the family farm or an acceptable union standard, a major objection or criticism based on social criteria would be ameliorated. Society would not need to be concerned about land reform per se. However, given certain goals of equity in income distribution and desires to build more viable rural communities, then land reform, tax reform, and unionization of farm labor, are seen as complementary policies. The assumed efficiency of the giant farm is based in large part on tax advantages and low wages, plus subsidies to irrigation in some cases. Agriculture can be made more competitive with little if any loss in efficiency by elimination of these special advantages. Land reform must be complementary to certain other tax and labor reforms if both efficiency and equity are to result.

[13]See Hiram M. Drache, *The Day of the Bonanza,* Fargo: North Dakota Institute for Regional Studies, 1964.

CONSERVATION AND LAND USE

Shortly after 1870, the basic beliefs in the laissez faire land policy began to be questioned by some government officials and a few magazine writers. In the following two decades, they were increasingly called into question by individual scientists and scientific societies until the challenge became resounding and a revolution in policy occurred.

The First Conservation Era

In 1891, Congress passed the famous Revision Act. This marked a fundamental shift in the nation's land policy away from laissez faire doctrines as applied to land and cast the federal government in a new role as the essential conservator of the nation's land resource. The Revision Act of 1891, among other things, incorporated the Forest Reserve Act, which provided for the original allocation of more than 150 million acres in the public domain to be set aside as forest reserves (done under Presidents Harrison, Cleveland, McKinley, and Theodore Roosevelt). Although the programs under the act ended in 1907, four years later Congress provided for additional national forests by purchase of private lands. After the National Conservation Congress in 1908, the withdrawal policy was extended to include public lands valuable for oil, potash, copper, phosphate, and other minerals. Finally, an overall leasing policy was written into the General Leasing Act of 1920.

The revolution in land policy beginning in the 1870s was initiated and importantly influenced by government officials, magazine writers, natural scientists, foresters, economists, and other professionals.[14] Henry George, who became famous as an advocate of a single tax to absorb the unearned increment in property appreciation and as a sponsor of other land reforms, called attention to the impending lack of land for settlement and the growth of farm tenancy. Other concerns about the exhaustibilty of land resources began to be expressed and, after the censuses of 1880 and 1890, there was growing concern about rising farm tenancy and the end of free land. Foresters played an early role in the crusade for a change in land policy through organization of the American Forestry Congress in 1881 and formation of the American Forestry Association in 1884. The American Economic Association, founded in 1885 by Professors Richard Ely, Simon N. Patten, and E. J. James, provided a voice for economists to protest against the dominant laissez faire attitude of the English and Austrian schools of economics. More in the tradition of German economists, they directed the country's attention to an array of pressing problems of public policy, including conservation and general land policy. The American Association for the Advancement of Science in 1890 petitioned the Congress to change the public land system to exert stronger control over land use in the interest of conservation

---

[14]For further discussion, see especially L. A. Salter, Jr., *A Critical Review of Research in Land Economics,* Minneapolis: The University of Minnesota Press, 1948, and discussion by Salter in Henry C. Taylor and Anne Dewees Taylor, *The Story of Agricultural Economics in the United States, 1840– 1932,* Ames: Iowa State College Press, 1952, chaps. 28, 29.

and more productive long-term use. The American Economic Association invited three outstanding leaders of the forestry crusade—B. E. Fernow, E. A. Bowers, and Gifford Pinchot—to prepare a comprehensive statement on the need for public action to conserve forests and other land resources and to deal with land use problems. In the ensuing years, the *American Economic Review* devoted considerable space to discussion of land resource and ownership problems, until other journals, such as the *Journal of Farm Economics* and the *Journal of Land and Public Utility Economics,* assumed greater responsibility.

Although the 30 years from 1891 to 1921 may properly be called the first conservation era in American history, it was by no means an era of unanimity in policy. Under three presidents—Harrison, Cleveland, and McKinley—46.8 million acres of forest lands were withdrawn from entry and designated as permanent national forests. But these actions, particularly that of Cleveland in setting up 13 new forest reserves just before he retired from office, were vigorously protested in some of the Western states and tended to crystallize anticonservation sentiment. During much of McKinley's first term, from 1896 to 1900, conservationists were on the defensive. The nomination of Theodore Roosevelt, a known conservation enthusiast, as McKinley's running mate in 1900, was a slap at Mark Hanna, the archly conservative, wealthy, and ruthless "boss" of the Republican party, an attempt by the Republican "Old Guard" to shunt Roosevelt into an innocuous role, and an effort by Republican liberals to balance and thus strengthen the ticket. Roosevelt's progressive leadership in the U.S. Civil Service Commission, the Navy Department, the New York Police Commission, and as Governor of New York was appealing to many voters.

The accession of Roosevelt to the Presidency after the assassination of President McKinley in September 1901 brought a new emphasis to conservation policy. Gifford Pinchot, a close friend of Roosevelt and an ardent conservationist, was named head of the new Forest Service. With Pinchot's far-sighted vision and enthusiastic support, Roosevelt vigorously began sequestering forest and mining lands still under government ownership. Opposition to his actions was so strong that congressmen from Western states were able to attach an amendment to an appropriation bill repealing the act of 1891. But, before Roosevelt signed the bill, he issued an order setting up 21 new forest reserves in 6 of the most important Western states. This action permitted him to reserve an additional 125 million acres by the time he left office. Although much of this land was rather poor, his prompt action blocked a plan to transfer to private parties the bulk of the remaining good timberland.

In March 1908, Roosevelt called the first National Conservation Conference, inviting state governors, Supreme Court justices, cabinet members, congressional leaders, businessmen, and technical experts. This resulted in the National Conservation Commission of 49 members, which brought out a three-volume report containing much valuable information on conservation.[15] With

[15]U.S. Congress, Senate Report of the *National Conservation Commission,* Senate Document 676, 60th Cong., 2d Sess., 1909.

this support, Roosevelt ordered the Secretary of the Interior to withdraw from entry some 80 million acres of coal lands, 1½ million acres of land adjacent to water-power sites, and nearly 5 million acres of land containing phosphate deposits.[16]

By moving to set aside forests, water power, coal, oil, and minerals, Roosevelt challenged the large lumber companies, the hydroelectric power industry, and the mining interests, all of whom bitterly opposed such interference with "free enterprise." Although 41 states set up state conservation commissions which helped to spread information and propaganda on the need for conservation, many newspapers were owned by lumber and mining interests, state legislatures and individual congressmen often were in debt or influenced by similar interests. Roosevelt found himself in bitter conflict with both the state legislatures and the Congress. His broad-ranging battle against trusts and monopolies sapped the energy of his administration and further efforts at conservation were largely a standoff. A series of measures was adopted to regulate removal of minerals by those who leased government land and finally an overall leasing policy was written into the General Mineral Land Leasing Act of 1920.

The first conservation era, beginning with the Revision Act of 1891, which Hibbard called in retrospect "the most signal act yet performed by Congress in the direction of a national land policy,"[17] came to a close with recognition that government had a proprietory interest and responsibility in use of the nation's natural resources. This marked a significant evolution in thinking about policy. But the major part of these resources long since had passed into private ownership, and many years would elapse before conservation of them would again hold center stage in the nation's policy.

As far as agriculture is concerned, the first conservation era scarcely touched the issue of soil conservation and the best use of soil. The government had moved to develop irrigation and, in passing the Federal Farm Loan Act of 1916, the initial act in the funding of the federal farm credit system, it made a significant move to implement the policy of family-farm ownership. But more general problems of soil conservation and land use policy were soon submerged in another overriding problem—that of farm-price collapse and excess capacity as revealed in the early 1920s.

The Broadening of Conservation and Land Use Policy

Shortly after the close of World War I, a basic change occurred in the national land problem, especially as related to agriculture and food supply. It was comparable in importance to the change exemplified by the Revision Act of 1891. After a 30-year period of increasing fears of food shortage, the agricultural plant suddenly appeared to be too large for the markets at hand. The early signal was the sharp drop in farm prices in 1920 and 1921, followed soon by a settling back in

---

[16]John D. Hicks, *The American Nation, op. cit.,* p. 398, and chap. 18.
[17]Hibbard, *A History of the Public Land Policies, op. cit.,* p. 532.

land values and a rising volume of farm-distress–farm-auction sales, property tax delinquencies, mortgage defaults and foreclosures, and farmer and rural business bankruptcies.

The general turning point in land policy was highlighted in a report published in the 1923 *Yearbook of Agriculture,* written by staff members of the Division of Land Economics in the Office of Farm Management and Farm Economics of the U.S. Department of Agriculture. The report presented the general thesis that there was no danger of a shortage of farm land and that a slow and cautious program of farm land development should replace that of eager expansion.[18] By that time 365 million acres of land were in crops and perhaps another 100 million acres of land might be brought into crop production without heavy investment in clearing, drainage, or other improvement. A modest improvement in the terms of trade for agriculture—maybe a 30 percent increase in farm prices—would bring much of these 100 million acres under cultivation. Another 500 million acres of land was considered physically capable of crop production, but much more favorable prices would have been required and much of the land would not be suitable for long-term cultivation because of its susceptibility to erosion. The problem was not to bring this land into use but to reduce crop production so as to bring output into balance with available markets. The report, based on studies of the nation's needs for land and a determination of the national land requirements, suggested that there was a continuing threat of a timber shortage and that greater attention should be given to protection and development of forest resources.

This view of land resources changed the course of professional attention and affected national policy in respect to conservation and land use for several years. Although, as early as 1910, the Commission on Country Life took note of the loss of soil fertility on land that had been farmed for several years, it did not give conservation a prominent place in its recommendations.[19] Although a few state experiment station economists and soil scientists, especially in Illinois and Wisconsin, began to give attention to what they called conservation farming, no national concensus developed. During the 1920s, farm journals and agricultural leaders began to emphasize the need to safeguard and build up soils. Finally, in 1929 the Congress appropriated $160,000 to investigate soil losses from erosion. Regional soil erosion experiment stations were set up under the Bureau of Chemistry and Soils in the Department of Agriculture in cooperation with the Bureau of Agricultural Engineering and the Forest Service.

In the meantime, many irrigation projects had been in financial trouble even before the postwar drop in farm prices. In the early 1920s, their difficulties were accentuated. On December 5, 1924, after a report by a special committee known as the Fact Finders, Congress enacted legislation which required careful advance

[18]L. C. Gray, O. E. Baker, F. J. Marschner, B. O. Weitz, W. R. Chapline, W. Shephard, and R. Zon, "The Utilization of Our Lands for Crops, Pasture, and Forest," *Yearbook of Agriculture,* Washington: U.S. Department of Agriculture, 1923, pp. 415–506.

[19]*Report of the Commission on Country Life,* Chapel Hill: The University of North Carolina Press, May 1944, pp. 83–90.

investigation of the land, the settlers, and the economic feasibility of proposed irrigation projects;[20] and later legislation further expanded the federal government's role in irrigation.[21]

Also in 1924 Congress passed the Clarke-McNary Act which greatly expanded the legislative basis for direct federal purchase and administration of land for forestry purposes.[22] This reaffirmed the role of the federal government as the essential conservator of forest resources and strengthened the basis for other policy action to be taken in the future.[23]

The tremendous shift in economic conditions of the 1920s from those prevailing in the conservation era, revealing in general the overexpansion of agriculture, had repercussions all along the line in terms of farm financial distress and economic studies relating to distress. But the shift did not lead immediately to a general change in agricultural land policy. For a decade in the 1920s, L. C. Gray and O. E. Baker, and their associates in the USDA's Division of Land Economics and other bureaus, worked over and over, constantly improving and refining, the national requirements for land in the light of changing population growth, dietary habits, and technology.[24] The studies gave a new direction to national thought about the relationship of the supply of land to prospective requirements. They formed a background for further consideration of land utilization potentials, such as that undertaken in a national conference called by Secretary of Agriculture Hyde in 1931. They also provided background for the Social Science Research Council study *Research in Agricultural Land Utilization,* published in June 1931. In retrospect, the studies of the 1920s, stimulated originally by concerns about population pressures on food supplies and later by farm financial distress, provided an orientation for the shifts in land policy that were to occur in the 1930s and a background for the second great conservation movement organized in the early years of the Roosevelt New Deal.[25]

The great period of agricultural expansion in America, extending from 1862 to the beginning of the Great Depression, came to an end with clear evidence: (1) Short of a revolutionary expansion in world trade, American agriculture had been overextended through the pressure of settlers for free land and by the acquiescence of government in this policy; and (2) a new policy in regard to land use for farm and forest production would be in the national interst. These conditions were the foundation for the next major era in land policy which we date from 1933 to 1972.

[20]U.S. Congress, House Committee in Irrigation and Reclamation, *Hearings on Extension of the Time of Payment for Settlers on Government Reclamation Projects,* 68th Cong., 1st Sess., 1923–24, May 1924.

[21]U.S. Department of the Interior, Committee of Special Advisers on Reclamation, *Federal Reclamation by Irrigation,* 1924.

[22]U.S. Congress, House Committee on Agriculture, *Hearings on Reforestation,* March 25–27, 1924, 68th Cong., 1st Sess., 1923–24, 1924.

[23]M. C. Calkins, "The Clarke Forestry Law," *Journal of Land and Public Utility Economics,* January 1925, pp. 125–128.

[24]M. M. Kelso, "Major Trends in Land Utilization Research in the United States," *New England Research Council on Marketing and Food Supply, Proceedings, 1941,* pp. 1–5; reproduced in part in Taylor and Taylor, *op. cit.,* pp. 852–855.

[25]Salter in Taylor and Taylor, *op. cit.,* pp. 864–870.

Agricultural Land Use Adjustment and Conservation, 1933–1972

Two general features mark the land policy of the 40-year period 1933–72. One was the decision, begun with the Agricultural Adjustment Act of 1933 and continued with every general agricultural act of the era, to provide a system for rationing seeded acreage of selected major crops among farm producers for the primary purpose of price support. The features of these acts varied from time to time from specific allotments for individual crops without regard to specific conservation objectives, to allotments linked with soil conservation require-ments, to so-called soil-bank programs in which land retirement was conceived as a system for storing the nutrients of the soil for future, presumably higher priority, use. The second feature was the development of a national system for soil conservation, reclamation, and land development, replete with a far-flung professional corps. a politically structured committee system, and an array of payment provisions to farmers for carrying out specified conservation practices.

In the beginning, studies initiated under the $160,000 appropriated by Con-gress in 1929 for investigation of soil losses from erosion soon led to a deeper appreciation of the extent of such losses from both wind and water erosion. Sheet erosion, the process by which soil is carried away without making noticeable changes in the appearance of the land, was found to be severe and of increasing significance, especially in the Great Plains. The condition was caused partially by overgrazing and cropping of dry-land soils. Losses through gullying and actual destruction of the land surface were found to be widespread in many of the older, more humid areas. The significance of the initial studies was highlighted by the droughts of the early 1930s, especially the drought of 1934 which affected practically the entire country and in which crops failed completely on several million acres. A study made in 1934 concluded that more than 280 million acres of crop and grazing land had been badly damaged by soil erosion and that some erosion damage was apparent on another 775 million acres of crop, grazing, and forest land.[26]

In spite of large crop surpluses, it was soon evident that (1) the future of the nation's food supply was endangered, and (2) national action of some kind would be required if such losses were to be checked and brought under control. The first action was the emergency conservation program initiated in 1933, organized under the Civilian Conservation Corps in the United States Forest Service. The objective of the CCC program was to provide healthful and useful work in the national forests for formerly unemployed young men. They lived in camps and were given food, lodging, and a small monthly wage. These efforts soon led to the idea of expanding the program to include erosion control on other types of land as well. Only a few months after the CCC was founded, the President, under emergency powers of the National Industrial Recovery Act, established the Soil Erosion Service in the Department of the Interior to develop conservation programs on public lands and demonstration projects partly or wholly on private

[26]As reported in *Our American Land, The Story of Its Abuse and Its Conservation*, U.S. Department of Agriculture, Soil Conservation Service, Miscellaneous Publication, No. 596, 1950, p. 4.

lands. Activities included sloping and terracing eroding lands, planting trees and grass, building check dams, and grassing waterways.

The Soil Conservation Service[27]

Recognition of the case for a more comprehensive attack on soil erosion, which was accelerated by the 1934 drought, led to transfer of the Soil Erosion Service to the Department of Agriculture in March 1935, and then to the design and passage of the Soil Conservation Act of 1935 (49 *Stat.* 163) on April 7. Support for the act was underlined by the fact that it was passed without a dissenting vote in either house of Congress. The act recognized wastage of soil and water resources as a menace to the national welfare and declared that provision for the permanent control of erosion was a policy of Congress. It directed that "the Secretary of Agriculture shall coordinate and direct all activities relating to soil erosion," and it authorized him (1) to conduct surveys, researches, and other studies, to distribute results, and to carry on demonstrations; (2) to carry out preventive measures; (3) to cooperate, or enter into agreements, with any agency or person concerned with soil conservation to give aid subject to the conditions necessary to carry out the purposes of the act. Finally, the act directed the Secretary to establish an agency to be known as the Soil Conservation Service to exercise the power conferred upon him, thus to confer on the new SCS a considerable status and power. The act, as amended by the Soil Conservation and Domestic Allotment Act of 1936 and other subsequent legislation, became the parent legislation for general soil conservation programs in succeeding years.

As a condition for granting benefits, the act provided that the Secretary may require (1) "The enactment and reasonable safeguards for the enforcement of State and local laws imposing suitable permanent restrictions on the use of such lands and otherwise providing for the prevention of soil erosion," (2) agreements or covenants respecting the use of such land, and (3) contributions, money or otherwise. Under the first of these provisions, the SCS, in collaboration with land grant college personnel, developed a model Standard State Soil Conservation Law, which was circulated to state governors, together with a letter from the President requesting that the states enact legislation authorizing the formation of soil conservation districts. The first state law was passed in 1937 and by 1952 all 48 states, Alaska, Hawaii, Puerto Rico, and the Virgin Islands had enacted laws. By 1952, there were 2,467 districts, organized mostly on a county basis containing nearly 5 million farms and 1.4 billion acres. By 1951 the SCS budget was $51 million. Texas had set up a $5 million revolving fund mainly to purchase machinery for terracing and the like. States, other than Texas, were appropriating $2.7 million annually for SCS work. The bulk of the nation's agricultural

[27]For more complete discussion, see Robert J. Morgan, *Governing Soil Conservation: Thirty Years of the New Decentralization,* Baltimore: Published for Resources for the Future, Inc., by the Johns Hopkins Press, 1965. For discussion concentrating on certain aspects of the political problem in soil conservation, see Charles M. Hardin, *The Politics of Agriculture, Soil Conservation and the Struggle for Power in Rural America,* Glencoe, Ill.: The Free Press, 1952.

land resource had been organized for cooperative effort in conserving and improving soils.

In the beginning, the SCS began a program of demonstration projects to teach and encourage the use of soil-conserving practices on farm lands, using as a basic method the whole-farm approach where soil conservation plans and programs were integrated with the total farm-home plan. In the summer of 1935, the 150 organized CCC camps and more than 300 newly formed camps were transferred to the SCS for an expanded program of conservation and demonstration projects. The Omnibus Flood Control Act of 1936 (49 *Stat.* 1570) directed the Department of Agriculture to institute investigations "of watersheds, measures for run-off and water-flow regulation and measures for the prevention of soil erosion on watersheds." The act provided that the upstream phase of flood control, including small watersheds, and various conservation measures on land should be administered by the Department and that the downstream phase, including dams and other engineering structures for control of flood damage, should be administered by the Army Corps of Engineers.

In the same year the President, by Executive order, established a Great Plains Committee to study and develop ways for controlling soil loss and erosion in the Great Plains. Then, in 1937, came the Pope-Jones Water Facilities Act (50 *Stat.* 869) to provide facilities for water storage and utilization in the arid and semiarid areas and to authorize the Secretary of Agriculture to undertake action programs in water facilities and water conservation. The Wheeler-Case Act of 1939, essentially a relief act, and the Flood Control Act of 1944 provided further authorization for flood control and water conservation activities.

Purchase of Submarginal Lands

For more than 300 years, land policy had emphasized methods of transferring public lands to private use, and now this policy was called into question. Studies developed the fact that vast areas, including a major part of the farmland in some states, would have to be taken out of production to conserve soils and to eliminate some of the most poverty-stricken areas. The policy proposal was not just to purchase lands for the purpose of land conservation; it really involved liquidation of assets of people living in submarginal dry-land areas. It was not intended that the lands so acquired would be retained by the federal agency making the purchase. Rather, the lands would be transferred to other operating or land-leasing agencies, such as the Grazing Service or the Forest Service. Thus the program was conceived as a means of adjusting agricultural resources to a type of organization and use more compatible with human and national interests.

The land purchase program never reached very large proportions in terms of its national impact. The bulk of some 11.3 million acres, which was purchased up to 1947, was acquired in 1936 and 1937. The program is of more significance to us now as a prototype for other land reforms that may be carried out in the future. The operating principle for such a program is that the government, through the grant of eminent domain, is able to undertake a reorganization of ownership of land parcels and, through lease or other measures, to direct the land into uses more compatible with standards of social or economic performance.

Management of Public Lands Used for Grazing[28]

Although nearly all the best farmland and most of the best grazing land in America has passed into private ownership, nearly one-third of all land is still in federal ownership, including more than one-half the land areas of the 11 Western states. About four-fifths of all public lands are held by the federal government and one-fifth by state and local governments. About one-fifth of all federal land and less than one-fifth of state and local land is used for grazing. The latter was acquired by tax foreclosures and other reversions or by original allocation under federal land disposal policies. In the early 1930s, much of this public land was being used by ranchers and stock producers largely on the basis of who was able to put livestock on the range and provide auxiliary feed, water, and other care. Much of the land was being grazed too heavily and the quality of the vegetation was deteriorating. Serious problems of excessive runoff and of wind erosion were becoming apparent. The lack of clearly defined rights made it unprofitable for ranchers to conserve the soils, build dams and reservoirs, control the grazing population, or make long-term plans for land improvements.

The Taylor Grazing Act (48 *Stat.* 1269) was passed to control the use of publicly owned grazing lands. It authorized grazing districts in which local ranchers would have rights to graze specified numbers of animals at a fixed fee per head. Local advisory boards elected by the ranchers were given legal recognition and permanent status by a 1939 amendment.[29] A National Advisory Board Council was established in 1940. Both state and federal advisory boards were made official in 1949, through an amendment to the Federal Range Code for Grazing Districts.[30]

When the Grazing Service was first established, about 166 million acres of grazing lands were in federal ownership. The original act limited to 80 million acres the land that might be organized in grazing districts. The specified area was raised to 142 million acres in 1936. In 1954, the limit was removed entirely.[31] Thus some 160 million acres of public grazing land were brought under control of the Division of Range Management, Bureau of Land Management, Department of the Interior. This land, added to the 160 million acres of national forest under the U.S. Forest Service on which some grazing is also permitted, constitutes the

---

[28]For extensive background discussion, see especially Wesley Calef, *Private Grazing and Public Lands, Studies of the Local Management of The Taylor Grazing Act,* Chicago: The University of Chicago Press, 1960; Phillip O. Foss, *Politics and Grass, The Administration of Grazing on the Public Domain,* Seattle: University of Washington Press, 1960; Marion Clawson, *The Western Range Livestock Industry,* New York: McGraw-Hill Book Company, 1950; and Clawson, *Uncle Sam's Acres,* New York: Dodd, Mead and Co., 1951.

[29]For further discussion, see J. Russell Penny and Marion Clawson, "Administration of the Grazing Districts," *Land Economics,* February 1953, pp. 23–34.

[30]See U.S. Bureau of Land Management, *The Federal Range Code for Grazing Districts,* 1949 and later revisions.

[31]Public Law 375, 83d Cong., May 28, 1954.

bulk of federally owned land that is used for food production in the 48 contiguous states. In addition, the federal government still owns about 98 percent of the 365 million acres of Alaska.

Since livestock ranchers normally try to maximize net returns from their operations and therefore tend to graze up to the maximum yield and since the government agencies are charged with regulating the use of the grazing lands to prevent excessive runoff and wind erosion, a conflict in policy continues and may be expected to do so indefinitely into the future. The system is well established, however, as a means to protect the major watersheds of the West, and it may be expected to survive. Public hearings and studies tend to stabilize the levels of grazing permitted, with revisions in the levels a matter for periodic evaluation.

Conflict and Compromise among the Implementers

The division of responsibility in the Omnibus Flood Control Act of 1936 between the Army Corps of Engineers and the Department of Agriculture Soil Conservation Service soon developed into a struggle for power, program, and influence between the two agencies. Where was the line to be drawn between the upstream responsibilities of the SCS and the downstream flood-control activities of the Army Corps of Engineers? Although the SCS was assigned overall responsibility for establishing policies, principles, procedures, and standards for the work to be conducted under the act, each agency was free to lobby for more appropriations and for expansion of its area of responsibility. How could priorities be established for the Corps and SCS activites? The upstream projects of the SCS included conservation programs to improve cover, increase absorbtion, and stabilize runoff as a means of protecting the lands upstream and aiding in the control of runoff that causes damage downstream. The fact that conflict did and still does occur should not be surprising. More unusual, perhaps, is the fact that compromises are continually reached and work goes on. A difficult problem in economic analysis, and in obtaining compromise among competing interests, runs throughout this area of policy.

The SCS program of whole-farm planning and demonstration also developed with conflict from two other sources: (1) the production control activities of the Agricultural Adjustment Administration (AAA), under the Soil Conservation and Domestic Allotment Act of 1936 and subsequent programs; and (2) the research and educational activities of the land grant colleges. In the first case, the act of 1936, its later amendments, and all subsequent acts, where crop production control is involved, have two purposes: crop production adjustment and soil conservation. Farmers are most often paid for two purposes: (1) to shift crop acreage from crops in surplus, which are generally soil-depleting, to conservation, soil-conserving uses; and (2) to adopt certain specified soil-conserving practices. The results do not necessarily conform with any overall plan of conservation for a farm as recommended by professional conservationists in the SCS or elsewhere. In the second case, the SCS program, emphasizing the whole farm plan, information, and education, is inherently in competition with the educational farm planning and management programs, sponsored by the Cooperative Extension Service of the nation's agricultural colleges. Consequently, it should come as no surprise that struggles for power, influence, and control of the conservation programs have erupted between the SCS and the agricultural colleges.

Efforts to resolve the conflicts inherent in conservation and production control were first attempted in a broad land use planning project organized in the Department of Agriculture's Bureau of Agricultural Economics (BAE). The project involved land grant universities, USDA personnel, and volunteer county land use planning committees of farmers and farm leaders. The program was initiated in the late 1930s and grew rapidly for a time. Land use plans were developed for entire counties, providing recommendations for land use and conservation, numbers and sizes of farms, development measures, community services, and the like. The effect was abortive, however, partially, we may judge, because of the pressure of the war effort in the early 1940s, the uncertain support of the land grant colleges, and, finally, the outright opposition of the American Farm Bureau Federation, whose leaders came to view the county land use planning committees, then established in some 1800 counties, as potentially competitive with county farm bureaus. Proposals for certain land reforms in the South were especially objectionable to the Farm Bureau, and in 1940 it launched a broad attack against "duplication and overlapping" in agricultural administration, the real goal being to stop the tendency for new organizations to stimulate new farm organizations.[32] Although the work of the AAA and the SCS could have been coordinated by the land use planning program, both agencies helped to kill it and the land grant colleges did not fight strongly for it. Funds for land use planning were discontinued and the program to this day has not been revived. In the political battles over the program, the position of the BAE was weakened, until the Bureau eventually broke up;[33] its economics work was reorganized and transferred into other agencies in the USDA, including the Economic Research Service (ERS) and the Agricultural Marketing Service (AMS).

The struggle for coordination and control of conservation programs deeply involved the land grant colleges through the Association of Land-Grant Colleges and Universities. In January 1948, an Association commitee recommended, before the House Committee on Agriculture, that the SCS program should be operated through the state agencies, that is, through the agricultural college experiment stations and extension services, insofar as educational, informational, and demonstrational work, including the extension of technical assistance to farmers, is involved. Opposition was expressed not only to the SCS organization but to the USDA programs rivaling those of the SCS, namely the Agricultural Conservation Program (ACP) of the Production and Marketing Administration (PMA). The Association recommended that any program should scrupulously avoid using conservation as a disguise for making payments to

---

[32]Hardin, *The Politics of Agriculture, op. cit.,* p. 136.
[33]Charles M. Hardin, "The Bureau of Agricultural Economics under Fire, A Study in Valuation Conflicts," *Journal of Farm Economics,* Vol. 28, No. 3, August 1946, pp. 635–668.

farmers to increase their incomes. Good soil conservation required—so the argument went—coordinated research and education. In short, the scope of research and educational work as developed in the land grant colleges should be broadened and strengthened to coordinate the major work to be done in conservation. As part of the proposal, it was recommended that payments for conservation should be made only when a large element of public interest is involved, when the practice is to yield returns only after a considerable time, when the practices are not likely to be carried out by farmers themselves without assistance, when the total annual payments to assisted farms are limited, and when payments do not exceed one-half the cost of the conservation practices. In the committee view, any system of payments should be merely supplemental to a vigorous program of education and research.[34]

In a long and involved struggle, however, the land grant colleges failed to carry their point. The program of the SCS remained administratively independent—sometimes competitive, sometimes cooperative with the colleges' teaching, research, and extension programs on soil conservation and land use. The issue of a more highly integrated policy for optimum conservation has not been successfully revived. The SCS program, as well as programs tied to land retirement for purposes of production control, is correlated, if at all, on an informal and ad hoc basis with other research and educational programs.

SCS programs have continued to emphasize complete farm planning according to SCS's philosophy of treating every acre according to its best "land use capabilities." Under the SCS provisions, landowners and operators who develop conservation plans that receive SCS approval may receive assistance from SCS technicians plus some soil conservation materials at near wholesale prices, such as seeds, seed innoculants, soil-conditioning materials, trees and plants, and, under appropriate circumstances, payments for carrying out the agreed conservation practices. Sometimes fertilizer and liming materials have been sold at reduced cost for purposes of trial and demonstration. In some districts, heavy machinery under control of the district has been made available for improvements such as terracing and waterway and dam construction. The emphasis is on self-help and local control coordinated under SCS district administration.

Although the SCS districts have considerable paper power, for example, to acquire and dispose of personal property, to sue and be sued, to ask and receive help from state and federal governments, and, in some states (with important qualifications), to pass land use regulations, their ability to wield power is highly restricted. The districts, defined as local units of government, have been created under state enabling acts, generally following the model Standard State Soil Conservation District Act prepared in 1936 by USDA and college personnel. Typically, farmers have petitioned to a state committee for formation of a district. A district may be formed on a favorable vote of registered farmland owners and at the discretion of the state committee. Although policy in a district is under control of a board, generally consisting of five elected farmers, in

---

[34]Hardin, *The Politics of Agriculture, op. cit.*, p. 27–31.

practice most of the leadership and program direction has been supplied by SCS personnel. Except in two states, Colorado and California, districts do not have the power to tax, and in these two the power is strictly limited. No district has the power of eminent domain.

In general, the SCS program consists of advice and some technical assistance given by SCS personnel to landowners or operators whose conservation plans are accepted as meeting the standards specified and published in the *ACP Handbook*. These standards specify the practices that can be funded on a cost-sharing basis, such as terracing or contouring, building tile drains and outlets, establishing reservoirs, sodding waterways, and digging diversion ditches. Specific limits are established for ACP or SCS funding at so much per acre for terracing and contouring—usually up to 50 or 75 percent of the actual cost, which is not to exceed an amount determined by the county committee. For tile drains, waterways, and diversion ditches, the limit may be so much per rod. A limit for tile outlets may be a flat amount as, for example, $45 per outlet. The major policy constraints, however, are those established by the budget allocated for the purpose. This raises the question of the priorities to be established and the constraints to be applied.

Constraints in Terms of Fund and Flow

Conservation yields two separate or distinguishable products: (1) the preservation or enhancement of a fund of soil or other resources, or (2) the enhancement of a flow of product by maintaining the productivity of the resource over a period of time. Erosion or sediment damage resulting from conservation failures can be viewed either as a reduction in benefits to the farmer or to society, or as an increase in cost of other activities. It may occur either on site (within a farm) or off site, as say, through silting of a drainage system. A prudent conservation policy will be to seek to invest in conservation according to the relative efficiency of the practices in building a fund or increasing a flow, up to that point where net additional investments in conservation are equated with net additional returns from conservation, while taking into consideration both public and private investment.

Conservation policy is complicated, however, in at least three ways: First, there are various choices or standards that may be used in estimating the future value of a fund. That is, how much do we want to spend to build the base for future food supplies? Or, how shall we value the product of the conservation practice in terms of food production at some time in the future? Second, fund and flow cannot be neatly separated. That is, an investment in conservation yields products that are spread over time. Some may be immediate. Others may be long term. In almost any project there are choices and alternatives between the two. These involve not only trade-offs between fund and flow but choices among various practices and systems for implementing them. Third, whereas a conservation program will generally yield marginal returns that are divided between off-site and on-site benefits, the costs are usually or largely incurred on site. Then, how much shall conservation of farmland be subsidized to reduce these off-site damages? An optimum might be for the government to invest up to the point where the value of the net reduction in off-site damages is equal to the subsidy incurred by the government.

Adjustment and Conservation, 1933–1972   All the agricultural adjustment acts, except the one of 1933, linked agricultural adjustment with conservation (1) by paying farmers for diverting cropland from production, and (2) by paying for specified conservation practices on at least part of the diverted land, or by a general statement supportive of conservation as a condition for receiving payments. The Agricultural Act of 1956, which initiated the Soil Bank Program, in essence primarily viewed conservation as the building of a fund of soil resources divided between the short-range acreage reserve and the longer-term conservation reserve. So subsidies to promote conservation were largely spent on idle land. In the 1960s, conservation expenditures under the Emergency Feed Grain Program, the Wheat-Cotton Act of 1964, and the basic Food and Agricultural Act of 1965 were largely allocated to idle land while the bulk of payments went to finance the land diversion. The Agricultural Act of 1970 continued this policy. In 1970, when land retirement was near the peak of 60 million acres, the net farm income of $15.9 billion included $3.7 billion in direct farm payments. Of this, $3.3 billion was to finance land diversion into the set-aside. The other $0.4 billion was paid as supportive of conservation under the Agricultural Stabilization and Conservation Service (ASCS) and the Great Plains conservation programs, or supportive of production under the Sugar Act and the Wool Act.

The emphasis on conservation of idled lands suggests that the Congress largely conceived of conservation as the building of a fund of resources rather than the maintenance or increase of a flow of productivity. Typically, the Act of 1970 read in part as follows:[35]

> The Secretary shall provide for a set-aside of cropland if he determines that the total supply of feed grains or other commodities will, in the absence of such a set-aside, likely be excessive taking into account the need for an adequate carryover to maintain reasonable and stable supplies and prices of feed grains and to meet a national emergency. If a set-aside of cropland is in effect under this subsection (c), then as a condition of eligibility for loans, purchases, and payments on corn, grain sorghums, and, if designated by the Secretary, barley, respectively, *the producers on a farm must set aside and devote to approved conservation uses an acreage of cropland* equal to (*i*) such percentage of the feed grain base for the farm as may be specified by the Secretary, plus (*ii*) the acreage of cropland on the farm devoted in preceding years to soil-conserving uses, as determined by the Secretary. The Secretary is authorized for the 1971, 1972, and 1973 crops to limit the acreage planted to feed grains on the farm to such percentage of the feed grain base as he determines necessary to provide an orderly transition to the program provided for under this section. . . .

[35]*Agricultural Act of 1970,* Public Law 91-524, 91st Cong., H. R. 18546, Nov. 30, 1970, Title V, section (c) (1), p. 11. Italics supplied.

Grazing shall not be permitted during any of the five principal months of the normal growing season as determined by the county committee established pursuant to section 8(b) of the Soil Conservation and Domestic Allotment Act, as amended, and subject to this limitation (1) the Secretary shall permit producers to plant and graze on the set-aside acreage sweet sorghum, and (2) the Secretary may permit, subject to such terms and conditions as he may prescribe, all or any of the set-aside acreage to be devoted to grazing or the production of guar, sesame, safflower, sunflower, castor beans, mustard seed, crambe, plantago ovato, flaxseed, or other commodity, if he determines that such production is needed to provide an adequate supply, is not likely to increase the cost of the price-support program, and will not adversely affect farm income. . . .

The act also allowed for substitutions among wheat, soybeans, and feed grains within the total allotment for such crops on an individual farm and it authorized additional land diversion payments to producers who:[36]

> . . . *devote to approved conservation uses an acreage of cropland on the farm in addition to that required to be so devoted* under subsection (c) (1) [and he shall] take such measures as the Secretary may deem appropriate *to protect the set-aside acreage and the additional diverted acreage* from erosion, insects, weeds, and rodents. Such acreage may be diverted to wildlife food plots or wildlife habitat in conformity with standards established by the Secretary in consultation with wildlife agencies. *The Secretary may provide for an additional payment on such acreage* in an amount determined by the Secretary to be appropriate *in relation to the benefit to the general public* if the producer agrees to permit, without other compensation, access to all or such portion of the farm as the Secretary may prescribe by the general public, for hunting, trapping, fishing, and hiking, subject to applicable State and Federal regulations.

The emphasis on conservation of idled lands, which highlights the fund concept of conservation and an apparent desire not to use conservation as a means to increase the flow of production, can be criticized on a number of grounds. First, in many cases it will reimburse farmers for practices that are no more conserving of soils than the practices they would normally employ. In this respect, it is in opposition to one of the recommendations of the land grant college committee in 1948. Second, since erosion and sediment damage is often positively correlated with high intensity of cultivation and with rotations emphasizing high-yielding row crops, the available funds are diverted from lands where they could have a higher efficiency for conservation. Third, land in a set-aside leads, in some instances, to more intensive cultivation of the remaining farm acreage, which sometimes adds to erosion damage.

The failure to provide more funds for reduction of erosion and sediment damage from cropped acreages is the most serious shortcoming of the entire program. Although this criticism may be related to the policies covering several decades, the problem became more acute in the early 1970s. Between 1972 and

---

[36]*Ibid.,* from sections (c) (2) and (c) (3), p. 12. Italics supplied.

1975, as funds for land diversion were withdrawn, funds for cost-sharing conservation practices, such as terracing and contouring, tilling and farm reservoirs, were drastically reduced. In many counties the 1975 budget allocation was only about half of what it was in 1974. This was sufficient to encourage only a very small fraction of the practices that might be required to achieve the optimum social welfare. To illustrate this last point, we consider some of the estimates that have been made of the economic losses from erosion and sediment damage.

Economic Analysis of Erosion and Sedimentation Damage

The economic losses from erosion and sediment damage are of two types: (1) the on-site losses in soil productivity on a farm or field, and (2) the off-site damages, including sedimentation of streams and reservoirs, downstream flooding from too rapid runoff or sedimentation, and pollution of streams and reservoirs. When these two losses are lumped together, they do not appear large when compared with the value of the farm product on most of the 400 milllion acres of cropland in America. Generally from the standpoint of the individual farmer, the on-site losses of soil productivity are not severe enough to justify shifting away from the more intensive systems of crop production. The off-site damages are generally much larger, however. Also, they are correlated with the on-site losses. The problem in public policy is to attain a crop rotation, tillage, and cultivation system where the net value of farm production, adjusted to reflect the off-site costs of erosion and sediment damage, is at or near a maximum. That is, the problem is to maximize net social income, defined as net income from farming including on-site losses in soil productivity, minus off-site damage costs.

Measuring On-Site Soil Losses   Earl R. Swanson and his associates at the University of Illinois have conducted an economic analysis of erosion and sedimentation on six watersheds in Illinois that cover a range of soil, slope, and erosion conditions.[37] They found that erosion and sediment damage was highly correlated with the intensity of cultivation and cropping. Continuous corn and rotations of corn-corn-soybeans or corn-soybeans, which are commonly the most profitable combinations over much of the cash-crop area of Illinois, had significantly higher rates of erosion and sediment damage than other rotations which included wheat and meadow crops. But the on-site soil losses, expressed as a reduction in net land rents per acre, were typically very low; so low, in fact, that they could almost be ignored by farmers in planning their crop rotation, tillage system, and conservation practices. In fact, among the six watersheds, the one that had the highest off-site damages had very low on-site losses, as indicated by reduction in net rent (Table 8-4).

[37]In addition to Swanson, the authors are A. S. Narayanan, M. T. Lee, Karl Gunterman, and W. D. Seitz. The general title of the series is *Economic Analysis of Erosion and Sedimentation,* University of Illinois at Urbana-Champaign, Department of Agricultural Economics, in cooperation with State of Illinois, Institute for Environmental Quality, AERR 126, 127, 128, 130, 131, and 135, April 1974 to April 1975. See also Karl Gunterman, M. T. Lee, A. S. Narayanan, and E. R. Swanson, *Soil Loss From Illinois Farms, Economic Analysis of Productivity Loss and Sediment Damage,* Chicago: Illinois Institute for Environmental Quality, IIEQ Document No. 74–62, December, 1974.

Table 8-4 Annual Dollar Loss in Net Land Rents per Acre Caused by Soil Erosion*

Crop rotation‡	Conventional tillage†			Plow-plant tillage†			Chisel plow tillage†		
	Up-and-down cultivation	Contouring	Contouring and terracing	Up-and-down cultivation	Contouring	Contouring and terracing	Up-and-down cultivation	Contouring	Contouring and terracing
Continuous corn	0.51	0.41	0.14	0.27	0.23	0.07	0.09	0.08	0.02
C-C-Sb	0.51	0.41	0.14	0.27	0.23	0.07	0.09	0.08	0.02
C-Eb	0.61	0.49	0.17	0.33	0.28	0.09	0.10	0.09	0.03
C-Sb-C-Wx	0.33	0.31	0.12	0.24	0.19	0.07	0.08	0.06	0.02
C-Sb-C-W-M	0.25	0.21	0.07	0.14	0.11	0.04	0.07	0.05	0.02
C-W-M-M-M	0.07	0.06	0.02	0.04	0.02	0.00	0.04	0.02	0.00
W-M-M-M	0.02	0.01	0.00	0.00	0.00	0.00	0.00	0.00	0.00

*The net rent is the net amount remaining for the landlord out of his share of the gross revenue after all his costs have been subtracted. The costs include the landlord's property taxes, depreciation, insurance, and repairs on improvements.

†The operations involved in the three tillage systems are as follows: (a) conventional tillage: shredding or disking residue, plowing (fall or spring), disking twice with harrow, and planting; (b) plow-plant tillage: shredding or disking residue, spring plowing with attached mulcher or clod buster, and planting; (c) chisel-plow tillage: chiseling residue, disking, harrowing, and planting.

‡Where C is corn, Sb is soybeans, O is oats, W is wheat, Wx is wheat with a catch crop, and M is meadow.

Source: Economic Analysis of Erosion and Sedimentation: Hambaugh-Martin Watershed University of Illinois at Urbana-Champaign, Department of Agricultural Economics, in cooperation with State of Illinois Institute for Environmental Quality, AERR 127, p. 17.

Further notes on the table:

1 Soil Conservation Service planning recommendations based on slope percentages are used in combining conservation practices for the watershed. For example, A (0–2 percent) and B (2–4 percent) slopes need only contouring. Slopes C (4–7 percent) and D (7–12 percent) need terrace treatment. Then a combined weighted average is computed.

2 The adjustment in the costs of field operations is as follows: 50 cents per acre per year increased cost for contouring and $4 per acre per year increased cost for terracing, over and above the conventional system costs, with no yield changes.

3 Total adjustments for the plow-plant system amount to $1.50 per acre per year less than for the conventional system.

4 For purposes of estimating the results of erosion over time, three erosion classes were used (1 = 7–14 inches of topsoil remaining; 2 = 3–7 inches of topsoil remaining; 3 = 0–3 inches of topsoil remaining).

5 Non-land crop production costs are subtracted from the adjusted gross income under high-level management to give net farm income per acre above non-land costs. Land costs are figured as under conventional tillage. Average prices of 1968–72 were used to estimate gross income (corn $1.18 per bushel, soybeans $2.65 per bushel, oats $0.63 per bushel, and meadow hay at $24.35 per ton on an average of 2 tons per acre).

6 A weighted average of net returns for each rotation is determined by weighting each crop according to the number of years it appears in the rotation, and these results are then aggregated to form a watershed average, with the soil-type/slope/erosion-class acreages used as weights.

368

Fortunately, however, the systems of tillage and conservation practices that reduce soil erosion to a low level are often the most profitable for the farmer. In some instances, chisel-plow tillage, which is generally most conserving of soils, is clearly more profitable than other types of tillage (Table 8-5).[38] Contouring or contouring and terracing are marginal practices for this watershed on the average, which means that they will be profitable on some fields but not on others, for a 20-year planning period. On something less than a 20-year annualized basis in this instance, it is generally not profitable for the farmer to substitute contouring or contour terracing for up-and-down cultivation, although plow-plant tillage and chisel-plow tillage would still be profitable.[39] In many instances, however, there typically are significant off-site damages associated with the highest-profit cropping system. The problem is to measure the off-site damage and develop policy that will result in highest net social income.

Measuring the Off-Site Sediment Damage Function   This measurement is made by first estimating the average soil loss from an acre of land by a rainfall factor for a region, a soil erodibility factor, slope and slope length, the crop management factor which includes rotations and tillage practices, and an erosion-control practices factor. All these measurements have been combined into what is called the Universal Soil Loss Equation.[40] This equation is as follows:

$$A = RKLSCP$$

where A is computed soil loss per acre per year
  R is the rainfall factor for the region
  K is the soil erodibility factor
  LS is the slope and slope length factor
  C is the cropping management factor
  P is the erosion control practice factor

Values for the factors in the Universal Soil Loss Equation may be developed for any situation where there are adequate data on rainfall, soils and slope, cropping systems, and conservation practices.

The next step is to place values on the damage that sediment causes as it is delivered off site by the drainage system. Another equation, such as the following, is required expressing aggregate sediment damage in dollars per year:

[38]A 12-year study conducted at the Ohio Agricultural Research and Development Center in Wooster, Ohio, found that growing corn on unplowed fields can increase yields on many types of soils with a reduction in soil erosion, increased retention of rainwater, quicker planting, and savings on tractor fuel. On poorly drained soils, the no-plow system generally led to reduced yields. See *Scientific American,* Vol. 233, No. 5, November 1975, p. 60.

[39]This is because terracing involves a considerable initial outlay involving several dollars per acre, and this expense must be amortized over several years in most instances to make it profitable. Further, contour cultivation involves some costs in terms of field convenience and loss of acreage.

[40]USDA Soil Conservation Service, *Universal Soil Loss Equation,* Agronomy Technical Note 1, Champaign, Ill.: 1970. For a more detailed description, see W. H. Wischmeier and D. D. Smith, *Predicting Rainfall Erosion Losses from Cropland East of Rocky Mountains,* USDA Agricultural Handbook 282, 1962.

Table 8-5 Net Income and Soil Loss per Acre in the Hambaugh-Martin Watershed Upland (20-Year Period Annualized Values) in West Central Illinois*

Crop rotation	Conventional tillage			Plow-plant tillage			Chisel plow tillage		
	Up-and-down cultivation	Con-touring	Contouring and terracing	Up-and-down cultivation	Con-touring	Contouring and terracing	Up-and-down cultivation	Con-touring	Contouring and terracing
Continuous corn									
Net income	$45.74	$46.32	$48.46	$51.07	$51.06	$53.13	$57.30	$56.95	$57.02
Soil loss, tons	60.53	49.10	12.03	33.63	27.28	6.68	9.62	7.64	1.87
C-Sb									
Net income	$39.61	$40.03	$41.72	$44.16	$44.29	$45.64	$49.81	$49.44	$49.32
Soil loss, tons	72.64	58.92	14.44	39.01	31.64	7.75	11.30	9.17	2.25
C-C-Sb									
Net income	$41.96	$42.35	$44.21	$47.04	$46.90	$48.47	$52.56	$52.17	$51.96
Soil loss, tons	60.53	49.10	12.03	32.38	26.19	6.42	9.42	7.64	1.87
C-C-Sb-Wx									
Net income	$35.84	$35.73	$37.03	$39.89	$39.64	$40.55	$44.87	$44.39	$43.76
Soil loss, tons	51.79	42.01	10.29	28.25	22.91	5.61	8.07	6.55	1.60
C-Sb-C-W-M									
Net income	$38.10	$38.19	$39.60	$41.83	$41.61	$42.35	$44.90	$44.57	$44.44
Soil loss, tons	29.78	24.18	5.91	16.24	13.19	3.22	8.12	6.59	1.61
C-W-M-M-M									
Net income	$38.30	$38.34	$39.08	$40.42	$40.29	$40.21	$41.63	$41.46	$41.10
Soil loss, tons	7.85	6.42	1.56	3.93	3.21	0.78	2.71	2.21	0.54
W-M-M-M									
Net income	$36.37	$36.30	$36.27	$36.81	$36.71	$36.57	$37.74	$37.33	$37.11
Soil loss, tons	2.71	2.21	0.54	2.17	1.76	0.43	1.76	1.44	0.35

*The technique of uniform end-of-the-period payments (R)—also called annuities—is used for calculating the 20-year period annualized values. The formula is

$$R = P\left[\frac{i(1 + i)^n}{(1 + i)^n - 1}\right]$$

where P is the present value of income streams over n periods and i is the interest rate. The interest rate used here is 7½ percent.
†Where C is corn, Sb is soybeans, O is oats, W is wheat, Wx is wheat with a catch crop, and M is meadow.
Source: Economic Analysis of Erosion and Sedimentation, Hambaugh-Martin Watershed, University of Illinois at Urbana-Champaign, Department of Agricultural Economics, in cooperation with State of Illinois, Institute for Environmental Quality, AERR 127.

$$D_S = A_N D_r E P_r$$

where D_S is sediment damage (dollars per year)
    A_N is the net drainage area
    D_r is the sediment delivery ratio
    E is soil loss (tons per acre)
    P_r is the cost of sediment damage per ton of sediment

In this equation, the net drainage area is defined to include a watershed or subwatershed. The sediment delivery ratio is expressed as the percentage of the total sediment that is actually delivered to the place where it causes damage, as in filling a reservoir or clogging a drainage system. The soil loss (tons per acre) is taken from the previously used Universal Soil Loss Equation. The cost of sediment damage per ton is estimated from costs of dredging; for example, for removal of a ton of sediment from a reservoir, the average cost of building a new reservoir, or dredging a new drainage system.[41]

In addition, we should also include the impact of soil erosion on flood damage and the probabilities of flooding. In many river valleys in the United States, it appears that floods—especially in the spring—have become more frequent and more damaging than they were years ago. A complete off-site damage function must take the costs of such flooding into account, even though an accurate estimate is very difficult to make.

Relating Policy to Off-Site Erosion and Sediment Damage

To develop a basis for policy goals, net farm incomes per acre should be related to the costs of off-site erosion and sediment damage arising from each crop-type situation. This relationship can be determined by subtracting these costs from net farm income per acre to yield a value called net social income. In respect to conservation, the public welfare is optimum when net social income is maximized. So the appropriate goal of public policy is to achieve such a maximum. This may be accomplished by a combination of education and payments to farmers sufficient to cause them to shift to the farming system that yields the highest net social income.

In essence, it is necessary to get the farmer to shift from the cropping system that yields the highest net farm income per acre to the system that gives the maximum net social income. In some cases where the land is very flat and runoff is normally small, no shift may be required. In other cases a significant change must occur. An example of the latter situation is shown in Table 8-6 for the Upper Embarras River Basin, which covers 896 square miles in Champaign, Douglas, Coles, Edgar, and Cumberland counties in East Central Illinois. The outlet of this watershed has been under investigation as a possible site for a flood-control reservoir to reduce the annual downstream flood and sediment damage.

---

[41]For further discussion of the procedure and functional relationships, see *Economic Analysis of Erosion and Sedimentation, op. cit.,* AERR 127, pp. 17–24. The cost of the damage was averaged at $4 per ton of sediment, not including possible costs of water-quality deterioration or flooding.

Table 8-6 Net Income and Sediment Damage per Acre per Year in the Upper Embarras River Basin Cropland, East Central Illinois

Crop rotation[a]	Tillage system[b] (1)	Conservation practice[c] (2)	Net farm income[d] (3)	Sediment damage[e] (4)	Net social income[f] (5)	Sediment damage, as percent of net income (6)
Continuous corn	Con	UD	$83.77	$3.04	$80.73	3.6
		CT	83.03	1.69	81.34	2.0
		CT/T	82.88	1.54	81.34	1.9
	PP	UD	82.70	1.63	81.07	2.0
		CT	81.98	0.90	81.08	1.1
		CT/T	81.84	0.82	81.02	1.0
	CP	UD	64.74	0.47	64.27	0.7
		CT	63.99	0.26	63.72	0.4
		CT/T	63.84	0.24	63.61	0.4
C-Sb	Con	UD	79.64	3.64	76.00	4.6
		CT	79.26	2.04	77.22	2.6
		CT/T	78.76	1.84	76.92	2.3
	PP	UD	78.59	1.93	76.66	2.6
		CT	77.86	1.07	76.79	1.4
		CT/T	77.72	0.99	76.73	1.3
	CP	UD	62.70	0.63	62.07	1.0
		CT	62.25	0.34	61.91	0.5
		CT/T	62.11	0.28	61.83	0.5
C-Sb-C-Wx	Con	UD	68.86	2.28	66.58	3.3
		CT	68.11	1.44	66.67	2.1
		CT/T	67.96	1.31	66.65	1.9
	PP	UD	67.80	1.42	66.38	2.1
		CT	67.04	0.78	66.26	1.2
		CT/T	66.91	0.70	66.21	1.0
	CP	UD	53.72	0.40	53.32	0.7
		CT	52.96	0.22	52.74	0.4
		CT/T	52.83	0.20	52.63	0.4
W-M-M-M	Con	UD	50.25	0.13	50.12	0.3
		CT	50.05	0.07	49.98	0.1
		CT/T	50.00	0.06	49.94	0.1
	PP	UD	49.96	0.11	49.85	0.2
		CT	49.77	0.06	49.71	0.1
		CT/T	49.72	0.05	49.67	0.1
	CP	UD	48.19	0.09	48.10	0.2
		CT	47.84	0.04	47.80	0.1
		CT/T	47.80	0.03	47.77	0.1

[a]Where C is corn, Sb is soybeans, W is wheat, Wx is wheat with a catch crop, and M is meadow.
[b]Con = conventional tillage, PP = plow-plant tillage, and CP = chisel-plow tillage.
[c]UD = up-and-down cultivation, CT = contouring, and CT/T = contouring and terracing.
[d]Net of non-land and costs, weighted average for the cropland.
[e]As discussed in *Economic Analysis of Erosion and Sedimentation,* University of Illinois at Urbana-Champaign, Department of Agricultural Economics, in cooperation with state of Illinois, Institute for Environmental Quality, AERR 135.
[f]Column 3 minus column 4.

A reduction in sediment damage is conceived as an increase in net social income under various farm tillage and cropping plans. Table 8-6 shows that net farm income is the highest for continuous corn ($83.77 per acre), with conventional tillage and up-and-down cultivation. But sediment damage is high for this and other corn-soybean rotations. Contouring or contouring and terracing reduces the damage substantially. The highest average net social income ($81.34 per acre) occurs with continuous corn, conventional tillage, and either contouring or contouring and terracing. The policy problem is how to achieve this type of tillage and conservation practice when such practices are beneficial or conducive to the highest net social income. Since net social income is much lower on average for the wheat and meadow rotations, we assume that they will have only limited use in this watershed. Also, in this instance, chisel-plow tillage is clearly not recommended to achieve either maximum net farm income or highest net social income.

There are a number of policy means or measures that may be conceived to affect land use, such as (1) an additional tax as a penalty for practices that cause erosion, (2) zoning against certain high-damage rotations, or (3) payments to induce the desired system and practice. They all are not equally acceptable, however. Taxing to induce a particular use may be judged unconstitutional as the taking of property without just compensation.[42] Even if it were constitutional, the problem of adjusting tax rates from year to year would be formidable, if not highly unpopular. Zoning is too crude an instrument for this purpose in most instances, even if it were politically acceptable, although government regulation of land use along streams, reservoir sites, and recreational areas may be part of a conservation plan or state land use program. Some lands may be purchased under eminent domain. A payment program is generally conceded to be the most practical and acceptable way to influence cropping plans, tillage systems, and conservation practices on farm lands.

The suggested goal for policy, that of maximizing net social income, may be achieved by paying farmers for shifting from the highest net farm income plan to one that gives the highest net social income. In Table 8-6, it may be noted that an average payment of 74 cents per acre is required under continuous corn to compensate for a shift from up-and-down cultivation to contouring ($83.77 − $83.03). An average payment of 89 cents, or 15 cents more, ($83.77 − $82.88), is required to add the optimum amount of terracing. Since there were some 525,370 acres in row crops, small grains, and pasture in this watershed,[43] this suggests that an annual appropriation of some $390,000 would be required to offset the costs of contouring and $79,000 to $80,000 more would be required to cover

---

[42]See Fred Bosselman, David Callies, and John Banta, *The Taking Issue, A Study of the Constitutional Limits of Government Authority to Regulate the Use of Privately-owned Land Without Payment of Compensation to the Owner,* Written for the Council on Environmental Quality, Washington: Government Printing Office, 1973.

[43]Illinois Conservation Needs Committee, *Soil and Water Conservation Needs Inventory,* University of Illinois at Urbana-Champaign, College of Agriculture, Cooperative Extension Service, 1970.

Table 8-7   Net Income and Sediment Damage per Acre per Year in the Polecat Creek Subwatershed Cropland

Crop rotation[a]	Tillage system[b] (1)	Conservation practice[c] (2)	Net farm income[d] (3)	Sediment damage[e] (4)	Net social income[f] (5)	Sediment damage percent of net income (6)
Continuous corn	Con	UD	$82.55	$10.20	$72.35	12.4
		CT	81.80	4.96	76.84	6.1
		CT/T	81.51	4.50	77.01	5.5
	PP	UD	81.50	3.84	77.66	4.7
		CT	80.75	2.31	78.44	2.9
		CT/T	80.46	1.88	78.58	2.3
	CP	UD	68.99	0.77	68.22	1.1
		CT	68.24	0.30	67.94	0.4
		CT/T	67.94	0.29	67.65	0.4
C-Sb	Con	UD	78.40	12.68	65.72	16.1
		CT	77.65	6.28	71.37	8.1
		CT/T	77.36	5.70	71.66	7.3
	PP	UD	77.35	5.94	71.41	7.7
		CT	76.60	2.76	73.84	3.6
		CT/T	76.31	2.56	73.75	3.4
	CP	UD	66.57	1.28	65.29	1.9
		CT	65.82	0.56	65.26	0.9
		CT/T	65.53	0.31	65.22	0.5
C-Sb-C-Wx	Con	UD	67.87	8.55	59.32	12.6
		CT	67.12	4.08	63.04	6.1
		CT/T	66.83	3.63	63.20	5.4
	PP	UD	66.82	3.88	62.94	5.8
		CT	66.07	1.77	64.30	2.7
		CT/T	65.78	1.44	64.34	2.2
	CP	UD	57.14	0.65	56.49	1.1
		CT	56.39	0.31	56.08	0.5
		CT/T	56.11	0.28	55.83	0.5
W-M-M-M	Con	UD	47.58	0.13	47.45	0.3
		CT	47.39	0.06	47.33	0.1
		CT/T	47.32	0.05	47.27	0.1
	PP	UD	47.32	0.12	47.20	0.3
		CT	47.13	0.05	47.08	0.1
		CT/T	47.06	0.04	47.02	0.1
	CP	UD	46.16	0.08	46.08	0.2
		CT	45.98	0.04	45.94	0.1
		CT/T	45.91	0.03	45.88	0.1

[a]Where C is corn, Sb is soybeans, Wx is wheat with a catch crop, W is wheat, and M is meadow.
[b]Con is conventional tillage, PP is plow-plant tillage, and CP is chisel-plow tillage.
[c]UD is up-and-down cultivation, CT is contouring, and CT/T is contouring and terracing.
[d]Net of non-land costs, weighted average for the cropland.
[e]As discussed in *Economic Analysis of Erosion and Sedimentation*, University of Illinois at Urbana-Champaign, Department of Agricultural Economics, in cooperation with State of Illinois, Institute for Environmental Quality, AERP 135.
[f]Column 3 minus column 4.

terracing, in addition to administration and technical assistance from the SCS. The cost is at least 10 times what has been appropriated for the SCS program in this watershed.

The importance of competent technical assistance, with cost-sharing payments based on approved farm plans, can scarcely be overemphasized, because the costs and returns on conservation practices vary widely. In the Polecat Creek subwatershed, which has about 15,000 acres in crops and pasture (Table 8-7), an average payment of $2.09 per acre ($82.55 − $80.46) will increase net social income by $6.23 per acre ($78.58 − $72.35). On some lands, even heavier expenditures on terracing, or subsidizing cover crops or small grains, would improve net social income. Each farm plan must be studied and approved in detail.

A Policy Conclusion

The appropriate guide for allocation of cost-sharing payments for conservation is equalization of net returns from investment expressed in terms of net social income. To define net social income more broadly, or rather to define it more accurately, estimates of marginal returns from conservation investments must include gains from reducing downstream flooding, improvements in water quality, and the like. Even without these additional considerations, the potential return from a more comprehensive conservation policy is very high in terms of net social income—so high as to suggest that the nation has greatly underinvested in this area of policy.

To optimize net social income through conservation policy, it is necessary to establish more precise goals. More work must be done to define the patterns of net social income in the various farm-crop situations on a watershed by watershed basis, so that the optimum farm systems can be identified.

To establish program levels and means, the costs of shifting from the highest net farm income situation to one that maximizes net social income must be identified. The actual costs are needed to tell how much can be accomplished by education and demonstration in comparison with other measures, such as zoning, tax, or subsidy.

The national appropriation for conservation must include a running inventory of the conservation situation to determine (1) the amount and location of land that is being depleted by soil erosion, (2) the land that has had treatment and its effectiveness, (3) the lands that will respond to further conservation measures, and (4) the costs of off-site damage and possible gains in reduction of this damage.

To implement conservation policy, activities of such agencies as the SCS, land grant colleges, the Bureau of Land Management, and the Army Corps of Engineers will require further definition and coordination.

Finally, to establish appropriate levels of policy constraints, conservation programs must be subjected to more independent study and public audit in the future than they have received in the past. As a general rule, most of this study and audit should be done by agencies that have no direct interest in spending funds for conservation. Thus, while there is a case for more coordination among agencies to implement programs, there also is a case for more rigorous and independent study of costs and benefits; that is the constraint to apply. Since the costs of erosion and sedimentation damage differ widely among watersheds as well as among farms and fields within a watershed, there is no substitute for more precise economic analysis as a basis for conservation programs. Although the argument for a much larger budget for conservation of agricultural lands appears to be strong, the efficient allocation of such a budget requires many discriminating and detailed decisions. For efficient performance, they must be based on accurate, detailed knowledge coordinated with other policies concerning land.

COORDINATING OTHER POLICIES RELATED TO LAND

Broadly speaking, the rising public concern over land and land-related policies is prompted by a belief that the nation is not making the best use of its land resources, either in terms of conservation or long-term best land use. The individual states and local governments are proving themselves inadequate to develop and implement the necessary policies. In addition to the problems in conservation, important shifts in land use are projected for the future. In the years from 1950 to 1970, urban areas accommodated an increase of 53 million people by taking 13.5 million acres of rural land, of which some 35 percent, or 4.7 million acres, were previously cropped.[44] This area was equivalent to about 1 percent of the 1950 cropland base, including cropland pasture. Projecting current trends, in the 30 years from 1970 to 2000 some 35 to 40 million acres of land will be converted to urban use, of which some 6 million acres might have been cropped in 1970. Highways, high-voltage transmission lines, and other rights-of-way will use an additional few million acres, as will plans for recreational areas, parks, and other uses. All together, the growth of cities and other nonagricultural uses is consuming about 2.7 million acres a year, while some 1.3 million acres are developed each year by irrigation, land clearing and drainage, leveling, and other means. The net loss to agriculture is estimated by the USDA, ERS at about 1.4 million acres a year, the impact of which is felt both locally and nationally.

As set against this resource demand, land use control traditionally has been a local experience, with zoning as the principal means or implement for carrying out policy. In most rural areas, zoning does not exist. But it has not had a trouble-free history in metropolitan areas, where it has created fragmented decision making and border conflicts. Fragmented decision making is also a problem in most states, with towns, cities, and counties encountering conflicts of interest in planning and funding changes in land use. Regional planning has brought some coordination of efforts of local governments in some states, but

[44]*Perspectives on Prime Lands,* Background papers for Seminar on the Retention of Prime Lands, July 16–17, 1975, sponsored by the U.S. Department of Agriculture Committee on Land Use (mimeographed). See especially Orville Krause and Dwight Hair, "Trends in Land Use and Competition for Land to Produce Food and Fiber," pp. 1–26.

generally the authority for implementing plans has not kept pace with the abilities of people and agencies to make them. Often, land use decisions at the state level are divided among several departments, each somewhat limited in its particular concern. A department of conservation may work at cross-purposes with a department of local government, for example; and a department of commerce may have another concern. Finally, individual states often work at cross-purposes with one another in matters of flood control, pollution abatement, and other functions. A coordinated national land use policy therefore requires action by the federal government.

A National Land Use Program

Development of a national land use program began in January 1970, when, in the 91st Congress, Senator Henry M. Jackson, Democrat from the state of Washington and chairman of the Committee on Interior and Insular Affairs, introduced a bill for national land use planning legislation (S. 3354). In December, after four days of hearings and many conferences, the committee reported the bill to the Senate. Since no floor action was taken, Senator Jackson introduced the proposal again early in 1971. The administration also proposed a similar measure which was featured in the President's environmental messages to the Congress in both 1971 and 1972. Ten days of hearings were held on the bill, then called the Land Use Policy and Planning Assistance Act, four in the Interior Committee and three each in Commerce and Banking, Housing and Urban Affairs. After numerous executive sessions and consultations with the National Governors' Conference, the National League of Cities and the United States Conference of Mayors, representatives of industry groups, and environmental citizen groups, the Interior Committee again reported the bill to the Senate. On September 19, 1972, after accepting several amendments, the Senate passed the bill (S. 632) by a vote of 60 to 18. Senator Jackson and others had unsuccessfully opposed two amendments striking certain sanctions from the bill and reducing the funding by two-thirds. But the House failed to act.

The bill (S. 268) was introduced again early in the 93d Congress and on February 6, 1973, the Interior Committee began a new set of hearings which lasted for six days.[45] The bill, virtually the same one that had passed the year before, again passed the Senate by a wide margin; but its companion bill (H.R. 10294) was defeated in the House in June 1974 by a few votes. It had appeared headed for passage in the House until President Nixon, in a move related to the threat of impeachment, announced his opposition to the bill. This action, combined with opposition from special interests throughout the country that felt threatened by the bill, were sufficient to prevent its adoption. The bill failed in spite of the fact that it had received the strong and often urgent support of such diverse groups as the National Governors' Conference (and nearly 30 individual

---

[45]See *Land Use Policy and Planning Assistance Act,* Hearings before the Committee on Interior and Insular Affairs, U.S. Senate, 93d Cong., 1st Sess., Feb. 6, 7, 26, 27, and April 2, 3, 1973, parts 1 and 2.

governors), the National Association of Counties, the League of Cities, and the United States Conference of Mayors, all the major environmental organizations, various water resources associations, the National Association of Manufacturers, and the Federation of Rocky Mountain States, Inc. The last-named organization particularly wished to strengthen the coordination of policy on public lands and in interstate or regional activities. The bill was also supported by such prestigious and varied publications as *Business Week, The New York Times, The Wall Street Journal,* both the *Washington Post* and the *Star,* the *Boston Globe,* the *St. Louis Post Dispatch,* the *Christian Science Monitor,* and the *Minneapolis Star.* The need for land use legislation also was recognized, as we noted in Chapter 5, by the National Commission on Food Marketing as well as the National Advisory Commission on Food and Fiber. It was also supported by such other groups as the Advisory Commission on Intergovernmental Relations.

The Land Use Policy and Planning Assistance Act of 1973 was designed to promote the general welfare, as a continuous responsibility of the federal government, by assisting states and local governments in land use planning, management, and development, and by providing grants for these purposes. The basic policy concept or goal was that intelligent land use planning and management can be coordinated in a national policy and should be a singularly important process for preserving and enhancing the environment, encouraging beneficial economic development, and maintaining conditions capable of improving the quality of life.

A new Office of Land Use Policy Administration was to be established in the Department of the Interior as the leading implementing agency to conduct a wide range of studies on land use, to administer a grant-in-aid program to the states and local governments, and to coordinate a range of assistance activities. There would be a new National Advisory Board on Land Use Policy drawn from related federal departments and agencies, state and local governments, and other public entities having land use planning and management responsibilities. To comply with grant-eligibility requirements, both the Senate and the House bills required the creation of a state land use planning agency and a state intergovernmental advisory council. The state planning agency would have authority and responsibility for the development of the state land use planning program. The state advisory council would be composed of elected officials of general-purpose local governments to participate in the development of the state planning program.

Both bills allowed exceptions for purely local and small-scale land use planning decisions. However, criteria must be provided for identifying and controlling certain land use planning activities. These were: (1) large-scale development (those private developments judged by the state, because of their magnitude or the magnitude of their environmental effect, to be likely to present issues of more than local significance); (2) land use proposals of regional benefit; (3) areas of critical environmental concern (areas where uncontrolled or incompatible development could result in environmental and other damage of more than local significance as judged by the state, or by the Secretary of Interior where the impact was considered to be of more than statewide concern); and (4) areas which are or may be impacted by key facilities (such as airports, major recreational lands, and facilities deemed by the state to tend to induce development of more than local impact).

The specific thrust of the grant assistance was twofold: (1) to subsidize development of a land use program, and (2) to financially support the operation of such a program, once developed and in operation. The Senate bill provided that during the first three years grants could be obtained for the development of a state land use planning process, to include data collection, technical assistance, training programs for local governments, and the establishment of criteria for identifying land use activities covered by the legislation. During the next two years, grants might be obtained for (1) the operation of a land use planning process, and (2) further development of a planning program in the areas covered by the legislation. After the end of the fifth year, grants could be obtained only by operation of a system that fully met the federal requirements of a land use planning process and program. Although the House bill differed in some details, the central thrust was the same. Both bills would have authorized $100 million annually for eight years following enactment.

A broader trend in national policymaking and a new lesson were signaled in February 1975, when Congressman Morris K. Udall, Democrat from Arizona, introduced a new bill (H.R. 3510). This bill, cited as the Land Use and Resource Conservation Act of 1975, authorized federal grants of $500 million to states over six years, to provide financial incentives and policy direction for development of state land use programs, and to increase coordination of federal agencies and states. This bill, with some provisions similar to the National Coastal Zone Management Act of 1972 (U.S. Code, section 1451 et seq.), would provide grants for development of state land use programs within three years and grants for three more years for implementation, once a program was approved by the Secretary of the Interior. It provided for assessments and regulations of developments of regional impact, large-scale subdivisions, and key facilities tending to induce growth. It established procedures to identify, designate, and regulate areas of critical environmental concern. It offered support for development of state policies to encourage energy conservation through efficient land use patterns, to formulate policies for commercial needs, housing, transportation, recreation, and open space. One section, possibly crucial for agriculture's political support, offered assistance for formulation of state policies for food and fiber production but distinguished lands used for this purpose from other critical lands.

The Role of the States

Although hundreds of billions—perhaps trillions—of dollars may have been lost by the failure of the federal government for many years to adopt a meaningful program supportive of comprehensive land use plans and development, it is fundamental in policy to recognize that the federal role is essentially supportive and contributory to the powers of the states. While the federal government may appropriate money for developmental plans and programs, it is the states that have the residual powers for public regulation of private land use and for direct administration of lands by a government agency. The federal government, lacking the statutory powers of the states, has used subsidies extensively to influence the use of land under private ownership, as in acreage control, soil conservation, and forest management programs. Education and technical services have been provided. In addition, the federal government has withheld large acreages from private ownership and has repurchased limited acreages of low-productivity lands, mainly in the Great Plains and Western states, in order to encourage conservation and to control their use more effectively. But, in terms of statutory powers to promote, influence, or regulate the development of private lands, the federal government must defer to the states.

State Planning and Zoning   The residual powers of state governments to promote public health, safety, and morals, and the general welfare include the powers to establish land use plans and controls, including the zoning of lands for use and development. The constitutional requirement is that (1) the objectives of the regulation must promote the general welfare, (2) the methods used must have a substantial relation to the ends or objectives to be sought, and (3) the regulation must not be arbitrary, unreasonable, or oppressive.[46]

Zoning ordinances adopted by local governments under state law generally describe the areas or districts to be zoned, the regulations applied to each, and the means of enforcing them. The districts are normally defined on maps available in local government offices. Certain land uses listed as nonconforming are either regulated and controlled, or forbidden entirely, under the theory that, by guiding or controlling economic development on private lands, the government will help to prevent the wastefulness of urban sprawl, pollution of the environment, and unnecessary or undesirable conflicts in land use.

Although zoning ordinances have long been used to control development of towns and cities, the zoning of rural lands has lagged far behind. Zoning was first tried in rural areas in Wisconsin in 1929 to prevent and control settlement of rural lands in the northern cut-over regions of the state. The success of zoning in these submarginal lands led to more general adoption of zoning laws, and, in recent years, almost all states have enacted legislation permitting local government units to zone rural lands. These ordinances are designed to prevent construction of undesirable buildings, mobile-home parks, and undesirable suburban developments, especially near lakes, streams, and other scenic areas.

In respect to agriculture, the trend has not been to use zoning to regulate the use of land for crops, but to adopt more broadly based laws for regulation and control of livestock enterprises, and for prevention of pollution through regulations concerning livestock waste and effluent, the use of farm chemicals, and the like. In Illinois, for example, the Environmental Protection Act (Public Act 76-2429), adopted in 1970, established (1) the Illinois Environmental Protection

---

[46]*State Legislation for Better Land Use,* Interbureau Committee Report, Washington: U.S. Department of Agriculture, April 1941, pp. xii–xv.

Agency, with a wide range of powers to study, investigate, promulgate regulations, contract, etcetera; (2) the Pollution Control Board, to define and implement standards established by the agency, to hold hearings, service petitions of variance, impose penalties, and so on; and (3) the Illinois Institute for Environmental Quality, to investigate practical problems, implement studies and programs relating to the technology and administration of environmental protection, to assemble data, recommend changes and developments of standards, and cooperate with other research and educational agencies.

The trend in the states has been to use the growing concerns for maintenance and improvement of the quality of the environment to set broad goals for protection of the environment and to establish agencies with both broad and specific powers to implement the policy. But, in many of the states, agricultural organizations have viewed this trend as an unnecessary and undesirable infringement on the freedom to farm. Thus, they have supported legislation such as that permitting farmers to join together to form special agricultural areas to keep agricultural land from being encroached upon; and that assessing agricultural land for tax purposes according to its current use in farming rather than its potential market value for development. The associations have also advocated laws limiting special assessments for urban-related purposes, restricting the jurisdiction of local governments to authorize or zone agricultural land for nonagricultural use, and strengthening the powers of private parties to challenge the right of eminent domain, and so on.

Preferential Taxation of Agricultural Lands In the mid 1970s, some 35 states had implemented programs for the preferential taxation of agricultural lands, and some 18 states had provisions for deferring part of the tax on land that was kept in farming.[47] A major goal in this legislation was to counteract the rising burden of taxes on farm real estate, which in aggregate had risen from an annual average of $405.3 million in 1940–45, to $811 million in 1950–54, to $1,671.3 million in 1960–65, and to $2,493.9 million in 1970. To this tax on farmland and improvements was added the aggregate tax on farmers' personal property of $66 million in 1940–45, $210.3 million in 1950–54, $307.8 million in 1960–65, and $445.8 million in 1970.[48]

Although farm real estate taxes as a percentage of net income from farming had not increased between the late 1950s and the mid 1970s, and taxes per $100 of market value had been steady since the early 1940s, the average property tax per acre of farmland had climbed steadily to more than six times as high in the mid 1970s as in the early 1940s. Expressed as a percentage of net income, in most

[47]David E. Hansen and S. J. Schwartz, "Landowners' Behavior at the Rural-Urban Fringe in Response to Preferential Property Taxation," *Land Economics,* Vol. 4, November 1975, pp. 341–354. See also Thomas I. Hady and Ann Gordon Sibold, *State Programs for the Differential Assessment of Farm and Open-Space Land,* U.S. Department of Agriculture, Economic Research Service, Agricultural Economic Report 256, 1974.

[48]Compiled from data in *Agricultural Finance Review,* Vol. 32, Supp., U.S. Department of Agriculture, Economic Research Service, January 1972; *Statistical Bulletin* No. 441, *ibid.,* July 1969; *Farm Income Situation,* FIS-218, *ibid.,* July 1971.

states property taxes paid by farmers were several times higher than those paid by nonfarmers. Although the property tax might be capitalized into the value of farm property,[49] being in this sense a burdenless tax, the increases in property taxes had to be paid out of net rent; and a projection of the 35-year trend from 1940 to 1975 had alarming implications for agriculture. If this trend were to be projected very far into the future, it would result in a restriction of farm output and higher prices for food. Up to 1970, some 4 or 5 times the quantity of cropland taken for urban uses was being shifted to lower-intensity agricultural or forestry uses or was idled because cropping it had become uneconomic.[50]

Preferential taxation or use-value assessment of agricultural land for purposes of tax relief and to prevent good farmland from being forced into other uses has had only limited effect on land use.[51] Use-value assessment was ineffective in preventing the more wasteful losses from urban sprawl. Many farmers have not made application to achieve what small benefits were obtainable from use-value assessment.[52] Although use-value assessment may encourage some farmers to stay in farming for a while, it does not appear to be capable of substantially altering either the timing or the pattern of development. To achieve the goals of more efficient use of land resources in economic development and to reduce the waste of urban sprawl, more comprehensive land use planning and more specific controls—such as large-area zoning—are required. These may do little, however, to control the growth of the burden of farm property taxes.

State and Federal Alternatives to Property Tax Increases

To significantly reduce or even contain the property tax burden on agriculture while still achieving an adequate level of funding for local government and elementary and secondary education, it is necessary to shift a larger portion of the total cost to state and federal tax sources. The policy issue has been highlighted not only by the alarming trends in farm property taxes but by court decisions based on constitutional arguments of equal protection and equal opportunity.

The first comprehensive court review of the issue was presented in a span of 18 months. On August 30, 1971, the California Supreme Court[53] ruled that the local property tax school funding scheme "invidiously discriminates against the poor because it makes the quality of a child's education a function of the wealth of his parents and neighbors." Although uniform education expenditures were not mandated by the California constitution, the court concluded "that the right

---

[49]See E. C. Pasour, Jr., "Capitalization of Real Property Taxes Levied on Farm Real Estate," *American Journal of Agricultural Economics,* Vol. 57, No. 4, November 1975, pp. 539–548.

[50]Robert C. Otte, "Farming in the City's Shadow: Urbanization of Land and Changes in Farm Output in Standard Metropolitan Statistical Areas, 1960–70," *Agriculture, Rural Development, and the Use of Land,* U.S. Senate, Subcommittee on Rural Development of the Committee in Agriculture and Forestry, 1974, p. 111.

[51]Hansen and Schwartz, *op. cit.,* p. 253.

[52]Franklin J. Reiss, "Taxation-Land Use Relationships," *Illinois Agricultural Economics,* University of Illinois at Urbana-Champaign, Department of Agricultural Economics, Vol. 15, No. 1, January 1975, pp. 1–7.

[53]*Serrano v. Priest,* cited in *The United States Law Week,* Vol. 40, Sept. 14, 1971, p. 2128.

to an education in our public schools is a fundamental interest which cannot be conditioned on wealth . . . that such a system cannot withstand constitutional challenge and must fall before the equal protection clause [of the Fourteenth Amendment, hence is unconstitutional.]"

The California decision was followed with similar rulings by United States district courts in Minnesota[54] and Texas,[55] and the Michigan Supreme Court.[56] Finally, the U.S. Supreme Court, in a 5 to 4 ruling on March 21, 1973, reversed the Texas decision, holding that education "is not among the rights afforded explicit protection under our federal Constitution."[57] But Justice Lewis F. Powell, Jr., writing for the majority, noted: "The need is apparent for reform in tax systems which may well have relied too long and too heavily on the local property tax. . . ." A minority dissenting opinion, written by Justice Thurgood Marshall, regarded the majority view "as a retreat from our historic commitment to equality of educational opportunity and as unsupportable acquiescence in a system which deprives children in their earliest years of the chance to reach their full potential as citizens."

The policy issue of equal funding of school systems can be related to school tax options affecting agriculture. In Illinois it has been found that the property tax for schools, which absorbs 65 percent of the total property tax receipts outside of Cook County, could be displaced by increased revenues from either state or federal income taxes with a substantial net gain to agriculture, with the greatest relative gains accruing to small and medium-sized family farms.[58] School funding would be made uniform over the state, as well as more equal between farm and nonfarm taxpayers in similar income situations. In Illinois, at least this would do much toward creating a uniform tax burden over the state and equalizing the funding of school districts. Also, it would help ease the financial problems of rural development and help to promote more general development based on economic criteria.[59]

A Policy Conclusion

To have a coordinated land use and development policy that will be most beneficial to agricultural efficiency and growth in the food supply, the residual powers of the state must be supplemented by federal appropriations and help in planning and development. The states, on the other hand, cannot best solve their more difficult problems of efficient land use by laws and regulations that are

[54]*Van Dusartz v. Hatfield,* cited in *The United States Law Week,* Vol. 40, Oct. 26, 1971, p. 2228.

[55]*Rodriguez v. San Antonio Independent School District,* 337 F. Supp. 280 (D.C. Tex. 1971).

[56]*Milliken v. Green,* Michigan Supreme Court, *The United States Law Week,* Vol. 41, Jan. 9, 1973, p. 2348.

[57]*San Antonio Independent School District v. Rodriguez, The United States Law Week,* Vol. 41, March 20, 1973, p. 4407.

[58]H. G. Halcrow, Folke Dovring, Arthur Eith, F. J. Reiss, J. T. Scott, Jr., W. D. Seitz, and R. G. F. Spitze, *School Tax Options Affecting Illinois Agriculture,* University of Illinois at Urbana-Champaign, College of Agriculture Agricultural Experiment Station, Bulletin 744, April 1973, especially pp. 8–10.

[59]See H. G. Halcrow, "Tax Changes for Rural Development," *Illinois Research,* University of Illinois Agricultural Experiment Station, Vol. 16, No. 4, Fall 1974.

essentially preferential in nature. The total land resource must be viewed in a comprehensive plan of development and environmental protection of which agriculture is an important part. The growth in tax burden imposed on farm land by the traditional property tax system must be contained or reversed by use of alternative tax sources to best promote agricultural prosperity in the future.

QUESTIONS FOR DISCUSSION

1 What were the goals in land distribution policy (a) in the colonial era, (b) from independence to passage of the Homestead Act, and (c) in the homestead era? What were some of the results of the Homestead Acts in terms of size of farm, land ownership, and tenure?

2 Discuss the current land problems resulting from early irrigation and reclamation policy, including the Desert Land Act of 1877, the Carey Act of 1894, the Reclamation Act of 1902, and the Omnibus Adjustment Act of 1926. Distinguish between problems of production efficiency and producer or farm worker equity; between farm producer problems and community problems. What would be some of the effects of strict enforcement of the 160-acre limitation on the sale of federal irrigation water?

3 What were the accomplishments of the first conservation era from 1891 to 1921? What were some of the conflicts in establishing policy goals? Appraise the effectiveness of the actions that were taken.

4 Discuss the shift in economic conditions for agriculture that occurred in the 1920s. How did it affect land policy? In respect to settlement? Conservation? Land use?

5 What were the major features of the land policies of the Roosevelt New Deal? The goals of the Soil Conservation Service? What goals were to be served by the purchase of submarginal lands? Distinguish between production and conservation goals.

6 Were the original goals of the AAA and the SCS complementary or conflicting? What were the goals of the Taylor Grazing Act, the Omnibus Flood Control Act of 1936, and the BAE program of land use planning? What conflicts emerged, and how were they settled? Are such conflicts continuing? What was the land grant college plan for conducting soil conservation? In your opinion, would this be an improvement? Discuss.

7 Define soil conservation in economic terms as contrasted with physical or chemical terms. Discuss the concept of fund and flow. What is an optimum conservation policy for the farmer? What various factors will the farmer need to estimate or measure in order to carry out an optimum policy? Conceptually speaking, how does the policy that is optimum for society differ from the one that is optimum for the farmer? Discuss the factors that must be taken into account in order to measure the social optimum.

8 How have the various agricultural adjustment acts linked conservation and production adjustment? Be specific. Comment and appraise or criticize in terms of (a) effects on production adjustment, (b) accomplishments in conservation, and (c) the effects on individual farm income and aggregate farm income. In what ways are conservation payments complementary to those for production adjustment? How are they conflicting? Does it make a difference if we count them as fund or flow?

9 Discuss or explain the methodology for developing (a) an off-site sediment damage function, and (b) estimates of net social income. Conceptually, what policy means

and constraints are available for achieving net social income? Comment on their relative efficiency and acceptability to farmers. Discuss the guides that may be used for cost-sharing payments. Summarize the steps that are necessary to develop conservation policy that is socially optimum.

10 Trace the history of efforts to develop a national land use program. Where do the political support and the political opposition originate? What would be the allocation of powers between states and the federal government? How would this allocation compare with the historical division of power for social control of land use?

Congressman Sam Steiger (Republican from Arizona), speaking before the annual AFBF meeting in January 1975, commented that the House had "wisely defeated" the federal land use bill. He argued that property owners were not adequately protected, under the just compensation provisions of the Bill of Rights, against the new concept of zoning to create "areas of environmental concern," in which commercial activities could be restricted. Discuss the implications for agriculture and possible compensation safeguards.

11 Discuss the general problems inherent in taxation of agricultural lands. What do tax theorists mean whan they say that the property tax is a "burdenless" tax? Do farmers consider it burdenless? Comment on the opposition of farmers to property tax increases. What alternatives are there? What would be their effects on agriculture?

REFERENCES

Bosselman, Fred P., and David Callies, *The Quiet Revolution in Land-Use Control,* Washington: Government Printing Office, 1972.

Calef, Wesley, *Private Grazing and Public Lands, Studies of the Local Management of the Taylor Grazing Act,* Chicago: The University of Chicago Press, 1960.

Clawson, Marion, *The Land System of the United States,* Lincoln: University of Nebraska Press, 1968.

Foss, Phillip O., *Politics and Grass, The Administration of Grazing on the Public Domain,* Seattle: University of Washington Press, 1960.

Hardin, Charles M., *The Politics of Agriculture, Soil Conservation and the Struggle for Power in Rural America,* Glencoe, Ill.: The Free Press, 1952.

Hibbard, Benjamin H., *A History of Public Land Policies,* New York: The Macmillan Press Company, 1924.

Morgan, Robert J., *Governing Soil Conservation: Thirty Years of the New Decentralization,* Baltimore: The Johns Hopkins Press, published for Resources for the Future, Inc., 1965.

Perspectives on Prime Lands, Background papers for Seminar on Retention of Prime Lands, Washington: U.S. Department of Agriculture, Committee on Land Use, 1975.

Robbins, Roy M., *Our Landed Heritage,* Princeton, N.J.: The Princeton University Press, 1942.

Salter, Leonard A., Jr., *A Critical Review of Research in Land Economics,* Minneapolis: The University of Minnesota Press, 1948.

U.S. Congress, *Agriculture, Rural Development, and the Use of Land,* Hearings, Subcommittee on Rural Development of the Committee on Agriculture and Forestry, 1974.

Capital and Credit Policy

I'm fed up with this endless How and When;
Since there's no money, let's make it Then.

Goethe
Faust, Part II

How does inflation affect the farm-food system, and can it be controlled in ways that are favorable to the system? How do the national farm credit programs affect farm-food production, economic structure, and income? What alternatives in credit, taxation, insurance, and similar factors will yield answers consistent with the goals inherent in the questions: What food shall be produced, how, and for whom? This chapter brings these questions and some of the answers together under the heading of capital and credit policy.

EFFECTS OF BUSINESS CYCLES AND INFLATION

The farm-food system is uniquely affected by business cycles and inflation because it does not increase or decrease output during the course of the cycle as much as most other industries. It tends to stay in full production. This is good for consumers; but it causes wide fluctuations in farm and food prices, thus bringing severe strain into the farm-food system, especially in the farm sector and the farm service industries. What policy can be followed to help in this situation is of fundamental interest in food policy for America.

The Effects of Inflation

Although the entire food system has been profoundly affected by inflation, the most severe effects appear to have fallen on the farm sector. During World War II the farm economy, which had suffered under a weak demand all during the Great Depression, benefited from increased food demand. The strong upward trends in farm and food prices were led by war-inflated earnings in the industrial sector and by additional transfers of purchasing power to food as money was diverted through price controls and restrictions on production of nonfood items. The farmers' windfall gains were large indeed, and farmers came out of the war in the strongest financial position ever attained. USDA data show that farmers' equities increased from $43.8 billion in 1940 to $90.0 billion in 1946. Between 1940 and 1946, demand deposits of country banks increased 3 to 4 times. Land prices rose. By 1946 the value of farm land was about double what it had been in 1940, while farm real estate debt fell to $7.8 billion in 1946 from $10 billion in 1940.

During this time and soon after, however, other changes occurred that were less favorable to farmers. Aggregate farm production expense was $6.5 billion in 1940, $12.6 billion in 1945, and $19.1 billion in 1950. The only major cost that did not increase was the annual outlay for farm mortgage interest. Aggregate farm operators' net income, estimated in constant 1945 dollars, reached a peak of $13.4 billion in 1946, but fell to $8.5 billion in 1950.

In the inflation of 1965 to 1971, although aggregate receipts from farm marketings rose from $39.4 billion to $52.9 billion, the net income from farming fell from $5.7 billion to $5.1 billion. Increases in government payments from $2.5 billion in 1965 to $3.1 billion in 1971, increases in nonmoney and other income from $3.7 billion to $4.6 billion, and a continued decline in the total farm population helped to raise average farm income from 67.4 percent of nonfarm income in 1965 to 72.4 percent in 1971. Thereafter, the unusual demand effects of 1972–76 submerged the impact of inflation on farm income.

The inflationary trend starting about 1965 or 1966, associated initially with federal deficits created to finance the Vietnam war, did not have a beneficial effect on agriculture. Although there was some growth in farmers' equities as land values continued to rise, most if not all of the real gains were wiped out by inflation. In the fall of 1970 the parity ratio was the lowest it had been since the early 1930s. The full-employment economy of the late 1960s, although contributing to a strong demand for food in the domestic market, did not bring a satisfactory level of prosperity to farmers.

The inflationary trends in farm and food prices beginning in 1972 were not solely the result of high-level business activity. Although this helped, farm prices were importantly affected by the shift in trade and by the demand-creating effects of other policies.

In essence, the strong effects of inflation and the ups and downs of the business cycle emphasize the importance, in making food policy for America, of being discriminating and judicious in the choices of policy means and implements to control inflation and influence the cycle. Policy is concerned with effects of various policy constraints placed on the government in taxing and spending, in management of prices and wages, and in regulating the money supply.

Taxonomy of the Business Cycle

For many years it was customary to classify the business cycle into four major phases of recession, depression, recovery, and prosperity.[1] In the 30 years following World War II, however, an inflationary trend overlay the cycle, making the traditional classification less than adequately descriptive. Consequently, suggestions were made for an alternate descriptive form or a new taxonomy, involving recession, recovery, demand-pull inflation, and stagflation, defined as follows:[2]

1 *Recession:* A period of some duration in which total aggregate activity actually declines from previous peaks and is widely diffused throughout the economy.
2 *Recovery:* Early expansion out of a recession in which unemployment is declining, prices are relatively stable, productivity is rising, and total output is expanding.
3 *Demand-pull inflation:* Equated with the classic inflationary situation in which "too much money chases too few goods." Production is forced up to capacity constraints, prices are rising rapidly, rates of improvement in productivity are declining, etcetera.
4 *Stagflation:* The economy stagnates at a high level of production, or fails to achieve further growth, even though prices and wages continue to rise at a relatively high rate. The slack among the unemployed is not taken up, even though the government may deliberately run a substantial deficit which is intended to stimulate business recovery.

According to this taxonomy, the business cycle can be dated as in Table 9-1.

Policies Related to Business-Cycle Taxonomy

Since the beginning of the Roosevelt New Deal in 1933 and the Keynesian revolution of the late 1930s,[3] it has been fashionable among economists to assume that a policy to hasten recovery from business recession or depression will contain important elements of monetary or credit expansion. Alternatively,

[1]For a list of references, see John R. Meyer and Daniel H. Weinberg, "On the Classification of Economic Fluctuations," *Explorations in Economic Research, Occasional Papers of the National Bureau of Economic Research,* Vol. 2, No. 2, Spring 1975, pp. 167–202.
[2]*Ibid.,* p. 172.
[3]John Maynard Keynes, *The General Theory of Employment, Interest and Money,* London: Macmillan & Co., Ltd., 1936.

Table 9-1 Classification of U.S. Business Cycles into a Four-Stage Scheme, February 1947–September 1973

Starting dates for			
Recession	Recovery	Demand-pull	Stagflation
?	?	?	May 1948
December 1948	November 1949	July 1950	January 1951
November 1953	August 1954	March 1955	—
September 1957	May 1958	—	—
June 1960	February 1961	May 1965	December 1967
January 1970	December 1970	January 1973	?

Source: John R. Meyer and Daniel H. Weinberg, "On the Classification of Economic Fluctuations," *Explorations in Economic Research, Occasional Papers of the National Bureau of Economic Research,* Vol. 2, No. 2, Spring 1975, p. 177.

recovery can be accomplished by printing money or by issuing federal bonds to cover a deficit, or by lowering the cost of credit through actions of the Federal Reserve. The federal deficit can be created by cutting taxes or by increasing spending, or both; and the force of the recovery may be associated with the vigor and consistency with which these policies are pursued.

But it is also recognized that a deficit or a monetary expansion under conditions of full employment will "overfuel" or "overheat" the economy, in which event the recovery phase of the cycle may shift into demand-pull, as apparently began to occur in May 1965, for example (Table 9-1). Also, a deficit or monetary expansion can feed inflation in the stagflation stage with high levels of unemployment, unless it is possible, through other avenues of policy, to get expansion in basic industry, such as steel making, coal production, and construction, to increase the aggregate supply of goods and services relative to money.

Government action—or rather inaction—initiated the 12-year inflation of 1965–76. In the calender year 1966, the federal budget was in balance, according to the National Income Accounts pioneered by the National Bureau of Economic Research. But military expenses were projected to increase rapidly, and this increase was expected to create excess demand in the civilian economy, unless this nonmilitary demand was restrained. In January 1967, President Johnson recommended a 6 percent surtax, to be effective by mid–1967, to at least partially offset these expenses. But Congress failed to act. The President repeated the request in the summer of 1967, raising it to 10 percent; but again Congress did not act. Again in January 1968, the President repeated the same request; but the new tax was not voted until mid 1968, more than three years after the demand-pull stage had been entered and almost six months after stagflation had begun. Although the wholesale price index was up only about 3 percent by mid 1968 from the early 1967 level, wage settlements announced in 1968 and industrial price increases programmed in 1968 and 1969 clearly marked the existence of stagflation.

President Nixon, on taking office in January 1969, announced that he would rely on the free market to determine prices and wages. For his administration, he rejected direct price controls and wage guidelines and declared that inflation would be controlled by the classic monetary and fiscal measures. The difficulty was that the federal budget was already running a surplus, and continued to do so throughout 1969. The President, to keep a campaign promise, recommended the removal of the surtax, thus leaving credit restraint as the only remaining policy means for control of inflation. Under these circumstances, however, credit restraint could have no other effect than to slow down the growth of industry and lead to more acute stagnation with rising levels of unemployment.[4]

Gardiner C. Means has called the Nixon approach to inflation control "a complete failure due to faulty diagnosis . . . [a] brutal plan [which] was indeed successful in creating stagnation."[5] Later the President attempted to freeze wages and prices and set up new guidelines. Although this effort was followed by some 16 months of only moderate price increases, the President did not request the necessary powers to implement a more comprehensive program. A belief in the self-correcting forces of the free market prevailed. Throughout the balance of the Nixon administration and the succeeding Ford Presidency, while the federal budget ran heavily in deficit, the main influence of government to control inflation was exerted through the Federal Reserve System under a restrictive credit policy.

Although credit restraint was a necessary measure for control of inflation in the absence of any other policy, it also restricted the growth of the economy, resulting in a huge loss in productive growth and in high-level unemployment. The lesson is that under the conditions assumed for stagflation, an inflation cannot be controlled simply by monetary or credit restraint, or by reductions in government spending, without accentuating losses in productivity and employment. Other policy means or measures are sometimes required.

Other Policy Means for Inflation Control

From 1965 on, the hypothesis of this critique is that the federal government relentlessly pursued almost all the wrong policies for control of inflation, given the policy goal of high-level production and employment.[6] From 1965 to mid 1968, the government failed to tax sufficiently to offset the increased outlays necessitated by the war policy. From December 1967 to 1970 when stagflation took over, inflation could not be controlled by the classic monetary-fiscal measures without incurring large losses in productivity and employment. For much

---

[4]A study by Arthur Smithies, which appears to apply to this situation, had concluded that "There appears to be no case where a simple policy of credit restraint will provide an adequate cure for persistent inflation." See Arthur Smithies, "The Control of Inflation," *Review of Economics and Statistics,* XXXIX, No. 3, August 1957, p. 282.

[5]Gardiner C. Means, "Simultaneous Inflation and Unemployment: A Challenge to Theory and Policy," *Challenge, the Magazine of Economic Affairs,* September/October 1975, p. 14.

[6]For a comparative discussion received after this section was written, see James R. Crotty and Leonard A. Rapping, "The 1975 Report of the President's Council of Economic Advisers: A Radical Critique," *The American Economic Review,* Vol. LXV, No. 5, December 1975, pp. 791–811.

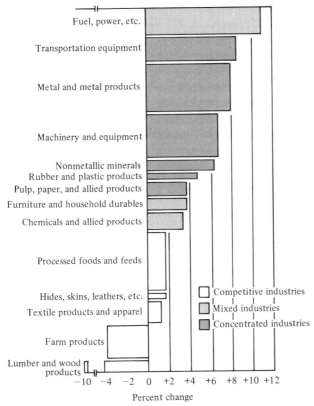

Wholesale price changes by product groups,
June 1969 to December 1970.
Average increase 4.0 percent.

Figure 9-1 Administrative inflation in stagflation and recession. Width of column represents weight of item in the index. *(Source: Bureau of Labor Statistics. Adapted from Gardiner C. Means, "Simultaneous Inflation and Unemployment: A Challenge to Theory and Policy," Challenge, the Magazine of Economic Affairs, September–October 1975, p. 15.)*

of this stage, since the federal budget was in balance or in surplus, the federal government was not directly adding to inflation.

Instead, this was what Gardiner Means has called "administrative inflation," a condition in which management is attempting to widen profit margins by price increases or labor is negotiating excessively large wage increases. Because of the continuing strong demand, both management and labor were successful in their policy, stagnation was occurring, and price increases were particularly strong in the concentrated industries where a few large firms wield market power (Figure 9-1).

The required policy means to control administrative inflation is not so much credit restraint as effective wage and price guidelines, especially in the concentrated industries. President Kennedy had used this policy with some success in the early 1960s; and, in 1971 when President Nixon tried wage and price guidelines, the policy was remarkably successful, as might be expected in the recovery stage (Table 9-1). But, starting in 1973, as the cycle moved into a strong demand-pull phase, which was compounded by devaluation and large-scale food exports, more direct measures to control wages and prices were still more urgently required.

The necessary policy was largely lacking. By emphasizing the reestablishment of a favorable trade balance, which accentuated the commodity inflation, additional pressure was exerted on prices.[7] In such conditions, inflation could not be controlled simply by credit restraint and by holding down on government expenditures without slowing economic recovery.[8] Measures to control wages and prices more directly were required.

Position of the Farm-Food Sector in Inflation Control

Policymakers in the farm-food sector have not reacted consistently toward a comprehensive view of the means to control inflation. Generally, as noted in Chapter 6, the farm organizations making policy have been most concerned with more directly expanding the farm-food market at home and abroad, with gaining the means for farm price support, and with credit expansion and income subsidy. Although farm organizations have—with consistent and almost religious regularity—passed resolutions favoring fiscal responsibility, balanced budgets, and control of government spending, they have not broadly supported more comprehensive policy to control inflation. As late as 1976, for instance, the American Farm Bureau Federation still believed that the best method of doing so was the elimination of federal deficits, while it opposed legislative authority for—presumably any—wage and price controls.[9]

In making policy it is crucial, however, to distinguish between the market position of the farm-food system and that of other more concentrated industries. Although the concentration in food marketing is considerable, as we noted in Chapter 5, the ability of the food industry to transmit administrative price increases is limited by the structure of the market and the stability of the supply of farm products. Throughout the last half of the 1960s, farm and food prices did not increase in proportion with the general wholesale index. The administrative inflation of 1969 and 1970 scarcely touched the food industry (Figure 9-1); and later, the food industry in essence merely reacted to the large demand increase of 1972 and 1973. To attempt to impose direct controls over food prices without effective rationing would have been to court disaster. In the concentrated

---

[7]For discussion of the role of agriculture in the 1973 inflation, see William Nordhaus and John Shoven, "Inflation 1973: The Year of Infamy," *Challenge, The Magazine of Economic Affairs,* May/June 1974, pp. 14–22.

[8]See Andrew F. Brimmer, "Alternative Monetary-Fiscal Policies and Sectoral Credit Flows," *The American Economic Review,* Vol. LXIV, No. 2, May 1974, pp. 112–120.

[9]*Farm Bureau Policies for 1976,* 57th Annual Meeting of the American Farm Bureau Federation, St. Louis, Mo., January 1976, p. 23.

industries it was a different matter, however, and a policy to encourage growth without price increase was required.

A Policy Conclusion

A growing body of theory suggests that the concentrated industries dominated by large firms do not initiate or spearhead inflation but actually delay the transmission of inflationary forces.[10] Similarly, the farm-food system does not initiate inflation and, largely lacking in ability to transmit administrative price increases, it also retards the transmission of inflationary forces. But the farm-food system is substantially influenced by inflationary forces largely initiated outside of it.

In the severe inflation of 1965–76, the initial impetus came from the unbalanced budgets of the federal government, and as the demand-pull force of this situation got underway, price increases were transmitted via the concentrated industries to a large area of the American economy. As demand-pull yielded to stagflation, a simple policy of money and credit restraint was insufficient to dampen down price increases in the industrial sector, in heavy industry especially, nor would further reductions in government spending have had the desired effect.

The lesson for policy is that a more broadly selective choice of policy means is required. The farm-food sector can be damaged by further inflation, both in terms of factor costs and in loss of foreign markets. In making food policy for America, the taxonomy of the business cycle must be taken into account. A more broadly based policy, especially in demand-pull and stagflation involving effective wage and price guidelines, tax incentives and rebates, as well as more selective credit policy, is required.

More specifically, the experience with inflation from 1965 to 1976 demonstrated the inadequacy of merely providing monetary and credit restraints, whether the federal budget was in deficit or surplus, and administrative inflation was occurring in the private sector, especially in the concentrated, heavy-industry manufacturing subsector.[11] Although this does not support the case for mandatory wage and price controls as a long-continuing policy, one may take the experience to suggest that a more direct income policy is generally required.[12] In addition to timely use of monetary-fiscal tools, a comprehensive income policy will include public guidelines for wage and price changes that adhere to broadly recognized standards of fairness and equity, an active public employment program, job training, and work incentives.[13] For extreme cases, the government will require residual powers of arbitration and wage or price roll back in clearly

[10]See Phillip Cagan, "Inflation and Market Structure, 1967–73," *Explorations in Economic Research,* Vol. 2, No. 2, Spring 1975, p. 204.

[11]See Ross E. Azevedo, "Phase III—A Stabilization Program that Could Not Work," *The Quarterly Review of Economics and Business,* Vol. 16, No. 1, Spring 1976, pp. 7–21.

[12]See Arthur F. Burns, "The Real Issues of Inflation and Unemployment," *Challenge, The Magazine of Economic Affairs,* January/February, 1976, pp. 6–11.

[13]See, also, remarks by Myron E. Sharpe, "Ten Rules for Full Employment without Inflation," *ibid.,* pp. 3–5.

specified circumstances. An alternative policy that fails to control inflation generally will not be beneficial to the farm-food sector. Even though certain windfall gains from inflation may be reflected in farm land prices, the case is strong for support of a comprehensive inflation-control policy by the farm-food sector. To be most successful, policymakers in the food and farm sector must support it as consistently as they have followed the long tradition of counteracting deflationary policy.

AGRICULTURE FIGHTS DEFLATION

While the record of food policymakers is spotty in regard to inflation, agriculture is traditionally the bastion of efforts to counteract deflation. The great deflations in the American economy, such as those between 1865 and 1896 and between 1929 to 1933, have been periods of acute discontent, as farm incomes fluctuated erratically and were generally low. Fixed debt charges, relatively fixed railroad rates, and sticky nonfarm prices rose in real terms, throwing a heavier burden on farmers and rural nonfarm people, who typically sought to have costs lowered or, failing in this, to reinflate the economy. The policy goal of agriculture and rural society generally is weighted against deflation, thus imparting an inflationary bias not only to American history but to the future as well.

The Nineteenth-Century Tradition

To see how this bias comes about, we may review some of the more important episodes relating to monetary and fiscal policy. In 1791, Alexander Hamilton, then Secretary of the Treasury, established the National Bank of the United States. During its first 20-year charter, it had a restraining influence on note issues of state banks and a vitally important and stabilizing effect on the monetary system. The charter was not renewed in 1811, and until the second bank was chartered in 1816, the state banks engaged in reckless expansion. The second bank did not follow the conservative policies of its predecessor, but it had to correct the badly expanded situation by a period of contraction. Even a modest contraction was unpopular in rural areas, however, and in 1836 President Andrew Jackson vetoed the act to renew the bank's charter because he feared that such concentration of monetary power would dictate policy for the country. From that time until passage of the National Banking Act of 1863, the state banks were in their heyday. Bank notes were issued sometimes without any idea of redemption and, particularly in the Western and Southern states, many banks violated all canons of sound banking practice. Sporadic panics—the most severe one, in 1837—occurred when banks were unable to meet the demands of their depositors.

Passage of the National Banking Act in 1863 ushered in a new era, a 30-year period of marked deflation culminating about the mid 1890s. Amendments to the act in 1865 drove state bank notes out of circulation by taxing them prohibitively, thus centering monetary control again in the federal government. Attempts to redeem the paper currency which had been printed to finance the Civil War also contracted the currency and had deflationary results. Farm people first tried to get railroad rates reduced to compensate, a policy that they tried to implement through the new National Grange of the Patrons of Husbandry (see Chapter 6). But, failing in this effort, they then turned to monetary policy, a trend which was greatly accelerated by the severe panic of 1873.

From the early 1870s to the presidential campaign of 1896, agricultural discontent, expressed in what is now called the Populist Revolt, was fanned by a number of grievances such as monopoly prices, high railroad rates and poor service, inadequate and unreliable high-cost credit, and low farm prices.[14] During this era wholesale prices dropped to one-third their previous level. The purchasing power of the dollar tripled. Evidence suggests that farm income rose in the 1860s, fell sharply in the 1870s, rose somewhat in the 1880s, and fell sharply again in the early 1890s, although it was roughly constant for the decade.[15] There was tremendous county-by-county variation, and, as the tide of settlement moved westward, increased demand for farm products was met by surges of settlement into new, rich lands of equal fertility, resulting in low prices for farm products and in productivity gains being passed on to consumers in the form of lower food prices.[16] The productivity gains that brought hardship to agriculture also contributed importantly to industrial development by their effect on food prices and trade.

Policy of Monetary Expansion

Although the difficulties of agriculture at the time of the Populist Revolt were due only partially to deflation, the political policy efforts to counteract these difficulties centered chiefly on monetary measures aimed at expansion of currency and credit. In the 1870s, goaded by the panic of 1873, the farmer turned from the question of railroad rates to that of the currency, embracing greenbacks and opposing redemption in silver or gold (specie). The National Greenback party was organized at Indianapolis in 1874 and nominated Peter Cooper as its presidential candidate. His platform in 1876 included a demand for a national paper currency, redeemable in interest-bearing bonds. The party lost, but it polled a large number of votes, particularly in the Midwest, and it attained sufficient influence to temporarily force abandonment of specie payment to retire the paper money that was in circulation. In 1878 the Greenback party polled at least a

---

[14]John D. Hicks, *The Populist Revolt, A History of the Farmers' Alliance and the People's Party,* Lincoln: University of Nebraska Press, 1968 (first published by The University of Minnesota Press, 1931).

[15]From John Bowman, "Trends in Midwestern Farm Values, 1860–1914," unpublished doctoral dissertation, Yale University, 1964, and Allan G. Bogue, *From Prairie to Corn Belt,* Chicago: The University of Chicago Press, 1963, as discussed by Douglass C. North, *Growth and Welfare in the American Past, A New Economic History,* Englewood Cliffs, N.J.: Prentice-Hall, Inc., 1966, pp. 145–148.

[16]From the hypothesis suggested by North, *ibid.,* p. 147.

million votes. Thereafter, although it ran candidates in 1880, 1882, and 1884, its total vote declined rapidly as the Democratic party adopted Greenback principles.[17]

Movement in the Populist Revolt coalesced around a campaign for coinage of silver. To review, silver had been underpriced by the federal government in the Coinage Act of 1834; that is, priced at less than its value in commercial markets. Accordingly, in the years following, little silver was purchased for coinage since silver commanded a higher price in other uses. By 1850 the silver dollar had virtually ceased to be used. In the Coinage Act of 1873, silver was dropped from coinage. This act received little opposition because silver was not being coined; but soon silver was discovered in several Western states. The Comstock Lode was developed in Nevada. Huge silver and copper deposits were found in Montana. The price of silver declined sharply.

Under populist pressure legislation, known as the Bland-Allison Act, was passed in 1878. It directed the Secretary of the Treasury to purchase a quantity of silver at a ratio of 16 to 1, that is, 1 ounce of gold for 16 ounces of silver, and to issue certificates redeemable in silver. The silver purchases, however, did not bring about the desired expansion. Silver coins and silver certificates seemed merely to displace other money.

The result was a growing popular support for free, unlimited coinage of silver. In 1890, the Silver Purchase Act provided that the Treasury must buy a larger amount of silver, equal to the annual output of all silver mines, by issuing Treasury notes redeemable in gold or silver. This act imposed a heavy drain on gold reserves, and by 1893, gold stocks were so reduced that President Grover Cleveland called Congress into special session to repeal the Silver Purchase Act, thus to save the gold standard. The action was contrary to populist counterdeflationary goals to raise prices and improve the debtor position of agriculture and rural society.

Repeal of the Silver Purchase Act created a major issue for the campaign of 1896: whether or not to take stronger measures to expand the currency. William Jennings Bryan stampeded the Democratic nominating convention with his "cross-of-gold" speech, calling for free coinage and a more expansive monetary-credit policy. But Republicans won again, supporting a sound money plank with limited expansion of paper money.

From 1896 onward, however, several factors combined to bring a substantial expansion in money and credit. The general index of wholesale prices began a long upward climb. Because of rapid industrialization from 1896 to 1910–14, which expanded employment and created good markets for food, farm product prices rose by 50 percent more than nonfarm prices. The populist agitation for counterdeflationary monetary policy died out, not to be revived again until the great contraction of the early 1930s.

[17]For further discussion, see Clara Eliot, *The Farmer's Campaign for Credit,* New York: D. Appleton & Company, 1927, pp. 1–64.

The Great Contraction

The severe contraction of the early 1930s revived interest in monetary policy to counteract deflation, and farm groups shifted back to the traditional positions favoring monetary expansion. The American Farm Bureau Federation (AFBF) led a campaign to revive inflation; and one mark of the Bureau's political effectiveness, in step with the feeling of the time and in league with other groups, is recorded in Title III of the Agricultural Adjustment Act of 1933, which authorized the President to issue greenbacks, to remonetize silver, and to alter the gold content of the dollar.[18] The National Farmers Union favored inflation. What we need, said Union President Simpson, is "a straight-out price-fixing measure on the basis of cost of production . . . the remonetization of silver, a good supply of paper money, and a sprinkling of counterfeit to take care of the situation."[19] The act of 1933 gave broad powers to the President to inflate the currency; but he did not favor the proposals that were made for printing money or for coining silver. He used the new powers chiefly to reduce the gold content of the dollar, thus devaluing the dollar in respect to other national currencies with subsequently great consequences for farm exports and trade.

Important for our study is the now well-documented observation that the great contraction of 1929–1933 was in fact greatly exacerbated by failure of the Federal Reserve System to take timely counterdeflationary action. According to Milton Friedman and Anna J. Schwartz,

> Throughout the contraction, the Federal Reserve System had ample powers to cut short the tragic process of monetary deflation and banking collapse. Had it used these powers effectively in late 1930 or even in early or mid 1931, the successive liquidity crises that in retrospect are the distinctive feature of the contraction could almost certainly have been prevented and the stock of money kept from declining or, indeed, increased to any desired extent. Such action would have eased the severity of the contraction and very likely would have brought it to an end at a much earlier date.[20]

Although the Federal Reserve did carry through a series of eight rate reductions to 1½ percent by May 1931, the result apparently had no stimulating effect.[21]

---

[18]Christiana M. Campbell, *The Farm Bureau and the New Deal, A Study of the Making of Farm Policy, 1933–40,* Urbana: The University of Illinois Press, 1962. According to Campbell (pp. 53–54), the ideas in all three titles of the act were urged on President Roosevelt by AFBF President Ed O'Neal by authority of the AFBF board. See also Arthur Schlesinger, Jr., *The Age of Roosevelt: The Politics of Upheaval,* Boston: Houghton Mifflin Company, 1960, pp. 144–161.

[19]*United States Daily News,* April 8 and 15, 1933.

[20]Milton Friedman and Anna Jacobson Schwartz, *The Great Contraction, 1929–1933,* A study by the National Bureau of Economic Research, Princeton, N.J.: Princeton University Press, 1965 (a reprint of Chapter 7 of *A Monetary History of the United States,* 1963).

[21]Melchior Palyi, *The Twilight of Gold, 1914–1936, Myths and Realities,* Chicago: Henry Regnery Company, 1972, p. 319.

A Policy Conclusion

The great contraction of 1929–33 was a historic milestone in monetary-fiscal policy that swung the balance strongly toward a more expansionist policy and program. The tradition within agriculture of counteracting deflation received powerful support. Clearly, in the perspective of history, the two great contractions, the era of the Populist Revolt and the severe contraction of the Great Depression, produced the years of greatest hardship for farm and rural people. Obviously, policies leading to deflation are not among the goals favored by farmers and food policymakers. The resistance in agriculture to deflation is of long standing and, for good reasons, it will continue to project into the future.

Support for monetary-fiscal stability and expansion goes beyond the tradition of counteracting deflation, however, to development of a comprehensive national policy to provide cheaper and more adequate credit for agriculture. The major implement for this policy is the federally sponsored farm credit system and related agencies.

FEDERALLY SPONSORED FARM CREDIT[22]

Federal credit services extended to agriculture are more complete than those made available to any other sector of the American economy. There is long-term farm mortgage credit of 5 to 40 years sponsored through 12 federal land banks (FLBs), one in each of the 12 Federal Reserve districts, which extend credit through more than 500 federal land bank associations (FLBAs). Intermediate-term or production credit is extended through 12 intermediate credit banks (ICBs), each coterminous with a FLB, which discount loan collateral presented to it by a local production credit association (PCA) to cover loans of a few months up to a maximum of seven years. The more than 400 PCAs make loans directly to farmers and farm-related businesses. At the local level, the FLBA and the PCA share facilities and staff resources to provide a complete line of credit to farmers. In addition, 12 banks for cooperatives and the Central Bank for Cooperatives in Washington, D.C., extend a full range of credit to agricultural cooperatives.

The general policy for these three systems is coordinated under the Federal Farm Credit Board, established as an independent agency in the federal executive, which directs the policymaking functions of the Farm Credit Administration (FCA). The President appoints 12 members of the board, one from each of the 12 Farm Credit districts, to serve a six-year term. One member is appointed by the Secretary of Agriculture and serves at his pleasure. The Governor of the FCA, who is the chief executive officer, is appointed by, and serves at the pleasure of the Board. In each FCA district, a board of seven members directs general loan

---

[22]This section draws on R. J. Saulnier, Harold G. Halcrow, and Neil H. Jacoby, *Federal Lending and Loan Insurance,* a study by the National Bureau of Economic Research, Princeton, N.J.: Princeton University Press, 1958.

policy for the district. One of the board members is appointed by the Governor of the FCA with advice and consent of the FCA board. The other six are elected by borrowers from local associations in the district, two by the FLBAs, two by PCAs, and two by borrowers from the district bank for cooperatives.

Development of Policy for Farm Mortgage Credit

Federally sponsored farm mortgage credit was initiated through the Federal Farm Loan Act of 1916 (39 *Stat*. 362; 12 U.S.C. 641-1012) with the policy goal "to provide capital for agricultural development, to create standard forms of investment based on farm mortgages and to equalize rates of interest on farm loans." A system of banks that would provide long-term farm mortgage credit had been a matter of some agitation since the years of the Populist Revolt, and several proposals had been studied. Two study groups, one appointed by President Theodore Roosevelt and the other by President Woodrow Wilson, studied the governmental and cooperative land bank systems of Europe and made proposals for a system of banks in the United States. But disagreements over two kinds of systems, a cooperative land bank system with government sponsorship and financial aid, and a system of privately organized and financed land banks under some type of government regulation, delayed legislative action.

Because of this disagreement, any special credit for agriculture was not provided in the Federal Reserve Act of 1914. When the Federal Farm Loan Act was passed in 1916, it, perhaps unfortunately, provided for two types of banks: joint stock land banks, which were privately organized and financed, and federal land banks, which were made subject to close government direction and supervision and whose original capital was supplied in the main by the federal government. Although 83 joint stock land banks were chartered by 1931, widespread defaults on their loans and their difficulties in raising funds put them in a precarious position, and in 1933 they were placed in liquidation. Only the federal land banks (FLBs) survived.

The policy role of the FLBs has varied through the years as needs and goals have changed. The banks started slowly and, from 1917 to 1932, furnished at a maximum only 6 to 7 percent of total farm mortgage credit. The 1932 and 1933 amendments to the Federal Farm Loan Act, which greatly expanded the loan powers of the banks, enabled them to help stem the high tide of foreclosures and bankruptcies brought on by the Great Depression. The 1933 amendment provided for extensions of farmers' loans and payment of farmers' overdue taxes, liens, and judgments, with these amounts added to the existing mortgages. A voluntary farm debt-adjustment program was initiated to scale down the debts of those farmers excessively in debt so that creditors could each receive at least a portion of the money due them. By the end of 1936, after three years of extensive farm mortgage refinancing, largely on an emergency basis, holdings of the land banks plus holdings of the Federal Farm Mortgage Corporation, which was established as an emergency supplementary program under the Federal Land Bank Commissioner, amounted to more than 40 percent of the total farm mortgage debt outstanding. The proportion held by the land banks remained close to 30 percent through 1943, then declined continuously through 1953, when it was only 15.3 percent of the $7.7 billion farm mortgages outstanding. From 1954 to 1960, the land banks increased their market share to more than 20 percent, and from 1960 to 1972 their share varied between 18 to 25 percent.[23] As of January 1, 1971, the land banks held $7.1 billion, or 24 percent, of the total $29.5 billion farm mortgages outstanding.

The Farm Credit Act of 1971,[24] which was based in large part on the work of a 27-member commission on agricultural credit appointed by the Federal Farm Credit Board in 1969, significantly broadened the role of the entire system. It authorized the FLBs to raise their lending limits from 65 to 85 percent of the appraised long-run market value of a farm property. Variable interest rates which had been used by federal land banks in a limited way since 1970 were made official. The maximum loan to a borrower, without prior FCA approval, was raised from $100,000 to $400,000. A FLB could participate in loans with another FLB. The act introduced loss sharing between an individual land bank, as agreed by the bank, and its local FLBAs, provided for open-end mortgages, and deleted mandatory personal liability in loans to family corporations and others. A FLB could own and lease property to an individual borrower. Lending power was expanded by authorizing FLBs to require stock investment up to $10 per $100 of loans, rather than the previous requirement of $5 per $100 of loans. The act permitted issuance of a unified security for all banks in the FCA system instead of each bank issuing its own. Finally, the act broadened the potential clientele and the range of services by authorizing loans on single-family, moderate-cost, nonfarm rural residences, not to exceed 15 percent of the outstanding loans of a bank, with acceptance of additional security other than first mortgages on real estate. It permitted financing of nonfarmers furnishing services related to farm operations, such as custom sprayers, custom harvesters, and other financially related services necessary to on-farm operations, such as electronic recordkeeping. It also permitted issuance of nonvoting stock and participation certificates to nonfarm borrowers.

A Policy Conclusion The federal land bank program has had a profound effect on the development of American agriculture. Initially, the introduction of long-term amortized loans at uniform rates of interest revolutionized the entire farm mortgage market and expanded the flow of long-term capital into agriculture. From 1917 through 1947, the federal government provided land banks with 1.6 billion "dollar-years" of interest-free capital through capital stock subscription.[25] An additional 1.7 billion "dollar-years" of interest-free capital in the form

---

[23]*Agricultural Statistics,* Washington: U.S. Department of Agriculture, 1972, table 710.

[24]Farm Credit Act of 1971, Public Law 92-181; 85 *Stat.* 583; 12 U.S.C. 2001. House Report No. 92-593.

[25]Dollar-years of capital were computed by adding the amounts of capital stock in the banks held by the government by year-ends over the period. G. K. Brinegar worked with the author in development of these estimates. See *Federal Lending and Loan Insurance, op. cit.,* chap. 6.

of paid-in surplus was provided in connection with mortgage extensions and deferments; and rather minor amounts of capital were provided in early years by using the banks for some government deposits. Through 1954, if an interest rate of 2 percent is assigned, the value is $67 million, or about one-fifth of cumulative net earnings.[26] In addition, as an aid to farmer borrowers in the Depression, the land banks were reimbursed by $277 million to compensate them for interest-rate reductions made at direction of the Congress in 1933–34. Also, some indirect aid was provided through purchase of land bank bonds by the Federal Farm Mortgage Corporation. Since 1947 the banks have been owned by borrowers through stock purchase, a policy which has continually added to their lending power. Revisions made in the act of 1971 assure that this power will be strengthened in the future. So the flow of long-term capital into agriculture will add to the production potential, an expectation that is also enhanced by the provision of federally sponsored production credit.

Development of Policy for Production Credit

The system of federal intermediate credit banks was created under the Agricultural Credits Act of 1923 (42 *Stat.* 1454; 12 U.S.C. 1021-1022), and $60 million was subscribed by the federal government, $5 million for each bank. In 1933 the Reconstruction Finance Corporation (RFC), one of the chief New Deal recovery agencies, was authorized by the Emergency Relief and Reconstruction Act (50 *Stat.* 704; 12 U.S.C. 1148) to establish and finance 12 regional agricultural credit corporations which were authorized to borrow from the FICBs, the RFC, and the Federal Reserve. These were transferred to the Farm Credit Administration by Executive Order 6084, March 27, 1933. The Farm Credit Act of 1933 (48 *Stat.* 257; 12 U.S.C. 1131 et seq.) authorized establishment of 12 production credit corporations (PCCs). The PCCs eliminated the need for the regional agricultural credit corporations, which were later consolidated. The PCCs were provided with $120 million of federal funds and authorized to act for the federal government in making subscriptions to Class A (nonvoting) capital stock of production credit associations (PCAs) to be organized as local lending agencies. This stock could be retired by PCAs out of earnings and the sale of Class B (voting) stock to borrowers, who were required to purchase Class B stock equal to 5 percent of their borrowed funds. An additional $40 million was provided by Congress in the Federal Farm Mortgage Corporation Act of 1934 (48 *Stat.* 348; 12 U.S.C. 1041) as a revolving fund for subscription, when needed, to their capital or paid-in surplus. The Farm Credit Act of 1953 required the Federal Farm Credit Board to develop a plan for retiring all government-owned capital in the FICBs and PCCs to make the entire system essentially borrower-owned through stock purchases by borrowers from PCAs. This was accomplished by 1968.

The Farm Credit Act of 1971 also, as in the case of the land banks, greatly expanded the lending powers of the FICBs and PCAs. The FICBs were

---

[26]The 2 percent interest rate is assumed simply for purposes of illustration and as consistent with the cost of federal money to some other programs, the Rural Electrification Administration, for example.

permitted to purchase stock or contribute to the surplus of PCAs, to participate in loans and loss-sharing plans with other FICBs and PCAs, to own and lease equipment to eligible borrowers, to offer financial services to farm operators, and to issue nonvoting stock to nonfarm borrowers. Additionally, as in the case of the FLBs, the FICBs were authorized to make loans through PCAs on single-family, moderate-cost, nonfarm rural residences of a short- and intermediate-term nature not to exceed 15 percent of the outstanding loans of the FICB. Also, financing was extended to nonfarmers rendering on-farm services to producers or harvesters of fish or other aquatic food products. Creation and maintenance of reasonable, unallocated contingency reserves were also permitted.

Authorizations directly to PCAs paralleled those to FICBs; and PCAs were additionally authorized to participate with local commercial banks in loans to farmers and ranchers, thus to meet the full credit needs of some of the larger farm operations. Most country banks have correspondent arrangements with larger city banks whereby they can get supplementary financing for a loan that is too large for them to handle alone, called an overline loan. Many city banks, however, have required a country bank to maintain deposits with them in the same ratio to the amount of overline loans carried. This requirement has reduced the financial resources of the country bank and made it more dependent on the city bank. By authorizing the PCAs to participate in overline loans through sharing the risk on the overline amount, the 1971 legislation created a more flexible situation for both lenders.

Unlike FLBAs, which function merely as intermediaries between farmer-member borrowers and the federal land banks, the PCAs actually extend credit to farmers and obtain funds in turn from the intermediate credit bank of the district. The extent to which the PCAs are permitted to use the facilities of the intermediate credit bank depends on the quality of the paper they originate and their net worth, which is generated by earnings and by stock purchase. Thus, the lending capacity of PCAs is influenced by the success of their experience locally and by their success in sale of bonds and debentures.

In the main, PCA borrowers are of the type that meets the credit standards of commercial banks and other private lenders, and evidence suggests that, consistently, loans have gone to well-established farm operators. Accordingly, loss experience on PCA loans has been about the same as that of commercial banks over similar periods, and the production credit system has been, on balance, self-supporting when full costs, including those for capital supplied interest-free by the federal government, are considered. The peak government investment of $90 million in the PCCs in the 1930s had been reduced to $3.6 million by mid 1954, less than 2 percent of the PCAs' aggregate net worth. Through mid 1954, the government had furnished 1.9 billion dollar-years of interest-free capital to the PCCs, and in addition, 1 billion dollar-years of government capital was used by PCAs through PCC holdings of their Class A stock. If the PCAs had been required to pay 2 percent interest for use of these funds, the total interest outlay would have been about $20 million, while net accumulated earnings for the PCAs were $90.8 million. In addition, the intermediate credit banks employed more than 1.8 billion dollar-years of interest-free capital, which at 2 percent interest would have cost $36 million. Against this, the banks paid $9.2 million in franchise taxes, earned surplus was $30.1 million, and reserves for contingencies were $17.1 million. Since 1954, with relatively much smaller holdings of government capital, the production credit system has grown and operated substantially without government subsidy.

A Policy Conclusion   By use of uniform interest rates and other conveniences, the PCA system has been highly stimulating to agricultural growth and development. For the country as a whole, it has acquired more than half the total non-real estate farm loan market. Although the federal government is no longer required to invest money in the system, the policy is still highly stimulative in regard to growth, which tends to favor large family farms and other large-scale operations. Thus, it is a growth-oriented policy with important implications for economic structure in farming.

Federally Sponsored Credit for Cooperatives

Lending to agricultural marketing and service cooperatives has been developed, as mentioned earlier, through the Central Bank for Cooperatives in Washington, D.C., and 12 district banks for cooperatives. The policy goal of this program is to provide credit with uniform rates and terms in three categories: (1) facility loans for constructing or acquiring buildings, equipment, or other goods to facilitate storing, handling, or marketing farm commodities and food products; (2) short-term operating loans on inventories, receivables, payrolls, and supplies; and (3) commodity loans to facilitate marketing farm commodities and buying farm supplies. The largest or heaviest borrowers have been cooperatives handling grains, fruits except for citrus, vegetables, cotton, and farm supplies, including petroleum. In most cases, loans to cooperatives are made by the district banks rather than by the Central Bank, which participates mainly in loans of national or broad interregional scope.

Policymaking was started under the Agricultural Marketing Act of 1929 (46 *Stat.* 11, 12 U.S.C. 1141 et seq.), under which the Agricultural Marketing Revolving Fund of $500 million was created to be loaned by the Central Bank for Cooperatives to farm marketing cooperatives, under the newly formed Federal Farm Board, with the general objective of supporting farm prices by storage of farm commodities. Such loans were transferred in 1933 to the newly created district banks, which obtained their original capital from the revolving fund. Later the banks obtained the major part of their loan funds by borrowing from, or discounting with, the FICBs and commercial banks.

Like the land banks and the PCAs, the banks for cooperatives lend largely to borrowers who meet credit standards of other lenders. Consequently, loan experience has been highly favorable and, especially since the early 1940s, the banks have been a growth factor in the farm-food system. The government supplied 3.3 billion dollar-years of interest-free capital up to mid 1954, which, at 2 percent, would have cost $67 million. In comparison, net profit to this date was

$78.4 million, with allocation of $50 million to earned surplus, $20.3 million to legal reserve, and $8.1 million to reserve for contingencies.

A Policy Conclusion In 1971 the operating constraints on the banks for cooperatives (BCs), like those on land banks and production credit, were loosened or made more flexible. The BCs are permitted to increase the maximum ratio of authorized debentures or similar obligations to the net worth of the BCs from the 8 to 1 limit before the act to a new statutory limit of 20 to 1, or to a prudent lesser ratio should it be established by FCA regulation. They have increased flexibility in the composition and management of their capital structure. They were granted additional authority to borrow money by issuing individual or consolidated BC notes, bonds, debentures, or other obligations as approved by the FCA. They were allowed to distribute a greater portion of patronage refunds in cash, to establish greater reserves against unexpected obligations, and to participate with other financial institutions in loans to eligible borrowers. All these provisions, by lessening the policy constraints on the BCs, add to their policy role in supplying credit funds to cooperatives. Again, as in the case of land banks and production credit, the result must be regarded as stimulative to agriculture, particularly the agricultural service, supply, and marketing sectors. As of June 30, 1972, the BCs had $2.1 billion of loans and discounts outstanding, compared with $8.4 billion for the federal land banks and $6.8 billion for PCAs.[27]

DIRECT FEDERAL LENDING, LOAN INSURANCE, LOAN GUARANTEE, AND GRANT PROGRAMS

A wide array of direct lending, loan insurance, loan guarantee, and grant programs has been developed under federal policy to serve the agricultural, food resource, and rural economy under three general goals: (1) to alleviate hardships for farm families in various types of emergency situations, (2) to aid low-income farm families that are unable to obtain satisfactory credit from other sources, and (3) to stimulate rural community resource development.

Policy Goals, Development, and Implementation

Although special credits and other aids to low-income farmers in certain emergency situations have been available since before World War I and were greatly expanded in the 1930s, new growth began in 1946 when the Farmers Home Administration was formed to implement all direct lending, loan insurance, and grant programs for low-income farmers. This role was broadened in 1949 to finance low-income farm housing, in 1968 to add loan insurance for farm and rural nonfarm housing, and again in 1972 to offer loan insurance, guarantees, and grants on rural housing, rural business enterprise, and community facilities. Under loan insurance, the FHA makes a loan to a borrower from a revolving

[27]*Agricultural Finance Statistics,* May 1973, p. 48.

fund and then in turn sells the paper to a bank or other investor while insuring the interest and principal repayment. Under loan guarantee programs a local bank or other lender makes a loan which, if falling within FHA guidelines, can be guaranteed up to 90 percent of the principle.

Under the Farmers Home Administration Act of 1946 (Chapter 964, Public Law 731, 60 *Stat.* 1062) almost all the direct lending to low-income farmers, which had been carried out for several years under a variety of programs and agencies, was placed under the newly formed FHA. The new agency was authorized to assume functions performed up to that time by the Farm Security Administration and by the Emergency Crop and Feed Loan Division of the FCA, namely, to make operating and production loans to farmers and stock producers, to finance purchase, improvement, or enlargement of family-size farms, to insure mortgages made by private lenders for purposes similar to those of the farm ownership loan program, and to make water-facility and disaster loans.[28] Under the Housing Act of 1949 (Public Law 171, Title V - Farm Housing; 42 U.S.C. 1471 et seq.), the role of the FHA was expanded to provide financial and technical assistance to low-income farm families for "decent" and "adequate" housing and farm buildings.[29] In 1953, authorization was given for a special program of loans to livestock operators in need of financing because of drought or low prices and for economic disaster loans in regions declared by the President under Public Law 875 to be disaster areas. The water-facility loan program was expanded to include loans for various conservation facilities and practices, a corresponding program of loan insurance was inaugurated, and authority was given under the farm ownership program to lend on second mortgage security.

By 1970 the FHA program included 23 separately identified activities: loan programs for farm ownership, insured loans to farmers and ranchers for outdoor income-producing recreation enterprises, direct and insured soil conservation and development loans, direct operating loans to farmers, emergency loans in designated areas, insured rural housing loans, and insured farm-labor housing loans, plus a variety of loan services to public and nonprofit associations for development and utilization of water supplies, grants for water and waste-disposal development costs, financial and technical assistance, and direct loans for manpower training centers in rural areas, direct loans from a revolving fund to organizations for purchase of land and development of rental cooperative

[28]The Resettlement Administration was formed in 1935 under Executive Orders 7027 and 7200, April 30, 1935, and was given responsibility for resettlement of low-income farm families and for a rehabilitation program that was started with grants under the Federal Emergency Relief Administration Act of 1933 (49 *Stat.* 115). All the duties and powers of the Resettlement Administration were transferred on Jan. 1, 1937, to the Secretary of Agriculture by Executive Orders 7530 and 7557. On Sept. 1, 1937, the name was changed to the Farm Security Administration, which continued until replaced by the FHA in 1946.

[29]There were special provisions for veterans under the farm ownership and farm housing programs of the FHA as authorized in the 1946 act. Also, the Veterans Administration had been authorized after World War II to guarantee or insure loans by other lenders to veterans for purchase, construction, or improvement of farm properties. Loans guaranteed or insured by the VA reached a peak of 19,793 in 1947 and thereafter declined to fewer than 2,000 per year after 1952. From *Agricultural Statistics*, Washington: U.S. Department of Agriculture, 1972.

housing. In addition, the FHA was assigned comprehensive planning responsibilities in helping local leaders in development planning and coordination of programs.

The Rural Development Act of 1972 (Public Law 92-419; 86 *Stat.* 657; 7 U.S.C. 1921 et seq.) swung the balance strongly toward loan guarantees for rural nonfarm housing, rural enterprise loans, and loan guarantees for small business enterprises, plus loans and grants for water and waste-disposal facilities, watershed protection and flood prevention, rural fire protection, and the like. The major policy goal, as expressed, was greatly enlarged from any previous one "to provide an effective program to enable rural America to offer living conditions and employment opportunities adequate to impede the steady flow of rural Americans to our nation's large population centers . . . to make it desirable for Americans to actually return to our rural areas, thereby lessening the burdens and problems of the modern big city" (Public Law 92-419, House Report No. 92-835, p. 3147).

The broad-purpose Rural Development Insurance Fund was established to displace the Rural Housing Insurance Fund of the 1968 act. Also, the assets and liabilities of the Agricultural Credit Insurance Fund applicable to loans for water systems and waste-disposal facilities were transferred to the Rural Development Insurance Fund. The maximum amount of new loans that could be held unsold in the Fund was raised from $100 million to $500 million and authority was given to pay interest subsidies to lenders who made guaranteed or insured loans where such payments were necessary to achieve a market rate of interest.

The FHA, under this broader grant of authority and increased funding, continued its farm loan and insurance programs and, in addition, began the following, giving first priority to loan guarantee rather than insurance programs: (1) rural enterprise loans on real estate up to $100,000 and 40-year term in rural areas and towns up to 50,000 population, (2) rural enterprise operating loans up to $50,000 and seven-year terms, (3) loans to rural youth up to seven-year term to participate in 4-H, Future Farmers of America, and like projects, (4) loans for terms up to 40 years for essential community facilities to public bodies and nonprofit associations in places having up to 10,000 population, (5) rural industrial assistance loans up to 40 years to finance businesses in towns up to 50,000 population, and (6) guaranteed loans for above-moderate-income housing in rural towns and towns up to 10,000, with interest rates as determined by the Department of Housing and Urban Development under the National Housing Act.[30]

Under FHA, the grant program included, most importantly, grants to public bodies or planning agencies to prepare comprehensive plans for rural development in places up to 10,000 population, grants for pollution-abatement control for farmers and industry, not to exceed 50 percent of the project costs, and grants to help communities attract business and industry up to 100 percent of costs of projects—all these provisions to be carried out in cooperation with local banks, planning agencies, and government bodies.

[30]From remarks by James V. Smith, Administrator of Farmers Home Administration, before the 21st National Agricultural and Rural Affairs Conference, Denver, Colo., Nov. 13, 1972.

A Policy Conclusion on Means and Constraints

Evaluations of the policy means and constraints in the types of programs implemented by the FHA have always been difficult and will remain so. The rural rehabilitation program, started in the early 1930s, served as a major source of relief throughout that decade. In 1935, with the formation of the Resettlement Administration, it became an integral and continuing part of the federal government's program for aid to agriculture. Farm and home advisement services were added to the loan service. The Farm Security Administration later continued the program. In 1946 under the FHA, a broader program of production and subsistence loans was developed to help low-income farm families improve their farms and homes. Public Law 878, approved August 1, 1956, changed the name from subsistence loans to operating loans, with the underlying purpose of putting greater stress on loans to farmers for making basic adjustments in their farming operations.

Operating loans were distributed among states roughly according to their number of low-income farms rather than to other measures, such as value of agricultural products produced or total number of farms. Loans were made for a specific purpose, such as purchase of livestock, machinery and equipment, land improvements, or specified expenses; they were generally limited to family-type farms, under plans covering more than a year, with an initial loan generally followed with subsequent loans based on the borrower's performance. Both operating and emergency loan programs have been supplemented by farm ownership loans and rural housing loans, emphasizing, since 1968, government insurance of loans by other lenders. This approach concentrated some loan programs very heavily in the Great Plains and some Southern states.

The policy means used by the FHA are a social invention of considerable significance, providing services that cannot be made available except through government facilities. The amount of technical aid given to borrowers is more than can be paid out of normal returns from interest payments. The losses are modest but higher than can be sustained by nongovernmental lenders. The programs are most fairly judged by setting these costs off against the social and economic progress made by individual borrowers and by their subsequent contribution to national growth and welfare. In the absence of such programs, relief costs would undoubtedly have been higher and human suffering greater.

In any evaluation, however, the acts of 1968 and 1972 must be regarded as landmark legislation with considerable potential for rural America. Adapting loan insurance to rural housing greatly expands the financial leverage exerted. To illustrate, just before the 1968 act was passed (January 1, 1968) the total loan volume of the FHA was only $1.4 billion. Three years later (January 1, 1971), it was still only $1.8 billion, of which a little more than $200 million was in rural housing loans; but loan insurance was $2.6 billion on rural nonfarm housing loans and $250 million on farm housing loans. On January 1, 1972, the amounts were $3.8 billion and $282 million respectively.[31] Adapting loan guarantees to a wider

[31]*Agricultural Finance Statistics,* May 1973, p. 31.

range of development investments will exert an even stronger financial leverage because the FHA is not limited by the size of the revolving fund as it is in the insurance programs.

It is clear, however, that no matter how these activities are evaluated, there is room for wide differences of opinion on what is the optimum scope and direction of policy constraints. In the House Report on the Rural Development Act of 1972 (Public Law 92-419, House Report No. 92-835), a minority view contended that the act was "both too expensive and too ineffective to be in the national public interest" (p. 3176), whereas other individual views and the majority views were generally supportive. In the end, the policy evaluation cannot be separated from the total view on what is the desired social and economic structure and how low-income people are to be subsidized and helped in respect to this structure. The special loan, insurance, and guarantee programs implemented under the FHA are, in the total picture, a rather modest effort— some may say too modest—to aid low-income farmers and others.

THE RURAL ELECTRIFICATION ADMINISTRATION

In contrast with the FHA and its broad and varied policy goals, one of the most specific of the federal lending programs in terms of goals, size, and effect on structure and development of food resources and the rural economy is the program of the Rural Electrification Administration (REA). The REA was started in 1935 by Executive orders of President Roosevelt to provide direct loans for rural electrification.[32] It was established as a permanent and independent agency by the Rural Electrification Act of 1936 (49 *Stat.* 1963; 7 U.S.C. 301 et seq.). Finally, it was transferred to the Department of Agriculture under Reorganization Plan II of 1939 (53 *Stat.* 561). On October 28, 1949, Public Law 423 amended the act to authorize loans for furnishing and improving rural telephone service. On May 11, 1973, new legislation (Public Law 93-32) provided for further expansion of the REA program, especially under loan insurance and guarantee programs to be financed through the Rural Electrification and Telephone Revolving Fund of about $5 billion, created and replenished through repayments from REA borrowers.

Policy Goals, Means, and Implementation

The policy goals of the REA program have been to accelerate and expand rural electric power development, primarily and most importantly through loans to local REA cooperatives, and secondly through loans to privately funded public power companies and other public bodies. Congress, in various acts, has directed how loan funds are to be allocated among the states and what terms are to be set for borrowers. Generally, loans have been made for a maximum term of 35 years, carrying low rates of interest (for several years the basic rate was 2

---

[32]Executive Order 7037, May 11, 1935, was issued under authority of the Emergency Relief Appropriation Act of 1935 (49 *Stat.* 115). Functions of the REA were further defined and redefined in Executive Order 7130, Aug. 7, 1935.

percent) and providing up to 100 percent of the cost of constructing generation, transmission, and distribution facilities.

The policy of "area coverage," adopted in the formative years of the REA, provided that once an area has been entered, service will be extended to substantially all users. This provision has resulted in extending electrification to almost all farms and rural communities in a service area, as compared with traditional policies of privately funded public power companies of extending power facilities only where marginal revenue is expected to equal or exceed marginal cost. The objective is to reach the so-called fringe areas and to serve relatively isolated families and communities as well as those located near main power lines.

The policy is implemented through rural electric cooperatives that are encouraged to borrow from the REA because of the favorable loan rates and services provided. The cooperatives in turn are required by terms of the loan agreement to provide service to all farm and rural customers within their assigned territory up to the limit of their power supply. One cooperative may buy power from another cooperative or from another power company to satisfy the demands of REA customers. Under the 1973 act (Public Law 93-32), the REA is authorized to make and issue interim notes to the Treasury, to sell or assign notes to the revolving fund, to insure loans, to provide financial assistance to borrowers, and to request loan applicants to apply for and accept concurrent loans from other lenders. By provisions of the 1973 act, the maximum loan ceiling is to be set by Congress, rather than by the administration. For 1974, ceilings of $618 million for rural electric insured loans, $140 million for rural telephone insured loans, and $30 million for capitalization of the Rural Telephone Bank, were considerably above previous loan levels. Appropriations of $16.7 million for REA salaries and expenses were the same as for fiscal year 1973. The House Report, commenting on Public Law 93-32, stated that "few programs . . . can equal the success of the rural electric and telephone programs in achieving the goals set out for them. . . . But, because of the dramatic changes in power requirements, the job is not finished. Providing electric and telephone service does play a fundamental role in enabling rural America to find jobs, and reduce the pressure on our urban environment." Noting, too, that many small towns were still "in dire need" of rural water and waste-disposal facilities, the committee also recommended $150 million in grants to FHA, $120 million of which would have been from funds previously frozen by the administration. Altogether, the Congress, in funding REA, made almost $1 billion available for rural power and telephone development in 1974, not counting its authorization to permit the REA to guarantee loans made by other lenders. Thus the REA, under congressional direction, as in the case of the FHA and the federally sponsored FCA, was given a strong leverage as a financial intermediary to speed the process of rural development.

The REA Policy Constraints

The policy authorized for the REA has accelerated the process of rural development and has had an output-increasing effect on agriculture, speeding up the substitution of capital for labor and replacing human labor and other types of power by cheaper sources of energy. In 1935 when the REA was started, only 11 percent of the farms in the United States were served by central-station electricity. By 1950, about 78 percent were so served, and by 1968, the number had risen to 98.4 percent. According to surveys of the REA, about half the farms in the nation and an increasingly high percentage of rural communities are served by cooperatives borrowing from the REA.

The REA program started slowly and accelerated. In the first decade, by the beginning of 1946, less than $½ billion had been advanced to borrowers. By the beginning of 1956, about $2.7 billion had been advanced. Ten years later, advances totaled $4.9 billion, with average advances of more than $300 million a year.[33] The 1973 legislation made an important break with the past by amending the Rural Electrification Act of 1936 under Title III of Public Law 93-32, to authorize use of the revolving fund to make and insure loans to be sold to private investors and to guarantee approved loans made by banks and other financial intermediaries. Perhaps most important for future policy was the provision for congressional guidance for loan guarantees instead of having the limits set in the Office of Management and Budget (OMB), which had in the previous year exercised "line item" vetoes for impoundment of a portion of the REA direct-loan funds appropriated by the Congress. The insured loan ceiling of $618 million for 1974, set by Congress in the 1974 Agriculture Environmental and Consumer Protection Appropriation Act, was about $200 million higher than REA had been lending earlier under its direct-loan program.

Under the 1973 act, all loan funds used by REA could be raised in the private money markets, with repayment insured through the revolving account in the U.S. Treasury. The difference between private money rates required to attract investors and the rates paid by REA borrowers was to be paid out of the revolving account, which in 1974 totaled more than $5 billion. The fund was being replenished by collections on outstanding REA loans, which in 1974 were running at about $25 million per month and increasing. The REA budget was thus separated from the federal budget subject to control of the Congress.

Two interest rates were provided for insured loans: a 2 percent rate, called the "special rate," and a 5 percent rate, called the "standard rate." Either one of two criteria might qualify a REA cooperative for the special rate: (1) an average consumer density of two or fewer to the mile, or (2) an average gross revenue per mile at least $450 below that of REA-financed electric systems, generally. This provided a subsidy to more sparsely settled areas and to low-density systems. In North Dakota, for example, there is just one consumer for every mile of power line.

In the early 1970s, REA systems averaged 3.9 consumers per mile and $849 gross revenue per mile of line, whereas, according to REA data, commercial utilities average 10 times as many customers and 15 times as much gross revenue

[33]*Agricultural Statistics, op. cit.,* 1969, pp. 517–521.

per mile of line.[34] Additionally, a cooperative may qualify for a special loan rate, to be decided solely at the discretion of the Administrator of the REA, on these conditions: If it has experienced extenuating circumstances or extreme hardships; if it cannot produce net income or margins equal to 150 percent of its total interest requirements at an interest rate higher than 2 percent; or if it cannot with good management provide its customers with services consistent with the purposes of the act. The 1973 act further provided that loans for generation and transmission should be given the same treatment as loans for distribution facilities, except when the REA determined that these loans did not need to meet the low-density requirements to qualify for the special rate. Thus, Congress, in writing the act, intended to further develop the REA program by greatly lessening the constraints, permitting the REA relatively unrestricted use of the $5 billion revolving fund to subsidize borrowing cooperatives at interest rates well below the current market.

Conflicts in Policy Making

Throughout the years of REA development, there have been continuing sharp conflicts of interest, some of which rose to a peak prior to passage of the 1973 amendments. The REA has received consistent political support from many farm organizations, especially the National Grange, the National Farmers Union, and the National Farmers Organization (NFO). Support from the American Farm Bureau Federation was strong in the early years and less vocal recently. Rural newspapers generally have acclaimed the rural electrification movement. Many consumer and labor groups have favored it. Farm and rural nonfarm people in most areas have strongly advocated its continued development. Powerful support has been generated in the Congress. To the supporters of the REA development, an original hero of the REA drama was Senator George W. Norris of Nebraska, one of the powerful liberals of the twentieth century, who waged a relentless campaign for extension of electric power into rural areas and who crowned his career with successful sponsorship of the Tennessee Valley Authority and the REA. But, without the skillful political maneuvering of President Roosevelt and his overwhelming New Deal majority in Congress, the REA might never have been created. Its establishment involved Roosevelt in a confrontation with the electric power utilities, which was one of the most intense political confrontations of his entire career.[35]

Opposition to REA has come from the privately funded public power companies and from various economy-minded constituents. Public power companies, through their lobbies in the Congress, have carried on vigorous and persistent war against the REA movement. Originally, in the early hearings on the proposals when they hoped that funds would be allocated to the existing companies to extend electrification into rural areas, their spokesman stated that

---

[34]Data from *Rural Electrification,* official monthly publication of the National Rural Electric Cooperative Association, February 1973, p. 23.

[35]Arthur M. Schlesinger, Jr., *The Age of Roosevelt: The Politics of Upheaval, op. cit.*

the federal government could provide new ways and means of performing an outstanding job of rural electrification. But when it became evident that the program was to become a new competitor in the power business, they marshaled their forces to fight it. In 1935, in a 14-page open letter submitted as a committee report to the Administrator of the REA, they argued that there were very few farms requiring power for the major farm jobs that were not already being served! They suggested a cooperative program, largely financed by federal funds, to help customers of existing power companies finance wiring, purchases of appliances, and the extension of utility lines into rural areas. But this program was opposed by most farm organizations as inadequate. It was not acceptable to Roosevelt or the Congress.

Funds appropriated by the government were first made available on a long-term cooperative-loan basis to public power companies, municipalities, and independent corporations. Early in 1935, however, most of the power companies decided, on advice of legal counsel, not to enter into cooperative agreements with the REA while important legal conflicts were pending or developing with the federal government over such issues as power sites, water-flow rights, and utility franchises. Therefore, if the program of rural electrification was to be carried through, it was necessary for Congress to choose between (a) lending money to existing power companies or to their customers, and (b) establishing cooperative-type organizations that would be independent of the companies. The farmers' choice between these two options was not difficult. The battle was joined, and REA was developed as an agency to finance and facilitate organization of rural electrification cooperatives for generation, transmission, and distribution of electrical power.

This program is what the public power companies have, at various times, called socialism, unfair competition, unnecessary and wasteful duplication of services. In the Congress they have lobbied against acts favorable to the REA, and in state legislatures they have lobbied for laws to further protect and expand their franchises, thus to restrict the growth of the REA programs. Generally, in most states, service territories are assigned by a regulatory commission or other body by issuance of an area certificate. Suppliers are given the right to construct specific facilities. Corridor protection is given to existing and potential consumers within a range of 300 to 2,000 or more feet from existing power lines; and outside of corporate limits, suppliers are generally given the right to serve existing consumers as of the date of an act and to make connections to new customers nearby.

Since, quite naturally, the power companies have tended to develop the most profitable territories first, the REA cooperatives have always had territorial problems, and various tactics have been used by power companies to block establishment of a successful cooperative. In the early years, REA spokespersons alleged that power companies would build lines into the more thickly settled portions of an area in an attempt to destroy the feasibility of a fledgling cooperative. This was called "cream skimming." Or, a power company might build lines into a territory to prevent it from becoming viable for REA development.

Sometimes these were called "spite lines." In most states the biggest battles over territory have taken place since World War II and especially since about 1960, as the growth of urban-surburban living has expanded into formerly rural areas. Territorial disputes continued in many states until more satisfactory laws were passed, and in other states wasteful duplication and pirating of territory still persists.[36]

The power companies organized the National Association of Electric Companies (NAEC), a major purpose of which was to fight further development of the REA as well as the construction of federal multiple-purpose dams, such as might be used by the REA. The NAEC has repeatedly argued in congressional hearings that further appropriations were not needed. In 1945, when about 50 percent of the nation's farms were electrified, representatives of NAEC and the Edison Electric Institute argued that further congressional appropriations were not needed because rural electrification was substantially complete. They contended that there would be unnecessary and wasteful duplication of generation, transmission, and distribution facilities, that the business of electric power supply should be in the hands of "business-managed, tax-paying enterprises," thus implying that the REA cooperatives were not soundly managed or did not pay their fair share of taxes. Throughout the years since 1945, this type of argument has continued.

The REA program reached and passed a policymaking crisis between December 29, 1972, and May 11, 1973, when the new REA act became law. On the first date, the Department of Agriculture, apparently without hearings or previous warnings, announced in a news release "that the REA electric and telephone 2% direct-loan programs are being converted to insured and guaranteed loan programs at somewhat higher interest rates effective January 1, 1973. This action was made possible by the enactment of the Rural Development Act of 1972 in which the Congress provided very broad authorities to make guaranteed and insured loans to finance all types of community development programs."[37] This action drew almost immediate criticism from leading members of the Congress who asserted that the administration had violated the intent of the 1972 act and had usurped the policymaking power of Congress. The general manager of the National Rural Electric Cooperative Association, Robert D. Partridge, immediately issued a statement calling the action "a shock and a disappointment," thereby initiating a campaign to fight against higher interest rates, to restore the direct loan program at existing loan rates, and to obtain support for expansion rather than curtailment of the REA system. During the ensuing 19 weeks of political activity centering in the Congress, the REA mounted an intense political campaign, the success of which may be judged by the fact that the 1973 act was passed by the Senate 93 to 3 and by the House 363 to 25. The vote was hailed by Partridge as "a smashing victory."[38] It was indeed

[36]For a summary of state legislation, see *RE* (formerly *Rural Electrification*), January 1974, pp. 30–33.

[37]*Rural Electrification*, February 1973, pp. 20–24.

[38]*Ibid.*, July 1973, p. 20.

one of the sharpest reversals in many years of a position taken by an administration. Perhaps the REA also gained from the desire of Congress to reassert itself.

The REA success in policymaking is enhanced by a national advertising program, called "Telling the Nation the Truth," or TNT, which has been supported by voluntary contributions from REA member systems since 1960. From 1968 through 1973, the annual budget averaged nearly $350 million from about 670 cooperatives in an average year, of which a major part was spent for advertising in newspapers, national journals, and other media to create a favorable public image for REA in a continuous and wide-ranging public relations effort. As stated editorially, "Vital to rural electrification's good image is understanding of the program's needs, problems and goals among those who may, or do, influence its future. Many audiences must be reached, each in an appropriate way; and this is TNT's job."[39] Policymaking in the REA is indeed a widespread effort and a considerable success must be ascribed to TNT.

A Policy Conclusion

The REA program, viewed as an important part of the national capital and credit policy affecting agriculture, has been broadly developmental in its impact. As a competitive element in the supply of power to rural areas, it has changed the structure of the electric power industry. Although the specific effects on competing sources of electric power cannot be documented here, the general conclusion is that development of the supply of power to rural areas has been accelerated. In this sense, the development of the REA program is consistent with the general support given to monetary expansion and the growth of capital and credit programs in agriculture. It is also consistent with the still more broadly based federal tax policy applying to agriculture.

TAX POLICY AFFECTING AGRICULTURAL INVESTMENT[40]

Federal tax policy and, to a lesser extent, some state policies encourage investment in agriculture by tax credits or write-offs for certain investments which appear as expenses and for which depreciation may be claimed. The provisions affect all investors—farm and nonfarm—with the general advantage going to large-scale investors and to some from outside agriculture. This situation has aroused fears among farm groups that the future of the family farm is threatened, and that the agricultural economy will be dominated in the future by large corporate firms, vertically or horizontally integrated. Specifically, it is charged that wealthy individuals and certain corporations can use high-level investment in agriculture to advantage as a cost or tax write-off while adding to their estate. Thus, they may escalate property accumulation, avoid considerable income tax in the process, and eventually pay only a capital gains tax on the accumulated estate.

[39]*Ibid.*, p. 10.
[40]This section draws on an unpublished term paper by Ronald Deiter, Ph.D. candidate in Agricultural Economics, University of Illinois at Urbana-Champaign, 1975.

Investments of High-Income Taxpayers in Agriculture

The federal income tax structure is progressive; marginal tax rates increase coincidentally with income, being based on the principle of ability to pay. At least two major features of the law provide a substantial preferential advantage, however, to the investments of high-income taxpayers.

First, progressive income tax rates do not provide an equal incentive to business spending for all taxpayers. Consider a proposed $100 business expenditure. If the taxpayer does not spend the $100, he must pay income tax on it. If the taxpayer is in the 70 percent tax bracket, $70 of the $100 would be paid in taxes. His real cost of making the investment is therefore only $30. Contrast this with a taxpayer in the 14 percent tax bracket. His taxes on the $100 would be $14, so the real cost of the business expenditure to him is $86. In essence, the graduated income tax system results in a tax subsidy for business expenditures, where the amount of the benefit is directly proportional to the level of the tax bracket. High-bracket taxpayers have more incentives to invest in agriculture (or other business) than do low-bracket taxpayers.

A second area of preferences deals with capital gains being taxed at more favorable rates than ordinary income, but again, taxpayers with high incomes receive a proportionately greater benefit. Compare two taxpayers: A, who is in the lowest, 14 percent bracket, and B, who is in a 70 percent bracket. Assume each has $1,000 worth of capital gains income.

Then: A will exclude one-half the capital gain from his income and will pay a tax of 14 percent on the remaining $500. His capital gains tax is $70. His tax savings are also $70, for without the opportunity to exclude one-half the capital gains income, his tax on the $1,000 would have been $140.

B may take advantage of the provision that individuals with capital gains up to $50,000 may either pay a capital gain tax of 25 percent on the total capital gain, or pay a rate equal to their ordinary income tax rate on one-half the capital gain, whichever is lower.[41] Agriculture is useful for such handling of capital gains because most farm real estate and most livestock held for draft, breeding, or dairy purposes is eligible for capital gain treatment when sold. The holding period for such purposes was increased from six to nine months in 1977 and to twelve months in 1978 and subsequent years.

B will pay a tax of 25 percent on the entire $1,000, since this tax will be $250, whereas it would have been $350 if the choice were to pay the tax on one-half the capital gains at the ordinary income tax rate ($500 × 70 percent). B would have to pay $700 in taxes on the gain if it were ordinary income. The tax savings are $700 minus $250, or $450, which is more than 6 times the savings accruing to A with the same level of capital gains income. The savings are again greater for taxpayers in high-income brackets.

[41]U.S. Department of Treasury, Internal Revenue Service, *Sales and Exchanges of Assets*, Publication 544, Washington: Government Printing Office, 1972. See also *New Provisions 1976 Tax Reform* (Public Law 94-455), Chicago: Commerce Clearing House, Inc., 2d printing, No. 5439, October 1976.

The greatest tax savings from use of the capital gains provisions go to tax payers in the higher brackets and to those who have substantial income from outside of agriculture. In the latter case farm investments reported on a cash basis may be used to establish losses for income-tax accounting purposes.

A type of tax-loss farming is perhaps most evident in large beef-breeding enterprises where it has been shown that under specified prices and input costs, with the capital gains provision, nonfarm investment in beef-cow herds is profitable; whereas, under the same prices and costs but without the provision of offsetting nonfarm income with farm losses, nonfarmer investors would realize substantial losses.[42] Furthermore, losses would occur even with much more favorable costs and prices. Without the capital gains provision and under the conditions specified, for taxpayers at or above the 50 percent tax bracket, for example, the yearly return to nonfarmer invested capital would be less than 4 percent, and then only under most favorable price and cost conditions. The conclusion is that given the current capital gains tax incentives for nonfarm capital to enter commercial beef-breeding enterprises, there is substantial loss to society in terms of excessive investment stimulation and heightened competition against family farms. Whereas the loss to the federal government in terms of revenues not received from high-income nonfarm investors is large, the tax value of the provisions to most family farm investors is around 15 percent of their income taxes.

The type of nonfarmer investor who has received the most publicity is the one who channels his investments through a farm management company. The management company usually purchases the cattle on behalf of the investor-client, cares for, feeds, and markets the cattle, and performs other management or financial services for specified fees and charges. The purpose is not to lose money through inefficient operations, and usually contracts guarantee the investor that the farm management company will be as efficient as possible.

But the Internal Revenue Code permits farmers to use the cash receipts and disbursements method of accounting in keeping their books for tax purposes; by using the cash basis of accounting, farmers can ignore year-end inventories of raised products, such as crops and livestock, for income tax purposes since such products are not considered income until actually sold.[43] Operating losses can occur quite often, especially in cattle operations, because only one-half the calf crop need be sold in a year if the heifer calves are converted into breeding stock; and after that year, the long-term buildup can be taxed as capital gain.[44] Either too large a loss in a given year or no loss is a condition to be avoided for most profitable income tax management.[45]

[42]U.S. Department of Agriculture, Economic Research Service, *Farm and Nonfarm Investment in Commercial Beef Breeding Herds: Incentives and Consequences of the Tax Law,* Report No. 497, Washington: Government Printing Office, 1972.

[43]James D. Keast, "Tax Loss Farming—Myths, Facts, and Loopholes," in National Farm Institute, *Corporate Farming and the Family Farm,* Ames: Iowa State University, 1970, pp. 50–57.

[44]Hoy F. Carmon, "Tax Shelters in Agriculture: An Example for Beef Breeding Herds," *American Journal of Agricultural Economics,* Vol. 50, No. 15, December 1968, pp. 1591–1595.

[45]William E. Martin and Jimmie R. Gatz, "Effects of Federal Income Taxes on Cattle-Ranch Prices," *American Journal of Agricultural Economics,* Vol. 50, No. 1, February 1968, pp. 41–55.

There is substantial evidence to indicate that tax-loss farming operations do exist. In 1966, for example, 108 individuals with annual incomes of more than $1 million were involved in some phase of farming, and 93 of them reported farming losses for income tax purposes.[46] In 1967 there were 113 individuals filing farm returns with annual incomes of $1 million or more, 101 of whom reported a net farm loss.[47] The 1969 federal income tax returns showed that 13,187 individuals with adjusted gross incomes between $50,000 and $100,000 reported $124 million in farm losses; in addition, about 75 percent of 7,614 individuals with farming activities and annual incomes over $100,000 reported farm losses totaling $117 million.[48]

Clearly, tax incentives not only attract nonfarmer capital into agriculture; they also influence the type of farm organization as well, with the ultimate impact being levied on the structure of the agricultural sector. At present, not enough is known about the costs and returns to producers and the impact on efficiency and resource allocation. More adequate policymaking in this area requires more information on the importance to agriculture of nonfarmer investments; on whether there should be efforts to replace such investments if possible; and on whether there are more tax advantages in agriculture than in other sectors of the economy. In considering such questions, it is appropriate to distinguish between impacts of a corporate form of organization (not necessarily nonfarmer) and the effects of truly nonfarmer investments in agriculture.

Corporations in Farming

In 1968 some 13,300 farming corporations operated 7 percent of all farm land in the 48 contiguous states, sold 8 percent of all farm produce, and owned or rented an average of 4,531 acres, which was about 8 times the average of all commercial farms.[49] The fear most often expressed is that this type of organization will expand to take over a progressively larger part of farm resources and will continue on to integrate other farm service and marketing firms into a small number of large conglomerates. Beginning in the 1930s, a number of states placed restrictions on corporate farming operations generally to limit either the amount of acreage a corporation could own or the range of agriculturally related investments that could be made.[50] Federal law does not place direct restrictions on corporations in farming. Recently, in the Farm Credit Act of 1971 (discussed above), restrictions were eliminated on lending to farm corporations by federally sponsored farm credit agencies, which had required personal as well as corporate

[46]Gaylord Nelson, "Summary of Remarks," by Cooperative Extension Service, University of Nebraska College of Agriculture and Home Economics, and U.S. Department of Agriculture, *Corporation Farming—What Are the Issues?* Report No. 53, Proceedings of North Central Workshop, Chicago: 1969, p. 13.

[47]U.S. Senate, statement of George Meany speaking on "AFL-CIO Program Urges Tax Justice and End to $17 Billion Loopholes," 91st Cong., 1st Sess., *Congressional Record*, April 14, 1969.

[48]U.S. Department of Agriculture, Economic Research Service, *Farm and Nonfarm Investments in Commercial Beef Breeding Herds, op. cit.*, 1972.

[49]U.S. Department of Agriculture, Economic Research Service, *Corporations with Farming Operations*, Report No. 209, Washington: Government Printing Office, 1971.

[50]Neil E. Harl, "Farm Corporations—Present and Proposed Restrictive Legislation," in *Corporation Farming—What Are the Issues?, op. cit.*

liability for loans. Loans to corporations under the act are a strictly credit decision. Thus the federal government not only encourages large-scale operation, both personal and corporate, by its handling of capital gains; its policy under the 1971 act offers more advantageous credit terms to corporations than were available previously. Although farm corporations are not eligible to borrow from the Farmers Home Administration, this restriction is of little importance since very few would qualify anyway.

Large-scale operations are often confronted with disadvantages in agriculture, such as greater labor difficulties, more risk and uncertainty, increased management complexity, waste-disposal and other environmental problems,[51] with undesirable effects on the social structure of the rural community.[52] Integration possibilities, however, undoubtedly account for many incentives for the incursion of corporations into agriculture. Coordination of the production process often gives the integrators a known market for their products. Or, on the other hand, a guaranteed supply of inputs of uniform and desired qualities gives advantage in the production process. Product control in terms of specified quantity, size, weight, quality, or color may be important to some agribusiness firms that are trying to produce large volumes of final products with homogeneous characteristics that will meet exacting demand specifications. In 1967, almost all broiler production, a large part of turkey and egg output, and more than half the fluid milk, vegetables, hybrid seed corn, sugar, and citrus fruits raised for processing in the United States were under some form of integrated and controlled arrangements.

Greater access to capital, more flexibility of resource use, advertising benefits, and sentimental reasons may be other explanations of corporate involvement in agriculture. Some corporations may also wish to invest in land for speculative purposes, as a hedge against inflation, or to meet possible future expansion needs. Be this as it may, what are the tax advantages and disadvantages accruing to corporations, and what are the alternatives for policy?

Farm Corporations as Taxpayers

As a separate legal entity, the corporation is also a separate taxpayer for most tax purposes. Two methods of taxing the income of farm corporations are available: the standard method, which taxes corporate income to the corporations; and a newer method, introduced in 1958, which permits shareholders of a closely held corporation to choose to have corporate income taxed to them.[53] If such a choice is made, the corporation is often described as a "corporation taxed like a partnership," a "pseudocorporation," a "tax-option corporation," or a "Sub-

[51]Howard W. Ottoson and Glen J. Vollmar, "The Nonfamily Corporation in Farming," in Gordon Ball and Earl O. Heady (eds.), *Size, Structure, and Future of Farms,* Ames: The Iowa State University Press, 1972, pp. 307–308.

[52]U.S. Senate, Select Committee on Small Business, *Corporation Farming, Hearings,* before a subcommittee of the Senate Select Committee on Small Business on the effects of corporation farming on small business, 90th Cong., 2d Sess., 1968, pp. 303–441.

[53]Cooperative Extension Service, *The Corporate Farm,* North Central Regional Extension Publication No. 11, Pamphlet 273, Ames: Iowa State University, 1960, pp. 10–11.

chapter S corporation." All shareholders of a Subchapter S corporation pay tax on their specific shares of corporate income at their individual tax rate whether they receive that income or leave it in the corporation. If the corporation loses money, the shareholders deduct their respective portions of the loss from their own returns. Likewise, the shareholders report their proportionate shares of capital gains or losses.

To qualify for the special status as a pseudocorporation:

1 The corporation must have only one class of outstanding stock.
2 There must be no more than 10 stockholders or up to 15 after five years as a tax-option corporation.
3 All shareholders must be individuals or estates (although some trusts qualify).
4 All shareholders must consent to election by the corporation.

Tax Rates Under the standard method of taxing the corporation, the first $25,000 of corporate income is taxed at 20 percent, the second at 22 percent, and the balance at 48 percent. These corporate marginal tax rates compare with individual tax rates of 14 percent on the first $1,000 of individual income up to as high as 70 percent on taxable income over $200,000 for married taxpayers filing jointly.[54]

The 1976 Tax Reform Act, Public Law 94-455 (signed October 4, 1976), extended these tax rates on corporations through 1977. This was a reduction from the "permanent" rate of 22 percent on the first $25,000 of taxable corporate income and 48 percent on all additional income.[55]

Deductions A farm corporation computes its taxable income in much the same way as an individual with one exception: It has no personal or nonbusiness deductions. Salaries paid to shareholder-employees, rent paid to shareholder-landlords, and interest paid to shareholder-creditors are allowable corporate deductions.

Some fertilizer and lime expenditures are deductible, and expenditures for clearing land for utilization in the farm business are also deductible. Both individuals and corporations are eligible for these operating-expense deductions.

Dividends Corporate income distributed as dividends is usually taxed twice. Dividends are not tax deductible to the corporation, and they are considered taxable income to the shareholders upon receipt. The double tax on dividends is partially offset by the fact that the first $100 of dividend income to the shareholder is not taxable.

Dividends received by one corporation from another domestic corporation

---

[54]Neil E. Harl, "Do Legal and Tax Rules Favor Large-Scale Agriculture?" *American Journal of Agricultural Economics,* Vol. 51, No. 5, December 1969, pp. 1381–1392.

[55]Donald R. Levi, "Federal Income Tax Law as an Incentive to Corporate Farming," in *Corporation Farming—What Are the Issues? op. cit.,* pp. 61–68. See *New Provisions, op. cit.,* p. 24.

are eligible for an 85 percent dividend-received credit, which reduces the effective rate on such income to 3.0 percent (20 percent × 15 percent) or 7.2 percent (48 percent × 15 percent). To discourage such use of a corporation, a personal holding tax of 70 percent is applied to the taxable income of a corporation if 60 percent or more of its adjusted gross income comes from investments (interest, dividends, annuities, royalties, rents, estate or trust income, and miscellaneous income) and if five or fewer people own 50 percent or more of the stock.

Since dividends are not tax deductible, the tax structure discourages a corporation from distributing them to shareholders and encourages it to keep them as retained earnings until they are liquidated and eligible for capital gains treatment. To pressure corporations not to retain earnings in excess of reasonable business needs in order to avoid paying tax on dividends, an accumulated earnings tax provision was enacted into law.

Operating Loss Deduction   Individuals and corporations, under similar rules, may apply operating losses from a trade or business to income of the three prior years and may deduct from the succeeding seven years' income any unabsorbed operating loss.

Capital Losses   Corporations may carry back and carry forward excess capital losses against capital gains. Individuals, in contrast, are allowed an unlimited carry-forward period and may also offset up to $2,000 of ordinary income in 1977 and $3,000 each year thereafter with excess capital losses.

Capital Gains   Special provisions apply to treatment of capital gains.[56] Corporations pay a maximum capital gains tax of 30 percent. Corporations, unlike individuals, are not entitled to a deduction of one-half of all long-term capital gains income for tax purposes.

Incorporating the Family Farm[57]

Although nearly two-thirds of all farm corporations are incorporated as family businesses, and another 14 percent are owned and controlled by individuals, family farm corporations are generally not regarded as part of the so-called corporate invasion of American agriculture. The corporation owner and farm operator remain one and the same—the farm family. Since these corporations are the predominant type in American agriculture today, however, the advantages and disadvantages of incorporation are a concern for policy.

Advantages   The advantages of incorporation may be listed under various categories as follows:

[56]*Corporation and the Federal Income Tax,* U.S. Department of Treasury, Internal Revenue Service, Publication 542, Washington: Government Printing Office, 1973. See also *New Provisions, op. cit.,* pp. 24–26, 42–43.

[57]N. G. P. Krausz, *Corporations in the Farm Business,* Urbana: University of Illinois Cooperative Extension Service, Circular No. 797, 1972.

1 *Limited liability.* A shareholder is liable for the debts of a corporation only to the extent of the shares of stock he or she owns. However, if the corporation becomes insolvent, the farmer whose total assets are in shares of the corporation loses all his or her property.

2 *Easy transfer of ownership.* The owner of a share of stock has the options of selling it, leaving it to designated persons by will, giving it away, or allowing it to go to heirs by law of descent, without breaking up the business. The oncoming generation can gradually buy into the farm business through shares of stock.

3 *Continuity of operation.* A corporation exists as long as the shareholders desire it and the requirements of the law are met. Changes in ownership caused by one generation's replacing another do not interrupt the functioning of the corporation because shares of stock, rather than farm land, livestock, and equipment are passed on to the next generation.

4 *Possible increased efficiency.* Adequate records, along with advance planning and reporting, are an essential part of incorporation and may tend to promote efficiency.

5 *Fringe benefits.* Shareholders can be employees of their corporation. As employees, they are eligible for fringe benefits such as retirement plans, tax-free medical benefits, group life insurance, and deferred compensation. Corporate employees, however, are subject to social security taxes at a higher rate than self-employed farmers.

6 *Means of improving credit status and pooling capital.* Incorporation may lead to increased financial strength for several reasons. First, the functioning and life of a corporation do not depend upon the lives of its employees or stockholders; that is, there is continuity of operation. Second, lenders and investors prefer to deal with more permanently based forms of business organization, such as the corporation, where they expect to find more unified and able management. Third, the credit and ability to pool assets of a corporation are not impaired by individual liabilities. And as farms have grown larger and as the adoption of new technology has spread, the demand for capital by farmers has accelerated at an unprecedented rate. Incorporation in many cases has helped to fulfill these needs.

7 *Tax advantages.* Although the legal and tax structure does not systematically discriminate against either corporations or noncorporations or against large-scale versus small-scale farmers, there frequently are tax advantages to incorporation, the specifics of which will vary among firms. To consider just one case, for example, using 1977 rates: Suppose a farmer has $60,000 of taxable income. Assume that $20,000 is used for personal living expenses and $40,000 is invested in the farm business. If tax is paid on the $60,000 as individual income, the tax will be $26,390. If the farm business is incorporated, however, the farmer may collect a $20,000 salary and leave the other $40,000 in the corporation or invest it in the farm business. The combined individual and corporate income tax would be $13,530, resulting in a tax saving by incorporation of $12,860.

Numerous other illustrations could be given, some of which might show no tax advantage to incorporation, but enough may be said to suggest that the possible tax-saving incentive, along with the other incentives or advantages of incorporating the family farm, may have contributed to the increasing number of corporate family farms.

Disadvantages   Incorporating the family farm may also have disadvantages, such as the following:

   1 *Initial cost of incorporation.* A corporation must pay certain fees and taxes which are not required for other types of business organization, such as filing fees paid to the Secretary of State for filing the articles of incorporation, an application to reserve a corporate name, and the annual report. There are also franchise taxes and license fees to be paid. Even a small corporation may have a $300 to $400 bill for initial taxes and charges.
   2 *Formality of incorporation and operation.* The law is quite specific about procedures required in operating a corporation. Shareholders, directors, and officers must perform the duties and exercise the powers granted to them by law in managing the corporation. Complete and accurate records of accounts, meetings, shareholders, and number and classes of stock must be kept at all times. Directors and officers must be elected, corporate policies and practices must be resolved, and, at a minimum, annual reports must be filed.
   3 *Restricted market for shares.* There may not always be a ready outside market for shares of a closely held family corporation. This could create a locked-in position for a minority shareholder where a majority of the shareholders are unwilling to purchase his or her shares. The stockholder's only alternative may be to sell the shares at less than actual value.

   Aforementioned advantages and disadvantages of incorporation undoubtedly explain, at least in part, the substantial increase in family farm corporations in recent years, especially among large family farms and those that are even larger.

A Policy Conclusion

Tax laws help to account for the growth of corporate farming, for the use of agriculture as a tax shelter for high-income taxpayers outside of agriculture, and for growth of large-scale enterprise relative to the family farm. Although efforts have been made to close the tax loopholes open to wealthy individuals and to reduce some of the advantages to large corporations, the results so far have been meager.[58] The tax law gives substantial advantages in farm investment to large-scale investors, especially to those having considerable income from nonfarm sources, and to some types of corporations. Given the progressive rate structure of the federal income tax, the small-scale or bona fide family farmer is disadvan-

---

[58]Senator Metcalf (Democrat of Montana), for example, introduced a bill to limit the use of farming losses to reduce taxes on nonfarm income, but it died in committee. See "Will Big Corporations Take Over Farming," *Farm Journal,* April 1968, pp. 36–37, 123.

taged to a far greater extent than apparently was intended by Congress in setting this rate structure.

Of specific importance, taxation of certain types of farm income as capital gain offers advantages to high-income taxpayers, especially individuals and corporations reporting significant income from both farm and nonfarm sources. Consequently, the family-sized farm suffers because the presence of nonfarm investors tends to inflate prices of farm and grazing land and to increase the competition for other inputs. Although the effects appear to be greatest in cattle production and other livestock enterprises, the effects are also spread widely over most of agriculture.

Although bona fide family farmers would gain competitive advantage from an amendment that strictly limits the tax losses that can be claimed on farm operations to reduce taxes on the combined farm and nonfarm income, the family farmer would benefit from the more fundamental reform of eliminating the capital gains provision completely. Additionally, if this reform were combined with shifts in emphasis away from property taxes and displacement by federal and state income taxes as discussed in Chapter 8, the bona fide family farmer would gain relatively more. These moves would, moreover, have other general beneficial effects on the efficiency of resource use, the cost of land, and other resources.

Inheritance: Gift and Estate Taxation as a Policy Issue

The taxation of inheritance raises additional issues of great importance to agriculture. The ways in which they are settled in the future will also have a great deal to do with concentration and the structure of agriculture. Since only about 2 percent of either federal or state revenues come from gift and estate taxes, and since taxes paid on farm property inheritance are only a very small fraction of this 2 percent, the issue is not primarily fiscal or significant for government revenues. Although the federal tax is, in toto, much more important than the state tax, the policy issue is mainly one of equity and economic structure of agriculture.

How Farm Inheritance Has Been Taxed   From 1941 through 1976, the federal estate tax on transfer at death, which became a permanent part of the federal revenue system in 1916, was computed on a "taxable estate" after deduction of a $60,000 specific exemption. The tax rate varied from 3 percent on taxable estates of $5,000 or less up to 77 percent on estates of $10 million or more. Before applying the $60,000 exemption, a marital deduction could be applied up to one-half of the adjusted gross estate. Under the gift tax on transfers during a person's lifetime, at three-fourths of the rates on transfers at death, an individual could give up to $3,000 a year to each of any number of individuals without incurring any gift tax. Furthermore, in addition to the annual gift, each individual had a $30,000 lifetime exemption and a marital exemption of one-half of the gift to a spouse.

The Tax Reform Act of 1976   This Act, which extended income tax reductions and made other changes, combined lifetime gifts and transfers at death into a single tax schedule. The new range was from 18 percent to 70 percent, and a system of tax credits was established, which provided an "equivalent" exemption, rising from 1977 through 1981, as follows:

Year	Credit	"Equivalent" Exemption
1977	$30,000	$120,666
1978	34,000	134,000
1979	38,000	147,333
1980	42,500	161,563
1981	47,000	175,625

In addition an increased marital deduction became available for transfers to a spouse: the greater of $250,000 or 50 percent of the qualifying property transferred to the spouse. Thus, an estate qualifying for the marital deduction would not be subject to any tax during 1977 until it exceeded $370,666. During and after 1981, the figure would be $425,625. Also, as from 1941 to 1976, an individual could give $3,000 a year to each of any number of individuals without incurring a gift tax.

The comparative taxes on estates of varying sizes, not counting the marital deduction, would be as follows:

	Estate taxes: 1941–1976		Estate taxes under the 1976 act[60]	
Taxable estate before the exemption	Estate tax if only $60,000 exemption is available	Estate tax using both $60,000 estate exemption and $30,000 lifetime gift tax	Estate tax 1977	Estate tax in 1981 and thereafter
$ 100,000	$ 4,800	$ 500	—	—
200,000	32,700	23,700	$ 24,800	$ 7,800
400,000	94,500	84,900	91,800	74,800
750,000	212,200	201,700	218,800	201,300
1,000,000	303,500	292,400	315,800	298,800

Special Provision Applying to Agriculture   Of considerable importance in many farm transfers, if certain conditions are met, real property used for farming

[59]For verification of some of the above data and for further discussion, see *Death and Taxes, Policy Issues Affecting Farm Property Transfers,* North Central Regional Extension Publication 40. W. Fred Woods, Harold D. Guither, Leonard R. Kyle, C. Allen Bock, Ralph E. Hepp, Gerald A. Harrison, Harold F. Breimyer, and Michael D. Boehlje prepared the publication under the cooperative extension project, Who Will Control U.S. Agriculture? University of Illinois at Urbana-Champaign, College of Agriculture, Cooperative Extension Service, Special Publication 38, September 1975.

[60]Public Law 94-455, Title XXII, Estate and Gift Taxes. See *Estate and Gift Tax Changes under 1976 Tax Reform,* Chicago: Commerce Clearing House, Inc., Federal Estate and Gift Tax Reports, extra ed., No. 270, October 7, 1976.

and some other trades or businesses may be valued on the basis of its use instead of, as had been the case, on the basis of "highest and best use." In general, to establish such value for tax purposes, the average annual gross cash rental for comparable farm property *less* the average annual state and local real estate taxes for comparable property is to be *divided* by the annual effective interest rate for all new federal land bank loans. At least 50 percent of the adjusted value of the decedent's gross estate must be composed of property to which the rule applies. Where this provision applies, it generally increases the amount of farm property escaping taxation and reduces the tax on the total property by moving the nonexempt property into lower tax brackets. This special valuation process will be available, however, to reduce the value of an estate up to $500,000.

A Policy Conclusion The case for reducing gift and estate taxes on farm inheritances rested largely on the proposition that, between 1941 (when rates were last adjusted) and 1976, the average size of farm about doubled and the average capital value per acre increased more than 10 times; so the taxable estate increased several times on individual operating units. It was argued that this accelerated the trend away from owner operation in favor of more tenancy, a condition inconsistent with the goals of American farm policy. Thus, some modification of gift and estate taxes applying to agriculture could be supported as consistent with more general goals.

Although a more liberal gift and estate tax policy will facilitate the transfer of farm properties intact, selective treatment of farm property will make ownership of farm land more attractive to investors from outside of agriculture. The special treatment of capital gains in farm-income-tax accounting and the use of tax-loss farming to reduce taxes on nonfarm income have already exerted a powerful force in this direction. The combined result may be to further reduce the number of opportunities for new operators to enter farming and further concentrate the ownership of farm property.

FEDERAL CROP INSURANCE AS A POLICY ISSUE

Federal crop insurance, conceived as a program under which farmers may insure their incomes against loss due to adverse weather and weather-related phenomena over which they have no control, has had a mixed experience in the United States. For this reason, crop insurance may be conceived as an issue relating to capital and credit policy and the financial security of farm owners and operators.

Experience with Federal Crop Insurance

Passage of the Federal Crop Insurance Act in 1938 (7 U.S.C. 1501) established the Federal Crop Insurance Corporation (FCIC), a wholly owned government corporation. The FCIC was to be the policy implementer to promote the national welfare by improving the economic stability of agriculture through a sound system of crop insurance, and by providing the means for the research and experience helpful in devising and establishing such insurance. Millions of farmers had suffered large losses or had been ruined financially in the drought years of the 1930s. The purpose of the act was to provide a nationwide program to offer security against such catastrophe. The FCIC was set up to insure crops against practically all causes of crop losses, including weather, insect infestations, and plant disease.

The FCIC was authorized to fix premiums, generally on a countywide basis, at so much per acre, to cover claims on insured crops, the insured levels being a certain percentage (such as 50 percent or 75 percent) of a farm's normal verified yield experience. Initially, the FCIC was authorized to fix premiums at rates sufficient to cover claims for crop losses and to establish a reserve against unforeseen losses, but not to cover operating and administrative expenses and the direct cost of loss adjustment—primarily crop inspections and loss determinations. The act of 1938 (Section 516, a) set a limit of $12 million per fiscal year to be appropriated for such costs. Management of the FCIC was vested in a board of five members, subject to appointment and general supervision of the Secretary of Agriculture.

The General Goal Federal all-risk crop insurance then had the goal of developing a self-sustaining operation with the premiums paid by farmers sufficient to cover both indemnities paid and administrative costs. The insurance would offset disaster losses, rather than the full value of a crop in a normal year, by insuring as an approximate minimum the return of money and expenses normally incurred in crop production. The ultimate goal then would be to stabilize the farmers' status on the land, to protect a minimum living standard, and to provide far greater stability in land tenure and farming operation.

Experience and Constraints The experience of the FCIC, as appraised in congressional hearings and government reports, is generally regarded as good, with net losses in years of poor crops and gains when crops have been good. In the first few years after the FCIC was organized, crop insurance was limited to wheat and cotton, and the experience was unfavorable to the FCIC. The 1944 Agricultural Appropriations Act provided only for liquidating the insurance on 1943 and earlier crops, and the 1945 Agricultural Appropriation Act provided only $350,000 for continued termination.[61] At this time, however, the House Committee on Agriculture considered amendments to the Federal Crop Insurance Act to improve the basic legislation and to reinstate the program on a basis that would provide more opportunity for successful operations. The FCIC was authorized to add additional crops to the program and to use experience rating in setting premium and indemnity levels. In six of the nine years from 1948, when the new authorizations began to be implemented on significant scale, to 1956, indemnities exceeded premiums. Then there were five years of good crops, and in 1961 the FCIC began to give primary consideration to expanded service to

---

[61]*Report of the Manager of the Federal Crop Insurance Corporation,* 1944. At the end of the commodity and crop year 1943, the totals for 1939 through 1943 were $38.7 million in premiums collected and $71.6 million in indemnities paid, on an insured production of 436.7 million bushels of wheat.

farmers. Its concern involved expanding the number of crops insured and getting more accurate data on insured levels. In 1958 and 1959, a new contract was instituted which permitted a farmer to add new crops to the initial coverages simply by endorsement. From 1948 to 1971, premiums ($654.8 million) exceeded indemnities ($620 million) by $34.8 million, an indemnity ratio of 95 percent. In 1972, the FCIC had a net gain from insurance operations of $17.2 million, less operating and administrative expense of $14.7 million. Insurance in force totaled $949 million, the highest since the program began, on 23 commodities in 1,422 counties.[62] Since 1972, generally there have been losses in years of poor crops, such as in 1974, and gains in years of good crops.

Although participation by farmers has been highest in the high-risk areas of the country, which demonstrates the need for insurance, at the high point of participation the FCIC contracts have covered less than 5 percent of the total value of the crops being grown in the country. Set against the stated goals, the program has fallen short. The failure to attract more farmers suggests that they have not looked with favor on the premium-indemnity schedules offered in the insurance contract, and if a major breakthrough is to be made in crop insurance policy, new systems must be developed.

New Systems for Crop Insurance[63]

To provide protection for a farmer against loss from crop failure due to conditions beyond his control, actuarial data must be based on the probable occurrence of these conditions. A farmer should not be compensated for losses resulting from the failure to farm efficiently in a given year. To be actuarially sound, the insurer must separate the risk of loss from factors that are not influenced by the individual farmer's performance and loss from those that are. The former, such as an area yield or certain weather phenomena, are insurable. The latter are not. Both premiums and indemnities must be based on criteria that are independent of the farmer's performance, or exogenous to the individual farm.

Area-Yield Insurance   Actuarially sound insurance protection can be provided by offering insurance on the yield record of a homogeneous area, such as a county or a specific type of farming area that may be either larger or smaller than a county. Premiums can be based to insure a certain percentage of the area yield, and indemnities would be paid to any insured farmer when the area yield in a year fell below the level specified in the insurance contract. That is, indemnities for insured farmers would be based on the index of yield of a previously selected sample of farms in the area, rather than on the specific yield experiences of the insured farm.

---

[62]Data from *Audit of Federal Crop Insurance Corporation,* Fiscal Year 1972.

[63]The balance of this discussion on insurance contract policy alternatives draws on Harold G. Halcrow, "Actuarial Structures for Crop Insurance," *Journal of Farm Economics,* Vol. XXXI, No. 3, August 1949, pp. 218–443; and Harold G. Halcrow, "The Theory of Crop Insurance," unpublished Ph.D. dissertation, The University of Chicago, 1948.

Any farmer in the area could be insured without resorting to a study of the farm's specific yield history or its year-to-year yield record. The yield trends on an individual farm would be a matter of indifference to the insuring agency, actuarially speaking. Farmers with increasing yields would not be penalized by use of insurance and farmers with decreasing yields would not be subsidized or indemnified because of their own poor performance. The insured level could be a percentage of normal area yield—such as 80 percent or 90 percent, for example—and farmers could be offered options as to the level at which they wished to purchase insurance. The insuring agency would have a simpler problem in defining normal yields and range of yields for an area than in setting individual normal yields and ranges of yields for hundreds of farms in an area. In addition, a weighted yield index could be developed for an area based on a composite of major crops, which would permit offering comprehensive coverage on any or all crops on an individual farm.

Weather-Crop Insurance   In the case of weather-crop insurance, premiums and indemnities could be based on indexes of weather performance. This insurance would be most easily adapted to areas, such as concentrated fruit and vegetable areas, where yields are closely correlated with such easily identified weather factors as frost and windstorm. It could also be adapted to range lands where a single factor, say, rainfall, is highly determining. Since payment of indemnities would depend on specified meteorological or weather data, the insurer would be actuarially indifferent about trends in yields on individual farms, the crops insured, or the consistency with which individual farmers insured. The important relationship would be the correlation of yields with the data determining the conditions for payment of indemnities and amounts to be paid. Where a significantly high correlation between specific weather data and crop yields is found, weather crop insurance could provide a valuable policy innovation.

Because of increasing knowledge about weather and new computer-assisted methods for more accurately correlating the various weather phenomena, the possibilities for weather crop insurance are much greater for the future than they were in the past. The possibilities for actuarial soundness are much better, more data that are significant in crop yields can be included in an insurance formula, and each datum can be measured with greater precision. In areas where crop yields are closely correlated with rainfall and temperature variations on specified dates in the season, or with specific phenomena such as the date of the first killing frost, such insurance could be used to almost completely stabilize farm incomes against crop failures caused by weather variations.

The insurance could be written to offer farmers a range of choices in respect to the amount of insurance they individually wish to carry per acre. Also, there could be a number of discrete choices expressed as a percentage of normal weather. In a cash grain area, a policy could be written to provide a specified amount of indemnity when rainfall, before a certain date, was a specified amount below normal, for example. Or, in a commercial fruit area, a policy could provide a range of indemnities based on degrees of frost on critical dates. An index could be developed to provide indemnities for crop diseases or insect infestations. With adequate data on weather, the insurance could be actuarially sound over a period of years. Because of the high probability of bunching poor crop years, however, the insurer would need to be a government agency or a private corporation underwritten by the federal government. Given these constraints, a new system of weather-crop insurance could be an innovation of considerable significance for broad areas of American agriculture.

Specific Risks More complete coverage for specific risks such as hail, windstorm, and flooding could be included as special riders attached to area-yield or weather-crop insurance policies. Indemnities would need to be based on specific appraisals of damage, as has become common in both hail policies and in the federal all-risk insurance contract. The indemnity covered by the specific risk would be the difference between the total crop loss and that covered by the area-yield or weather-crop contract. This recognizes that losses may be caused from hail, windstorm or flood regardless of whether a year is otherwise good or bad for crops. The important thing is to base the actuarial calculations for indemnity on events that are beyond the individual farmer's power to control.

Finally, in the event that certain organized programs, such as hail suppression, should have an impact on crop yields or their distribution, crop insurance premiums would need to be adjusted downward to reflect the probable reductions in crop losses.[64] This is a complex matter beyond the scope of our current discussion, however, in which much of the basic research is still to be done.

QUESTIONS FOR DISCUSSION

1 Discuss the effects of inflation on the farm-food system, distinguishing among the effects on farmers, farm service industries, and food marketing and processing.
2 Traditionally, farm organizations have favored fiscal responsibility or balanced budgets to control inflation. Account for this position. What alternatives are there for control of inflation? Are each of them equally applicable to the various stages of the cycle? If not, how would you discriminate among them?
3 How has deflation tended to affect farm and rural people? What policies have been advocated for offsetting or counteracting deflation? Would these have been effective? Comment.
4 What are the general policy goals of the federally sponsored farm credit system? How does the system work to carry out these goals? Distinguish between long-term farm mortgage credit, production credit, and credit for farm cooperatives, as to the

[64]See S. A. Changon, Jr., "Recent Studies of Urban Effects on Precipitation in the United States," *Bulletin of the American Meterological Society,* Vol. 50, 1969, pp. 411–421; J. Lear, "Home-brewed Thunderstorms of La Porte, Indiana," *Saturday Review,* April 6, 1968, pp. 53–55; T. F. Malone, "Weather Modification Implications of the New Horizons in Urban Areas on the Distribution of Thunder Rainfall 1951–1960," *Transactions of Institute of British Geographers,* Vol. 44, 1967, pp. 97–118; and Newsweek editors, "Heavy Industry in Chicago Means More Rain in La Porte," *Newsweek,* April 19, 1968, p. 2.

means for implementation and the constraints that apply in development of lending programs. Appraise the impact of the Farm Credit Act of 1971 on the quantity of farm output, the economic structure of agriculture, and the distribution of income.

5 Distinguish among the direct lending, loan insurance, and guarantee programs in agriculture as to goals and the means for their implementation. How do these programs compare in magnitude with the federally sponsored farm credit programs? How do the means and implementing agencies differ? How do the policy constraints compare in terms of program costs and benefits to the people served?

6 The program of the Rural Electrification Administration has always involved considerable conflict with certain groups and interests. Account for this antagonism by appraising the REA program goals, means, implements, and constraints. What has been the effect of the REA program on growth and development of agriculture? On rural economic development?

7 Discuss the effects of progressive income taxes on investments in agriculture. How do the tax provisions for capital gains affect the aggregate levels of investments in agriculture? Compare the advantages of capital gains provisions to high- and low-bracket taxpayers, especially those regarding crops and livestock and those involving farmers and investors from outside agriculture. What are some of the rules to obtain maximum benefit from tax-loss farming? What are the inferences for policy?

8 Some study groups have recommended that corporate farming should be made illegal because of alleged unfair competition with the family farm. What policies in credit and taxation are favorable to corporate growth? More specifically, how are farm corporations taxed as compared with individuals? What advantages are given to individuals with high nonfarm incomes to invest in farming either as individuals or as a farm corporation? What are the advantages and disadvantages of incorporating the family farm? What are the inferences for policy?

9 It has been suggested that there should be higher exemptions or lower rates to facilitate inheritance of farm property. Discuss the pros and cons of this suggestion. What would be the effects on farm efficiency? On economic structure of the farm economy? On the distribution of income?

10 What has been the goal of federal crop insurance? By review of the experience of the Federal Crop Insurance Corporation, comment on how well this goal may have been achieved. What are the comparative advantages and disadvantages of area-yield insurance and weather-crop insurance?

REFERENCES

Azevedo, Ross E., "Phase III—A Stabilization Program that Could Not Work," *The Quarterly Review of Economics and Business,* Vol. 16, Spring 1976, pp. 7–21.

      Andrew F., "Alternative Monetary-Fiscal Policies and Sectoral Credit Flows," *The American Economic Review,* Vol. LXIV, No. 2, May 1974, pp. 112–120.

Burns, Arthur F., "The Real Issues of Inflation and Unemployment," *Challenge, The Magazine of Economic Affairs,* January/February 1976, pp. 6–11.

Crotty, James R., and Leonard A. Rapping, "The 1975 Report of the President's Council of Economic Advisers: A Radical Critique," *The American Economic Review,* Vol. LXV, No. 5, December 1975, pp. 791–811.

Halcrow, Harold G., "Actuarial Structures for Crop Insurance," *Journal of Farm Economics,* Vol. XXXI, No. 3, August 1949, pp. 218–443.

Means, Gardiner C., "Simultaneous Inflation and Unemployment: A Challenge to Theory and Policy," *Challenge, The Magazine of Economic Affairs,* September/October, 1975, pp. 6–20.

Meyer, John R., and Daniel A. Weinberg, "On the Classification of Economic Fluctuations," *Explorations in Economic Research, Occasional Papers of the National Bureau of Economic Research,* Vol. 2, No. 2., Spring 1975, pp. 167–202.

Nordhaus, William, and John Shoven, "Inflation 1973: The Year of Infamy," *Challenge, The Magazine of Economic Affairs,* May/June, 1974, pp. 14–22.

Saulnier, R. J., Harold G. Halcrow, and Neil A. Jacoby, *Federal Lending and Loan Insurance,* a study by the National Bureau of Economic Research, Princeton, N.J.: Princeton University, 1958, chap. 6.

Chapter 10

Human Resource
and Income Policies

A man educated at the expense of much labour and time to any of those employments which require extraordinary dexterity and skill may be compared to one of those expensive machines. The work which he learns to perform, it must be expected, over and above the usual wages of common labour, will replace in him the whole expense of his education, with at least the ordinary profits of an equally valuable capital.

Adam Smith
Wealth of Nations[1]

Human resource and income policies applied to the farm food system have increased the supply of management and labor while other policies in the areas of science and technology have decreased the demand, especially in the farm sector. This imbalance has depressed marginal rates of return to management and labor in farming, causing widespread and sometimes catastrophic adjustments in both farming and the rural community. Although the policies have been less depressing or more rewarding to high-level management than to low-

---

[1]Modern Library edition, p. 101.

level management, and to highly skilled workers than to unskilled workers, the shock of adjustment has been felt throughout agriculture.

In summary, in human resource terms there have been high rates of product yield from investments in education, management, and vocational training. This return is equivalent to an expansion in supply of management and labor, which tends to depress the marginal rate of return to management and labor. Because of difficulties in adjustment, the policies have created a chronic excess supply of low-level management and unskilled labor, which is reflected in a substantially large poverty sector in the farm and rural community. Although the high rates of yield from investments in human resources are desired, some of the income consequences are not. The purpose of this chapter is to set the goals in broader perspective and to analyze some of the policy alternatives.

HUMAN RESOURCE GOALS AND CAPITAL THEORY

Under the concept of human capital, people are viewed as a unique product of investment.[2] Starting with innate ability, they develop their capacity to make a contribution to production by a process of investment in which current resources are sacrificed for future returns through formal education, migration, private effort, and on-the-job training. This investment, combined with investments in other resources, yields returns over the lifetime of the individual, which may be consumed, saved, or given to others. This concept can consistently explain various phenomena in the markets for management and labor, or human capital, in general and in our area of concern.

Efficiency and Equity

Returns to human capital investment are generally high in the American economy. Although we do not have ways of identifying the aggregate return to human capital investment or the composite rate of return for the total economy, the estimated average private rates of return that characterize United States education—one of the main forms of human capital investment—are high, compared with returns from other investments (Table 10-1). The inference is that the efficiency of the economy—the rate of output to input—is increased by shifting investments toward education and other investments in human capital until the private rates of return, including money and other satisfactions, equate at the margin with returns from other nonhuman capital investment. Equalization of marginal rates of return among alternative investments is the general criterion of efficiency.

The general criterion of equity, applied to human capital investment, is that a just or equitable society will attempt to offer to each individual an equal opportunity to be productive through publicly supported schools and other

[2]For a more general discussion on human capital, see Theodore W. Schultz, "Human Capital: Policy Issues and Research Opportunities," in *Economic Research: Retrospect and Prospect. Human Resources,* 50th Anniversary Colloquium VI, New York: National Bureau of Economic Research, 1972.

Table 10-1   Estimates (Percentages) of Private Rates of Return to Investments
in the United States in Education, Corporate Manufacturing, and the Private
Domestic Economy

Year	High school graduates (white males, after personal taxes)*	University graduates (white males, after personal taxes)*	Corporate manufacturing firms (after profit taxes but before personal taxes)†	U.S. private domestic economy (implicit rates of return after profit taxes but before personal taxes)‡
1939	16	14.5		
1949	20	13.+		12.6
1956	25	12.4	7.0 (for period 1947–57)	14.4 (1955–56)
1958	28	14.8		12.3 (1957–58)
1959	Slightly higher than in 1958			9.7
1961	Slightly higher than in 1958			11.2 (1960–61)
1963–65	—	—		13.3

*From Gary S. Becker, *Human Capital: A Theoretical and Empirical Analysis, with Special Reference to Education,* New York: National Bureau of Economic Research, 1964.
†*Ibid.,* p. 115 and n. 2.
‡D. W. Jorgenson and Zvi Griliches, "The Explanation of Productivity Change," *Review of Economic Studies,* Vol. 34, July 1967, p. 268.
Source: Theodore W. Schultz, "Human Capital: Policy Issues and Research Opportunities," in *Economic Research: Retrospect and Prospect. Human Resources,* 50th Anniversary Colloquium VI, New York: National Bureau of Economic Research, 1972, p. 29, and Schultz, "Resources for Higher Education: An Economist's View," *Journal of Political Economy,* May/June 1968, p. 337.

means. Since human capital in the form of innate ability is more equally distributed than nonhuman capital (income-producing property), improvements in educational opportunity equally available to all will provide for improvements in equity. This proposition, when applied to the national economy, has led to two hypotheses:[3] (1) Improvements in elementary and secondary education which (theoretically, at least) have been made available to all have been somewhat progressive in their income effects (tending to make the distribution of income more equal). (2) Improvements in higher education, because of restrictions on entry, cost, etc., have not been so widely available or so broadly utilized, and the general results have tended to be regressive in their income effects (tending to make the distribution of income less equal).

These two hypotheses have led to what has been called the "equity-efficiency quandary" in policy for investments in higher education.[4] The basic thesis is that the allocation of resources to provide instruction in higher education is neither socially equitable or efficient. On the side of equity, generous subsidies

[3]Schultz, *ibid.,* p. 26.
[4]See Theodore W. Schultz (ed.), "Investment in Education: The Equity-Efficiency Quandary," Workshop at the University of Chicago, June 7–10, 1971, sponsored by the Committee on Basic Research in Education of the National Research Council, *Journal of Political Education,* Vol. 80, No. 3, part II, May/June 1972.

are extended to all college students by general tax support of public colleges and universities, thus subsidizing in measure relatively affluent and high-income families. Some of the children in large families in the middle-income brackets, children from broken homes, and children of the poor or otherwise disadvantaged more frequently do not participate, or are not able to enjoy the opportunities that are made available. On the efficiency side, appropriate signals are not sufficiently available or given to enable students to make socially efficient choices in regard to citizenship and careers, which in large measure determine lifetime incomes and satisfaction. Categories of opportunity are not neatly arranged according to each individual's comparative ability, ambition, aptitude, etcetera, so people are not drawn to them. The losses from the failure to achieve one's best career opportunity increase as the economy advances in its complexity and in its use of specialized skills. The benefits from counseling, career guidance, and similar aids gain importance as a result of the growing diversity of career choices.

Fortunately, in terms of both equity and efficiency, however, growth itself is not an equilibrium state. In the United States, investment in education has occurred at a higher rate than investment in nonhuman capital. Education has become less elite and more mass oriented. The markets for management and labor have become more systematized. In many occupations, standardization and automation have reduced the benefits to be derived from heavy investments in human capital. Because of the structure of the labor market, union rules, and regulations, many jobs that pay well do not require much general skill and the specialty requirements can be quickly learned. As a result, among the major industrial occupations the inequality of income has been reduced, to be replaced by another problem—that of creating and maintaining a sufficient incentive for quality performance and high productivity. At the same time, there is a growing need for a broader and deeper understanding of the functioning of democracy and the economic organization that is the foundation of civilization.

Efficiency of Human Capital Investment in Agriculture

A first approximation of the efficiency of human capital investment in American agriculture can be approached by estimating the net output per man-year by direct (on-farm) and indirect (off-farm) labor used for agricultural production.[5] According to this yardstick, the annual rate of productivity gain of labor in American agriculture was about 1.5 percent around 1920, close to 3 percent around 1940, and 6 percent around 1960.[6] Earlier, the productivity increment was ¾ percent around 1900, ⅜ percent around 1880 and just over ¼ percent in 1870.[7]

---

[5]See Folke Dovring, *Productivity of Labor in Agricultural Production*, University of Illinois at Urbana-Champaign, College of Agriculture, Agricultural Experiment Station Bulletin 726, September 1967. See also W. Gossling and F. Dovring, "Labor Productivity Measurement: The Use of Subsystems in the Interindustry Approach, and Some Approximating Alternatives," *Journal of Farm Economics,* Vol. 48, 1966, p. 375.

[6]Dovring, *op. cit.,* p. 15.

[7]*Ibid.,* p. 18.

Constant 1954 dollars

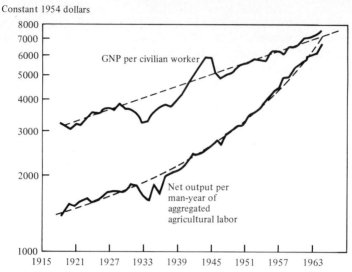

Figure 10-1 Aggregated labor productivity of the civilian labor force and the agricultural labor force in the United States. *(Source: Adapted from Folke Dovring, Productivity of Labor in Agricultural Production, University of Illinois at Urbana-Champaign, College of Agriculture, Agricultural Experiment Station Bulletin 726, September 1967, p. 14.)*

Since 1960, data indicate the possibility (unconfirmed because the new trend is too short) of a deceleration in productivity increase at 3.5 percent per year.[8] With such a deceleration, the rate of productivity gain would be halved in 20 years, but the gains would still be substantial in the years ahead (Figure 10-1).

Figure 10-2 compares gross, net, and aggregated labor productivity in American agriculture, drawn on different absolute scales to make them more readable, although the scales are the same and the slopes of the curves are therefore comparable. The broken lines are all part of the same function, mentioned above, which reflects accelerated productivity gains of 3.5 percent annually. Increase in the productivity of aggregated labor consists of a rising ratio of output to labor used. Given the slow rate at which aggregate agricultural output may increase, reduction of manpower, particularly in farming, is the obvious prerequisite for rapid productivity increase. The fast exodus from farming that has occurred is not an explanation of the phenomenon of rising productivity; it is the main part of the process. Without the migration from farming, especially since the late 1930s, the subsequent increase in farm labor productivity would have been impossible.

The trend over time in aggregated farm labor productivity thus is a function (1) of the trend in farm input technology (increasing leverage of more and more systematic knowledge, allowing a more efficient approach to the problems of mastering nature), (2) of educational, financial, and other allied factors that, together, promote or retard the application of new technology, and (3) of the accelerating tendencies in the economic system as a whole, which determine the

[8]*Ibid.*, pp. 22–23.

opportunities for people migrating from farming. The rate of productivity increase may be said to reflect rates of advancement in technology; but, since output of technology is also a result of human capital investment, the aggregative change in labor productivity reflects wide degrees of complementarity among the various forms of capital. The sum or aggregative effect has been to bring labor productivity in agriculture near to that of the total civilian labor force.

Equity of Human Capital Investments in Agriculture

Because of the differential effects of human capital investments in agriculture, increasing the level of such investment has tended to make the income distribution more skewed in agriculture than in the total economy, with a proportionately larger low-income poverty sector in both the farm and the rural nonfarm population than among metropolitan populations (Table 10-2). Furthermore, in the farm and rural nonfarm populations there are fewer families with incomes over $12,000. Black families (as well as some smaller minority groups) are disadvantaged, compared with the white population. As was noted in Table 7-1, among the smallest farm classes, where less than $10,000 of farm produce is sold annually, the income from off-farm sources exceed that from farm sales. Further, although off-farm income has increased greatly, especially since 1960 (Table 7-2), as late as 1971, income of farm and rural nonfarm families was still unfavorable (Table 10-2). We may note that in 1971, for example, to equalize the income distribution of farm families and white metropolitan families, the number of white

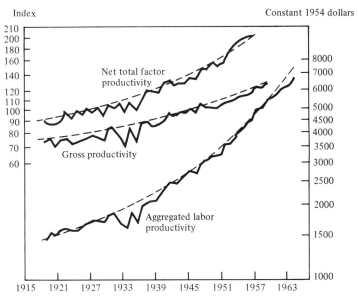

Figure 10-2 Comparison of productivity indexes for American agriculture. (*Source: Adapted from Folke Dovring, Productivity of Labor in Agricultural Production, University of Illinois at Urbana-Champaign, College of Agriculture, Agricultural Experiment Station Bulletin 726, September 1967, p. 14.*)

Table 10-2 Money Income of Families: Farm, Rural Nonfarm,* and Metropolitan, by Race, 1971

Race and residence of families	Total	Percentage distribution by income level					
		Under $2,000	$2,000–$3,999	$4,000–$6,999	$7,000–$11,999	$12,000–$24,999	$25,000 and over
White							
Farm	1,976	9.6	15.3	24.5	29.8	17.9	2.8
Rural nonfarm	13,496	4.4	10.6	19.3	33.8	28.7	3.2
Metropolitan	32,169	2.5	6.4	13.7	30.8	39.7	7.0
Black							
Farm	133	28.5	30.9	19.9	14.2	6.6	0.0
Rural nonfarm	1,073	14.3	24.4	30.7	22.1	8.1	0.3
Metropolitan	3,951	7.7	16.9	23.3	28.9	20.9	1.3

*Rural nonfarm is nonfarm outside metropolitan areas.

Source: Constructed from *Statistical Abstract of the United States, 1973,* U.S. Department of Commerce, Bureau of the Census, table 538, p. 331.

farm families with incomes of less than $7,000 (49.4 percent of all white farm families) would have to be reduced by more than one-half (to 22.6 percent of all white metropolitan families), and the number of black farm families with less than $7,000 in income (79.3 percent of all black farm families) would need to be reduced by more than two-thirds. Further, the percentage of families with annual incomes of $12,000 or more is much lower among both farm and rural nonfarm families than among metropolitan families.

George Tolley, in rationalizing this income distribution, has developed the hypothesis that farms under high-level management have experienced favorable cost-curve shifts and that the number of farm operating units declines as many farm firms with low-level management are displaced by a smaller number of firms under high-level management.[9] This hypothesis leads him to conclude that the agricultural income problem, rather than being caused by an excess supply of resources, is a problem of income distribution caused by differences in earnings between high-level and low-level management. The basic contention is that low-level management is outmoded, being displaced or disappearing from agriculture. The goal of policy should be to compensate outmoded management for obsolescence while moving toward a situation where high-level managers neither need income supplements nor are subject to production control.[10]

Although wide differences in the quality of management in agriculture are readily admitted and the process of adjustment is in the direction that Tolley indicates, the problem of goals raises important questions of value.[11] To what extent shall the poorer managers be displaced rather than having their human capital and other resources upgraded? What special programs shall be implemented to help low-level managers either move with some hope of bettering their condition or stay where they are in agriculture? How much shall society put into such programs? The problem is conceived here as involving basic values to place on human life.

Efficiency in Agricultural Adjustment

According to criteria of efficiency, however, the problem is not just to displace low-level managers. High-level farm managers may be underpaid by just as much as low-level managers in terms of their alternative opportunities elsewhere, or their opportunity cost of staying in farming.[12] Hathaway and Perkins found that, in the long run, among off-farm migrants there is a strong positive correlation between their former earnings in agriculture and their subsequent nonfarm earnings.[13] The inference is that low-level farm managers are not less well paid

---

[9]G. S. Tolley, "Management Entry into U.S. Agriculture," *American Journal of Agricultural Economics,* Vol. 52, No. 4, November 1970, pp. 485–493.

[10]*Ibid.,* p. 492.

[11]Harold F. Breimyer, "Tolley and Management: Unreliable Returns and Nonimputable Costs," *ibid.,* Vol. 53, No. 3, August 1971, pp. 522–523, and Tolley's reply, pp. 523–525.

[12]This point is emphasized by Breimyer in his comment on the Tolley article.

[13]Dale E. Hathaway and Brian E. Perkins, "Occupational Mobility and Migration from Agriculture," in *Rural Poverty in the United States,* Washington: National Advisory Commission on Rural Poverty, 1968, p. 207.

than high-level farm managers in terms of their nonfarm opportunities and that displacement of low-level farm managers by high-level managers contributes little to the total efficiency of the economy, even though the number of operating units declines. Criteria of efficiency call for continuing adjustments at all levels of efficiency until marginal rates of return are equalized between or among the various alternatives.

Human Capital Improvement and Transfer

The general goal combining equity and efficiency calls for two kinds of policies: (1) policies to upgrade or improve human capital, and (2) policies to facilitate migration or transfer of human capital. Both are required because if the supply of human capital is upgraded in farming, *ceteris paribus,* or without migration, the marginal value product of a given amount of human capital in farming is depressed. If migration occurs without upgrading the human resources, the relatively unattractive opportunities available to farm families outside of agriculture will add little to their incomes or to the value of their product to society.

In the past, the income gains of families migrating from farming have been small, especially in times of less than full employment. In three pairs of years, for example, 1957–58, 1958–59, and 1959–60, the average (mean) income gains to first-year off-farm migrants were, respectively, $37, $234, and $212.[14] Approximately 40 percent of those who changed from farm to nonfarm occupations had lower incomes in their nonfarm occupations. Average earnings of migrants did not increase with distance migrated. The long-run earnings of mobile farm workers were strongly correlated with the magnitude of gain or loss in income in the first year of off-farm employment.

The aggregate real wealth of the nation can in fact be reduced by encouraging untrained workers to move into unfamiliar surroundings, and there is considerable evidence that this has occurred in the past. Leon Keyserling (former chairman of the Council of Economic Advisers, consulting economist and attorney, and president of the Conference on Economic Progress) testified, for example, that in his analysis, "uprooted farm workers have contributed maybe half, maybe 60 percent, of the total excess unemployment problem in the United States since 1947 or since 1953, although they are now only 6 percent of the working population." The cost of progress in American agriculture, in other words, is partially embedded "in the taxes which they (consumers) pay to support relief, in the cost of recessions and stagnation, and in the competition in the job market of dispossessed farmers."[15]

As we noted in Chapter 4, however, the earnings of farm managers and laborers have been depressed by low opportunity costs, high transfer costs, and some people's psychic preferences for farming as a way of life (Figure 4-3). The way to improve the general situation is not to discourage transfer of human

[14]*Ibid.,* p. 203.
[15]*Farmworkers in Rural America, 1971–1972,* Hearings, Subcommittee on Migratory Labor, Committee on Labor and Public Welfare, U.S. Senate, 92d Cong., part 1, p. 36.

capital from one occupation to another, but to improve the human capital that is available for transfer and to assist in perfecting the markets for management and labor.

Nature and Magnitude of Human Capital Transfer

Reduced entry of new farm operators, rather than increased migration of older operator families, accounts for the major reductions in the aggregate farm population. This fact can be seen by a study of cohorts (groups of persons born within the same time interval). To illustrate, in 1910 there were 419,000 farm operators between 15 and 24 years of age. The number in this cohort increased rapidly so that by 1920, when the cohort covered operators 25 to 34 years of age, there were 1.33 million. By 1930, as a result of further entry, there were 1.42 million 35 to 44 years of age. Then death, retirement, disability, and change of occupation (not necessarily in that order) began to balance entry into agriculture; so by 1950, when the cohort was 55 to 64 years of age, the number was only 1.43 million. Thereafter it declined rapidly, mostly by retirement rather than by transfer to jobs, so that by the 1959 census date, only 617,000 were in the cohort. By 1969 nearly all were partially or completely retired.

In comparison, in the 1949 census only 164,000 farm operators were under 25 years of age. By 1959, there were 403,000 in the 25-to-34 age cohort, and by 1969, there were 523,000 in the 35-to-44 age group. In 1959, only 62,000 farm operators were under 25 years. By 1969, there were 274,000 in the 25-to-34 age cohort. In 1969, only 53,000 farm operators were under 25 years of age.[16]

Thus, progressively over the last several decades, substantially fewer operators have been entering farming. The average age of the farm population has therefore tended to be high. So, even if entrants continued at the 1970 level, there would be a continued reduction in the farm population, assuming an employment rate at the level of the 1950s or 1960s.

Net migration from farming depends on employment. Thus the total population in farming is a function of both entry and migration. Net migration of people from farms, which was restricted during the Great Depression through lack of off-farm employment opportunity, rose to more than 1 million persons annually during the 1940s and 1950s. Then net migration trended downward to the early 1970s (Table 10-3).

Gross outward migration has been offset by (1) an excess of births over deaths among the farm population, (2) a reverse migration back to farms, and (3) entry of formerly nonfarm people into farming. During 1957–63, gross off-farm mobility, measured as the percentage of farm-employed individuals in one year who changed to nonfarm employment in the following year, averaged 14 percent of the total farm population for each of the six possible periods. The reverse flow, or the in-farm mobility rate, averaged 12 percent.[17] The annual rate of net migration was most importantly affected by the level of employment on a year-

---

[16]*Statistical Abstract of the United States* 1974, table 1007, p. 597.
[17]Hathaway and Perkins, *op. cit.*

Table 10-3 Farm Population and Components of Change, by Decades 1920–1969, and Annual 1970–1973

Year	Farm population, April 1* (millions)	Average annual change by decades 1920–69 and annually 1970–73		Farm population as percentage of total population in year indicated	Annual percentage rate of net migration†
		Births minus deaths† (thousands)	Net migration† (thousands)		
1920	32.0	485	−630	30.1	−2.0
1930	30.5	385	−382	24.9	−1.2
1940	30.5	390	−1,139	23.2	−4.4
1950	23.0	271	−1,013	15.3	−5.3
1960	15.6	116	−744	8.7	−5.7
1970	9.7	47	−642	4.8	−6.6
1971	9.4	43	−330	4.6	−3.5
1972	9.6	29	157	4.6	1.6
1973	9.5	26	−164	4.5	—

*Beginning 1960, April-centered annual averages.
†Averages by decades and annual.
Source: Statistical Abstract of the United States, 1974, table 1004, p. 596.

to-year basis, rather than by major fluctuations in annual farm income. The highest rate of net migration was in 1955–64, a decade of low unemployment. Apparently, migration was not appreciably slowed by the massive farm programs then in existence. But migration was appreciably slowed in the early years of the 1970s as the levels of unemployment rose to new highs, unprecedented since the Great Depression.

The declining farm population resulting from reduced entry has important policy implications. The average age of farm operators, although rising in the past several decades, will return to a more normal distribution. The problem of maintaining adequate farm income will shrink in terms of its national budget implications. But the case for human capital investment per capita for those migrating as well as for those staying in agriculture remains strong. In fact, as the farm economy becomes more capital-intensive, the case for increased human capital investment is strengthened.

Conclusion on Goals

To reach acceptable goals of efficiency and equity, it is necessary to have a diversity of policies that will both upgrade human resources and facilitate broad adjustment or readjustment of these resources. It is not logical to expect, when farming is experiencing continuous upgrading in productivity and displacement of human capital, that real incomes in farming will equal those of the nonfarm population solely as a result of migration unaided by education, information, health programs, subsidies for housing or migration, and the like. The policy means or measures must be broad and inclusive.

POLICY MEANS AND PROGRAMS

The policy means and programs for efficiency and equity in human resource and income programs include, but are not restricted to, the following: (1) improvements in elementary and secondary schooling, including vocational programs; (2) broadening some programs of higher education, especially those of the land grant colleges and universities; (3) special programs for overcoming poverty, including rural community development; and (4) more general programs for human capital investment and mobility.

Elementary and Secondary Education

Rural residents in all regions of the United States, including those living on farms, have shared in the general rise in the nation's educational levels in recent years. Among white people outside metropolitan areas, in March 1970 two out of three persons aged 25 to 44 had completed high school, whereas not quite two out of five persons aged 45 or older had done so. Among black persons, the improvement was more pronounced in relative terms, but their education still lags far behind that of whites. For black farm residents, 90 percent of whom live in the South, more than half those 25 to 44 years of age had had 8 years of schooling or less, and less than one-fourth had had 12 years of schooling or more. Furthermore, among many of the rural schools, especially in the South, the quality of education is inferior.[18] In general, in educational attainment as measured solely by years of schooling, persons in the nonmetropolitan areas of the nation lag behind those in the metropolitan centers. Farm lags behind rural nonfarm, and black lags behind white (Table 10-4).

The policy goal is intrinsically that of correcting some of these inequalities by upgrading school programs in rural areas and equalizing opportunities for farm and nonfarm and for black and white. Its importance is illustrated by the fact that labor income from farming—after eliminating, through regression analysis, the effects of age, capital owned, quality of schooling, and nonlabor inputs used in farming—is significantly affected by years of schooling. Based on 1959 data, for white persons (largely male) living on farms, the increase in income due to increasing the years of schooling from 8 years to 9-11 years was $750, and the increase from 5 to 9 years to 9 to 11 years was approximately $1,200.[19] For nonwhites in the South, however, the difference in farm labor incomes between 5 to 7 and 9 to 11 years of schooling was only about $330.[20] The smaller difference for nonwhites may further reflect the quality of schooling and general lack of farm resources. The general inference is that no more than two additional years of schooling affects income of people living on farms at least as much as does

[18]*Equality of Educational Opportunity,* Washington: U.S. Department of Health, Education, and Welfare, Office of Education, OE-38000, 1966, pp. 20–21.

[19]Finis Welch, "Measurement of the Quality of Schooling," *American Economic Review,* Vol. 56, No. 2, May 1966, p. 384.

[20]*Ibid.*

Table 10-4 Educational Attainment of Persons 25 Years of Age and Over, by Color and Residence, March 1970

	Percentage of population			
	8 years of school or less		12 years of school or more	
Age and residence	White	Black	White	Black
Total	26.1	43.0	57.4	33.7
Metropolitan areas	22.1	36.0	61.5	38.8
Nonmetropolitan areas	33.2	60.9	50.0	20.6
Nonfarm	31.7	59.1	51.2	21.6
Farm	43.1	74.5	42.0	11.9
25 to 44 years	11.8	22.4	71.6	47.9
Metropolitan areas	9.4	18.0	74.7	52.2
Nonmetropolitan areas	16.5	36.3	65.9	34.2
Nonfarm	15.9	34.3	66.2	35.3
Farm	21.8	54.1	62.3	23.7
45 years and over	36.8	63.1	46.6	19.9
Metropolitan areas	32.1	55.7	51.2	24.2
Nonmetropolitan areas	44.9	78.9	38.7	10.5
Nonfarm	43.4	77.9	40.0	11.3
Farm	53.5	86.4	31.9	4.6

Source: U.S. Department of Commerce, Bureau of the Census, Statistical Abstract of the United States, 1971, 1972.

migration from farms to urban areas. Improved schooling in rural areas is one of the most important policy means for investing in human resources in rural areas and, at the same time, reducing the skewness of the farm and rural nonfarm income pattern.

State and Federal Funding as a Policy Means To overcome some of the wide variation in financial support of elementary and secondary schools and to equalize tax burdens among school districts, many states have actively moved to increase state funding; and, starting with passage of the Elementary and Secondary Education Act of 1965, the federal government has moved rapidly to expand its share of the cost. Still, in most states as late as 1974, local property taxes were the main source of support for elementary and secondary schools and more than half of all property taxes went for this purpose. This fact has prompted many students and study commissions to recommend more state and federal funding of regular school programs plus specific grants for designated purposes.[21] Furthermore, beginning in 1971, a series of court decisions brought into question the traditional system of school support based on local property taxes and sought to force (1) more equal support for elementary and secondary schools among school

[21]See, for example, The President's Commission on School Finance, Washington, 1972; State-Local Revenue Systems and Education Finance, Advisory Commission on Intergovernmental Relations, Washington, 1971; National Education Finance Project (5 Vols.), Gainesville, Fla.

districts, and (2) equalization of tax burdens among taxpayers in different districts.

In the initial, path-breaking case in this series, on August 30, 1971, the Supreme Court of the State of California held that in California the local property tax school-funding scheme "invidiously discriminates against the poor because it makes the quality of a child's education a function of the wealth of his parents and neighbors." The court held that, although uniform education expenditures were not mandated by the California constitution (Article IX, No. 5) requiring the legislature to provide for a system of common schools, judicial review under the equal protection clause required active and critical analysis of legislation involving suspect classifications or touching on fundamental interests. The court concluded, "Recognizing as we must that the right to an education in our public schools is a fundamental interest which cannot be conditioned on wealth, we can discern no compelling state purpose necessitating the present method of financing. We have concluded, therefore, that such a system cannot withstand constitutional challenge and must fall before the equal protection (of the Fourteenth Amendment, hence is unconstitutional)."[22]

On October 12, 1971, the United States District Court of Minnesota, in another class action suit brought by and for public school children, stated,

> The rule is that the level of spending for a child's education may not be a function of wealth other than the wealth of the state as a whole. . . . In a number of decisions over the past fifteen years the United States Supreme Court has made it plain that classifications based upon wealth are suspect . . . the variations in wealth are state created . . . the poverty is that of a governmental unit the state itself has defined and commissioned. . . . [It is concluded] that a system of public school financing which makes spending per pupil a function of the school district's wealth violates the equal protection guarantee of the 14th Amendment to the Constitution of the United States.[23]

Hence, the state is responsible for developing a system which does not so discriminate.

Also in December 1971, a United States district court in Texas ruled that the current system of financing public education in Texas discriminates on the basis of wealth by permitting citizens of affluent districts to provide a higher-quality education for their children while paying lower taxes; and that the plaintiffs who brought suit on behalf of all Texas children living in school districts with low property valuations were being denied equal protection of the laws by operation of the Education Code sections relating to the financing of education, including the minimum foundation program. Accordingly, some new form of financing had

[22]*Serrano v. Priest,* cited in *The United States Law Week,* Vol. 40, September 14, 1971, p. 2128.
[23]*Van Dusartz v. Hatfield,* cited in *The United States Law Week,* Vol. 40, October 26, 1971, p. 2228.

to be utilized, with the sole restriction that the program adopted not make the quality of education a function of wealth other than the wealth of the state as a whole.[24] Finally, in a somewhat similar decision, on December 29, 1972, the Michigan Supreme Court, with two justices dissenting, ruled that the Michigan school financing system, which admittedly resulted in revenue inequalities among school districts, could not survive constitutional challenge unless the state could prove that there was no less onerous alternative to achieve the objective of school finance.[25]

On March 21, 1973, the United States Supreme Court, in a five to four decision, held the Texas system of financing schools constitutional, in effect reaffirming use of local property taxes for school financing.[26] The Court held that education "is not among the rights afforded explicit protection under our Federal Constitution." But Justice Lewis F. Powell, Jr., writing for the majority, noted: "The need is apparent for reform in tax systems which may well have relied too long and too heavily on the local property tax. . . ." A minority dissenting opinion, written by Justice Thurgood Marshall, regarded the majority view "as a retreat from our historic commitment to equality of educational opportunity and as unsupportable acquiescence in a system which deprives children in their earliest years of the chance to reach their full potential as citizens. . . ."

Although the United States Supreme Court decision reaffirming the legal use of the property tax for schools permitted various inequalities to continue, more equal funding for schools and equalization of tax burdens must be regarded as a fundamental policy measure for greater efficiency and equity in human capital investment that is especially important for rural areas. It has been shown that the property tax for schools can be displaced by increases in income taxes or sales taxes with general benefits for farmers.[27] This shift also can bring a more uniform standard for school funding and can equalize school finance burdens within and among states and various regions of the country. The initial benefit of such a trend in finance may accrue most importantly to the South and to rural rather than urban areas, but productivity benefits are spread nationwide through the effects of migration and mobility in employment. Although agriculture receives a modest windfall gain by equalization of tax burdens, and although small farms gain relatively more than large farms when property taxes are displaced by income taxes, the greater gains in the general welfare occur through equalizing and therefore enriching the investment in human capital.

---

[24]*Rodriguez v. San Antonio Independent School District,* 337 F. Supp. 280 (D.C. Tex. 1971). For further discussion of the United States Supreme Court review of this case, see *The United States Law Week,* Vol. 41, October 17, 1972, p. 3197.

[25]*Milliken v. Green,* Michigan Supreme Court, *The United States Law Week,* Vol. 41, January 9, 1973, p. 2348.

[26]*San Antonio Independent School District v. Rodriguez, The United States Law Week,* Vol. 41, March 20, 1973, p. 4407.

[27]H. G. Halcrow, Folke Dovring, Arthur Eith, F. J. Reiss, J. T. Scott, Jr., W. D. Seitz, and R. G. F. Spitze, *School Tax Options Affecting Illinois Agriculture,* University of Illinois at Urbana-Champaign, College of Agriculture, Agricultural Experiment Station Bulletin 744, April 1973.

Federally Financed Education and Training   In the United States, as we have noted, elementary and secondary education was traditionally the special right or prerogative of the individual states. The pattern was broken in 1917 when Congress passed the Smith-Hughes Act, which established federal support for the teaching of vocational agriculture in high schools. Although many supplementary acts have been passed, the Smith-Hughes Act set the basic framework for vocational training in agriculture and, in important respects, it was a forerunner of broader vocational training in high schools and in the more recently developing junior colleges. Vocational training for agriculture received a major boost in the 1930s as part of the New Deal programs for expansion of employment. The organization named "Future Farmers of America" was organized to give a voice to the program and to carry out a variety of activities, such as debates, public speaking contests, farm projects, and other competitions. In 1940, one-third of the federal appropriation for vocational education went to agriculture. By 1964, the figure was 23.2 percent. Since then the expansion of vocational education in other areas and the development of junior colleges have reduced this share to a much lower figure. In 1962, enactment of the Manpower Development and Training Act (MDTA) set a new pattern for vocational training for unemployed and underemployed workers. Members of farm families with less than $1,200 annual income were defined as "unemployed" under the act, and were eligible for training allowances. Training was in either farm or nonfarm skills, with monetary allowances for subsistence and transportation for those who needed them during training. Under this act, 1.7 million persons were enrolled in various work-training programs between March 15, 1962, and June 30, 1971, under a total federal obligation of $2.4 billion. Program data list 1.1 million persons as having completed training, with 879,000 having obtained posttraining employment.[28] Institutional and on-the-job training programs conducted under the MDTA enrolled about 42,000 unemployed and underemployed persons in rural areas in 1970, about one-fifth the total number of first-time enrollments in that year. Relatively few were training for skilled jobs in mechanized farming operations. Training covered a wide variety of occupations, oriented mostly toward nonagricultural industries.[29]

The Vocational Education Act of 1963 provided federal grants to states on a matching basis for construction of area vocational-technical schools to supplement the regular public schools and to encourage a broad expansion of vocational training, closely meshed with job-market opportunities. The rural schools responded mainly by redirecting their offerings to agricultural business, or agribusiness occupations—food processing, ornamental horticulture, agricultural mechanics, farm management, and vocational home economics. Amend-

---

[28]Garth L. Mangum, "MDTA: A Decade of Achievement," Seymour L. Wolfbein (ed.), *Manpower Policy: Perspectives and Prospects* (papers on the occasion of the 10th anniversary of the Manpower Development and Training Act of 1962), Philadelphia: Temple University, 1973, p. 42.

[29]U.S. Department of Labor, *Manpower Report of the President,* Washington: April 1971, p. 131.

ments to the act in 1968 authorized a substantial increase in support and greater flexibility in programs. By 1969, more than 200,000 students were enrolled in the broadened program. In the 13 states in the Appalachian region, an Appalachian Regional Commission was formed for a special intensive effort to deal with high levels of rural unemployment. As of 1970, 122 new schools were operating in this region, and eventually 204 would be built to provide schooling for 114,000 students each year.

The Elementary and Secondary Education Act of 1965 offered federal help for rural areas to improve their educational facilities. Aid to deprived children was the largest program under the act, with additional provisions for funds for libraries, supplementary education centers, and research, and for strengthening state departments of education. Initially, the aid to each school district within each state was determined by the state's expenditure per school child and the number of school-age children in the district who came from families with annual incomes of less than $2,000, or from families with more than $2,000 that were receiving assistance under Aid to Families with Dependent Children (AFDC). Although it was admitted as late as 1971 that "direct evidence regarding the effectiveness of programs made possible by the Elementary and Secondary Education Act of 1965, the chief source of Federal aid to regular education, is not yet available . . . ,"[30] it was suggested that "the progress recently made in rural education lends hope that rural people will be increasingly well prepared educationally for urban as well as rural life and work."[31] Additional problems to be overcome were (1) the limited financial resources of many predominantly rural states and local areas and the consequent inadequate financing of rural education, (2) the failure of schools to cope with the problems of minority-group education in either segregated or desegregated institutions, and (3) the lack of up-to-date vocational training.

Enactment of the Economic Opportunity Act of 1964 (EOA) began a new emphasis by the federal government in vocational and educational training programs. The Office of Economic Opportunity (OEO) was established to implement and, it was hoped, to coordinate a number of programs. Title I of the EOA authorized the Neighborhood Youth Corps program for paid-work experience for youths 16 to 21 years of age, later amended to 12 to 21 years of age, of whom about one-fourth were rural. Young people in the program remained in their home environment while gaining job proficiency through full-time work or while supplementing their income with part-time work in order to remain in school. The Job Corps was authorized to provide youth characterized by low income, lack of employment, and inadequate job preparation with some education, vocational training, and work experience in urban training centers or rural conservation centers. To be eligible, applicants had to be between 16 to 21 years of age, undereducated, and jobless.[32]

[30]*Manpower Report of the President, ibid.,* p. 133.
[31]*Ibid.*
[32]*Ibid.,* p. 134.

Title II of the EOA authorized Operation Head Start to provide assistance to preschool centers for children of limited opportunity who would later enter kindergarten or first grade. The program involved teachers, parents, doctors, and social workers in an effort to overcome deficiencies that would lead to underperformance in school and society. A Community Action program was begun to offer support to projects operated by welfare agencies, schools, churches, and other groups to deal with problems of inadequate job opportunities, housing, education, and health. These projects were largely confined to cities. The Adult Basic Education programs were established under Title IIB for persons 18 years of age and over who lacked the basic skills necessary to qualify for better jobs or for occupational training. This program was replaced under Title III of the Elementary and Secondary Education Act, and its administration shifted to the Secretary of Health, Education, and Welfare.

Title III of the EOA included financial assistance for migrants and other seasonal farm employees and their families. Programs included accelerated school programs to shorten the school year for children of migrants, adult education in reading and other basic skills, remedial summer programs for youth, vocational training for adults, and day-care centers for preschool children.

Title V of the EOA contained a work experience program for the needy and unemployed, including part-time and seasonal farm workers, who were receiving public assistance. The projects were conducted by state and local government agencies with the aid of federal financing. Illiterates participated in a basic education program before receiving experience in an occupation. Length of training averaged about nine months and, altough the projects were generally unavailable or inconvenient for most farm families, they were helpful to seasonal farm workers who were supported by public assistance part of the year.

Some of the programs were given descriptive names by the Office of Economic Opportunity, in the Department of Labor. Operation Mainstream, a small program about two-thirds rural, was organized to give unemployed workers, typically displaced farmers or other older rural workers, experience in work that would, for example, enhance the beauty of rural areas, expand recreational and other community facilities, rehabilitate housing, and provide care for the elderly. Projects were sponsored by such organizations as the National Farmers Union, the National Council of Senior Citizens, the National Retired Teachers Association, and the National Council on the Aging. Concentrated Employment programs (CEPs) were designed to provide supportive services in local areas with high rates of poverty and unemployment. In late 1970, of 82 CEPs in operation, 13 were in rural poverty areas. The Concerted Services in Training and Education program was organized to provide a broader approach to coordination of manpower and educational and economic development. Projects were underway or planned for 20 rural areas in 17 states by the end of 1971. Altogether, in fiscal 1970 more than a million persons were enrolled in training or work-experience programs administered by the Department of Labor, of whom one-fourth were from rural areas (Table 10-5).

Table 10-5   Enrollees in Training and Work-Experience Programs Administered by the Department of Labor, by Urban and Rural Areas, Fiscal Year 1970

Program	Total (in thousands)	Urban areas		Rural areas	
		Number (in thousands)	Percentage of total	Number (in thousands)	Percentage of total
Total	1,051.4	799.9	76	251.5	24
Manpower Development and Training Act:					
Institutional training	130.0	105.3	81	24.7	19
On-the-job training	91.0	73.7	81	17.3	19
Neighborhood Youth Corps:					
In school	74.4	43.2	58	31.2	42
Out of school	46.2	31.9	69	14.3	31
Summer	361.5	245.8	68	115.7	32
Operation Mainstream	12.5	4.1	33	8.4	67
Public Service Careers (New Careers)	3.6	3.2	89	.4	11
Concentrated Employment Program	110.1	98.0	89	12.1	11
JOBS (federally financed)	86.8	86.8	100		
Work Incentive Program	92.7	74.2	80	18.5	20
Job Corps	42.6	33.7	79	8.9	21

Source: U.S. Department of Labor, *Manpower Report of the President,* Washington: April 1971, p. 130.

Conclusion It has been estimated that as many as 3 million poor rural residents need some training and other services to upgrade their skills and increase their employability.[33] Manpower programs served only 8 percent of this number in 1970, while serving over 10 percent of the much larger number of urban residents in need of help. But, in broad vision, the manpower problems confronting rural America are reflecting the failure of nonfarm employment to grow rapidly enough in or near rural areas to absorb workers displaced from agriculture and to provide jobs for new entrants into the labor force. A comprehensive program, therefore, is required involving increased employment opportunities as well as education and training for employment. The lesson of the past experience is that training has to be linked to jobs. Before turning to the question of employment expansion—in our case, Rural Community Development—let us consider the role of higher education as human resource policy.

Higher Education as Human Resource Policy[34]

Two policy goals have greatly influenced higher education and research in the United States, especially in the land grant colleges and the U.S. Department of Agriculture. One is an extension of the principle inherent in public education in the nation's elementary and secondary schools, that all children shall have free opportunity for as complete an education as their individual tastes and abilities warrant. The other is that science shall be used to increase the efficiency and progress of agriculture and industry. Consequently, in spite of all the diversities in form and emphasis among states and localities, historians agree that "there is a *system*" in which "the essential features of method, of curriculum, of organization, of purpose . . . can be identified as American, distinct from those of any other people."[35] This sytem importantly affects the entire structure of agriculture and rural society. In respect to human resources or human capital resources, it is the cutting edge.

The Land Grant College Act[36] Development of the land grant system and related institutions in the Department of Agriculture is highlighted in policymaking legislation dating back to 1862. In that year the Congress passed and President Lincoln signed what is now called the Land Grant College Act, or the First Morrill Act, in reference to the sponsor of the legislation, Justin Smith

---

[33]Leonard Lecht, *Poor Persons in the Labor Force: A Universe of Need* (Washington: National Planning Association), as reported in *Manpower Report of the President, op. cit.,* p. 130.

[34]For further philosophical and historical development of this subject, see, especially, Richard Gordon Moores, *Fields of Rich Toil, The Development of the University of Illinois College of Agriculture,* Urbana: The University of Illinois Press, 1970; Allan Nivens, *The State Universities and Democracy,* Urbana: The University of Illinois Press, 1962; Earle D. Ross, *Democracy's College, The Land-Grant Movement in the Formative Stage,* Ames: Iowa State College Press, 1942; and, for a more general history, Fred A. Shannon, *The Farmers' Last Frontier, Agriculture, 1860–1897, Vol. V, The Economic History of the United States,* New York: Farrar & Rinehart, Inc., 1945.

[35]Paul Monroe, "Historic Foundations of American Education," *Essays in Comparative Education,* as quoted by Ross, *op. cit.,* p. 1.

[36]For a summary of laws, see *United States Code, Annotated, Title 7, Agriculture,* chaps. 13 and 14, sections 301–390k.

Morrill, Representative from Vermont. An earlier bill, passed by the Congress in 1859 after extensive debate, had been vetoed by President Buchanan on grounds of its possible high cost, possible confusion between state and federal governments, dangers of land speculation, and other reasons, including possibly opposition from the Southern states. Of the 22 senators who voted against the bill, 18 were from the South.

The 1862 act appropriated to each state and territory a quantity of land—or scrip which could be used in purchase of land—equal to 30,000 acres for each senator and representative in Congress, based on the census of 1860. Each state and territory were to use receipts from ownership or sale of this land to establish a college or university in compliance with the principles embodied in the legislation. According to Morrill, the teaching of science should be the leading responsibility, and opportunity should be broadly available to children in all walks of life. No longer should higher education be limited to the few, the fortunate elite, as in Europe and other parts of the world.[37]

One of the basic ideas in the act—free education for the people—was as old as the American colonies themselves, and public lands had been granted for educational purposes since the ordinances of 1787.[38] The first ordinance, on July 13, 1787, did not make a specific grant but declared, "Religion, morality, and knowledge being necessary to good government and the happiness of mankind, schools and the means of education shall forever be encouraged." Ten days later, Congress provided, in the second ordinance, for the sale of public lands to the Ohio Company, that section 16 in each township should be set aside for common schools, and "not more than two complete townships . . . be given perpetually for the purpose of a university." In 1841 in what appears to be a clear forerunner of the Morrill Act, Captain Alden Partridge of Vermont asked Congress to appropriate $40 million for education from the sale of public lands, the money to "be distributed among the States . . . in proportion to their representation on the floor of Congress." All but four of the states admitted to the Union before the Civil War received land grants for education. By 1854 the federal government had donated more than 60 million acres of public lands for schools and more than 4 million acres for state universities.[39]

Industrial Education   The idea of industrial education, although contrary to educational practice throughout the colonial era, also has its roots in the events of the early 1800s. The general idea was aptly expressed by de Tocqueville after his travels in America. "It is evident," he wrote, "that, in democratic communities the interests of individuals, as well as the security of the commonwealth, demands that the education of the greater number should be scientific, commercial, and industrial, rather than literary."[40] Others followed this theme. The idea

[37]Nivens, *op. cit.,* p. 15.
[38]Moores, *op. cit.,* pp. 5–7.
[39]Moores, *op. cit.,* and Nivens, *op. cit.,* pp. 15, 16.
[40]Alexis de Tocqueville, *Democracy in America,* as quoted by Ross, *op. cit.,* p. 11.

grew and was taken up by some of the very active agricultural societies for promoting agriculture, of which there were an estimated 1,000 by 1858.[41] These societies published magazines, newspapers, journals, almanacs, and books. They promoted fairs, meetings, socials, debates, and other activities. In 1851, Jonathan Baldwin Turner, a teacher of rhetoric, Greek, and Latin at Illinois College in Jacksonville from 1833 to 1847, proposed a plan to establish "a University for the Industrial Classes in each of the States. . . ."[42] These new universities, which would teach every science and art known to man, would elevate the farmer and mechanic to that exalted position in human society that God meant for them to occupy. No student above a fixed age would be excluded, and he could attend for as long—"whether for three months or seven years"—as he wished. A few months later in the *Prairie Farmer* for March 1852, Turner published a letter asserting his belief that if "farmers and their friends" will "exert themselves they can speedily secure for this State, and for each State in the Union, an appropriation of public land adequate to create and endow in the most liberal manner, a general system of popular Industrial Education, more glorious in its design and more beneficent in its results than the world has ever seen before."[43] Turner's ideas gained wide attention in Illinois and across the nation; and the next year the Illinois legislature sent to Congress a set of resolutions declaring that a system of industrial universities, liberally endowed in each state, would develop the people and "tend to intellectualize the rising generation."[44]

These ideas, incorporated nine years later in the Morrill Act, were both the foundation and the inspiration, in an otherwise discouraging situation, for evolution of the system of land grant colleges and universities. In almost all states except New York and Minnesota, receipts from the land grant were disappointing and grossly inadequate. Land prices were depressed and the grant was generally poorly managed. State legislatures were for the most part penurious, lacking the vision of the educational proponents. Farm and rural people generally, to say the least, only mildly supported the basic ideas. Industrial education was often ridiculed, especially in respect to its application to agriculture.

Agricultural Research Largely through the perseverance of a few far-sighted university and political leaders, however, the ideas not only survived; by the late 1880s many of the state universities had both begun teaching and established agricultural experiment stations. A number of congressmen had called for federal support for agricultural research in addition to support for agricultural and industrial education. In 1887, Representative William H. Hatch of Missouri successfully sponsored a bill that would grant $15,000 annually to

[41]Herman E. Kroos, *American Economic Development*, 2d ed., Englewood Cliffs, N.J.: Prentice-Hall, p. 109.
[42]Mary Turner Carriel, *The Life of Jonathan Baldwin Turner* (Urbana, Ill.: 1961), as quoted by Moores, *op. cit.,* pp. 5, 6.
[43]*Prairie Farmer,* March 1852, p. 114, as quoted by Moores, *op. cit.,* p. 6.
[44]Nivens, *op. cit.,* p. 14.

each state that would establish an agricultural experiment station in connection with a land grant college or university. The stations were "to aid in acquiring and diffusing among the people of the United States useful and practical information on subjects connected with agriculture, and to promote scientific investigation and experiment respecting the principles and applications of agricultural science." The United States Department of Agriculture was raised to cabinet status; and a spirit of mutual respect and trust began to develop between scientists in the department and the experiment stations.

Direction of Federal Support   The second Morrill Act in 1890 expanded support for the land grant colleges and, although it prohibited payment of funds to any state or territory "where a distinction of race or color is made in the admission of students," it defined compliance as the provision of separate colleges for white and black students. Thus a dual system arose in most of the Southern states, and it was not successfully challenged until the historic Supreme Court decision of 1954.

The Adams Act of 1906 attempted to lead the experiment stations (already 52 at that time) into more fundamental or original scientific research by providing that the funds were "to be applied only to paying the necessary expenses of conducting original researches or experiments bearing directly on the agricultural industry of the United States." Experiment station directors were required to keep separate accounts for funds appropriated under the Adams Act to assure their expenditures for original work.

The Nelson amendment in 1907 granted a further appropriation for the endowment and maintenance of land grant colleges, with the provision that a portion of the money could be spent in providing courses especially to prepare instructors for teaching the elements of agriculture and the mechanic arts. In 1914 a bill sponsored by Representative Lever of South Carolina and Senator Smith of Georgia was enacted into law. The legislation, known as the Smith-Lever Act, or Acts, of May 14 and 22, 1914, provided federal funds to initiate

> agricultural extension work . . . in order to aid in diffusing among the people of the United States useful and practical information on subjects relating to agriculture and home economics, and to encourage the application of the same . . . including practical demonstrations in agricultural and home economics and subjects relating thereto to persons not attending or resident in said colleges in the several communities, and imparting information on said subjects through demonstrations, publications and otherwise . . . in such manner as may be mutually agreed upon by the Secretary of Agriculture and the State agricultural college or colleges receiving the benefits of the Act.

The Purnell Act of 1925 authorized the more complete endowment of the agricultural experiment stations, and stated, "funds . . . shall be applied to . . . such economic and sociological investigations as have for their purpose the development and improvement of the rural home and rural life. . . ."

The Bankhead-Jones Act of June 29, 1935 (amended in June 1952 and July 1960) provided additional funds for basic research into the laws and principles relating to agriculture, the further development of cooperative extension work, and the more complete endowment and support of the land grant colleges.

The Agricultural Marketing Act of 1946 provided for extensive research in conjunction with the experiment stations and cooperative extension services on a state matching-fund basis, to provide for "an integrated administration of all laws so that marketing is improved, costs reduced, dietary and nutritional standards improved, and wider markets developed resulting in the full production of American farms being disposed of usefully, economically, profitably, and in an orderly manner."

In 1955, in an act appropriating funds for the agricultural experiment stations, the Congress consolidated all the previous laws as an amendment to the Hatch Act (84th Congress, 1st Session, Chapter 790, Public Law 352). The policy of Congress was declared

> to continue the agricultural research at the State agricultural experiment stations . . . to promote the efficient production, marketing, distribution, and utilization of products of the farm as essential to the health and welfare of our peoples and to promote a sound and prosperous agriculture and rural life as indispensable to the maintenance of maximum employment and national prosperity and security . . . to assure agriculture a position in research equal to that of industry, which will aid in maintaining an equitable balance between agriculture and other segments of our economy. It shall be the object and duty of the State agricultural experiment stations . . . to conduct original and other researches . . . , including researches basic to the problems of agriculture in its broadest aspects . . . , the development and improvement of the rural home and rural life and the maximum contribution of agriculture to the welfare of the consumer, as may be deemed advisable, having due regard to the varying conditions and needs of the respective states.

Ever since 1862 the Congress has specified how appropriations for the land grant system shall be allocated to the states and, within general guidelines, has specified how this money shall be used. In the 1946 act, it was specified that not less than 20 percent of the research money appropriated to each state should be used for marketing, in the apparent belief that research in marketing would further improve the efficiency of marketing services, reduce the price spread between producers and consumers, and thus help farmers and consumers as well. Some experiment station directors apparently had difficulty in developing sufficient marketing research projects to utilize 20 percent of their allotted funds, and in the amendments submitted to Congress by the Department of Agriculture in 1955, it was recommended that this requirement be reduced. The House Committee on Agriculture reinserted the requirement stating that "the committee believes that the present agricultural situation, with surpluses plaguing the producers of many commodities, is a clear indication of the need for continued emphasis in marketing of agricultural products and the research connected therewith.''[45] Thus the emphasis continued on scientific production and management research, marketing, and distribution.

Policy Constraints on Higher Education   It may be said that the federal legislative history, through its emphasis on broadly based industrial education, vocational training, scientific research, and cooperative extension, is a grand design for a policy in development of human capital. In broad perspective, this may be true. The productivity of human resources has been greatly upgraded, as much of our entire discussion suggests. But the effects and the benefits are not evenly distributed among people of different abilities and material endowments. High-level managers and those with substantial material endowment have progressed rapidly and the marginal rate of return has been high. Low-level managers and those with low material wealth have been disadvantaged. Not only have low-level managers been harder to reach with educational programs; until very recently, the land grant colleges and the U.S. Department of Agriculture have not received a clear policy directive to do so; and when this instruction was given, the resources to support such programs have been clearly inadequate for the task at hand. The competitive position of low-level managers has been worsened by the rising productivity of high-level managers. The land grant colleges and the Department of Agriculture have been criticized on occasion for contributing to poverty and low incomes in farming and the rural community.[46] The suggestion has been made that the resources of higher education, including agricultural research and extension, should be reallocated to deemphasize scientific research and education, particularly as they apply to the agribusiness sector of large farms and agricultural business firms. This would—so the argument goes—slow down the rate of productivity gain, reduce input costs for low-level managers through reduced competition for farm inputs, upgrade the productivity of their resources, and improve the terms of trade for farm output.

The rebuttal to this argument takes several forms: To the extent that the rates of productivity gain were slowed, there would be higher food prices. Further, it is not clear that low-level managers would gain significantly by such a shift in emphasis, or that higher education and research are the best way to help them. The problem of adequate employment for the economically disadvantaged is a broader and less tractable problem, as our following discussion will emphasize.

PROGRAMS FOR OVERCOMING POVERTY

Adequate employment for those disadvantaged by the "green revolution" is both a value-laden policy goal based on concepts of equity and distributive justice,

[45]U.S. Code Congressional and Administrative News, 84th Cong., 1st Sess., House Report No. 1298, p. 2977.
[46]See Jim Hightower, Hard Tomatoes, Hard Times, The Failure of the Land Grant College Complex, Preliminary Report of the Task Force on the Land Grant College Complex, 1972. Agribusiness Accountability Project, Washington, D.C.

and a pragmatic goal of a society seeking to maximize its output of goods and services. This fact is demonstrated in the policymaking legislation that deals with the problem and in the various efforts that are made for social and economic reform.

Legislative Acts and Programs

On April 27, 1955, President Eisenhower submitted to Congress a special report recommending that the state cooperative extension service be given additional appropriations to develop in problem areas a more effective program for the assistance of farm people with low incomes. The report, "Development of Agriculture's Human Resources," stated that educational programs in low-income farm areas must differ from those in other areas. Special methods and techniques are needed. In many cases, communitywide interest and effort are required. The extension services, as a result of many years' experience in planning and conducting programs with other agencies, were the best qualified to carry out such programs. The President followed this report with an executive memorandum and a proposed bill, which was passed by the Senate without amendment. The House, however, rejected it as too broad or vague, and passed a more specific bill, technically an amendment to the Smith-Lever Act.[47]

The new law authorized additional funds for cooperative extension services to do one or more of the following: (1) provide intensive on-the-farm educational and counseling assistance to farm families in appraising and resolving their problems; (2) offer assistance and counseling to local groups in appraising resources to improve the capability of agriculture, or to develop industry designed to supplement farm income; (3) cooperate with other agencies and groups in furnishing all possible information on existing employment opportunities, particularly to farm families having underemployed workers; and (4) in cases where the farm family, after analysis of its opportunities and existing resources, found it advisable to seek a new farming venture, to provide information, advice, and counsel regarding the change. The law authorized additional funds not to exceed 10 percent of the funds appropriated for cooperative extension work by colleges.[48]

Although research, extension, and technical assistance were to be concentrated to a greater extent than in the past on low-income problems and on opportunities to develop agriculture's low-income human resource, the programs that emerged fell far short of the implied policy goals. During the rest of the Eisenhower administration, the Congress allocated only $2 million to operate the Rural Development Program and gave the FHA only a small amount of additional lending authority. By 1960, only 210 counties were participating in the program, and it was estimated that only 18,000 new full-time jobs had been created as a direct result of industrial growth and new business. In all fairness,

---

[47]*U.S. Code Congressional and Administrative News,* 84th Cong., 1st Sess., 1955, pp. 779–780, 3014–3016, Agricultural Development—Educational and Other Assistance, chap. 798—Public Law 360 (an act to amend Public Law 83, 83d Cong.).

[48]*U.S. Code Annotated,* Section 341, 67 *Stat.* 83.

the program was little more than a pilot effort. It scarcely scratched the unemployment-underemployment poverty problem of rural areas.

In 1961 under President John F. Kennedy's administration, the Rural Development Program was reorganized and renamed Rural Areas Development (RAD). Although considerable publicity was provided, the new program, like its predecessor, was mainly a planning and coordinating effort. It did not receive a significant budget increase and, although some 20,000 projects, ranging from community facilities through industrial parks, were promoted through 1966, the result can be appraised as little more than a continuation of the pilot effort.[49]

The Rural Community Development Service was formed in February 1965 as a policy implementer, specifically to organize and coordinate the resources of the Department of Agriculture in rural development programs. At the state level, a coordinating committee was generally formed, consisting of representatives of such agencies as the FHA, the Soil Conservation Service, the Agricultural Stabilization and Conservation Service, and the Federal-State Cooperative Extension Service. At the local or county level, representatives of these agencies and others were frequently organized into technical action panels.

In addition to the RAD, the Accelerated Public Works Program was funded to stimulate economic activity in depressed rural areas, primarily through subsidies for improvements in administrative and social overhead. Congress appropriated about $850 million for 1962 and 1963; and improvements in public facilities provided direct employment for about 100,000 people. One chief result of this was to make some depressed areas more attractive.

The Area Redevelopment Administration (ARA) was established in the Department of Commerce by the Area Redevelopment Act of 1961 to provide (1) loans to support job-creating commercial and industrial enterprises, (2) grants and loans to build or improve public facilities, (3) technical assistance to bridge the knowledge gap, and (4) retraining programs to fit workers to new jobs. By 1965 the ARA claimed that it had been instrumental in starting 1,487 community industrial development projects and that it had stimulated investment of $260 million in rural areas. An estimated 65,000 jobs were created in rural areas under the program. Greater emphasis was placed on regional development plans. Top priorities for assistance went to those areas and districts which had high unemployment and low family incomes.[50]

In the Manpower Act of 1965, the Economic Development Administration (EDA) absorbed the programs of the Area Development Administration. The national Office of Economic Opportunity (OEO) was formed. Economic development regions were established under the Public Works and Economic Development Act of 1965, and within each region, economic development districts were formed, each having an economic development center to organize a range of economic assistance in development. Redevelopment areas in a district were

[49]*Rural People in the American Economy,* U.S. Department of Agriculture, Economic Report No. 101. Washington: Government Printing Office, 1966.
[50]The White House and U.S. Department of Labor, *Manpower Report of the President,* 1967.

eligible for a 10 percent bonus on grants for public works projects. Initial action in creating a district had to be taken by a state or state agency. Technical assistance took the form of (*a*) studies to identify area needs or to solve industrial or economic problems, (*b*) grants-in-aid amounting to 75 percent of the costs of planning and administering local economic development programs, and (*c*) management and operational guidance for private firms. In addition, low-interest, long-term loans were offered to encourage and help private businesses establish plants in redevelopment areas. Loans could cover up to 65 percent of the total project cost and could run for 25 years at interest rates commensurate with federal borrowing costs. Also, under some of the work-training programs previously discussed, funds were appropriated to hire the chronically unemployed. In some of the programs, such as Operation Mainstream noted earlier, federal funds were to provide permanent jobs at decent wages for workers to improve rural towns and depressed rural areas. This program provided public employment for only about 8,100 in 1967, however, with about half the funds going to rural areas. Later, the program called "New Careers" was designed for trainees to take over some of the routine tasks in hospitals and other public facilities. In 1967, this program had funds for only 2,706 work opportunities with only 12 percent in rural areas. In summary, in 1967 public service employment totaled about 500,000 persons, not more than one quarter of whom could be regarded as being from rural areas.[51] Although federal efforts to relieve rural poverty were often imaginative and forward-looking, the scarcity of funds restricted development. The programs were sometimes regressive, aiding middle- and upper-income people, yet helping only a small number of the rural poor.[52]

Problems of Employing the Disadvantaged

By the mid 1960s, when economic expansion had generated more plentiful employment opportunities and unemployment had fallen below 4 percent—the figure used by the Department of Labor to define full employment—the national focus of manpower concerns moved away from overall unemployment levels to the special labor market problems of those broadly designated as disadvantaged.[53] New legislation included the Civil Rights Act, the Public Works and Economic Development Act, the Economic Opportunity Act, Model Cities legislation, the Vocational Education Act and amendments, new provisions for work incentives in the Social Security Act, and amendments to the Manpower Development and Training Act of 1962. The legislation provided new directions and some increased funding for programs for disadvantaged persons—primarily youth and the undereducated and unskilled members of various minority groups. Federal funding for state employment service (ES) agencies increased as follows:

[51]National Advisory Commission on Rural Poverty, *The People Left Behind,* Washington: Government Printing Office, 1967.

[52]Marion Clawson, "Rural Poverty in the United States," *Journal of Farm Economics,* Vol. 49, No. 5, December 1967, pp. 1227–1234.

[53]U.S. Department of Labor, *Manpower Report of the President,* Washington: March 1973, p. 46.

Fiscal year	Obligations (in millions)
1962	$146.9
1963	163.0
1964	172.7
1965	200.0
1966	248.7
1967	276.9
1968	298.7
1969	316.7
1970	347.6
1971	374.4
1972	378.8

Emphasis shifted from the traditional ES labor exchange functions to provide more intensive individual service to those having the most difficulty in finding productive work. But inflation reduced the effectiveness of this service, so that between 1966 and 1970, although the number of nonfarm jobs rose by 10 percent, the number of nonfarm job placements by ES agencies dropped by 30 percent. In 1969–71, as the total number of new jobs began to shrink and the number of unemployed rose, the number of placements of disadvantaged workers also fell. Total ES nonfarm placement were only 3.4 million in 1971, fewer federal placements than in any year since the Great Depression. As unemployment rose in succeeding years, the normal migration out of farming was reversed. Increases in the farm population in 1972 (Table 10-3) can be taken as an early warning of the worsening plight of the economically disadvantaged as well as an indication of the shortfalls in the programs for overcoming poverty in the rural community. Some may argue that the migration into farming also signaled a slide toward depression in the industrial economy. Either way or both ways, it serves as a background for our more specific review of programs.

Manpower Programs of the Department of Labor

Manpower programs of the Department of Labor continued to expand after 1968 (Table 10-6) as the federal government expanded its training of the economically disadvantaged. Federal outlays for manpower programs were estimated at $3,446 million for 1974 (Table 10-7).

Those enrolled in the programs (Table 10-8) were identified by the Department of Labor as mostly from the disadvantaged population in both rural and urban areas. In fiscal year 1972, an estimated 85 percent were disadvantaged, and the figure would have been higher except for preferences given to veterans, as directed by Congress, in the Public Employment Program (PEP).

Almost 70 percent of all enrollees were under 22 years of age. Women, who accounted for 44 to 46 percent of the unemployed during 1970–72, made up 40 percent of total enrollees in the program administered by the Department of Labor. Blacks accounted for 45 percent of all trainees. Over 60 percent of the trainees in the CEP and the JOB Corps, 23 percent in PEP, and 19 percent in Operation Mainstream were black (Table 10-8).

About 45 percent of the slightly more than 750,000 persons who terminated training in 1972 were placed in jobs. Of the other 55 percent, most had dropped out before completing training. Fewer than 10 percent of those who completed training failed to obtain jobs:

Program	Terminations	Employed completers	Employment rate (percentage)
All programs	751,400	336,800	45
MDTA, institutional	153,800	81,500	53
JOBS	91,300	44,200	48
MDTA, JOBS-Optional	50,600	28,000	55
MDTA, OJT (national contract)	29,200	23,300	80
PSC	68,500	26,200	38
CEP	88,000	39,300	45
Job Corps	48,600	35,000[a]	72
WIN	110,200	33,300	30
PEP	57,400	17,800	31
Construction Outreach	53,800	8,200	15

[a] Job Corps obtains follow-up placement data on both completers and noncompleters.

Hourly earnings of those hired out of the federal programs varied by sex, age, and race suggesting the degree to which concepts of equal opportunity are or are not achieved in practice:

Characteristic	Hourly earnings			
	MDTA		CEP	WIN
	Institutional	On-the-job		
All trainees	$2.49	$3.16	$2.24	$2.46
Sex				
Men	2.75	3.44	2.38	2.92
Women	2.23	2.12	2.03	2.11
Race or ethnic group				
White	2.55	3.27	2.14	2.59
Black	2.32	2.71	2.28	2.26
Spanish speaking	2.25	2.96	2.23	2.48
Age				
Under 22 years	2.27	2.77	2.15	2.22
22 to 44 years	2.57	3.26	2.31	2.49
45 years and over	2.71	3.41	2.15	2.66

It may be inferred that up to the end of fiscal 1972 at least, the Department of Labor programs ranked high in cost-effectiveness, the generally recognized criterion for such programs. In succeeding years, as unemployment increased,

Table 10-6 Enrollments in Manpower Programs Administered by the Department of Labor, Selected Months, 1968–1972 (in Thousands)

Program	April 1968	April 1969	April 1970	April 1971	1972 April	1972 November
Total	355.3*	433.6*	455.7	508.4	696.4	649.1
Institutional training under Manpower Development and Training Act	60.4	56.7	53.7	62.4	61.2	43.5
JOBS (federally financed) and other on-the-job training (OJT)†	38.9	57.3	87.9	86.3	90.9	104.1
Neighborhood Youth Corps:						
In-school and summer	131.9	101.6	104.6	106.3	126.2	104.1
Out-of-school	57.6	47.5	33.3	38.4	41.2	42.1
Operation Mainstream	9.0	10.2	13.0	21.6	21.6	28.6
Public Service Careers‡	3.8	3.4	4.2	26.2	26.8	20.7
Concentrated Employment Program§	19.8	70.5	53.3	38.8	36.4	30.0
Job Corps	32.5	29.8	20.7	22.1	22.8	22.2
Work Incentive Program§		56.2	84.9	106.2	121.0	111.0
Public Employment Program					148.2	142.3

*Includes Special Impact projects.

†Includes the MDTA-OJT program which ended with fiscal 1970 (except for national contracts) and the JOBS-Optional Program which began with fiscal 1971; also Construction Outreach, with 68,900 enrollees in fiscal 1972.

‡Data relate only to New Careers segment until mid 1970 when the Supplemental Training and Employment Program (STEP) was initiated. STEP was phased out over the first half of 1972. Enrollments in other PSC options were first reported in November 1970.

§Exclusive of enrollees in "suspense"; that is, enrolled in other programs such as MDTA institutional training.

Note: Detail may not add to totals because of rounding.

Source: U.S. Department of Labor, *Manpower Report of the President*, March 1973, p. 53.

policymakers could scarcely hope for as good a record. Still, the programs could be needed even more and continue to be beneficial if jobs were available. This underscores the need in policymaking to look not only at the systems of training but also at the programs for job creation. Of most interest in our concern is that of rural development, or as it is sometimes called, rural community development.

Concepts of Rural Development Related to Policy

Various publications[54] have documented that in nonmetropolitan areas and rural communities, as compared with metropolitan, urban, and suburban areas, (1) population growth rates are lower, (2) the rate of business expansion is generally lower, (3) average family earnings are lower, and (4) there is a larger percentage of people in low-income or poverty classes (as noted in Table 10-2, for example).

[54]See, for example, *The Economic and Social Conditions of Rural America*. Prepared by the Economic Development Division, Economic Research Service, U.S. Department of Agriculture, for the Committee on Government Operations, United States Senate, 92d Cong., 1st Sess., Part I, Washington: Government Printing Office, May 1971.

Table 10-7   Estimated Outlays and New Enrollments in Federal Manpower Programs, Fiscal Year 1974

Activity	Expenditures (millions)	New enrollees (thousands)
Institutional training	$ 771	981
Manpower revenue sharing	303	162
Job Corps (national program)	111	38
Work Incentive Program	164	61
Social service training	120	692
Other	73	29
On-the-job training (OJT)	**566**	**371**
Manpower revenue sharing	159	120
JOBS (basic)	96	117
Work Incentive Program	97	56
OJT for veterans	203	69
Other	11	9
Vocational rehabilitation	**824**	**573**
Vocational rehabilitation	707	560
Veterans rehabilitation	117	13
Work support	**1,285**	**632**
Manpower revenue sharing	481	464
Emergency employment assistance	574	14
Work Incentive Program	102	27
High school work-study	9	57
Other	119	71
Total	**3,446**	**2,558**

Note: Detail may not add to totals because of rounding.
Source: Office of Management and Budget, *Special Analyses, Budget of the United States Government, Fiscal Year 1974.*

These facts lead to the hypothesis that the general welfare will be improved if the appropriate steps are taken to expand the rural economy relative to the urban. Then a more satisfactory geographic pattern of population will emerge. There will be less congestion in urban areas. Incomes will be more equitably distributed. The quality of living will be enhanced. So rural development is proposed as a policy goal, or a means for improving the general welfare.[55]

There are, of course, several concepts of what rural development means, or of what it consists, what the goals should be, and what the appropriate means, implementers, and constraints are. But all goals and program evaluations come back sooner or later to the concept of cost-effectiveness. Within this concept, however, there are two somewhat opposing views: One is that the main purpose of rural development is, or should be, to help the economically disadvantaged in the rural community. The main emphasis should be on interpersonnel income

[55]See George Brinkman, et al., *The Development of Rural America,* Manhattan: University Press of Kansas, 1974; John T. Scott, Jr., et al., *Rural Community and Regional Development: Perspectives and Prospects,* University of Illinois at Urbana-Champaign, AE-4336, June 1974.

Table 10-8 Characteristics of Enrollees in Federally Assisted Work and Training Programs, Fiscal Year 1972 (by Percentage of Total Employees)

Program	Women	Blacks*	Spanish-speaking	Age		Years of school completed		On public assistance†
				Under 22 yrs	45 yrs and over	8 years or less	9–11 years	
Institutional training under Manpower Development and Training Act	37	33	12	38	8	10	32	15
JOBS (federally financed) and other OJT‡	27	34	18	38	7	15	35	12
Neighborhood Youth Corps								
In-school and summer	43	53	12§	100		19	77	30
Out-of-school	50	43	16§	94	3	25	72	38
Operation Mainstream	31	19	10§	4	44	42	29	24
Public Service Careers	65	45	16	21	18	7	23	20
Concentrated Employment Program	41	61	20	45	5	16	42	14
Job Corps	26	62	10	100		30	61	39
Work Incentive Program	60	36	19	28	5	17	41	99
Public Employment Program	28	23	7	14	16	9	16	11

*Substantially all the remaining enrollees were white except in Operation Mainstream, JOBS, and Job Corps. In these programs 4 to 15 percent were American Indians, Eskimos, or Orientals.

†The definition of "public assistance" used here varies somewhat among programs (e.g., it may or may not include receipt of food stamps and "in kind" benefits). In the NYC program, it may relate to enrollees' families as well as enrollees themselves.

‡Data relate only to New Careers segment until mid 1970 when the Supplemental Training and Employment Program (STEP) was initiated. STEP was phased out over the first half of 1972. Enrollments in other PSC options were first reported in November 1970.

§Includes Mexican Americans and Puerto Ricans only; data on "other" Spanish-speaking Americans are not available.

Source: Manpower Report of the President, U.S. Department of Labor, March 1973, p. 54.

distribution. The other is that the purpose is, or should be, to accelerate the income growth of the rural community with little, if any, attention to problems of equity in income distribution. Internal community savings or external capital would be used to maximize economic growth without regard to changes in employment or the distribution of benefits. Between these two views, important compromises must be made; this requirement is reflected in the policymaking legislation and the programs that have developed.

Rural Development Legislation   In the Agricultural Act of 1970 (Public Law 91-524; 84 *Stat.* 1358, Section IX), the Congress committed itself "to a sound balance between rural and urban America . . . the highest priority must be given to the revitalization and development of rural areas." All executive departments and agencies were directed "to establish and maintain insofar as practicable, departmental policies and procedures with respect to the location of new offices and other facilities in areas or communities of lower population density. . . ." The Secretaries of HEW and Agriculture were directed to report annually on their efforts to provide assistance to states to develop economically depressed areas and the information and technical assistance given to small communities and less populated areas in regard to rural development. The law states that the President shall report (1) on the availability of telephone, electrical, water, sewer, medical, educational, and other government or government-assisted services to rural areas; (2) on efforts of the executive branch to improve these services; and (3) on the possible utilization of the Farm Credit Administration and other agricultural agencies to fulfill rural financial assistance requirements not filled by other agencies.

The Rural Development Act of 1972   This act (Public Law 92-419), having the stated purpose, "To provide for improving the economy and living conditions in rural America," combined a number of related programs into the first generally comprehensive program of rural development.[56] Title I, which may be cited as the Consolidated Farm and Rural Development Act, presented amendments to the Consolidated Farmers Home Administration Act of 1961. It contained 26 sections specifying various loans and grants that may be made covering a wide range of farm and rural enterprise. Title II covered amendments to the Watershed Protection and Flood Prevention Act (Public Law 83-566, 68 *Stat.* 666), for improving the nation's land and water resources and the quality of the environment by means of expanded planning under both short- and long-term agreements, loans and grants, implemented by federal cost sharing in conservation and water facility projects. Title III was a broad amendment to the Bankhead-Jones Farm Tenant Act. Title IV provided for cooperative agreements with state officials for rural community fire-protection facilities. Title V authorized

[56]*Guide to the Rural Development Act of 1972,* prepared by the Subcommittee on Rural Development, Committee on Agriculture and Forestry, U.S. Senate, 93d Cong., 1st Sess., Dec. 10, 1973.

rural development and small farm research and education, including cooperative extension, to provide "the essential knowledge necessary for successful programs of rural development." To assure national coordination with programs under the Smith-Lever Act of 1914 and the Hatch Act as amended in 1955, the administration of each state program was assigned to the university accepting the benefits of the Morrill Act of 1862, but any private or publicly supported college or university might submit a project proposal. Title VI set the rules for general administration of rural development.[57]

The intent of the Congress in passing the 1972 act was to have the federal government play a strong and affirmative role in revitalizing rural America. The lead responsibility in the executive boards was vested in the Secretary of Agriculture, who was charged with organizing the Department so that its many bureaus and offices would work effectively together in promoting the development of rural America. State and local government were to share responsibility and functions but not to be given carte blanche in the use of federal funds and assistance for rural areas.[58]

Development, passage, and implementation of the act were hampered from the beginning, however, by the fact that the administration sought a different solution. In 1971, President Nixon had called for adoption of special revenue sharing for rural community development "with the discretion of how [the federal money] will be used . . . strictly a State and local matter."[59] At the same time, as part of a general administrative reorganization, the President proposed legislation that would have merged seven departments and several administrative agencies into four major departments. The Department of Agriculture would have been reduced and the functions relating to rural development would have been placed in a new Department of Community Development. Just how this new department would function effectively in the public interest if the discretion for spending federal money were to be strictly a state and local matter was never made clear. The Congress held hearings on these proposals but declined to adopt them, adding, instead, new specific forms of assistance such as community facility loans and guaranteed private business loans.

Although the President signed the bill into law on August 30, 1972, he reiterated his preference for federal revenue sharing "to provide additional financial resources to State and local governments without counterproductive Federal strings attached," and for "new loan authority for commercial, industrial, and community development under a credit-sharing system which would allow the States themselves to select most of the loan recipients."[60] In other words, instead of having a coordinated federal plan with conditions attached, there would be various state plans and numerous local options, offering a broad invitation to various interpretations and types of administrative actions.

[57]*Ibid.,* pp. 156–176.
[58]*Ibid.,* p. 5.
[59]*The Budget of the United States Government,* Fiscal Year 1972, pp. 12, 5.
[60]*Weekly Compilation of Presidential Documents,* Vol. 8, No. 36, Sept. 4, 1972, pp. 1313, 6.

The initial draft regulations of the Department of Agriculture that were prepared to implement the act followed the President's spirit of revenue sharing, stating: "Federal implementation of the act will be consistent with the President's policy of decentralized decision making and administrative responsibility to State and local elected officials to the maximum extent practicable. Unless specified otherwise by the State government, Federal agencies will look to the State Governors to speak for the State governments in all matters pertaining to the administration of the act."[61] Loan and grant funds would be allocated to states on a formula basis, but there would be no further federal regulation below that level. To the contrary, the intent of the Congress was to use the already established federal and federally sponsored agencies to decide on business loans and related grants according to federal guidelines. To make this clear, seven senators, under leadership of Carl T. Curtis (Republican of Nebraska), proposed an amendment that: "No grant or loan authorized to be made under this act shall require or be subject to the prior approval of any officer, employee, or agency of any State." And this was finally adopted in the Agriculture and Consumer Protection Act of 1973 as an amendment to the Consolidated Farm and Rural Development Act, Section 310 B.

It would be an understatement to say that rural development was merely retarded by the President's view. Title I of the 1972 act authorized $465 million in annual grants for planning and constructing water and waste-disposal systems, for development of rural industries, and for rural development planning activities; but the bulk of water and waste-disposal grant funds appropriated for fiscal 1973 were impounded, and the President's budget included only $10 million in grant funds for rural industries. The President's budget request for fiscal 1974 did not identify any of the funds requested for the additional Soil Conservation Services activities in these fields, except $8 million for a land inventory and monitoring program. The total SCS budget recommended for 1974 was $285 million, a decrease of $89 million from 1973. Cost sharing to improve protection against fires in rural areas was passed over in both the President's request and the congressional appropriations for 1974. Under Title V, whereas, up to $10 million was authorized for fiscal 1974, up to $15 million for 1975, and up to $20 million for 1976, the President's request for 1974 was only for $5 million, and only $3 million was authorized by Congress. Under this level of funding, only two states would receive as much as $100,000 and 23 states would each receive less than $40,000, clearly a level of appropriation that would be more frustrating than productive of real substantive work. Only the FHA and the REA, as noted in Chapter 9, received more than token support sufficient to progress toward implementing the broad goals expressed in the legislation. And, as we noted, expansion of the REA was accomplished over the strong objections of the administration.

Discouragement and dismay over implementation of the 1972 act were

[61]Rural Development Coordination, Notice of Proposed Rule Making (7 CFR pt. 22), Office of the Secretary, Department of Agriculture (mimeographed).

recorded in a number of public documents.[62] Richard Longmire, representing the National Association of Conservation Districts (NACD) in Senate hearings in early 1973, expressed dismay at the slow pace of implementation of the act and at the low funding levels proposed. One year later, the NACD council noted, "The Congress of the United States enacted the Rural Development Act of 1972, but this new legislation has never been adequately funded. The act provides many of the tools needed in the protection and development of our resources, and the enhancement of our rural economy."[63] Although there was increased funding for FHA under Title I, and the SCS had implemented provisions permitting the use of other federal funds for acquisition of land rights in watershed projects and other technical measures, "implementation of most other significant authorities, and especially those in titles II, III, and IV of the Act, is at a standstill."[64]

Dr. Clay L. Cochran, executive director, Rural Housing Alliance, described the RHA as a nonprofit educational and informational organization dedicated to the expansion of housing opportunities for lower-income people in rural areas and small towns. He argued that, although almost 60 percent of the substandard housing in the nation is outside of metropolitan areas, rural areas have received "only about 20 percent of the public housing units built to date and only about a third of all federal housing subsidies."[65]

A progress report by a senior specialist in the Library of Congress on rural housing programs begins with the statement: "Inadequate housing is one of the most serious problems of rural America. Of the 20 million households in rural communities, almost 2.5 million lacked complete plumbing at the start of the 1970's. . . . Four out of five families without full plumbing facilities in their homes had incomes in 1969 of less than $6,000 and more than half had deep-poverty incomes of less than $3,000. A disproportionate number of elderly people occupy inferior shelter."[66] Under the 1972 act and others, the bulk of FHA loans are insured. The FHA collects monthly payments and otherwise services the loans while new loan funds are raised by the sale of certificates of beneficial ownership to private investors, with interest and capital insured by the federal government. Appropriations are required to cover insufficiencies and administrative expenses. Although the volume of rural housing loans rose steadily from 1969 through 1973 and funds obligated annually increased from about $500 million to almost $1.9 billion, the number of families assisted grew from only 50,000 to 120,000. In 1973, about 99,000 loans were made for construction of new housing, about 9,000 were for assisted rental housing, and the balance were for home repair.

Although, at this rate, it would take more than 20 years merely to replace the

---

[62]See, for example, *Implementation of the Rural Development Act,* Hearings, Subcommittee on Rural Development, Committee on Agriculture and Forestry, U.S. Senate, 93d Cong., 2d Sess., May 8 and 9, 1974.

[63]*Ibid.,* p. 295.

[64]From statement by Richard G. Longmire, *ibid.,* p. 295.

[65]*Ibid.,* p. 249.

[66]Morton J. Schussheim, "Rural Housing Programs—A Progress Report," Library of Congress, Congressional Research Service, *ibid.,* pp. 345 ff.

2.5 million homes not having plumbing (if all loans were for this purpose, there were no other deficiencies, and no other loan sources were available), the administration's proposed budget for fiscal 1974 (submitted to the Congress in January 1973) provided no new loan obligations for subsidized homeownership, rural housing, or housing for farm laborers.[67] The only programs to be continued were the moderate-income building loans (Section 502 without interest credits, 33-year term with interest at or near the market level). Only $618 million was proposed for this purpose, and $10 million was requested for direct loans for home repairs to very low-income families. The Congress, however, went well beyond this, approving $2.1 billion for rural housing, of which $1.3 billion was earmarked for subsidized homeownership loans to very low-income families (median income of $5,941 in 1973), $144 million was allocated for the rental housing program, and $10 million was provided for farm labor housing loans. The administration's request for rural housing for 1975 was for $2,139 million. However, the number of new homes actually funded under the program would— according to the administration report—drop from almost 59,000 in 1973 to about 27,000 in 1975.[68]

An Appraisal of Implements and Constraints   Any appraisal of how well the 1972 act was implemented or constrained by congressional and administrative action is a matter of judgment. The Assistant Secretary for Rural Development of the Department of Agriculture, William Irwin, testified that the aggregate of FHA and REA loans and grants would be more than $4.9 billion in fiscal 1974, compared with $1.8 billion in fiscal 1969.[69] In fiscal 1973, 15,492 families received farm ownership loans under FHA. By January 1974, the FHA had outstanding 9,783 sewer, water, and other community facility loans, and 611,451 rural housing loans of which 75 percent had been made in the previous 4½ years. In the calendar year 1973, foreclosures and voluntary conveyances of FHA properties numbered only 3,961 against an outstanding inventory of 517,000 properties at the beginning of the year, a remarkably low rate of 0.77 percent.[70]

In the matter of new loans for business and industrial development in rural areas, a loan level of $200 million had been set by the Congress in October 1973. Secretary Irwin, apparently reflecting the administration viewpoint, saw no "established need" for more than $400 million, or $200 million for insured loans and $200 million for guaranteed loans. His view was that " . . . this additional assignment of going into business and industrial loans gets into an area where we want to move with real responsibility. We are not anxious to . . . [make] loans that not only waste the taxpayers money but really disadvantage the community that is involved. . . ."[71] Senator Dick Clark, chairman of the Subcommittee on Rural Development, observed that " . . . it would seem with the problem in rural

[67]*Ibid.*, p. 347.
[68]*Ibid.*, p. 349.
[69]*Ibid.*, pp. 3, ff.
[70]*Ibid.*, p. 14.
[71]*Ibid.*, p. 10.

development and the need for development that $400 million wouldn't be a very significant figure. . . . When you think of a budget of $300 billion. . . ."[72] The $400 million would provide 40 to 50 thousand jobs in fiscal 1975, using the same job-cost ratio as in 1974.[73] In other words, with the number of unemployed in the nation rising rapidly to the 5 million level and beyond, the administration was proposing an expanded loan program for the entire rural area of the United States that could offset perhaps 1 percent of this, and members of Congress were only mildly agreeing or disagreeing with this policy.

How much is enough? Or what is the lesson for the future? Almost 19 years after President Eisenhower and the Congress, noting the need for rural development, had adopted a significant law with broad policy goals, the program was still at a pilot level. The administrations of four presidents had come and gone without offering what one would call reasonably strong leadership toward rural development, nor had the Congress moved with broad vision to implement its well-stated policy goals. The necessary preliminary research to lend rigor to an expanded investment program had been given only token funds. Although broad macroeconomic studies—generally done with a high degree of capability—were at hand,[74] the many, more detailed, and costly microeconomic studies that would provide a firm foundation for development had not been funded. As of May 1974, the administration of the Rural Development Service was asking for only $10 million "for comprehensive planning."[75] And in the opinion of the senior specialist on rural affairs, Library of Congress, "after about 2 years of the Rural Development Act of 1972, it has been partially implemented but is truly just beginning. . . . to date it is accurate to say that virtually nothing has been done in the field that has helped rural people. . . . The paramount problem remains one of funding. . . ."[76]

Senator Herman E. Talmadge, chairman, Senate Committee on Agriculture and Forestry, described the bill which became the Rural Development Act of 1972 as "probably the single most significant rural development legislation ever considered by the Congress." And he asserted, "The executive branch must do an aggressive, dedicated job of implementing and administering the law if the

[72]*Ibid.*, p. 11.
[73]*Ibid.*, p. 12.
[74]See, for example, *Rural Development: Research Priorities; Communities Left Behind: Alternatives for Development; Rural Industrialization: Problems and Potentials,* collections of papers from three symposia, under general sponsorship of the North Central Regional Center for Rural Development, Iowa State University, and other cooperating institutions, the Farm Foundation, South Dakota State University, and Purdue University, 1973 and 1974.

See, also, reports sponsored by or prepared for the Subcommittee on Rural Development, Committee on Agriculture and Forestry, U.S. Senate: *Library Services in Rural Areas,* Oct. 5, 1973; *Getting a Hand on Rural Development: The Colorado Approach,* Oct. 10, 1973; *Where Will All the People Go?* Oct. 23, 1973; *Training and Employment Programs Serving Rural America,* Oct. 31, 1973; *Proceedings of A National Conference on Rural Development* (Nov. 25–27, 1973), Jan. 2, 1974; *The Transportation of People in Rural Areas,* Feb. 27, 1974; *Rural Industrialization: Prospects, Problems, Impacts and Methods,* April 19, 1974.

[75]*Implementation of the Rural Development Act, op. cit.,* p. 15.
[76]From oral testimony of Morton J. Schussheim, *op. cit.,* p. 352.

intent of Congress is to be honored.''[77] Other senators and representatives joined in this sentiment. If we assume that this is the intent of the Congress and the will of the people, what needs to be done?

First, of course, is the matter of funding, which in our view must go far beyond the limits originally authorized by Congress. Not only must there be large expansions in loans and grants; there must be more adequate funds for detailed microeconomic research and commensurate increases in budgets of the implementing organizations, the FHA, and other cooperating agencies. Constraint of the program on grounds that its expansion would be inflationary runs counter to the economic hypothesis that expansion of the output of rural industry and improvement of rural community facilities, including housing, will make an important contribution to national growth, in economic terms creating a marginal product of greater value than the marginal cost. As we argued in Chapter 9 and consistent with the expressed intent of Congress, inflation must be controlled more effectively through appropriate tax policy and other measures, not by restricting growth of the rural community.

Second, various studies have suggested that many firms can reduce costs by locating plants in depressed rural areas. To achieve the desired level of rural growth, the government must largely abandon the policy of emphasizing loans to industries that cannot get credit from commercial sources and, instead, must enlarge the inducements to industries that are more viable. In determining location, it has been found that firms consider (1) proximity to the relatively immobile factors of production, such as bulky raw materials, available land, and labor; (2) transportation costs and proximity to markets; and (3) possible economies in centralization and decentralization.[78] Given convenient, efficient transportation, space, and labor supply, the rural economy can provide many superior opportunities for industrial growth. To maximize the returns from such opportunities, it is necessary to offer inducements to firms that have high probabilities of financial success, rather than to concentrate on marginal or inefficient industries, as is suggested by the legislation underlying many of the federal funding programs for rural business and industry.[79]

Third, a distinction must be made between helping poor people and subsidizing poor—that is, inefficient—firms and industries. To the extent that people are poor because they have not had equal opportunity, the solution is to make the investments in human capital according to equity and efficiency criteria, after maximizing the productivity from special loan, grant, insurance, and other programs designed to encourage rural business and industry.

How much of the income inequality among regions can be corrected by

---

[77]*Guide to the Rural Development Act of 1972, op. cit.,* p. 152.

[78]Harold G. Halcrow, "A General Comment on Rural Community Development," *Rural Community and Regional Development,* University of Illinois at Urbana-Champaign, Department of Agricultural Economics, AE-4336, June 1974, pp. 10–12.

[79]See John A. Baker and Sue Baker, *Guide to Federal Programs for Rural Development,* Community Development Services, Arlington, Va. 22205.

increased human capital investment and expansion of employment opportunities is suggested by a study relating regional differences in incomes of male workers to differences in the distribution of schooling, age (experience), and employment.[80]

> Interstate differences in the distribution of schooling and age explain 65 to 70 percent of interstate differences in the earnings of all males and all white males in the United States, but these variables perform less well where income data are used. For non-white males, however, schooling and weeks worked account for a high proportion (80 percent) of interstate differences in the level of income and earnings . . .[81] White–non-white differences in the level of earnings across states are found to be due largely (80 to 90 percent) to racial differences in the explanatory variables [particularly the lower levels for nonwhites in schooling and weeks of employment during the year].[82]

The inference for rural development policy can be made explicit. The spread of human capital investment across all economic sectors of the rural society, especially farm and rural nonfarm, and among the races, white, black, and other minorities, will close the earning and income gaps between rural and urban, farm and rural nonfarm, *provided* that the rural employment opportunities keep pace with the advances in education and vocational training. This provision is not so important for college graduates because, there is, in effect, a national labor market for them. Because of the high mobility of college graduates, their wages vary very little across the states.[83] For those with less schooling, the tendency to migrate is weaker and wage rates show significant differences between and among states.[84] Thus there are higher rates of return from schooling in the poorer states.[85] Then, as these higher rates of return are exploited, the income differences will tend to narrow between farm and rural nonfarm, rural and urban, and white, black, and other minority groups. The differences between high-level management and low-level management in the farm economy will narrow because of (1) increased mobility and (2) expanded nonfarm job opportunities, rather than by significantly greater upgrading of low-level farm managers. This is the general implication of more broadly based human capital investment and more successful rural development programs.

[80]Barry R. Chiswick, *Income Inequality: Regional Analyses within a Human Capital Framework,* New York: National Bureau of Economic Research; distributed by Columbia University Press, 1974.

[81]Weeks worked was found to be not a significant variable for white males because it varies too little across the states, and age is not significant for nonwhite males because of the low slope—or low variation by age or experience—of the nonwhite experience-earnings profile. *Ibid.,* pp. 10, 27.

[82]*Ibid.,* p. 27.

[83]*Ibid.,* p. 22.

[84]Rashi Fein, "Educational Patterns in Southern Migration," *Southern Economic Journal, Supplement* (Part 2), July 1965, pp. 106–124.

[85]Chiswick, *op. cit.,* chap. 5; W. Lee Hanson, "Total and Private Rates of Return to Investment in Schooling," *Journal of Political Economy,* April 1963, pp. 128–140; and Giora Hanoch, "An Economic Analysis of Earnings and Schooling," *Journal of Human Resources,* Summer 1967, pp. 310–329.

In conclusion, although rural development has had rather far-reaching goals, the program has been retarded by the very low levels of funding and by uncertainty in regard to the choices of policy means and implementing institutions. In broad vision, a more clear-cut goal is required in respect to the optimum distribution of population over the country; whether or not, for example, it will be national policy to have a higher percentage of people living and employed in the presently more rural areas. This has implications for transportation policy, for example, such as the kind of investments to make, the amount to invest in upgrading and modernizing the nation's railways, and the aid to be given in subsidizing rural roads. It has implications for the Rural Electrification Administration. Is it desired to finance more integrated developments similar to the Tennessee Valley, for example? The direction for this policy must come from a national administration and the Congress. A truly integrated plan for rural development based on consistent macroeconomic theory cannot be developed until the answers to such questions are made more explicit.

The Hired Farm Working Force

The formation of policy for the hired farm working force (HFWF) can be treated as a special problem in human resource and income policy involving policy measures to achieve both efficiency and equity. The HFWF is composed of about 2.5 to 2.7 million workers, of whom 500,000 to 700,000 are regular or year-round workers working 150 days or more; about 1 million are seasonal workers who work 25 to 149 days; and more than 1 million are casual workers who work less than 25 days a year. The number in each category has declined rather consistently for a long time, and especially since the late 1950s, as farm automation and capital-intensive technology have been developed and become more economical than human labor. Sometimes the number in the HFWF has tended to increase, particularly when the level of unemployment in the nation has risen, and farming has provided limited employment for a small percentage of the unemployed work force (Figure 10-3).[86]

The general condition for earnings and employment among the HFWF has left much to be desired. Until the early 1970s, the HFWF was almost totally unorganized, as the employer groups had successfully beaten back the wage earners' attempts at unionization. Wages were generally low, averaging a little less than $15 per day for all farm workers in 1973; they worked an average of 95 days per year. Although additional fringe benefits were often provided, such as housing, meals, and other family perquisites, almost all the HFWF had been excluded from effective wages and hours legislation, social security benefits, unemployment insurance, retirement programs, and the like. Only about one-fifth of all farm workers were covered by minimum-wage legislation set at $1.30 per hour in 1970; but review and enforcement were spotty and far from complete.

[86]The data for discussion of the HFWF are from Robert C. McElroy, *The Hired Farm Working Force of 1973—A Statistical Report,* U.S. Department of Agriculture, Economic Research Service, Economic Development Division, Agricultural Economic Report No. 265, July 1974.

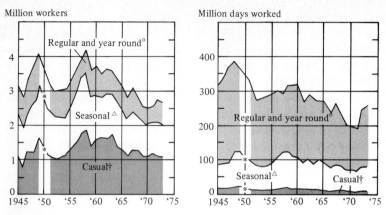

Million workers

Million days worked

*Not available.   △Worked 25–149 days.
°Worked 150 or more days.   †Worked less than 25 days.

Figure 10-3 Trends in hired farm work force, 1945–1974. *(Source: USDA, ERA, Negative 3120, 1974.)*

Despite the rise in hourly wages for farm work over several years, they were still estimated to be as low as 40 to 45 percent of factory wages, and there had been no improvement relative to factory workers in 20 years. There was no federal law to protect workers' rights to organize and to bargain collectively. The necessary enabling legislation had been stalled or defeated in the Congress by the more dominating interests of farm employer groups.

A great variation has existed within the HFWF. Among many of the regular or year-round workers, earnings and working conditions have compared favorably with those of the majority of farm owner-operators. Traditionally on family farms in the United States, the so-called hired man has shared in most, if not all, of the family privileges enjoyed by farm-operator families. Even so, in 1973, the 1.6 million noncasual workers, who averaged 154 days of work, earned only $14.93 per day, or an average for the year of $2,303. Among these workers there were 400,000 who averaged 310 days of farm work and earned $4,696 in cash wages. Another 250,000 averaged 205 days of farm work and earned $3,474. About 950,000 averaged 68 days of farm work and earned $889. The balance of the HFWF, about 1.1 million casual workers, averaged 9 days of work and earned an average of $12.10 a day from farm work.

In 1973, of the total HFWF of 2.7 million workers, 1.6 million persons did farm work only, working an average of 123 days and earning $1,850, and 1.1 million persons averaged 55 days of farm and 118 days of nonfarm wagework for total earnings of $3,097. Those who did farm wagework earned only about $15 per day. Those who did both farm and nonfarm work averaged $14.40 per day from farm work and $19.45 from nonfarm wagework.

Although for many years farm wage workers had agitated for the rights to bargain collectively and for other improvements, little progress had been made. Finally, under the pressure of more militant farm labor leadership, a few collective bargaining contracts began to be written. In 1975, in what is clearly a landmark law, the California legislature adopted a new Agricultural Labor Relations Act.[87] It guaranteed farm workers certain rights to organize and to bargain collectively, and included the right to strike as well as the right to refrain from union organization. It established procedures for elections and labor representation, and made it unlawful for an employer to pay (that is, to bribe) any representative of an employee group or any official of a union organization. The act also set standards for regulation of secondary boycotts. Finally, it established an agricultural labor relations board with broad powers to implement the law and provided for judicial review and enforcement.

Since California employs more farm labor than any other state, its 1975 law is highly significant, perhaps the beginning of a new era in farm worker legislation. It is important, therefore, for us to review the policymaking history and carefully consider further alternatives for the future. We shall begin with some of the congressional hearings.

Congressional Hearings and the Condition of the HFWF   On July 22, 1971, the Senate Subcommittee on Migratory Labor of the Committee on Labor and Public Welfare, under the chairmanship of Senator Adlai E. Stevenson III, Democrat from Illinois, began a series of hearings on farmers and farm workers in the rural United States.[88] In an opening statement, inserted in the record, Stevenson noted that large, well-financed farms appeared to be doing reasonably well; some were obviously prospering. But rural poverty was chronic in some areas and acute in others. The social costs were high and growing higher. Too often the picture of rural America was one of weathered and empty stores, broken windows, collapsed or unpainted barns, rusted gas pumps, boarded-up houses, unkempt farms, and eroded soil. Too many rural towns were shabby, declining, poignant symbols of a continuing human tragedy in rural America, a result of human choices—and failures to choose—over the years.

The committee hearings had the purpose to examine those past choices in the hope that choices and decisions in the future would be more rational and more compassionate, that all rural Americans would share in the decisions that deeply affected their lives. For those Americans who still lived on the land—small farmers and farm workers—Senator Stevenson held that Thomas Jefferson's vision of a rural economy in which citizens "reserve to themselves a wholesome control over their public affairs" was still worth striving for. And, he maintained, there should be a standard of living which ensures that the fruit of a citizen's labor will bring fulfillment, not penury and dispossession.

By June 20, 1972, when the last of the hearings in this series was held, some 4,046 pages of hearings, papers, and supporting documents had been assembled

---

[87]See *Topical Law Reports,* 1975, Commerce Clearing House, Inc., New York; and *Labor Law Reporter,* State Laws, California 47,200, June 13, 1975.

[88]*Farmworkers in Rural America, 1971–1972,* Hearings before the Subcommittee on Migratory Labor of the Committee on Labor and Public Welfare, U.S. Senate, 92d Cong., 1st and 2d Sess., Part I, July 22, Sept. 21 and 22, 1971; Part II, Nov. 5, 1971; Part III, A, B, and C, Jan. 11, 12, and 13, 1972; Part IV A and B, June 19 and 20, 1972; and Part V, A and B, appendices.

or solicited, and the most complete record of the status of farm workers in the United States became available for public use. In general, the committee found that there was indeed a still chronic, and in some places acute, low-income problem. Advancing farm mechanization and other technologies had continued to displace farm workers. Wages generally were low and the bargaining position of workers was weak. Housing generally was far below acceptable standards although it varied widely over the country. On a large proportion of family farms, hired workers had good facilities, often comparable in comfort, if not in style or pretentiousness, to that of the farm operator family. On some large farms comfortable, sound accommodations had been built for the hired help. As other studies had shown, however, in numerous cases, especially in the South and in concentrated large-farm and vegetable areas, farm wage laborers were poorly housed, sometimes in conditions worse than in most big-city ghettos.[89] Often, especially for migrant workers, the living condition was almost minimal, without sanitary facilities and with the barest essentials for modern living.

The Stevenson hearings as well as other studies show that farm work has continued to be one of the most hazardous of all occupations. Agriculture ranked third, behind only mining and construction, in work-related deaths in 1970. Partially because of continuing expanding use of the range of chemical poisons, as we discussed in Chapter 4, threats to fieldworkers' health are widespread.[90] Dr. Joel Schwartz, a biophysicist at the University of California at Berkeley, has noted that the replacement of chlorinated hydrocarbons (DDT and others) by the more acutely toxic organophosphate pesticides, such as parathion, has been exposing farm workers to increased dangers of poisoning.[91] Farm workers have been allowed to enter fields too soon after spraying, and no safe reentry interval has been established by law. According to his estimate, the number of hours lost by farm workers to pesticide-related illness per 1,000 hours worked may be higher than 5.25. If true, this would make some farm work riskier than even construction, which generally has been regarded as the most dangerous. Farming apparently ranks as high as, if not higher than, any other major industry—with the likely exception of mining—in nonfatal accidents and work-related sicknesses.[92]

[89]The titles of these studies are generally descriptive. See, for example, Ruth Holland, *The Forgotten Minority, America's Tenant Farmers and Migratory Workers,* London: Crowell-Collier Press, Collier-Macmillan Ltd., 1970; Truman E. Moore, *The Slaves We Rent,* New York: Random House, Inc., 1965; Ronald B. Taylor, with foreword by Carey McWilliams, *Sweatshops in the Sun, Child Labor on the Farm,* Boston: Beacon Press, 1973; Dale Wright, with foreword by Senator Harrison A. Williams, Jr., of New Jersey, *They Harvest Despair, The Migrant Farm Worker,* Boston: Beacon Press, 1965.

[90]Taylor, *op. cit.,* chap. 2, notes, for example, that according to *The Miami Herald,* Florida has had an average of 428 pesticide poisonings and 7 deaths annually, and health officials admit that their records do not reflect all the poisonings. Most of the victims are children below the age of 10. In 1963, a California worker died and 94 others were seriously poisoned in picking peaches. A newspaper in the Rio Grande valley in Texas reported that 14 farmhands were felled by parathion sprayed on a cotton field where they worked.

[91]See *Smithsonian,* Vol. 6, No. 3, August 1975, pp. 13, 14.

[92]See, for example, "Farm Resident Accidents" in *Accident Facts,* an annual report of the National Safety Council, Chicago.

Finally, a large part of the farm sector has still depended on child labor, a condition almost unique among the nation's major industries. According to a survey by the American Friends Service Committee, as reported in the Stevenson hearings, more than one-fourth of all farm wage workers—as many as 800,000—were under 16 years of age in 1970. In Aroostook County, Maine, the largest of the commercial potato counties, 35 percent of all potato acreage was harvested by children. In the Willamette Valley of Oregon, a concentrated fruit and vegetable area, 75 percent of the strawberry and bean harvesters were children. And the survey of child abuse by the American Friends Service Committee frequently found shocking conditions for child labor. A 10-hour day, or more, was common at the height of the harvest season, when the heat may go over 100 degrees. Children of farm workers suffered serious educational disadvantages. Generally there was little or no assurance of adequate diets or other health care.[93]

The condition of child labor in farming has been the subject of critical review for some time. In 1950, a presidential commission established by President Harry Truman reported that there were 395,000 children between the ages of 10 and 15 working on farms, including children of both farm operator families and of wage laborers. The children about which the commission members were most concerned were not those doing the chores and vacation jobs children often do on a family farm, but those who were

> to be seen in large acreages of peas, snap beans, or cotton where children, sometimes as young as 5 or 6 years, work along with the adult members of the family at stoop labor.
>
> Children work in agriculture because of the need to supplement their parents' earnings and because compulsory school attendance laws are not enforced. They also work, however, because their parents have no other place for them during their own work hours. A third factor is that some employers prefer children as workers.[94]

Two decades later, the American Friends Service Committee reported:

> Children from the age of six work in the fields, harvesting the food we all eat. . . . The use of children as industrial laborers was outlawed under the Fair Labor Standards Act of 1938. Yet in 1970 one-fourth of the farm wage workers in the United States are under 16 years of age. Except for a change in locale—the work is done outdoors—the child labor scene in 1970 is reminiscent of the sweatshop scene of 1938 . . . children who work in agriculture are, for the most part, exempted from

---

[93]Again there were no complete records. Taylor, *op. cit.,* p. 43, reports that in 1969 a pediatrician who had established a farm worker medical clinic in the San Joaquin Valley ran some cholinesterase tests as part of a larger study of farm children. He found that, of 58 children studied, 27 had abnormally low cholinesterase levels when compared to normal values established for adults. When he asked other scientists what these levels meant, he was told that he was the first in the United States to analyze rural children's blood in this way. To him it was tragically absurd that such a study by a rural country doctor in 1969 should be the first ever done on children. Cholinesterase is an essential body enzyme or catalyst of the nervous system which may be destroyed by phosphate and carbonate pesticides. A single drop of the most toxic phosphates will kill a person within hours.

[94]Taylor, *op. cit.,* p. 183–184.

child labor laws and are practically abandoned to the discretion or whim of whoever's farm they are working on.[95]

Farm producers have been permitted to use children heavily in hand labor and other jobs, and the parents of these children—being paid sweatshop wages—have needed this additional income to keep their poverty level of living from falling further.

Ronald Taylor concluded his study of child labor on the farm with the following observation:

> Children should not *have* to work. They should not be used to depress the labor market, should not be used to take the place of breadwinners. . . . Child labor on the farm must be stopped. The cost in human lives is too great, the waste of human potential too much to throw away. . . . The myths must be put to rest once and for all. The farm is not a good place for children to work, just as no factory, no mine, no cotton mill is a good place for children to work. To argue that the farm is different, to call the fields lush and cool and the air unpolluted, is a callous effort to mask the truths of child labor. It is time to put such nonsense aside, it is time that we all—the urban and rural communities—begin to seek solutions that will guarantee these children a healthy, productive future.[96]

Migrant farm workers and especially their children generally have been the most abused and disadvantaged. Not only have they suffered from the usual disadvantages of an unorganized or nonunion labor market; as we noted, the federal minimum wage standards have been modest and enforcement has been spotty. Migrant workers have been exploited by unscrupulous crew bosses. Their bargaining position has been undercut by small farm operators seeking off-farm work, by active recruitment by employer organizations to create an economic surplus of workers, and by overt encouragement by some large-scale farm producers to bring Mexican nationals and other minority groups into the farm labor market. Any protection of their position by either state or federal government has been weak and ineffective. Local, state, and federal governments have given their support to employers rather than to the migrant employees. Dale Wright, who was awarded the highest distinction bestowed annually by the American Newspaper Guild for his reporting of the migrant workers' status, characterized the migrant worker as "unwanted in the farm community which purchased his labor so cheaply; he is a misfit, often a burden on the urban center nearby. He is inarticulate, the possessor of few skills, disorganized, rootless; and because of his migrancy and the accident of his birth as a Negro, a Puerto Rican, a Mexican or West Indian, he is a minority within a minority."[97]

Congressional concern over the plight of farm labor did not start with the hearings of the Stevenson committee nor will it end there. In 1969 the U.S.

---

[95]Taylor, *op. cit.,* p. 184.
[96]Taylor, *op. cit.,* pp. 200–202.
[97]Dale Wright, *They Harvest Despair, op. cit.,* Preface.

Senate Migratory Labor Subcommittee, under the chairmanship of Senator Walter Mondale, Democrat of Minnesota, held extensive hearings on the subject.[98] It learned that farm wage workers, especially in fruits and vegetables, were frequently exposed to dangerous chemicals used in pesticides. In 1969, USDA investigators found proof of 150 to 200 deaths each year from pesticides, and under cross-examination they estimated that the real number was at least 4 times that many. Also, it was possible that 80,000 were injured each year by pesticides.[99] Children as young as nine or ten were found with severe depressions from overwork, malnutrition, and other causes.[100] Almost everywhere the picture was the same. Children of various ages, in a few cases as young as five or six, were working with their parents. Crew leaders were taking 10 to 25 percent off the top of the wage structure, which in many cases went below $1 an hour, and in some cases averaged as low as 30 to 40 cents. A doctor testifying before the Mondale subcommittee had found living conditions for migrant farm workers in Florida and Texas "horrible and dehumanizing to the point of our disbelief. . . . Without heat, adequate light or ventilation, and containing no plumbing, or refrigeration, each room no larger than 8 by 14 feet . . . the living space of an entire family, appropriately suggesting slave quarters of earlier days."[101]

In both the House of Representatives and the Senate, a Select Committee on Nutrition and Human Needs held extensive hearings in the late 1960s.[102] Hunger and malnutrition were found to be widespread, especially among the hired labor force in agriculture, most commonly among migrant workers. Conditions concerning hunger in the United States had been documented earlier.[103] Through the widely seen CBS-TV documentary "Hunger U.S.A.," the fact of considerable hunger, exploitation, and human abuse was brought to a large sector of the American public. Although Secretary of Agriculture Orville Freeman criticized the CBS staff for distorting the facts, later hearings and other investigations and reports seemed to more than substantiate the TV presentation.[104]

Thus, the facts of poverty in American agriculture and rural society have been brought to the attention of all those who have a desire to know. The Congress responded by broadening the coverage and increasing the funding for the food stamp program (as noted in Chapter 3), by setting a minimum wage at

---

[98]U.S. Congress, Senate Committee on Labor and Public Welfare, *Migrant and Seasonal Farmworkers Powerless,* Hearings before the Subcommittee on Migratory Labor of the Committee on Labor and Public Welfare (16 vols.), Washington: Government Printing Office, 1970.

[99]Taylor, *op. cit.,* p. 38.

[100]From testimony of Robert Coles, author of *Children of Crisis: Migrants, Sharecroppers, Mountaineers* (4 vols.), Boston: Little, Brown and Company, 1971. See Taylor, *op. cit.,* p. 58.

[101]Taylor, *op. cit.,* pp. 169–170.

[102]U.S. House of Representatives, Select Committee on Nutrition and Human Needs, *The Food Gap: Poverty and Malnutrition in the United States;* and U.S. Senate, Select Committee on Nutrition and Human Needs, *Nutrition and Human Needs,* Hearings before the Select Committee on Human Needs (in five parts), Washington: Government Printing Office, 1969.

[103]*Hunger, U.S.A.: A Report by the Citizens' Board of Inquiry into Hunger and Malnutrition in the United States,* Boston: Beacon Press, 1968.

[104]See, for example, Taylor, *op. cit.,* chap. 7, Hunger: Knock on Any Door, pp. 150–178, and more recent congressional hearings. See also Robert Coles, *Children of Crisis, op. cit.*

$1.30 per hour in 1970 for hired farm labor on larger farms, a provision which has been ignored or circumvented by payment of piece rates or other measures, and by requiring registration of leaders of farm work crews, a law which also appeared to be easily ignored or only sporadically enforced. In the Department of Labor, the Rural Manpower Service (RMS) was formed ostensibly to help farm and rural nonfarm workers find jobs and to offer other information on employment, transportation, social services, and the like. Upon examination, however, the RMS was found to be grower oriented and grower dominated. It expanded the supply of laborers to meet the seasonal demand for labor on farms; thus it had a depressing effect on farm wage rates and otherwise failed to serve the interests of the farm workers and their families.

In 1972, a special study group, formed in the Department of Labor at the urging of migrant legal aid lawyers, reported:

> Without the economic and political power which comes from organization and solidarity, farm workers' interests suffered accordingly. They did not have the same protection under the minimum wage legislation enjoyed by other workers, and their hourly wages consequently were normally lower. Their coverage under unemployment insurance, social security, and workmen's compensation was nonexistent or restricted compared to coverage of nonagricultural workers . . . farm workers are susceptible to exploitation by careless, insensitive and even unscrupulous employers and social service workers. Yet individual workers generally are afraid to press their complaints because of the strength of the forces working against them— language barrier, fear of losing jobs, fear of eviction from bad but scarce, housing and other problems. . . . Few states set minimum age for children employed in agricultural work outside of school hours and those that do are sometimes lax about enforcement or are grossly understaffed.[105]

The enforcement of labor regulations has never been the traditional role of government without the bargaining power exerted by labor unions. This fact is sometimes, but not always, well understood. In 1971, Representative B. F. Sisk, from California, introduced a bill in Congress that would have ended the exemption of farm workers from the provisions of the National Labor Relations Act of 1935, as amended. The Sisk bill would have provided legal protection for farm workers to organize and to choose their union and union leaders by secret ballot. The intent, according to Sisk, was also to protect farmers from unauthorized strikes, compensate them for unfair labor practices in critical times such as at harvest, and assure the consumer of stable supplies of food through regulation of labor-management procedures. The basic thesis presented by Sisk was, "Farm labor legislation is necessary for order, stability and progress in the farm economy."[106]

Although the California Farm Bureau led important opposition to the Sisk

[105]As reported by Taylor, *op. cit.,* pp. 185–187.
[106]Statement of B. F. Sisk in *Farmworkers in Rural America, op. cit.,* p. 1197.

bill and the American Farm Bureau Federation also opposed it, by June 1972 the AFBF had taken the position that

> the time has come to enact legislation governing the relationships of farmers and farm workers. . . . such legislation should involve the following: Administration by an independent farm labor relations board—Secret balloting by workers on representative questions—Essentially the same list of unfair labor practices as are set forth in the National Labor Relations Act, and particularly the prohibition of secondary boycotts—An exemption for small farmers—The preservation of state laws relating to compulsory unionism—The right to such damages for unlawful boycotts—Availability of an arbitration procedure. [It was believed] . . . that a small specialized board, which could develop simplified, fast, and innovative procedures and give special handling where circumstances warrant, is an absolute essential of a workable farm labor relations program in agriculture.[107]

The Sisk bill did not become law, however, and the first major break in legislation pertaining to the organization of the HFWF was the California Agricultural Labor Relations Act of 1975.[108] This act declared it to be

> the policy of the State of California to encourage and protect the right of agricultural employees to full freedom of association, self-organization, and designation of representatives of their own choosing, to negotiate the terms and conditions of their employment, and to be free from the interference, restraint or coercion of employees of labor, or their agents, in the designation of such representatives, or in self-organization, or in other concerted activities for the purpose of collective bargaining, or other mutual aid or protection [47,405, Sec. 1140.2].

The act also provided for an Agricultural Labor Relations Board, as we noted, and for regulations such as hearings, rights of witnesses, publicity, free speech, "good faith" bargaining, and reduction of court testimony to writing. It was a significant step in the long policymaking struggle to organize the HFWF. To see how significant it was and what might be the further outcome in the new third era of food policy, it is important for our study to review some highlights of this struggle.

Highlights of the Policymaking Struggle to Organize the HFWF   Representatives of farm labor unions are quite agreed that unionization of farm workers is necessary for an equitable income distribution in agriculture and the food economy.[109] Stated policy goals are: (1) freedom to continue the organization and

---

[107]Statement of the American Farm Bureau Federation presented by Matt Triggs, Assistant Legislative Director, June 20, 1972, in *Farmworkers in Rural America, op cit.,* p. 2560.

[108]*Topical Law Reports, Labor Law Reporter,* California Par. 47, 200-47,488, June 13, 1975.

[109]See, for example, statement of Delores Huerta, vice-President, United Farm Workers Organizing Committee, Delano, Calif., in *Farmworkers in Rural America, op. cit.,* pp. 1766–1797; and statement of John Henning, executive secretary-treasurer, California AFL-CIO, San Francisco, *ibid.,* pp. 872–893.

unionization of farm workers without legislative restraints; (2) protection from too fast a rate of farm mechanization, causing displacement of wage workers; and (3) other aids, such as enforcement of laws against assault and battery, credit aids like those that have been available to some low-income farm operators, special medical and educational programs, and the like.[110]

To achieve these goals, it has been proposed that, as a basic minimum, Congress take action to (1) extend the National Labor Relations Act to farm workers; (2) require all states to provide unemployment insurance and workmen's compensation coverage for farm workers (in 1971 only 17 states covered farm workers under workmen's compensation); (3) extend federal minimum-wage coverage to all farm workers (about one-third were covered in 1971); (4) end illegal alien entrance into farm labor markets; (5) expand rural housing programs; and (6) develop federally funded educational programs for children of migratory workers.[111]

Against these viewpoints there have long been arrayed a substantial political force and an organization of landowners and large farmers to prevent farm workers from organizing or otherwise bargaining to improve their lot. In July 1939, Carey McWilliams, then newly appointed chief of California's Division of Immigration and Housing, an agency directly concerned with the problem of migrant workers, published his study of migratory farm labor in California.[112] This book, appearing soon after John Steinbeck's *Grapes of Wrath* told the shocking story of dust-bowl migrants from Oklahoma, so vividly documented and portrayed the misery of farm migrant labor in California that it became the center of a storm of protest and vilification led by the Associated Farmers of California. In his book McWilliams traced the farm labor problem to land monopolization in California. This has its roots in the large-scale Mexican land grants. By the terms of the cession of California to the United States, it was provided that previously issued Mexican land grants would be respected; at that time, as we discussed more fully in Chapter 8, more than 8 million acres of California land were held by some 800 grantees. The grants were generally large. Titles were vague and boundaries were often poorly defined. But the grantees survived most court tests and the grants were not broken up. In addition, by 1870 the railroads held some 20 million acres of California land.

The process of land monopolization was given early impetus by a carelessly conceived state land policy, by wholesale corruption of state officials, and by widespread and sometimes fraudulent trading of land scrip. In less than one decade, most of almost 11 million acres of land granted by the federal government to the state of California had been given away or acquired by a small number of individuals and firms for a nominal fee. Federal land laws, such as the Swamp Act, were further exploited to accentuate land monopolization. In 1935,

---

[110]From statement of Delores Huerta, *ibid.*, pp. 1771, 1772.

[111]From statement of John Henning, *ibid.*, pp. 884, 885. Issues of land ownership and water distribution were also linked to the welfare of workers and family farms, as noted in Chapter 8.

[112]Carey McWilliams, *Factories in the Field, The Story of Migratory Farm Labor in California,* Boston: Little, Brown and Company, 1939.

Paul Taylor of the University of California reported that, as a result, "Of all farms in the United States whose product is valued at $30,000 or above, nearly 37 percent are found in our own State. California has within its borders 30 percent of the large-scale cotton farms of the country, 41 percent of the large-scale dairy farms, 44 percent of the large-scale general farms, 53 percent of the large-scale poultry farms, and 60 percent of the large-scale fruit farms of the United States."

The consistent policy of the large landowners of California has always been to obtain farm labor at the lowest possible cost. At an early date, growers began to look eastward, to the Orient, and south to Mexico for coolie and peon labor. Chinese, Japanese, Americans, Eastern Europeans, Mexicans, and Filipinos were imported or domestically recruited to swell the ranks of unskilled farm wage labor. And, by almost every means at their disposal, the organizations of large land holders stopped the efforts of farm workers to form unions and to obtain laws that would protect them from exploitation.

In 1942, McWilliams published a study of farm migratory labor in the United States, finding a similar pattern of workers' exploitation, low wages, unregulated work conditions, poor diets and malnutrition, generally minimum housing, and poor health provisions.[113] Commonly, wherever there was employment of farm labor on large-scale farms, and apart from the family-farm hired-hand situation, there was a pattern of low wages, child labor, and exploitation of workers, especially in fruit and vegetable production, cotton picking, tobacco, grapes, and onions. Although the lowest wages and the most widespread exploitation was in the South, the conditions were general over most of the United States.

In 1965, Truman Moore listed nine major strike activities in the West between 1947 and 1961.[114] Some of them involved several actions extending over a number of years. They were all broken up by farmers' associations and government officials, typically by highway patrolmen or local police escorting braceros (Mexican nationals) through union lines. In 1959, at a meeting of the National Advisory Committee in Washington, it was pointed out that sugarcane plantation workers in Louisiana were still being paid only 40 to 50 cents per hour. Promises made by the AFL-CIO to the union's Agricultural Workers Organizing Committee (AWOC) four years earlier, to help them organize the sugarcane workers, had not been fulfilled. And three years later, the AFL-CIO, apparently under pressure from other quarters, shut off funds for the AWOC.

About 1964, an important new element entered the drive for recognition of farm workers' unions. Fred Ross, a field worker for the Community Service Organization (a community action group in California), met Cesar Chavez, a Mexican-American born in Brawley, California. Ross hired Chavez, and together they toured California on a CSO membership drive.

At that time, a growers' association and the California Farm Placement Service (FPS) had a worker-referral system under which a worker who applied to the FPS would be referred to an association; but that association would hire

---

[113]Carey McWilliams, *Ill Fares the Land, Migrants and Migratory Labor in the United States,* Boston: Little, Brown and Company, 1942.
[114]Truman E. Moore, *op. cit.,* pp. 156, 158.

workers only in the carrot fields where wages were very low. Domestic workers could not get work in other crops because of grower preferences for Mexican nationals, even though, according to Public Law 78, which was supposed to regulate entry of Mexican workers, American workers were to be given preference. For several months Chavez met a group of 20 to 30 workers each morning and went to the FPS, got referral cards, and applied at the growers' association for employment. Their applications would be refused and Chavez would return to the CSO office and file a complaint with the FPS. Finally, after getting newspaper and television coverage, a complete investigation of the FPS was obtained. An assistant chief was fired for taking bribes from growers, the head of the agency and two others resigned, and several employees received "official letters of censure and reprimand." Chavez was well on his way to organizing the Farm Workers Association. By September of 1964, more than 1,000 families belonged to the FWA, paying $3.50 per month membership dues.[115]

In 1965, the organization, now the United Farm Workers Association (UFWA), led a strike of Filipino and Chicano table-grape workers at Delano, California. The action was more successful in obtaining worker demands than any previous effort had been. More importantly, it provided the opening wedge for a five-year nationwide effort to bring pressure for the acceptance of labor organization in table grapes, about 95 percent of which are produced in California. The UFWA joined with the AFL-CIO's Agricultural Workers Organizing Committee to form the United Farm Workers Organizing Committee (UFWOC) and to forestall an organizing drive by the Teamsters Union, which the UFWOC accused of offering "sweetheart contracts" to growers, and consequently of being preferred by the larger growers. The growers resisted organization by importing Mexican nationals who carried so-called green cards, really visas permitting resident aliens to work in the United States.

To force growers to accept organization of farm workers, the UFWOC organized a nationwide boycott of table grapes. By the beginning of 1970, it was claimed that consumption of table grapes had been cut by 30 percent, and 20 percent of the 1969 harvest—6 million boxes—were in cold storage.[116] The boycott, the first successful nationwide boycott in the history of American labor organization, had succeeded because some of the message had gotten through to the American people, the justice of the workers' position was emphasized, the workers had shown remarkable patience, and there had been considerable community tolerance of the boycott.[117] By 1972, the UFWOC had signed a number of contracts, the first of which had been with the vast DiGiorgio Corporation, where the UFWOC won an election over the Teamsters Union. Additionally, in the lettuce industry a number of contracts had been signed with such large growers as United Fruit, Inter-harvest, Purex, and D'Arrigo, a large, family-owned corporation. In the wine industry also, the large producers, such as Shenley, Paul Masson, Seagram, Almadén (National Distillers), Gallo, Hueblein,

---

[115]Truman E. Moore, *op. cit.,* pp. 130–133.
[116]Victor Salandini, in *Farmworkers in Rural America, 1971–1972, op. cit.,* pp. 1438–1445.
[117]*Ibid.,* p. 1445.

and Christian Brothers, had signed labor contracts. Smaller growers were more resistant.

The initial successes of the UFWOC led to reentry of the Teamsters into farm labor organization and to a jurisdictional fight between the Teamsters and the UFW. Starting in April 1973, the Teamsters signed all but 2 of the 31 growers of table grapes in the Coachella Valley in Southern California. Although this valley provided only about one-eighth of the 25 million boxes of table grapes produced in California, it supplied about 80 percent of the grapes brought to market in late June and July. Under the Teamsters' contract, the minimum wage for pickers was $2.30 per hour, rising in four years to $2.70, plus 30 cents extra per box picked. A fast worker might fill 10 to 11 boxes an hour. Under the UFW, the minimum contract for 1973 was $2.40 per hour. Warfare between the Teamsters and the UFW had been signaled in November 1972 when the Teamster locals across the country warned local merchants that "members of this local will not unload any lettuce bearing the United Farm Workers label." Then, in December, Frank Fitzsimmons, president of the Teamsters, speaking at the convention of the American Farm Bureau Federation, proposed an alliance between labor and agriculture to fight Chavez and "his revolutionaries." Quickly the Teamsters, who already had organized cannery workers and the transportation of some other farm crops, negotiated new contracts with lettuce growers in Arizona and California and then turned to grapes. The UFW threatened a new boycott, this time against the Teamsters. George Meany, president of the AFL-CIO, pledged that the federation "will do everything that's necessary to keep (UFW) alive," and he promised $1.6 million in cash and "substantial manpower" to help in the fight against the Teamsters. Chavez, who had received the inspirational blessing of Robert Kennedy in 1966, the continued support of the National Conference of Catholic Bishops, and new support from the powerful Seafarers' International Union, was not to be deserted now to fight alone.[118]

The times for farm labor organization had changed more than dramatically. Walter J. Stein, who did the most thorough study of the migration of farmers from the Dust Bowl to California in the 1930s, concluded that the Okies, as they were called, did not make good prospects for farm labor organization.[119] Their values were too close to those of their potential employers. They did not understand labor organization. They greatly oversupplied the farm labor market and were discouraged from organizing by the united opposition of large-scale farmers. In 1939, for example, when Senator Robert La Follette of Wisconsin brought his committee on civil rights and labor bargaining to California, he was met by the outspoken hostility of the Associated Farmers of California.[120] Later, a committee chaired by Representative John H. Tolan, liberal Democrat of

[118]*Chicago Daily News,* June 22, 1973.

[119]Walter J. Stein, *California and the Dust Bowl Migration,* Westport, Conn.: Greenwood Press, Inc., 1973.

[120]U.S. Senate, Subcommittee of the Committee on Education and Labor, 74th Congress, Pursuant to Senate Resolution 266, *A Resolution to Investigate Violations of the Right of Free Speech and Assembly and Interference with the Right of Labor to Bargain Collectively.* See also Carey McWilliams, *op. cit.,* chap. 1 on Senator La Follette in California, pp. 13–29.

California, met similar hostility.[121] Although these committees prevailed to develop the most extensive record of testimony and studies ever assembled in these areas, no farm labor unions were formed. The Congress turned in another direction.

In World War II, as the Okie migrants were drawn into defense industries, their place in agriculture was taken by Mexican nationals. In 1951 Congress passed Public Law 78, the so-called bracero program, which was continued to 1964. In its peak year, about 500,000 Mexicans were admitted for farm work under temporary permits—the green cards mentioned earlier. When this program was finally discontinued, the farm labor market continued to be oversupplied by small farmers and the perennial migrants as well as by aliens, many of whom had entered the United States illegally.

In November 1974, Attorney General William B. Saxbe noted that estimates of permanently ensconced aliens in the United States ranged from 4 to 7 million, but that the number could be as high as 12 million.[122] Saxbe and Representative Peter J. Rodino, Jr. (Democrat of New Jersey), chairman of the House Judiciary Committee, favored a federal statute making it a federal offense to knowingly hire an alien who had entered the United States illegally. If all workers were registered, their legal status could be checked through the Social Security Administration. As of 1974, such a bill had passed the House of Representatives twice; but Senator James O. Eastland (Democrat of Mississippi), chairman of the Senate Judiciary Committee, had refused even to call a hearing on the bill. Various estimates suggested that as many as 1 million illegally entered aliens might be denied work if the bill were to become law. Senator Eastland, who was also one of the nation's largest cotton producers, insisted that in any crackdown on illegal aliens, growers and other employers should not be hurt because of a shortage of workers. Throughout the Cotton Belt and the South generally, farm wage rates were about two-thirds or less of what they were in the highest-wage states.[123]

Thus, the farm labor market was supplied up to the end of our second great era for food policy and beyond by low-wage, unorganized workers, who were also relatively unprotected by federal programs and other worker benefits commonly provided in other parts of the American economy. Early in the new third era of food policy, however, although the Congress had not acted, the policy process for farm labor began to change as a result of the first successful labor union organizing activity. This was followed, as we have noted, by an apparent shift in the position of the American Farm Bureau Federation. Then came the California Agricultural Labor Relations Act. Farm labor unions, which had been

---

[121]U.S. House of Representatives, Select Committee to Investigate the Interstate Migration of Destitute Citizens, Pursuant to House Resolution 63 and House Resolution 491, 76th Congress. Under the 77th Congress, the committee was retitled the Select Committee to Investigate National Defense Migration. See also Stein, *California and the Dust Bowl Migration, op. cit.*

[122]*Chicago Daily News,* Nov. 20, 1974.

[123]See *The Migratory Farm Labor Problem in the United States,* the annual reports of the Committee on Labor and Public Welfare, U.S. Senate, Subcommittee on Migratory Labor pursuant to S. Res. 188 (89th Cong., 2d Sess.).

so bitterly opposed for years, had become a viable policy alternative. What might be the major economic consequences?

Economic Consequences of Organization in the HFWF   Based on an assumption of 2.5 million farm wage earners working an average of 95 days per year for an average of eight hours per day (1.9 billion farm wage hours), a $2 an hour average increase in national farm wage rates, which might have brought the real wage for farm wage earners near to that of factory workers in the early 1970s, would have cost about $3.8 billion, *ceteris paribus*. If this cost were passed on to the retail and restaurant level, the national food budget of, say, $160 to $190 billion would be increased by 2 to 2.4 percent. This cost increase would not be realized under actual circumstances, however, for several reasons: (1) Farm labor in a given crop would become more productive—for example, by substitution of adult workers for children, by introduction of more laborsaving technology, and by general upgrading of worker efficiency. (2) The number of farm wage workers would decline as mechanization was accelerated and output per worker increased. (3) Farm labor would become more settled and generally more productive, as has already been demonstrated where labor conditions have improved. (4) There would be shifts among certain crops and marketing processes to take advantage of various cost-reducing innovations. (5) Production of family farms would expand in response to improved markets that might result from output reductions on farms formerly using large amounts of wage labor.

Because of the highly seasonal nature of farm wage employment, the annual earnings of those who did only farm work, however, would still lag far behind those of most industrial workers. In 1971, for example, the farm wage earners in California worked only 1,200 hours, whereas industrial workers averaged more than 2,000 hours.[124] To make real incomes comparable, either farm wage rates would have to be still higher or alternative sources of off-season employment would need to be more available to farm workers. As the number of farm wage earners dropped relative to the volume of nonfarm employment, however, the opportunities for farm workers to earn additional income from nonfarm sources would increase.

Part of the solution also lies in expansion in the number of family-sized farms. *The California Farmer,* published by the California Farm Bureau, noted this in its issue of September 18, 1971. Under the title of "Is This a New Era in California Agriculture?" it concluded that enforcement of the 160-acre limitation on water supplied by a new federally funded irrigation project in Tulare County was resulting in "a new glamor . . . or so it would seem. In this operation, efficiencies usually attributed to large acreage can be met and perhaps surpassed for an owner of less than 160 acres, while the quality of living is increased. The barren land of southeast Tulare County is fast becoming a profitable garden with high-quality living."

Although there is immense variety in American agriculture, which is part of

---

[124]*Ibid.,* p. 872.

its strength, it seems safe to conclude with the hypothesis that changes in policy for hired farm labor are critical for elimination of poverty in the farm and rural nonfarm community. Many other things can be done to help the family farm, such as closing tax loopholes and eliminating special treatment for capital gains, as discussed in Chapter 9. Enforcement of certain land laws is important, such as enforcement of the 160-acre limitation on sale of water on federally irrigated land, as noted in Chapter 8. More can be accomplished by education, upgrading of worker skills, and more effective rural community development. But the critical policy condition for elimination of poverty among farm wage workers is unionization under effective state and federal law.

In some cases, farm labor union bargaining will hasten further mechanization, whereas, in other cases, the mechanization that will be practical is already complete, or will be completed whether or not labor is organized. In either instance, such "technological displacement," as it is sometimes euphemistically called, creates some of our greatest social problems. Andrew Schmitz and David Seckler have shown that in some cases—such as that of the tomato harvester— the gains in efficiency are so great that the large-scale adopters of the harvester could put the displaced workers on a terminal pension for a few years and still gain from use of the machine.[125] In other cases, although the gains may not be so great, labor union bargaining will hasten mechanization. What shall be the policy to compensate displaced laborers? The extension of wages-and-hours legislation into agriculture will make displaced farm laborers eligible for unemployment compensation and other benefits while expansion of nonfarm employment will provide more rewarding opportunities. Continued expansion of the nonfarm labor force is essential.

A Policy Conclusion

To return to the main subject of this chapter, we may conclude that there are a number of choices for human resource and income policy that can enhance the general welfare and result in improved efficiency and equity in the investment of human capital. The concepts of human capital investment and development are now more applicable to the broad realm of human resource and income policies appropriate for the food economy. The minimum policy requirements are a broadening of human capital investment, research and education, a much more adequate funding for rural community development programs, and a new law protecting and regulating farm labor organization.

Alternative sources of employment need to be opened up if the rural society is to maintain a desirable economic balance. Thus, community and regional development is emphasized as a policy alternative to promote growth in other sectors. As Varden Fuller has pointed out, however, this approach involves a different political interest than that of programs primarily for commercial farm-

---

[125]Andrew Schmitz and David Seckler, "Mechanized Agriculture and Social Welfare: The Case of the Tomato Harvester," *American Journal of Agricultural Economics,* Vol. 52, No. 4, November 1970, pp. 569–577.

ers.[126] New agencies are required as policy implementers. Policy constraints must be set that are more consistent with the general goals of national policy. Fortunately, with judgment, understanding, and timely policy action, they can be coordinated and made complementary to other policies outside the food economy.

QUESTIONS FOR DISCUSSION

1 Discuss the concepts of efficiency and equity as applied to human capital investment. What is the criterion of optimum efficiency in such investment? Assuming that optimum efficiency is a policy goal, what are some of the means or measures that will help to bring it about? Will they be equitable? Comment.

2 Discuss the basic thesis of the equity-efficiency quandary in higher education. Is higher education becoming more or less equitable? Comment. In general terms, what are some policy measures that will make higher education both more equitable and more efficient? What are some of the difficulties with such policies? Does the same quandary apply in elementary and secondary education? In adult education programs? Comment.

3 Based on the efficiency criterion, what is an optimum for human capital investment in agriculture? What are the necessary trends in policy to achieve such a situation? Would the result be equitable? Comment.

4 In terms of opportunity costs, are low-level managers in agriculture more or less underpaid than high-level managers? Comment, stating your concept of underpayment. What policy measures are required for further improvements in efficiency and equity (a) within agriculture, and (b) between agriculture and the rest of the society? Distinguish between the necessary and the sufficient policy actions.

5 Compare educational attainments in metropolitan and nonmetropolitan regions in the United States, between farm and rural nonfarm persons, and between blacks and whites. What are some of the inferences for educational policy aimed at efficiency and equity?

6 Comment on the federally financed programs for education and training, stating (a) the general hypothesis or hypotheses of these programs, (b) the adequacy of the programs as related to the goals, and (c) the general experience. What are the policy alternatives for the future? Evaluate.

7 Discuss the basic concepts and theory underlying the land grant college movement, industrial education, and federal-state support for agricultural research and education. How have these movements affected (a) the efficiency of capital investment in agriculture, and (b) the equity of such investment?

8 Review the federal legislative history relating to programs to overcome rural poverty. What are the necessary conditions for overcoming rural poverty? The sufficient conditions?

9 Leonard Goodwin, in his study *Do the Poor Want to Work?* (Brookings Institution, 1972), concluded that poor people have as high life aspirations as the nonpoor and

[126]Varden Fuller, "Political Pressures for Income Distribution," *Journal of Farm Economics,* Vol. 47, No. 5, December 1965, pp. 1245–1251. Reprinted in Vernon W. Ruttan, Arley D. Waldo, and James P. Houck (eds.), *Agricultural Policy in an Affluent Society,* New York: W. W. Norton & Company, Inc., 1969.

want the same things, among them a good education and a nice place to live. They express as much willingness to take job training and in general reveal no differences when it comes to life goals and desire to work. Discuss the implications of these findings for federal job-training and related programs.

10 In the Agricultural Act of 1970, the Congress stated that the highest priority should be given to revitalization and development of rural areas, a policy that was repeated in the Rural Development Act of 1972. What new provisions were included in the latter? Were they generally consistent with the goals? Evaluate the accomplishments under this legislation.

11 Suppose that you were given the task of defining an optimum development policy for the nation's rural areas. What conditions would you take into account? What would be your criteria of equity and efficiency? On what basis would you choose between alternative policies? What groups might be most advantaged by your policy? Most disadvantaged?

12 Review the status of the HFWF in respect to the following: (a) changes in aggregate levels of employment, (b) hours worked and annual earnings, (c) competitive structure in bargaining and changes in this structure since the late 1960s, and (d) work conditions, housing, etc.

13 Several congressional hearings have depicted a rather sorry existence for much of the HFWF, yet the legislation developed by the Congress in this area generally lags behind that for industrial workers. Account for this. In general macroeconomic or theoretical terms, what has been the effect of low wages in agriculture (a) on aggregate net farm-operator income, (b) on returns to the smaller family farm, (c) on returns to larger-than-family farms?

14 What are the general provisions of the California Agricultural Labor Relations Act of 1975? What would be the structural effects within agriculture if similar provisions were adopted nationwide? That is, what would be the effects (a) on aggregate net farm-operator income, (b) on the distribution of net income among farm-operator families, (c) on farm service and marketing firms, and (d) on consumer food prices?

15 Discuss the possible interrelated effects on net farm-operator income of heavier human capital investment in agriculture, more effective rural development programs, and more complete organization of the HFWF. Distinguish between effects on efficiency and equity, on small farms versus large farms, and on the returns to human capital versus returns to land and other capital resources.

REFERENCES

Brinkman, George, et al., *The Development of Rural America,* Manhattan: University Press of Kansas, 1974.

Chiswick, Barry R., *Income Inequality: Regional Analyses Within a Human Capital Framework,* New York: National Bureau of Economic Research, 1974.

Coles, Robert, *Children of Crisis: Migrants, Sharecroppers, Mountaineers,* Boston: Little, Brown and Company, 1971.

Dovring, Folke, *Productivity of Labor in Agricultural Production,* University of Illinois at Urbana-Champaign, College of Agriculture, Agricultural Experiment Station Bulletin 726, September 1967.

Halcrow, H. G., et al., *School Tax Options Affecting Illinois Agriculture,* University of Illinois at Urbana-Champaign, College of Agriculture, Agricultural Experiment Station Bulletin 744, April 1973.

Hathaway, Dale E., and Brian E. Perkins, "Occupational Mobility and Migration from Agriculture," in *Rural Poverty in the United States,* Washington: National Advisory Commission in Rural Poverty, 1968.

Hightower, Jim, *Hard Tomatoes, Hard Times,* Washington: Agribusiness Accountability Project, 1972.

Marshall, Ray, *Rural Workers in Rural Labor Markets,* Salt Lake City: Olympus Publishing Company, 1974.

McElroy, Robert C., *The Hired Farm Working Force of 1973—A Statistical Report,* U.S. Department of Agriculture, Economic Research Service, Economic Development Division, Agricultural Economic Report No. 265, 1974.

Schultz, Theodore W. (ed.), *Human Resources, Economic Research: Retrospect and Prospect,* 50th Anniversary Colloquium VI, General Series 96, New York: National Bureau of Economic Research, 1972.

——(ed.), "Investment in Education: The Equity-Efficiency Quandary," *Journal of Political Economy,* Vol. 80, No. 3, Part II, May/June, 1972.

Scott, John T., Jr., *Rural Community and Regional Development: Production and Prospects,* Urbana: University of Illinois, AE-4336, 1974.

Taylor, Ronald B., *Sweatshops in the Sun, Child Labor on the Farm,* Boston: Beacon Press, 1973.

U.S. Senate, *Farmworkers in Rural America, 1971–1972,* Hearings, Committee on Labor and Public Welfare, Subcommittee on Migratory Labor, 92d Cong., 1st and 2d Sess., 1971 and 1972.

——, *Implementation of the Rural Development Act,* Hearings, Committee on Agriculture and Forestry, Subcommittee on Rural Development, 93d Cong., 2d Sess., 1974.

——, *The Economic and Social Condition of Rural America in the 1970's,* Prepared by U.S. Department of Agriculture, Economic Research Service, Economic Development Division, for the Committee on Government Operations, 92d Cong., 1st Sess., 1971.

Chapter 11

Coordinating
Nutrition Policy

Malnutrition may just be the most serious problem to face even the most affluent nations.

Georg Borgstrom
The Hungry Planet, 1965

All solutions are going to be difficult and costly. . . . we need both more production and more distributive justice. . . . Nutrition must play a major role. . . . the need for responsible food and nutrition policies can only grow in urgency in the months and years ahead.

Jean Mayer
National Nutrition Policy Study, 1974[1]

This chapter coordinates food and nutrition policy, in which we conceive of *nutrition* as the science of food as it relates to optimal health and performance, and *nutrition policy* as those aspects of food policy that most directly influence human nutrition. We shall discuss problems and goals in nutrition policy, the efforts and alternatives in policy for improving nutrition, and the recognized needs in research and development of such policy. Observations on these

---

[1]Hearings, Select Committee on Nutrition and Human Needs, United States Senate, 93d Cong., 2d Sess., June 14, 19–21, 1974, Parts 1–7. This study is a major source of material for this chapter.

subjects are combined with other observations to conclude with a general view of food policy for America that can be most effective in the future.

SETTING THE GOALS IN NUTRITION POLICY[2]

As we have noted, modern science and agriculture have freed the people of the United States and many persons in other countries from the age-old threat of serious food shortages. Since early in the nineteenth century when this progress really began, there have been important gains in diet and nutrition for a world population that is now more than 5 times as large as at the beginning of that century. Much has been learned about nutrition, and policies are available to extend these gains with ever-growing equity and efficiency.

But modern science and the food industry have also freed people from the traditional diets based on natural farm products, hunting, and fishing. Although this development has resulted in improvements in nutrition for many people in this country and around the world, it has not been universally beneficial. In many countries it is doubtful that the average diet has improved very much in terms of nutritive values, if at all. In the United States, although the rising levels of athletic performance and the more general gains in human growth and longevity might suggest that substantial advances have been made in nutrition among all groups, other evidence suggests that, on balance, our diets and state of health as related to nutrition have not changed for the best.[3] Many people have poor diets.

Studies show that education usually increases dietary adequacy and that people with family incomes above $10,000 have more nutritious diets than those with lower incomes.[4] In recent decades as real incomes have risen, however, it is possible that the overall dietary quality has fallen. In 1965, for example, only 50 percent of all households consumed the recommended allowances for seven designated nutrients, a full 10 percent lower than in 1955, despite a 25 percent rise in per capita real disposable income between 1955 and 1965.[5] The proportion of poor diets, containing less than two-thirds of the recommended allowances of one or more of these seven nutrients, rose from 15 percent in 1955 to 21 percent in 1965. These declines in diet adequacy were generally attributed to increased consumption of bakery goods and other foods high in sugar and fat, increasingly high consumption of grain-fed beef, and lower consumption of fresh fruits and vegetables, milk and milk products, and some other foods necessary for a well-

---

[2]The general sources used for information on nutrition are: Helen Andrews Guthrie, *Introductory Nutrition*, 3d ed., St. Louis: The C. V. Mosby Company, 1975; and L. Jean Bogert, George M. Briggs, and Doris Howes Calloway, *Nutrition and Physical Fitness*, 9th ed., Philadelphia: W. B. Saunders Company, 1973.

[3]See Michael Jacobson, "Our Diets Have Changed, But Not for the Best," *Smithsonian*, April 1975, pp. 96–102.

[4]Corinne Le Bobit and Faith Clark, "Are We Well Fed?" *Food: Yearbook of Agriculture*, Washington: Government Printing Office, 1959, p. 624

[5]*Poverty, Malnutrition and Food Assistance Programs: A Statistical Summary*, U.S. Senate, Select Committee on Nutrition and Human Needs, 91st Cong., 1st Sess., p. 5.

balanced diet.[6] More recent surveys do not as yet show a reversal of this trend. In hospitals, where good diets may be especially desirable, the average diet has been described as presenting one of the most serious nutritional problems of our time.[7]

The state of nutrition is only partially reflected in data on health and longevity. Although the average life expectancy of a baby born in the United States is almost twice what it was in the early nineteenth century, the main gains have come from drastically lowered rates of infant mortality and from almost complete control or eradication of such highly contagious diseases as scarlet fever, diptheria, and tuberculosis. Just since 1950, the rate of infant mortality under one year has dropped spectacularly from 29.2 per 1,000 live births to 26.0 in 1960, to 20.0 in 1970, and to 16.5 in 1974. Also, there was a sharp drop in the maternal death rates per 100,000 live births from 83.3 in 1950, to 37.1 in 1960, to 21.5 in 1970, and to 20.8 in 1974. Both infant and maternal mortality is significantly lower among white and well-to-do Americans than among minority groups and the less well-to-do. Between the 1930s and the 1970s there were a number of significant declines in deaths from the infectious and communicable diseases, such as acute bronchitis and bronchiolitis, influenza, and pneumonia. The crude death rates per 1,000 persons annually dropped from around 11 in the decade of the 1930s, to 9.5 in the 1950s and 1960s, and averaged between 9.4 and 9.1 in the 1970s. The average life expectancy rose from about 60 years in 1930 to 69 by 1955. Then it rose slowly to an even 70 in 1960, to 70.2 in 1965, to 70.9 in 1970, and to an estimated 72 in 1974. In 1973, the life expectancy was 67.6 years for males and 75.3 for females, a wider difference than in the 1930s.[8] The United States ranked seventh among world nations in life expectancy for women and nineteenth for men. In annual reports by the Department of Health, Education, and Welfare (HEW), a barrier to further improvement was related to the American life-style, which included excessive use of alcohol and tobacco, lack of proper exercise, and inadequacies in diet and nutrition.

Surveys of the Status of Nutrition in America

Until 1968, attempts to evaluate the nutritional status of the American population were confined to small, selective groups. The results of the surveys were summarized first in *Nutritional Status, U.S.A.,* which reported on the work of more than 200 professional nutrition investigators from 1947 through 1958, covered earlier in 178 publications.[9] About 4,000 people in each of three age

[6]*Dietary Levels of Households in the United States, Spring 1965: A Preliminary Report,* U.S. Department of Agriculture, Economic Research Service, No. 67-17, January 1968, p. 9.

[7]Charles E. Butterworth, "The Skeleton in the Hospital Closet," *Nutrition Today,* March/April 1974, pp. 4–8; and George L. Blackburn and Bruce Bistrian, "A Report from Boston," *ibid.,* May/June 1974, p. 30.

[8]For annual summaries for the United States, see the *Monthly Vital Statistics Report,* U.S. Department of Health, Education, and Welfare, Public Health Service, Health Resources Administration, National Center for Vital Statistics, Rockville, Md.

[9]Agnes Fay Morgan (ed.), *Nutritional Status, U.S.A.,* An Interregional Research Publication, University of California at Berkeley, Division of Agricultural Sciences, California Agricultural Experiment Station Bulletin 769, October 1959.

groups—5 to 12, 13 to 20, 20 and over—and from 39 of the 48 states, were studied; and, on the whole, their nutritional status was found to be good, probably the best that had ever been reported for similar population groups. The average nutrient intakes by both boys and girls up to age 12 in all regions were estimated to be adequate, even deluxe, except that the calcium intake of the girls was slightly low. Boys aged 13 to 20 averaged more than adequate amounts of all nutrients except vitamin C, or ascorbic acid. Girls aged 13 to 20 were adequate or high in only three essential nutrients, vitamin A, riboflavin, and niacin. Among adults aged 20 and over, in spite of some deficiencies in total calories, a usually good intake of vitamins, minerals, and proteins pointed to generally wise food choices. Among both children and adults in all regions, the nutrients most often lower than recommended amounts were vitamins A and C, calcium and iron. The standards for adequacy were those set or reaffirmed in 1958 by the National Research Council of the National Academy of Sciences for recommended daily allowances of nutrients.[10]

In *Nutritional Status, U.S.A.,* the quality of nutrition was generally related to economic status and level of education. Children from the lower socioeconomic levels were below average in height and weight, indicating generally poor nutrition; but 15 to 20 percent of all adolescents were obese as a result of overeating and too little exercise, and many older people were also overweight. One-quarter to one-half of all the women examined in widely separated parts of the country were 10 percent or more overweight, and more than one half of these were in turn more than 20 percent overweight. Among a sample of men from three states, the number that were 10 percent or more overweight varied from 24 percent in California and Colorado to 39 percent in New Jersey, with about half of them excessively overweight. Among the nutrient inadequacies, iron was commonly limited in diets of pregnant women and small children. Ascorbic acid or vitamin C, vitamin A, calcium and iron were the nutrients most often consumed at levels below the recommended dietary allowance (RDA); but other biochemical evidences of more general vitamin insufficiencies were rare.

In 1965, the USDA surveyed 7,500 households, selected to represent all households in America, based on a seven-day dietary recall by the homemaker of all food available for consumption at home, with adjustments for food eaten away from home. Only one-half the households had diets rated good in that they provided the RDA for all nutrients. One-fifth of the families had diets rated poor in that they provided less than two-thirds of the RDA for one or more nutrients. Dietary adequacy improved as income increased; but an adequate income provided no assurance of a good diet, since 9 percent of the households with

---

[10]Recommended daily allowances of nutrients were derived from recommended dietary allowances (RDA) first published by the National Academy of Sciences in 1943 with the objective of providing standards for good nutrition for people of all ages. To simplify calculations of daily nutritional needs, the RDA were then presented as daily allowances. In 1973 the Food and Drug Administration developed the United States Recommended Daily Allowances (USRDA) as standards for nutritional labeling. See *Recommended Dietary Allowances,* 8th ed., rev., National Academy of Sciences, National Research Council, Food and Nutrition Board, Committee on Dietary Allowances and Committee on Interpretation of the Recommended Dietary Allowances, Washington: 1974.

incomes of more than $10,000 had poor diets and a much larger proportion had diets that were either deficient or excessive in terms of total calories, or below the RDA for one or more nutrients.

On December 5, 1967, Congress provided, in the Partnership for Health Amendments of 1967, for the first comprehensive nutrition survey of the American people, subsequently identified as the Ten-State Nutrition Survey.[11] The study was designed to examine the dietary practices and nutritional status of a representative sample of persons heavily weighted toward people living in low-income areas, in three social and ethnic groups—Black, White, and Spanish-American. Although the primary interest in each state was malnutrition among the poor, the target population also included middle- and upper-income individuals living in the selected enumeration districts. The sample was divided into two parts to make comparisons between five high-income and five low-income ratio states (Figure 11-1).

The nutritional status of people in the ten-state survey was assessed on the basis of physical and anthropological measurements, biochemical determinations on blood and urine, a dental examination, and dietary evaluations. Dietary intake was determined on the basis of a 24-hour recall by the homemaker and selected nutritionally vulnerable members of the household. Since this recall technique did not allow for the normal day-to-day variation in food intake, it tended to overestimate the proportion of the population with "inadequate" diets.[12] The study, however, still yielded useful results based on extensive measurements and evaluations.

The data revealed important differences in the relative importance of nutritional problems between the populations of the two five-state groups and among the three ethnic groups (Figure 11-1). Iron was the nutrient most generally classed as a high nutritional problem among all groups, while low intake of vitamins A and C and of riboflavin was related more closely to age or ethnic groups. Low vitamin A levels were found in the serum of children (particularly Spanish-Americans); low levels of vitamin C were found in the serum of mothers, and evidence of growth retardation was found in each state and ethnic group. Low hemoglobin levels existed in 11 percent of the total population and in 30 percent of the black population. Obesity was reported among adult females in 50 percent of the survey group, and among a high proportion of adult white males, especially in the high-income states. Poor dental health was associated with poor nutrition.

In 1971–72, DHEW began its Health and Nutrition Examination Survey (HANES) of a planned sample of 30,000 people, from 1 to 74 years of age in 65 primary sampling areas in the United States, which the department planned to repeat every two years. The first preliminary findings of 10,126 people from 35

---

[11] *Ten-State Nutrition Survey,* 1968–1970, DHEW Publication No. (HSM) 72-8120, 5 vols., Washington, 1972.

[12] For a more general criticism of dietary standards and survey techniques see D. Mark Hegested, "Dietary Standards," *Journal of the American Dietetic Association,* Vol. 66, No. 1, January 1975, pp. 13–19.

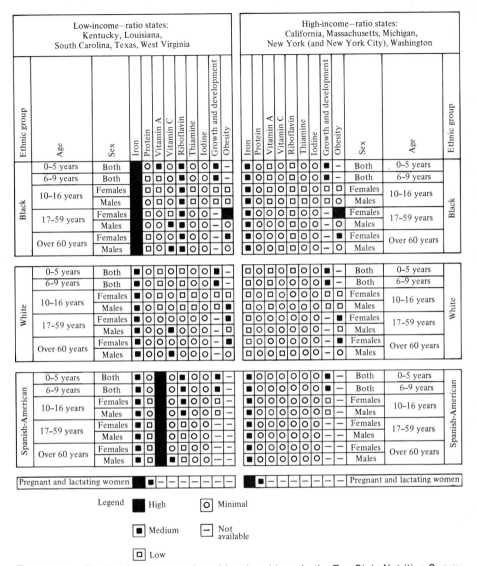

Figure 11-1 Relative importance of nutritional problems in the Ten-State Nutrition Survey, 1968–1970. (*Source: Washington: Department of Health, Education and Welfare, DHEW Publication No. 72–8120, 1972.*)

sampling areas revealed that a high percentage of persons of all ages, both above and below the poverty line, both sexes, and both white and black, had nutrient intakes less than the recommended standard levels for the four most critical nutrients—calcium, iron, and vitamins A and C. The average intake of iron was especially low for children and women aged 18 to 24. Although the average mean intake of most nutrients except iron was generally above the recommended levels, the survey data suggested a high incidence of nutrient inadequacies as well as considerable dietary excesses (Table 11-1).

HANES also showed that, although undernutrition and malnutrition were not confined to any one socioeconomic, cultural, or ethnic group, several groups have more intense or critical nutritional problems than others. They include Indians, migrant agricultural workers, Eskimos, Spanish-Americans, the poor, and the elderly. American Indians, numbering less than one-half million and having per capita incomes averaging less than $1,000 per year, consume a generally cheap and inadequate high-carbohydrate diet that is more often than not nutritionally poor, being especially low in ascorbic acid and Vitamin A.

The migrant agricultural workers, as we noted in Chapter 10, have had virtually no financial security. In addition to poor educational opportunities, generally poor housing, and lack of medical or dental attention, they have been unable to buy normal amounts of good food and have often lacked adequate facilities for food storage, preparation, or adequate sanitation. Several studies have shown that diets of the migrant families are low in vitamins A and C, calcium, and riboflavin, reflecting chief reliance on carbohydrates and limited use of meat and poultry products, milk and milk products, fresh fruits, and green and leafy vegetables.

Eskimos traditionally have lived chiefly by hunting and fishing, and so have had a diet high in fat and protein and low in carbohydrate. As they have lost their traditional food resources and food-gathering skills, many have shifted to a high-carbohydrate diet with a growth in dental and other health problems.

More generally, the poor in America have been identified as a group with less than adequate diets. This hallmark is due in part to their limited resources for all necessities and in part to their generally low levels of education and lack of knowledge in food choice and preparation. The rise in food prices in the early 1970s was especially hard on the poor, who normally have to spend a high percentage of their income on food. This, of course, was an important factor taken into account by the Congress in voting for rapid expansion in the food stamp and school lunch programs.

The nutritional problems of the elderly are especially noted because not only are the stresses that affect the aged subtle and insidious, but diet deficiencies or excesses are cumulatively detrimental over the years. Physiologically, the elderly suffer from decreased ability to absorb and transport nutrients through the digestive-circulatory system and therefore have a relatively increased need for an attractive, palatable, and nutritious diet. Their nutritional problems and goals are particularly important in our view of policy.

In summary, although the surveys of the status of nutrition show that a high proportion of the nation's total population have good to excellent diets, and that the average food intake is perhaps the highest of any nation, signs of malnutrition, hunger, and poor eating habits are evident all around us. At least 30 percent of our total population show some evidence of malnutrition in the form of inadequate intake of food and nutrients (especially iron, calcium, vitamin A, vitamin C, and riboflavin), or in the form of anemias, obesity, or diseases closely associated with poor nutrition, such as the circulatory diseases (heart disease, hypertension, stroke, and so on), diabetes, severe dental and periodontal disease, and alcoholism. Many health problems stem from overeating—that is, too high consumption of total calories even in a well-balanced diet—as well as from eating too freely of certain types of food (sugar, fats, and alcohol), with the inevitable overweight and the diseases often associated with overweight, such as diabetes, high blood pressure, and heart disease. According to these surveys and supporting health data, appropriate nutrition intervention activites could reduce morbidity and mortality from heart disease by 25 percent, respiratory and infectious diseases by 20 percent, cancer by 20 percent, and diabetes by 50 percent.[13] Clearly, if uniformly good health is an accepted goal for America, there is much yet to do in improvement of the nutritional status of many people and groups.

Nutritional Goals and Dietary Trends

The general goal of good nutrition, which should need no further defense, is related to a vast, complex, and rapidly expanding knowledge of more than 40 essential nutrients. Recommended intakes have been established as United States Recommended Daily Allowances (USRDA) in 18 categories which must be supplied by food for good health and bodily functioning.[14] The deficiencies and excesses that have developed in American diets are not due to a lack of scientific knowledge in regard to these nutrients, even though we will argue that much more research needs to be done. Neither are they due to a lack of recommendations from nutritionists and food scientists, public health officials, and others who are generally knowledgeable in food policymaking. Nor are they due to a lack of supply of the basic food stocks.

The deficiencies and excesses that must be reduced to achieve the goal of good nutrition in America are related more to the lack of purchasing power among the poor, the general ignorance or lack of motivation of consumers in regard to nutrition principles, and the health-damaging preferences of some consumers; and they are related to the decisions of business executives and investors who manufacture and supply food. As food technology has developed it has become profitable to fabricate and sell many foods that are low in essential nutrients or high in other nutrients, such as fats and sugars, which are already excessively high in the national food mix.

Some of the dietary changes that must be achieved to reach the major goals of national nutrition policy can be observed by the trends in consumption of fats and fat-rich foods, carbohydrates, and proteins. Although other factors are also important, we shall first concentrate on these three.

[13]Guthrie, *op. cit.*, p. 8.

[14]Thus, the USRDA is a standard set of daily quantities of specified vitamins, minerals, and protein judged to be essential in human nutrition by the U.S. Food and Drug Administration (FDA). Values are taken from the Recommended Dietary Allowance (RDA) developed by the Food and Nutrition Board of the National Academy of Sciences, National Research Council, as published by FDA on March 14, 1973. The USRDA, as periodically revised, has replaced the other measures previously used as a standard for good nutrition.

Table 11-1   Comparison of Percentage of Persons with Nutrient Values Less than the Standards, and Mean Nutrient Intakes as a Percentage of Standard by Race, Age, and Sex for Income Levels, United States, 1971–1972.

Age, sex, and nutrient	White		Negro	
	Percentage of persons with intakes less than standard	Mean intake as percentage of standard	Percentage of persons with intakes less than standard	Mean intake as percentage of standard
	Income below poverty level*			
1–5 years, both sexes				
Calcium	14.42	197	35.26	149
Iron	94.46	67	93.61	60
Vitamin A	51.51	160	46.07	187
Vitamin C	58.23	138	48.54	161
18–44 years, female				
Calcium	56.39	110	74.50	80
Iron	94.24	57	94.66	49
Vitamin A	73.54	82	64.42	149
Vitamin C	72.26	108	59.37	132
60 years and over, both sexes				
Calcium	40.43	121	44.67	108
Iron	62.66	95	67.31	93
Vitamin A	61.45	108	62.40	163
Vitamin C	59.16	119	54.65	141

Income above poverty level*

1–5 years, both sexes				
Calcium	12.14	210	24.96	166
Iron	94.88	69	95.29	66
Vitamin A	36.91	157	51.01	199
Vitamin C	42.82	189	52.91	160
18–44 years, female				
Calcium	55.59	110	71.69	77
Iron	91.13	59	94.70	55
Vitamin A	64.90	114	67.36	116
Vitamin C	49.04	150	56.81	127
60 years and over, both sexes				
Calcium	34.41	142	47.71	117
Iron	46.97	114	64.57	109
Vitamin A	55.56	196	52.24	226
Vitamin C	38.96	174	43.78	165

*Excludes persons with unknown income.

Source: From preliminary findings of the first Health and Nutrition Examination Survey, United States, 1971–1972, Dietary intake and biochemical findings, Washington: Department of Health, Education, and Welfare, 1974.

Consumption of Fats and Fat-rich Foods   Fats and fat-rich foods of either animal or vegetable origin are required as a source of essential fatty acids for the growth and well-being of all species of higher animals, including man. They are also useful, but not essential, as carriers of fat-soluble vitamins A, D, E, and K, as a concentrated and dietary efficient source of energy, and as means of making foods appetizing and satiating. Because of their high energy content, they play a critical role in weight control. A diet that is low in fat either supplies less energy than the body needs, thereby causing weight loss, or is much more bulky than the usual American or European diets. One that is high in fat will likely provide food energy in excess of bodily needs, thus contributing to undesirable weight gains or obesity. Excess energy taken either in the form of fat, carbohydrate, or protein will be converted into body fat and stored in fatty tissues in various parts of the body.

Over a considerable period of time, the average fat content of the American diet has increased steadily, thus placing fat in the most critical role as a suspect nutrient in the nationwide high incidence of obesity, heart trouble, and other complications. In 1910, it was estimated that fat provided only 32 percent of the total calories available in the American diet. By 1935, the figure had risen to 35 percent, and by 1972 to 41 percent. About 40 percent of total fat was visible fat—such as butter, margarine, vegetable fat such as in salad dressing, and the layer of fat on meat—and 60 percent was invisible—such as marbling throughout meat fibers, in egg yolk, homogenized milk and milk products, nuts, and whole-grain cereals. In 1972, the total available fat, not counting losses in cooking or other obvious waste, was 127 pounds per capita, considerably higher than in all but the most affluent of other countries. It was estimated that, on the basis of trend projections, per capita consumption of visible fat would rise from 53 pounds in 1972 to 60 pounds in 1985.

Some nutritionists believe that a drastic modification of fat in the American diet would be unwise, except for middle-aged men with high blood cholesterol and triglyceride levels, especially those who work under emotional tension and have a family history of heart disease; but, in most cases, there would be no harm and important benefits if the amount of fat in the diet were reduced to less than 35 percent of total calories, if the amount of dietary cholesterol were correspondingly reduced, and if there were a further shift to polyunsaturated fat of vegetable origin and away from saturated (animal) fat. This shift toward use of vegetable fats has been related to expansion of soybean production and improvement of extraction techniques. This trend is generally considered desirable both for nutrition and for more efficient food production, and many people may have reached the state of optimum balance between fats of animal and vegetable origin, even though total consumption of fat is still considerably higher than optimum for good health. (See Table 11-2.)

Carbohydrate Consumption   Carbohydrates, another important source of energy which is supplied almost exclusively (except for milk) by foods of plant origin, have declined about 25 percent in per capita consumption over the past 60

Table 11-2 Approximate Sources of Nutrients in the Average American Diet* (in Percentages)

Food groups	Food Energy	Protein	Fat	Carbo-hydrate	Calcium	Phos-phorus	Iron	Magne-sium	Vitamin A value	Thiamin	Ribo-flavin	Niacin	Vitamin B-6	Vitamin B-12	Vitamin C
Meat (including pork fat cuts), poultry, and fish	21.1	42.0	36.0	0.1	3.7	26.7	31.4	14.1	23.8	31.2	25.9	47.7	47.6	70.4	1.1
Eggs	2.2	5.8	3.2	0.1	2.6	6.0	6.0	1.4	6.8	2.5	5.8	0.1	2.2	9.2	0
Dairy products, excluding butter	11.2	22.2	12.3	7.0	76.1	36.1	2.3	22.1	11.2	9.5	42.4	1.7	9.4	20.4	4.4
Fats and oils, including butter	17.7	0.1	41.6	†	0.4	0.2	0	0.4	8.5	0	0	0	0.1	0	0
Citrus fruits	0.8	0.4	0.1	1.8	0.9	0.7	0.8	2.0	1.4	2.6	0.5	0.8	1.2	0	25.3
Other fruits	2.3	0.6	0.3	5.0	1.2	1.1	3.6	4.0	6.3	1.9	1.6	1.8	5.7	0	11.6
Potatoes and sweet potatoes	2.8	2.4	0.1	5.6	0.9	4.0	4.7	7.4	5.0	6.6	1.8	7.5	12.1	0	20.3
Dark green and deep yellow vegetables	0.2	0.4	†	0.5	1.5	0.6	1.6	2.0	21.1	0.8	1.1	0.6	1.7	0	8.2
Other vegetables, including tomatoes	2.4	3.2	0.4	4.7	4.8	4.8	9.2	10.3	15.4	6.9	4.5	6.0	9.2	0	29.1
Dry beans and peas, nuts, soya flour	2.8	4.7	3.5	1.9	2.5	5.4	5.9	10.4	†	5.1	1.7	6.7	3.9	0	†
Flour and cereal products	19.3	17.7	1.3	35.6	3.3	12.3	26.2	17.9	0.4	32.8	14.1	22.2	6.8	0	0
Sugars and other sweeteners	16.4	†	0.0	37.2	1.1	0.2	5.7	0	0	†	†	†	0	0	†
Coffee and cocoa‡	0.7	0.4	1.2	0.6	1.0	1.8	2.5	7.7	†	0.1	0.7	4.9	0.1	0	0
Total§	100.0	100.0	100.0	100.0	100.0	100.0	100.0	100.0	100.0	100.0	100.0	100.0	100.0	100.0	100.0

*From U.S. Department of Agriculture, *National Food Situation*, Washington: November 1971. Percentages were derived from nutrient data which include quantities of iron, thiamin, and riboflavin added to flour and cereal products; quantities of vitamin A value added to margarine and milk of all types; and quantities of vitamin C added to fruit juices and drinks.
  †Less than 0.05 percent.
  ‡Chocolate liquor equivalent of cocoa beans.
  §Components may not add to total due to rounding.

years; but the consumption of sugar, which in its modern highly refined state is a pure-energy carbohydrate with no other nutritive value, has remained almost constant, at near 100 pounds per capita except during the World Wars. It supplies between 15 to 20 percent of the total calorie intake of the American population.[15] Formerly, carbohydrate was thought to be the only energy source for physical work. Present information indicates, however, that carbohydrate plays a dominant role only in heavy exercise when oxygen supply to the muscles becomes limiting. During steady-state work, fat provides about half the energy. The fat utilized comes from lipid pools in the muscle tissue and fatty acids mobilized from adipose tissue and transported to the working muscle by the blood. Protein is not used for work energy to any great extent.

Sucrose, which is the most common of the various sugars and is obtained from either sugarcane or sugar beets, is consumed at high level in the American diet. This level of sugar consumption, when combined with the generally rising consumption of fat, means that the excessive dietary sugar or fat is converted to body fat unless intake is balanced by exercise which utilizes the excess calories. The combined high level of sugar and fat consumption contributes to obesity as the diet remains high in total calories, and to poor nutrition as other foods that are necessary for a more optimally balanced diet are displaced. Poor nutrition may occur even though the diet is high in total calories. Among at least one-fifth of the teenage and adult population, high levels of alcohol consumption further aggravate the nutrient deficiencies. Although sugar has an important place in the diet as an economical source of food energy, the high level of American sugar consumption, when combined with the long upward trend in fat consumption and other factors, has important adverse effects on health.

Meats and Other Protein Foods   Protein consumption is generally high in the American diet and, together with fat, has been increasing in recent years and decades. Protein is supplied mainly by meats and other protein-rich foods such as poultry, eggs, fish, and milk, all containing high-quality protein in concentrated form, B vitamins, especially riboflavin, thiamine, niacin, and iron. Food grains and soybean products are also an important source of protein to supplement the other foods, although they do not supply considerable amounts of calcium, vitamin A (except for yellow corn), and C, or riboflavin. Also, to be satisfactory for growth and reproduction, proteins in grains must be supplemented to a moderate extent by other proteins that are richer in the essential amino acids, lysine and tryptophan. Several foods, including leguminous plants such as peas and beans, milk and other animal proteins, meet this need.

Although protein is essential for good health and vigor, many well-to-do Americans consume considerably more than is required for continued best health. The high protein consumption, often added to high consumption of fat and sugar or alcohol, results in a diet that is too high in total calories for optimum

---

[15]F. J. Stare (ed.), "Sugar in the Diet of Man," *World Review of Nutrition and Dietetics,* Vol. 22, 1975, pp. 237–326.

health. How to regulate the total calorie intake to achieve the desired balance with total energy use, and yet achieve a well-balanced diet, is a major problem for nutrition education and other policy. Because a protein-rich diet is generally not cheap, however, the poor usually do not have this problem to such a degree; and a different policy problem prevails, that of supplying a diet at modest cost that is sufficiently high in protein to meet recommended allowances.

Dental Ill Health as Related to Diet

The two major causes of the all too common problems of dental ill health and subsequent tooth loss are dental caries, more generally known as cavities, and periodontal disease, or disease of the gums and jaws that hold the teeth. The first stage of this disease is gingivitis, or gum inflammation, and the advanced stage is pyorrhea, or severe inflammation and deterioration that may lead to loss of all the teeth. Tooth loss prior to age 35 is primarily due to dental caries, whereas, in later years, in addition to caries, periodontal disease increases as a hazard to oral health. Mainly as a result of these two health hazards, more than 20 million Americans have lost all their teeth, by age 45 one out of five will need dentures, and at least half of those age 65 or over have no natural teeth left.

The dental caries is basically a local disease caused mainly by a streptococcal type of bacteria that ferment dietary carbohydrates to form chiefly lactic acid which, at susceptible sites in the teeth, initiates the carious lesion by demineralizing the enamel surface. The bacteria also deposit a layer of foreign material, called "plaque," which accumulates over a period of weeks on some of the tooth surfaces to which it attaches tenaciously. The plaque is colonized by several types of bacteria, some of which are cariogenic and live mainly on sucrose and other food carbohydrates. Thus, the sequence of tooth decay is affected by diet, especially the availability of sugars, most importantly sucrose to feed the bacteria (Table 11-3).

The incidence of dental caries has been found to be greatly affected by the presence of fluorine in drinking water. This element, which in its natural state is found chiefly as the mineral fluorite or fluorspar, is calcium fluoride, $Ca F_2$, and as cryolite, $Na_3 AlF_6$. Use of water containing an amount equal to 1 part per million (1.0 ppm) during the years of tooth development has been found sufficient to reduce tooth decay or dental caries by as much as 60 percent in both the deciduous (baby) teeth and the permanent (or adult) teeth. But if the presence of fluorine goes above 2.5 parts per million for a period of time, the tooth enamel, which normally contains a small percentage of fluorine, will contain an excess amount, and a discoloration known as mottled teeth will result.

Fluorine is the only element that has been found effective in producing decay-resistant teeth in humans. The effects of 10 years of fluoridation on the dental health of children in certain communities are shown in Table 11-4. Many municipalities, after a period of education and policy explanation, have voted to add fluorine to their drinking water. But, although the cost of doing so is very small, generally between 20 cents and $1.15 per person annually, and although there are no known deleterious effects, the U.S. Public Health Service estimated

Table 11-3 **"Caries-Potentiality" of Representative Foods***

Food	Total sugar content (percent)	"Caries potentiality"
Caramel	64.0	27
Honey + bread + butter	19.0	24
Honey	72.8	18
Sweet cookies (biscuits)	9.0	18
Marmalade	65.3	10
Marmalade + bread + butter	16.3	9
Ice Cream	2.4	9
Potatoes (boiled)	0.8	7
Potatoes (fried)	3.9	7
White bread + butter	1.5	7
Coarse rye bread + butter	2.3	7
Milk	3.8	6
Apple	7.5	5
Orange	6.5	3
Lemonade	9.3	2
Carrot (boiled)	2.4	1

*Adapted from J. M. Dunning, *Principles of Dental Public Health,* Cambridge: Harvard University Press, 1970. Calculated from sugar concentrations in saliva and how long they remained high after eating each specific food. In general, those with the lowest scores should be used instead of those with highest scores, if optimal dental health is desired.

that at the end of 1970, only 92 million out of 206 million Americans had access to fluoridated water. Of the 92 million, 8 million were receiving it naturally (the beneficial effects of fluorine were first discovered among this type of population).

A restriction on the spread of public fluoridation programs arises out of the strength of antifluoridation movements, which traditionally have been based on a number of mistaken notions or premises; for example, that so much fluorine will be added to the water that mottling or discoloration of the teeth will result; that since fluorine in its elementary state is a poisonous gas, fluoridation will cause increases in mortality and morbidity rates and in the birth rates of mongoloids or other abnormalities; or that fluoridation is an undesirable and unwarranted infringement on the individual's freedom of choice. Because of such opposition, policy toward fluoridation has varied widely over the country in spite of strong endorsements by the U.S. Public Health Service and other such knowledgeable and prestigious organizations as the American Dental Association, the American Medical Association, the World Health Organization, the American Public Health Association, the American Institute of Nutrition, and the Food and Nutrition Board of the National Research Council. At the end of 1971, the U.S. Public Health Service reported that the percentage of the population on public water supplies with natural or controlled fluoridation varied from 100 percent in Washington, D.C., and 98.1 percent in Illinois to 2.7 percent in Utah.

Table 11-4 Reductions in Decayed, Missing, and Filled Permanent Teeth (DMF Index) Reported among Children in Communities after 10 Years of Fluoridation*

Community	Age studied	Percentage reduction
Grand Junction, Colo.	6	94.0
New Britain, Conn.	6–16	44.6
District of Columbia	6	59.1
Evanston, Ill.	6–7–8	91.3–64.6–62.6
Fort Wayne, Ind.	6–10	>50.0
Hopkinsville, Ky.	? (Children)	56.0
Louisville, Ky.	First 3 grades	62.1
Hagerstown, Md.	7, 9, 11, and 13	57.0
Grand Rapids, Mich.	6–7–8	75.0–63.0–57.0
Grand Rapids, Mich.	9–10	50.0–52.0
Newburgh, N.Y.	6–9	58.0
Newburgh, N.Y.	10–12	57.0
Newburgh, N.Y.	13–14	48.0
Newburgh, N.Y.	16	41.0
Charlotte, N.C.	6–11	60.0
Chattanooga, Tenn.	6–14	70.8
Marshall, Texas	7–15	54.0
Brantford, Ont.	6–7–8	60.0–67.0–54.0
Brantford, Ont.	9–10	46.0–41.0
Brantford, Ont.	11–13	44.0
Brantford, Ont.	14–16	35.0

*From J. M. Dunning, "Current Status of Fluoridation," *New England Journal of Medicine,* 272:30, 1965.

In respect to dental care, there are an estimated 1 billion unfilled cavities in the American population today, an average of nearly six per person for those who have teeth. Among children under the age of five, one out of ten has eight or more unfilled cavities; the incidence of decayed, missing, or filled teeth then rises rapidly in the ages six to nine, less rapidly to age 15, and more rapidly again in the late teens and early twenties. One half the children under 15 never have been to a dentist, and up to 80 percent of this group live in poorly served rural areas or poverty-impacted urban communities. Thus, there is a pattern of widespread dental neglect, which ultimately greatly increases the economic cost or loss from caries and periodontal disease, to say nothing of the pain and discomfort; and, although much of it is positively related to poverty, this neglect affects an unnecessarily large proportion of the total population.

In respect to diet and nutrition, an extensive volume of studies shows that a well-balanced diet, in addition to good and regular dental care, is essential for good oral health or a low incidence of dental caries and periodontal disease. Although the level of sugar consumption is especially important, the form in which sugar and other starches are consumed is even more so.[16] Sweet and

[16]See, especially, S. B. Finn and R. B. Glass, "Sugar and Dental Decay," *World Review of Nutrition and Dietetics, op. cit.,* pp. 304–326.

sticky foods, including chewing gum, candies, and high-sugar, between-meal snacks that stay in the mouth for some time—thus to maintain an extended food source for the streptococcal bacteria—are most conducive to tooth decay. The level of sugar consumption is important because it is positively related to the maintenance of the bacterial food source. Thus, for example, widely different cavity counts have been found among countries in the Western Hemisphere, and total sugar consumption has followed the same pattern, with the highest incidence of caries being in the United States and seven countries in Central and South America.[17] England has documented increases in consumption of sugar from 20 to 110 pounds per capita over the past 100 years, and there has been a nearly parallel rise in the prevalence of caries. During World War II, sugar consumption in Europe was severely restricted, and caries dropped significantly two years thereafter. When sugar consumption returned to a higher level, caries also increased to the previous high levels.

A Policy Conclusion   A major problem for nutrition policy centers on the best ways to achieve a shift in some of the dietary trends that are incompatible with optimal human health and performance and how best to develop the dietary and eating habits that are more generally beneficial. Our general view is that education must play a much more dominant role than it has in the past, that certain reforms must occur in food advertising and labeling, that government standards for food grading, purity, and nutritive value must become more realistic and effective, and that a higher degree of cooperation must be achieved between consumer groups and various interests in the food industries. To understand how these steps may be consistent with general policy goals, we next consider eating and related health habits, or the status of nutrition as related to eating habits in America.

INFLUENCING EATING HABITS

Although the essentials of a good diet are known or can be taught, the observations that we have made suggest that much of the available information has been ignored or rejected. It has been observed that 30 to 50 percent of the families in America have one or more members who fairly regularly skip breakfast, and three out of four families do not eat breakfast as a family unit.[18] Often the first food of the day is at coffee-break time. While most school children now have lunch at school, the blue-collar father is having a bag lunch, which is apparently poorly balanced nutritionally, and the white-collar father may have a hurried and nutritionally inadequate lunch or an entirely too heavy business lunch. Frequently, the mother, at home or in the office, may have no lunch or something merely to retard the appetite, because skipping meals may be one of her ways of

---

[17]J. M. Dunning, *Principles of Dental Public Health,* Cambridge, Mass.: Harvard University Press, 1970.
[18]See P. A. Lachance. "The Vanishing American Meal," *Food Product Development,* Vol. 7, No. 9, or *Medical Dimensions,* Vol. 2, No. 10, 1973.

dieting. The children almost invariably eat something after school, too often taking a snack that is high in sugar or fat and low in terms of balancing the daily food intake. Then the main meal in the evening may be too high in total calories, or sometimes too small, with the degree of convenience foods served depending on the time available for its preparation. The family dinner eaten at home with good and competent food preparation may occur as seldom as three days a week or less. Then, there often are all sorts of drinking and snacking during the prime-time evening television and/or a substantial snack before bed.

On the average, about 70 percent of all meals are eaten at home and up to 60 percent of the family's food dollar is spent on food that is eaten at home. Although there are millions of good to excellent cooks in the nation and a considerable portion of families are known to have diets that are very good to excellent, the combination of home cooking and eating out results in diets rated as poor for at least one-half of all families. There is apparently too heavy reliance on the types of foods served by many drive-in, fast-food services, too high in fat and sugar and poorly balanced in terms of other essential nutrients. Too many home-cooked meals are just as bad if not worse. Some foods lose nutrients because of the typical home-storage methods, and more nutrients are lost in cooking.[19] Therefore, nutritionists have become increasingly concerned not only with the nutrient values of particular foods but of food in the combinations used by consumers—by the meal and by the day—including snacks.

How do these food combinations evolve or come about? How does an individual's diet and nutrition pattern develop? We consider these questions as a further background to the development of nutrition policy by viewing diets and eating habits as related to age and the life cycle.

Infants and Young Children Eating habits start young, even in infancy. Under normal conditions, most pediatricians agree that breast feeding is the best way to start a baby's healthy development. Human milk is specifically adapted to the nutritional requirements of human infants. But only one of every five babies born in the United States enjoys the nutritional and psychological benefits of breast feeding. The other four begin with bottle feeding. Evaporated milk, which used to be the mainstay of bottle-fed babies except for a few who were raised on cow's milk, has been almost completely displaced by prepared formulas. (See Table 11-5.)

The most common commercial formulas are modified from cow's milk to approximate the known chemical composition of human breast milk so that feeding either by breast or by a properly prepared infant formula will be a satisfactory way to meet the baby's complete nutritional needs until the age of four to six months. Although a baby receiving bottle feeding with gentle and loving care may be just as secure and happy as a breast-fed infant, it is not

[19]See Paul A. Lachance and John W. Erdman, Jr., "Effects of Home Food Preparation Practices on Nutrient Content of Foods," in Robert S. Harris and Endel Karmas (eds.), *Nutritional Evaluation of Food Processing*, 2d. ed., Westport, Conn.: The Avi Publishing Co., Inc., 1975, chap. 17, pp. 529–567.

Table 11-5   A Sample of the Variety of Milk Formulas

			Examples of:		
	Human milk	Cow's milk, fresh whole	Modified infant formula, based on cow's milk*	Soy-based formula	Hydrolyzed protein formula
Calories per 100 milliliters	67–72	67	67	67	67
Linoleic acid as percent of fatty acids	10.6	2.1	—	—	—
Grams, per 100 milliliters of:					
Protein	1.1–1.2	3.3	1.5	2.5	2.2
Carbohydrate	6.8–7.2	4.8	7.0	6.8	8.5
Fat	3.3–4.5	3.7	3.7	3.4	2.6
Water	87	87	87	87	87
Calcium: phosphorus ratio (milligrams per liter)	340:140	1250:960	550:430	800:630	1000:700
Vitamins per liter					
A, international units	1660–1898	1025–1425	1600	1500	1500
C, milligrams	51	11	50	50	50
D, international units	4–21	13–31*	400	400	400
B-1, milligrams	0.16–0.2	0.44	0.4	0.5	0.46
B-2, milligrams	0.36–0.4	1.75	0.6	1	1.8
B-6, milligrams	0.1	0.64	0.3	0.4	0.5
B-12, micrograms	0.3	4	1.5	2	4.5
Pantothenic acid, milligrams	1.8	3.4	2	2.5	3.2
Niacin, milligrams	1.5	0.94	7	7	4
Folacin, micrograms	25	27–100	50	170	50
K, micrograms	15	60	35	80	18
E, international units	6.6	1.0	5	5	5
Iron, milligrams	0.3	—	1.4 (with iron-8–12 mg)	8–10	12

*400 international units (IU) when fortified.

Source: From L. Jean Bogert, George M. Briggs, and Doris Howes Calloway, *Nutrition and Physical Fitness*, 9th ed., Philadelphia: W. B. Saunders Company, 1973, p. 461.

possible to duplicate the protective effect of human milk against infections, specifically certain infantile diarrheas. Moreover, proper breast feeding may have important psychological gains for the infant resulting from a close and harmonious relationship with the mother.[20]

The bottle feeding of babies has more subtle implications, however, for nutrition education policy. The bottle-fed baby often finds it easy to gorge itself, which may begin to establish a pattern of overfeeding with subsequent allergic reactions and tendencies toward obesity. Frequently it appears that a bottle-fed baby is encouraged to finish the bottle, rather than to stop at a more voluntary point. Even more important, from early in the twentieth century up to the early 1960s, infants in America were being shifted to solid foods at earlier ages. Although this trend has leveled off, and although, subsequently, the Academy of Pediatrics recommended that 2½ to 3 months is the optimal time for introducing solid foods into the infant's diet, many mothers—apparently influenced by their desire for convenience, by the gains in social status of having a precocious child, or by the advertisements of baby-food manufacturers—have been shifting to solid foods sometimes as early as three to six weeks of age for cereals, and adding other solid foods soon thereafter. According to available information, as many as 90 percent of American infants are on solid foods before three months of age.[21]

Although the findings in the literature are not unanimous, such feeding habits apparently can have a number of adverse consequences. Many studies report an increased incidence of food allergy among infants who are introduced to a variety of solid foods at an early age; and, if the total calorie intake is too high, this will lead to rapid gain in weight, which is equally undesirable in infants and adults. It has been postulated, and there is suggestive evidence, that the number of fat cells in the body is determined within the first year of life, and that the number of cells created is proportionately larger in the overfed infant who, in later life, will find it more difficult to control weight because these fat cells will tend to remain filled. Similarly, atherosclerosis, a major cause of heart failure and death in males, is a condition in which high levels of blood cholesterol and lipids in the walls of the arteries may be influenced by early feeding. Although a certain amount of fat is required in the diet of the young, excessive amounts should be avoided. Finally, it has been established that the sodium or salt intake of an infant at four months may be 3 times the recommended level if it is eating a full complement of baby foods, many of which contain salt or to which the mother adds salt. High levels of salt before the child's kidneys are mature enough to excrete the excess sodium may increase the risk of hypertension (high blood pressure) in adulthood, even though this disease is also conditioned by other factors. In 1970, the National Academy of Sciences recommended to the Food and Drug Administration that the level of salt in infant foods be restricted to 0.25 percent instead of the 1 percent previously found in many commercially prepared

[20]Bogert, Briggs, and Calloway, *op. cit.,* p. 460.
[21]Guthrie, *Introductory Nutrition, op. cit.,* p. 397.

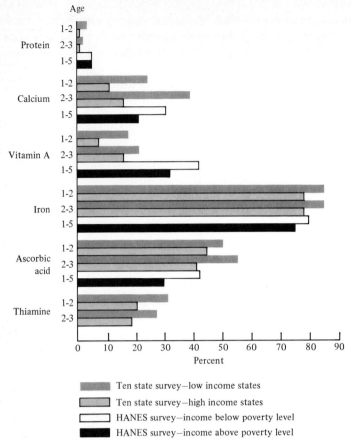

Figure 11-2 Percentage of preschool children with intake below 2/3 RDA by age and income level. *(Source: Helen Andrews Guthrie, Introductory Nutrition, 3d ed., St. Louis: The C. V. Mosby Co., 1975.)* Data based on results of Ten-State Nutrition Survey (1968–1970) and preliminary findings of first Health and Nutrition Examination Survey (HANES) (1971–1972).

foods. But even though this level is maintained, a too early complement of commercial foods, either alone or combined with other foods to which salt has been added, perhaps for the benefit of other family members, can lead to an undesirable diet pattern.

In summary, results of nutritional surveys have confirmed the fact that, although physical symptoms of nutritional deficiency tend to be nonspecific, three-fourths of all children up to six years of age have had diets that provide less than two-thirds of the RDA for iron. One-third to one-half of all children had similarly low intakes of vitamin C. One-fourth had low intakes of calcium. One-tenth to one-half had low intakes of vitamin A; and more than one-fifth had low intakes of thiamine (Figure 11-2). A much higher percentage of all children, of course, receive below 100 percent of the recommended daily allowances.

Evidently there is still much to be done in upgrading the nutritional knowledge and expertise of parents, from whom infants and small children obtain their direction on eating habits and diets. Improvements in selection and preparation of foods must be accomplished with more knowledge of the effects of the combinations that result. Although additional scientifically selective fortification of some foods can help to prevent some nutritional deficiencies, it is basically the homemaker-parent and those who serve as proxies for parents who must be willing objects of more generally available nutritional knowledge and education.

Older Children in Pubescence and Adolescence As children grow older, much of the message that they receive from the adult world, from television, movies, newspapers and magazines, and from the examples of adults continues to lead them into bad eating habits and poor diets. School cafeterias frequently serve meals too rich in fat and sugar, too low in whole grains, fresh fruits, and vegetables. Although requirements for federal funds under the National School Lunch Act (Public Law 396, 79th Congress, June 4, 1946) provide that the most common type of lunch must provide one-third or more of the daily nutrient intake of the 10- to 12-year-old child, with adjustments for both younger and older children, concern has been expressed that many lunches have failed in this regard. The USDA, over the objection of many nutritionists, has allowed schools to serve nutrient-fortified cupcakes for breakfasts in place of cereal and orange juice. Although the school lunch program has been expanded greatly, as we have noted, this improvement has not been accompanied by equivalent emphasis on a national nutrition-education program.

Outside the schools, television commercials employ the latest ad-agency techniques promoting sweet and fatty foods, sugar-coated cereals sometimes higher in percentage of sugar than a typical candy bar, and high-sugar drinks and snacks. Many eating habits are conditioned by what is advertised and served at public celebrations—baseball games and other athletic contests, picnics, and carnivals. A large part of this diet is based on a hot dog and bun, which occupies a doubtful position in the average diet of fatty hamburgers and french fries; deep-fried foods that are high in fats and starches; peanuts, popcorn, and Cracker Jack; beer and soft drinks. The high-calorie level of this snack-type of diet may lead to obesity or overnutrition if combined with good food at home and additional calorie-laden food and drink; yet, the combination can still be inadequate in terms of essential diet-balancing nutrients. Food-vending machines typically invite children—as well as adults—to buy soda pop, candy, and gum. Fast-food outlets often feature meals that are very low in vitamins A and C and well below one-third of RDA for other important nutrients.[22] Although the typical burger and french-fry meal is less deficient in several nutrients if a good milk shake is substituted for a soft drink, almost all are still low in vitamin A and C.

As a consequence of these diet habits, many of the important nutrient

---

[22]Li-Fang Chem and P. A. Lachance, "An Area of Concern: The Nutritive Profile of Fast-Food Meal Combinations," *Food Product Development*, Vol. 8, October 1974. For a general summary see "How Nutritious Are Fast-Food Meals," *Consumer Reports*, A Publication of Consumers Union, May 1975.

deficiencies found in infants and young children are accented in the years of pubescence, the period from the beginning of sexual development up to about 15 years for boys and 13 years for girls, and in the subsequent years of adolescence, averaging from 15 to 21 for boys and 13 to 17 years for girls. Consequently, many of the deficiencies noticed in preschool children are more pronounced by adolescence, indicating very serious deficiencies in diets up to adulthood (Figure 11-3).

As a policy conclusion in regard to nutritional goals, we cannot overstress the high priority of an educational program in schools and the public media, coordinated with school lunch and other programs, not only to teach the essentials of good nutrition but also to deal with other aspects of good health. A conference sponsored by the Growth and Development Branch of the National Institute of Child Health and Human Development, attended by some 50 scientists in nutrition, anthropometry, clinical endocrinology, pediatrics, and related biomedical fields, concluded with these fundamental policy recommendations:[23] Studies of the nutrition of adolescents should embody more sophisticated procedures, including bone growth measurements combined with biochemical and clinical measures of fitness; more refined estimates of nutrient requirements; correlation of body composition and sexual characteristics with plasma hormone levels; and identification of specific medical groups with obesity, diabetes, and elevated blood cholesterol levels, followed by studies of their future nutrition and health, with the goal of improving diet habits. The relationship between body composition of the adolescent and the incidence of illness and mortality in later life is still to be adequately explored and is a matter of high priority. All these steps must be combined with a broader educational program on nutrition.

Young Adults and the Middle-Aged   Most young and middle-aged Americans have a diet that is generally adequate in most vitamins, minerals, and protein; but, since this diet reflects habits formed in earlier years, it is often hazardously high in total calories, fats, sugars, and starch, and too high in salt. This diet, combined in many cases with excessive consumption of alcohol, contributes to poor health, obesity, and related health problems.The syndrome of diet-related health problems gradually becomes more severe as people progress through middle age until, as old age approaches, undesirable conditions that were chronic now frequently become acute (Figure 11-4).

People in Old Age   As old age approaches, many of the diet-related ailments that were merely contributory to poor health become more critical. The functional changes in aging that are due to loss of cells rather than to poorly functioning cells help to account for steady declines in energy requirements for bodily functions. But, as the loss of cells reduces the energy requirement with age, the necessity for good nutrition for the remaining cells remains essentially as high as before. Therefore, as certain vital organs progressively lose efficiency from about age 30 on, chiefly as the number of cells of an organ, and hence its

[23]John I. McKigney and Hamish N. Munro, *Nutrient Requirements in Adolescence,* U.S. Department of Health, Education, and Welfare, National Institutes of Health, Publication No. 76-771.

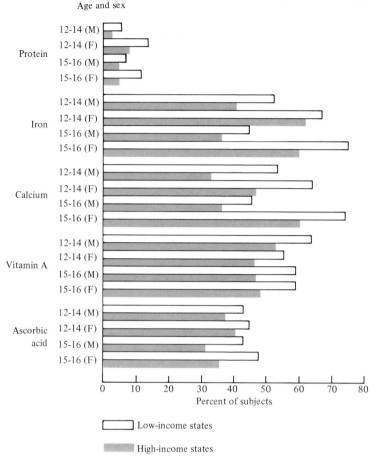

Age and sex

Figure 11-3 Percentage of adolescents (ages 12–16) in the United States with dietary intakes below 2/3 RDA by age, sex, and income level. *(Source: Helen Andrews Guthrie, Introductory Nutrition, 3d ed., St. Louis: The C. V. Mosby Co., 1975.)* Data from Ten-State Nutrition Survey (1968–1970).

size and functional capacity, are reduced, the intake of most essential nutrients must remain high to provide adequate nourishment for the remaining cells.

Because of the reduced efficiency of vital organs, including the loss of taste buds and its effect on appetite—on the average, a 75-year-old person has only 36 percent as many taste buds as a 30-year-old—diets tend to become more deficient, in terms not only of vital nutrients but of total calories as well. The ability to retain and utilize calcium is especially important, and special precautions must be taken in old age to maintain consumption of foods high in calcium that are compatible with the reduced efficiency of the digestive system (Figure 11-5).

A Policy Conclusion   To meet national goals of adequate nutrition, which means a much higher proportion of the population near the RDA but not excessively above, a really substantial change must occur in diets and eating

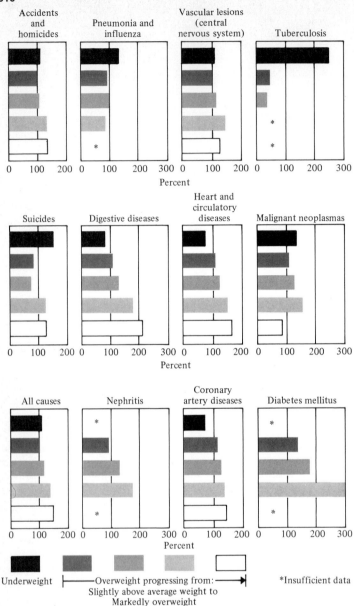

Figure 11-4 Relationships of body weight to mortality from specific diseases in humans. *(Source: E. Weir, Human Nutrition Report No. 2, Washington: USDA, 1971.)*

habits from infancy through to old age. There must be significant developments in nutrition policy, including nutrition education and a wide range of other activity, affecting the food industry and the general public. Special measures, including income supplements or food subsidies for nutritionally vulnerable groups, must be made more efficient and must be administered with a knowledge of their nutritional efficiency as well as concepts of equity.

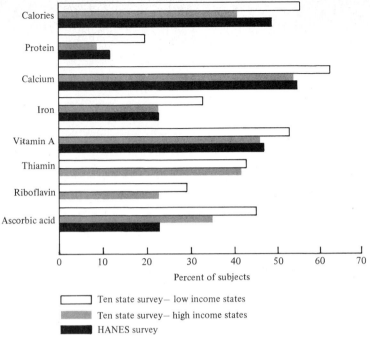

Figure 11-5 Percentage of persons over 60 years of age with dietary intakes below 2/3 RDA for selected nutrients. *(Source: Helen Andrews Guthrie, Introductory Nutrition, 3d ed., St. Louis: The C. V. Mosby Co., 1975.)* Data based on results of the Ten-State Nutrition Survey (1968–1970) and the first Health and Nutrition Examination Survey (HANES) (1971–1972).

How these policies may or can evolve is perhaps best understood by first reviewing the efforts that have been made to develop them. After that, we can look at more specific requirements of nutrition policy and the alternatives in how it may be implemented and constrained.

EFFORTS TO DEVELOP NUTRITIONAL POLICY[24]

Efforts to develop nutritional policy for America have been underway for a long time, and recently the basis for more effective policies to improve nutrition has greatly broadened. Still, there are long-standing habits, cultural heritages, and powerful interests tending to retard the development of a more effective national policy. The efforts that have been made contain lessons that must be recognized and understood if an optimum policy is to be achieved in the future.

The Background

The first efforts on a national scale to improve nutrition were made during World War I. The high rejection rate under Selective Service was partly attributed to

[24]Among the major sources, this section draws on a study by Mary C. Egan, U.S. Department of Health, Education, and Welfare, Health Services Administration, Bureau of Community Health Services, for the *National Nutrition Policy Study,* 1974, *op. cit.,* pp. 2084–2108.

malnutrition. In April 1917, the Secretary of Agriculture called two conferences of state commissioners of agriculture, representatives of land grant colleges, and the press to develop recommendations for food conservation and nutrition. In June and July, the United States Food Administrator called several agencies into conferences to familiarize the American people with nutrition concepts.

In 1918, the Children's Bureau and the Council of National Defense launched "the Children's Year Campaign" to formulate "minimum standards for the public protection of the health of mothers and children." It was recommended:

    1   that adequate diets be taught by home visits to mothers of infants and preschool children

    2   that centers for child health supervision be established to include a nutrition clinic

    3   that open-air classes and rest periods be established for certain children thought to be suffering from malnutrition or susceptible to tuberculosis

    4   that schools with more than 1,000 children have a full-time school nurse who would give instruction in personal hygiene and diet and make home visits to instruct mothers in principles of hygiene

    5   that funds should be appropriated to provide treatment for all remediable defects of children, diseases, deformities, and cases of malnutrition

    6   that nutrition classes should be conducted for physically subnormal children and mid-morning lunches or noon meals provided when necessary and

    7   that adolescents should have an ample diet with special attention to growth-producing foods

Few if any of these recommendations, however, were incorporated into national policy.

During the 1920s these recommendations were largely ignored as far as a national policy was concerned, and in 1930 the White House Conference on Child Health and Protection was called "to make recommendations as to what ought to be done and how to do it, in order to make optimal nutrition possible for the children of our country." Eleven specific recommendations were made for establishment of nutrition and related programs in schools and communities. Ten of these were, in essence, suggestions for action by state and local agencies. One recommended: "That nutrition service be made available to communities unable to finance a complete nutrition service through stimulation of private and public agencies." Except for this, no recommendations were made for general funding of nutrition programs.

During the winter of 1932–33, as the Depression deepened, evidence indicated an increase in the number of undernourished children and a decrease in the amount of medical care being given in some states and local communities. In October 1933, a national conference was called by the Secretary of Labor "to consider plans for stimulating nationwide interest in health of children in families affected by the economic depression." It recommended a nationwide program to locate undernourished children and to formulate methods of overcoming malnutrition by more adequate feeding and medical care. But it was left to the states to modify suggestions "in accordance with their individual needs." In spite of the presumably wide-ranging programs of the Roosevelt New Deal, federal funds were not appropriated to share the costs or otherwise support educational programs in nutrition or to fund school lunches or other general nutrition programs. In the late 1930s, direct distribution of food and food stamps affected not more than 1 or 2 percent of the nation's population and a special school milk program affected only a small percentage of the school children.

Policies in the 1940s

The 1940s were highlighted by more conferences and committee reports but little action. In 1940, the White House Conference on Children in a Democracy emphasized the interplay of the concept of democracy and the particular needs of children. It recommended that "nutrition service when needed should be provided as a part of a service of maternity care and care of newborn infants." More effective nutrition services should be included in preventive, curative medical services for all infants and children through private resources or public funds.

In May 1941, the National Nutrition Conference for Defense was convened by the President to "make recommendations to solve nutrition problems at national, state and community levels as an essential part of defense and as a part of a continuing national health and welfare program." During the conference a "state of unlimited national emergency" was proclaimed. The conference pledged its full support for mobilizing national resources and recommended 12 lines of attack on malnourishment. These included use of the FDA's Recommended Dietary Allowances as a general goal and yardstick for nutrition, more research and education, full production by agriculture, more production for home use, and full use of any practical devices such as food stamps, school lunches, and low-cost milk distribution. The food stamp program was discontinued in 1943, however. The school lunch was not expanded or put on a continuing basis until passage of the National School Lunch Act on June 3, 1946.

In 1942, the National Research Council's Committee on Nutrition in Industry developed several recommendations relating to the diets and nutrition of defense workers to improve food services related to in-plant meals and snacks. Many of these recommendations were adopted in defense plants.

In 1945, a study entitled a Survey of Nutrition Programs and Organization in Federal Agencies, conducted by the Bureau of the Budget, explored the questions of the type of work the federal government should undertake and how it should do it. Emphasizing the need for coordination of programs, it suggested that national food industry advertising should be submitted for clearance, preferably on a voluntary basis, to a central point in the federal government. No action was taken on this recommendation.

Policies in the 1950s

The 1950s saw a growing awareness of the influence of nutrition and health on the productivity of population groups. In 1950, a committee of the National Academy of Science, focusing on diagnosis and pathology of nutrition deficiencies, recommended expansion of nutrition education through state and local health agencies for both medical practitioners and the lay population. All nutrition activities should be coordinated in a specific unit of the health department. Such units should assume responsibility for initiating and directing programs assisted by a state nutritional council. In the same year, the Midcentury White House Conference on Children and Youth recommended that school lunches be provided for all children and be provided free for children unable to pay for their lunches without differentiation between children who can and cannot pay.

In 1952, the National Food and Nutrition Institute held in Washington, apparently basking in the nutritional advances made in the previous decade, heard a report from representatives of the medical profession that it was difficult to find a clinical case of a nutritional disease to study. The incidence of vitamin deficiency disease had begun to decline soon after a national program for the enrichment of white bread was inaugurated, and the conference turned its attention to obesity, the degenerative diseases, and combating food quackery. It acknowledged the need for more research and educational effort, especially among school children. It recommended that more attention be given to multiple approaches to achieving good nutrition, such as adequate income, continued enrichment of flour and food fortification, good health care, and adequate therapeutic services. But, the medical report saying that cases of nutritional diseases were hard to find received wide publicity. People wanted to believe it; and, apparently for several years, it had a profoundly negative effect on their concern for a stronger national policy on nutrition.

In April 1957, the Third National Nutrition Education Conference focused on the theme of increasing the effectiveness of nutrition education. In a number of sessions, participants were appalled to see how much parents' selection of various foods was determined by children's requests, based on what they had seen or heard on television and radio. The Conference recommended that the U.S. Office of Education encourage states to make nutrition education a part of the elementary teacher's preparation, that conferences of teachers be called to increase the effectiveness of nutrition education, that each state's Nutrition Council serve as a clearing house on information and education, that state and local committees sponsor refresher courses, etcetera.

In 1958, the U.S. Public Health Service convened the National Conference on Nursing Homes and Homes for the Aged. This step reflected a rising concern about the increasing number of the chronically ill and infirm aged who were being committed to these homes. The conference emphasized, in 14 specific recommendations, that a licensing agency should assume responsibility for education and training in all phases of food service for all personnel in the nursing homes and homes for the aged, that a national project should be conducted to develop a cost accounting system specifically for such facilities, that further studies of nutritional requirements of the aged be encouraged, that standards be established to assure that food meets nutritional standards, and so on.

Policies in the 1960s

As contrasted with the somnolence of the 1950s, the decade of the 1960s saw a reawakening to the problem of poverty in the United States, and with this, came a more general awareness of the problems of hunger and malnutrition. But this movement was slow to develop.

In 1960, the White House Conference on Children and Youth was called "to promote opportunities for children and youth to realize their full potential for a creative life in freedom and dignity." Rather mild recommendations were made to include health education and nutrition in school curricula, to develop information programs to educate adolescents in sound nutritional attitudes and priorities, to emphasize to adolescent girls the importance of nutrition in preparation for motherhood, to inform parents and others in charge of feeding children of nutritional requirements as recommended by professional authorities, and to alert parents and others to the dangers of fad diets and excessive use of certain "health foods."

In 1961, the first White House Conference on Aging was held to direct attention to "the problems and potentials of older Americans." Dietary, feeding, and dental services—including public education programs—should be considered among the services in organized community programs. It was concluded that there should be special nutrition programs for the aged, education to help older adults better to understand their peculiar health needs, and more effective means for the Public Health Service and the Office of Education to distribute information on nutrition. The impact of advertising on the "habits of nutrition" should be more fully assessed. All health personnel (including nutritionists) should have more knowledge of the process of aging and its health implications.

In 1961, the American Public Health Association and the Association of State and Territorial Public Health Nutrition Directors sponsored the conference called "The Role of State Health Departments in Nutrition Research." It explored the needs in nutrition research as related to public health and the role of state health departments in such research. It recommended that nutrition should enter into many health programs and receive appropriate consideration, that nutrition research should be integrated with ongoing or proposed health programs, and that well-qualified nutrition research personnel should be prepared for leadership and training.

In 1963, the Food and Nutrition Board of the National Research Council issued "Recommendations on Administrative Policies for International Food and Nutrition Programs." This document recognized the need for effective action programs to meet urgent food and nutrition deficiencies in developing areas of the world. It recommended several steps for the U.S. Agency for International Development (AID) and other federal agencies, including a primary focus on United States foreign policy to help prevent serious malnutrition among children, particularly from the age of weaning to five years. In the ensuing years, there was a substantial increase in AID programs and large-scale shipment of wheat, especially to India following failures of the monsoon rains in 1964–66. But, except for this emergency food shipment and modest support by AID for nutrition programs, there was little, if any, more action on a national nutrition policy late in the 1960s than there had been in the 1950s.

As we noted in Chapter 3, although the pilot programs of the Kennedy administration awakened many people to the fact that there was hunger in America, it was not until 1967 or 1968 that the issue began to make front-page news. In 1967, the President's Commission on Rural Poverty, in its publication *The People Left Behind,* presented a shocking account of the extent of poverty and malnutrition in rural areas, which served as an opening wedge for increased concern.

In 1969, President Nixon called the White House Conference on Food, Nutrition, and Health to direct national attention and resources to the country's remaining and changing nutrition problems. The full conference, attended by more than 3,000 people ranging from high-level industry and government representatives to the poor themselves, directed its concern to five major questions:

1   How do we assure continuing surveillance of the state of nutrition?
2   What should be done to improve the nutrition of our more vulnerable groups?
3   How do we monitor the continued wholesomeness and nutritional value of our foods?
4   How do we improve nutrition teaching in our schools, and what programs of popular education do we need to better inform the public of proper food buying and food consumption habits?
5   What should be done to improve federal programs that affect nutrition?

There were literally hundreds of recommendations in response to these five questions, which may be summarized under five points, namely,

1   Establish a system for surveillance and monitoring of the state of nutrition of the American people, including better coordination of nutrition at the national level and a national nutrition policy with responsibility at a high level.
2   Give more attention to feeding programs and income support among vulnerable groups—the poor, the aging, the sick, and special disadvantaged population groups; provide nutritional care in health programs and nutrition education (but not as a replacement for food or money).
3   Provide more product information to the public and improve the adequacy, quality, and safety of the food supply. The call was for simplifying legislation to ensure better protection of the consumer through improved food labeling, standardization of sizes and shapes of containers, and similar steps. Support was expressed for the food industry to be more innovative in development of new and improved foods.
4   Expand nutrition education programs in the curriculum of every school, to developing a large-scale nutrition information campaign with improved use of mass media techniques, to improved preparation of all disci-

plines responsible for nutrition education, to more effective involvement of parents and the community.

5   Improve the system and support for federal food delivery programs, and more specifically, to improve and expand the school feeding programs to reach all children and to coordinate and unify operations; encourage and support voluntary action by private groups and community-based organizations; establish an Office of Nutrition in the Department of Health, Education, and Welfare to formulate and carry through policies on nutrition; and reestablish the Food Council of America to conduct nutrition education campaigns.

Policies in the 1970s

The 1970s saw an acceleration of the efforts toward a national nutrition policy but with important constraints on funding at almost all levels of government. The 1970 White House Conference on Children, which was preceded by 24 preconference forums and attended by 4,000 delegates, recommended (1) a more comprehensive family assistance program, based on a family income standard that would assure reasonable economic security, plus expansion and improvement of existing food programs; (2) vigorous enforcement of standards for nutritive value of foods, using nutritionists in direct service or consultant roles; and (3) promotion of mandatory legislation in each state for health and safety education (including nutrition) to be included in the regular instruction in all schools, public and private, from kindergarten through high school. Provision of family life education for parents or prospective parents, including information on child development, nutrition, and home management.

The White House Conference on Youth held in April 1971 included several recommendations related to hunger and health care. Among them were: that the President declare a national hunger emergency and use his authority to assure that no American in need should go without federal food assistance; that the food stamp program be expanded to every appropriate political subdivision in the nation; that the budget request for the fiscal 1972 food stamp program be increased to $2.75 billion to accomplish the preceding recommendations, and that $3.5 billion be requested for fiscal 1973; that the Department of Agriculture henceforth base food stamp value of coupon allotment on the low-cost food plan ($134 per month for a family of four); and that "cash-out" of food stamps in a guaranteed income proposal be opposed unless the cash-out is on a dollar-for-dollar basis.

Also in 1971, the National Nutrition Education Conference, the sixth in a series on high school age youth and community nutrition, recommended consideration of the adolescent in terms of growth and development, rather than age; special attention to those disease problems of youth which have special complications and risks and to those which hold important consequences for later life; greater appreciation and understanding of the many factors that influence decision making by youth relative to nutrition, for example, the prevalence of misinformation and the distrust of certain youth and adults of the science of nutrition and technology as related to the food supply; more involvement of youth in planning and presenting nutrition programs and more effort to reach youth not in school with nutrition information; inclusion of nutrition in the school curriculum in a sequential manner; and more nutrition education of teachers.

In addition to these conferences, which strongly advocated more government involvement in support of food aid and nutrition, many other influential groups were calling for expanded programs. The Committee on Maternal Nutrition of the National Academy of Science, concerned about the nation's high neonatal and infant mortality rates, recommended a broad expansion of community health and nutrition programs more specifically related to the role of nutrition in human reproduction. Medical school curricula should be strengthened to provide more scientific education on nutrition; more qualified nutrition personnel should be available in community health services; there should be a single standard of high-quality maternity care, including more emphasis on nutrition for all pregnant women; those planning and implementing food programs should give infants, children, adolescents, and pregnant women top priority.

In 1971, the White House Conference on Aging sought to crystallize in national policy the dimensions of a society in which older Americans might "fitly live" while completing the "adventure of life" with fulfillment and serenity. A major proportion of federal funds should be allocated for programs to rehabilitate the malnourished aged and to prevent malnutrition among those approaching old age. More specifically, all programs should establish and enforce high standards with specific regulations for the food and nutrition services provided by institutions and home-care agencies that receive any direct or indirect federal funds. Nutrition services and nutrition counseling should be components of all health delivery systems, including such plans as Medicare, Medicaid, health maintenance, health services, extended care facilities, and disease prevention programs.

Nutrition programs should concentrate government nutrition resources on providing food assistance to those in need, with a significant portion of these resources designated for nutrition education of all consumers, especially the aged, and education by qualified nutritionists of those who serve the consumer. They should also offer a variety of options for meals for older persons and require all federally assisted housing developments to include services or to ensure that sources are available for the feeding of elderly residents and those who have access to the development. The federal government should assume responsibility for making adequate nutrition available to all elderly persons. (Minimum adequate incomes were suggested, with food assistance used in the interim.) The federal government should also establish and enforce such standards as are necessary to ensure the safety and wholesomeness of the national food supply, as well as improve nutritive value.

In 1972, the Study Commission on Dietetics, using the contributions of many people to arrive at specific recommendations related to the problems, opportunities, and needs of the field of dietetics, made six major recommendations. Among them were that the basic education of dietetics be designed as a four-year curriculum resulting in a bachelor's degree and include both the didactic learning and introductory clinical experience necessary for beginning practice as a dietitian; and that the undergraduate curriculum be built around the central theme of the human life cycle.

EMERGING NATIONAL POLICY ON NUTRITION

By the mid 1970s, some major elements of a national policy on nutrition were beginning to emerge, although the response at the federal level to the diligently conceived recommendations was disappointing.[25] No action had been taken, as recommended in 1969, to establish a federal system to develop national guidelines for nutrition policy, defining the various responsibilities for improving nutrition, including assessment of accountability, and authority for program management and evaluation. Neither the recommended office of Special Assistant to the President for Nutrition nor the recommended Office of Nutrition, in HEW, to implement national policy had been established, perhaps because, in essence, there was no national policy to implement. It was not until October 1972, more than three years after the previous White House Conference, that HEW moved to establish a Departmental Nutritional Coordinating Committee to develop an integrated nutritional policy for HEW, to improve information exchange within HEW and with other agencies, to develop and review proposed legislation, to identify research and program needs, to assess nutrition activities in HEW, and develop guidelines for nutrition programs.

But, in spite of these disappointments and others, by the mid 1970s some of the main elements of an expanded policy on nutrition began to emerge more clearly. Important new advances began to be made in expanding nutrition education and improving food advertising, in getting more precise food standards and product labeling, and in supporting research and development of new food products.

Policy for Nutrition Education

The basic policy concepts underlying the support for increases in nutrition education are that good nutrition is essential for good health at all stages of life, and that, without a major effort in public education, the desired improvements in nutrition will not be achieved. An adult population that had shown itself to be remarkably resistant to the new knowledge concerning the dangers of cigarette smoking and the damages from excessive use of alcohol would also be hard to convert from a lifetime of bad eating habits and poor nutrition.

Studies by nutritionists had shown that school children without nutrition education were not capable of selecting a good and nutritious diet from among an array of food items. To combat the deleterious effects of food advertising on

---

[25]See "Federal Response to Date to the Recommendations of the White House Conference on Food Nutrition and Health, Pertaining to Education, Advertising and Labeling," *National Nutrition Policy Study, 1974, op. cit.*, pp. 2048–2083.

television and radio and in the public press, and other misinformation in respect to diet and nutrition, nutrition education should start with the schools. The thesis was that good nutrition had to be learned, and the earlier the learning occurred, the better.

The Federal Response In 1969, the White House Conference had recommended a unified, sequential nutrition education curriculum, designed for prekindergarten children through adults, to be distributed to every school in the nation. The Office of Education (OE), through the new Office of Coordinator of Education Services, should fund a national series of regional conferences for all chief school officers and staff, development of state and local curricula and associated items, and three to five years of surveillance and communication to strengthen and enlarge nutrition education and services in the schools.

In 1974, five years after these recommendations had been made, there was still no official unified curriculum and the recommended conferences had not been held. Although the Comprehensive School Health Act (S. 3074), which was supported by the national Parent Teachers Association, and although the National Health Education Policy and Development Act (H.R. 13,537) to set up a health education administration in HEW had been introduced, the bills did not reach a vote. The HEW programs, including Headstart, Follow Through, and the community feeding services, offered nutrition education in varying degrees. Education under the HEW Administration for the Aging (based on Public Law 92-258, 1972) had been postponed because of delays in appropriations. In the six years from fiscal year 1969 through fiscal year 1974, the Public Health Service of HEW made total grants of slightly less than $10 million for training nutritionists and dietitians.[26] None of the recommended Community Nutrition Centers, which were to provide public education, consultation, and advanced training in nutrition, had been established.

Educational Progress, Government, and Industry Only the Department of Agriculture, under the Expanded Food and Nutrition Extension Program (EFNEP), had been funded for a significantly expanded program. More than 22,000 program aides had been trained to teach nutrition education to adults in low-income families. In 1971, an Economic Research Service study of a sample of 10,000 of these EFNEP families showed that, prior to their beginning in the program, these families were spending 35 percent of their total income on food. Diets were generally most deficient in fruits, vegetables, and milk products. The poorest initial diets were among the urban families who were the least educated, often on welfare, and with the lowest total income. Following participation in the EFNEP, most families made marked improvements in their diets as measured by the number of daily servings of food from each of the four basic food groups. Some families were able to reduce their expenditures on food by $5 to $10 per week.

[26]*Ibid.*, p. 2058.

The Cooperative Extension Service was prepared to extend the EFNEP to some 10 million homemakers through paraprofessionals trained by home economists in the Extension Service. Within USDA, the National Agricultural Library and the Food and Nutrition Service were jointly participating in operation of the Food and Nutrition Information and Educational Materials Center to provide informational materials to nutrition and school lunch personnel and thus to help improve the quality and acceptance of school food programs. In addition, HEW's National Institute of Education was operating the Education Resource Information Center (ERIC), which maintains data storage and retrieval on materials for nutrition education.

In December 1973, a national effort was begun to extend nutrition information through public media. The Office of Consumer Affairs Coordination, USDA, HEW, and the Grocery Manufacturers of America sponsored a National Advertising Council food, nutrition, and health campaign, implemented by various publications, television, and radio broadcasts. A new booklet, *Food Is More than Just Something to Eat,* was published; and, in March 1974, 1 million copies were included in *Family Health* magazine, the cost of which was underwritten by General Foods. By June 1974, "Mulligan Stew," a 4-H nutrition education television and participation program developed in USDA, had enrolled more than 3 million young people in 35 states. Two leaflets, "Money Saving Meals" and "The Cost of Meats and Meat Alternatives," were featured in a television presentation. The Food and Nutrition Service of USDA developed a 10-part television course on food and nutrition for school food service workers and parents. But, recommendations for legislation to require all radio and television stations to devote at least 10 percent of their broadcast time for public service announcements and programs, of which food and nutrition would be a part, had not been funded or otherwise supported. The mass media effort fell far short of the recommendations of the 1969 conference.

The Massachusetts In-Service Teacher Workshops in Nutrition   In 1972–73, the Massachusetts Department of Education began a program in nutrition education for public school teachers that might serve as a model for the nation. In 1969, as a background to this campaign, it had been found that, in testing a sample of 80,000 school children in Massachusetts, only 53 percent of the children (on the survey day) consumed a satisfactory or good lunch.[27] Projected, this finding meant that almost half the public school children in Massachusetts, or more than 500,000 boys and girls, had an inadequate meal that day. In fact, 6 percent had no lunch at all. Of the children buying à la carte items in school, bringing lunch from home, buying lunch in a neighborhood store, or going home for lunch, almost two-thirds ate an inadequate meal. Continuing the projection, 257,000 (24 percent of those surveyed) came to school with an inadequate breakfast. More than

[27]Massachusetts Department of Education, Bureau of Nutrition Education and School Food Service, *Focus on Nutrition, You Cannot Teach a Hungry Child, A Report of 80,000 Massachusetts Public School Children,* Boston, 1969.

139,000 had had no breakfast. Only 5 percent of the more than 1 million public school children in Massachusetts had had a good breakfast that morning.

The Massachusetts program was built around in-service teacher workshops to upgrade the capability of classroom teachers as a prelude to an expanded school program in nutrition education.[28] These were generally 6 to 12 hours in total length, with instruction sessions spaced a week or so apart, depending on local educational agency policy. The workshops were action oriented, with enrollment generally limited to 15, using visual aids and well-prepared instruction materials.

The workshop program was based on the fact that sheer numbers made it impossible for a qualified nutritionist or dietitian to do the necessary teaching on a one-to-one or classroom basis. National surveys showed that, if every dietitian in America were employed in public school teaching, with none left over for hospitals, clinics, or other jobs, the nation would have only one dietitian per 2,900 school children. The teacher/pupil ratio is about 1 teacher per 25 children. Therefore, training allied professionals was the most practical solution.

In 1970, the Massachusetts Department of Education published 10 educational goals, of which physical and emotional well-being was listed first, with the statement that without these basic attributes, achievement of other goals would be more difficult. In a 1972 statewide assessment of educational programs, Massachusetts school administrators listed health education as a "major" need and regarded present educational programs in this area as only "fair." The 1968–70 Ten-State Nutrition Survey, in which Massachusetts was one of the states studied, gave added credence to their evaluation. Funding under the USDA food service program gave nutrition education top priority, and the Massachusetts legislature added supplemental funds.

The Massachusetts Department of Education issued a detailed and specific set of guidelines for the workshops: to develop and coordinate the activities in nutrition education, direct and evaluate performance, coordinate budgets in conformance with state law, set standards for teacher participation, and so on. Workshop supervisors were generally required to have at least eight years of full-time, or equivalent part-time, experience in the field of education, nutrition, and food delivery systems, have experience as a teacher, and hold a Massachusetts teaching certificate. Workshop assistants must have working knowledge of principles, practices, and techniques in the nutrition education, plus other qualifications. Adequate funding was recognized as essential for the program, not only in Massachusetts but throughout the country.

Proposed National Nutrition Education Act The National Nutrition Policy Study hearings of June 19–21, 1974, were followed on July 31 with introduction of a bill (S. 3864, 93d Congress, 2d Session) entitled the "National Nutrition Education Act of 1974." It was submitted by Senator George McGovern,

---

[28]Dorothy L. Callahan, "Inservice Teacher Workshops," *Journal of Nutrition Education,* Vol. 5, No. 4, October-December 1973, and *National Nutrition Policy Study,* 1974, pp. 2282–2285.

chairman of the Select Committee on Nutrition and Human Needs, for himself and for Senators Abourezk (Democrat of South Dakota), Case (Democrat of New Jersey), Cranston (Democrat of California), Hart (Democrat of Michigan), Kennedy (Democrat of Massachusetts), Mondale (Democrat of Minnesota), Percy (Republican of Illinois), and Schweiker (Republican of Pennsylvania). This was proposed as a three-year pilot effort in nutrition education. The policy goal was to make available federal funds, with a small state matching share, to introduce a comprehensive nutrition education program into the curricula of the nation's schools. The legislation would stress technical assistance, teacher training, planning, and organization in the state and federal office, and curriculum development.

Each state would have a nutrition education coordinator, who would be responsible for developing and enacting a state plan for nutrition education, and an advisory council for nutrition education. The plan would include ways to incorporate nutrition education into all subjects, insofar as practical, using both professional and community resources. A national nutrition center would be established to coordinate education in nutrition education, compile latest materials, develop recommended curricula, and evaluate efforts in nutrition education. It would use existing and expanded facilities in HEW and USDA.

This bill, drafted in consultation with officers of the Society for Nutrition Education, the American School Food Service Association, the National Dairy Council, and officials of federal agencies and state departments of education, authorized federal funds of $75 million for the first year. The states would share 40 percent of the federal funds equally, with 60 percent distributed on the basis of student enrollment. The bill required that each state appropriate for its nutrition education programs a minimum of 25 percent of the federal funds received under the act. Teacher training and pilot programs, however, would be funded entirely by the federal appropriation. The federal Commissioner of Education would be responsible for general administration, with each state program headed by a state coordinator.

In short, the bill generally followed the thesis of the Society for Nutrition Education that "Nutrition education should be viewed as the means to develop each individual's nutritional knowledge in such a way that he will be motivated to choose a nutritionally adequate diet. . . ."[29] It would have authorized initial support for the recommended "vastly improved nutrition education programs in the schools which provide nutrition education for every school child . . . , a strong nutrition training program . . . , and the development of a national nutrition education council to guide and coordinate a multitude of nutrition education efforts."

This first bill never reached a vote, and in June 1975, Senator McGovern introduced it again. Citing "the misuse of abundance" as the cause for the "new misnourished," McGovern called for new action to develop a comprehensive

---

[29]From the "Statement on the Needs for Nutrition Education, May 1974," submitted by the Board of Directors, Society for Nutrition Education, *National Nutrition Policy Study,* 1974, *op. cit.,* pp. 2286–2290.

nutrition education program. The bill would have authorized grants for teacher training, pilot demonstration programs, and state program development and implementation. Of the proposed authorized amounts—$75 million in 1976, $80 million in 1977, and $85 million in 1978—$50 million each year would go to the states to help them establish programs in nutrition education.

The proposals for federal aid in nutrition education, however, continued to fail to attract significant political support. In October 1975, more than 14 months after the introduction of the first bill, hearings on the second Senate bill still had not even been scheduled. The myths that the states were providing good education in nutrition, or that education was not essential for good nutrition, were dying hard.

For the national goals of nutrition policy to be achieved, a much higher priority for nutrition education must be established and consistently supported in the future.

Food Advertising and Nutrition Policy

Food advertising is both the hope and despair of nutrition policymakers. On the one hand, some groups, such as the Milk Packaging Group of the Paperboard Packaging Council and the Dairy Industry Task Force of the Milk Industry Foundation, have made significant progress in combining advertising with information on nutrition.[30] The labeling of milk and milk products has improved in accuracy, and advertising campaigns for these products will contribute to improvements in nutrition, especially among children. On the other hand, it has been estimated that at least 70 percent of the advertising claims on television for products relating to health are unsatisfactory or misleading; and food ads must be at least as high in this regard.[31] Since about $4 billion is spent on food advertising annually, if this proportion were projected to the total advertising media, some $2.8 billion in food advertising would be judged to be unsatisfactory in regard to health and nutrition.[32] Some 15 percent of commercial television is allocated for advertising, a large part of which is about food. On the Saturday morning children's programs especially, a large part of the advertising is on food, and much of it promotes manufactured products that are of doubtful nutritional value in the average diet. Sometimes as many as 10 attractive messages an hour have urged the child to eat or drink extremely sweet products.[33] If the child is persuaded to do so and the parent does not intervene, the advertising contributes to poor eating habits, generally inadequate nutrition, obesity, and tooth decay.

The percentage of all children who are adversely affected by such programs is not known. The advertiser must assume that a substantial number are influ-

---

[30]*National Nutrition Policy Study, 1974, op. cit.,* pp. 2294– 2425.

[31]F. A. Smith, G. Trivax, D. A. Zuehlke, M. D. Lowinger, and L. N. Nghiem, "Health Information during a Week of Television," *New England Journal of Medicine,* Vol. 286, No. 5, 1972, pp. 6–520.

[32]J. D. Ullrich and G. M. Briggs, "The General Public," in Jean Mayer (ed.), *U.S. Nutrition Policies in the 1970's,* San Francisco: W. H. Freeman Co., 1973, chap. 17.

[33]F. A. Smith et al., "Health Information during a Week of Television," *op. cit.*

enced, or the investment in advertising is not profitable. Although more nutrition education in the schools and on mass media might be a significant counterforce, without industry reform or adoption and enforcement of a code toward good nutrition, or even a complete ban on food advertising in children's programs, as some nutritionists have recommended, the deleterious effects are overwhelming.

The money spent in the mass media that is devoted to improved nutrition is very small in comparison with the $4 billion budget for food advertising. The Nutrition Foundation, which is partially funded by industry groups and which has sound nutrition education as its major goal, has spent only about $100,000 annually, and the money spent by such groups as the National Dairy Council and the National Livestock and Meat Board, which in its way contributes to good nutrition, is also small in comparison. The other efforts that we have mentioned, although of considerable significance and help, do not eliminate the case for policy to regulate food advertising. Food marketing firms that operate in an oligopoly type of setting must advertise to survive and prosper. Some questions are: What type of policy toward advertising will be in the public interest? What controls can industry accept, or what is practical? What policy constraints shall be applied?

Regulating Food Advertising   A unified policy to regulate food advertising has been slow to develop. Both the Food and Drug Administration and the Federal Trade Commission have responsibility for issuing and enforcing regulations on food, the FDA especially in the areas of food purity and sanitation standards, and the FTC in the areas of information, advertising, and certain trade practices. In regard to advertising, the FTC is charged with promulgating and enforcing trade regulation rules (TRRs) concerning advertising claims for food. Typically, a TRR not only prohibits making untrue claims; specific levels of nutrient content may be required before certain nutrition information can be included in ads. Additionally, certain limited nutrient information may be required in virtually all food advertisements.

Because of improvements and advances in the food industry, however, the specific limits to FTC authority in writing and enforcing a TRR have been increasingly much in doubt, and, to help in clarifying these limits, the Congress passed the Magnuson-Moss Warranty—FTC Improvement Act, which the President signed on January 5, 1975. This act more specifically authorized the FTC to define unfair acts or practices and required it to issue TRRs to prevent them. It strengthened the FTC requirements to hold informal hearings on a proposed TRR and to establish procedural rules for the public input and hearings, and to allow appropriate time for comments and criticism from the public, professional nutritionists and industry representatives.

The FTC has authority to appoint a presiding officer for a hearing, who has broad and extensive powers. This officer must designate the issues of fact to be covered at hearings and publish them together with notices of proposed rulemaking. The presiding officer may or may not choose to allow any petitioner's appeal, add or modify any designated issue of specific fact, and consider petitions from persons to add or modify any issues. The officer has power to identify the disputed issues of fact, to control the conduct of hearings, and to rule on the disputed issues of law or policy. At the termination of a set of hearings on a proposed TRR, the presiding officer is required to prepare a summary of the record, which the FTC staff uses to develop final recommendations for action by the full Federal Trade Commission.

On completion of this process, which will take at least five to six months and perhaps longer, the FTC may issue the TRR, ask for more information, table the entire effort, or substantially modify the original proposal and begin the entire procedure again. If the proceeding is reopened, it will be limited to those issues not already covered. Throughout the process, the public has an open opportunity to submit (1) comments on the entire proposal, (2) issues of specific fact, which should be included in the public hearing, (3) petitions for additions, deletions, or modifications to the published issues of fact, (4) statements of interest on specific issues, and (5) comments and/or requests for review.[34]

In summary: The FTC has broad powers granted to it to regulate food advertising. But these powers are also limited to the prohibition of untrue claims and to certain other requirements, such as warnings to be included in advertisements. A proposed TRR on protein supplements, for example, would require disclosure of the percentage and major sources of protein in the supplement in addition to the following statements: "Warning. Serious illness can result from improper use of this product: Not to be used for feeding of infants (birth to 1 year of age) or by persons with chronic or acute liver or kidney disease, except under medical supervision. Use of this product by children 1 to 3 years of age increases their need for liquids other than milk." Also, "Protein supplements are unnecessary for most Americans. The U.S. Public Health Service has determined that the daily diet of most Americans provides adequate protein." The rule also restricts claims that protein supplements provide quick energy, remedy fatigue, counteract or delay signs of aging, and so on.[35]

Regulating Food Labeling   The General Accounting Office (GAO), in its publication *Food Labeling: Goals, Shortcomings, and Proposed Changes,* issued by the Comptroller General in 1975, noted that although most food products comply with federal packaging and labeling laws and regulations, improvements are needed so that labels tell consumers what they need to know to select products that are most suited to their needs. The GAO recommended:

1   *Full disclosure* of all ingredients on packaged food products, to displace the provisions of the then active Food, Drug and Cosmetic Act, which exempted some food products and required only a general ingredient listing.

2   *Percentage labeling,* to show the amounts of various ingredients that

[34]Mahlon A. Burnette III, "The Food Advertising TRR Proceedings: A Scenario," *Food Product Development,* Vol. 9, September 1975.
[35]From *The Federal Register,* Sept. 5, 1975.

make up a product, because various manufacturers use different formulas for the same product.

3 *Nutrition labeling,* to overcome the lack of nutritional and educational information on food labels, because Americans suffer dietary and health problems due in part to lack of good nutrition.

4 *Quality grading* on a mandatory basis, in lieu of the voluntary USDA quality grading system, to provide more complete information for consumers to judge the comparative quality and value of alternative products.

5 A *uniform dating system* for perishable and semiperishable goods, because the variety and types of dates then in use were generally not well understood, which resulted in limited consumer use.

6 A *federal unit pricing program* to help consumers compare prices because, although unit pricing was available on about 50 percent of the items in chain-operated grocery stores, use of the system often required complicated mathematical calculations.

Studies showed that, increasingly, consumers wanted to know more exactly what they were eating.[36]

Following the GAO report, several bills were introduced in Congress to implement these recommendations and others. A main policy goal of the Consumer Food Act of 1975 (S. 641, 94th Congress, 1st Session), similar to the Food Surveillance Bill (S. 2323, 93d Congress, 2d Session) which passed the Senate in 1974, was to "enhance the health and the nutritional and economic welfare of the consumer" by means of increased authority for the FDA with respect to regulations regarding the labels on food products (S. 641, Title III). In regard to *open dating,* the FDA would be authorized to establish regulations requiring dating information on packages and labels of perishable and semiperishable foods, together with a statement of the storage conditions, such as humidity and temperature, if they differed from ordinary room temperatures. In regard to *nutrition labeling,* the label would be required to carry nutrition information, but only if nutrients had been added or a claim of nutritional value was made on the label or in advertising or promotion. For those foods that required labeling, the label should show the percentage of each ingredient that was significant with respect to the value, quality, nutrition, flavor, or acceptability of the product.

In addition to the Senate bill (S. 641), the Consumer Food Labeling Act (H.R. 42, 94th Congress, 1st Session), entirely devoted to food labeling, would go somewhat further. In addition to percentage ingredient labeling, spices, flavorings, and colorings would have to be listed separately by their common or usual name. In addition to nutrient labeling, for canned and frozen foods the label would have to include a statement of the net and drained weight. Every perishable or semiperishable food, as defined by the FDA, would have to show the pull date (the latest permissable date for sale) and the optimum temperature and

---

[36]For additional discussion, see Nancy Harvey Steorts, "Some Consumer Concerns Regarding Food Labeling and Packaging," *Food Technology,* October 1975.

humidity conditions for storage. All manufactured foods would have to show the name of the manufacturer, packer, and distributor, instead of just one of the three, as formerly. Quality grading and unit pricing would be required.

A Policy Conclusion   The maturing of policy in regard to advertising and consumer information apparently will emphasize the disclosure of basic facts about food in terms that consumers can understand. The legislation will not change the basic economic structure of food processing and marketing; but disclosure of more factual information can have a salutary effect on the food industry and, especially if combined with new and improved programs on nutrition education, it can provide the basis for more healthful diets and eating habits.

Drawing attention to nutritional factors apparently has some educational benefits for consumers.[37] It acts as a stimulant for the industry to improve the quality of some manufactured foods, and it provides a disciplinary factor for food advertising. The consumer benefits from nutrition labeling tend to increase with program duration as consumer food habits change to make more use of the information. Most consumers see nutrition labeling as having a positive or desirable effect on food advertising and on the nutritional accountability of food manufacturers. Hypothetical benefits include the potential of the labels to inspire consumer confidence in the food industry, to encourage the production and manufacture of more nutritious foods, to stimulate consumer education concerning nutrition, and to satisfy the consumers right and desire to know.[38] Although evidence that consumers' purchasing decisions may be altered by nutrition labeling is extremely scarce and superficial, some 85 percent of the consumers queried indicated agreement with these stated benefits.[39]

Consumer advocacy has been an important force in the evolution of policy in food advertising and nutrition information. In 1969, participants in the White House Conference on Food, Nutrition, and Health gave their support to improvement of national nutrition as a goal of prime importance. They endorsed encouraging advertisers of food products to "reserve space on packages or on inserts for explanatory material on nutrition" and persuading regulatory agencies "to permit more voluntary labeling dealing with the major nutritional components of food products."[40] Industry responded by creating its own forms for such information while it developed new foods and altered others; In 1970, Massachusetts enacted a law requiring unit pricing on many products and in 1971 other

[37]See R. J. Lenehan, J. A. Thomas, D. A. Taylor, D. L. Call, and D. I. Padberg, "Consumer Reaction to Nutrition Information on Food Product Labels," *Search Agriculture,* Ithaca, N.Y.: Cornell Agricultural Experiment Station, Vol. 2, No. 15, Agricultural Economics 4, September 1972, pp. 1–28, especially p. 23.

[38]Daniel I. Padberg, "Non-use Benefits of Mandated Consumer Information Programs," *Proceedings of the Second Workshop on Consumer Action Research,* Berlin, Germany, April 9–12, 1975.

[39]Lenehan et al., "Consumer Reaction to Nutrition Information on Food Product Labels," *op. cit.,* pp. 20–21.

[40]*White House Conference on Food, Nutrition and Health, Final Report,* p. 300.

states and cities followed. In addition, many food chains voluntarily experimented with unit pricing in areas where it was not mandated, so that in five years time it became relatively common.[41] Although it was estimated that in the aggregate no consumer savings were realized by the policy of unit pricing, consumers generally reacted positively to the practice. Costs were lower than originally estimated, especially in large stores. Consumers liked the idea of basic information to be provided by the food distributor.[42]

Simultaneously and for several years, various proposals were made for a specific agency to serve as an advocate for consumers and provide protection for their interests. In 1975 the Senate passed a bill to provide for an Agency for Consumer Advocacy (S. 200, 94th Congress, 1st Session), and on June 30 a similar bill was introduced in the House. The agency (ACA) would advocate consumer interests, and *only* consumer interests, in proceedings before federal agencies, such as the FTC, FDA, and USDA. It would receive consumer complaints, transmit them to appropriate agencies, and make them publicly available. It would publish a consumer register concerning actions by Congress, agency hearings, and other information useful to consumers; it would adopt and expand consumer education programs and encourage meaningful action by consumers in its activities.

The ACA would be empowered to intervene in the proceedings of any agency as an adversary to protect the interests of consumers, and if the results were not satisfactory, to use its own legal staff to seek review in federal court. Any business or corporate enterprise engaged in activities that would substantially affect the interests of consumers might be required to file a report with the ACA in reply to written questions relating to such activities. Each federal agency, before adopting any rule affecting consumers, would be required to file a report with the ACA concerning the estimated benefits and costs of the proposed rule.

Many policy questions concerning consumer advocacy, nutrition information, unit pricing, and the like cannot be answered, however, except through a continuous flow of research having to do with realized and potential costs and benefits. In regard to further government regulation and control, such as proposed for the ACA, will benefits exceed costs if adopted throughout the food industry? The long lag that has occurred in response to many recommendations suggests that there still is a paucity of policy-oriented economic research on which to proceed.

Recognized Research Priorities

In 1972, a Committee of Future Planning was established by the Agricultural Research Service (ARS) of the USDA at the Western Regional Research Center

---

[41]*Progressive Grocer,* April 1972, pp. 98–99; April 1973, p. 106; April 1974, p. 82.

[42]T. David McCullough and Daniel I. Padberg, "Unit Pricing in Supermarkets. Alternatives, Costs, and Consumer Reaction," *Search Agriculture,* Ithaca, N.Y.: Cornell University Agricultural Experiment Station, Vol. 1, No. 6, Agricultural Economics 2, January 1971, pp. 1–28.

at Berkeley, California, to develop research and development (R&D) priorities in agriculture-related fields.[43] The approach itself was viewed as an experiment based on a multistep survey to develop a guide for R&D workers, to identify neglected areas of research, and to improve cross-communication and fertilization among research fields and organizations. From a list of 136 scholars and scientists in industry, universities, and government, 112 agreed to serve as panelists. In the first step, each individual was asked to respond anonymously to the request: "List present and future research and development needs related to providing abundant, high-quality food at minimum cost while protecting the environment." The responses from the 70 panelists who replied were grouped into categories and, in the second step, the panel of 112 was asked to: "Rate the importance of the statements of need, collected from Step 1 of the survey, in terms of research and development priorities . . . on a balance of social desirability and technical/economic feasibility. Use the scale: 5 = highest priority, urgently needed; 4 = important; 3 = some advantage; 2 = little or no impact; 1 = problem already solved."

Replies were received from 86 members of the panel in eight categories of research involving a number of areas in each category (Table 11-6). The top-rated needs in each category reflected the increased concerns over the safety and environmental aspects of food production, as well as some of the frustrations or difficulties that had been encountered in dealing with these concerns (Table 11-7). The high rating of social, political, and psychological needs in the ranking of research categories (Table 11-6), and the particularly high rating given to the need for synthesis of the regulations and programs of the Department of Agricul-

[43]J. M. Krochta, T. R. Rumsey, and D. F. Farkas, "Defining Food R&D Needs as a Guide for the Future," *Food Technology,* October 1975.

Table 11-6   Rankings of Categories of Needed Research and Number of Items Ranked in Each Category

Ranking	Category	Average priority rating	Number of research areas ranked in each category
1	Social, political, psychological	3.51	15
2	Agricultural production	3.41	34
3	Systems analysis	3.22	15
4	Harvesting	3.17	10
5	Transportation, storage, and distribution of new products	3.16	19
6	Processing	3.10	81
7	Packaging, storage, and distribution of processed foods	3.04	40
8	New foods	2.92	31

Source: J. M. Krochta, T. R. Rumsey, and D. F. Farkas, "Defining Food R&D Needs as a Guide for the Future," *Food Technology,* October 1975.

Table 11-7 The Ranking of the Highest Priority Research Needs in R&D

Ranking	Need	Average priority rating
1	Synthesis of USDA, FDA, and EPA regulations regarding water use, sanitation, and pollution into a system with common objectives	4.21
2	Plant and equipment design and operation for greater reduction and recycling of water, and for reduced waste and pollution	4.16
3	Alternate sources of fertilizer to replace petrochemical fertilizers	4.06
4	Rational, acceptable risk/benefit considerations for foods and food additives	4.03
5	Improved yields without increasing chemical fertilizer requirements	4.02
6	Insect and disease control which limits or eliminates use of chemicals	3.98
7	Methods for converting food-processing-plant effluents into feeds, fertilizers, energy, useful chemicals, etc.	3.96
8	Total systems study to compare energy demand, water usage, nutritional value, packaging costs, etc., of the various processing and preservation methods	3.95
9	Systems for recovering, purifying, and utilizing plant proteins to give functional and acceptable (nutrients, flavor, texture, cost) engineered food for human consumption	3.92
10	Breeding of varieties which will extend harvest and processing season	3.90
11	Improvement in food distribution efficiencies	3.90

Source: J. M. Krochta, T. R. Rumsey, and D. F. Farkas, "Defining Food R&D Needs as a Guide for the Future," *Food Technology*, October 1975.

ture, the Food and Drug Administration, and the Environmental Protection Agency. (Table 11-7), reflects the policy-related issues in food and nutrition. Almost all the 15 items rated in this category have important implications for national food and nutrition policy (Table 11-8).

Research for Nutrition Policy

One goal for nutrition policy is indicated in the high priorities given for research to synthesize the regulations of the USDA, FDA, EPA, FTC, and other agencies to deal with food and food resources. Comparatively little is known about the cost-benefit ratios inherent in the many proposals for legislation to regulate food advertising, food labeling, food additives, and the like. The major expense of more rigorous and precise standards, which appears as a cost to the food industry, must be passed on to the consumer. For nutrition policy to be optimum from the consumer's standpoint, research must establish the most important cost and benefit relationships, not only for the regulations that are proposed from time to time but for changes in nutritional values and other attributes resulting from the alteration of foods and diets by food processing and additives.

Nutritional Values, Food Alteration, and Additives. More than one-half the total food intake of Americans as measured by dry weight now comes from foods that are highly processed or fabricated from the original food forms, such as flour and prepared cereals, sugars, reconstituted fats and oils, and some of the

Table 11-8   Ranking of Research Needs in the Social, Political, and Psychological Category

Ranking	Need	Average priority rating
1	Synthesis of USDA, FDA, and EPA regulations regarding water use, sanitation, and pollution into a system with common objectives	4.21
2	Rational, acceptable risk/benefit considerations for foods and food additives	4.03
3	Improvement in food distribution efficiencies	3.90
4	As a national food insurance policy, plans and methods for producing a larger proportion of foods locally for largely local consumption—striving for independence from outside sources of energy, fuels, fertilizers, and transportation	3.89
5	Solution to the balance-of-payment problems and high cost of import oil	3.84
6	More efficient utilization of agricultural grains than feeding to beef cattle	3.70
7	Transfer of small-plant technology to developing countries	3.56
8	Solution of problems with increasing use of standards of identity and guidelines (for example, requirement that ice cream and milk contain only butterfat)	3.51
9	Development of incentives to cause farmers to produce the best and most needed products	3.49
10	Better communication system for transfer of information to small processors	3.31
11	Relationship whereby the cost of developing equipment would be shared by the user and a new ethical position would be developed between the manufacturer and the user	3.09
12	Dating of all packaged foods	3.09
13	Reduction of sugar used in canning fruit	3.07
14	A joint industry committee to establish a series of standards enabling a host of supply items to be quickly and easily interchanged	3.07
15	Reduction of amount of packaging media in canned products	2.94

Source: J. M. Krochta, T. R. Rumsey, and D. F. Farkas, "Defining R&D Needs as a Guide for the Future," *Food Technology,* October 1975.

proteins and other carbohydrates. The balance of the diet is composed of the more traditional foods. These are often processed in ways that may alter their nutritive values.

Many of the highly processed foods as well as the more traditional foods are altered by food additives. Used for a variety of purposes, the additives include food preservatives, dyes for coloring, flavor enhancers, physical or biological stabilizers, nutrient enrichers, and so on. Acidulants accentuate the naturally tart taste of fruits in jellies and preserves. Antioxidants inhibit oxidation. Dyes for artificial coloring make certain foods more appealing; they give color to margarine, for example. Also, they reduce the costs in manufacturing some foods. Artificial colors make chocolate cake or ice cream look like chocolate without the expense of chocolate. Almost all flour is bleached to produce the whiteness desired by consumers. Artificial flavoring is used for many commercial food products; and stabilizers turn many preparations into a physically stable state. Stabilizers keep processed cheeses firm for a long time, although some of the original flavor may be lost. Nutritive agents are added to highly advertised breakfast foods, flour, and various drinks and other foods. Surfactants bind the ingredients of many processed foods into a stable consistency. The average American consumes some 6.7 pounds of food additives annually, and the gross value of sales, which was $636 million in 1971 and $900 million in 1975, will, according to estimates, reach $1,109 million in 1980 (Table 11-9).

If we take the position that additives and food alterations are an essential part of the nation's food supply, the task of research is to determine whether such procedures contribute to good nutrition and whether other foods that are more economical, nutritious, palatable, and otherwise more satisfactory can be produced. Concurrently, research is also required to discover whether or not there are deleterious effects or dangers in certain processes and additives. The National Nutrition Consortium has recommended that such research should be supported in colleges and universities, qualified nutrition centers, health-care facilities, special institutes, industry, and the federal agencies.[44] Research support should be provided for all areas of food production, processing, and use.

Research for Nutrient Identification As we shift from a generally static commodity type of natural food supply to one based more fully on ready-to-eat prepared and fabricated foods, the issue of nutritive value becomes paramount and the importance of research to identify the nutritional impact of dietary alteration is imperative. Research sponsored by both government and industry is necessary to determine not only the nutritional content of such foods, but also the true biological availability of nutrients. The interactions of ingredients from combined food sources, which may result in imbalances and poor absorption, must be determined. The availability of iron, for example, is a function of both the source of iron and the other nutrients in the diet.

Although education can tell people how best to utilize a given food supply once the necessary research is done, in the evolutionary type of food supply to which we are committed, research must continually evaluate the risk of nutritional deficiency from dietary data and appraise the nutritional consequences of various alternatives in diets. Dietary instruction then must take account of

[44]From a special report, "Guidelines for a National Nutrition Policy," *Nutrition Reviews,* Vol. 32, No. 5, May 1974. The National Nutrition Consortium, Inc., includes the American Institute of Nutrition, the American Society for Clinical Nutrition, the American Dietetic Association, and the Institute of Food Technology. Together, these organizations have a membership of 40,000 scientifically trained professionals.

Table 11-9 Food Additive Market-Value Estimates for 1971, 1975, and 1980

Class	1971	1975	1980
	(in millions)		
Acidulants	$ 55.84	$ 69.92	$ 98.19
Antioxidants	12.73	15.55	19.82
Preservatives	10.64	12.58	16.06
Colors	16.77	19.37	27.38
Flavor and flavor enhancers	254.00	326.90	476.40
Enzymes	21.63	27.84	40.84
Stabilizers, etc.	98.80	128.40	151.30
Nutritive agents	61.11	91.40	146.60
Surfactants	53.71	62.05	71.64
Miscellaneous	50.74	56.18	60.58
Totals	$635.97	$800.19	$1,108.81

Source: "Prospects in Food Additives." Unpublished speech by Dr. Ferdinand B. Zienty (Manager of Food Research and Development, Monsanto Company) before the American Institute of Chemical Engineers, March 19, 1974.

cultural and esthetic phenomena to best meet recommended dietary allowances. Although fabricated foods are desired that are generally at least as nutritious as the naturally occurring counterpart they are designed to replace, the correct policy response to a food that is deficient is rarely that of encouraging a race among food fabricators to enrich the food by fortification. Rather, the object of research policy should be to determine how deficiencies can be best overcome either by fortification and food additives or by identifying the suitable food substitutes to achieve a balanced and nutritious diet.[45]

Research for New Foods For the most efficient development of future food supplies using science and technology, there must be continuous research on development of new foods. The objective is to create a food that is as nutritious as, or more nutritious than, the food it might displace, that is, more economical to produce and more acceptable to the consumer.

Soybean milk, which may become economically important as a new source of protein, illustrates the possible needs and benefits of such research. Although soybean milk has been a food staple in the Orient for several centuries, it has a distinct painty flavor that is objectionable to many people. In 1975, it was announced that this off-flavor can be prevented through an 11-step process that converts the major soybean nutrients to a palatable food.[46] The process starts

[45]For further discussion, see Helen A. Guthrie, "Concept of a Nutritious Food," and D. M. Hegested, "Dietary Allowances and Nutrition Policy," papers presented at a symposium on *Translating Nutrition Concepts Into Policy,* sponsored by the Food and Nutrition Board of the National Academy of Sciences, Washington, Dec. 4, 1975.

[46]L. S. Wei, M. P. Steinberg, and A. I. Nelson, "A New Illinois Soybean Beverage: Tasty, Smooth, Nutritious, and Economical," in *Illinois Research,* University of Illinois at Urbana-Champaign, College of Agriculture, Illinois Agricultural Experiment Station, Vol. 17, No. 4, Fall 1975.

with soaking or hydrating and then cooking good-quality soybeans in water containing baking soda. This process inactivates the enzyme that generates the painty flavor and a palatable beverage can be produced. Or the process can be interrupted in mid-stage to produce a soybean beverage base which can be used as a high-protein dairy analog in milk, yogurt, and ice cream, or which can be frozen or dried for future use as protein-enriched flour, meat extender, and other purposes. Soybean milk also offers a specific alternative for individuals who cannot tolerate cow's milk.

Although this soybean product will provide an economical source of protein to displace or enrich some of the more conventional proteins, its use as a major protein source, as in flour, milk, or other products, may cause loss of essential minerals. Soy contains constituents, such as phytic acid and fiber, which bind and thus make such minerals as calcium and zinc unavailable. How to replace such minerals or prevent the nutrient losses from such binding action is an important area for research. Additionally, in composing well-balanced diets, it is essential to recognize, as a USDA study concluded in 1972, that "Because of essential amino-acid imbalance, most plant proteins are less efficient, have lower digestibility, and a lesser biological value than animal proteins."[47] In other words, the question for nutrition research is not just to find a new ingredient to substitute for another, but to identify the comparative nutritive values of foods in respect to their final efficiency in utilization.

Fabricated Foods as a Solution to Nutritional Problems   The modern food supply is critically dependent on food manufacturing and processing techniques, including the additives that contribute to these processes. Although only a small portion of the additives contributes directly to nutrition (Table 11-9), additives will continue to play a critical role in efficient use of foods as conditioners, preservers, extenders, flavor enhancers, and so on. In the wise use of fabricated foods, it will continue to be important and even essential for them to contribute to good health, or at least not be damaging to health. What are some changes to guard against?

We have already commented on the undesirably high levels of sugar and fat in the typical American diet; but since some two-thirds of total sugar consumed in the United States is delivered in prepared foods and beverages, the problem of reducing the high sugar consumption requires both education to direct consumers away from high-sugar foods and research to develop alternative foods, as well as more accurate food labeling and regulation of advertising. Invisible sugar is delivered not only in most manufactured beverages, cakes, and candies, but also in such originally sugar-free products as ketchup, peanut butter, pickles, cheese dips, soups, and biscuit mixes. Many canned fruits and juices have a very high sugar content, and some of the prepared cereals contain even more sugar, proportionately.

[47]William W. Gallimore, *Synthetics and Substitutes for Agricultural Products: Projections for 1980,* U.S. Department of Agriculture, Economic Research Service, Market Research MR Report No. 947, March 1972.

Although very little research is required to verify the high sugar levels in many food products, the real question for a nutrition policy is more subtle. Since sugar is generally the cheapest source of calories, closely followed by many fats, the research problem is not to find simple substitutes for sugars and fats, but to encourage use of traditional foods that are lower in sugar and fat. The educational problem is to make the information about these foods more widely known and thus to counteract some of the more diet-degrading advertising of products that are high in sugar and fat.

In Chapter 4, we discussed at some length the problem of obtaining the optimum use of pesticides, which includes education in regard to proper use as well as regulation and control. A somewhat similar policy problem exists in regard to the optimum use of food additives and, although knowledge concerning their effects is essential for a good and safe food supply, it has not been possible to fully test them all before they came into general use. The problem is to determine their long-term effects on human health and metabolism.

Although nearly all are believed to be harmless in normal use, a number of food additives that formerly received the FDA rating of GRAS (generally regarded as safe) have been withdrawn from use. Thus, for example, Violet No. 1, a food coloring used for 22 years by the USDA to stamp meat as USDA "prime" or "choice" was banned in 1973 by the FDA as possibly linked to cancer. Until 1966, breweries had been permitted, both by the FDA and the Canadian Food and Drug Directorate, to add a small quantity of cobalt salts to beer to increase the amount of foam. After a number—possibly as many as 100—heavy beer drinkers had died of apparent heart attacks, the combination of cobalt and beer was suspected as toxic and its use was banned. Cyclamates, which had been permitted in soft drinks as a substitute for sugar, were banned when it was suspected that they might be linked to cancer if used extensively over a long period. The hypothesis in this regard is not universally accepted, and the issue of the use of cyclamates may be regarded still as a moot question in food additive policy.

Food additives and allergies pose another difficult problem. It has been claimed or hypothesized that some 12 to 15 percent of the American population are allergic to one or more of the food additives.[48] But, since allergies are very subtle, varying among food combinations and even in respect to one individual from time to time, the issue remains in doubt. It has been claimed that at least 50 percent of the hyperkinesis (a form of overactivity) and learning disabilities in children are caused by food coloring and other additives in the food supply.[49] But other scientists have found no support for the hypothesis that food additives do produce behavioral hyperactivity in children. Although it is conceded that within

[48]Claude Frazier, *Coping with Food Allergy*, New York: Quadrangle Books, Inc., 1974.

[49]B. Feingold, "Food Additives and Child Development," *Hospital Practice*, Vol. 8, No. 11, 1973; Feingold, "Recognition of Food Additives as a Cause of Symptoms of Allergy," *Analytical Allergy*, Vol. 26, 1938, p. 309; and Feingold, "Adverse Reactions to Food Additives with Special Reference to Hyperkinesis and Learning Disability (H-LD), "*Congressional Record-Senate*," S-19738-42, October 1973.

the vast group of "hyperactive children" there may be a subgroup whose basic underlying allergies become manifest as behavior symptoms resembling hyperactivity, the relationship of hypersensitivity or allergy to food additives has not been demonstrated convincingly.[50]

For our purposes, we may conclude with the authors of "Nutrition Update" that the continuous unraveling of new information about nutrition and food components has important implications for nutrition education and good health.[51] Human immunity to infection is importantly related to a well-balanced diet and is usually impaired by deficiencies of protein and other components of a good diet, especially vitamins A, B-12, C, iron, and so on. One's susceptibility to different types of cancer is affected by diet. Human intestinal cancers have been associated with high consumption of animal protein and fat, and with lack of dietary fiber, even though causation is not necessarily implied. Although certain food additives may be carcinogenic, they may have no demonstrated role in human carcinogenesis under conditions of normal use. It is believed, in fact, that some of the most hazardous carcinogens are naturally occurring food toxicants, such as, for example, aflatoxins, which are produced by molds that grow readily on peanuts and grains; and it is recommended that people take precautions to avoid eating moldy peanuts, nuts, seeds, legumes, and cereal products. New information is being developed relating nutrition—or rather, poor nutrition—to other diseases, such as diabetes, heart disease, and hyperkinesis. New roles are being established for certain nutrients, such as linoleic acid and related fatty acids. The general conclusion is that a diet chosen wisely from a wide variety of foods continues to be the best health protection.

A More General Conclusion

Our more general conclusion is that an improved national policy for nutrition, depending more heavily on research and education, is vital to reach the highest goals in food policy for America. Although agreed standards are necessary for food production from the farm through to the consumer-household and therefore some regulation is essential, regulation alone is not necessarily productive. Only by a greater commitment to research needs in nutrition, and to integration of this research with a national program in nutrition education, will we fully realize the improved diet potentials of the future.

In still broader vision of food policy, nutrition policy can be coordinated with the other policy elements so that the future demands of the United States population for food can be met with greater efficiency and equity. The food resource sector can be an even greater source of national wealth in international commerce and trade. Our nation can maintain at least the tradition of the immediate post-war decades in food aid to other countries.

---

[50]Sushma Palmer, Judith L. Rapoport, and Patricia O. Quinn, "Food Additives and Hyperactivity," *Clinical Pediatrics,* Vol. 14, No. 10, October 1975, pp. 956–959.

[51]Jean Weininger and George M. Briggs, "Nutrition Update, 1975," *Journal of Nutrition Education,* the Official Journal of the Society for Nutrition Education, Vol. 7, No. 4, October–December 1975, pp. 141–144.

To achieve these goals, however, not only must judicious choices be made in food policy, but also there must be a new measure of cooperation among the nations. The trade channels must be opened more widely for the mutual benefits of comparative advantage to be more generally enjoyed. In no major economic sector is this more important than in food and agriculture. In addition, all nations, and the rich ones especially, must cooperate in helping, on a nation-by-nation basis, to achieve the indigenously desired balance between population and food resources. Many believe that the time for this is already past. Clearly, the food-population problem in many developing nations will become more severe before it gets better. But this need not be cause for despair. We view it rather as a challenge for strong policymakers in our area of study to try to be helpful as opportunity occurs.

The future of food policy should not be viewed with either despair or unfounded optimism. Some progress is being made in population control, and in the food economy, many important advances in both efficiency and equity still lie ahead. But, in a sophisticated food economy, the maximum human welfare never occurs automatically. The appropriate policy requires both broad vision and detailed study, leading to future implementation of the more generally socially preferred options.

Thus, an optimum food policy for America requires a broad national commitment and understanding, a new level of rural-urban cooperation, a balanced approach in answer to the three questions: What to produce? How? For whom? It requires a new commitment to the future, a continuing new appraisal of accomplishments and national priorities or goals, an evaluation of means and the best ways to implement them, and finally, a judicious application of policy constraints. Success in this policy will yield advances for human welfare in this country and around the world.

QUESTIONS FOR DISCUSSION

1 Some people consider it paradoxical that, as many people have become more affluent, their diets have deteriorated nutritionally. Is such a result consistent with the income elasticities shown in Chapter 3? Is such a trend reversible? Comment.

2 Summarize the early recommendations for nutrition policy in America comparing them with actual accomplishments and results. How did they differ from those of the 1950s? What were the significant policy developments of the 1960s? Summarize the response in the 1970s to the 1969 White House Conference on Food, Nutrition, and Health.

3 Outline the arguments for federal support for a national policy for nutrition education. Account for the apparent weakness of political support for such a policy.

4 Trace the evolution of federal support for the school lunch and related programs. What are the arguments for the program? The arguments against it?

5 Food advertising is both the hope and the despair of food policymakers. If improved nutrition is the major policy goal, what changes must be made in food advertising programs? How may these be brought about? What forces have prevented these changes?

6 Discuss the roles of the FDA and the FTC in regulating food advertising. What is a TRR? How is it promulgated? What are some of the objections to having more stringent regulation through a TRR?

7 Discuss the recommendations of the General Accounting Office in *Food Labeling: Goals, Shortcomings, and Proposed Changes*. What are the assumed costs and benefits? Discuss the problem of identifying such benefits and costs.

8 What is the policy argument for an Agency for Consumer Advocacy? The argument against? Appraise the pros and the cons.

9 Comment on the rankings of the highest priorities in food research needs for R&D. Do you have other priorities to suggest? Comment.

10 Outline a general plan for coordinating future food and nutrition policy, indicating where you will place the greatest emphasis or priority and your reasons for doing so.

REFERENCES

Berg, Alan, *The Nutrition Factor: Its Role in National Development,* Washington: The Brookings Institution, 1973.

Berg, Alan, Nevin S. Scrimshaw, and David L. Call (eds.), *Nutrition, National Development, and Planning.* Proceedings of an International Conference held at Cambridge, Mass., October 19–21, 1971. Cambridge, Mass.: The M.I.T. Press, 1973.

Bogert, L. Jean, George M. Briggs, and Doris Howes Calloway, *Nutrition and Physical Fitness,* 9th ed., Philadelphia: W. B. Saunders Company, 1973.

Dunning, J. M., *Principles of Dental Public Health,* Cambridge, Mass.: Harvard University Press, 1970.

Guthrie, Helen Andrews, *Introductory Nutrition,* 3d ed., St. Louis: The C. V. Mosby Company, 1975.

Harris, Robert S., and Endel Karmas (eds.), *Nutritional Evaluation of Food Processing,* 2d ed., Westport, Conn.: The Avi Publishing Co., Inc., 1975.

Mayer, Jean (ed.), *U.S. Nutrition Policies in the 1970's,* San Francisco: W. H. Freeman and Company, 1973.

Rosenthal, Benjamin, Michael Jacobson, and Marcy Bohm, "Professors on the Take: Financial Ties to Huge Food Corporations May Shade the 'Expert Testimony' of Nutritionists, *The Progressive,* Vol. 40, No. 11, November 1976, pp. 42–47.

U.S. Senate, *National Nutrition Policy Study,* Hearings, Select Committee on Nutrition and Human Needs, 93d Cong., 2d Sess., parts 1–7, 1974.

Name Index

Abel, Martin E., 23*n*.
Abelson, Philip H., 140, 331
Achorn, Frank P., 105*n*.
Adams, Dale W., 39*n*.
Aders, Robert O., 177*n*.
Allen, George C., 99*n*.
Andrilenas, Paul, 109*n*., 113*n*.
Angly, Edward, 289*n*.
Arthur, Henry B., 167*n*., 170*n*.
Aull, George H., 167*n*.
Azevedo, Ross E., 393*n*., 430

Babcock, Howard E., 237*n*.
Bachman, Kenneth L., 134
Baker, John A., 471*n*.
Baker, O. E., 355*n*.
Baker, Sue, 471*n*.
Ball, Gordon, 128
Balz, Dan, 195*n*.
Banta, John, 373*n*.
Barker, R. J., 118*n*.
Barker, Randolph, 39*n*.

Barletta, Ardito, 3*n*.
Barnes, Peter, 346*n*.
Bartlett, R. W., 274*n*., 276*n*., 279*n*., 280*n*.
Bates, Thomas H., 262*n*.
Baumol, W. J., 10*n*.
Beal, G. M., 96*n*.
Beale, Calvin L., 43*n*.
Bean, L. H., 133*n*.
Becker, Gary S., 434
Beckett, Grace, 153*n*.
Behrens, William W., III, 32*n*.
Bell, Patrick, 94
Benedict, Murray R., 160*n*., 167*n*., 168, 197,
    286*n*., 331, 335*n*.
Bennett, Merrill K., 34*n*.
Benson, Ezra T., 230
Berg, Alan, 545
Berg, Sherwood O., 183*n*.
Bever, Wayne, 110*n*.
Bistrian, Bruce, 494*n*.
Black, John D., 34*n*., 133*n*., 143*n*., 147*n*., 154,
    156*n*., 158*n*., 160*n*., 163*n*., 168*n*., 197, 343*n*.
Blackburn, George L., 494*n*.

Subject Index